AN INTRODUCTION TO
MACROECONOMICS

■ ■ ■

■ ■

This copy of MACROECONOMICS
by Blomqvist, Wonnacott, and Wonnacott
is from the library of

_____

■ ■ ■

AN INTRODUCTION TO
MACROECONOMICS

THIRD CANADIAN EDITION

■■■■■■■■■■■■■■■■■■■■■■■■■■■■■■■■

ÅKE BLOMQVIST

University of Western Ontario

PAUL WONNACOTT

University of Maryland

RONALD WONNACOTT

University of Western Ontario

McGRAW-HILL RYERSON LIMITED

Toronto   Montreal   New York   Auckland   Bogotá
Caracas   Hamburg   Lisbon   London   Madrid   Mexico
Milan   New Delhi   Paris   San Juan   São Paulo
Singapore   Sydney   Tokyo

■ ■ ■

■ ■

AN INTRODUCTION TO MACROECONOMICS, Third Canadian Edition

Copyright © McGraw-Hill Ryerson Limited, 1990, 1987, 1983. Copyright © 1990, John Wiley and Sons, Inc. Copyright © McGraw-Hill, Inc. 1986, 1982, 1979. All rights reserved. No part of this publication may be reproduced, stored in a data base or retrieval system, or transmitted, in any form or by any means, electronic, mechanical, photocopying, recording, or otherwise, without prior written permission of McGraw-Hill Ryerson Limited.

ISBN: 0-07-549917-7

1 2 3 4 5 6 7 8 9 0   D   9 8 7 6 5 4 3 2 1 0

Printed and bound in Canada

Care has been taken to trace ownership of copyright material in this text. The publishers will gladly take any information that will enable them to rectify any reference or credit in subsequent editions.

Canadian Cataloguing in Publication Data

Blomqvist, Åke G., date —
    An introduction to macroeconomics
3rd Canadian ed.

Includes bibliographical references and index.
ISBN 0-07-549917-7

1. Macroeconomics.   I. Wonnacott, Paul, date —
II. Wonnacott, Ronald J., date —   .   III. Title.

HB172.5.B56 1990   339   C90-093250-3

Sponsoring Editor: Jackie Kaiser

Senior Supervising Editor: Carol Altilia

Copy Editor: Edie Franks

Cover and Text Design: Daniel Kewley

Technical Artist: Lynda Powell

Typesetting: Compeer Typographic Services Limited

Printing and Binding: John Deyell Company

Cover Painting:
MACDONALD, J.W.G. (Jock)   Canadian 1897–1960
Fleeting Breath, 1959
ART GALLERY OF ONTARIO, TORONTO
Canada Council Joint Purchase Award, 1959

∞   This book was manufactured in Canada using acid-free paper.

■ ■ ■

To my mother, Ingrid Blomqvist

■ ■

INTERESTED IN A NEW STUDY AID?

Economics is one of the most challenging introductory-level courses in the curriculum. In recognition of this, we have developed a *Study Guide* to accompany the Blomqvist/Wonnacott/Wonnacott text. Its features include:

■ *Crossword Puzzles*
An innovative way to reinforce important new terminology.

■ *Chapter Highlights*
A useful refresher for exam preparation.

■ *Answers to Text Questions*
Approximately half the end-of-chapter questions from the text are answered here.

■ *Self-Test Questions and Exercises*
An opportunity to monitor your own progress throughout the course.

The *Study Guide* is available through your campus or local bookstore. Please refer to ISBN 0-07-551007-3. If the item is not in stock, it can be ordered by the bookstore manager.

■ ■ ■

Summary of Contents

Contents

■ ■

PART 3 THE MANAGEMENT OF AGGREGATE DEMAND

PART 4   AGGREGATE SUPPLY: THEORY AND POLICY ISSUES

PART 5   THREE GREAT MACROECONOMIC CONTROVERSIES

■ ■ ■

Preface

■ ■

TO THE STUDENT

Economics is like the music of Mozart. On one level, it holds great simplicity: Its basic ideas can be quickly grasped by those who first encounter it. On the other hand, below the surface, there are fascinating subtleties that remain a challenge—even to those who spend a lifetime in its study. Therefore, we hold out this promise: In this introductory study, you will learn a great deal about how the economy works—the basic principles governing economic life that must be recognized by those in government and business who make policy decisions. At the same time, we also can promise that you won't be able to master it all. You should be left with an appreciation of the difficult and challenging problems of economics that remain unsolved.

HOW TO USE THIS BOOK

Our objective has been to make the basic propositions of economics as easy as possible to grasp. As each new topic is encountered, essential definitions are printed in coloured type and key steps in the argument are emphasized with boldface type. These highlights should be studied carefully during the first reading and during later review. (A glossary is provided at the end of the book. It contains a list of definitions of terms used in this text plus other common economics terms that you may encounter in class or in readings.) The basic ideas of each chapter and new concepts that are introduced are summarized in the Key Points section at the end of the chapter.

When you read a chapter for the first time, concentrate on the main text. Don't worry about the boxes, which are optional. They are set aside from the text to keep the main text as simple and straightforward as possible. The boxes fall into two broad categories: First are the boxes that provide levity or colour—for example, Kurt Vonnegut's tale in Box 38-2 of the Handicapper General whose aim is to ensure that people will not only start out equal but also finish that way. Second are the boxes that present detailed theoretical explanations that are not needed to grasp the main ideas in the text. If you want to glance at the boxes that are fun and easy to read, fine. But when you first read a chapter, don't worry about those that contain more difficult material. On the first reading, you also may skip starred (*) sections of the text, along with the footnotes and appendices; these also tend to be more difficult.

Economics is not a spectator sport. You cannot learn just from observation; you must work at it. When you have finished reading a chapter, work on the problems listed at the end; they are designed to reinforce your understanding of important concepts. [The starred (*) problems either are based on material in a box, or are more difficult questions designed to provide a challenge to students who want to do more advanced work.] Because each chapter builds on preceding ones and because the solution to some of the problems depends on those that came before it, remember this important rule: Don't fall behind in a problem-solving course. To help you keep up, we recommend the *Study Guide* (Third Canadian Edition), which is specifically designed to assist you in working through each chapter. It should be available in your bookstore.

TO THE INSTRUCTOR

The starting point of this book is the U.S. edition of *Economics* by Paul Wonnacott and Ronald Wonnacott. As we have revised and updated the text, we have continued to keep in mind the two major questions (posed in earlier editions) that have long concerned us as teachers of introductory economics.

For *macroeconomics*, what we asked ourselves was this: After studying introductory economics, are students able to understand public controversies over such topics as the level of government spending, taxation, and debt; the relation between inflation and unemployment; and the interdependence between U.S. and Canadian interest rates and monetary policies? Are we training our students to understand the front pages of the newspaper?

For many years, the introductory course was aimed at teaching students how policy should be run; that is, at providing a cookbook of "right" answers. In our exposition, we emphasize instead a balanced treatment of conflicting approaches and conclusions, so as to impress on the student that, in many areas, there is still great uncertainty about what policies should be pursued.

In this edition, the material on macroeconomics has been somewhat reorganized. Following an introduction to national income accounting and other basic macroeconomic concepts, the main discussion of macroeconomic theory and policy is contained in Parts 3, 4, and 5. Part 3 deals with issues in aggregate demand management and focuses on the relative effectiveness of monetary and fiscal policies in different circumstances. In Part 4 we discuss aggregate supply problems, including the unemployment-inflation trade-off, and the determinants of productivity growth in both advanced and developing countries. Part 5, finally, discusses three long-standing macroeconomic controversies: (1) Should the policy makers attempt to fine-tune the economy, or would we be better off if they followed stable policy rules? (2) What methods can be used to improve our ability to deal with the inflation-unemployment dilemma; in particular, should we use wage and price controls for this purpose? (3) What have been the problems of the international monetary system, and should we attempt to reform it?

While there are no simple, indisputably "correct" answers to the great macroeconomic questions, we believe that the major issues can be presented clearly to beginning economics students, thereby providing them with an understanding of important, recurring public debates over macroeconomic policy.

For *microeconomics*, what we asked ourselves was this: Does the introductory study of microeconomics lack coherence? To the student, does microeconomics tend to become merely one thing after another — a guided tour through the economist's workshop, introducing as many polished pieces of analytical machinery as possible for later use in more advanced courses? Most students do not continue to advanced economics courses. For them, there is little point in concentrating on analytical techniques for their own sake, when time could be spent studying interesting policy issues instead. Even though a comprehensive survey of techniques may give a head start to those students who do continue in economics, it also increases the risk that they will be bored by repetition, and will miss some of the forest while concentrating on the trees. Therefore, in deciding which analytical concepts to emphasize, we have followed a simple rule of thumb: focus on those most useful in studying policy issues.

In the Third Canadian Edition, as in the first two, we have attempted to make microeconomics more interesting by organizing our discussion in Parts 6 to 9 around two continuing themes: efficiency and equity. In Parts 6 and 7, we provide the analytical foundation, leading up to the discussion of the efficiency of a system of competitive markets, and the problems introduced by monopoly and oligopoly. In this discussion we emphasize the interpretation of the demand curve as a marginal benefit curve and the supply curve as a marginal cost curve. In emphasizing marginal concepts, we have tried to give students an appreciation of the meaning of allocative efficiency — why it is desirable to produce the goods that consumers demand. But we have tried to show also why it is not the last word. In particular, we believe that it is possible for first-year students to grasp fairly easily what many in the past discovered only in a graduate school: There is a different efficient solution for each income distribution; hence, a solution that is efficient is not necessarily "best."

In Part 8, we deal with a set of microeconomic policy issues that relate primarily to efficiency: regulation of business and the environment (including anti-pollution laws, and health and safety regulations); the efficient exploitation of natural resources; the provision of public goods; and the problems and opportunities of international trade policy, both at the multilateral and bilateral levels. In Part 9, the emphasis is on equity: We discuss how the returns to factors of production and the distribution of income are determined, and how policies may be designed to reduce inequality and fight poverty. But, of course, the issues of efficiency and equity are interrelated. In our discussion of efficiency in Parts 7 and 8, we show how policies that are primarily aimed at improving efficiency (such as the allocation of property rights in a common property resource) also may influence income distribution and, thus, equity; and, in Part 9, we discuss how policies that are intended primarily to improve equity (such as social assistance programs) also may have side effects on efficiency.

Thus, the most important objective we set ourselves in our discussion of both macroeconomics and microeconomics is to provide students with an understanding of *current policy issues*. Our second objective is to meet the challenge of providing comprehensive and relatively rigorous coverage of the many topics that may be introduced in an introductory course, without making the basic material in the book too difficult for the average student. To accomplish this, we have continued to keep the exposition of the main ideas in the text as simple and systematic as possible. (To reinforce the text, key ideas are repeated frequently in the captions that accompany the illustrations.) Thus, we believe that we have made it relatively easy for most students to understand the fundamental concepts. The more demanding material, which appears in the appendices, the optional boxes, and the starred (*) sections, can be used by the instructor to provide a further challenge to particularly well-prepared and ambitious students.

OTHER POINTS OF INTEREST

Finally, we draw your attention to a number of ways in which our treatment differs from that of many other texts and also to some changes that we have made in this edition.

■ In the preparation of any Canadian economics text, an important issue that must be faced is how to incorporate the material on international economic relations. It could be discussed all in one section (for a more unified treatment), or the interplay between domestic and international factors may be discussed throughout the book (to reflect the fact that, in virtually all policy discussions in Canada, the repercussions of policies on international economic relations must be taken into account). We have chosen the second alternative, because we felt that almost no Canadian policy issue can be adequately discussed without taking international repercussions into account.

As in previous Canadian editions, much of the core material on international trade and finance is contained in three chapters: Chapter 14 in the macroeconomics half, which deals with exchange rates, the balance of payments, and stabilization policy and, in the microeconomics half, Chapters 33 and 34, which deal with the gains from trade and international trade policy, respectively. (The trade policy chapter has been extensively rewritten to reflect both the 1988 Canada-United States Free Trade Agreement and the multilateral issues under the Uruguay Round of trade negotiations.) In this edition we have introduced a new chapter that deals with (1) the question of how the international monetary system should be organized, and (2) the LDC debt crisis of the 1980s.

In addition to these chapters, the text incorporates international material throughout both the macro and micro halves. For example, we discuss how Canada's high marginal propensity to import influences the value of the investment multiplier (Chapter 10); the effect of Bank of Canada foreign currency transactions on the money supply and the role of foreign interest rates and exchange rates in influencing Canadian monetary policy; and the problem of dealing with import prices when designing a program of wage and price controls in Canada. In Parts 8 and 9, the role of foreign capital in Canada is discussed in relation to the determination of the return to capital in general (Chapter 37). In Chapter 30, our treatment of pollution includes an examination of transboundary pollution, in the form of acid rain and water pollution in the Great Lakes basin.

Furthermore, we have added to the international content in this edition by including a lengthy section on productivity growth in developing countries (with emphasis on the ''success stories'' of the newly industrializing countries in Southeast Asia), as well as a number of short sections (identified by the words ''Living in a Global Economy'' in the headings) that give non-North American illustrations of various economic principles discussed in the text.

■ In emphasizing efficiency and the gains from specialization, we continue to give more than usual attention to economies of scale. In Chapters 3 and 33, economies of scale are given billing almost equal to comparative advantage in explaining the efficiency effects of specialization and trade; also, in Chapter 34 we emphasize the potential gains from exploitation of scale economies as an important reason for Canada to enter into a free trade agreement with the United States.

Economies of scale are especially important for a small country such as Canada, and the topic should not be avoided because of the difficult analytical problems that it raises at a more advanced level.

■ As noted above, the discussion of macroeconomic policy has been substantially reorganized and now contains separate sections dealing with issues relating to aggregate demand and aggregate supply. Because two new chapters have been added, it has been possible to provide a fuller discussion of some important issues (the theory and policy of relating to the unemployment-inflation trade-off—including a brief introduction to the idea of rational expectations—the organization of the international monetary system, and the LDC debt crisis) that were given only brief treatment in earlier editions.

■ The functions of capital markets and their institutions, and the problem of financial instability, are often given very brief treatment in introductory texts. As in previous editions, we deal with these issues in some detail in several places: in the discussion of business finance in Chapter 23; in the treatment of the functioning and regulation of the monetary system in Chapters 11 and 12; and in our discussion in Chapter 20 of the breakdown of the international gold standard in the interwar period. (Many students are fascinated by the gold standard. Like most economists, we don't believe that proposals to go back to the gold standard should be taken seriously. But we also believe it is important that students of economics know why.)

■ Substantial changes have also been made in the microeconomics half of the book. The material on different forms of business organization and capital markets that previously appeared in the introductory Part 1 of the book now has been moved to Part 6, immediately before the chapters on the costs of production and competitive supply. The result is a more complete integration of the theory of the firm with a discussion of the institutional environment in which real-world firms operate. Another change is that the material on health and safety regulations and on anti-pollution legislation has been put together in a new chapter (Chapter 30), providing a more unified treatment of various types of government regulation to protect our quality of life. There is also a fairly detailed discussion of Canada's recently revamped competition legislation in Chapter 29, which now is devoted mainly to various aspects of competition policy.

■ Should indifference curves be introduced in the main text discussion of consumer theory? We are of two minds on this matter. On the one hand, we share the view that the indifference-curve derivation of an individual demand curve provides the most intellectually satisfying basis for the later interpretation of market demand curves as marginal benefit curves. But, on the other hand, the indifference-curve derivation tends to be cumbersome and is not, in our view, strictly necessary to justify this interpretation. As a compromise, we have put the discussion of indifference curves in the appendix to Chapter 22. Moreover, and more importantly—in an application not typically attempted in a book at this level—we use indifference curves (in an appendix to Chapter 26) to demonstrate the efficiency of perfect competition. However, we also illustrate this result more simply in the text itself, using supply and demand curves.

■ As in the previous edition, we show how conflicts can exist not only between objectives such as equity and efficiency, but also between groups of people in the economy. For example, the main result from the theory of comparative advantage is that foreign trade can increase a nation's real income. But in explaining this result, we think it's important to go behind the scenes to emphasize how trade affects various groups differently: Low-cost imports benefit consumers, but they hurt competing domestic producers. It is easy for students to identify such winners and losers. They thereby can appreciate the irony of complaints about agricultural price supports from business executives who benefit from tariffs that prop up the prices of the goods they produce. Moreover, this identification of different groups — and the differences in their political power — helps the student to answer one of the basic questions raised by the theory of public choice: Why is there a difference between what the government should do, and what it does do?

■ ■ ■

WE WISH TO THANK . . .

In developing this book, and earlier editions, we have been helped by many friends and colleagues with whom we have had discussions over the year about Canadian economic problems and policy. Though we cannot list them all, we wish to acknowledge our indebtedness to them. Several persons also helped by commenting on parts of the manuscript or by providing information on specific matters relating to Canadian institutions and policy. They are:

Ronald Bodkin	University of Ottawa
Michael Bradfield	Dalhousie University
Jim Brander	University of British Columbia
Kevin Burley	University of Western Ontario
Thomas F. Chambers	Canadore College
Avi J. Cohen	York University
Thomas Courchene	University of Western Ontario
Jim Davies	University of Western Ontario
Don Gilchrist	University of Saskatchewan
Hugh Grant	University of Winnipeg
Christopher Green	McGill University
Morley Gunderson	University of Toronto
Jim Hatch	University of Western Ontario
Stephen Hemphill	McLeod, Young and Weir, Ltd.
Paul B. Huber	Dalhousie University
Derek Hum	University of Manitoba
Ernie Jacobson	Northern Alberta Institute of Technology
Susan Johnson	University of Western Ontario
Susan Kamp	University of Alberta
Edward Ketchum	Health and Welfare Canada
Harvey B. King	University of Regina
David Laidler	University of Western Ontario
John McDougall	University of Western Ontario
Gary McMahon	Laurentian University
John Palmer	University of Western Ontario
Michael Parkin	University of Western Ontario
Tom Powrie	University of Alberta
David Robinson	Laurentian University
Gideon Rosenbluth	University of British Columbia
Ron Shearer	University of British Columbia
Ian Skaith	Fanshawe College
Larry Smith	University of Waterloo
Maurice Tugwell	Acadia University
Jack Vermeeren	The Royal Bank
Tom Wilson	University of Toronto
Ron Wirick	University of Western Ontario
Hugh Young	Department of Finance, Ottawa

Furthermore, we would like to acknowledge the research assistance provided by Ken Stanton. We also are grateful to the editorial and production staff at McGraw-Hill Ryerson in Toronto. In particular, we would like to thank Jackie Kaiser, Carol Altilia, and freelance editor Edie Franks.

Åke Blomqvist
Paul Wonnacott
Ron Wonnacott
London, Ontario, and
College Park, Maryland

Part 1

■ ■

Basic Economic Concepts

Chapter 1

■ ■

Economic Problems and Economic Goals

Economy is the art of making the most out of
life.
George Bernard Shaw

Some years ago, a Japanese mass circulation newspaper, the *Mainichi*, conducted a survey of 4000 people, asking them what they thought of first when they heard the word *takai* (high). Twelve percent responded, "Mount Fuji." The overwhelming majority — 88% — said: "Prices."

In Canada, economic issues have played a crucial role in recent federal elections. In 1979, the victory of Joe Clark's Conservatives could be explained in large part by the hostility that the Liberals' energy policy had created in the Western provinces, and by public disappointment with the failure of their anti-inflation policy (the rate of inflation was 9.2% in 1979). After only nine months, Clark's government fell when its budget was defeated in Parliament, largely because of its proposed increases in the prices of gas and oil. And when the Conservatives won a landslide victory over the Liberals in 1984, the record-high unemployment rate that had prevailed in 1982/83 was an important factor in explaining the massive swing in the popular vote. Finally, the 1988 election in which the Mulroney government won its second majority was almost completely dominated by a single economic question: Whether or not Canada should enter into a free trade agreement with the United States. Issues, such as the cost of living and the security of their jobs are of immediate concern to almost all Canadians. With the rare exception of the individual who inherits great wealth, most of us spend a large part of our energy in the struggle to make a living.

In the words of Alfred Marshall, a great teacher and scholar of a century ago, "economics is a study of mankind in the ordinary business of life."

Under this broad definition, economics addresses many specific questions. To list but a few:

■ Why is it so difficult to get a job at some times, and so easy at others?

■ What jobs will be available when we finish university? What will they pay?

■ What determines the relative prices of goods? Why is water cheap, even though it is necessary to life itself? Why are diamonds expensive, even though they are an unessential luxury?

■ Will continued economic growth cause the destruction of our natural environment?

■ Why has the value of the Canadian dollar fallen so low relative to the U.S. dollar?

■ What are the long-term consequences of large deficits in the federal government's budget?

■ Why did our economy produce so much more in 1988 than in 1948?

Economics is a study of success, and it is a study of failure.

ECONOMIC PROGRESS

From the vantage point of our comfortable homes of the late twentieth century, it is easy for us to forget how many people, throughout history, have been losers in the struggle to make a living. Unvarnished economic history is the story of deprivation, of 80-hour work weeks, of child labour—and of starvation. But, it is also the story of the slow climb of civilization toward the goal

3

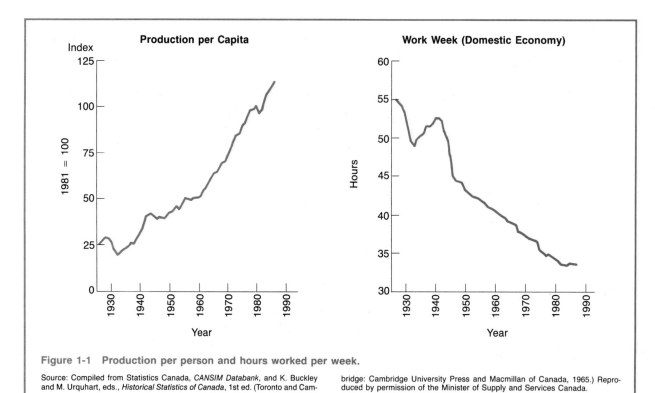

Figure 1-1 **Production per person and hours worked per week.**

Source: Compiled from Statistics Canada, *CANSIM Databank*, and K. Buckley and M. Urquhart, eds., *Historical Statistics of Canada*, 1st ed. (Toronto and Cambridge: Cambridge University Press and Macmillan of Canada, 1965.) Reproduced by permission of the Minister of Supply and Services Canada.

of relative affluence, where the average person as well as the fortunate few can have a reasonable degree of material well-being and leisure.

One of the most notable features of the Canadian economy has been its growth. Although there have been interruptions and setbacks, economic progress has been remarkable. Figure 1-1 shows one of the standard measures of success—the increase in total production per person. (The measure of production in this diagram is gross domestic product, or GDP for short. This concept will be explained in Chapter 6.) The average Canadian now produces nearly three times as much as the average Canadian of 1945, and more than five times as much as the average Canadian at the turn of the century. Furthermore, the higher output is produced with less effort. The average work week has declined by almost 40% since 1926. Thus, economic progress in Canada has been reflected both in an increase in the goods and services that we produce and enjoy, and in a greater amount of leisure time.

A similar tale of success has occurred in many other countries, as illustrated in Figure 1-2. Between 1960 and 1986, output grew at an average annual rate of 3.3% in the United States, 3.9% in France, 3.3% in Germany,

and 3.7% in Italy. Nor has growth been confined to the countries of Europe and North America. Particularly notable has been the growth of the Japanese economy. From the ashes of the Second World War, Japan has emerged as one of the leading nations. As a result of a rapid growth averaging 6.7% per year between 1960 and 1987, Japan now ranks with Switzerland, the United States, Canada, and Norway as one of the highest income countries in the world.[1] Other stories of success have come from the middle income countries of East Asia, such as South Korea, Hong Kong, and Singapore.

■ ■ ■ ■ ■

[1] The success of the Japanese economy has made that country the subject of good-natured humour. In a lecture, U.S. economist Paul McCracken of the University of Michigan recalled that on his first trip to Japan in the fifties, he had gone to offer the Japanese advice on economic growth policy. Added McCracken, ''I've been trying to remember ever since what we told them.''

There are substantial problems in comparing output per person in various countries. See Irving *B*. Kravis and others, *A System of International Comparisons of Gross Product and Purchasing Power*, United Nations International Comparison Project: Phase One (Baltimore: Johns Hopkins University Press, 1975), p. 231.

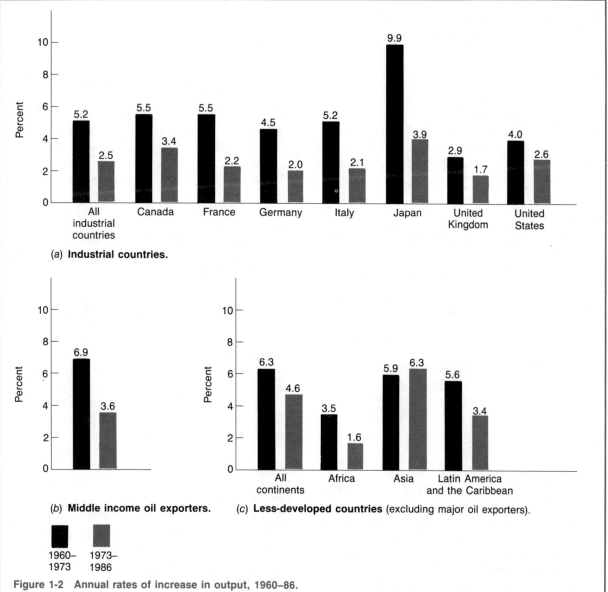

Figure 1-2   Annual rates of increase in output, 1960–86.

Growth has been rapid in many countries. Growth was particularly fast in Japan between 1960 and 1973, when output increased at an average annual rate of 9.9%. Note that for most countries, growth slowed down after 1973 — with the rapidly developing economies of Asia being an exception.

The slower growth may be traced in part to the disruptions caused by the rapid increase in the price of oil.

Source: Compiled from data in International Monetary Fund (IMF), *Annual Report*, 1984, pp. 32–34; IMF, *Annual Report*, 1987, pp. 43–46.

ECONOMIC PROBLEMS

Although rapid growth has occurred in many countries, it has been neither universal nor automatic. In a number of countries, the standard of living remains abysmally low, with an average income per person of less than $300 *per year*. The World Bank—an international institution whose major purpose is to lend to the less developed countries (LDCs) — estimates that, between 1965 and 1986, output per person rose at an average annual rate of only 1.25% in the 30 poorest countries (excluding

China). The record is even bleaker in the poorest of the poor, where the increase in population has outrun the increase in production, and output per person has actually declined.[2] In the large cities of Asia, Latin America, and Africa, millions of people are crowded together in makeshift housing, with barely enough income to feed themselves and with little access to things like basic health care and education for their children. Many have moved there to escape even worse poverty in the countryside.

Even in a relatively prosperous country, such as Canada, substantial economic problems remain. For example, we may wonder:

- Why are so many unable to find work, when so much needs to be done?

- Why do pockets of poverty remain in an affluent society?

- Why have prices kept marching upward?

- Why is the average income so much lower in the Atlantic provinces than in the rest of Canada?

- Are we really producing the right things? Should we produce more housing and fewer cars? Or more medical services and fewer sports spectaculars?

- Why is pollution such a problem? What should be done about it?

ECONOMIC POLICY

Why? and *What should be done?* are the two key questions in economics. The ultimate objective of economics is to *develop policies to deal with our problems.* However, before we can formulate policies, we must first try to understand how the economy has worked in the past, and how it works today. Otherwise, well-intentioned policies may go astray and lead to unforeseen and unfortunate consequences.

When economic policies are studied, the centre of attention is usually the policies of the government—policies, such as taxation, government spending programs, international trade policy, and the regulation of particular industries, such as telephone companies, airlines, and railroads. However, the policies of private businesses are also important. How should they organize production in order to make their goods at the lowest possible cost? What prices should a business charge? When should

a supermarket increase the stocks of goods in its warehouse?

The Controversial Role of Government

For more than two hundred years, economics has been dominated by controversy over the proper role of government. In what circumstances should government take an active role? When is it best for government to leave decisions to the private participants in the economy? On this topic, the giants of economics have repeatedly met to do battle.

In 1776, Scottish scholar **Adam Smith** published his pathbreaking book, *An Inquiry into the Nature and Causes of the Wealth of Nations.*[3] Modern economics may be dated from that year. Smith's message was clear: Private markets should be liberated from the tyranny of government control. In pursuit of their private interests, individual producers would make the goods that consumers want. It is not, said Smith, "from the benevolence of the butcher, the brewer, or the baker that we expect our dinner, but from their regard to their own interest." There is an "invisible hand," he wrote, that causes the producer to promote the interests of society. Indeed, "by pursuing his own interest he frequently promotes that of the society more effectually than when he really intends to promote it." In general, said Smith, the government should be cautious in interfering with the operations of the private market.

According to Smith, the best policy is generally one of *laissez-faire* — leave it alone. Government intervention usually makes things worse. For example, government imposition of a tariff is generally harmful. (A tariff or duty is a tax on a foreign-produced good as it enters the country.) Even though a tariff generally helps domestic producers who are thereby given an advantage over foreign producers, the country as a whole loses. Specifically, a tariff increases the cost of goods available to consumers, and this cost to consumers outweighs the benefits to producers. Smith's work has been refined and modified during the past 200 years, but many of his laissez-faire conclusions have stood up remarkably well. For example, there is still a very strong economic argument against high tariffs on imported goods. In recent decades, one of the principal areas of international coop-

---

■ ■ ■ ■ ■
[2] World Bank, *World Development Report 1988*, pp. 222–23.

■ ■ ■ ■ ■
[3] Available in Modern Library edition (New York: Random House, 1937). Smith's book is commonly referred to as *The Wealth of Nations.*

eration has been the negotiation of lower tariffs and, in the late 1980s, this argument was an important reason why Canada decided to enter into an agreement with the United States to eliminate all tariffs on trade between the two countries by 1999.

However, during the Great Depression of the 1930s —a century and a half after the appearance of *The Wealth of Nations*—the laissez-faire tradition in economics came under attack. In 1936, *John Maynard Keynes* published his *General Theory of Employment, Interest and Money* (also known, more simply, as the *General Theory*). In this book, Keynes (which rhymes with Danes) argued that the government has the duty to intervene in the economy, to put the unemployed back to work. Of the several ways in which this could be done, one stood out in its simplicity. By building public works,, such as roads, post offices, and dams, the government could provide jobs directly, and thus provide a cure for the Depression.

With his proposals for a more active role for government, Keynes drew the ire of many businessmen. They feared that, as a result of his recommendations, the government would become larger and larger and private enterprise would gradually be pushed out of the picture. But, Keynes did not foresee this result. He believed that, by providing jobs, the government could remove the explosive frustrations caused by the mass unemployment of the 1930s, and could make it possible for Western political and economic institutions to survive. His objective was to modify our economic system and make it better. Unlike Karl Marx, he did not believe that the system would have to be destroyed and replaced by a different one in order to solve these problems. (For a brief introduction to the revolutionary ideas of Marx, see Box 1-1.)[4]

Thus, Smith and Keynes took apparently contradictory positions — Smith arguing for less government, and Keynes for more.[5] It is possible, of course, that each was

right. Perhaps the government should do more in some respects, and less in others. Economic analysis does not lead inevitably either to an activist position or to a passive, laissez-faire stance on the part of the government. The economist's rallying cry should not be, ''Do something.'' Rather, it should be, ''Think first.''

ECONOMIC GOALS

We have already noted that the ultimate goal of economics is to develop better policies to minimize our problems and to maximize the benefits from our daily toil. More specifically, there is widespread agreement that we should strive for the following goals:

1. *A low rate of unemployment*. People willing to work should be able to find jobs reasonably quickly. Widespread unemployment is demoralizing and it represents an economic waste. Society forgoes the goods and services that the unemployed could have produced.
2. *Price stability*. It is desirable to avoid rapid increases — or decreases — in the average level of prices.
3. *Efficiency*. When we work, we want to get as much as we reasonably can out of our productive efforts.
4. *An equitable distribution of income*. When many live in affluence, no group of citizens should suffer stark poverty.
5. *Growth*. Continuing growth, which would make possible an even higher standard of living in the future, is generally considered an important objective.

The list is far from complete. Not only do we want to produce more, but we want to do so without the degradation of our environment; the *reduction of pollution* is important. *Economic freedom* — the right of people to choose their own occupations, to enter contracts, and to spend their incomes as they please—is a desirable goal. So, too, is *economic security* — freedom from the fear that chronic illness or other catastrophe will place an individual or a family in a desperate financial situation. The objective of economic security has played a large and increasingly important part in Canadian policy in the last few decades.

Another long-standing (but more controversial) goal is more *economic independence*. Some people feel that

---

■ ■ ■ ■ ■

[4] Throughout this book, the boxes present illustrative and supplementary materials. They can be disregarded without losing the main thread of the discussion.

[5] Conflicting views over the proper role of government may be found in the works of two retired professors: the University of Chicago's Milton Friedman (for laissez-faire) and Harvard's John Kenneth Galbraith (who argues for more government). See John Kenneth Galbraith, *The Affluent Society* (Boston: Houghton Mifflin, 1958), and Milton Friedman and Rose Friedman, *Free to Choose* (New York: Har-

court Brace Jovanovich, 1980). (We strongly recommend that if you read one of these books, you read them both. Each of the books puts forth a convincing case. Nevertheless, they are flatly contradictory.)

Box 1-1

■ ■ ■ ■ ■ ■ ■ ■ ■ ■ ■ ■ ■ ■ ■ ■ ■ ■ ■ ■

Karl Marx

The main text refers to two towering economists — Adam Smith and John Maynard Keynes. In the formation of the intellectual heritage of most British and North American economists, Smith and Keynes have played leading roles. But, if we consider the intellectual heritage of the world as a whole, Karl Marx is probably the most influential economist of all. The current economic systems in a number of countries — most notably, the Soviet Union and China — were founded on Marx's theories.

Many business executives viewed Keynes as a revolutionary because he openly attacked accepted economic opinion and proposed fundamental changes in economic policy. But, by revolutionary standards, Keynes pales beside Marx. The Marxist call to revolution was shrill and direct: "Workers of the world, unite! You have nothing to lose but your chains."

Why did they have nothing to lose? Because, said Marx, workers are responsible for the production of all goods. Labour is the sole source of value. But, workers get only part of the fruits of their labour. A large — and in Marx's view, unjustified — share goes to the exploiting class of capitalists. (Capitalists are the owners of factories, machinery, and other equipment.) Marx believed that, by taking up arms and overthrowing capitalism, workers could end exploitation and obtain their rightful rewards.

On our main topic — the role of government — Marx was strangely ambivalent. Who would own the factories and machines once the communist revolution had eliminated the capitalist class? Ownership by the state — by all the workers as a group — was the obvious solution. And, in fact, this has been the path taken by countries, such as the Soviet Union: The revolution has led to state ownership of the means of production. Yet, Marx also believed that the revolution would eventually lead to the "withering away" of the state. There has been no perceptible sign of this withering away in Marxist societies.

Courtesy of Canapress Photo Service

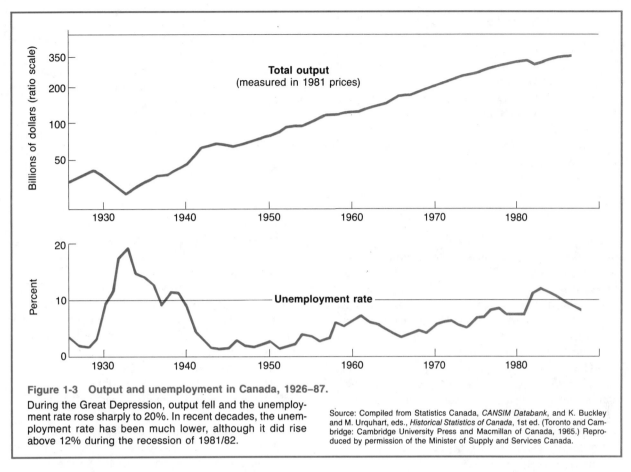

Figure 1-3 Output and unemployment in Canada, 1926–87.
During the Great Depression, output fell and the unemployment rate rose sharply to 20%. In recent decades, the unemployment rate has been much lower, although it did rise above 12% during the recession of 1981/82.

Source: Compiled from Statistics Canada, *CANSIM Databank*, and K. Buckley and M. Urquhart, eds., *Historical Statistics of Canada*, 1st ed. (Toronto and Cambridge: Cambridge University Press and Macmillan of Canada, 1965.) Reproduced by permission of the Minister of Supply and Services Canada.

too many decisions which affect the welfare of Canadians are made by foreign firms and that increased control by Canadians over our own economy is an important objective.

The achievement of our economic goals provides the principal focus of this book. As a background for later chapters, let's look at the major goals in more detail.

1. A Low Rate of Unemployment

The importance of the objective of full employment was illustrated most clearly during the Great Depression of the 1930s, when Canada and many other countries conspicuously failed to achieve it. During the sharp contraction from 1929 to 1933, total output in Canada fell by 30% and spending for new buildings, machinery, and equipment declined by more than 85%. As the economy slid downward, more and more workers were thrown out of jobs. By 1933, almost 20% of the labour force was unemployed. (See Figure 1-3.) Long lines of the jobless gathered at factory gates in the hope of work;

disappointment was their common fate. Nor was the problem quickly solved. The downward slide into the depths of the Depression went on for a period of four years, and the road back to a high level of employment was even longer. It was not until the beginning of the 1940s, when our industry began working around the clock to produce weapons and war materials, that many of the unemployed were able to find jobs. During the decade 1931–1940 unemployment averaged above 11% of the labour force in every year except one.

A *depression* exists when there is a very high rate of unemployment over a long period of time.

Something had clearly gone wrong — disastrously wrong. Large-scale unemployment represents tremendous waste; time lost in involuntary idleness is gone forever. The costs of unemployment go beyond the loss of output; unemployment involves the dashing of hopes. Those unable to find work suffer frustration and a sense of worthlessness, and their skills are lost as they remain idle.

The term **unemployed** is reserved for those who are willing and able to work, but are unable to find jobs. Thus, those of you who are full-time university students are not included among the unemployed. Your immediate task is to get an education, not a job. Similarly, the 70-year-old retiree is not included in the statistics of the unemployed. Nor are those in prisons or mental institutions, since they are not available for jobs.

A person is *unemployed* if he or she is available and looking for work, but has not found it.

The unemployment rate is calculated as a percentage of the total labour force — the labour force being the sum of those who are actually employed, plus those who are unemployed. (Labour force and employment statistics are tied to the traditional definition of "jobs." Thus, for example, a mother who stays at home to raise her children is neither "in the labour force" nor "employed," although she certainly works.)

At the end of the Second World War, the Great Depression was still a fresh memory. The public, the politician, and the economist shared a common determination that a repeat of the 1930s could not be permitted. And, so far, we have been largely successful in our efforts to prevent a repetition of the prolonged period of very high unemployment of the 1930s.

But, the postwar years have certainly not been an unbroken story of success. From time to time, there have been downturns in the economy — much more moderate, it is true, than the slide of 1929 to 1933, but downward movements nonetheless. These more moderate declines, or **recessions**, have often been accompanied by a substantial increase in the unemployment rate. In December 1982, during the worst recession of the past four decades, the unemployment rate rose to a peak of 12.9%. While we have been successful in preventing big depressions, the problem of periodic recessions has not been solved.

A *recession* is a general slowdown of economic activity, usually involving a decline in total output, income, and employment, lasting six months or more, and marked by contractions in many sectors of the economy. (The slowdown is not confined to just one or two industries,, such as forest products or car manufacturing.)

2. Stability of the Average Price Level

During the Depression of the 1930s, unemployment was the overwhelming problem, and in the first half of the 1980s joblessness once again became the dominant economic issue. But, during the late 1970s, **inflation** became a severe problem; following the economy's recovery from the 1982 recession, the re-emergence of inflationary pressures again became a concern in the late 1980s.

Inflation is an increase in the average level of prices. (Deflation is a fall in the average level of prices.)

Observe in Figure 1-4 how the average of prices paid by consumers has risen through most of our recent history, with the period 1920–33 being a notable exception. Prices rose most rapidly after World War I and, for a brief period, after World War II. Between 1973 and 1981, inflation was unusually severe for peacetime periods. (Details on how to draw and interpret diagrams may be found in the appendix to this chapter and in the Study Guide which accompanies this text.)

While unemployment represents sheer waste — society loses the goods which might have been produced by those out of work — the problem with inflation is less obvious. When a price rises, there is both a winner and a loser. The loser is the buyer who has to pay more. However, there is a benefit to the seller, who gets more. On balance, it is not clear whether the society is better or worse off.

It is true, of course, that there is much resentment against inflation. But, perhaps at least some of this resentment reflects a peculiarity of human nature. When people find the goods they *sell* rising in price, they see the increase as perfectly right, normal, and justified. On the other hand, when they find the goods they *buy* rising in price, they often view the increase as evidence of the seller's greed. When the price of wheat rises, farmers see themselves at last getting a reasonable return from their toil. When the price of oil increases, the oil companies argue that they are getting no more than the return necessary to finance the search for more oil. When the price of books rises, authors feel that they are getting no more than a "just" return for their creative efforts and book publishers insist that they are no more than adequately compensated for their risks.

However, when the farmer, the oil company, the author, and the book publisher find that the prices of the

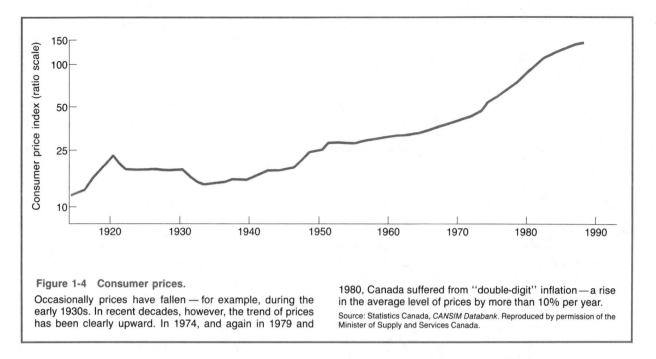

Figure 1-4   Consumer prices.

Occasionally prices have fallen — for example, during the early 1930s. In recent decades, however, the trend of prices has been clearly upward. In 1974, and again in 1979 and 1980, Canada suffered from "double-digit" inflation — a rise in the average level of prices by more than 10% per year.

Source: Statistics Canada, *CANSIM Databank*. Reproduced by permission of the Minister of Supply and Services Canada.

goods they buy have increased, they believe they have been cheated by inflation. We all may be the victims of an illusion — the illusion that each of us can and should have a rise in the price of what we sell, but that the price of what we buy should remain stable. For the economy as a whole, this is not possible.

This two-sided nature of price increases — a gain to the seller but a loss to the buyer — means that it is difficult to evaluate the dangers of inflation. Indeed, there has been considerable controversy as to whether a low rate of inflation (with prices increasing at a rate of, say, 2% or 3% per annum) is dangerous or whether, on the contrary, it may actually be beneficial to society. (Some say that a small rate of inflation makes it easier for the economy to adjust to changes and to maintain a high level of employment.)

However, when inflation gets beyond a moderate rate, there is widespread agreement that it becomes a menace. It becomes more than a mere transfer of money from the buyer to the seller; it interferes with the production and exchange of goods. This has most clearly been the situation during very rapid inflations, when economic activity was severely disrupted.

Hyperinflation — that is, a skyrocketing of prices at annual rates of 1000% or more — occurs most commonly during or soon after a military conflict, when government spending shoots upward; for example, in Germany during the early 1920s, in China during its Civil War in the late 1940s, and in the southern states during the U.S. Civil War. Hyperinflation means that money rapidly loses its ability to buy goods. People are anxious to spend money as quickly as possible while they can still get something for it.

Clearly, hyperinflation of 1000% or more per year is an extreme example. However, lower rates of inflation, amounting to 10% or less per year, can also have serious consequences:

1. Inflation hurts people living on fixed incomes and people who have saved fixed amounts of money for their retirement or for "a rainy day" (future illness or accident). The couple who put aside $1,000 in 1960 for retirement has suffered a rude shock. In 1988, $1,000 bought no more than $225 bought in 1960.

2. Inflation can cause business mistakes. For good decisions, businesses need an accurate picture of what is going on. When prices are rising rapidly, the picture becomes obscured and out of focus. Decision makers cannot see clearly. (For example, business accounting is done in dollar terms. When there is rapid inflation, some businesses may report profits but, using a more accurate calculation, they might actually be suffering losses. Consequently, inflation can temporarily hide

problems.) Our economy is complex. It depends on a continuous flow of accurate information. *Prices are an important link in the information chain.* For example, a high price should provide a signal to producers that consumers are especially anxious to get more of a particular product. But, in a severe inflation, producers find it difficult to know whether this is the message, or whether the price of their product is rising simply because all prices are rising. In brief, *a severe inflation obscures the message carried by prices.*

Here, it is important to distinguish between a rise in the **average level of prices** (inflation) and a change in *relative* prices. Even if the average level of prices were perfectly stable (that is, no inflation existed), some *individual* prices would still change as conditions change in specific markets. For example, new inventions have cut the cost of producing computers, and computer companies have as a result been able to cut prices sharply. At the same time, energy prices (for oil, gasoline, electricity, etc.) have risen substantially during the past 20 years in response to the sharp increases in the world price of oil that occurred in 1973 and 1979. The resulting fall in the price of computers relative to the price of oil has performed a useful function. It has encouraged consumers and businesses to use more of the relatively cheap computers and to conserve on the relatively expensive oil. (Of course, this is not to deny that the rise in the price of energy was painful, particularly to those living in the coldest areas of the country.)

3. Efficiency

This illustration—of how consumers and businesses use more computers when they become cheaper — is one example of **economic efficiency**.

In an economy, both the unemployment rate and the inflation rate may be very low, but performance may still be poor. For example, fully employed workers may be engaged in a lot of wasted effort and the goods being produced may not be those which are most needed. In this case, the economy is inefficient.

> *Efficiency* is the goal of getting the most out of our productive efforts.

Under this broad definition, two types of efficiency can be distinguished: **technological efficiency** and **allocative efficiency**.

To illustrate technological efficiency (also known as technical efficiency), let us consider two bicycle man-

ufacturers. One uses a large number of workers and many machines to produce 1000 bicycles. The other uses fewer workers and fewer machines to produce the same number of bicycles. The second manufacturer is not a magician; he is simply a better manager. He is technologically efficient, whereas the first manufacturer is not. Technological inefficiency exists when the same output could be produced with fewer machines and fewer workers, working at a reasonable pace. (Technological efficiency does not require a sweatshop.) Technological inefficiency involves wasted effort and sloppy management; better management is the solution.

Allocative efficiency, on the other hand, involves the production of the best combination of goods, using the lowest-cost combination of inputs. How much food should we produce, and how many houses? Suppose we produce only food, and do so in a technologically-efficient way, with no wasted effort. We will still not have achieved the goal of allocative efficiency, because consumers want both food and housing.

Or consider another question: How much newsprint should Canada produce, and how much wine? If we produce just enough of each to meet the demand of Canadian wine drinkers and newspaper readers, we will probably not reach allocative efficiency. A better solution would be to produce more newsprint and less wine, and then to trade newsprint for imported wine in the world market.

Thus, allocative efficiency involves the choice of the right combination of outputs. It also involves using the best (lowest-cost) combination of inputs. Consider our earlier illustration. The cost of computers is coming down while the cost of oil has risen. If businesses fail to adjust — that is, fail to conserve oil and to use computers more — then there is allocative inefficiency.

Relative prices perform a key role in encouraging allocative efficiency. As we have noted, the decrease in the price of computers encourages businesses to use more computers, and less of other relatively more expensive inputs. And low costs of producing newsprint in Canada encourages foreigners to buy paper from us, while we are encouraged to buy wine from Italy and Spain because of the low wine prices in those countries. While it is undesirable to have large changes in the *average* level of prices (inflation or deflation), changes in *relative* prices may perform a very useful function by encouraging businesses and consumers to conserve on scarce goods and use cheaper alternatives.

4. An Equitable Distribution of Income

Ours is an affluent society. Yet many people remain so poor that they have difficulty in buying the basic necessities of life,, such as food, clothing, and shelter. In the midst of plenty, some live in need. The moral question must then be faced: Should some people have so much, while others have so little?

When the question is put this way, the compelling answer must surely be no. Our sense of justice is offended by extreme differences, and compassion requires that assistance be given to those crushed by illness and to those born and raised in cruel deprivation.

Our sense of equity, or justice, is offended by extreme differences. Thus, most people think of *equity* as a move toward *equality*. But, not all the way. The two words are far from synonymous. While there is widespread agreement that the least fortunate should be helped, there is no consensus that the objective of society should be an equal income for all. Some individuals are willing to work overtime; it is generally recognized as both just and desirable for them to have a higher income as a consequence. Otherwise, why should they work longer hours? Similarly, it is generally considered "right" for the hardworking to have a larger share of the pie. After all, they have contributed more to the production of the pie in the first place.

There is no agreement on how far we should go toward complete equality of incomes. The "best" division (or *distribution*) of income is ill defined. Therefore, much of the discussion of income distribution has been focused on narrower questions,, such as: What is happening to those at the bottom of the ladder? What is happening to the families who live in poverty?

Poverty is difficult to define in precise dollar terms. For one thing, not everyone's needs are the same. The sickly have the greatest need for medical care. Large families have the most compelling need for food and clothing. Those who live in cities, where the costs of food and shelter are high, need a larger annual income to pay for basic necessities than do those who live on farms, where they can grow some of their own food. There is no simple, single measure of the "poverty line" below which families may be judged to be poor. Reasonable standards may, however, be established by taking into consideration such obvious complications as the number of individuals in a family. For example, the National Council of Welfare — a government advisory body—has defined poverty standards for families in large cities and rural areas. (See Table 1-1.)

There are two ways of raising people above the poverty line. The first is to increase the size of the national "pie." As the level of income rises throughout the economy, the incomes of those at the lower end will also generally rise. In the words of former U.S. President, John Kennedy, "A rising tide lifts all boats."

A second way to reduce poverty is to increase the share of the pie going to people with the lowest incomes. Thus, poverty may be combatted by a ***redistribution of income***. For example, the well-to-do may be taxed in order to finance government programs aimed at helping the poor.

Since World War II, the Canadian federal government has organized or helped finance many major programs designed to raise the incomes of poor families. During the 1960s and 1970s, these programs helped bring about a very substantial reduction in the number of people living in poverty. As Figure 1-5 shows, there was a steady decline in the percentage of Canada's population classified as poor, from over 35% in the early 1960s to a low of 12% in 1981. During 1982–84, under the influence of the deep 1981/82 recession, the percentage rose to as high as 14.5%. However, as the economy expanded in the later 1980s, the downward trend resumed and by 1987 the figure had fallen to 11.3%.

We are still far short of the objective of eliminating poverty. Why is this task so difficult?

One major reason is unemployment. As unemployment rates rose in the early 1980s, many of those who lost their jobs fell into poverty. Other possible explanations include the tendency for workers to retire early (at which time they tend to drop into the low income group), and the increased frequency of marriage breakdowns.

Table 1-1 Poverty Standards in Large Cities and Rural Areas, 1988 (Annual Family Income)

Number of people in the family	Large cities	Rural areas
1	$11,564	$ 8,553
2	15,258	11,178
3	20,411	14,967
4	23,521	17,303
5	27,408	20,120
6	29,935	21,966
7 or more	32,950	24,202

Source: 1988 Poverty Lines—Estimates by the National Council of Welfare (Ottawa: Minister of Supply and Services, 1988).

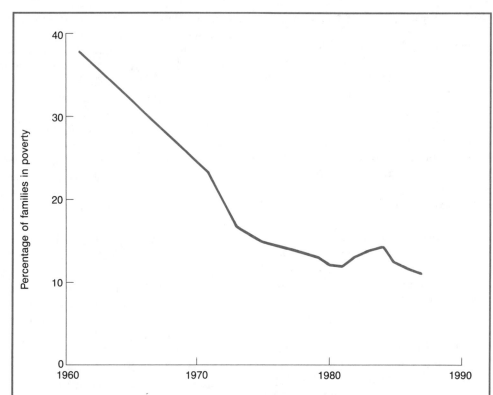

Figure 1-5   The percentage of the population living in poverty.

By Statistics Canada's poverty standard, the proportion of the population living in poverty declined substantially until 1981. Following an increase in the early 1980s, it fell again in 1985/86.

Source: Estimated by authors from data in F. Vaillancourt, *Income Distribution and Economic Security in Canada*, Vol. 1 (Toronto: University of Toronto Press in cooperation with the Royal Commission on the Economic Union and Development Prospects for Canada, 1985) and Statistic Canada, *Income Distribution by Size*, various years. (To account for a change in Statistics Canada's definition of poverty, we have raised earlier estimates relating to years before 1979 by 2.7 percentage points.)

When one family with an income above the poverty line splits up, it often creates a one-parent family (usually headed by the mother) with an income below the poverty line.

The design of policies to further reduce the extent of poverty remains a challenging problem.

5. Growth

In an economy with large-scale unemployment, output can be increased by putting the unemployed back to work. Slack in the economy can be reduced and productive capacity used more fully. Once the economy approaches its capacity, however, additional increases in output require an increase in the productive capacity itself. Capacity can be raised either by an addition to the available resources (for example, an increase in the number of factories and machines), or an improvement in technology (that is, the invention of new, more pro-

ductive machines or new ways of organizing production). When economists speak of growth, they typically mean an *increase in the productive capacity* of the economy that results from technological improvement and additional factories, machines, or other resources.

The advantages of growth are obvious. If the economy grows, our incomes will be higher in the future. We and our children will have higher standards of material comfort. Moreover, some of the rising production can be used to benefit the poor without reducing the incomes of the rich.

During the early 1960s, growth became a prominent national goal in most Western countries, both because of its economic advantages and because expansion of productive capacity was seen as an important part of Western security; the West had to "keep up with the Russians." During the late 1960s and early 1970s, doubts began to develop. While its advantages are obvious, growth comes at a cost. If we are to grow more rapidly, more of our current efforts will have to be directed toward the production of machines and away from the production of consumption goods. In the future, of course, as the new machines begin operating, they will turn out more consumption goods — more clothing, radios, or cars. Thus, current policies to stimulate growth will make possible higher consumption in the future. But, for the moment, consumption will be less. Thus, to evaluate a high growth policy, we have to compare the advantage of higher *future* consumption with the sacrifice of lower *current* consumption.

Seen in this light, it is not clear that the faster the rate of growth, the better. Why, for example, should I live modestly, just so my children may at some future date live in luxury? The future generations should be considered, but so should the present one.

Even if we were concerned solely with the welfare of coming generations, it would not be so clear that the more growth, the better. Increasing levels of production use increasing quantities of raw materials. A moderate rate of growth may be in the best interests of future generations because it allows us to conserve raw materials.

Furthermore, very rapid rates of growth may harm the environment. If our primary objective is to produce more and more newsprint, steel, and automobiles, we may pay too little heed to the belching smoke of the pulp and paper mills, to the pollution of our lakes and rivers, or to the effect of the automobile on the quality of the air we breathe. Thus, during the 1970s, there was less emphasis on growth than there had been during the early 1960s and more emphasis on other goals, such as preservation of the environment. In the late 1980s, new problems once more brought environmental protection to the forefront: the worsening of the acid rain situation, and the global threats posed by the depletion of the atmosphere's ozone layer and the warming of the earth's climate through the greenhouse effect.

INTERRELATIONSHIPS AMONG THE GOALS

The achievement of one goal may help in the achievement of others. As we have noted, growth may make it easier to solve the poverty problem. Additional income may be provided to the poor out of the growth in total income without reducing the income of those at the top. Thus, social conflicts over the share of the pie may be reduced if the size of the pie is increasing.

Similarly, the poverty problem is easier to solve if the unemployment rate is kept low, so that large numbers of unemployed do not swell the ranks of the poor. When goals are *complementary* like this (that is, when achieving one helps to achieve the other), economic policy making is relatively easy. By attacking on a broad front and striving for several goals, we can increase our chances of achieving each.

Unfortunately, however, economic goals are not always complementary. In many cases, they are in conflict. For example, when the unemployment problem is reduced, the inflation problem tends to get worse. There is a reason for this. Heavy purchasing by the public tends to reduce unemployment, but it also tends to increase inflation. It reduces unemployment because, as the public buys more cars, unemployed workers get jobs again in the auto factories; and when families buy more homes, construction workers find it easier to locate jobs. At the same time, heavy purchasing tends to increase inflation because producers are more likely to raise their prices if buyers are clamouring for their products.

Another example of such *conflicts among goals* in economic policy making is the relationship between efficiency and economic independence. Allocative efficiency in a relatively small economy, such as we have in Canada, requires a large amount of international trade and investment. But, there are many who feel that as our economic relations with foreign countries, particularly the United States, become more extensive, we will ultimately become too dependent on the policies and attitudes in those countries. The price of allocative efficiency may be a partial loss of Canada's political and economic independence. Such conflicts among goals test the wisdom of policy makers, and exacerbate the political controversies over economic policy.

A PREVIEW

These, then, are the five major objectives of economic policy: *low unemployment*, *price stability*, *efficiency*, an *equitable distribution of income*, and *growth*. The first two goals are related to the *stability* of the economy. If the economy is unstable, moving along like a roller coaster, its performance will be very unsatisfactory. As it heads downhill into recession, large numbers of people will be thrown out of work. Then, as it heads upward into a runaway boom, prices will soar as the public scrambles to buy the available goods. The first two goals may, therefore, be looked on as two aspects of a single objective: that of achieving an *equilibrium* with stable prices and a low unemployment rate. This will be the major topic in Parts 2, 3, 4, and 5 (Chapters 6 through 17) of this book.

Equilibrium is the first of three main "E's" of economics. The second E — *efficiency* — will be studied in Parts 6, 7, and 8 (Chapters 21 through 34). Are we getting the most out of our productive efforts? When does the free market — where buyers and sellers come together without government interference — encourage efficiency? Where the free market does not encourage efficiency, what (if anything) should be done?

Part 9 (Chapters 35 through 40) deals primarily with the third E — *equity*. If the government takes a laissez-faire attitude, how much income will go to workers? To the owners of land? To others? How do labour unions affect the incomes of their members? How can the government improve the lot of the poor? The final objective —growth—cuts across a number of other topics, and thus appears periodically throughout the book. However, before we get into the meat of policy issues, we must first set the stage with some of the basic concepts and tools of economics. To that task we now turn (in Chapters 2 through 5).

KEY POINTS

1. During the twentieth century, substantial economic progress has been made in Canada and many other countries. We are producing much more, even though we spend less time at work than did our grandparents.

2. Nevertheless, substantial economic problems remain: problems, such as poverty in the less developed countries and at home; high rates of unemployment; and inflation.

3. One of the things we study in economics is how we can deal with our problems, either through private action or through government policies.

4. In the history of economic thought, the role of government has been controversial. Adam Smith in 1776 called for the liberation of markets from the tyranny of government control. By 1936, John Maynard Keynes was appealing to the government to accept its responsibilities and to undertake public works in order to get the economy out of the Depression.

5. Important economic goals include the following:

(a) An equilibrium with high employment and price stability.

(b) Efficiency. *Allocative efficiency* involves the production of the right combination of goods, using the lowest cost combination of inputs. *Technological efficiency* occurs when goods are produced with the smallest feasible quantity of inputs (while working at a reasonable pace).

(c) Equity in the distribution of income.

(d) A satisfactory rate of growth.

6. Large changes in the *average* level of prices are undesirable. However, changes in *relative* prices may be desirable as a way of encouraging people to conserve scarce goods and use more plentiful, cheaper alternatives.

7. Goals are complementary if the achievement of one helps in the achievement of the other. For example, a reduction in unemployment also generally reduces poverty. However, goals may be in conflict. An increase in spending works to reduce unemployment, but it also can increase the rate of inflation.

KEY CONCEPTS

economics	*hyperinflation*	*equal distribution of income*
laissez-faire	*the average level of prices*	*equitable distribution of income*
depression	*relative prices*	*redistribution of income*
recession	*allocative efficiency*	*growth*
unemployment	*technical efficiency*	*complementary goals*
inflation	*poverty*	*conflicting goals*

PROBLEMS

1-1. According to Smith's "invisible hand," we are able to obtain meat, not because of the butcher's benevolence, but because of his self-interest. Why is it in the butcher's self-interest to provide us with meat? What does the butcher get in return?

1-2. Suppose another depression occurs like the Depression of the 1930s. How would it affect you? (Thinking about this question provided a major motivation for a generation of economists. They were appaelled at the prospect and determined to play a role in preventing a repeat of the Great Depression.)

1-3. The section on an equitable distribution of income reflects two views regarding the proper approach to poverty:

(a) The important thing is to meet the basic needs of the poor; that is, to provide at least a minimum income for the purshase of food, shelter, and other necessities;

(b) The important thing is to reduce inequality; that is, to reduce the gap between the rich and the poor.

These two views are not the same. For example, if there is rapid growth in the economy, objective (a) may be accomplished without any progress being made toward (b). Which is the more important objective? Why? Do you feel strongly about your choice? Why?

1-4. Explain how an upswing in purchases by the public will affect (a) unemployment and (b) inflation. Does this result illustrate economic goals that are complementary or in conflict?

1-5. In Figure 1-1, you saw that the length of the average work week in Canada has declined more or less continuously since World War II. In the United States, the decline has been less sharp, whereas in Sweden the length of the work week has fallen even more than in Canada.

(a) Can you think of some reason for this difference?

(b) How would you expect these trends to have affected the growth rates of total production and worker incomes? Is it necessarily true that people in a country where total income is growing rapidly are better off than people in another country where income is growing more slowly?

Appendix

■ ■ ■ ■ ■

Diagrams Used in Economics

Chapter 1 contains diagrams which illustrate important points,, such as the increase in production per person since 1926 (Figure 1-1), and the fact that economic growth has slowed down since 1973 (Figure 1-2). In the study of economics, diagrams are frequently used—as you may see by flipping through this book. A picture is often worth a thousand words. Diagrams can fix important ideas in our minds. They present information in a vivid and eye-catching way. But, unfortunately, they can also mislead. The first and lasting impression may be the wrong impression. This appendix explains some of the major types of diagram used in economics. It also explains some of the ways in which diagrams may be used to impress or mislead, rather than inform.[6]

Three major types of diagrams will be considered:
1. Diagrams that present and compare two facts.
2. Diagrams that show how something changes through time. For example, Figure 1-4 illustrates how the average level of prices has usually risen, but has sometimes fallen.

■ ■ ■ ■ ■

[6] For more detail on how readers may be misled, see the sprightly book by Darrell Huff, *How to Lie with Statistics* (New York: Norton, 1954).

3. Diagrams that show how two variables are related to one another; for example, how an increase in family income (variable 1) results in an increase in spending (variable 2).

1. A SIMPLE COMPARISON OF TWO FACTS

The simplest type of diagram brings together two facts for comparison. Often, the best method of presenting two facts — and the least likely to mislead — is to use a bar chart like the one in Figure 1-2. In the top left corner, the first bar shows that the average rate of growth of industrial countries between 1960 and 1973 was 5.2% per year, while the second bar shows that the rate was only 2.5% in 1973–86. By comparing the heights of the two bars, we immediately see how growth rates have changed.

Things to Watch

Even such a simple diagram may carry a misleading message. There are several "tricks" which an unscrupulous writer can use to fool the reader.

Suppose, for example, that someone wants to present the performance of a country or a corporation in the most favourable light. Consider an example—a country whose steel production rose from 10 million tonnes in 1980 to 20 million tonnes in 1990.

Figure 1-6 is a bar chart illustrating this comparison in the simplest, most straightforward way. Glancing at the height of the two bars in this diagram, the reader gets the correct impression—steel production has doubled.

This is a very good performance, but not a spectacular one. Suppose someone wants to "gild the lily," and make things look even better. Two easy ways of doing so — without actually lying—are illustrated in Figure 1-7.

The left panel is designed to mislead because part of the diagram is omitted. The heights of the bars are measured from 5 million tonnes rather than zero. Thus, the 1990 bar is three times as high as the 1980 bar, and the unwary reader may be left with the wrong impression— that steel production is three times as high in 1990, whereas, in fact, it is only twice as high. This, then, is the first thing to watch out for: Do the numbers on the vertical axis start from zero? If not, the diagram may give the wrong impression.

The right panel shows another way in which the reader may be fooled. The bars of Figure 1-6 are replaced with something more interesting — pictures of steel mills.

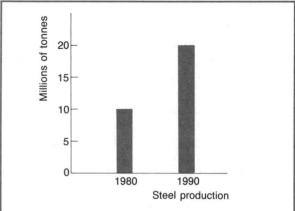

Figure 1-6   A simple bar chart.
The simplest bar chart provides a comparison of two numbers — in this case, the production of steel in two years. We see correctly that steel production has doubled.

Because production has doubled, the steel mill on the right is twice as high as that on the left. But, notice how this picture gives the wrong impression. The mill on the right is not only twice as high. It is also twice as wide, and we can visualize it as being twice as deep, too. Therefore, it isn't just twice as large as the mill on the left; it is many times as large. Thus, the casual reader again may be left with the wrong impression—that steel output has increased manyfold, when, in fact, it has only doubled. This, then, is the second reason to be wary. Look carefully and skeptically at diagrams using silhouettes or pictures. Do they leave you with an exaggerated impression of the changes that have actually occurred?

A third way to mislead is illustrated in Figure 1-8. In both panels, the facts are correct regarding the average price of common stock in Canada. (Each share of common stock represents part ownership of a company.) The left panel shows that, between 1929 and 1952, the average price of stocks changed very little. The right panel shows facts which are equally true. Between 1932 and 1952 — almost the same period of comparison — stock prices increased more than threefold. How can these panels both be correct? The answer: Between 1929 and 1932, the most spectacular stock-market collapse in history occurred, with stocks losing two-thirds of their value. (The bar for 1932 is only one-third as high as the bar for 1929.)

Notice the contrast between the two panels. The left one implies that not much is to be gained by entering the stock market. The right panel gives exactly the opposite impression: The stock market is the place to get rich.

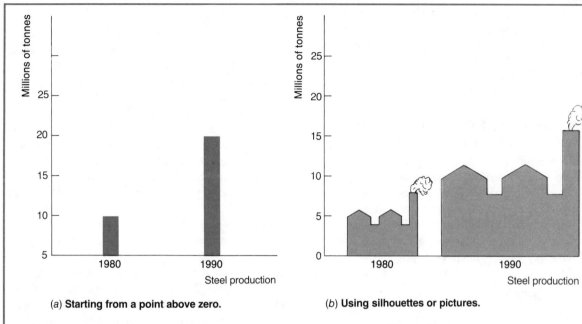

(a) **Starting from a point above zero.**

(b) **Using silhouettes or pictures.**

Figure 1-7   Variations on the simple bar chart.
Readers may be misled by variations on the simple bar chart. Both of the above panels present the same information as in Figure 1-6. In the left panel, the vertical axis begins with 5 million tonnes, rather than zero. In the right panel, pictures are used instead of bars. In each case, the reader may be left with the erroneous impression that steel production has more than doubled.

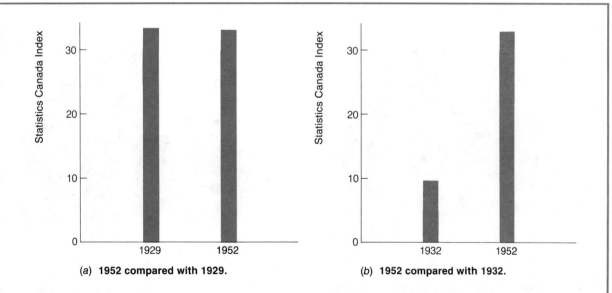

(a) **1952 compared with 1929.**

(b) **1952 compared with 1932.**

Figure 1-8   Comparisons depend on the times chosen.

Comparisons may change even when seemingly minor changes are made in the dates. In 1952, stock prices were no higher on average than in 1929 (left panel). However, they were three times as high in 1952 as they had been in 1932.

Source: Statistics Canada, *CANSIM Databank*. Reproduced by permission of the Minister of Supply and Services Canada.

Thus, an author can give two completely different messages, depending on the choice of the initial "base" year (1929 or 1932). So, beware. In any diagram showing how something has changed over time, ask yourself: Has the author slanted the results by selecting a base year designed to mislead?

2. TIME SERIES: HOW SOMETHING CHANGES THROUGH TIME

That last problem can be avoided by providing more information to the reader with a *time series* diagram, showing stock prices *every* year, not just a beginning and final year. Even better is to show stock prices every month. With a more detailed figure, the reader can see a much more complete story, including both the collapse of 1929 and the way in which stock prices have risen since 1932.

> A *time series diagram* shows how something (such as the price of stocks, the output of steel, or the unemployment rate) has changed through time.

However, even when we provide a detailed time series, a number of issues remain. Here are some of the most important.

Should We Measure from Zero?

In discussing a simple comparison between two facts, we seem to have settled the question of how we should measure up the vertical axis of a diagram. To start at any figure other than zero can be misleading—as in the left panel of Figure 1-7, when steel production was measured up from a starting point of 5 million tonnes.

However, once we provide the detailed information of a time series, we should reopen the question of how to measure along the vertical axis. The problem is that we now have two conflicting considerations. We would like to start from zero to avoid misleading the reader. On the other hand, starting from some other point may make the details of a diagram much easier to see.

This is illustrated in Figure 1-9, which shows the rate of unemployment in each year from 1975 to 1988. In the left panel, the unemployment rate is measured vertically, starting from zero. This gives us the best picture of how the overall unemployment rate compares in any two years we might like to choose (for example, 1981 and 1982). Contrast this with the right panel, where the measurement of unemployment starts above zero. Like Figure 1-7, this panel *can* be misleading. For example, the bars for 1981 and 1982 might leave the impression that the unemploy-

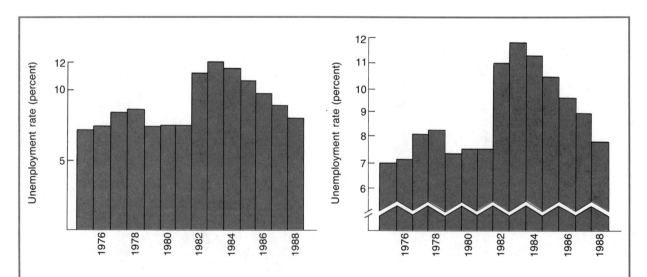

Figure 1-9   A time series: The unemployment rate, 1975–88.
The reader is provided with much more information with a time series showing every year or every month rather than just two years. In this diagram, there is an advantage in starting the vertical measurement above zero. Observe that the detailed year-to-year changes stand out more clearly in the right panel than in the left. To warn the reader that something has been left out, a gap is left in the vertical bars.

Source: *Bank of Canada Review* (July 1988). Reproduced by permission of the Minister of Supply and Services Canada.

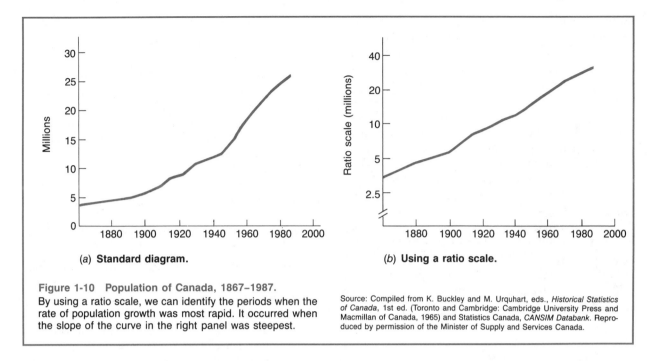

Figure 1-10   Population of Canada, 1867–1987.
By using a ratio scale, we can identify the periods when the rate of population growth was most rapid. It occurred when the slope of the curve in the right panel was steepest.

Source: Compiled from K. Buckley and M. Urquhart, eds., *Historical Statistics of Canada*, 1st ed. (Toronto and Cambridge: Cambridge University Press and Macmillan of Canada, 1965) and Statistics Canada, *CANSIM Databank*. Reproduced by permission of the Minister of Supply and Services Canada.

ment rate more than doubled between those years, whereas, in fact, it increased by far less.

However, the right panel has a major compensating advantage. It provides a much clearer picture of how the unemployment rate *changes* from year to year; the year-to-year differences are much more conspicuous. These year-to-year changes are very important, since they are one measure of fluctuations in the economy. Consequently, the right-hand diagram can be more informative.

If the right panel is chosen, readers must be warned that we have not started from zero. One way is to leave a gap in the vertical bars, to show that something has been left out. Alternatively, we can leave a gap in the vertical axis itself, as illustrated.

How Should Growth Be Illustrated?

Some time series — such as a nation's population — have a strong tendency to grow through time. If we measure in the normal way along the vertical axis, the curve becomes steeper and steeper through time, as shown in the left panel of Figure 1-10. There is nothing necessarily wrong with this presentation — the increase in the population between 1970 and 1980 (2.7 million) was, in fact, much greater than the increase between 1870 and 1880 (0.6 million).

However, there are two related problems with this figure. First, the numbers in the early years — prior to 1900, say — are so small that details are hard to see. Second, we may be interested not just in the *absolute numbers*, but in the *rate* at which population is growing. Thus, the 0.6 million increase in population in the 1870s represents a much greater rate of increase (1.8% per year) than the 2.7 million increase of the 1970s (1.2% per year).

To highlight the *rate* of growth, a ***ratio*** or ***logarithmic*** scale is used on the vertical axis (Figure 1-10, panel (*b*)). On such a scale, equal *percentage* changes show up as equal distances. For example, the distance from 5 million to 10 million (an increase of 100%) is the same as the distance from 10 million to 20 million (also an increase of 100%). In such a diagram, if something grows at a *constant rate* (for example, by 2% per year), it shows up as a *straight line*. By looking for the steepest sections of the time series in the right panel of Figure 1-10, we can identify the periods when population has grown at the most rapid rate. Similarly, back in Figure 1-4, the steepest parts of the curve show when the most rapid rates of inflation occurred.

A ratio scale is appropriate for a time series — like population — where the emphasis is on proportional rates of growth (or decline). However, it is inappropriate for a series that does not have a strong tendency to grow (or decline) at a proportional rate. For example, there is no reason to expect the unemployment rate in the economy to either grow or decline systematically over time, and there is no particular reason to use a logarithmic scale in a diagram showing the unemployment rate.

Finally, note that when a logarithmic scale is used, the question of whether the vertical axis is measured from zero becomes irrelevant, since zero cannot appear on such a diagram. By looking at Figure 1-10(*b*), we can see why. Each time we go up 1 centimetre (one notch on the vertical axis), the population doubles — from 5 to 10 million, and then to 20 million. We can make exactly the same statement the other way around: Each time we go down 1 centimetre, the population falls by half — from 5 million to 2.5 million, then 1.25 million, and so on. No matter how far we extend the diagram downward, each additional centimetre will reduce the population by one half. Therefore, the population can *never* reach zero on such a diagram.

Real or Monetary Measures?

People often complain that the federal government is getting "too big." Suppose we wanted to look at the size of the government. How would we do so?

The most obvious way is to look at the amount the government spends. Measured in dollars, the growth of government spending has been truly stupendous over the past half century or so (Figure 1-11). But, there are several shortcomings to this simple measure.

The first has to do with prices, which have risen substantially during the past half century. Inflation means that even if the government had remained exactly the same size — building the same number of schools and roads, and keeping the same number of soldiers in the army — it would have spent many more dollars. That is, its expenditures in dollar or *nominal* terms would have gone up rapidly. In order to eliminate the effects of inflation, government statisticians calculate *what government expenditures would have been if prices had not gone up* — that is, if prices had remained at the level existing in a single year. Such a measure of government expenditures — in *constant-dollar* or *real* terms — is shown in panel (*a*) of Figure 1-12. Observe how much more slowly government expenditures have grown when the effects of inflation are eliminated. (Further details on how real expenditures are calculated will be presented in a later chapter.)

Relative Measures

Even when measured in real terms, government expenditures have risen substantially. Does this, in itself, mean that the government is "too big"? The answer is, not necessarily. One reason is that, as the government has grown, so has the overall economy. Thus, we may ask the question: has the government grown *relative to the economy*? (As in Figure 1-1, the size of the economy is measured by gross domestic product or GDP.) In Figure 1-12(*b*), observe that government expenditures have not grown much relative to the economy (that is, as a percentage of GDP) in recent decades.

3. RELATIONSHIPS BETWEEN VARIABLES

Frequently, economists want to keep track of the relationship between two variables. Table 1-2 provides an illustration — the relationship between the incomes of households and their expenditures for the basic necessities (housing, food, and clothing). The top row (Row *A*) indicates that a hypothetical family with an income of $10,000 spent $7,000 on the basic necessities. Similarly, Row *B* shows that a family with an income of $20,000 spent $11,000 on these basics.

The data in Table 1-2 may be graphed as Figure 1-13, where income is measured along the horizontal axis and

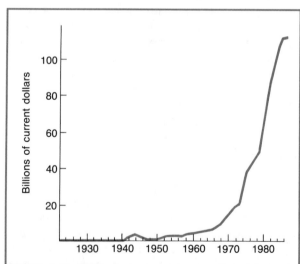

Figure 1-11 Federal government expenditures, measured in dollars.

As measured by the number of dollars spent, the size of the federal government has expanded very rapidly.

Source: Statistics Canada, *CANSIM Databank*. Reproduced by permission of the Minister of Supply and Services Canada.

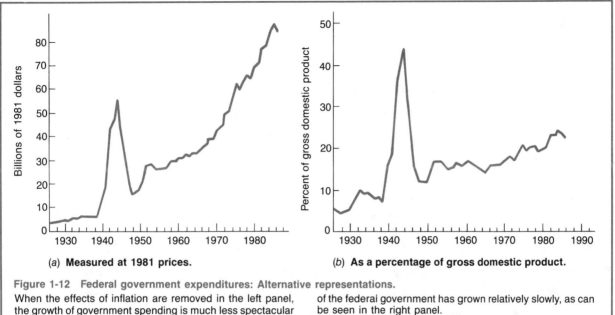

(a) **Measured at 1981 prices.**   (b) **As a percentage of gross domestic product.**

Figure 1-12   Federal government expenditures: Alternative representations.

When the effects of inflation are removed in the left panel, the growth of government spending is much less spectacular than in Figure 1-11. As compared to the overall size of the economy (as measured by gross domestic product), the size of the federal government has grown relatively slowly, as can be seen in the right panel.

Source: Compiled from Statistics Canada, *CANSIM Databank*. Reproduced by permission of the Minister of Supply and Services Canada.

expenditures for basics up the vertical axis. (The lower left corner, labelled "0," is the *origin*—the starting point from which both income and basic expenditures are measured. To plot the data in row *A* of the table, we measure $10,000 in income along the horizontal axis, and $7,000 in spending for basics up the vertical axis. This gives us point *A* in the diagram. Similarly, points *B*, *C*, and *D* represent corresponding rows *B*, *C*, and *D* in Table 1-2.

One question which can be addressed with such a diagram is how expenditures on the basics *change* as income increases. For example, as income increases from $10,000 at point *A* to $20,000 at point *B*, basic expend-

itures rise from $7,000 to $11,000. That is, expenditures on the basics rise by $4,000 in response to the $10,000 increase in income.

This relation can be illustrated by drawing a line between points *A* and *B*, and looking at its *slope* — the slope being defined as the *vertical change* or *rise* (*HB*) divided by the *horizontal change* or *run* (*AH*). In this example, the slope is $4,000/$10,000 = 4/10. As incomes increase from point *A* to point *B*, families spend 40% of the increase on the basics.

Observe in this diagram that the slope becomes smaller and smaller as we go further and further to the right; — that is, as we move to larger and larger incomes. Whereas the slope is 4/10 between *A* and *B*, it is only $3,000/$10,000, or 3/10, between *C* and *D*. This smaller slope makes sense. Families with high incomes already have good houses, food, and clothing. When their income goes up another $10,000, they don't spend much more on the basics; they have other things to do with their income.

Nevertheless, no matter how far to the right this diagram is extended, the line joining any two points will always slope *upward* ;—that is, the slope is always *positive*. The reason is that, as people's incomes rise, they always want somewhat better houses, food, and clothing.

Table 1-2
Household Income and Expenditures for Basics

	(1) Household income (after taxes)	(2) Expenditures for basics
A	$10,000	$ 7,000
B	20,000	11,000
C	30,000	14,500
D	40,000	17,500

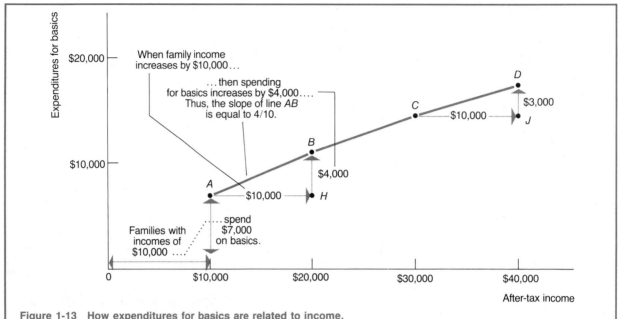

Figure 1-13   How expenditures for basics are related to income.

As family income increases (along the horizontal axis), the family's expenditures for the basics increase (as measured up the vertical axis). The slope of the line between any two points—such as A and B—shows how strongly expenditures for basics respond (*HB*) to an increase in income (*AH*).

However, in some relationships, there may be a downward-sloping curve. Figure 1-14 illustrates the situation facing a company producing a small business aircraft. The costs facing such a company are high — it has the expense of designing the aircraft and it requires an expensive plant for production. If the firm produces only a few units each year (say, 10 aircraft, measured along the horizontal axis), it will operate at point *A*. It will be unable to charge a price high enough to cover its costs and it will, therefore, suffer a loss. That is, its profit (measured along the vertical axis) will be negative. As it sells more, its revenues will rise, and it will begin to make profits to the right of point *B*.

Nevertheless, profits do not rise indefinitely. If the company were to produce a large number of planes — 200, say — it would have to slash prices in order to sell them. This would reduce its profits. Thus, the profit curve at first slopes upward, reaches a peak at *C*, and then slopes downward.

Point *C* is very significant for the firm. At this point, the firm *maximizes its profits*. At this point, the curve ceases to slope upward, and is just about to slope downward. That is, the slope is just about to switch from being positive to becoming negative. Thus, at the point of maximum profit, the slope of the curve is *zero*.

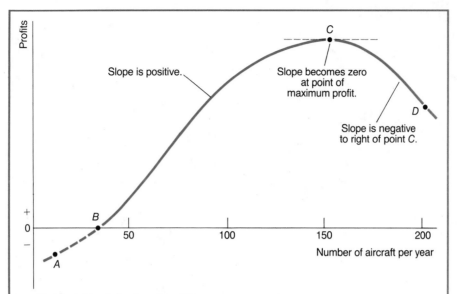

Figure 1-14 Output and profits.

If the firm produces only a few planes, it cannot cover its costs. It suffers losses. (Profits are negative.) As production increases, its losses shrink as it approaches point *B*. Then, to the right of *B*, the firm begins to make profits. As long as output is less than 150 units, the profits curve has a positive slope — that is, it slopes upward. Profits reach a peak at point *C* and thereafter begin to decline. Thus, to the right of *C* the curve has a negative slope. At the point where the curve reaches its peak, the curve is horizontal — that is, its slope is zero.

Chapter 2

■ ■

Scarcity and Choice: The Economic Problem

*Economics studies human behaviour as a
relationship between ends and scarce means.*
Lionel Robbins

In the early 1980s, U.S. President Reagan launched the Strategic Defence Initiative. The SDI (popularly referred to as Star Wars) was a huge program of research and development to create a system of defensive weapons that would make the United States virtually impenetrable to outside attackers. Closer to home, in 1987 the Mulroney government outlined plans to spend some $12 billion on a fleet of nuclear submarines to strengthen Canada's capability to defend our coastal waters and patrol the vast Arctic oceans.

As it turned out, spending on the Star Wars program during Reagan's eight years in office was much less than what was originally planned. In Canada, the nuclear submarine program became a very controversial issue and, in the April 1989 federal budget, the government announced that it had been postponed indefinitely.

The resistance against these spending proposals did not develop because military officials had a change of heart. Instead, the opposition came from others: from politicians and government officials in charge of other kinds of programs, as well as from the general public. Their concern was with the cost.

How do countries pay for things like Star Wars or a nuclear submarine fleet? The answer: through additional taxes that require the public to give up income that they could otherwise have spent on other things, such as better housing or faster cars; or through cutbacks in other kinds of government spending, such as transfers to help the provinces finance their programs in health care and post-secondary education. These military spending proposals have run directly into the central *economic problem*. We must make *choices*. We cannot have everything we want because:

1. Our material *wants* are virtually unlimited; and
2. Economic *resources* are *scarce*.

If we use our productive capacity to make nuclear submarines, we will have less resources for other things.

> The *economic problem* is the need to make choices among the options permitted by our scarce resources.
>
> *Economics* is the study of how scarce resources are allocated to satisfy alternative, competing, human wants.
>
> To *economize* is to achieve a specific benefit at the lowest cost in terms of the resources used.

UNLIMITED WANTS . . .

Consider first our wants. If we can survive in a simple one-bedroom apartment, why do we aspire to much larger homes filled with gadgets? Why do our material wants never seem to be satisfied?

Material wants arise for two reasons. First, each of us has basic biological needs: the need for food, shelter, and clothing. But, there is also a second reason. Clearly, we are prepared to work more than is required to meet our minimum needs. We want more than the basic diet of vegetables and water needed to sustain life. We want more than the minimum clothing to protect us from the cold. In other words, we want not only the essential goods and services that make life possible, but also some of the non-essentials that make it pleasant. Of course, the two basic reasons for material wants cannot be sharply separated. When we sit down to a gourmet meal in a restaurant, we are getting the food essential for satisfying our biological requirements. But, we are getting something more as well. When we savour exotic foods in a comfortable and stylish atmosphere, we are getting luxuries too. Such non-essentials are sufficiently pleasant that we are willing to work to obtain them.

The range of consumer wants is exceedingly broad. We want *goods*, such as houses, cars, shirts, and tennis rackets. Similarly, we want *services*, such as medical care, haircuts, and laundry services. When we get what we want, it may whet our appetites for something more. We may become dissatisfied with the old lawn mower and want a self-propelled one instead. After we buy a house, we may wish to replace the carpets and drapes. Furthermore, as new products are introduced, we may want them too. We want video recorders, home computers, and a host of other products that earlier generations never even dreamed of. Even though it is conceivable that, some day, we will say, "Enough," that day seems far away. Our material wants show no sign of being completely satisfied.

. . . SCARCE RESOURCES

Because of the second fundamental fact, not all wants can be satisfied. Although our productive capacity is large, it is not without limit. There are only so many workers in the labour force, only a given amount of land, and we have only a certain number of machines and factories. In other words, our resources are limited.

Resources are the basic inputs used in the production of goods and services. Therefore, they are also frequently known as *factors of production*. They can be categorized under three main headings: land, capital, and labour.

1. *Land*. Economists use the term land in a broad sense, to include not only the arable land used by farmers and the city land used as building lots, but also the other gifts of nature that come with the land. The abundance of such *natural resources* constitutes an important explanation for the prosperity of the Canadian economy. Early economic development was based to a large extent on our fur-bearing animals and fish resources, as well as on our fertile agricultural land. Other resources, such as minerals, petroleum and natural gas, forestlands and rivers from which we can produce hydroelectric power, have become more important in the present era. All are classified as part of Canada's vast land resource.

2. *Capital* refers to buildings, equipment, and materials used in the productive process. An automobile assem-

bly plant is "capital," and so are the machines in the plant and the steel with which automobiles will be built. In contrast to land, which has been *given* to us by nature, capital has been *produced* at some time in the past. This may have been the distant past; the factory may have been built 15 years ago. Or it may have been the recent past; the steel may have been manufactured last month. The process of producing and accumulating capital is known as *investment*.

Unlike *consumer goods* (such as shoes, cars, or food), capital goods or "investment goods" (such as tractors, factories, or machinery in the factories) are not produced to satisfy human wants directly. Rather, they are intended for use in the production of other goods. Capital produced now will satisfy wants only indirectly and only at a later time when it is used in the production of consumer goods. The production of capital, therefore, means that someone has been *willing to wait*. When a machine is produced rather than a car, the choice has been made to forgo the car now in order to produce the machine, thereby making it possible to produce more cars or other goods in the future. Thus, capital formation involves a choice between consumption *now* and more consumption *in the future*.[1] We should emphasize one point of terminology. Unless otherwise specified, economists use the term "capital" to mean *real capital*, not financial capital. In previous paragraphs, we've been referring to real capital — the factories and machinery used to produce other goods. *Financial capital*, on the other hand, consists of financial assets, such as common stocks, bonds, or bank deposits. Such assets are important. The holder of a stock or bond, for example, has a form of wealth that is likely to produce income in the future in the form of dividends on the stock or interest on the bond. But, while an individual might consider 100 shares of Hiram Walker stock as part of his or her "capital," they are not capital in the economic sense. They are not a resource with which goods and services can be produced.

Similarly, when economists talk of investment, they generally mean *real investment* — the accumulation of machines and other real capital — and not

▪ ▪ ▪ ▪ ▪

[1] Note that the one who is willing to wait (forgo present consumption in exchange for an expected future return) may be a foreign capitalist. A substantial proportion of the capital resources used in Canada is indeed owned by foreigners; the implications of this are discussed later in this chapter.

financial investment (such as the purchase of a Canada Savings Bond).

3. *Labour* refers to the human resource — the physical and mental talents that people apply to the production of goods and services. The construction worker provides labour, and so does the university professor and the physician. (The professor produces educational services and the doctor produces medical services.)[2]

One particular human resource deserves special emphasis: ***entrepreneurial ability***. Entrepreneur is a French word that means "someone who undertakes." More specifically, it means someone who

(a) organizes production, bringing together the factors of production — land, labour, and capital — to make goods and services.

(b) makes business decisions, figuring out what goods to produce and how to produce them.

(c) takes risk. (There is no guarantee that business decisions will turn out to be correct.)

(d) innovates, introducing new products, new technology, and new ways of organizing business.

In order to be successful, an entrepreneur needs to be aware of changes in the economy. Is the market for adding machines declining, while that of computers expanding? If so, the successful entrepreneur will not build a new assembly line for adding machines, but will instead consider the production of computers. Some entrepreneurs are spectacularly successful: for example, Steve Jobs and Steve Wozniak, who set up Apple Computer while still in their twenties. Their mushrooming sales helped to make the microcomputer a common household appliance—and made them multimillionaires in the process (Box 2-1). Other entrepreneurs are engaged in much more prosaic, everyday tasks. The mechanic who runs his own garage and filling station is an entrepreneur, as is the university student who runs a house-painting

■ ■ ■ ■ ■

[2] The preceding paragraphs have presented the traditional division of the factors of production into the categories of land, labour, and capital. While still popular, this traditional division is not universally used by present-day economists. In particular, some economists now talk of "human capital." This is the education and training which add to the productivity of labour. Human capital has two of the important characteristics of physical capital: (1) a willingness to wait during the training period, when the trainee does not produce goods or services; and (2) the increase it brings about in the productive capacity of the economy, since a trained worker can produce more than an untrained one.

business during the summer months. The key questions facing an entrepreneur are these: Are people willing to pay for what I can produce? Can I sell the good or service for enough to cover costs and have some profit left over?

Because entrepreneurs are the ones who undertake the production of new goods, they play a strategic role in determining the dynamism and growth of the economy.

SCARCITY AND CHOICE: THE PRODUCTION POSSIBILITIES CURVE

With unlimited wants and limited resources, we face the fundamental economic problem of *scarcity*. We cannot have everything we want; we must make *choices*.

The problem of scarcity — and the need to make choices — can be illustrated with a ***production possibilities curve*** (PPC). This curve shows what can be produced with our existing resources (land, labour, and capital) and with existing technology — that is, methods of production. Although our resources are limited and our capacity to produce is likewise limited, we have an option as to what goods and services we produce. We may produce fewer cars and more aircraft, or less wheat and more corn.

In an economy with thousands of products, the choices before us are complex. In order to reduce the problem to its simplest form, consider a very basic economy with only two goods: woollen clothing and wheat. If we decide to produce more food (wheat), then we will have to produce less clothing.

The options open to us are shown in the hypothetical production possibilities table (Table 2-1) and the corresponding production possibilities curve (Figure 2-1).

Table 2-1   Production Possibilities

Options	Clothing (billions of metres)	Food (millions of tonnes)	Units of food that must be given up to produce one more unit of clothing (opportunity cost of clothing)
A	0	20	
B	1	19	1
C	2	17	2
D	3	13	4
E	4	8	5
F	5	0	8

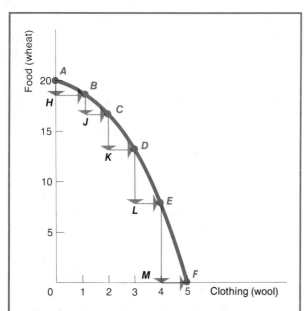

Figure 2-1 The production possibilities curve.
The curve shows the combinations of two goods that can be produced with limited resources of land, labour, and capital.

The Shape of the Production Possibilities Curve: Increasing Opportunity Costs

More reasonable cases are those in which we produce some of each good. Consider how the economy might move from point *A* toward point *F*. At point *A*, nothing is produced but food. It is grown on all types of arable land throughout the nation. In order to begin the production of clothing, we would raise sheep in the areas which are comparatively best suited for wool production — on hilly meadowland in the Atlantic provinces and British Columbia, say. From these lands, we would get a lot of wool, while giving up just a small amount of food that might have been grown there. This is illustrated as we move from point *A* to point *B* on the production possibilities curve. Only one unit of food is given up in order to produce the first unit of clothing.

As we decide to produce more wool, however, we must move to land which is somewhat less suited to wool production. As a result, we do not get the second unit of clothing quite so easily. To produce it, we must give up more than one unit of food. This is illustrated in the move from point *B* to point *C*. As clothing production is increased by one more unit (from one unit to two), food production falls by two units (from 19 to 17). Thus, the ***opportunity cost*** of the second unit of clothing — the food we have to give up to acquire it — is greater than the opportunity cost of the first unit.

> The *opportunity cost* of a product is the alternative that must be given up to produce that product. (In this illustration, the opportunity cost of a unit of clothing is the wheat that must be given up when that unit of clothing is produced.)

Further increases in the production of clothing come at higher and higher opportunity costs in terms of lost food. As we move to the third unit of clothing (from point *C* to *D*), we must start grazing sheep on good corn land in Southern Ontario. A lot of food must be given up to produce that third unit of clothing. Finally, as we move from point *E* to point *F*, all our resources are switched into the production of clothing. The last unit of clothing comes at an extremely high opportunity cost in terms of lost output of food. Wheat production is stopped on the farms of Manitoba and Saskatchewan, which are no good at all for producing wool. The wheat lands remain idle, and prairie farmers migrate to the Atlantic region and B.C., where they can make only minor contributions to wool production. Thus, the last

Consider first an extreme example, where all our resources are directed toward the production of food. In this case, illustrated by option *A*, we would produce 20 million tonnes of food, but no clothing. This clearly does not represent a desirable composition of output. Although we would be well-fed, we would be running around naked. However, no claim has been made that the points on the production possibilities curve are necessarily *desirable*; the only claim is that they are *possible*. And point *A* is possible.[3]

At the other extreme, if we produced nothing but clothing, we would make five billion metres, as illustrated by point *F*. Again, this is a possible outcome, but not a desirable one. We would be well-dressed as we faced starvation.

■ ■ ■ ■ ■

[3] It may be advantageous for a country to specialize by devoting most of its resources to producing one good only (wheat, say) when it can sell this good (wheat) to foreign countries in exchange for all other goods (such as clothing). The possibility of specialized production and international trade is likely to be especially important for a relatively small country, such as Canada.

unit of clothing (the move from point *E* to *F*) comes at a very high cost of eight units of food.

Thus, *the increasing opportunity cost of wool is a reflection of the specialized characteristics of our resources*. Our resources are not completely adaptable to alternative uses. The lands of New Brunswick and Saskatchewan are not equally well suited to the production of wool and wheat. Thus, the opportunity cost of wool rises as its production is increased.

As a result of increasing opportunity cost, the production possibilities curve bows outward. Technically, this kind of curve is described as *concave to the origin*. The arrows in Figure 2-1 illustrate why. The horizontal increases in clothing production — from point *H* to *B*, from *J* to *C*, from *K* to *D*, and so on — are each one unit. The resulting reductions in food production — measured vertically from *A* to *H*, *B* to *J*, *C* to *K*, and so on — become larger and larger, making the curve slope increasingly steeply as we move to the right.

While opportunity costs generally increase, as shown in Figure 2-1, it is not logically necessary that they must do so. In some cases, it is possible for opportunity costs to be constant. For example, beef cattle and dairy cattle can graze on similar land; it is possible that the resources used to raise beef are equally suited for dairy cattle. Thus, the opportunity cost of beef in terms of milk may be constant. If so, a production possibilities curve drawn with milk on one axis and beef on the other would be a straight line.

THE PRODUCTION POSSIBILITIES CURVE IS A ''FRONTIER''

The production possibilities curve in Figure 2-1 illustrates what an economy is capable of producing. It shows the maximum possible combined output of the two goods. In practice, actual production can fall short of our capabilities. Obviously, if there is large scale unemployment, labour resources are being wasted. The same is true if workers are employed, but are wasting their time on the job. In either case, the result is a point like *U*, inside the production possibilities curve in Figure 2-2. Beginning at such a point, we could produce more food *and* more clothing (and move to point *D*) by putting the unemployed back to work. (With full employment, we alternatively could choose any other point on the production possibilities curve,, such as *B*, *C*, or *E*.)

Thus, while the production possibilities curve represents options open to the society, it does not include all conceivable options. The attainable options include not only the points on the curve, but also all points in the shaded area inside the curve.

The production possibilities curve, therefore, traces out a *frontier* or *boundary* of the options open to us. We can pick a point on the frontier if we don't waste resources and maintain a high level of employment. Or we can end up inside the curve if we use resources in a wasteful way or mismanage the economy into a depression. But, points (such as *T*) outside the curve are currently unattainable. We cannot reach them with our present quantities of land, labour, and capital, and with our present technology.

In summary, the production possibilities curve illustrates three important concepts: scarcity, choice, and opportunity cost.

1. *Scarcity* is illustrated by the fact that combinations outside the curve cannot be attained. Even though we

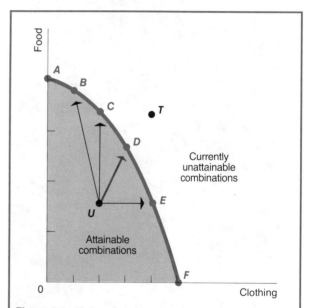

Figure 2-2 Unemployment and the production possibilities curve.

Point *U* represents a position of large-scale unemployment. If people are put back to work, the economy can be moved to point *D*, with more food and more clothing.

With its limited resources, the society can choose any point along the production possibilities curve, or any point within it. Points in the shaded area within the curve are undesirable; the society could do better by moving out to the curve. Points beyond the curve are unattainable with the resources currently at our disposal.

Box 2-1

■ ■ ■ ■ ■ ■ ■ ■ ■ ■ ■ ■ ■ ■ ■ ■ ■ ■ ■ ■

A Tale of Two Dreams

One task of the entrepreneur is to identify new opportunities and potential new products. In the business world, it is the entrepreneur who dreams dreams. But, the entrepreneur must also be practical and hard-headed. Will the public share the dream? Will the new product sell? Can the entrepreneur produce it at a price low enough to attract customers?

Apple Computer

For Steve Jobs and Steve Wozniak, the answer was a resounding "yes."

In the mid-1970s, the two college dropouts were employed in the electronics industry — Wozniak at Hewlett-Packard and Jobs as a designer of video games at Atari. In their spare time, they tinkered. In 1976, Wozniak built the first Apple — a small, easy-to-use computer. Jobs recognized its promise. They put together their available financial resources — $1,300 — to start production in Jobs' garage.

For a fledgling electronics company, California's Silicon Valley was the place to be. An early task for the new entrepreneurs was to get funds for expansion by tapping into the local pool of venture capital. They were not immediately successful. One of their first prospects was put off by Jobs' cutoff jeans, sandals, and wispy beard. Then they made contact with A.C. Markkula, a former marketing manager at Intel (a maker of computer chips), who was delighted with the new machine. He put up $250,000, joined the company, and persuaded two venture capital firms to put up more money. Apple Computer was ready to go.

Wozniak quickly redesigned the original model. The trim, attractive Apple II was born. Sales surged: 800 thousand dollars in 1977, $7.9 million in 1978, 100 million dollars by 1980, and $500 million by 1982. The pace was frenetic. To Markkula, the problem was to "keep the race car on the track."

Apple's break-neck growth created a major problem: how to keep the creative ferment and raw enthusiasm of a small company, while developing the structure and discipline needed in a large business. The team which developed Apple's Macintosh model — mostly young people in their 20s — wore T-shirts with their motto: "Working 90 hours a week, and loving every minute of it." The creativity of that group was remarkable, but the slightly madcap atmosphere exacted a toll. Many of Apple's young engineers burned out and left the company in their 30s. To create a more structured company, Apple in 1983 brought in as president a professional manager and marketing expert, former president John Sculley of Pepsi-Cola. In the next two years, both Wozniak and Jobs left Apple.

The Avro Arrow*

The Apple dream generally has been happy, if somewhat surreal. In contrast, the dream of the pilots, engineers, and executives who, for a short time, put Canada in the spotlight as a world leader in aircraft technology, ended in disappointment.

Courtesy of Apple Canada Inc.

* This box is based on material in Greig Stewart's *Shutting Down the National Dream: A. V. Roe and the Tragedy of the Avro Arrow* (Toronto: McGraw-Hill Ryerson Limited, 1988).

Canadian Warplane Heritage Archives

A. V. Roe of Canada Ltd. was started in 1945 in a Malton, Ontario, plant that had been used to build bombers during World War II. By 1947, the young company had won two important contracts, one to develop a jet-powered transport plane for Trans-Canada Airlines (TCA, which later became Air Canada), the other to build jet fighters for the Canadian Air Force.

The transport plane project ended in failure. Even though many international aviation experts were impressed with ''the Jetliner,'' TCA engineers decided its fuel consumption was too high, and none was ever produced beyond the original prototype.

But, on the military side, Avro (as the company was commonly known) was successful. Some 700 of its CF-100 fighters were eventually produced. By the early 1950s, Avro engineers had already designed a successor to the CF-100, a delta-winged fighter capable of flying at 1.5 times the speed of sound. The federal government agreed to pay for the development of several prototypes of this plane, the legendary ''Avro Arrow.''

Under the leadership of its dynamic young president, Crawford Gordon, the company grew rapidly in the 1950s. It diversified its business, and in 1957 had become the third largest in Canada. But, its biggest project by far was the Arrow. In 1958, some $300 million had already been spent on developing the Arrow and the Iroquois engine that would power it, and it was estimated that the cost of just 100 combat-ready planes would bring the total to well over $1 billion. (In relation to Canada's GDP at the time, this was considerably larger than the cost of the nuclear submarine program proposed in the late 1980s.)

By the time the first prototype of the Arrow was flying, however, there was already concern over both the high cost of the program and the need for advanced fighter planes in an age of un-manned missiles. After the Conservative election victories in 1957 and 1958, it became clear that the project was in trouble. At Avro, work continued at a frantic pace to get more planes ready, and Gordon went to Ottawa for a personal meeting with Prime Minister Diefenbaker to try to get a commitment to continued funding. But, it was too late. In February 1959, Diefenbaker rose in the House of Commons to announce the termination of the project. The six completed Arrows were cut up for scrap, and almost 10 000 people at Avro lost their jobs. A few months later, Crawford Gordon (whose business difficulties had been compounded by a variety of personal problems) was gone from the company. The Avro Arrow dream was dead.

might want such combinations, we cannot have them with the resources available to us.

2. Because we cannot have combinations outside the curve, we must settle for a *choice* of one of the attainable combinations outlined by the PPC.

3. *Opportunity cost* is illustrated by the downward slope of the production possibilities curve.

GROWTH: THE OUTWARD SHIFT OF THE PRODUCTION POSSIBILITIES CURVE

As time passes, a point, such as T (Figure 2-2) may come within our grasp as our productive capacity increases and the economy grows. There are three main sources of growth:

1. technological improvement, representing new and better ways of producing goods;
2. man increase in the quantity of capital;
3. an increase in the labour force.

Consider a change in technology. Suppose a new type of fertilizer is developed that substantially increases the output of our land, whether wool or wheat is being produced. Then we will be able to produce more wheat and more wool. The production possibilities curve will shift out to the new curve (PPC$_2$) shown in Figure 2-3.

> *Growth* is defined as an increase in the productive capacity of the nation. It is illustrated by an outward movement of the production possibilities curve.

Although the new fertilizer illustrated in Figure 2-3 increases our ability to produce both wheat and wool, other types of technological improvement may increase our ability to produce only one of them. For example, the development of a new disease-resistant strain of wheat will increase our ability to produce wheat, but not wool. In this case, illustrated in Figure 2-4, nothing will happen to the place where the production possibilities curve meets the axis for clothing. If we direct all our resources to the production of clothing, we can still produce no more than shown by point F. However, if we direct all our resources to wheat, we can produce more; the other end of the PPC moves upward along the food axis, from A to B. Thus, the development of the new strain of wheat causes the PPC to move upward, from PPC$_1$ to PPC$_3$.

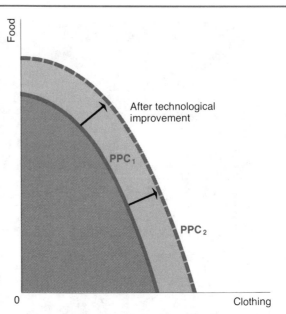

Figure 2-3   Technological improvement.
As a result of the development of a new fertilizer, our productive capabilities increase. The production possibilities curve moves outward.

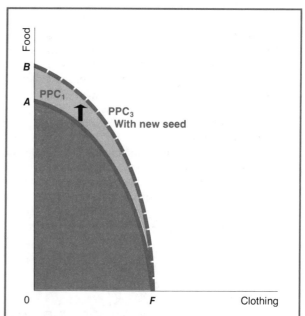

Figure 2-4   Technological improvement in a single good.
When a new, improved strain of wheat is developed, the production possibilities curve moves out to PPC$_3$.

GROWTH: THE CHOICE BETWEEN CONSUMER GOODS AND CAPITAL GOODS

As an alternative to technological change, consider the second source of growth listed above: an increase in the quantity of capital. The capital we have today is limited. However, capital itself can be produced. The quantity of capital that we will have in the year 2000 will be determined in large part by how much of our resources we choose to devote this year and in coming years to producing capital rather than consumer goods.

In order to study this choice, we must look at a different production possibilities curve—not one showing food and clothing but, rather, one showing the choice between the production of capital goods (such as machines and factories) and the production of consumer goods (such as food, clothing, and TV sets).

In Figure 2-5, two hypothetical economies are compared. Starting in 1990, these two countries faced the same initial production possibilities curve (PPC_{today}). The citizens of Extravagania (on the left) believe in living for the moment. They produce mostly consumption goods and very few capital goods (at point A). As a result, their capital stock will be not much greater in 2000 than it is today, so their PPC will shift out very little. In contrast, the citizens of Thriftiana (on the right) keep down the production of consumer goods in order to build more

capital goods (at point B). By the year 2000, their productive capacity will be greatly increased, as shown by the large outward movement of the PPC. Because they have given up so much consumption today, their income (and ability to consume) will be much greater in the future. Thus, any society faces a choice: How much consumption should it sacrifice now in order to be able to consume more in the future?

Capital Imports and Growth

In the example illustrated by Figure 2-5, we have assumed that the increase in the capital stock of a country is made possible because its citizens are willing to wait—that is, to forgo a certain amount of present consumption. But, a country's own citizens do not necessarily have to forgo consumption in order for the country's capital stock to increase. For example, an increase in Canada's capital stock may be financed by residents of *foreign* countries, either through their lending money to Canadians, or through foreign direct investment in Canada. (An example of foreign lending to Canadians would be if foreigners bought $10 million worth of bonds issued by B.C. Hydro, with the proceeds being used to finance the building of a new generating station. Direct investment occurs when foreigners control the capital created in Canada—for example, if Suzuki of Japan spends $100 million to construct an assembly plant near Woodstock, Ont.) When increases in Canada's capital stock are

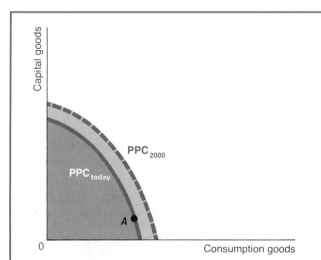

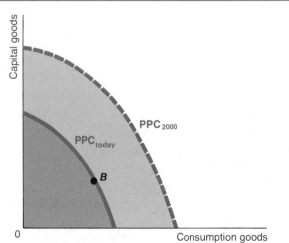

Figure 2-5   Capital formation now helps to determine future productive capacity.
(*a*) **Extravagania**. Most productive capacity is directed toward the production of consumer goods (point *A*). Little investment takes place. The result is slow growth.

(*b*) **Thriftiana**. Much of current (1990) capacity is used to produce capital goods (point *B*). The result is rapid growth, illustrated by a large outward movement of the production possibilities curve by the year 2000.

financed by foreigners in either of these ways, it is foreigners, not Canadians, who are forgoing present consumption in order to make the increased capital formation possible: This process is referred to as a *capital inflow* or *capital imports* into Canada.

> When foreigners finance a part of the increase in a country's capital stock, the country is said to have a *capital inflow*, or to be *importing capital*.

Although capital inflows can help to move the production possibilities curve outward at a rapid pace, not all of this benefit goes to Canadians. Some goes to the foreigners who have to be paid a return on their investment. To illustrate this, suppose that Canada's production possibilities curve has expanded from PPC_{today} to PPC_{2000} in panel (*b*) of Figure 2-5 through large-scale capital imports. While it will still be true that the large capital stock in the year 2000 will make it possible for us to produce a large amount of goods and services in that year, some of our output will have to go to the foreign capitalists as a return on their capital. (The very important issues faced by a country which has large capital imports will be further discussed in Chapter 37.)

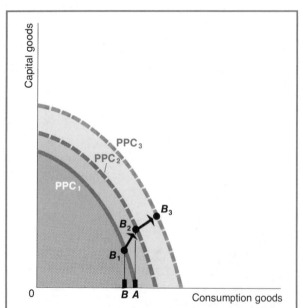

Figure 2-6 "Takeoff" into economic growth.

If point B_1 is initially chosen (on PPC_1), then growth will occur. The economy can move progressively to B_2, B_3, and beyond. However, the initial choice of B_1 rather than A will require people to forgo some consumption goods, as measured by the distance AB. The problem therefore is: What short-term miseries will be caused by the choice of B_1 rather than A?

Economic Development: The Problem of Takeoff

For some countries, the question of growth may be approached in a relatively relaxed manner. For countries, such as Canada or the United States, the issue is not a matter of life or death. Even if we consume most of our current output and grow only slowly, we will still be comfortable in the year 2000. The same is true for Japan and for the countries of Western Europe. (However, Japan conspicuously has not taken a relaxed approach to the growth question. Japan has been "Thriftiana" *par excellence*, investing a large share of national output in new plant and equipment, and growing rapidly.)

Some other countries, however, face a much more critical situation. They are so poor that they can scarcely take a relaxed view either of the present or of the future. Unless they can import capital, they face a cruel dilemma (illustrated in Figure 2-6). If they consume all their current output (at point A), then they will remain stuck on PPC_1. Their future will be just as bleak as the present.[4] On the other hand, if they want to grow, they will have to produce capital, and this means cutting back on their production of consumer goods. (If they choose the growth strategy and move initially to point B_1, then the production of consumer goods will decrease from A to B.) Since the already low level of consumption is depressed further, more people may starve.

In the long run, the growth strategy pays off. Because capital is produced at B_1, productive capacity grows. The production possibilities curve shifts out to PPC_2. Now the nation can pick point B_2, where it not only produces capital goods, but also consumes as much as it originally did at A. (B_2 is directly above point A.) The economy has achieved a *takeoff*. Because it is now producing capital goods, its PPC is continuously moving out. Consequently, the nation can produce ever increasing amounts of both consumer and capital goods.

■ ■ ■ ■ ■

[4] In this simplified example, it is assumed that only capital changes, and that technology and population remain constant. In fact, all three major determinants of growth (capital, labour, and technology) may change. If technology improves, growth may occur even in the absence of investment; the outlook is not as bleak as suggested above. On the other hand, population pressures may make the outlook even worse. As population grows, output must grow if the already low standard of living is not to fall even lower. Thus, just to maintain the present standard, some capital formation may be required.

However, the long-run process does not solve the painful problem of the present: Should consumption be depressed, at the possible risk of starvation, in order to initiate the growth process? How can the economy take off without the danger of a crackup halfway down the runway? (The danger may be political as well as economic. If a government chooses point B_1, the population may be unimpressed with "pie in the sky"—the promise of a brighter future. They may vote the government out, or rebel.)

One possible solution to this difficult dilemma lies in capital imports from other countries. Richer countries can provide the resources for the early stages of growth, either by granting aid or through private investment. (For example, a Canadian clothing manufacturer might build a plant in the developing country.) In this way, economic takeoff might occur without the sacrifices that capital formation otherwise requires.

AN INTRODUCTION TO ECONOMIC THEORY: THE NEED TO SIMPLIFY

The production possibilities curve is the first piece of theoretical equipment which the beginning economics student typically encounters. There will be many more. At this early stage, it is appropriate to address directly a problem that often bothers both beginning and advanced students of economics. The production possibilities curve, like many other theoretical tools that will be introduced in later chapters, represents a gross *simplification* of the real world. When the PPC is drawn, it is assumed that only two types of goods can be produced food and clothing, or consumer goods and capital goods. (Diagrams are limited to two alternatives because the printed page has only two dimensions.) Yet obviously, there are thousands of goods produced in the modern economy. This raises a question: With our simple approach, can we say anything of relevance to the real world?

Theory Necessarily Involves Simplification

If we wished to describe the real world in detail, we could go on without end. A complete description would be useless as a guide to private behaviour or public policy; it would be too complex. In a sense, theory is like a map. A road map is necessarily incomplete. In many ways, it is not very accurate, and, indeed, downright wrong. Towns and villages are not round circles. Roads of various qualities do not really come in different col-

ours. If a road map were more realistic, it would be less useful for its intended purpose. If it tried to show every house and every tree, it would be an incomprehensible jumble of detail. A road map is useful precisely because it *is* a simplification that shows in stark outline the various roads that may be travelled. Similarly, the objective of economic theory is to draw in stark outline the important relationships among producers and consumers.

When details are left out of a road map, it becomes more useful as a guide for the auto traveller. However, it becomes less useful for other purposes. A road map is a poor guide for airplane pilots, for example, who instead need a map with the height of mountains marked clearly. A road map is also a poor guide for sales managers, who need a map showing regional sales targets and staff assignments. The way in which a map is constructed depends on its intended use. Various maps are "true," but they do not represent the "whole truth." An important question for a map user thus becomes: Do I have the best map for my purpose?

The same generalization holds for economic theory. If we wish to study long-run growth, we may use quite different theoretical tools from those we would use to study short-term fluctuations. If we want to study the consequences of price controls on the housing market, we may use different tools from those we would choose to investigate the economic consequences of a cut in Old-Age Security benefits. Just as in the case of the map, the "best" theory cannot be identified unless we know the purposes for which it is to be used.

The production possibilities curve is a theoretical tool whose purpose is to illustrate the concept of scarcity. If we begin on the PPC, with our resources fully employed, then we can come to a significant conclusion: To produce more of one good, we will have to cut back on the production of some other good or service. The "if" clause is important. It tells us that when we consider points along the PPC, we are making an assumption — that resources are fully utilized. When the "if" clause is violated—when the economy begins with large-scale unemployment — then we reach quite a different conclusion: The economy *can* produce more consumer goods and more capital goods at the same time. Thus, the "if" clause acts as a label on our theoretical road map. It makes clear what assumptions we are making and tells us when the map can be used.

For the novice and old hand alike, it is essential to recognize and remember such "if" clauses. We must pay attention to the assumptions underlying any theory that we use. If we don't, we may use the wrong theory, and make serious policy mistakes—just as the pilot who uses the wrong map may fly a plane into the nearest mountain top.

The Distinction between Positive and Normative Economics

The uses of theory are many, but they may be divided into two main families. *Positive* or *descriptive* economics aims at understanding how the economy works. It is directed toward explaining the world as it is, and how various forces can cause it to change. In contrast, *normative* economics deals with the way the world (or some small segment of it) *ought* to be.

A debate over a positive statement can often be settled by an appeal to the facts. For example, the following is a positive statement: "Canadian newsprint production last year was 100 million tonnes." By looking up the statistics, we can find out whether this was true. A more complicated positive statement is: "There are millions of barrels of oil under the Beaufort Sea." With a geological study, we can discover whether this is likely to be so. A third positive statement is this: "If one cubic metre of tar sands is passed through steam, five litres of oil will flow out of the sand." By experimentation, we can discover whether this is generally true.

A *normative* statement is more complex: for example, "We ought to extract oil in large quantities from the Beaufort Sea." Facts are relevant here. If there is no oil under the Beaufort Sea (a positive conclusion), then the normative statement that we ought to extract oil must be rejected for the very simple reason that it can't be done. However, facts alone will seldom settle a dispute over a normative statement since it is based on something more —on a view regarding appropriate goals or ethical values. A normative statement involves a value judgement, a judgement about what ought to be. It is possible for well-informed individuals of exemplary character to disagree over normative statements, even when they agree completely regarding the facts. For example, they may agree that there is, in fact, a large quantity of oil under the Beaufort Sea. Nevertheless, they may disagree over whether it should be extracted. These differences may develop, perhaps, over the relative importance of a plentiful supply of heating oil as compared with the damage to the Arctic environment which might accompany the extraction of oil; or from a difference of opinion over whether the Canadian taxpayer should be required to provide a subsidy necessary for this development.

Although some positive statements may be easily settled by looking at the facts, others may be much more difficult to judge. This is particularly true of statements making claims about causation. They may be quite controversial because the facts are not easily untangled. For example: "If there is no growth in the money stock next year, then inflation will fall to zero"; or, "If income tax rates are increased by 5%, government revenues will increase by $20 billion next year"; or, "Rent controls have little effect on the number of apartments constructed each year."

In evaluating such statements, economists and other social scientists have two major disadvantages as compared with natural scientists. First, experiments are difficult or impossible in many instances. Society is not the plaything of economists. They do not have the power to conduct an experiment in which one large city is subjected to rent control while a similar city is not, simply to estimate the effects of rent control. Nevertheless, economists do have factual evidence to study. By looking at situations where rent controls have actually been imposed by the government, they may be able to estimate the effects of those controls. Moreover, in special situations, economic experiments are possible, particularly when the government is eager to know the results. For example, experiments have been undertaken to determine whether people work less when they are provided with a minimum income by the government. (Some results from these studies will be discussed in Chapter 39.)

The second disadvantage is that the social sciences deal with the behaviour of people, and behaviour can change. Suppose we estimate corporate profits next year to be $20 billion. We might carelessly conclude that, if the profits tax is raised by 10%, the government will receive an additional $2 billion in revenues. But, this is not necessarily so. With a higher tax rate, businesses may behave differently, in order to reduce the taxes they have to pay. Furthermore, even if we have evidence on how businesses have responded to a 10% tax increase in the past, we cannot be certain that they will respond the same way in the future. They may have become more imaginative in finding ways to avoid taxes. The possibility that people will learn and change their behaviour has been one of the most interesting areas of research in economics in recent years.

In contrast, physical scientists study a relatively stable and unchanging universe. Gravity works the same way today as it did in Newton's time.

KEY POINTS

1. *Scarcity* is a fundamental economic problem. Because wants are virtually unlimited and resources are scarce, we are faced with the need to make *choices*.

2. The choices open to society are illustrated by the *production possibilities curve*. This illustrates the concept of the *opportunity cost* of a good *A*, which is the amount of another good *B* that must be given up to produce *A*.

3. Not all resources are identical. For example, the land of Manitoba is different from the land of Nova Scotia. As a consequence, opportunity cost generally increases as more of a good is produced. For example, as more wool is produced, more and more wheat must be given up for each additional unit of wool. As a result, the production possibilities curve normally bows outward.

4. The production possibilities curve is a frontier, representing the choices open to society—if there is full utilization of the available resources of land, labour, and capital. If there is large-scale unemployment, then production occurs at a point *within* this frontier.

5. The economy can grow and the production possibilities curve can move outward if:
(a) technology improves;

(b) the capital stock grows;
(c) and/or the labour force grows.

6. By giving up consumer goods at present, we can produce more capital goods, and thus have a growing economy. The production of capital goods (investment), therefore, represents a choice of more future production instead of present consumption.

7. Through capital imports, a country may achieve economic growth without reducing its present consumption. However, some of the extra production which results from capital imports has to be used to pay foreign capitalists for the use of their capital.

8. For the poorest countries, a choice between present consumption and growth is particularly painful. If consumption is suppressed in order to grow more rapidly, people may starve. But, growth is essential to raise a low standard of living.

9. Like other theoretical concepts, the production possibilities curve represents a simplification. Because the world is so complex, theory cannot reflect the "whole truth." Nevertheless, a theory—like a road map—can be valuable if it is used correctly. In order to determine the appropriate uses of a theory, it is important to identify the assumptions on which the theory was developed.

KEY CONCEPTS

goods
services
resources
scarcity
factors of production
land

labour
capital
investment
entrepreneur
production possibilities curve
increasing opportunity cost

growth
takeoff
capital imports
positive economics
normative economics
theory

PROBLEMS

2-1. Some economists like to define economics broadly, as the study of how people make their living, of the problems they encounter in doing so, and of the ways in which they can reduce these problems. Another common definition of economics is tied closely to the idea of scarcity. Economics is "the study of the allocation of scarce resources to satisfy alternative, competing human wants."

Clearly, scarcity is an important part of economics. We cannot have all the goods and services we want. However, one of the central economic problems defined in Chapter 1 cannot be attributed to a scarcity of resources. Which one? Why is this problem not attributable to a scarcity of resources? Is this problem covered by the broader definition of economics?

2-2.   ''Wants aren't insatiable. The economic wants of Peter Pocklington have been satisfied. There is no prospect that he will spend all his money before he dies. His consumption is not limited by his income.'' Do you agree? Does your answer raise problems for the main theme of this chapter: that wants cannot all be satisfied with the goods and services produced from our limited resources? Why or why not?

2-3.   ''The more capital goods we produce, the more the Canadian economy will grow, and the more we and our children will be able to consume in the future. Therefore, the government should encourage capital formation.'' Do you agree or disagree? Why?

2-4.   Does your answer to question 2-3 fall under the heading of ''positive'' or ''normative'' economics? Why?

Chapter 3

■ ■

Specialization, Exchange, and Money

*Money . . . is not of the wheels of trade: it is
the oil which renders the motion of the wheels
smooth and easy.*

David Hume

The early French colony at Quebec was a forbidding place in winter, when temperatures often fell to $-30°$ Celsius. Keeping warm was the first problem. Getting supplies from France was a close second. During the winter, the St. Lawrence River was clogged with ice.

Of the many things that the colony lacked, money was one. Not only did ships have difficulty sailing up the river but, even when they did come, they had little currency; the colony's sponsors in France were reluctant to send money. The colonists found that barter was very cumbersome; even in a simple economy, money was essential. What could they do? They hit upon an ingenious solution. They used playing cards as money. The man with an ace in his pocket often had a smile on his face.

In the modern economy, as in the early colonies, money plays a central role. Over the decades, production has become increasingly specialized with the development of new machinery and equipment. Specialization contributes to efficiency; often, workers can produce more by specializing. But, specialization necessitates exchange. A farmer who produces only beef wants to exchange some of that beef for clothing, cars, dental care, and a whole list of other products.

This chapter will explain:

■ The two types of exchange:
  1. barter
  2. exchange for money

■ Why exchange is so much simpler with money than barter

■ How people can gain from specialization and exchange

EXCHANGE: THE BARTER ECONOMY

In a *barter* system, no money is used: One good or service is exchanged directly for another. The farmer specializing in the production of beef may find a hungry barber and thus get a haircut, or find a hungry tailor and thus exchange meat for a suit of clothes, or find a hungry dentist and thus obtain dental treatment. A simple barter transaction is illustrated in Figure 3-1. In a barter economy, there are dozens of such bilateral (two-way) transactions: between the farmer and the tailor; between the farmer and the dentist; between the dentist and the tailor; and so on.

Clearly, barter is inefficient. Farmers might spend half their time producing beef, and the other half searching for someone willing to make the right trade. Barter requires a *coincidence of wants*: Those engaged in barter must each have a product that the other wants. The farmer not only must find someone who wants beef, but that someone must also be able to provide something in exchange that the farmer wants. Furthermore, with barter, there is a problem of *indivisibility*. A suit of

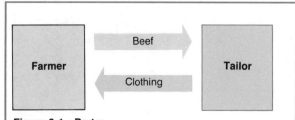

Figure 3-1 Barter.
With barter, no money is used. The farmer exchanges beef directly for clothing. Transactions involve only two parties—in this case, the farmer and the tailor.

clothes — or an automobile, or a house — should be bought all at once, and not in pieces. To illustrate, suppose that a beef farmer who wants a suit of clothes has been lucky enough to find a tailor who wants meat and is willing to make a trade. The suit of clothes may be worth 50 kg of beef, and the farmer may be quite willing to give up this amount. The problem is that the tailor may not be *that* hungry, perhaps wanting only 25 kg. In a barter economy, what is the farmer to do? Get only the jacket from this tailor, and set out to find another hungry tailor in order to obtain a pair of pants? If the farmer does so, what are the chances that the pants will match?

EXCHANGE WITH MONEY

With money, exchange is much easier. It is no longer necessary for wants to coincide. In order to get a suit of clothing, the farmer need not find a hungry tailor, but only someone willing to pay money for the beef. The farmer can then take the money and buy the suit of clothes. Money represents *general purchasing power—*that is, it can be used to buy any of the goods and services offered for sale. Therefore, complex transactions among many parties are possible with money. Figure 3-2 gives a simple illustration with three parties. Actual transactions in a monetary economy may be very complex, with dozens or hundreds of participants.

Money also solves the problem of indivisibility. The farmer can sell the whole carcass of beef for money, and use the proceeds to buy a complete set of clothes. It doesn't matter how much beef the tailor wants.

In the simple barter economy, there is no clear distinction between seller and buyer, or between producer and consumer. When bartering beef for clothing, the farmer is at the same time both a seller (of beef) and a buyer (of clothing). In a monetary economy, in contrast, there is a *clear distinction between seller and buyer*. In the beef market, the farmer is the seller; the hungry tailor is the buyer. The farmer is the producer; the tailor is the consumer.

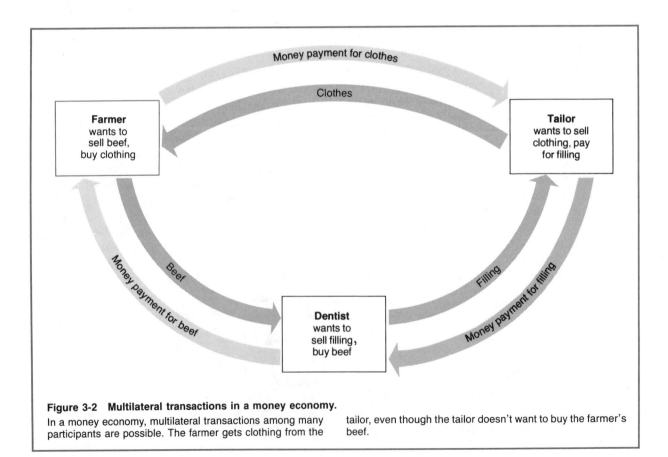

Figure 3-2 Multilateral transactions in a money economy.
In a money economy, multilateral transactions among many participants are possible. The farmer gets clothing from the tailor, even though the tailor doesn't want to buy the farmer's beef.

The Circular Flow of Expenditures and Income

The distinction between the producer and consumer in a money economy is illustrated in Figure 3-3. Producers — or *businesses* — are put in the right-hand box; consumers — or *households* — in the left. Transactions between the two groups are illustrated in the loops. In the top loops, consumers' expenditures for goods and services are shown. Beef, clothing, and a host of other products are bought with money.

In the lower loops, transactions in economic resources are shown. In a complex exchange economy, not only are consumer goods bought and sold for money; so are resources. In order to be able to buy food and other goods, households must have money income. They acquire money by providing the labour and other resources which are the inputs of the business sector. For example, workers provide their labour in exchange for wages and salaries, and owners of land provide their property in exchange for rents.

Figure 3-3 is simplified. For example, it does not include government, which is a major purchaser of goods and services. (Remember the purpose of simplification discussed in Chapter 2: to show important relationships in sharp outline.) Figure 3-3 shows the circular flow of payments—that is, how businesses use the receipts from sales to pay their wages, salaries, and other costs of production, while households use their income receipts from wages, salaries, etc., to buy consumer goods.

THE MONETARY SYSTEM

Because barter is so inefficient, people turn naturally to the use of money. One example was the early colony at Quebec, with its playing card money.

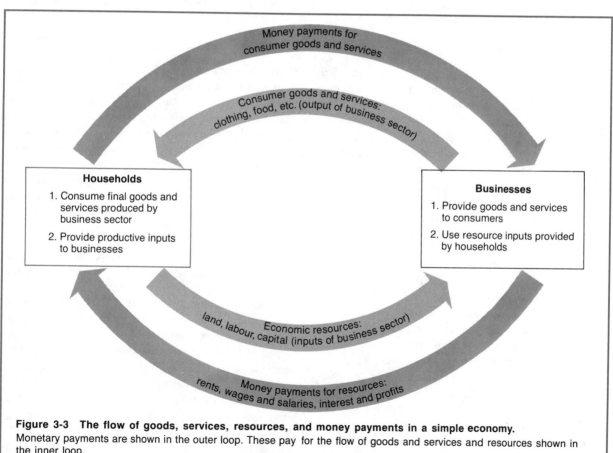

Figure 3-3 The flow of goods, services, resources, and money payments in a simple economy.
Monetary payments are shown in the outer loop. These pay for the flow of goods and services and resources shown in the inner loop.

Box 3-1

■ ■

Early Money on the Island of Uap†

On the south-sea island of Uap, the medium of exchange is called fei. This currency consists of large, solid, thick stone wheels ranging in diameter from one to twelve feet, and in the center a hole, so that the stones may be slung on poles and carried. They are not found on Uap itself, but are quarried in Babel-thuap, some four hundred miles away. Size is the most important factor, but also the fei must be of a certain fine, white, close-grained limestone. A traveler to Uap described the fei as follows:

> A feature of this stone currency, which is also an equally noteworthy tribute to Uap honesty, is that its owner does not need to actually possess it. After concluding a bargain which involves a fei too large to be conveniently moved, its new owner is quite content to accept the bare acknowledgment of ownership; and without so much as a mark to indicate the exchange, the coin remains undisturbed on the former owner's premises.
>
> There was in a village nearby a family whose wealth was unquestioned — acknowledged by everyone, and yet no one, not even the family itself, had ever laid eye on this wealth; it consisted of an enormous fei lying at the bottom of the sea! Many years ago an ancestor of this family, on an expedition after fei, secured this remarkable stone, which was placed on a raft to be towed homeward. A violent storm arose and the party, to save their lives, were obliged to cut the raft adrift, and the stone sank out of sight. When they reached home, they all testified that the fei was of magnificent proportions and extraordinary quality, and that it was lost through no fault of the owners. Thereupon it was universally considered that the mere accident of its loss overboard was too trifling to mention. The purchsing power of the stone remained, therefore, as valid as if it were leaning visibly against the side of the owner's house.

†Abridged, from Norman Angell, *The Story of Money* (New York: Garden City Publishing Co., 1929), pp. 88–89.

The powerful tendency for money to appear may also be illustrated by an example of an economy that began without money: the prisoner-of-war camp of World War II.[1] Economic relations in such a camp were primitive; the range of goods was very limited. But, some things were available: rations supplied by the German captors, and the Red Cross parcels which arrived periodically. These parcels contained a variety of items, such as canned beef, jam, margarine, and cigarettes. Nonsmokers who received cigarettes were eager to trade them for other items. The basis was established for exchange.

At first, trading was rough and ready, with no clear picture of the relative values of the various items. In one instance, a prisoner started around the camp with only a can of cheese and five cigarettes, and returned with a complete Red Cross parcel. He did so by buying goods where they were cheap, and selling them where they were dear. However, as time went by, the relative prices of various goods became more stable, and all prices came to be quoted in terms of cigarettes. For example, a can of cheese was worth seven cigarettes. Not only did cigarettes become the measuring rod for quoting prices, but they were used as the common medium of exchange — that is, cigarettes were the item used to buy goods. Cigarettes became the money of the POW camp. This was a natural evolution; there was no government to decree that cigarettes were money, and no authority to enforce that choice. At other times and in other societies, other items have been used as money: items as diverse as beads, porpoise teeth, rice, salt, wampum, stones, and even woodpecker scalps. (Box 3-1 tells about another example.)

Monetary Problems in the POW Camp

Cigarette money made the primitive economy of the prisoner-of-war camp more efficient. But, problems occurred, including problems quite similar to those of more advanced monetary systems. As part of the natural trend toward simplification, distinctions among different brands of cigarettes became blurred. Although all cigarettes were not equally desirable to smokers, all were equal as money. In paying for beef or other items, a cigarette was a cigarette. What was the consequence? Smokers held back the desirable brands for their personal use and spent the others. The less desirable cigarettes, therefore, were the ones used as money; the "good" cigarettes were smoked. This illustrates *Gresham's law*. This law, first enunciated by Elizabethan

■ ■ ■ ■ ■
[1] This illustration is based on *R. A. Radford*, "The Economic Organization of a P.O.W. Camp," *Economica* (November 1945): 189–201.

financier Sir Thomas Gresham (1519–1579), is popularly and loosely abbreviated: "Bad money drives out good." In this case, "bad" cigarettes drove "good" cigarettes out of circulation as money. (The good cigarettes were smoked instead.)

Gresham's law: If there are two types of money whose values in exchange are equal while their values in another use (like consumption) are different, the more valuable item will be retained for its other use while the less valuable item will continue to circulate as money. Thus, the "bad" (less valuable) money drives the "good" (more valuable) money out of circulation.

The tendency for every cigarette to be treated as equal to every other cigarette caused another monetary problem. As a cigarette was a cigarette, prisoners often pulled out a few strands of tobacco before passing a cigarette along. This corresponds precisely to a problem when gold coins circulate: There is a temptation to "clip" coins by chipping off bits of gold. Furthermore, the cigarette currency became "debased": Some enterprising prisoners rolled cigarettes from pipe tobacco or broke down cigarettes and rerolled them, reducing the amount of tobacco in each. Similarly, governments have from time to time given in to the temptation to debase gold coins by melting them down and reissuing them with a smaller gold content. (Private entrepreneurs have had a strong incentive to do the same, but they have been discouraged throughout history by severe punishments against counterfeiting.)

However, it was not clipping or debasement that led to the greatest monetary problems in the POW camp. As long as there was a balanced inflow of both cigarettes and other goods, the exchange system of the camp worked reasonably well. But, from time to time, the weekly Red Cross issue of 25 or 50 cigarettes per prisoner was interrupted. As the existing stock of cigarettes was consumed by smokers, cigarettes became more and more scarce. Desperate smokers had to offer more and more to get cigarettes; their value skyrocketed. To put the same point another way: Other goods now exchanged for fewer and fewer cigarettes. A can of beef which previously sold for 20 cigarettes dropped in value to 15, 10, or even fewer cigarettes. Thus, there was a *deflation*—a decline in the prices of other goods, measured in terms of money.

As cigarettes became increasingly scarce and prices continued to fall, prisoners began to revert to barter in exchanging other goods. Smokers who had the few remaining cigarettes were reluctant to give them up to make purchases. Then, from time to time, thousands of cigarettes would arrive at the camp during a brief period. Prices soared; in other words, the value of cigarettes fell. Prisoners became reluctant to accept cigarettes in payment for other goods. Once again, barter became common. Thus, *the monetary system worked smoothly only so long as a reasonable balance was kept between the quantity of money (cigarettes) and the quantity of other goods*.

Several characteristics of a good monetary system may be drawn out of this story of the "cigarette standard":

1. A smoothly operating monetary system should be made up of money whose value is **uniform**. Non-uniform money will set Gresham's law into operation, with "bad" money driving "good" money out of circulation. In our economy, the Bank of Canada has the responsibility to assure that money is uniform. It is the institution that issues paper currency. It matters not whether the bills I have in my pocket are crisp and new, or whether they are tattered and soiled. The Bank of Canada will replace a two-dollars bill, say, with a new bill of equal value when it becomes excessively worn. This means that it represents two dollars in value to anyone. And because the Bank guarantees that I can exchange a two-dollar bill for coins any time I want to do so, I don't care whether I get a two-dollar bill or two loonies or eight quarters in change when I make a purchase at the variety store, even though the metal in the coins is more valuable than the paper in the two-dollar bill.

   This uniformity in the value of each dollar obviously adds to the ease of exchange—and it means that Gresham's law does not operate in our modern economy.

2. A second important characteristic of a good monetary system is that there be the **proper quantity of money**, neither too much nor too little. In Canada, the responsibility for controlling the quantity of money also lies with the Bank of Canada. This important topic will be studied in Part 3 of this book.

COMPARATIVE ADVANTAGE: A REASON TO SPECIALIZE

Money, the development of markets, and — perhaps equally important — the development of a sophisticated transportation and communications system, all make possible a high degree of specialization of production. They make specialization possible and relatively smooth, but they don't provide a reason why specialization is advantageous in the first place. Near the beginning of the chapter, an answer was suggested: Specialization can add to efficiency. Specialization generates *gains*. It is now time to explain just how. A key concept in the explanation is the ***principle of comparative advantage***. To understand this principle, it is useful to look first at the simpler concept of ***absolute advantage***.

A good is often made in the place that is best suited for its production: wood products in British Columbia, corn in Iowa, bananas in the tropical lands of Central America, coffee in the cool highlands of Colombia, and so on. In technical terms, there is some tendency for a good to be produced in the area that has an *absolute advantage* in its production.

A country (or region or individual) has an *absolute advantage* in the production of a good if it can produce that good with fewer resources (less land, labour, and capital) than can other countries (or regions or individuals).

Note that this principle applies to specialization among individuals within a city or town. Consider the case of the lawyer and the professional gardener. The lawyer is better at drawing up legal documents and the gardener generally is better at gardening, so it is in the interest of each to specialize in the occupation in which he or she has an absolute advantage.

However, the truth is often more complicated than this. By looking at the complications, we will be led to the idea of comparative advantage. Suppose a certain lawyer is better at gardening than the gardener; she's faster and more effective—in short, she has a "greener thumb." She has an absolute advantage in both the law and gardening. If absolute advantage were the key, she would practice law and do her own gardening as well.

Does this necessarily happen? The answer: No. Unless this lawyer positively enjoys gardening as a recreation, she will leave the gardening to the professional. Why? Even though the lawyer, being an excellent gardener, can do as much gardening in one hour (let us say) as the gardener could in two, she will be better off to stick to law and hire the gardener to work on the flowers and shrubbery. Why? In one hour's work, the lawyer can draw up a will, for which she charges $50. The gardener's time, in contrast, is worth only $5 per hour. By spending the hour on the law rather than gardening, the

lawyer comes out ahead. She earns $50, and can hire the gardener for $10 to put in two hours to get the gardening done. The lawyer gains $40 by sticking to law for that one hour. (This is explained in more detail in Box 3-2.)

The gardener also gains through specialization. Although he has to work 10 hours in order to earn the $50 needed to hire the lawyer to draw up his will, it would take him much more time to draw up the will himself. He would have to spend many hours—as many as 100, perhaps—poring over law books just to learn the basic traps to avoid in drawing up a will. (Even after spending the 100 hours, he could not be sure that he might not have missed something very simple that the lawyer learned in her many years of study.) Thus, by spending 10 hours on gardening and using the income to buy the lawyer's time, the gardener gains: He gets a better will than he could have gotten by struggling with legal books for a full 100 hours.

This example leads to two important conclusions:

1. There are ***mutual benefits*** from specialization and exchange. The lawyer gains by specializing and hiring someone else to do the gardening. The gardener likewise gains, getting a better will in less time than by trying to do it himself.
2. Absolute advantage is *not* necessary for mutually beneficial specialization. The lawyer has an absolute advantage in both gardening and law; the gardener has an absolute disadvantage in both. But, the lawyer has a *comparative advantage* in law; the gardener has a *comparative advantage* in gardening. Both gain from specialization.

British economist **David Ricardo** enunciated the principle of comparative advantage in the early nineteenth century to illustrate how countries gain from international trade. But, comparative advantage provides a general explanation of the advantages of specialization; it is just as relevant to domestic as to international trade. Nevertheless, it is customary to follow Ricardo and consider this principle as part of the study of international economics. We follow the custom, and put off our detailed analysis of comparative advantage to the chapter on international trade. For the moment, we note that the concept of comparative advantage is related to opportunity cost.

If two individuals (or cities or nations) have different opportunity costs of producing a good or

Box 3-2

■ ■

Illustration of Comparative Advantage

A. Assume the following:
  1. In one hour, the lawyer can plant 20 flowers.
  2. In one hour, the gardener can plant 10 flowers. (Therefore, the lawyer has the absolute advantage in gardening.)
  3. The lawyer's time, in the practice of law, is worth $50 per hour.
  4. The gardener's time, in gardening, is worth $5 per hour.

B. Question: How should the lawyer have 20 flowers planted?

  Option 1: Do it herself, spending one hour.
  Cost: She gives up the $50 she could have earned by practising law for that hour.
  Option 2: Stick to the law, and hire the gardener to plant the 20 flowers.
  Cost: Two hours of gardener's time at $5 per hour, making a total of $10.

C. Decision: Choose option 2.
  Spend the available hour practising law, earning $50. Hire the gardener to do the planting for $10. Net advantage over option 1: $40.

D. Conclusion: The lawyer has the comparative advantage in law.

Courtesy of Miller Comstock Inc./Roberts

---

service, the individual (or city or nation) with the lower opportunity cost has the *comparative advantage* in that good or service.

The opportunity cost is the alternative forgone. To prepare a will, the lawyer's opportunity cost is the 20 flowers that she could have planted instead. (Details are in Box 3-2.) In contrast, the gardener would have faced a much higher opportunity cost to prepare a will. It would take him 100 hours, in which he alternatively could plant 1000 flowers. Since the lawyer's opportunity cost of drawing up a will is lower than the gardener's (20 flowers vs. 1000), the lawyer has the comparative advantage in law. She will specialize in this, leaving the flowers to the gardener. Furthermore, it follows directly that the gardener has the comparative advantage in gardening. To plant a flower, he gives up only one-thousandth of a will, compared to the one-twentieth forgone by the lawyer. Accordingly, the gardener will stick to his gardening, and leave the drafting of the will to the lawyer.

Comparative advantage, then, provides one reason to specialize. It may be considered the first great propellant driving the wheels of commerce, while money acts as the grease, making the machine run with less friction. But, there is also a second fundamental reason to specialize.

ECONOMIES OF SCALE: ANOTHER REASON TO SPECIALIZE

Consider two small cities that are identical in all respects. Suppose that the citizens of these cities want both bicycles and lawn mowers, but that neither city has any basic advantage in the production of either good. Will each city then produce its own, without any trade existing between the two? Probably not. It is likely that one city will specialize in bicycles, and the other in lawn mowers. Why?

The answer is, *economies of scale*. To understand what this term means, first assume that there is no specialization. Each city directs half its productive resources into the manufacture of bicycles and half into the manufacture of lawn mowers, thus producing 1000 bicycles and 1000 lawn mowers. But, if either city specializes by directing all its productive resources toward the manufacture of bicycles, it can acquire specialized machinery and produce 2500 bicycles. Similarly, if the other city directs all its productive resources toward the manufacture of lawn mowers, it can produce 2500. Note that each city, by doubling all inputs into the production of a single item, can *more* than double its output of that item from 1000 to 2500 units. Thus, economies of scale exist.

> *Economies of scale* exist if an increase of $x\%$ in the quantity of every input causes the quantity of output to increase by more than $x\%$. (For example, if all inputs are doubled, then output more than doubles.)

Even though neither city had any fundamental advantage in the production of either product, they can gain by specialization. Before specialization, their combined output was 2000 bicycles and 2000 lawn mowers. After specialization, they together make 2500 bicycles and 2500 lawn mowers.

While Ricardo's theory of comparative advantage dates back to the early nineteenth century, the explanation of economies of scale goes back even further—to Adam Smith's *Wealth of Nations* (1776). In Smith's first chapter, "Of the Division of Labour," there is a famous description of pin-making:

> A workman not educated to this business . . . could scarce, perhaps, . . . make one pin in a day, and certainly not twenty. But, in the way in which this business is now carried on, not only the whole work is a peculiar trade, but it is divided into a number of branches. . . .

> One man draws out the wire, another straightens it, a third cuts it, a fourth points it, a fifth grinds it at the top for receiving the head. . . . Ten persons, therefore, could make among them upwards of forty-eight thousand pins in a day. Each person, therefore, . . . might be considered as making four thousand and eight hundred pins in a day.[2]

What is the reason for the gain that comes from the division of pin-making into a number of separate steps? Certainly, it is not that some individuals are particularly suited to drawing the wire, while others have a particular gift for straightening it. On the contrary, if two individuals are employed, it matters little which activity each is assigned. Adam Smith's "production line" is efficient because of economies of scale which depend on:

1. The introduction of specialized machinery.
2. Specialization of the labour force on that machinery.

Modern corporations also derive economies of scale from a third major source:

3. Specialized research and development, which make possible the development of new equipment and technology.

In the modern world, economies of scale are very important as an explanation of specialization. They are a major reason why the manufacturers of automobiles, aircraft, and mainframe computers are few in number and large in size. It is partly because of economies of scale that the automobile industry is concentrated in central Canada, with cars being shipped to other areas in exchange for a host of other products. And economies of scale help explain why Canada's petro-chemical industry is concentrated in the Lake St. Clair region of Southern Ontario.

However, economies of scale explain much more than the trade among the regions, provinces, and cities within a country. They also are an important explanation of trade between countries. For example, economies of scale in the production of large passenger aircraft go on long after the U.S. market is met. Thus, there is a major advantage to Boeing in producing aircraft for the world market. There are gains to the aircraft buyers, too. For example, Norway can buy a Boeing 747 for a small fraction of the cost of manufacturing a comparable airplane.

■ ■ ■ ■ ■

[2] Adam Smith, *An Inquiry into the Nature and Causes of the Wealth of Nations* (Modern Library edition, New York: Random House, 1937), pp. 4–5.

LIVING IN A GLOBAL ECONOMY: ECONOMIES OF SCALE AND THE CANADA/UNITED STATES FREE TRADE AGREEMENT

Even the huge U.S. market is not large enough for some producers to capture all the economies of scale — for example, the manufacturers of aircraft and mainframe computers. But, it is large enough for the producers of many other goods,, such as automobiles. In fact, U.S. auto firms can offer a wide variety of models and still produce most of them at the high volume needed to gain substantially all the economies of scale. Thus, these producers can achieve low cost and at the same time provide a wide choice of models to consumers.

However, the United States is unique, since it is so large. Smaller economies — like Canada's — cannot produce a wide range of cars and at the same time achieve the high volume output necessary to lower costs. Thus, Canada has a choice among three options. It can:

1. Produce a variety of models, each on a small scale and, therefore, at high cost, for the domestic Canadian market. This option would provide car buyers with a choice among models, but at high cost.
2. Produce a small number of models, each at high volume, for the domestic market. This would provide the advantage of low cost, but consumers would not have much choice.
3. Gain both advantages (high-volume, low-cost production and a wide variety of models) by engaging in international trade. (Produce only a few models in Canada, at high volume and low cost. Export many of these cars in exchange for a variety of imported models.)

Historically, up to the early 1960s, Canadian automotive policy was based on the first choice. But, the twin advantages of option 3 are clear, and can come only through international trade. In order to gain these advantages, Canada in 1965 entered a special agreement with the United States, allowing duty-free passage of cars both ways across the border.

The favourable experience with the auto agreement was part of the reason the Canadian government finally decided, in the late 1980s, to negotiate a free trade agreement with the United States. Under the agreement, all tariffs between the two countries will be phased out by 1999. In addition, it provides for more open trade in services (such as banking services) and in energy, and for greater freedom of investment across the border.

For Canada, economies of scale provide one of the main advantages of the free trade agreement. As the treaty came into effect at the beginning of 1989, Canadian businesses had started a process of reorganization, cutting down the number of products and models but increasing the output of the goods they did continue to produce. Much of the output from the longer production runs is destined for the U.S. market. U.S. businesses likewise gain freer access to Canada, which is the most important market for U.S. exports.

The free trade agreement is highly complex, and raises many controversial issues that go beyond economic efficiency; we will discuss some of these issues in detail in Chapter 34. But, the increase in productivity and the possibility that many new jobs would open up in Canada's export industries were important elements in the debate that took place over free trade in the mid-1980s.

In this chapter, the advantages of specialization and exchange have been studied. Exchange takes place in markets; how markets operate will be the subject of the next chapter.

KEY POINTS

1. Specialization requires exchange. The most primitive form of exchange is barter. This has the disadvantage that it requires a coincidence of wants.
2. Complex exchange, with many participants, is feasible in an economy with money. Because exchange is so much easier and more efficient with money, money will evolve even in the absence of government action — as happened in the prisoner-of-war camp.
3. In the prisoner-of-war camp, some cigarettes were more desirable than others. The desirable cigarettes were smoked, leaving the less desirable cigarettes to circulate as money. This illustrated Gresham's Law: "Bad money drives out good." In the modern Canadian economy, the Bank of Canada provides a *uniform* currency. Every dollar is worth the same as every other one; there is no "bad" money to drive "good" money out of circulation.

4. Specialization contributes to efficiency. There are two major reasons why there are gains from specialization and exchange:
    (a) comparative advantage
    (b) economies of scale

5. If two individuals (or regions or countries) have different opportunity costs of producing a good or service, then the individual (or region or nation) with the lower opportunity cost has the *comparative advantage* in that good or service. An example is the lawyer who is better than the gardener at both the law and gardening. Even so, she does not do her gardening herself, because she gains by specializing in the law (her comparative advantage) and hiring the gardener to do the gardening (his comparative advantage).

6. Economies of scale exist if an increase of $x\%$ in the quantity of every input causes the quantity of output to increase by more than $x\%$.

7. Economies of scale is an important argument in favour of freer international trade. Because of scale economies, Canada's auto industry was able to grow rapidly after the 1965 Canada-United States agreement on duty-free trade in autos, and the hope that Canadian industry will be able to take advantage of scale economies was one of the reasons why Canada was willing to enter into a comprehensive free trade agreement with the United States in 1989.

KEY CONCEPTS

specialization
exchange
barter
coincidence of wants
indivisibility

general purchasing power
medium of exchange
Gresham's law
debasement of the currency

deflation
absolute advantage
comparative advantage
economies of scale

PROBLEMS

3-1. (a) Among the goods Canada exports are newsprint and sawn timber, farm machinery, and agricultural products, such as wheat. Why are these goods exported?
      (b) Imports include automobiles, computers, oil, and agricultural products, such as wine, coffee, and bananas. Why are these goods imported?
      (c) Canada exports some agricultural products, and imports others. Why? Canada exports many cars, but it also imports some. Why are we both exporters and importers of cars?

3-2. Suppose that one individual at your college is outstanding, being the best teacher and a superb administrator. If you were the college president, would you ask this individual to teach or to become the administrative vice-president? Why?

3-3. Most jobs are more specialized than they were 100 years ago. Why? What are the advantages of greater specialization? Are there any disadvantages?

3-4. Draw a production possibilities curve (PPC) for the lawyer mentioned in Box 3-2, putting the number of wills drawn up in a week on one axis and flowers planted on the other. (Assume that the lawyer works 40 hours per week.) How does the shape of this PPC differ from that in Chapter 2?

*3-5. Draw the production possibilities curve of one of the two identical cities described in the section on economies of scale. Which way does the curve bend? Does the opportunity cost of bicycles increase or decrease as more bicycles are produced?

* Problems marked with asterisks are more difficult than the others. They are designed to provide a challenge to students who want to do more advanced work.

Chapter 4

■ ■

Demand and Supply: The Market Mechanism

Do you know,
Considering the market, there are more
Poems produced than any other thing?
No wonder poets sometimes have to *seem*
So much more business-like than business men.
Their wares are so much harder to get rid of.

Robert Frost, *New Hampshire*

Although some countries are much richer than others, the resources of every country are limited. Choices must be made. Moreover, every economy involves some degree of specialization. In every economy, therefore, some mechanism is needed to answer the fundamental questions raised by specialization and by the need to make choices:

1. *What* goods and services will be produced? (How do we choose among the various options represented by the production possibilities curve?)
2. *How* will these goods and services be produced? For example, will cars be produced by relatively few workers using a great deal of machinery, or by many workers using relatively little capital equipment?
3. *For whom* will the goods and services be produced? Once goods are produced, who will consume them?

THE MARKET AND THE GOVERNMENT

There are two principal mechanisms by which these questions can be answered. First, answers can be provided by Adam Smith's ''invisible hand.'' If people are left alone to make their own transactions, then the butcher and baker will provide the beef and bread for our dinner. In other words, answers may be provided by transactions among individuals and corporations in the *market*.

In a *market*, an item is bought and sold. Markets where transactions between buyers and sellers take place with little or no government interference are often referred to as *private* or *free* markets.

The ***government*** provides the second method for determining what goods and services will be produced, how they will be produced, and for whom. The government affects the economy in four principal ways: by ***spending***, by ***taxation***, by running ***public enterprises***, and by ***regulation***.

1. *Spending.* When the government pays Old-Age Security benefits to retirees, it influences who gets society's output; the recipient of the benefit is able to buy more goods and services. When the government buys ships for the navy, those ships are produced; the government affects *what* is produced. When the government spends money for agricultural research, it influences *how* food will be produced.
2. *Taxes.* When the government collects taxes, it influences *who* gets society's output. When I pay taxes, I have less left to buy goods and services. Taxes also affect *what* is produced. For example, a tax on gasoline encourages people to buy smaller cars. More small cars are produced, and fewer large ones. Finally, the tax system may also influence *how* goods are produced. Incentives built into the tax law encourage businesses to use more machinery in producing

goods. When they buy machinery, their taxes are reduced.

3. *Public enterprises.* The government owns and operates some businesses, including Crown corporations, such as Air Canada or Canada Post. It decides what these enterprises will produce, and how they will produce it.

4. *Regulation.* Governmental regulations may also influence what, how, and for whom goods and services are produced. For example, the government prohibits the production of some pesticides, and requires seat belts and other safety equipment in cars. It thereby affects what is produced. It requires producers of steel to limit their emissions of smoke into the atmosphere, thereby influencing how goods are produced. The government also regulates some prices—for example, the price of telephone services. This keeps down the incomes of shareholders, as well as executives and workers, in private phone companies. With less income, these people can buy less. Thus, the government influences *who* gets society's product.

In addition to the market and the government, there are other institutions which help to answer the three basic questions: *What? How?* and *For Whom?* For example, when a relief organization collects voluntary contributions of clothing or money for distribution to the poor or to the victims of a natural disaster, it is influencing who gets the output of society. Similarly, within the family, a mechanism other than the market or the government is used to determine how the budget for clothing, etc. is divided among the family members. Nevertheless, economists concentrate on the market and the government when they study the way in which society answers the three basic questions.

Conceivably, a nation might depend almost exclusively on private markets to make the three fundamental decisions. The government might be confined to a very limited role, providing defence, police, the courts, roads, and little else. At the other extreme, the government might try to decide almost everything, specifying what is to be produced, and using a system of rationing and allocations to decide who gets the products. But the real world is one of compromise. In every actual economy, there is some *mixture* of markets and government decision making.

In Canada, the United States, Japan, and the Western European nations, most choices are made in the market.

In these countries, the government plays a relatively limited role by international standards. This is especially true in the United States, where public enterprise accounts for a very small share of total economic activity, and where there has been a tendency in recent years toward *reduced* regulation of private markets. In Canada, the role of government and public enterprise is more prominent than in the United States. However, in comparison with countries at the other end of the spectrum, it still appears very limited. In the economies of the Soviet Union and China, decision making is very heavily concentrated in the government.

As *Marxist* nations, they reject the idea that the market should determine *for whom* goods will be produced. They do not permit individuals to own large amounts of capital. Individuals may of course own small capital goods, but the major forms of capital—factories and heavy machinery—are owned by the state. Therefore, individuals do not receive large dividend payments with which to buy a considerable fraction of the output of the economy. In contrast, most capital is privately owned in *capitalist* or *free enterprise* countries, such as Canada, the United States, and Britain.

In a Marxist nation, not only does the government own most of the capital, it also is involved in detailed decisions as to which products will be produced with this capital. For example, the Soviet Union has a central planning agency which issues directives to the various sectors of the economy to produce specific quantities of goods. It would, however, be a mistake to conclude that government planning is a rigid and all-pervasive method of answering the three basic questions. Markets for goods exist in all Marxist countries, and some — particularly Hungary and Yugoslavia — allow many decisions to be made through the market. China is now engaged in a major experiment in which more reliance is being placed on the market.

A *capitalist* or *free enterprise* economy is one in which individuals are permitted to own large amounts of capital, and decisions are made primarily in markets, with relatively little government interference.

A *Marxist* economy is one in which the government owns most of the capital, and makes many of the economic decisions. Political power is in the hands of a party pledging allegiance to the doctrines of Karl Marx.

Because the market is relatively important in Canada, it will be our initial concern. (Later chapters will deal in detail with the economic role of the government in Canada and with the Marxist economic system.) This chapter explains how the market answers the three basic questions: What will be produced? How? For whom?

THE MARKET MECHANISM

In most markets, the buyer and the seller come face to face. When you buy a suit of clothes, you talk directly to the salesclerk; when you buy groceries, you physically enter the seller's place of business (the supermarket). However, physical proximity is not required to make a market. For example, in a typical stock-market transaction, a widow in Medicine Hat puts in a call to her broker to buy 100 shares of Suncor common stock. About the same time, someone in Fredericton calls his broker to sell 100 shares. The transaction takes place on the floor of the Toronto Stock Exchange, where representatives of the two brokerage houses meet. The buyer and the seller of the stock do not leave their respective homes in Alberta and New Brunswick.

Some markets are quite simple. For example, a barbershop is a "market," since haircuts are bought and sold there. The transaction is obvious and straightforward; the service of haircutting is produced on the spot. In other cases, markets are much more complex. Even the simplest everyday activity may be the culmination of a complicated series of market transactions.

As you sat at breakfast this morning drinking your cup of coffee, you were using products from distant areas. The coffee itself was probably produced in Brazil. The brew was made with water that perhaps had been delivered in pipes manufactured in Quebec and purified with chemicals produced in Sarnia, Ontario. The sugar for the coffee may have been produced in the Caribbean. Perhaps you used artificial cream made from soybeans grown in Southern Ontario. Possibly, your coffee was poured into a cup made in Britain, and stirred with a spoon manufactured in Taiwan from Japanese stainless steel which used nickel from Sudbury in its production. All this was for one cup of coffee.

In such a complex economy, something is needed to keep things straight, to bring order out of potential chaos. **Prices** bring order by performing two important, interrelated functions:
1. Prices provide **information**.
2. Prices provide **incentives**.

To illustrate, suppose we start from the example of chaos. Most of the coffee is in Vancouver and most of the sugar in Montreal. Coffee lovers in Montreal would clamour for coffee, even at very high prices. The high price is a signal, providing *information* to coffee owners that there are eager buyers in Montreal. It also provides them with an *incentive* to send coffee to Montreal. In any market, the price provides the focus for interactions between buyers and sellers.

PERFECT AND IMPERFECT COMPETITION

Some markets are dominated by a few large firms; others have thousands of sellers. The "big three" automobile manufacturers (G.M., Ford, and Chrysler) make most of the cars sold in Canada and the United States, with the rest provided by Japanese, European, and other foreign firms. Such an industry, which is dominated by a few sellers, is an **oligopoly**. (The word "oligopoly" means "a few sellers," just as "oligarchy" means "rule by a few.") Some markets are even more concentrated. For example, there is just one supplier of local telephone services to homes in your area; the local telephone company has a **monopoly**. On the other hand, there are thousands of wheat producers.

> A *monopoly* exists when there is only *one seller*. An *oligopoly* exists when a *few sellers* dominate a market.

The number of participants in a market has a significant effect on the way in which the price is determined. In the wheat market, where there are thousands of buyers and thousands of sellers, no individual farmer produces more than a tiny fraction of the total supply. No single farmer can affect the price of wheat. For each one, the price is given; the individual farmer's decision is limited to the number of bushels of wheat to sell. Similarly, the millers realize that they are each buying only a small fraction of the wheat supplied. They realize that they cannot, as individuals, affect the price of wheat. Each miller's decision is limited to the number of bushels to be bought at the existing market price. In such a **perfectly competitive** market, *there is no pricing decision* for the individual seller and the individual buyer to make. Each buyer and seller is a **price taker**.

Perfect competition exists when there are so many buyers and sellers that no single buyer or seller has any influence over the price. (Sometimes, this term is shortened simply to "competition.")

In contrast, individual producers in an oligopolistic or a monopolistic market know that they have some control over price. For example, IBM sets the prices of its computers. That does not mean, of course, that it can set *any* price it wants and still be ensured of making a profit. It can offer to sell at a high price, in which case it will sell only a few computers. Or it can charge a lower price, in which case it will sell more. A *buyer* may also be large enough to influence price. C.P. Rail is a large enough purchaser of steel to be able to bargain with Canadian steel companies over the price of steel. When individual buyers or sellers can influence price, **imperfect competition** exists.

Imperfect competition exists when any buyer or any seller is able to influence the price. Such a buyer or seller is said to have *market power*.

Note that the term "competition" is used differently in economics and in business. Don't try to tell someone from Chrysler that the automobile market isn't competitive; Chrysler is very much aware of the competition from General Motors, Ford, and the Japanese. Yet, according to the economist's definition, the automobile **industry** is far *less* competitive than the wheat industry.

An *industry* refers to all the producers of a good or service. For example, we may speak of the lumber industry, the wheat industry, or the accounting industry. Note that the term "industry" can refer to *any* good or service; it need not be manufactured.

A *firm* is a business organization that produces goods and/or services. A *plant* is an establishment at a single location used in the production of a good or service; for example: a factory, mine, farm, or store. Some firms — such as General Motors—have many plants. Others have only one; for example, the local independent drug store.

Because price is determined by impersonal forces in a perfectly competitive market, the competitive market is simplest, and will, therefore, be considered first. The perfectly competitive market is also given priority because competitive markets generally operate more efficiently than imperfect markets, as we shall eventually show in Chapters 26 to 28.

THE PERFECTLY COMPETITIVE MARKET: DEMAND AND SUPPLY

In a perfectly competitive market, price is determined by **demand** and **supply**.

Demand

Consider, as an example, the market for apples, in which there are many buyers and many sellers, with none having any control over the price. For the buyer, a high price acts as a deterrent. The higher the price, the fewer apples buyers purchase. Why is this so? As the price of apples rises, consumers switch to oranges or grapefruit, or they simply cut down on their total consumption of fruit. Similarly, the lower the price, the more apples are bought. A lower price brings new purchasers into the market, and each purchaser tends to buy more. The response of buyers to various possible prices is illustrated in the **demand curve** in Figure 4-1. Points *A*, *B*, *C*, and *D* correspond to rows *A*, *B*, *C*, and *D* in the **demand schedule** shown beside the figure.

A *demand curve* and a *demand schedule* show the quantities of a good or service which buyers would be willing and able to purchase at various market prices.

Note carefully that the demand schedule or demand curve applies to a *specific population* and to a *specific time period*. Clearly, the number of apples demanded during a month will exceed the number demanded during a week, and the number demanded by the people of Nova Scotia will be less than the number demanded in the whole of Canada. In a general discussion of theoretical issues, the population and time framework are not always stated explicitly, but it nevertheless should be understood that a demand curve applies to a specific time and population.

Supply

While the demand curve illustrates how buyers behave, the supply curve illustrates how sellers behave; it shows how much they would be willing to sell at various prices. Needless to say, buyers and sellers look at high prices

Table 4-1   The Demand Schedule for Apples

	(1) Price P ($ per bushel)	(2) Quantity Q demanded (thousands of bushels per week)
A	10	50
B	8	100
C	6	200
D	4	400

Table 4-2   The Supply Schedule for Apples

	(1) Price P ($ per bushel)	(2) Quantity Q demanded (thousands of bushels per week)
F	10	260
G	8	240
H	6	200
J	4	150

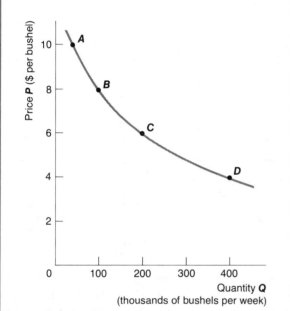

Figure 4-1   The demand curve.

At each of the possible prices specified, there is a quantity of apples that people would be willing and able to buy. This information is provided in Table 4-1 and is reproduced in this diagram. On the vertical axis, the possible prices are shown. In each case, the quantity of apples that would be bought is measured along the horizontal axis. Since people are more willing to buy at a low price than at a high price, the demand curve slopes downward to the right.

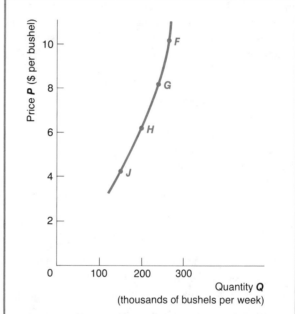

Figure 4-2   The supply curve for apples.

For each of the possible prices specified, the supply schedule (Table 4-2) indicates how many units the sellers would be willing and able to sell. This information is illustrated graphically in this figure, which shows how the supply curve slopes upward to the right. At a high price, suppliers will be encouraged to step up production and offer more apples for sale.

in a different light. Whereas a high price discourages buyers and causes them to switch to alternative products, a high price encourages suppliers to produce and sell more of the good. Thus, the higher the price, the higher the quantity supplied. This is shown in the **supply curve** in Figure 4-2. As in the case of the demand curve, the

points on the supply curve (*F*, *G*, *H*, and *J*) are drawn from the information given in the corresponding rows of the **supply schedule** above the figure.

A *supply curve* and a *supply schedule* show the quantities of a good or service which sellers would be willing and able to sell at various market prices.

The Equilibrium of Demand and Supply

The demand and supply curves may now be brought together in Figure 4-3. (See also Table 4-3.) The **market equilibrium** occurs at point E, where the demand and supply curves intersect. At this equilibrium, the price is $6 per bushel, and weekly sales are 200 000 bushels.

> An *equilibrium* is a situation where there is no tendency to change.

To see why E represents the equilibrium, consider what happens if the market price is initially at some other level. Suppose, for example, that the initial price is $10; — that is, it is above the equilibrium price. What happens? Purchasers buy only 50 000 bushels (shown by point A in Figure 4-3), while sellers want to sell 260 000 bushels (point F). There is a large **excess supply**, or **surplus**, of 210 000 bushels. Some sellers are disappointed: They sell much less than they wish at the price of $10. Unsold apples begin to pile up. In order to get them moving, sellers now begin to accept a lower price. The price starts to come down — to $9, then $8. Still, there is a surplus, or an excess of the quantity supplied over the quantity demanded. (However, the surplus is now a smaller amount, BG). The price continues to fall. It does not stop falling until it reaches $6, the equilibrium. At this price, buyers purchase 200 000 bushels, which is just the amount the sellers want to sell. Both buyers and sellers are now satisfied with the quantity of their purchases or sales at the existing market price of $6. Therefore, there is no further pressure on the price to change.

> An *excess supply*, or *surplus*, exists when the quantity supplied exceeds the quantity demanded. (The price is above the equilibrium.)

Now consider what happens when the initial price is below the equilibrium, at, say, $4. Eager buyers are willing to purchase 400 000 bushels (at point D), yet producers are willing to sell only 150 000 bushels (at point J). There is an **excess demand**, or **shortage**, of

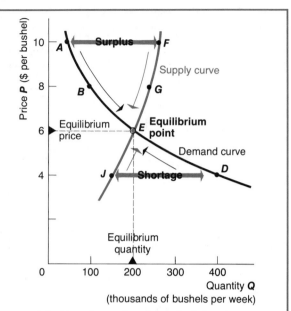

Figure 4-3   How demand and supply determine equilibrium price and quantity.
Equilibrium exists at point E, where the quantity demanded equals the quantity supplied. At any higher price, the quantity supplied exceeds the quantity demanded. Because of the pressure of unsold stocks, competition among sellers causes the price to be bid down to the equilibrium of $6. Similarly, at a price less than the $6 equilibrium, forces are set in motion which raise the price. Because the quantity demanded exceeds the quantity supplied, eager buyers clamour for more apples, and bid the price up to the equilibrium at $6.

250 000 bushels. As buyers clamour for the limited supplies, the price is bid upward. The price continues to rise until it reaches $6, the equilibrium where there is no longer any shortage because the quantity demanded is equal to the quantity supplied. At point E, and only at point E, will the price be stable.

> An *excess demand*, or *shortage*, exists when the quantity demanded exceeds the quantity supplied. (The price is below the equilibrium.)

Table 4-3   The Equilibrium of Demand and Supply

(1) Price P ($ per bushel)	(2) Quantity Q demanded (thousands of bushels per week)	(3) Quantity Q supplied (thousands of bushels per week)	(4) Surplus (+) or shortage (−) (4) = (3) − (2)	(5) Pressure on price
10	50	260	Surplus + 210	Downward
8	100	240	Surplus + 140	Downward
6	**200**	**200**	**0**	**Equilibrium**
4	400	150	Shortage − 250	Upward

SHIFTS IN THE DEMAND CURVE

The quantity of a product which buyers want to purchase depends on the price. As we have seen, the demand curve illustrates this relationship between price and quantity. But, the quantity which people want to purchase also depends on other influences. For example, if incomes rise, people will want to buy more apples—and more of a whole host of other products, too.

The purpose of a demand curve is to show how the quantity demanded is affected by price, **and by price alone**. When we ask how much people want to buy at various prices, it is important that our answer not be disturbed by other influences. In other words, when we draw a demand curve for a good, we must *hold constant incomes and everything else that can affect the quantity demanded*—with the sole exception of the price of the good. We make the **ceteris paribus** assumption — that other things remain unchanged. (*Ceteris* is the same Latin word that appears in '' *et cetera*,'' which literally means ''and other things.'' *Paribus* means ''equal'' or ''unchanged.'')

Of course, as time passes, other things do not remain constant. Through time, for example, incomes generally rise. When that happens, the quantity of apples demanded at any particular price increases. The whole demand curve shifts to the right, as illustrated in Figure 4-4. Since *economists use the term ''demand'' to mean the whole demand curve or demand schedule*, we may speak of this rightward shift in the curve more simply as an *increase in demand*.

Demand Shifters

A shift in the demand curve—that is, a change in demand—may be caused by a change in any one of a whole host of ''other things.'' Some of the most important are the following:

1. Income

When incomes rise, people are able to buy more. And people do, in fact, buy more of the typical or **normal good**. For such a good, the number of units demanded at each price increases as incomes rise. Thus, the demand curve shifts to the right with rising incomes, as illustrated in Figure 4-4.

Not all goods are normal, however. As incomes rise, people may buy *less* of a good. For example, they switch away from margarine and buy more butter, which they can afford now. When this happens—when the increase in income causes a leftward shift of the demand curve for margarine—the item is an **inferior good**.

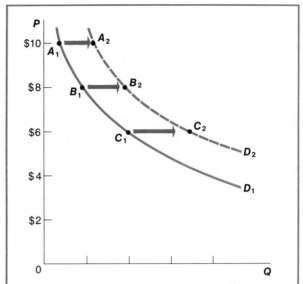

Figure 4-4   A change in the demand for apples.
When incomes rise, there is an increase in the number of apples that people want to buy at any particular price. At a price of $10, for example, the quantity of apples demanded increases from point A_1 to A_2. At other prices, the increase in incomes also causes an increase in the number of apples demanded. Thus, the whole demand curve shifts to the right, from D_1 to D_2.

If an *increase* in income ⬆	Shifts the demand curve for a good to the *right* ➡	It is a *normal* good (or a *superior* good)
If an *increase* in *income* ⬆	Shifts the demand curve for a good to the *left* ⬅	It is an *inferior* good

2. Prices of Related Goods

A rise in the price of one good can cause a shift in the demand curve for another good.

For example, if the price of oranges were to double while the price of apples remained the same, buyers would be encouraged to buy apples instead of oranges. Thus, a rise in the price of oranges causes a rightward shift in the demand curve for apples. Goods, such as apples and oranges — which satisfy similar needs or desires—are **substitutes**. Other examples are tea and coffee, butter and margarine, bus and train tickets, and heating oil and insulating materials.

For *complements* or *complementary goods*, exactly the opposite relationship holds. In contrast to substitutes — which are used *instead* of each other — complements are used *together*, as a package. For example, gasoline and automobiles are complementary goods. If the price of gasoline spirals upward, people become less eager to own automobiles. The demand curve for cars, therefore, shifts to the left. So it is with other complements,, such as tennis rackets and tennis balls, or formal clothing rentals and tickets to a formal dance.

Finally, many goods are basically *unrelated*, in the sense that a rise in the price of one has no significant effect on the demand curve of the others. Thus, bus tickets and butter are unrelated, as are coffee and cameras.

| If an *increase* in the *price* of A | ↑ | Shifts the demand curve for B to the *right* → | Then A and B are *substitutes* |
| If an *increase* in the *price* of C | ↑ | Shifts the demand curve for D to the *left* ← | Then C and D are *complementary goods* |

3. Tastes

Tastes change over time. Because of increased interest in physical fitness, more people are jogging. This increases the demand for running shoes. Tastes and, therefore, demand are quite volatile for some products, particularly for fads like video games.

The above list covers some of the most important demand shifters, but it is far from complete. To see how it might be extended, consider the following questions:
1. If the weather changes, how will the change affect the demand for skiing equipment? For snow tires?
2. If people expect cars to be priced $2,000 higher next year, what effect will this have on the demand for cars this year?
3. As more and more families get videocassette recorders, and thereby become able to skip through the commercials with the fast scan button, how will this affect the demand by companies buying TV ads? (A.C. Nielsen, an American firm which rates TV shows as a service for advertisers, has found

that when people watch taped shows half of them do, in fact, "zap" the commercials.)[1]

WHAT IS PRODUCED: THE RESPONSE TO A CHANGE IN TASTES

At the beginning of this chapter, three basic questions were listed. To see how the market mechanism can help to answer the first of these — *What* will be produced? — consider what happens when there is a change in tastes. Suppose, for example, that people develop a desire to drink more tea and less coffee. This change in tastes is illustrated by a rightward shift in the demand curve for tea and a leftward shift in the demand curve for coffee.

As the demand for tea increases, the price is bid up by eager buyers. With a higher price, growers in Sri Lanka and elsewhere are encouraged to plant more tea. At the new equilibrium, shown as point E_2 in Figure 4-5, the price of tea is higher than it was originally (at E_1), and the consumers buy a larger quantity of tea. In the coffee market, the results are opposite. At the new equilibrium (F_2), the price is lower and a smaller quantity is bought.

Thus, competitive market forces cause producers to "dance to the consumers' tune." In response to a change in consumer tastes, prices change. Tea producers are given an incentive to step up production, and coffee production is discouraged.

SHIFTS IN SUPPLY

While the market encourages producers to "dance to the consumers' tune," the opposite is also true. As we shall now show, consumers "dance to the producers' tune" as well. The market involves a complex interaction: sellers respond to the desires of buyers, and buyers respond to the willingness of producers to sell.

Just as the demand curve reflects the desires of buyers, so the supply curve illustrates the willingness of producers to sell. In an important respect, the two curves are similar. The objective of each is to show *how the quantity is affected by the price of the good, and by this price alone*. Thus, when we draw the supply curve, once again we make the *ceteris paribus* assumption. Everything except the price of the good itself is held constant.

■ ■ ■ ■ ■

[1] Answer: It will reduce the demand. It has been estimated that this resulted in a yearly loss of $200 million in advertising revenue in the United States in 1987.

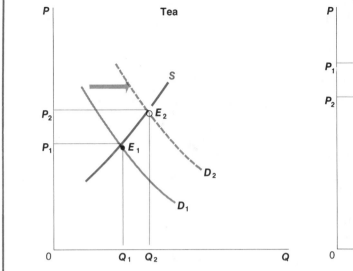 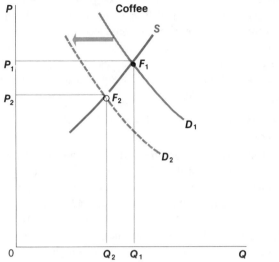

Figure 4-5 A change in tastes.

A change in tastes causes the demand for tea to increase and the demand for coffee to decrease. As a result, more tea is bought at a higher price. Less coffee is bought, and the price of coffee falls.

Supply Shifters

As in the case of demand, the "other things" that affect supply can change through time, causing the supply curve to shift. Some of these "other things" are the following:

1. The Cost of Inputs

For example, if the price of fertilizer goes up, farmers will be less willing to produce wheat at the previously prevailing price. The supply curve will shift to the left.

2. Technology

Suppose that there is an improvement in technology that causes costs of production to fall. With lower costs, producers will be willing to supply more at any particular price. The supply curve will shift to the right.

3. Weather

This is particularly important for agricultural products. For example, a drought will cause a decrease in the supply of wheat (that is, a leftward shift in the supply curve), and a freeze in Florida will cause a decrease in the supply of oranges.

4. The Prices of Related Goods

Just as items can be substitutes or complements in consumption, so they can be substitutes or complements in production.

If an *increase* in the *price* of A	Shifts the supply curve for B to the *left*	Then A and B are *substitutes in production*
If an *increase* in the *price* of C	Shifts the supply curve for D to the *right*	Then C and D are *complements in production*, or *joint products*

We saw earlier that substitutes in consumption are goods which can be consumed as *alternatives* to one another, satisfying the same wants (for example, apples and oranges). Similarly, **substitutes in production** are goods which can be produced as *alternatives* to one another, using the same factors of production. Thus, corn and soybeans are substitutes in production; they can be grown on similar land. If the price of corn increases, farmers are encouraged to switch their lands out of the production of soybeans and into the production of corn. The amount of soybeans they are willing to supply at any given price decreases; the supply curve for soybeans shifts to the left.

We also saw earlier that complements in consumption are used *together* (for example, gasoline and automobiles). Similarly **complements in production** or **joint**

products are produced together, as a package. Beef and hides provide an example. When more cattle are slaughtered for beef, more hides are produced in the process. An increase in the price of beef causes an increase in beef production that, in turn, causes an increase in the production of hides — that is, a rightward shift of the supply curve of hides.

The Response to a Shift in the Supply Curve

To illustrate how ''consumers dance to the producers' tune,'' suppose that there is a frost in Brazil that wipes out part of the coffee crop. As a result, the quantity of coffee available on the market is reduced. That is, the supply curve shifts to the left, as illustrated in Figure 4-6. With less coffee available, the price is bid upward. At the new equilibrium (G_2), the price is higher and the quantity sold is smaller.

How do consumers respond to the change in supply? Because of the higher price of coffee, consumers are discouraged from buying. For example, some may decide to drink coffee only once a day, rather than twice. Anyone who is willing and able to pay the high price will get coffee; those who are unwilling or unable to pay the price will not get it. Thus, the *high price acts as a way of allocating the limited supply among buyers*. The coffee goes only to buyers who are sufficiently eager to be willing to pay the high price, and sufficiently affluent to be able to afford it.

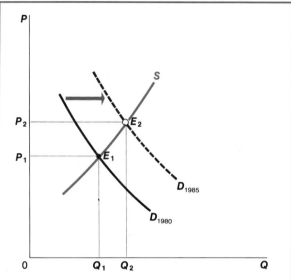

Figure 4-7   A shift in the demand for tea.
This diagram, based on the left panel of Figure 4-5, shows that there is an increase in the quantity of tea supplied as the equilibrium moves from E_1 to E_2. However, supply does not change, since the supply curve does not move.

SHIFTS IN A CURVE AND MOVEMENTS ALONG A CURVE

Because the term ''supply'' applies to a supply schedule or a supply curve, a ''change in supply'' means a *shift* in the entire curve. Such a shift took place in Figure 4-6 as a result of a freeze in Brazil.

In this figure, observe that the demand curve has not moved. However, as the supply curve shifts and the price consequently changes, there is a movement *along* the demand curve from G_1 to G_2. At the second point, less is bought than at the original point. The quantity of coffee demanded is less at G_2 than at G_1.

The distinction between a *shift in a curve* and a *movement along* a curve should be emphasized. What can we say about the move from G_1 to G_2?

1. It is correct to say that ''supply has decreased.'' Why? Because the entire supply curve has shifted to the left.
2. It is *not* correct to say that ''demand has decreased.'' Why? Because the demand curve has not moved.
3. It is, however, correct to say that ''the quantity demanded has decreased.'' Why? Because a smaller quantity is demanded at G_2 than at G_1.

A similar distinction should be made when the demand curve shifts. This is shown in Figure 4-7, based

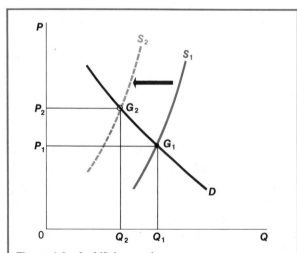

Figure 4-6   A shift in supply.
A freeze in Brazil causes a leftward shift in the supply curve of coffee. The result is a movement of the equilibrium along the demand curve from G_1 to G_2. At the new equilibrium, there is a higher price, and a smaller quantity is sold.

on the left panel of Figure 4-5, where the demand for tea increases because of a change in tastes. The rightward movement of the demand curve causes the equilibrium to move *along* the *supply* curve, from E_1 to E_2. It is not correct to say that supply has increased, since the supply curve did not move. However, the *quantity supplied* did increase as the price rose. (Quantity Q_2 is greater than Q_1.)

THE INTERCONNECTED QUESTIONS OF *WHAT, HOW,* AND *FOR WHOM*

We have explored how two tunes are played. Demand is the tune played by consumers, and supply the tune played by producers. We have also seen how each group dances to the tune played by the other.

If we now want to go beyond the question of what will be produced to the other questions—*how?* and *for whom?*—we must recognize that the world is even more complex. We don't merely have two tunes being played. We have a whole orchestra, with the tune played on any one instrument related to the tunes played on all the others.

The major segments of the economy are illustrated in Figure 4-8, which adds detail to Figure 3-3. The *product markets* for apples, coffee, bread, housing, etc., are represented by the upper box; we have concentrated on product markets thus far. The box at the bottom indicates that there are similar *markets for factors of production*, with their own demands and supplies. For example, to produce wheat, farmers need land; they create a demand for land.

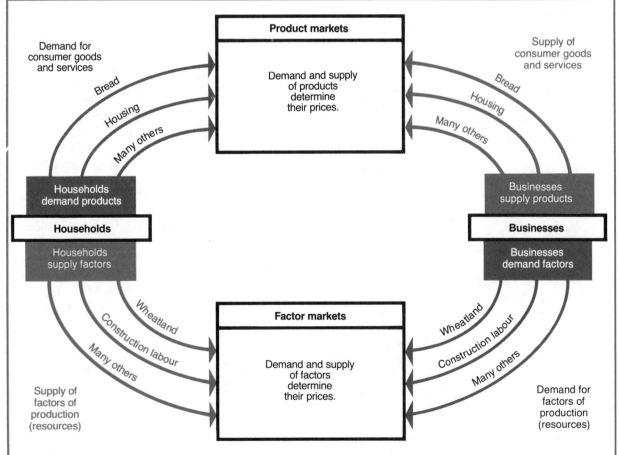

Figure 4-8 Markets answer the basic questions of *what*, *how*, and *for whom*.

The product markets (top box) are most important in determining *what* is produced, and the factor markets (lower box) in determining *how* goods are produced, and *for whom*. However, there are many interrelationships among the two boxes. For example, incomes change in response to changing demand and supply conditions in the lower box, and these changing incomes, in turn, influence the demand for products in the upper box.

At the same time, those with land are willing to sell or rent it if the price is attractive; they create a supply of land.

In answering the question, *What* will be produced? we begin by looking at the top box, where the demand and supply for products come together. If there is a large demand for bread, we may expect a lot of it to be produced. But, eventually we will also have to look at the lower box, where the demand and supply for the factors of production come together. Why are the factor markets relevant? Because the demand and supply in the upper box are influenced by what happens in the factor markets in the lower box.

As an example, consider what happens when oil is discovered in Northern Alberta. To build the pipeline needed to get the oil out, workers had to be hired. As a consequence, the demand for construction labour in Alberta increased sharply. The price of labour (that is, the wage rate) in Alberta shot up, and construction workers flocked in from the other provinces. The spiraling wage payments in Alberta (lower box) had repercussions on the demands for goods and services in Alberta (upper box). For example, the demand for housing in Alberta (in the upper box) increased as a result of the higher earnings of construction workers in the lower box.

How? and *For Whom?*

To answer the question, "*What* will be produced?" we began by looking at the product markets in the upper box of Figure 4-8. To answer the questions *How?* and *For whom?* we begin by looking at the lower box.

The factor prices established in the lower box help to determine *how* goods are produced. During the Black Death of 1348–50 and subsequent plagues, an estimated quarter to a third of the Western European population died. As a consequence, labour supply was substantially reduced and wages rose sharply — by 30% to 40%. Because of the scarcity of labour and its high price, wheat producers had an incentive to farm their lands with less labour. Wheat was produced in a different way, with a different combination of labour and land. In those days —as today—the market mechanism was the way in which the society conserved its scarce supply of a factor (in this case, labour).

The answer to the question, "*For whom* is the nation's output produced?" depends on incomes, which are determined by the interplay of supply and demand in factor markets (lower box in Figure 4-8). For example, the

supply of accountants is small compared with the demand for accountants. The price of their "labour" is, therefore, high; accountants generally have high incomes. On the other hand, unskilled labour is in large supply, and is, therefore, cheap. Consequently, the unskilled worker receives a low income.

LIVING IN A GLOBAL ECONOMY: RENTING AN OFFICE IN TOKYO, LONDON, OR HONG KONG

While Japan is rich, the Japanese are not.

Clyde Prestowitz[2]

In real estate, so the saying goes, three things are important: location, location, and location. Prime office space is similar in design and quality in all of the major financial capitals of the world. But, the price it commands depends very much on the location. Demand and supply can differ greatly between cities, resulting in quite different rentals.

Buoyant demand and limited supply combine to make Tokyo the most expensive city in the world to rent an office. In 1988, office space in downtown Tokyo rented for an average of $1,750 per m^2 per year. For a space 4 m x 3 m, that meant an annual rental of $21,000. Not surprisingly, many junior executives found themselves cramped in offices that were little bigger than closets.

New York was far behind, with an annual rental of "only" $450. That was cheaper than London ($1,550), Paris ($700), or Hong Kong ($650). Hong Kong is often classified as a less developed area. How can offices be so expensive? One reason is the short supply of land: Hong Kong has 5.5 million people crowded in an area about 52 km^2. Another reason is the booming economy. Hong Kong is one of the best places to do business in all of East Asia, and firms are willing to pay the high rents.

THE MARKET MECHANISM: A PRELIMINARY EVALUATION

Some see private enterprise as a predatory target to be shot, others as a cow to be milked; but few are those who see it as a sturdy horse pulling the wagon.

Winston Churchill

■ ■ ■ ■ ■

[2] *Trading Places: How We Allowed Japan to Take the Lead* (New York: Basic Books, 1988), p. 311.

There are thousands of markets in Canada, and millions of interconnections among the markets. Changes in market conditions are reflected in changes in prices. As we have seen, prices provide information to market participants; they provide them with incentives to respond to changing conditions; and they bring order out of a potentially chaotic situation—even though there is no individual or government bureaucracy in control.

Strengths of the Market

In some ways, the market works very well. Specifically:

1. The market *gives producers an incentive to produce the goods that consumers want*. If people want more tea, the price of tea is bid up, and producers are encouraged to produce more. (However, see Box 4-1 for a special case where producers offer a "bad" rather than a "good," and where a strong case can be made for the government to suppress the product.)

2. The market *provides an incentive to acquire useful skills*. For example, the high incomes that doctors earn give students an incentive to undertake the long, difficult, and expensive training necessary to become a physician.

3. The market *encourages consumers to use scarce goods carefully*. For example, when the coffee crop is partially destroyed by bad weather, the price is driven up, and people use coffee sparingly. Those who are relatively indifferent are encouraged to switch to tea. Even those who feel they must have coffee are motivated to conserve. With a high price of coffee, they are careful not to brew three cups when they intend to use only two.

4. Similarly, the price system encourages producers to *conserve scarce resources*. In the pasturelands of Alberta, land is plentiful and cheap; it is used to raise cattle. In Japan, in contrast, land is relatively scarce and expensive; few cattle are raised. At full-sized golf courses, fees are astronomical; most golfers have to be content with driving ranges.

5. The market involves a *high degree of economic freedom*. Nobody forces people to do business with specific individuals or firms. People are not directed into specific lines of work by government officials; they are free to choose their own occupations. Moreover, if people save, they are free to use their savings to set themselves up in their own independent businesses.

6. Markets *provide information* on local conditions. For example, if an unusual amount of hay-producing land in a specific county is plowed up to grow corn, then the price of hay in that county will tend to rise. The higher price of hay will signal farmers that they should put some of the land in this county back into hay. No government agency can hope to keep up-to-date and detailed information on the millions of localized markets like this one, each with its own conditions. (Note the amount of information that is relevant, even for this simple decision on whether hay or corn should be planted: the quality of the land, particularly its relative productivity in hay and corn; the number of cattle and horses that eat hay; the cost of fertilizer for hay and for corn; the cost of seed for each; and so on.)

In evaluating how well a market works, we should keep in mind the most important question of all: *Compared to what?* Even a poor market may work better than the alternatives. Thus, one of the strongest arguments for the market parallels Winston Churchill's case for democracy: It doesn't work very well, but it does work better than the alternatives that have been tried from time to time.

The Alternative of Price Controls: Some Problems

Consider what happens if the government tries to keep a price down by setting a price ceiling. Specifically, suppose it sets the price at P_1, below the equilibrium at E in Figure 4-9. The result is a shortage AB. Eager buyers have trouble finding the good. Thus, when the United States had a ceiling on gasoline prices in 1979, drivers had to wait in long lines at gas stations. Obviously, they wasted time—not to speak of the gasoline they wasted while waiting in line. The nations of Eastern Europe, where governments regulate many prices, have chronic shortages. The Soviet Union is a "queuetopia."

Moreover, as a result of price controls, goods may disappear from regular distribution channels, and flow instead into illegal black markets. In this case, the scarce goods go to those willing to break the law. Furthermore, the public may end up paying more for black market goods than it would pay in a free market. Black marketeers charge higher prices to compensate for the risks, and because they have to use informal, inefficient marketing arrangements.

A *black market* is one in which sales take place at a price above the legal maximum.

Box 4-1

■■■■■■■■■■■■■■■■■■■■■■■■■

The Controversy Over Heroin

Kurt Schmoke used to be a prosecutor. He sent hundreds of felons to jail for drug-related crimes. But, when he became Mayor of Baltimore, he created a national furor by calling for a debate on the legalization of heroin. The present system, he argued, is a failure. For drug dealers, ''going to jail is just part of the cost of doing business. It's a nuisance, not a deterrent.''

Proponents of legalization do not condone the use of heroin and other hard drugs. But, they pose a question: Why are the social costs of the present system so high? Much of our crime is associated with drugs. Addicts steal to support their habit, and dealers fight over turf. If heroin were legalized, its price would fall, reducing the compulsion of addicts to steal. If drugs were distributed by hospitals or clinics, they would be less attractive; they would be associated with sickness, not with the defiance of authority. Most of the $8 billion spent each year in the United States on the war against drugs could be diverted to treatment, which now receives less than $1 billion.

Proponents of legalization also point out that the drug trade has led to corruption and bribery at home and abroad, because it is both lucrative and illegal. In at least one country—Colombia—the government is engaged in a shooting war with drug barons; two cabinet officers have been assassinated in drug-motivated crimes in recent years.

The undisputed fact that heroin kills people is not sufficient reason to keep it illegal. Tobacco kills people too, and so does alcohol—particularly when used by drivers. Prohibition of alcohol was a failure, and was repealed in the 1930s as a way to reduce the power of organized crime. The same argument can be applied to heroin and many other illegal drugs. So say the advocates of legalization.

Opponents point out that heroin and alcohol are very different. Only 10% of alcohol users become addicts, whereas most heroin users do. If heroin were legalized, its falling price would attract new users. The costs of medical care for addicts would soar. Further-

Price controls can create other problems. For example, in its desire to prevent labour unrest, the Polish government kept bread fixed at a low price—so low that is was less than the price of wheat that went into making the bread. Farmers found that it was cheaper to feed their livestock bread rather than grain. This represented a waste of the resources that had been used to make wheat into bread.

The Market Mechanism: Limitations and Problems

While the market has impressive strengths, it is also the target of substantial criticisms:

1. While the market provides a high degree of freedom for participants in the economy, *it may give the weak*

more, the legalization of heroin, cocaine, and such drugs might lead to a much greater use of new synthetics and derivatives like crack, whose long-term effects are poorly understood. Removing the legal prohibition might be taken as a signal that hard drugs are now socially acceptable.

The British experience underlines just how difficult it is to foresee the long-term consequences of legalization. Beginning in the 1950s, Britain made heroin available to addicts by prescription. Doctors provided small doses — enough to prevent withdrawal symptoms, but not enough to create highs. The objective was to stabilize doses and, if possible, to wean addicts away from the drug. For many years, the program worked; the number of addicts remained about the same. But, the worldwide drug boom of the 1970s created a flood of heroin. Addicts found that they could easily get enough heroin to produce highs, and that, after all, is why they started taking the drug in the first place. Because they could get only limited quantities from doctors, most addicts stopped going. The prescription system died out.

Like many other countries, the Netherlands found drug use increasing in the early 1970s. They responded with a program designed to separate the markets for heroin and marijuana. Jail terms for heroin dealers were tripled. At the same time, the government announced that they would not prosecute people with small amounts of marijuana, although laws against marijuana remained on the books. The idea was to keep a small market in soft drugs, which young people could use in relative safety without going to criminals who might also offer samples of hard drugs. The Dutch were originally concerned that this would lead to an upsurge in the use of marijuana, but consumption has actually fallen. And the policy of separating the two markets seems to be working. The overall use of heroin has fallen, especially among young people. In 1981, 14% of Dutch addicts were under 22; by the end of the decade, less than 5% were.

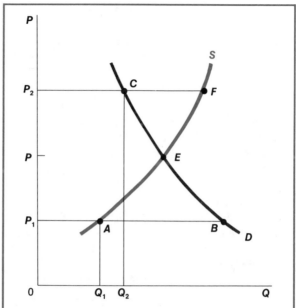

Figure 4-9 Price-setting by the government.
If the government sets a price ceiling at P_1 to keep the price below the equilibrium at E, the result is a shortage, AB. Observe that the consumers end up with less: the quantity supplied at A is less than at equilibrium E.

On the other hand, if the government sets a price floor at P_2, the result is a surplus. The government can keep the price at P_2 if it is willing to buy the surplus, CF. Again, the public ends up with less—at C—than it would get at equilibrium E. Thus, when the government sets the price, consumers get a smaller quantity, *whether the price is set above or below its equilibrium.*

and the helpless little more than the freedom to starve. In a market, producers do not respond solely to the needs or the eagerness of consumers to have products. Rather, they respond to the desires of consumers that are backed up with cash. Thus, under a system of laissez-faire, the pets of the rich may have better meals and better health care than the children of the poor.

2. Markets *simply won't work* in some areas. Where there is a military threat, individuals cannot provide their own defence. An individual who buys a rifle has no hope of standing against a foreign power. Organized military forces, financed by the government, are needed. The police and the judicial system are other services that can best be provided by the government. No matter how well the market works in general, people can't be permitted to "buy" a judge.

3. In a system of laissez-faire, *prices are not always the result of impersonal market forces.* In many markets, one or more participants have the power to influence price. *The monopolist or oligopolist may restrict production in order to keep the price high*, as we shall see in detail in later chapters.

4. Activities by private consumers or producers may have undesirable *side effects*. Nobody owns the air or

the rivers. Consequently, in the absence of government restraints, manufacturers use them freely as garbage dumps, harming those downwind or downstream. The market provides no incentive to limit such negative side effects.

5. An unregulated system of private enterprise may be *quite unstable*, with periods of inflationary boom giving way to sharp recessions. Economic instability was a particularly severe problem in the early 1930s, when the economies of many countries collapsed into a deep depression.

6. In a system of laissez-faire, businesses may do an excellent job of satisfying consumer wants as expressed in the marketplace. But, should the businesses be given high marks, if they have *created the wants in the first place* by advertising? In the words of John Kenneth Galbraith, "It involves an exercise of imagination to suppose that the taste so expressed originates with the consumer."[3] In this case, the producer is sovereign, not the consumer. According to Galbraith, the consumer is a puppet, manipulated by producers with the aid of the advertising industry's bag of tricks. Many of the wants which producers create and then satisfy are trivial: for example, the demands for automobile chrome and junk food.

Without arguing the merits of each and every product, defenders of the market system make a countercase, based in part on the question: Compared with what? If market demands are dismissed, who then is to decide which products are "meritorious" and which are not? Government officials? Should not people be permitted the freedom to make their own mistakes? And why

■ ■ ■ ■ ■
[3] John Kenneth Galbraith, "Economics as a System of Belief," *American Economic Review*, May 1970, p. 474. See also Galbraith, *The New Industrial State* (Boston: Houghton Mifflin, 1967).

should we assume that created wants are without merit? After all, we are not born with a taste for art or good music. Our taste for good music is created when we listen to it. Galbraith certainly wouldn't suggest that symphony orchestras are without merit simply because they satisfy the desire for good music which they have created. But, who then is to decide which "created" wants are socially desirable?

If these criticisms of the market are taken far enough, they can be made into a case for replacing the market with an alternative system. Marxist economists lay particular emphasis on points 1, 5, and 6 in their argument that the market should be replaced with central planning and government direction of the economy.

However, these criticisms are also often made by those who seek to reform, rather than replace, the market system. The recent economic history of Western Europe, North America, and many other parts of the globe has been written to a significant extent by such reformers. If the market does not provide a living for the weak and the helpless, then its outcome should be modified by private and public assistance programs. If monopolists have excessive market power, they should be broken up or their market power should be restrained by the government. If an unregulated market means that only American television programs would be shown in Canada, the government should regulate the television industry to protect Canadian culture. Where there are undesirable side effects,, such as pollution, they should be limited by taxation or control programs. In defence, justice, the police, and other areas where the market won't work or works very poorly, the government should assume responsibility for the provision of services.

Although the market is a vital mechanism, it has sufficient weaknesses to provide the government with a major economic role. This role will be the subject of the next chapter.

KEY POINTS

1. Every economy has limited resources and involves specialization and exchange. In every economy, a mechanism is needed to answer three fundamental questions:
   (a) *What* will be produced?
   (b) *How* will it be produced?
   (c) *For whom* will it be produced?

2. There are two principal mechanisms for answering these questions:
   (a) The market, where individuals are free to make their own contracts and transactions.
   (b) The government, which can use taxation, spending, regulation, and government-owned enterprises to influence *what, how*, and *for whom*.

In the real world, all countries rely on a mixture of markets and government action. However, the mixture differs among countries. Canada and other Western countries place a relatively heavy reliance on the market. In the U.S.S.R. and other countries of Eastern Europe, the government has a much more pervasive influence.

3. *Prices* play a key role in markets, providing information and incentives to buyers and sellers.

4. Markets vary substantially, with some being dominated by one or a few producers, while others have many producers and consumers. A market is *perfectly competitive* if there are many buyers and many sellers, with no single buyer or seller having any influence over the price.

5. In a perfectly competitive market, equilibrium price and quantity are established by the intersection of the demand and supply curves.

6. In drawing both the demand and supply curves, the *ceteris paribus* assumption is made — that "other things" do not change. Everything that can affect the quantity demanded or supplied — with the sole exception of price — is held constant when a demand or supply curve is constructed.

7. If any of these "other things" — such as consumer incomes or the prices of other goods — do change, the demand or supply curve will shift.

8. *What* the economy produces is determined primarily in the market for goods and services in the upper box of Figure 4-8. On the other hand, *how* and *for whom* are determined primarily in the factor markets (the lower box). However, there are numerous interactions among markets. The answer to each of the three questions depends on what happens in both the upper and lower boxes.

9. There is a substantial case to be made for the market system, because it encourages firms to produce what people demand, and because it encourages the careful use of scarce goods and resources. Nevertheless, the market also has significant weaknesses, which provide the government with an important economic role.

KEY CONCEPTS

market	*industry*	*inferior good*
central planning	*firm*	*normal or superior good*
capitalist economy	*plant*	*substitutes*
free enterprise	*demand*	*complementary goods*
mixed economy	*supply*	*supply shifter*
monopoly	*equilibrium*	*joint products*
oligopoly	*surplus*	*price control*
perfect competition	*shortage*	*black market*
imperfect competition	*ceteris paribus*	
market power	*demand shifter*	

PROBLEMS

4-1. Figure 4-6 illustrates the effect of a Brazilian freeze on the coffee market. How might the resulting change in the price of coffee affect the tea market? Explain with the help of a diagram showing the demand and supply for tea.

4-2. The relatively high incomes of doctors give students an incentive to study medicine. Other than the expected income and costs of training, what are the important things which affect career decisions?

4-3. It is often said that "the market has no ethics. It is impersonal." But, individual participants in the market do have ethical values, and these values may be backed up with social pressures. Suppose that in a certain society, it is considered not quite proper to be associated with a distillery. With the help of demand and supply diagrams, explain how this view will affect:

(a) The demand and/or supply of labour in the alcohol industry.

(b) The willingness of people to invest their funds in the alcohol industry, and the profitability of that industry?

4-4. Suppose that social sanctions are backed up by law, and that people caught selling marijuana are given stiff jail sentences. How will this affect the demand and supply of marijuana? The price of marijuana? The quantity sold? The incomes of those selling marijuana?

*4-5. In distinguishing between substitutes and complements, the text listed a number of simple cases. Tea and coffee are substitutes, while cars and gasoline are complements.

However, it is worth looking more closely at one example that may not seem quite so simple: heating oil and insulation. How would you correct or rebut the following *erroneous* argument:

> Heating oil and insulation are complements, not substitutes, because they are used together. In Winnipeg, Manitoba they use a lot of heating oil and a lot of insulation. In Miami, Florida they don't use much of either.

Try to answer this question without looking at the following hints. But, if you have difficulty, consider these hints:

(a) Think about the market for heating oil and insulation in a single place, say, Winnipeg. When the price of heating oil goes up in Winnipeg, do you think that this causes the demand curve for insulation to shift to the right or to the left? Does this make insulation a complement or substitute for heating oil, according to the definitions in the text?

(b) Are natural gas and oil substitutes or complements? Suppose the erroneous statement given above had mentioned heating oil and natural gas, rather than heating oil and insulation.

(c) If we accept the erroneous statement shown above, can't we argue in a similar manner that there are no such things as substitutes? For example, wouldn't we also accept the following incorrect conclusion: "In the Niagara region, more apples and more cherries are sold than in the Northwest Territories. Therefore, apples and cherries are used together. They are complements, not substitutes." Do you see that this statement is incorrect, because it departs from the standard assumption that "other things remain unchanged?" In identifying complements and substitutes, we must not switch from one location and population (Northwest Territories) to another (Southern Ontario); we must look at a single set of people, such as the Winnipeg example in part (a). Do you see why economists emphasize the assumption that "other things remain unchanged" (*ceteris paribus*)?

Chapter 5

■ ■

The Economic Role of the Government

> In answering that question [on the role of the
> State] it would be necessary to enter into a
> large consideration of what the Government
> can do for the benefit of those subject to it,
> and that is a very wide question, on which
> people may differ.
>
> John Stuart Mill, in evidence before
> the Select Committee on the Income and
> Property Tax, 1852

The defects and limitations of the market system, outlined at the end of Chapter 4, provide a reason for the
government to play an important role in the economy.
In the words of Adam Smith, there are economic functions "... which, though they may be in the highest
degree advantageous to a great society, are, however,
of such a nature, that the profit could never repay the
expence to any individual, or small group of individuals''; consequently, these functions must be undertaken
by the government.

In Chapter 4, we described briefly how the government affects the economy in four principal ways: by
spending, by **taxation**, by **regulation**, and by running
public enterprises. For example, when the government
spends for roads or for ships for the navy, then production is affected: More roads and ships are built. The
primary function of *taxation* is to raise revenue for the
government; taxes are an unpleasant necessity. But taxes
may also be used for secondary purposes. For example,
if the government wants to discourage the production of
some goods, it can put a tax on them. (This will raise
their price and lead consumers to buy less.) The government also influences economic behaviour through
direct regulation. Regulations regarding seat belts and
other safety equipment have affected the design of automobiles; safety requirements affect the way in which

coal is mined; and government regulations limit the
amount of pollution that manufacturers can discharge
into the air and water. Finally, the government indirectly
affects many sectors of the economy through the activities of *public enterprises*. For example, because the
CBC has a policy of favouring Canadian programming,
more Canadians have jobs in symphony orchestras or in
the television industry, and TV viewers spend less of
their time watching foreign programs.

In contrast with the private market, where people
have an option of buying or not, government activities
generally involve compulsion. Taxes must be paid; people are not allowed to opt out of the system when the
time rolls around for paying income taxes. Similarly,
government regulations involve compulsion; car manufacturers must install safety equipment. And compulsion sometimes exists even in a government spending
program. Young people must go to school (although
their parents do have the option of choosing a private
school rather than one run by the government).

Later sections of this chapter will consider how the
government can use spending, taxation, regulation, and
public enterprise, to improve the outcome of the private
market. As a preliminary, it is necessary to look at some
facts showing how the government's role has expanded,
and what the government is currently doing.

THE GROWTH OF GOVERNMENT EXPENDITURES

During the nineteenth and early twentieth centuries, government expenditures covered little more than the expenses of the army and police, a few public works, and the salaries of judges, legislators, and a small body of government officials. Except for wartime periods when spending shot upward to pay for munitions, weapons, and personnel, government spending was small. As late as 1928, all levels of government (federal, provincial, and local) together spent less than $800 million a year. Of this total, about two-thirds was spent by provincial and local governments. Highway maintenance and education were typical government programs. This does not mean, however, that a rigid policy of laissez-faire was followed. Even during the nineteenth century, the Canadian government participated in some important sectors of the economy, notably railroad building.

With the Depression of the 1930s, there came a major increase in government activity. Distress and unemployment were widespread, and it was increasingly hard to believe that the workings of the private market would lead to the best of all possible worlds. Public sector spending increased rapidly as all levels of government tried to alleviate the burden on the unemployed and to create new jobs for them in the public sector. Then, as Canada became heavily involved in the Second World War, huge federal government spending was required to pay for military equipment and for the salaries of military personnel.

When the war ended in 1945, the nation demobilized and government spending fell by about 30%. But the decline was only temporary. Over the past three decades, spending at all levels of government has increased rapidly, to total no less than $267 billion by 1988 (Figure 5-1).

Government Expenditures in Perspective

Clearly, government spending has become very large. It is hard for the average citizen, accustomed to dealing with a family budget measured in hundreds or thousands of dollars, to comprehend government budgets measured in billions. A billion dollars may be more meaningful if it is reduced to a personal level: A billion dollars represents about $40 for every man, woman, and child in Canada. Thus, with total annual budgets amounting to $267 billion, our federal, provincial, and local governments spent more than $10,000 per Cana-

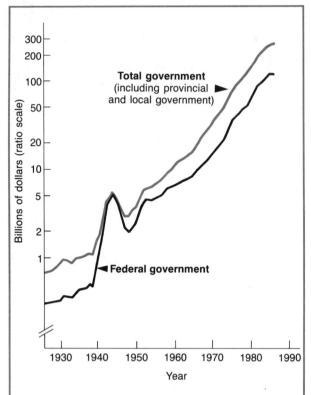

Figure 5-1 Government expenditures, 1926–86.
The most rapid rate of increase in government spending came during 1940–45, as the federal government had to spend enormous sums to pay for the war. In the last two decades, government spending has again increased rapidly; most of this increase has been accounted for by non-defence expenditures at all levels of government (federal, provincial and municipal).

Source: Statistics Canada, *CANSIM Databank*. Reproduced by permission of the Minister of Supply and Services Canada.

dian in 1988. The magnitude of a billion dollars may be illustrated in another way. When the government borrows $1 billion at an interest rate of 10% per annum, its interest payments amount to more than $270,000 *per day.*

But the expenditures shown in Figure 5-1 can give a misleading impression of the size of the government. While the government is spending more and more, so are private individuals and businesses. For both the government and the private sectors, these rising expenditures reflect two major trends: More and more goods and services are being bought, and at higher and higher prices. We can see government expenditures in better perspective by examining them, not in dollar terms

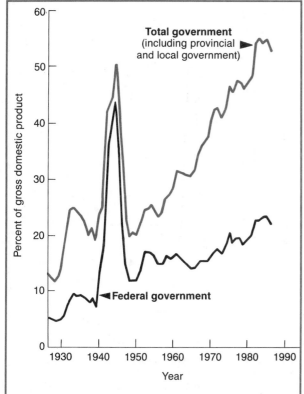

Figure 5-2   Total government expenditures (including transfers).
If we look at what the government takes for itself plus what it takes to redistribute in the form of transfers, then the government has laid claim to a larger and larger share of total output and spending in Canada.

Source: Statistics Canada, *CANSIM Databank*. Reproduced by permission of the Minister of Supply and Services Canada.

(as in Figure 5-1), but rather as a percentage of total spending in Canada.[1]

When we do this in Figure 5-2, the increase in government expenditures does not look quite as dramatic. Following the wartime peak of about 50% of total Canadian spending, government spending fell to less than 25% in the mid-1940s, and the percentage then rose only slowly until the mid-1960s. However, since then it has again risen at a rapid pace and, by the late 1980s, total government spending had surpassed the wartime level of more than 50% of total spending.

-----

[1] The measure of total spending — gross domestic product (GDP) — will be explained in Chapter 6.

Government Purchases versus Transfers

A further complication in measuring the size of the government arises because of the two major categories of government expenditures: (1) *purchases of goods and services* and (2) *transfer payments*.

Government purchases of goods include items such as typewriters, computers, and army trucks. The government purchases services when it hires schoolteachers, police officers, and employees for government departments. When the government purchases such goods and services, *it makes a direct claim on the productive capacity of the nation.* For example, when it spends $600 for a typewriter, then steel, plastic, rubber, and labour are used to manufacture the typewriter. Similarly, the purchase of services involves a claim on productive resources. The police officer hired by the government must spend time on the beat, and thus becomes unavailable for work in the private sector.

Government transfer payments, on the other hand, are payments for which the recipient does not provide any good or service in return. Family allowances and social assistance payments to low-income families are examples of transfer payments, as are Old Age Security (OAS) and Unemployment Insurance benefits.

In contrast with government purchases, transfer payments represent no direct claim by the government on the productive capacity of the nation. For example, when the government pays OAS benefits to retired people, there is no reallocation of the nation's product away from the private sector toward the government sector. Unlike the typewriter company that manufactures a typewriter and ships it to the government to get the payment of $600, the OAS benefit recipient does not use up productive resources to provide the government with a good or a service in return for the benefit. This does not mean, of course, that the Old Age Security program is unimportant. When the government collects taxes[2] to finance it and pays benefits to retirees, the pattern of consumer spending is affected. The old have more to

-----

[2] Payments into social insurance funds such as the Canada Pension Plan or Unemployment Insurance are sometimes called *contributions*, on the grounds that individuals acquire a right to pensions and other benefits as a reward for their payments. But it is also correct to label these contributions as taxes, since they are involuntary payments which must be made to the government. (Furthermore, while benefits bear some relation to the "contributions" which an individual has made, they are not closely tied to previous "contributions.")

spend, and those of working age who pay taxes, have less. As a consequence, producers find themselves faced with greater demands for the things that old people want, and with smaller demands for the products desired by the working population. Therefore, although the system of government transfer payments affects the amount of the nation's product that various individuals can purchase, it does not redirect the economy toward production for the government.

> A *transfer payment* is a payment by the government to an individual, for which the individual does not provide a good or service in return.

Figure 5-2 showed total government expenditures, including transfers. Another way of measuring the size of the government is to look only at government purchases of goods and services; that is, expenditures excluding transfers, as shown in Figure 5-3. These are the expenditures that make a direct claim on the productive resources of the economy. As a share of total Canadian spending, government purchases of goods and services stayed relatively constant between the early 1950s and the mid-1960s. Even though the percentage has risen in the last 20 years, the late 1980s it had risen to only about 20% — no more than half its wartime peak.

We can thus get two somewhat different impressions of the government's size, compared with the size of the economy. If we look only at purchases of goods and services, then the percentage of national product going to the government has been rising fairly slowly over the past two decades. If, on the other hand, we include transfers, the government's percentage has been increasing much more rapidly. Thus, the principal reason for the government's increasing share of the economy is not that it is directly claiming more and more of the nation's output for itself. Instead, the increasing share is mostly due to the claiming of more revenue by the government to be redistributed in the form of transfer payments such as family allowances and social welfare assistance.

While the government is a major participant in the Canadian economy, the governments in some European countries assume an even larger role. In a country such as Sweden, taxes have to be very high to pay for the cradle-to-grave welfare system. But, in other countries, the role of the government is smaller, and tax collections are a smaller percentage of income. In spite of its rapid achievement of a standard of living similar to Western Europe's, Japan has remained a low-tax country, col-

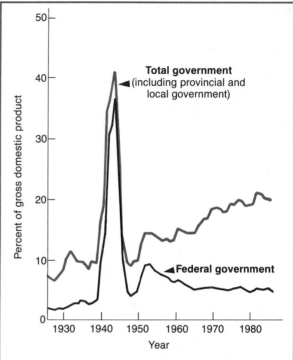

Figure 5-3   Government purchases of goods and services.

However, as a percent of total spending, government purchases of goods and services have changed much more slowly over the past two decades.

Source: Statistics Canada, *CANSIM Databank*. Reproduced by permission of the Minister of Supply and Services Canada.

lecting only about half as large a share in taxes as do the Western European countries. It is also the case that the U.S. government collects a significantly smaller share of total income as taxes than does Canada.

THE BUDGETS OF THE CANADIAN GOVERNMENTS

Federal Government Expenditures

Details on federal government expenditures in Canada, and on the taxes that finance these expenditures, are provided in panel (*a*) of Table 5-1. This table includes both purchases of goods and services and transfer payments to persons as well as to other levels of government. In Canada's federal system, the share of the federal government in total government spending on goods and services is comparatively small. Thus, expenditures on current goods and services in Table 5-1 are a relatively

**Table 5-1   Federal Government Expenditure and Revenue
Fiscal Year Ending March 31, 1986**

(a) **Expenditure**	**Billions of Dollars**	**Percentage**
1. General Services	5.6	5
2. Protection of Persons and Property	11.9	10
3. Transportation and Communication	3.5	3
4. Health	7.1	6
5. Social Services	39.2	34
6. Education	4.0	3
7. Resource Conservation & Industrial Development	8.1	7
8. General-purpose transfer to other levels of government	6.8	6
9. Debt Charges	19.8	17
10. Other Expenditure	10.6	9
Total	116.6	

(b) **Revenue**	**Billions of Dollars**	**Percentage**
1. Personal Income Tax	34.8	39
2. Corporation Income Tax	9.2	10
3. Non-Resident Income Tax	1.1	1
4. General Sales Tax	9.4	10
5. Excise Duties and Special Taxes	3.4	4
6. Unemployment Insurance Contributions	8.8	10
7. Universal Pension Plan Levies	4.4	5
8. Other Tax Revenue	5.3	6
9. Return on Investment	6.2	7
10. Miscellaneous Non-tax Revenue	7.6	8
Total	90.2	

Source: Statistics Canada, *Federal Government Finance*, 1985. Reproduced by permission of the Minister of Supply and Services Canada.

small portion of the expenditures shown (around one-fifth of the total). Included in this share is defence spending, as well as the cost of maintaining the federal civil service in Ottawa and elsewhere in Canada.

"Social services" is now the single largest expenditure item, accounting for just about a third of the federal budget. This item includes Old Age Security and Guaranteed Income Supplement payments to retired people, family allowances, and Unemployment Insurance benefits.

The federal government also transfers a large share of its revenue to provincial and local governments: In addition to item (8) — "general purpose transfers" — items (4), (5), and (6) also include federal transfers to help cover provincial costs for health care, education, and social welfare.

By far the fastest-growing expenditure category in recent years has been "Debt Charges," that is, interest on the public debt. The main reason for this rapid growth is that the size of the debt itself has grown rapidly. In 1975, the federal debt was less than $40 billion; at the end of 1988 it was just about $270 billion. (We will discuss the public debt in more detail in Chapter 10.)

Provincial and Local Government Expenditures

As can be seen from Figure 5-2, the share of total public expenditure accounted for by provincial and municipal governments is about as large as the federal government's share, thus reflecting Canada's relatively decentralized system of government. (In the United States, federal government spending is closer to 2/3 of total public sector spending.) Panel (*a*) in Table 5-2 gives a breakdown of provincial/local expenditure. The largest expenditure items at this level of government are the costs of education (26%) and health care (20%). These costs have been growing rapidly in the past several decades. Spending on social services other than education and health account for a smaller share in the provincial/local budget than in the federal budget. While provincial and local governments pay the cost of social assistance to families or individuals with low income, the expenditures on such welfare programs are not nearly as high as the federal government's expenditures on programs such as family allowances, Old Age Security and Unemployment Insurance.

Government Receipts

Details on the revenue derived from taxation at the federal and provincial/municipal levels are shown in panel (*b*) of Tables 5-1 and 5-2.

The federal and provincial *income taxes on individuals* yield the largest share of tax revenue at both levels of government: 39% of total federal tax revenue and 17% for provincial/local governments. Collection of the federal and provincial income taxes has been largely centralized, so that (except in Quebec) both are computed on the basis of the same income tax return prepared by the taxpayer at the end of April, and the actual taxes are paid to the federal government which then remits the provinces' shares to the provincial treasuries.

Table 5-2   Consolidated Provincial-Local Government Revenue and Expenditure
Fiscal Year Ended Nearest to December 31, 1984

(*a*) **Expenditure**	**Billions of Dollars**	**Percentage**
1. General Services	7.3	5
2. Protection of Persons and Property	6.2	5
3. Transportation and Communication	9.5	7
4. Health	26.7	20
5. Social Services	17.8	13
6. Education	35.7	26
7. Resource Conservation & Industrial Development	6.8	5
8. Debt Charges	13.1	10
9. Other Expenditure	12.7	9
Total	135.8	

(*b*) **Revenue**	**Billions of Dollars**	**Percentage**
1. Personal Income Tax	19.7	17
2. Corporation Income Tax	3.6	3
3. Non-Resident Income Tax	—	—
4. General Sales Tax	10.2	9
5. Other Consumption Taxes	5.4	5
6. Health and Social Insurance Levies	7.6	7
7. Other Tax Revenue	17.1	15
8. Natural Resource Revenue	8.1	7
9. Return on Investment	12.7	11
10. Miscellaneous Non-tax Revenue	9.8	9
11. Total transfer from the federal government and government enterprises	20.4	18
Total	114.6	

Sources: Compiled from Statistics Canada, *Local Government Finance 1984* and *Provincial Government Finance 1984*. Reproduced by permission of the Minister of Supply and Services Canada.

Table 5-3   Federal and Provincial Income Tax, Ontario Residents, 1988†

(1) Taxable Income	(2) Income Tax	(3) Income Tax as Percent of Income	(4) Marginal Tax Rate
$ 15,000	$ 1,833	12.2%	26.2%
25,000	4,451	17.8	26.2
40,000	10,110	25.3	40.0
80,000	27,280	34.1	46.0
150,000	59,482	39.7	46.0

†We have assumed that the taxpayer has a non-refundable tax credit of $1,360.
Source: Compiled from Revenue Canada, *General Tax Guide for Residents of Ontario*, 1988.

In all provinces except Quebec, a person's provincial income tax liability is computed as a percentage of his or her federal income tax, but the percentage varies: In 1988, it ranged from a low of 43% in the Northwest Territories to a high of 60% in Newfoundland and New Brunswick.[3] For the same taxable income, the percentage paid as income tax therefore varies from province to province.

In Table 5-3, column 2, we have computed the 1988 federal and provincial income tax payable for a taxpayer living in Ontario where the provincial tax was 51% of the federal tax. The *average tax rate*, shown in the third column, is simply the total tax divided by income. Observe that the income tax is *progressive*: the average percentage tax increases as taxable income increases.

Note also the concept of the **marginal tax rate** shown in the last column; this is the percentage tax payable on *additional* income. For example, in the tax bracket with income of less than $27,500, the marginal tax rate is 26.2%. Within this bracket, if income rises by $100 (from $25,000 to $25,100, say), an extra $26.20 must be paid in taxes. The marginal tax rate becomes higher as taxable income rises: It is the higher marginal tax rate that pulls up the *average* tax rate as income rises.

If a tax takes a larger percentage of income as income rises, the tax is *progressive*.

If a tax takes a smaller percentage of income as income rises, the tax is *regressive*.

If a tax takes a constant percentage of income, the tax is *proportional*.

The *corporate income tax* represents the second largest source of tax revenue for the federal government, and is an important source of revenue for the provincial governments as well. Like the personal income tax, the total corporation income tax is collected by the federal government, which then remits the provinces' shares to the provincial treasuries.[4] The basic corporation income tax schedule has only two rates for a given type of corporation. For example, for small Canadian-controlled corporations in the manufacturing sector, it is about 20%, while for a large corporation it is around 43% (the rates vary somewhat from province to province). Business income (or ''net income'') of corporations is computed by deducting all business expenses from total revenues; in other words, the tax is levied on corporate profits.

Municipal governments raise almost nine-tenths of their tax revenue from *property taxes*, i.e., taxes imposed on the ownership of land and houses. (Property taxes are included in item (7) in Table 5-2 (*b*)). Various kinds of *sales taxes* are levied by the federal and provincial governments. Sales taxes are generally levied as a uniform percentage of the price of all goods and services, with specified exceptions. (For example, food is exempted from federal sales tax.) In addition, there are various federal and provincial excise taxes on specific commodities (such as tobacco, beer and liquor, cosmetics, gasoline, and fuel oil). The federal government also collects customs duties on goods imported into Canada. While the customs duties are imposed partly to raise revenue, they also have the function of protecting Canadian producers from foreign competition by making

■ ■ ■ ■ ■

[3] In Quebec, the provincial income tax is computed directly from the individual's taxable income, and the tax is collected directly by the province.

[4] There are two exceptions to this procedure: Quebec and Ontario, where the tax is collected directly by the provincial governments.

imported goods more expensive. (Tariffs will be discussed more fully in Chapter 34.)

With expenditures of $116.6 billion and tax revenues of $90.2 billion, the federal government ran a *deficit* of more than $26 billion in 1985/86. By historical standards, this was very large. In part, the size of the deficit may be attributed to the delayed effects of the 1982 recession: Between 1981 and 1982, the deficit doubled as the amount of revenue from various kinds of taxes fell and government spending on Unemployment Insurance benefits increased. But the federal deficit continued to increase during 1983–85, even though the economy was then pulling out of the recession. Provincial and municipal governments have not had deficits on anywhere near the same scale as the federal government in recent years and, in some years, they have even registered small budget *surpluses.*

> If a government's revenues exceed its expenditures, it has a budget *surplus.*
>
> If a government's expenditures exceed its revenues, it has a budget *deficit.*
>
> If a government's revenues are approximately equal to its expenditures, its budget is *balanced.*

INTERGOVERNMENTAL FISCAL RELATIONS IN CANADA

> . . . the number of federal-provincial disputes in any one year varies in direct proportion to the number of federal-provincial meetings multiplied by the cube of the number of federal-provincial coordinating agencies in the respective governments.
>
> Gordon Robertson, formerly Clerk of the Privy Council and Secretary to the Cabinet

The total expenditures of provincial and municipal governments in recent decades have been substantially larger than the amounts of *tax* revenue collected by these governments. To make up for the shortfall, they have had to rely on financial support from higher levels of government.

Municipal governments, whose expenditures have been growing rapidly and whose only substantial source of tax revenue is the property tax, have been receiving large transfers from the provincial governments. The provincial governments, in turn, have also needed large amounts of revenue, not only to pay for the transfers to the municipal governments, but also to finance the rapidly growing cost of health care, post-secondary education, and social welfare. (Under the Constitution, and formerly under the British North America Act, programs in these areas are the responsibility of the provincial governments.) Historically, the federal government has helped meet the provinces' financial requirements in several ways:

1. It has made large transfer payments to the provincial governments.

2. By decreasing its share of the total revenue from the personal income tax, the federal government has made it easier for the provinces to increase their revenue from this source.

3. Federal transfer payments to various groups of individuals (such as the retired, the unemployed, and families with children) have reduced the need for provincial expenditures on social welfare.

Canada's complicated system of federal-provincial transfer payments is largely governed by two Acts of Parliament: the Federal-Provincial Fiscal Arrangements Act and the Established Programs Financing Act. The system includes several types of transfers. One type is referred to as *equalization payments.* These are payments from the federal government to the "have-not" provinces, i.e., the low-income provinces that have a relatively small tax base. Without such payments, "have-not" provinces wanting to raise the same per capita *revenues* as the average for Canada would be able to do so only by levying very high tax *rates.* To avoid this, the federal government makes equalization payments, so as to "ensure that all provinces are able to provide reasonably comparable levels of public services without resorting to unduly high levels of taxation."

Equalization payments represent *unconditional transfers* with no restrictions on how they are to be spent. Even more important are *conditional transfers* —payments that are made with "strings attached," that is, only if the provinces meet certain conditions imposed by the federal government. Prior to 1977, most of the conditional transfers consisted of federal cost sharing for a number of important provincial programs, including social assistance, hospital insurance, medicare, and post-secondary education. Under the cost-sharing approach, the provincial governments would make the decisions on how much to spend on these programs. However, the province would pay no more than roughly half the cost — the other half was paid by the federal government. This cost sharing was designed to meet two objectives—to increase the provinces' revenues and to encourage them to follow federal guidelines in designing their health insurance and educational systems, thus providing a certain uniformity in these systems across Canada.

There is no doubt that this conditional transfer scheme made the provincial governments more willing to spend money on such programs as health care and higher education; for each dollar they spent, they had to raise only 50 cents from taxpayers in their own province. In fact, the federal government became concerned that the system made the provinces *too* willing to spend money in these areas, especially those provinces that had comparatively large revenues to spend on their own half of the cost. To solve this problem, the federal government tried to control expenditures by limiting the grants to *some* kinds of health services only. But, in turn, they found that this "solution" distorted the system. For example, instead of building more convalescent homes (which were less expensive but were not subsidized by federal grants), the provinces enlarged the acute-care hospitals (which were more expensive but were subsidized).

Because of these problems, the system was substantially modified in 1977. The existing conditional transfers in health care and post-secondary education were abolished. As compensation, the provinces received two things: an increase in their share of the revenue from the personal income tax and a federal undertaking to transfer predetermined amounts to the provinces as *block grants* to help offset provincial spending on health and education. The block grants were still conditional in the sense that the provincial health and post-secondary education programs had to conform to the existing federal guidelines. However, the amounts to be transferred were no longer determined by the amounts spent by the provinces themselves.

Federal-provincial fiscal relations are complicated and sometimes spark considerable controversy. A recent example was the long and acrimonious debate over the 1984 Canada Health Act which authorized the federal government to withhold transfers from provinces which allowed extra billing by physicians or imposed hospital user charges. Many provincial politicians and officials saw the Act as an unwarranted federal intrusion in an area of provincial jurisdiction and complained that it was going to make it harder for them to finance their health care systems.

In a federal system, there will always be controversy over programs and policies for which jurisdiction and financial responsibility are divided among the federal, provincial, and local governments. As Ottawa struggles to control the federal deficit, federal-provincial friction is likely to increase. By 1989, the federal government was trying to reduce its spending by shifting more of the fiscal burden of health care, education, and social welfare assistance to the provinces.

GOVERNMENT REGULATION

The billions of dollars that governments spend or collect in taxes have a substantial effect on the types of goods produced and on who gets those goods. But the size of budgets cannot be taken as the sole measure of the government's economic impact. Business behaviour is significantly influenced also by various regulatory programs, even though the costs of administering these programs show up as comparatively small items in the government's budget.

For example, regulations imposed by the government of Ontario have forced the International Nickel Corporation (INCO) to install complicated anti-pollution equipment in order to reduce the emissions of sulphur dioxide from its plant in Sudbury, Ontario. The cost of the equipment, which will be borne by INCO, will be much higher than the government's cost of administering the anti-pollution program.

Government measures to limit various abuses of private business have a long history in Canada. In 1889, a section was put into the Criminal Code which provided sanctions against attempts by business to limit competition in order to raise prices and profits in an industry. This section was the predecessor of the present Competition Act, which outlaws agreements between firms not to undercut each others' prices.

There are many other forms of government regulation. For example, the Department of Health and Welfare tests the effectiveness and safety of drugs before they are permitted into the market. Government regulation is especially detailed in financial markets: Canada's chartered banks are supervised and controlled by the Bank of Canada. In those provinces with privately-owned telephone companies, rates are regulated by the provincial government. Radio and television communications are regulated by the Canadian Radio-Television and Telecommunications Commission (CRTC). The Canadian Transport Commission regulates the railroad and airline industries, while provincial Highway

Transport Boards are responsible for supervising and controlling the trucking industry. The regulatory activities of the National Energy Board were at the forefront in the conflict between the federal government and the Western provinces over energy policy in the 1970s and early 1980s. Another area of rapidly growing regulation has been agriculture, where federal and provincial agencies have been created to control and supervise the marketing of a wide variety of farm products ranging from wheat to eggs, dairy products, and even asparagus.

The role of government regulation over the economy grew at a particularly rapid pace in the 1960s and 1970s. In the 1970s, there was particular emphasis on regulation affecting the environment, health and safety, transportation, product standards, business licensing, and land use planning.

Problems with Government Regulation

In many areas, regulation is relatively uncontroversial. For example, few people complain about a government agency that certifies the airworthiness of aircraft. Similarly, there is widespread support for government regulation to keep unsafe drugs off the market. For each of these cases, regulation was established to deal with a problem area where the free market had been tried and found wanting.

However, by the late 1970s, many observers began to feel that in some areas, regulation was becoming very cumbersome or too restrictive. Business executives were complaining over long delays in obtaining regulatory approval for major projects; such delays, they said, can add substantially to the cost of projects. There were suggestions that the standards used to evaluate the safety of drugs may be too restrictive. For example, when saccharin was temporarily banned after experiments showed that massive doses of saccharin appeared to increase the risk of cancer in laboratory animals, critics pointed out that more lives might be lost from problems caused by overweight (as people could no longer use saccharin instead of sugar to keep their weight down) than from an increased incidence of cancer. Provincial marketing boards for agricultural products have had their policies questioned with increasing frequency. True, unregulated markets for agricultural products or transportation may have various disadvantages; for example, they might lead to large fluctuations in the prices of foodstuffs. But regulation may also have disadvantages: It might cause waste and higher consumer prices, and be unfair to individual producers.

As a result of these criticisms, the 1980s saw a trend toward reduction of the extent of regulation in various sectors, both in Canada and the United States. While regulation in agricultural markets was largely left intact, major steps were taken toward deregulation in the Canadian airline, rail, and trucking industries. In the United States, the Reagan administration substantially deregulated the airline industry. More ominously from a Canadian point of view, the Reagan administration also deemphasized environmental regulation. As a result, little was done to reduce the amount of acid rain pollution that U.S. power plants were allowed to create.

What is needed is a sense of balance. The private market mechanism has substantial defects. But government agencies also have defects; they are not run by superhumans capable of solving all our problems. In some cases, such as acid rain, we should give them more effective regulatory power. But in other cases, such as air transportation or some types of farm products, it may be better to live with the defects of the market. The cure of regulation may be more costly than the defects themselves.

Regulation in the public interest is made particularly difficult because of the political clout of producers. When regulations are being developed, the affected industry makes its views known forcefully. But the views of consumers and taxpayers are diffuse and often remain underrepresented.

The predominance of producer influence is not simply the result of a conspiracy of wealth. Rather, it is an intrinsic feature of a highly specialized economy. Each of us has a major, narrow, special interest as a producer; and each of us has a minor interest in a wide range of industries whose goods we consume. We are much more likely to react when our particular industry is affected by government policy; we are much less likely to express our diffused interest as consumers. Narrow producer interests are expressed not only by business, but also by labour. For example, some of the loudest early criticism of airline deregulation came from representatives for unions of flight attendants and employees of the Canadian Transport Commission. Unions concentrate their attention on events in their particular industry, even though the union members are also consumers using a wide range of products. We repeat: This prevalence of producer influence is primarily a result of modern technology and a high degree of specialization; it is not primarily a result of our particular system. It exists in a wide variety of political-economic systems, including those of the United States, Britain, France, Germany, Japan, and the Soviet Union.

PUBLIC ENTERPRISE

In addition to the influence they exert over the economy through their regulatory activities, Canadian governments also participate directly in many markets through government-owned firms. Petro-Canada, the CBC, and Quebec Hydro are all examples of *Crown corporations*. Most Crown corporations are similar to private business firms in the sense that they derive most of their revenue from selling various goods or services to the public. The economic significance of such government enterprises is much greater in Canada than in the United States. For example, it has been estimated that Crown corporations accounted for about 15% of all capital investment in Canada in the early 1980s; the corresponding figure for the United States was less than 5%.

> *Crown corporations* are government-owned firms that derive most of their revenues from selling goods or services to the public, sometimes in direct competition with privately owned firms in the same market.

Crown corporations exist in a wide variety of markets. Many of them are *natural monopolies*, where economies of scale are substantial so that the market can support no more than one firm large enough to exploit these economies of scale. (Natural monopoly is explained in more detail in Chapter 27.) In the United States, most firms in naturally monopolistic markets are privately owned but heavily regulated by the government; in Canada they are often government-owned instead — for example, corporations producing electric power or telephone companies in the Prairie provinces. Crown corporations also exist in more competitive markets — for example, in transport and communication where government-owned corporations such as Air Canada, CN, and CBC operate in direct competition with privately owned firms.

Part of the function of the government-owned companies is to serve various submarkets that private companies are reluctant to serve—air and rail service to small remote communities, television transmissions to the Arctic, or radio programs featuring classical music, for example. In other cases, they undertake tasks that may be potentially profitable in the long run but require very large initial investments and involve such a high degree of risk that private firms are unwilling to invest. An

example of such a "pioneer enterprise" is Atomic Energy of Canada which developed the CANDU nuclear reactor.

Not all ventures into new technology are financial successes. For example, Canadair Ltd. of Montreal, which until 1986 was a federal Crown corporation, was subsidized to the tune of several *billion* dollars by the Canadian taxpayer when it developed the technologically advanced Challenger executive jet in the early 1980s. When Canadair was sold to private interests, the government was able to recover only a small fraction of the amount that had been invested in developing the Challenger.

In many provinces, there are government-owned development corporations that provide financial support for industrial development and, in many cases, governments also create Crown corporations by taking over firms that otherwise would close down. Thus, the B.C. government owns and operates a newsprint mill at Ocean Falls; Nova Scotia owns a steel mill in Sydney; and a federal Crown corporation is responsible for the operation of Cape Breton coal mines. Often, government "bailouts" of failing private firms are undertaken to protect communities in which the firm provides a large share of total employment.

In recent years, there has been considerable debate over possible reforms that might improve the efficiency of government firms. The debate has focused on two main issues: accountability and privatization.

Accountability

While most Crown corporations cover most of their costs using revenue they earn from the sale of goods and services, they usually don't cover them all. As the owner, the government is often called on to pay subsidies for certain tasks the corporations undertake, to provide guarantees for repayment of money they borrow, or simply to cover operating deficits of the firms. This is not surprising. Most Crown corporations are established because governments want to use them to do things that are not privately profitable (such as providing air and rail service to distant communities) and that require a subsidy. But once it is clear that a Crown corporation is not necessarily expected to cover *all* its costs, the question arises: Where does one draw the line? If the corporation's managers are given a blank cheque, they are likely to spend too much. The managers must be *accountable* to someone and, since it is the government that owns the firm, their accountability must ultimately to be the politicians who decide about government spending. Thus, the reform proposals in this area have focused on ways of strengthening the political control over Crown corporations by providing more precise definitions of the objectives that they are expected to serve and by providing the politicians with better information about current and future spending plans.

Privatization

In some cases, the original reason for establishing a public enterprise may disappear over time. For example, an unprofitable firm that has been taken over by a provincial government in order to preserve jobs may become profitable again, or a new technology developed by a Crown corporation may become ready for commercial application. In such cases, one possible strategy is to *privatize* the public enterprise — that is, to turn it over to private ownership.

At the federal level, a program for reducing the scope of government enterprise through privatization was an important part of the platform of the 1979/80 Conservative government under Joe Clark; their proposal to privatize Petro-Canada gave rise to considerable controversy. While Petro-Canada remained in the public sector, the privatization policy was revived when the Mulroney government came to power in the mid-1980s. A number of Crown corporations were sold, including Canadair and deHavilland, another government-owned aircraft manufacturer. In 1988, the decision was made to partially privatize Air Canada by selling 45% of its share capital to the public.

To some extent, the arguments for privatization are ideological. They are generally supported by private firms that object to competition from government-subsidized Crown corporations. But there is also another argument based on the idea that managers of private firms have stronger incentives to perform efficiently than managers of public enterprises. The reason is that if managers of private firms perform inefficiently, this is quickly reflected in a reduction in the value of the firms' shares. To prevent this, the firms' owners (shareholders) will put pressure on the managers to perform better or will even replace the management. On the other hand, if managers of publicly owned firms perform inefficiently, the incentive to improve performance is less strong — for two reasons. First, the managers may be able to claim that they are losing money because the government is forcing them to continue various unprofitable activities, not because they are inefficient. Second, since shares of publicly owned firms are not traded in the market, the taxpayers (who are the ones that ultimately will carry the burden of an inefficient performance) may be only very imperfectly aware of the firms' performance.

The evidence on the relative efficiency of managers in public and private firms is mixed. Some studies have shown that private firms operating in a heavily regulated market are no more efficient than public firms in the same market. On the other hand, evidence suggests that private firms providing electricity and water to municipalities in the United States are able to produce these services at a significantly lower cost than government-owned ones.

THE ECONOMIC ROLE OF THE GOVERNMENT: What Should the Government Do?

With budgets of governments and Crown corporations reaching billions of dollars and with an extensive list of government regulations, the Canadian economy is clearly a substantial distance away from a pure market system of laissez-faire. What principles and objectives guide the government when it intervenes?

In part, government intervention is based on deep social attitudes that are often difficult to explain. Consider, for example, the contrasting attitudes in the United States and Britain. Several decades ago, Americans looked askance at government-financed, "socialized" medicine in Britain. Yet, at the same time, they could consider British education "undemocratic" because many well-to-do Britons sent their children to privately financed elementary and secondary schools. The British, on the other hand, were proud of their educational system and puzzled by what they considered a quaint, emotional American objection to public financing of medical care. During the past three decades, the gap between the two societies has narrowed, with increasing governmental involvement in medicine in the United States and a decline in the importance of privately financed education in Britain.

The government intervenes in the economy for many reasons; it is hard to summarize them all. But we will look at five of the main ones.

1. The Government Provides What the Private Market Can't

Consider defence expenditures. For obvious political reasons, defence cannot be left to the private market. The prospect of private armies marching around the country is too painful to contemplate. But there is also a compelling economic reason that defence is a responsibility of the government.

The difference between defence and an average good is the following. If I buy food at the store, I get to eat it; if I buy a movie ticket, I get to see the film; if I buy a car, I get to drive it. In contrast, if I want a larger, better equipped army, my offer to purchase a rifle for the army will not add in any measurable way to my own security. My neighbour and the average person in New Brunswick or Manitoba will benefit as much from the extra rifle as I do. In other words, the benefit from defence expenditures goes broadly to all citizens; it does not go specifically to the individual who pays. If defence is to be provided, it must be financed by the government, which collects taxes to ensure that everyone contributes.

Such goods — where the benefit goes to the public regardless of who pays — are sometimes known as ***public goods***.

2. Externalities

An ***externality*** is a side effect — good or bad — of production or consumption. For example, when individuals are immunized against an infectious disease, they receive a substantial benefit: They are assured that they won't get the disease. But there is an ***external benefit*** as well, because others gain too: They are assured that the inoculated individuals will not catch the disease and pass it along to them. Similarly, there is an external benefit when people have their houses painted: The neighbourhood becomes more attractive.

An ***external cost*** occurs when a factory pollutes the air. The cost is borne by those who breathe the polluted air.

> An *externality* is a side effect of production or consumption. Persons or businesses other than the producer or consumer are affected.
>
> An externality may be either positive (for example, vaccinations) or negative (for example, pollution).

Because of the effects on others, the government may wish to encourage activities which create external benefits, and to discourage those with external costs. It can do so with the use of any of its four major tools: expenditures, public enterprise, regulation, or taxation. The government spends money for public health programs for the immunization of the young. In order to reduce pollution, it may pass regulations on the types of auto-

mobiles which can be built. And taxes on gasoline or on pollution-producing factories might likewise be used to discourage pollution.

The existence of an externality does not in itself make a compelling case for government action; the government should not be concerned with insignificant externalities or other trivial matters. Thus, private incentives are generally enough to ensure that homes will be painted; the government does not usually intervene. However, there is growing concern over more serious externalities: While little was done about pollution two decades ago, major efforts are now directed toward cleaning up the air and water and preventing further environmental deterioration.

3. Merit Goods

Government intervention may also be based on the paternalistic view that there are cases in which people are not the best judges of what is good for them. According to this view, the government should encourage ***merit goods*** — those that are deemed particularly desirable — and discourage the consumption of harmful products. People's inability to pick the "right" goods may be the result of short-sightedness, ignorance, addiction, or manipulation by producers. (Recall the brief discussion in Chapter 4 of Galbraith's views on created wants.)

In some cases, the government attempts merely to correct ignorance in areas where the public may have difficulty determining (or facing?) the facts. The requirement of a health warning on cigarette packages is an example. But, in other instances, the government goes further: to outright prohibition, as in the case of heroin and other hard drugs.

The view that "the government knows best" is generally greeted with skepticism; the government intervenes relatively sparingly to tell adults what they should or should not consume. (Children are, however, another matter; they are not allowed to reject the "merit" good, education.) However, substantial government direction does occur in welfare programs, presumably on the ground that those who get themselves into financial difficulties are least likely to make wise consumption decisions. Thus, part of the assistance to the poor consists of subsidized day-care centres and housing programs rather than outright grants of money. In this way, the government attempts to direct consumption toward housing, food and care for the children, rather than (perhaps) toward liquor for an alcoholic parent.

4. Helping the Poor

The market provides the goods and services desired by those with the money to buy, but it provides little for the poor. In order to help the impoverished and move toward a more humane society, programs have been established to provide assistance for old people, the handicapped, and the needy in general.

With few exceptions, Canadians agree that the government must be responsible for providing the poor with a decent living standard. However, there continues to be a good deal of controversy over the issue of whether the current system does a good job of meeting this responsibility. Part of the problem is that there is a large number of agencies and programs that affect the well-being of the poor; indeed, it is perhaps inaccurate to speak of a welfare "system" at all. The result may be a lack of consistency. Some of the money being spent may go to people who are not really poor while some who are poverty-stricken may "fall between the cracks" and get little or no help. Another difficulty lies in how to reconcile conflicting objectives. How can help be given to the needy without weakening the incentive to work? How can assistance be guaranteed to abandoned mothers without weakening the incentives of fathers to stay with their families? How can we provide affordable housing for low-income families without creating ghettos of the poor? There are no easy answers to such questions.

5. The Government and Economic Stability

Finally, if we go back to the beginning of the upswing in government activity—to the Depression of the 1930s —we find that the primary motivation was not to affect the kinds of products made in the economy nor specifically to aid the poor. Rather, the aim was to increase the quantity of production. With unemployment rates exceeding 15% of the labour force year after year, the problem was to produce more — more production of almost anything would help put people back to work. Since the dark days of the 1930s, a major responsibility of the government has been to promote a high level of employment and stability in the economy.

TAXATION

The art of taxation consists of plucking the goose so as to obtain the largest amount of feathers with the least possible amount of hissing.

Jean Baptiste Colbert
Seventeenth-century French statesman

The major objective of taxation is to raise revenues— to obtain feathers, without too much hissing. But other objectives are also important in the design of a tax system.

1. Neutrality . . .

In many ways, the market system works admirably. Adam Smith's "invisible hand" provides the consuming public with a vast flow of goods and services. As a starting point, therefore, a tax system should be designed to be neutral. That is, it should disturb market forces as little as possible, unless there is a compelling reason to the contrary.

For the sake of illustration, consider a far-fetched example. Suppose that blue cars were taxed at 10% and green cars not at all. This tax would clearly not be neutral regarding blue and green cars. People would have an incentive to buy green cars; blue cars would practically disappear from the market. A tax which introduces such a distortion would make no sense.

While this illustration is silly, real taxes do introduce distortions. For example, several centuries ago, houses in parts of Europe were taxed according to the number of windows. As a result, houses were built with fewer windows. To a lesser degree, the current property tax introduces a perverse incentive. If you have your house painted and your roof repaired, the government's evaluation of your house (the assessed value) may be raised and your taxes increased as a consequence. Therefore, property taxes encourage you to let your property deteriorate.

The problem is that every tax provides an incentive to do something to avoid it. So long as taxes must be collected, complete neutrality is impossible. The objective of the tax system must therefore be more modest: to *aim* toward neutrality. As a starting point in the design of a tax system, the disturbance to the market that comes from taxation should be minimized.

2. . . . and Nonneutrality: Meeting Social Objectives by Tax Incentives

There is, however, an important modification which must be made to the neutrality principle. In some cases, it may be desirable to disturb the private market.

For example, the government might tax polluting activities, so that firms will do less polluting. The market is disturbed, but in a desirable way. Another example is the tax on cigarettes, which, in addition to its prime objective of raising revenue for the government, also discourages cigarette consumption.

Taxation and regulation can be used to correct the failures of the private market. But the two approaches are quite different in one respect. Regulation aims at *overriding* the market mechanism, forbidding or limiting specific behaviour on the part of business. Taxation aims at *using* the market mechanism, but making it work better. When there are externalities, such as pollution, the signals of the market are incomplete; businesses or individuals who pollute the air do not have to pay the cost. Taxation of externalities can improve the outcome of the market by making the signals facing businesses and individuals more complete: Taxation makes polluters pay a penalty and gives them an incentive to reduce pollution.

3. Simplicity

To anyone who has wasted several spring weekends sweating over an income tax form, simplicity of the tax system is devoutly desired. Of course, we live in a complex world and the tax code must to some degree reflect this complexity. Even so, it is difficult to avoid the impression that the Canadian tax code is more complicated than is necessary. In part, this is due to the fact that simplification of the code would involve the abolition of various special rules which have been legislated over the years in order to provide tax relief for certain particular types of income or for particular ways of spending or investing it. When simplifying changes are proposed, there will be vocal opposition from those taxpayers or firms who will lose from the changes. An example of this problem was provided in the mid-1960s, when a comprehensive set of revisions of Canada's tax laws were recommended by the Carter Commission on Taxation.[5] If all of the Commission's proposals had been adopted, the structure of the Canadian tax system would have been greatly simplified with a much more uniform tax treatment of different sorts of income. As it turned out, however, many of the special rules in the existing tax laws were in fact retained and, while some of the Commission's recommendations for change were accepted by the government, they were only partially implemented.

4. Equity

Taxation represents coercion; taxes are collected by force if necessary. Therefore, it is important that taxes

■ ■ ■ ■ ■

[5] *The Royal Commission on Taxation Report* (Ottawa: Queen's Printer, 1966). The Commission derived its popular name from its chairman, K.L. Carter.

both be fair and give the appearance of being fair. There are, however, two different principles for judging fairness.

The Benefit Principle

This principle recognizes that the purpose of taxation is to pay for government services. Therefore, let those who gain the most from government services pay the most. If this principle is adopted, then a question arises: Why not simply set prices for government services which people can voluntarily pay if they want the services? In other words, why not charge a price for a government service, just as Via Rail charges for railway tickets?

This approach may work in some cases—for example, for a toll road from which drivers can be excluded if they do not pay. But it will not work for public goods that benefit people even if they do not pay; for example, defence, disease-control programs, or air traffic control. Everyone will enjoy them, but no one will want to pay for them. It is the function of the government to determine whether such programs are worthwhile. Once the decision is made to go ahead, people must be required to support the program through taxes.

If the benefit principle of taxation is followed, it is up to the government to estimate how much various individuals and groups benefit, and to set taxes accordingly. (Individual citizens cannot be allowed to provide the estimates of how much they benefit personally; they have an incentive to understate their individual benefits in order to keep their taxes down.)

Ability to Pay

If the government sets taxes according to the benefit principle, it does not redistribute income. People are simply taxed in proportion to their individual benefits from government programs. But while it might make sense to apply the benefit principle of taxation to the financing of programs to provide public goods or merit goods (such as education and health services), it cannot very well be applied to government programs to help the poor. The purpose of these programs is to transfer resources from those who are relatively well off—that is, whose *ability to pay* is greater—to those who have lower income and wealth, and therefore are less able to pay.

If the only taxes were a progressive income tax and an inheritance tax and if at the same time the government provided assistance to those at the bottom of the economic ladder, it would substantially redistribute income from the rich to the poor. But the world is not so simple. There are different levels of government and each one levies several different kinds of taxes. When all the taxes are taken together, it is not so clear that government is taking a substantially larger percentage of income from the rich than from the poor, as we shall see in the next section.

THE BURDEN OF TAXES:
Who Ultimately Pays?

It is difficult to determine who bears the burden of many of our taxes. For example, consider the relatively simple case of the Canada Pension Plan contribution. (As we noted in footnote 2, even though it is called a "contribution" it is essentially equivalent to a tax.) Part of this tax is deducted from the take-home pay of the worker. In 1988, it was deducted at the rate of 4% of the worker's gross income, subject to a maximum contribution of $478. This maximum was reached at an income of $26,500. Therefore, the same $478 was paid by employees with an income of $27,000 or, say, a $54,000 income. Thus, this tax is regressive: The employee earning $27,000 per year pays twice as large a percentage of gross income as the employee earning $54,000 per year.

The burden in this case is simple to see. However, it is not so clear for the other portion of this tax which was levied on the *employer* (4% of gross income). Does that tax come out of the employer's profits? Or is it passed on to the consumer in the form of higher prices? Or, possibly, this half may also fall on the worker: If there were no unemployment insurance contributions, the employer might be willing to pay a higher wage.

As another example, consider the corporation income tax. It is sometimes maintained that this tax is a relatively painless way of raising government revenue because it is levied on corporate profits and not on the incomes of individuals. However, this argument is suspect for at least two reasons. First, corporations' profits influence the individual incomes of shareholders, so that a profits tax does directly affect the income of some individuals. Second, a higher rate of corporation income tax may be "passed on" in the form of higher prices, so that the tax is, in effect, "paid" by the buyers of the corporations' products. When we recognize this, we cannot even tell whether the corporation income tax is ultimately progressive or regressive!

As these examples show, the question of tax burden — of who ultimately pays — is complicated, even when

we are looking at only a single particular tax. Needless to say, estimating the burden — or *incidence* — of *all* Canadian taxes, federal, provincial, and municipal, is even more difficult. Nevertheless, the problem of the incidence of the tax system as a whole *has* been studied by a number of economists, each using a somewhat different method and different assumptions. Figure 5-4 illustrates a set of recent incidence estimates by Professor John Whalley of the University of Western Ontario; the data refer to the early 1970s. The solid black curve in the middle refers to his "central case"; it implies that the system was progressive, since total taxes paid as a fraction of income rises from 27% for the lowest income group to 43% as it reaches the highest income group. What is somewhat surprising, though, is that the curve is relatively flat in the intermediate range. When most of us think of taxes, we think first of the income tax with its definitely progressive rate structure. But as the estimates by Whalley and others have shown, a large part of

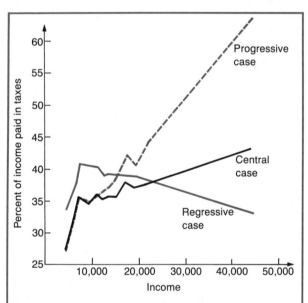

Figure 5-4 Estimates of the overall incidence of Canadian taxes.

Many estimates of the overall incidence of Canadian taxes suggest that the system is neither highly progressive (except in the lowest income brackets) nor highly regressive, as illustrated by the solid black curve. However, with different assumptions concerning the burden of taxes on the income of those who own capital (who earn profits or interest), the estimated incidence pattern may become quite different, as shown by the solid and broken colour curves.

Source: John Whalley, "Regression or progression: the taxing question of incidence analysis", *Canadian Journal of Economics*, November 1984, Table 5 and Table 6.

the progressive effect of the personal income tax is offset by other taxes (such as sales and excise taxes and social security contributions) that are regressive.[6]

The incidence estimates of Whalley and others have to be very carefully interpreted. As Whalley notes, they all depend on both the precise definition of income and several somewhat arbitrary assumptions concerning the incidence of the burden of particular taxes (such as social security contributions or the corporation income tax). By changing these assumptions, one can produce a significantly different picture of the overall pattern of tax incidence. As an example, consider the two colour curves in Figure 5-4. The solid colour line implies a highly regressive distribution of the tax burden. It results from assuming that the burden of taxes on business profits and interest income is "shifted forward" to consumers in the form of higher prices (rather than resulting in lower income of the owners of capital). The broken colour line, in contrast, shows a more progressive incidence pattern; it results from taking into account not just taxes this year, but also taxes in future years — in particular, how taxes will reduce income on the future return on present savings.

While this discussion illustrates that the estimates of total tax incidence must be taken with more than a grain of salt, most of those who have worked on the incidence problem agree on one thing: The degree of progressivity in the overall tax system is considerably smaller than one would be led to believe if one simply looked at the structure of tax rates in the personal income tax. This is true not only because many other types of taxes are regressive, but also because of a variety of "loopholes," some of which provide particularly attractive opportunities for rich people to reduce their taxes.

TAX LOOPHOLES

Loopholes are provisions of the law which permit the reduction of taxes. Thus, those who use loopholes are acting perfectly legally to *avoid* taxes and should be sharply distinguished from those who act illegally

■ ■ ■ ■ ■
[6] Earlier work by W. Irwin Gillespie indicated a much less progressive tax system than implied by Whalley's estimates. As Whalley points out, however, the difference is largely due to the fact that Gillespie measures taxes as a proportion of income *before government transfers*. Since such transfers constitute a relatively large proportion of the income of people in the lower income classes, this substantially raises the estimate of taxes as a proportion of income in these classes.

to *evade* taxes, perhaps by padding their deductions or understating their income. The term loophole clearly implies that the tax provision is unfair and, as there can be strong disagreement over just what is fair, there is likewise some disagreement over just what constitutes a loophole. However, here are some of the items that often are put on the list.

1. Capital Gains

When an asset is sold for more than it cost, the seller has made a capital gain. For example, if you buy stock in MacMillan Bloedel for $1,000 and the value of the stock later rises to $1,500, you have made a capital gain of $500. Until 1985, if you actually "realized" your capital gain by selling the stock, you had to pay tax on the gain, but only at half the percentage you would pay on ordinary income such as wages and salaries. In the first budget introduced by the Mulroney government, this loophole was made even bigger. A provision was introduced that completely exempted capital gains from income tax up to a lifetime maximum of $500,000 (later reduced to $100,000) per person. This rule clearly was of great benefit to taxpayers who receive a large portion of their income as capital gains, such as those who sell large blocks of common stock.

2. Imputed Income from Owner-Occupied Housing

The Canadian tax system favours home owners, for the following reason. For people who have a substantial amount invested as equity in their own homes, out-of-pocket housing costs (i.e., costs of maintenance, property taxes, and mortgage payments) are lower than the amount of rent paid by people who live in rental housing of a comparable standard. The difference represents a return on the home owner's equity. While most other income from capital (such as interest on bonds) is taxed, the implicit return on home owners' equity is not. The benefits of this loophole are greater for people with high incomes — and, thus, high marginal tax rates — and expensive homes. (In some countries, including the United States, home owners also are allowed to deduct mortgage interest from taxable income. This is a *second* big tax advantage of home ownership. Mortgage interest has never been deductible in Canada, although the Conservative government of Joe Clark was planning legislation to introduce such a provision at the time the Liberals returned to power in 1980.)

3. Preferences to Some Corporations

For small business corporations (those with less than $200,000 of taxable income) the rate of federal corporation income tax in the late 1980s was less than half the rate for large corporations. All corporations engaged in manufacturing and processing in Canada are treated more favourably than other firms for tax purposes: Their federal income tax rate was some six percentage points lower than for other firms. Manufacturing firms also benefit from special rules that allow them to reduce their taxable income by writing off the cost of new capital equipment in a relatively short time. (This is called "accelerated depreciation.") In addition, many of them have been protected against competition from abroad by tariffs on imported foreign goods. Since 1978, corporations investing in new productive facilities have been given an *investment tax credit*; in 1987, it was in the range of 5% to 7% of the actual cost of the investment for most firms, but higher credits were given in so-called "slow growth areas" and in the Atlantic provinces.

4. Special Rules for Resource Industries

Industries based on natural resources — such as mining and production of oil and natural gas — benefit from special rules that reduce their effective cost of finding and exploiting new resource deposits. In addition, other provisions in the tax law have reduced the effective tax rate on their profits. Until 1988, they were permitted a special deduction called a *depletion allowance*, amounting to 25% of their net taxable income. They could also issue *flow-through shares*. Owners of such shares could deduct part of the firm's exploration and development expenditures from their personal taxable income. (While this meant that the firm itself lost these tax deductions, there could still be a substantial net reduction in total taxes if the shareholders' marginal tax rate was higher than the rate that applied to the corporation.)

5. Farms and Films

To support the Canadian film industry, there is special legislation that allows taxpayers to deduct from their taxable income a substantial portion of any money they invest in the film industry. Many individuals with high incomes have used these rules to "shelter" a portion of their income from taxes. Until the late 1980s, special rules also made it possible to use investments in Multiple Unit Residential Buildings (MURBs) as a tax shelter. Similarly, the income tax law contains a number of provisions to reduce the tax burden on Canadian farmers.

For example, while there was a $100,000 lifetime limit on the amount of capital gains that a taxpayer could shelter from tax, a higher limit applied to capital gains on farm property. In addition, farmers were allowed to reduce their taxable income by deducting part of their mortgage interest payments and the costs of various kinds of land improvement and by making use of rules that allowed rapid write-offs (depreciation) of farm buildings. While there is widespread support in Canada for assisting farmers, much of the benefit of these rules has gone to individuals such as doctors and lawyers with high off-farm incomes: By buying a farm and becoming "part-time farmers," they have been able to use these rules to create large accounting losses on their farming operations, and deduct these losses from their off-farm incomes. As a result, they have been able to shelter a substantial portion of their income from taxes.

TAX REFORM IN THE 1980s

The proliferation of special rules and loopholes has made the Canadian tax system increasingly complex over the years. Moreover, it has contributed to making it less effective in redistributing income from the rich to the poor. It is not surprising, therefore, that proposals for reform of the tax system has been a regular feature of the Canadian political landscape for a long time.

Even though the Carter Commission recommended drastic changes to the tax system, there was little in the way of major reform during the 1960s and 1970s. (An important exception was a move in the mid-1970s to *index* the tax system — that is, to make the system less sensitive to the distortionary impact of inflation; we will discuss tax indexing further in a later chapter.) Partly as a result of tax reductions and tax reform in the United States in the early 1980s, interest in tax reform picked up in Canada as well at that time.

While there were many different reform proposals, most participants in the debate gradually came to agree on three elements that should be part of an effective tax reform package.

1. The tax base should be broadened.

That is, many existing deductions and loopholes which reduce the taxes of particular individuals or groups should be reduced or eliminated. Not only would this simplify the tax structure. It would also make the tax system fairer. Under the existing system, people with the same income often end up paying very different amounts of tax depending on the deductions and exemptions they are allowed.

With a broader tax base, more revenue could be collected at existing tax rates. This leads to the second type of reform proposal.

2. There should be a reduction in income tax rates.
In the 1980s, there was increasing evidence from various countries that high marginal income tax rates might do considerable damage to a country's economic performance by reducing individuals' willingness to work and save, and by causing a great deal of energy and resources to be wasted in the search for ways to avoid taxes. In a number of countries, including Britain and the United States (Box 5-1), marginal tax rates were decreased considerably.

The proposals for reducing tax rates often went together with suggestions to simplify the tax structure by reducing the number of tax brackets in the income tax schedule. A particularly simple proposal was for a *flat tax*, which would have a single tax rate (say, 20%) applied to all income over and above some basic exemption.

3. Deductions should be replaced by tax credits.
Before 1988, the income tax law allowed taxpayers in particular categories (such as those with dependants, those who were over 65, or those who were disabled) to deduct certain amounts when calculating their taxable income, thereby reducing the tax they had to pay. A problem with such deductions is that their value to the taxpayer — that is, the amount by which they reduce the tax payable — depends on the taxpayer's marginal tax rate. For example, the 1987 deduction of roughly $2,600 for an elderly person led to a tax saving of $1,300 for a person with an income of, say, $60,000, whose combined marginal rate of federal and provincial income tax was 50%. On the other hand, for a retired person with an income of only $20,000 and a combined marginal rate of 30%, the tax reduction would be only $780.

This problem can be overcome by replacing tax deductions with provisions for **tax credits**. For example, instead of allowing taxpayers over 65 to deduct $2,600 when calculating taxable income, one might simply allow them to deduct a fixed sum from their tax liability.

A *deduction* (or *exemption*) reduces the tax payable by the amount of the deduction times the taxpayer's marginal tax rate. A *tax credit* reduces the tax payable by the amount of the credit — that is, by the same dollar amount for every taxpayer who can claim it.

The 1988 Tax Reforms

Discussions of a set of tax reforms that would incorporate these three elements took place throughout the 1980s. An early set of reform proposals that focused on broadening the tax base by closing a number of tax loopholes was introduced by Finance Minister Allan McEachen in 1981. However, this "tax reform budget" was heavily criticized for imposing retroactive penalties on those who had been using loopholes that were perfectly legal before the budget. As a result of the criticism, many of the reform proposals were withdrawn, and McEachen was replaced as Finance Minister.

The next set of major reform proposals came in a 1987 White Paper which outlined specific suggestions for changing both the personal and corporate income taxes as well as the manufacturers' sales tax. After extensive consultations, some of the proposals were modified and the first stage of the reform (changing the personal and corporate income taxes) was introduced in 1988; the second stage (reform of the manufacturers' sales tax) was scheduled to follow later.

The 1988 reform reflected all three of the elements discussed above. The tax bases for the personal and corporate income taxes were broadened by the elemination of a number of loopholes. For example, an earlier rule that had exempted the first $1,000 of interest and dividend income from personal income tax was abolished, and the rules governing "tax shelter investments" (such as Canadian films and hobby farms) were tightened. The effective rate of tax on capital gains (above the $100,000 exemption) was increased. With respect to the corporation income tax, the preferences given to firms in the manufacturing and resource sectors were reduced. (The depletion allowance was scheduled to be abolished altogether.) At the same time, the rates of federal personal and corporate income taxes were generally reduced, and the structure of tax rates was simplified. For example, the number of tax brackets in the personal income tax schedule was reduced from ten to just three. The highest marginal rate of federal personal income tax was reduced by five percentage points; for a taxpayer living in a province where the provincial income tax is 50% of the federal tax, the combined federal/provincial marginal rate fell from 51% to 43.5%. The rates of corporation income tax were also reduced. Finally, a number of existing deductions and exemptions in the personal income tax law were converted to tax credits. They included the "basic personal exemption," the

Box 5-1

■ ■ ■ ■ ■ ■ ■ ■ ■ ■ ■ ■ ■ ■ ■ ■ ■ ■ ■ ■

Reaganomics: Any Verdict Yet?

Government is not the solution to our problems. Government is the problem.

Ronald Reagan

In the 1980 presidential campaign in the United States, the basic election promise of the Republican candidate Ronald Reagan was that if elected, he would fundamentally change the economic strategy of his Democratic predecessor Jimmy Carter. He stated two goals. First, he was going to restore fiscal responsibility by eliminating, or at least sharply reducing, the federal government deficit. His second promise was a reflection of his strongly held view that government in the United States had gone far beyond its appropriate role of providing protection from external enemies, and providing domestic law and order. One of his objectives, said Reagan, was to "get the government off the backs of the people." By loosening the heavy hand of government, the administration hoped to invigorate the private enterprise economy, and to unleash a strong economic expansion.

When he took office in January 1981, these objectives were translated into an economic program which was quickly given the label "Reaganomics." It included the following strategic components:
1. Increase defence expenditures.
2. Restrain, and where possible reduce domestic (non-defence) spending by the federal government.
3. Restrain the growth of government regulation.
4. Cut tax rates.

Reagan and his advisors were convinced that this strategy, and especially the tax cuts and reductions in regulation, would produce an unprecedented rate of economic growth. Such a strong expansion would help increase revenues, since people must pay more in taxes when their incomes rise. Cuts in domestic programs would also help to lower government deficits. In the early budget projections made in 1981, the administration forecast a balanced budget by the end of President Reagan's first term in 1984.

Reality turned out very differently. In fiscal 1979, Jimmy Carter's last year in office, the federal deficit was estimated at less than $30 billion. During Reagan's first four years, the deficits were $74 billion, $79 billion, $126 billion, and $202 billion. What went wrong with the early predictions? Several factors can be cited.
1. Economic expansion was much less vigorous than the administration had hoped. It is true that the economy grew at a very healthy rate in 1983/84. But this came only after the severe recession of 1981/82. Because the whole economy grew less

"married exemption," and the exemptions for dependent children and for persons over age 65.

The plans for the second stage of reform include a substantial broadening of the tax base for the federal manufacturers' sales tax that in the past has applied to only about one-third of all goods and services. The broadening of the tax base will yield a substantial increase in revenue from this source; alternatively, it will make possible a reduction in the tax rate.

Since a sales tax tends to be regressive, an increased reliance on sales tax revenue by the federal government would, by itself, tend to make the tax system as a whole less progressive. To offset this tendency, the reform plans call for the introduction of a relatively large sales tax credit (in the personal income tax) that would compensate the poor for the burden of increased sales taxes. The full amount of the credit would be available only to individuals with incomes below a specific threshold

level. For people with higher incomes, the credit would be gradually reduced, until it would disappear altogether at another, higher, income level.

The 1988 reform package has been criticized by some observers for not going far enough in making the tax system more efficient and fair. Nevertheless, most economists agree that it takes us a considerable distance in the right direction: The new system will be simpler than the old and the substitution of tax credits for many earlier exemptions and deductions will reduce the share of the total tax burden born by the poor.

Why Can't We Get Rid of All the Loopholes?

While the 1988 reforms went some distance toward reducing the size of various loopholes in the tax system, there were only a few that were eliminated altogether. Why is it so difficult to get rid of the loopholes and rapidly than expected for the four years as a whole, tax revenues were much less than expected.

2. Domestic spending was a great deal more difficult to cut than expected. In particular, interest on the debt was much higher than the projections made in 1981.

During the second Reagan administration, the size of the deficit, and what should be done about it, continued to dominate the debate over economic policy. Although the deficit fell somewhat in 1984, it again rose above $200 billion in 1985 and 1986, and remained above $150 billion in 1987.

The seriousness of the American deficit problem should not be exaggerated. In relation to the size of the economy as a whole, the U.S. deficit was less than half as large as the Canadian federal deficit in the late 1980s. Nevertheless, because it is so large in absolute terms, it can have significant effects on the world economy as a whole, and there is concern in many countries that the continued popularity of the simple precepts of Reaganomics is going to make it hard for President Bush to bring it down further. One of the reasons he beat Governor Dukakis in the 1988 election was that he promised to continue Reagan's commitment to no major tax increases. Since expenditure cuts are also difficult and painful, it remains to be seen how successful he will be in further deficit reduction.

Courtesy of Canapress Photo Service/Barry Thumma

create a simple and fair tax system once and for all? There are several possible reasons.

First, there will always be disagreement over precisely what is fair. For example, most economists would probably agree that fairness would require some taxation of imputed income from owner-occupied housing, but that feeling is unlikely to be shared by the majority of the population who own homes. Indeed, many Canadians agreed with Joe Clark's proposals to give even *more* tax relief to home owners by permitting deduction of mortgage interest from taxable income.

A second complication is the political problem. Clearly, those who benefit from loopholes have an incentive to lobby for their continuation. Moreover, reform is complicated by the fact that fairness is only one of the major objectives in a tax system. Most of the loopholes were put in expressly to promote national goals which the proponents considered important. For

example, the investment tax credit was introduced to stimulate capital investment in Canada. It was made larger in the Atlantic provinces and in certain other areas with high unemployment in order to create more industrial capacity and job opportunities there. The depletion allowance and the favourable tax treatment of capital gains have been justified as incentives for entrepreneurs to take risks. Accelerated depreciation, lower corporate tax rates, and tariff protection of manufacturing industry are defended on the grounds that they will create a more diversified economy in Canada and reduce our tradtional dependence on resource-based industries. (The pros and cons of such tariff protection are discussed later in Chapter 34.)

Therefore, many of the activities that the loopholes encourage contribute to long-standing Canadian goals such as industrialization, regional equalization, and so on. But some of the arguments for special tax treatment are more convincing than others. Furthermore, the question should be asked: Is the tax system the best way to promote diverse national goals?

Unfortunately, there is no all-purpose answer to this question. Many economists favour the use of taxes to achieve some goals — to discourage pollution, say. But few believe in using the tax system to favour the manufacturing industry through a whole host of preferential tax rules. In taxation, as in so many areas of economics, the policy maker is left with the problem of balancing conflicting national goals.

KEY POINTS

1. The defects and limitations of the market provide the government with an important economic role. The government affects the economy through expenditures, taxation, and regulation.

2. In dollar terms, government spending has sky-rocketed since 1926. However, as a percentage of national product, the growth of government spending has been much slower.

3. Of the federal expenditures, transfer payments have risen much more rapidly than expenditures for goods and services. Provincial government spending has been rising especially fast in the areas of health care and education.

4. Personal income taxes, sales and excise taxes, and corporate income taxes are the main sources of revenue for the federal and provincial governments. For local governments, property taxes are the most important. Provincial governments also benefit from revenue sharing by the federal government and local governments receive large transfers from provincial governments.

5. Government regulatory agencies are active in many areas, regulating many activities of private firms in order to protect the public against monopolies, and from business practices such as the sale of unsafe products or destruction of the environment.

6. Federal and provincial governments operate a large number of Crown corporations. There are many reasons for establishing government-owned businesses. In markets which are natural monopolies, government ownership may be a better alternative than a regulated monopoly under private ownership, or government ownership may be the best way to meet a social objective such as the provision of television programming in remote areas. Sometimes, government takes over private firms as a way of protecting jobs in particular communities.

7. The primary reasons for government intervention in the economy are to:
   (a) Provide public goods that cannot be supplied by the market because individuals have no incentive to buy them; individuals get the benefits regardless of who buys.
   (b) Deal with externalities, such as pollution.
   (c) Encourage the consumption of "merit" goods, and discourage or prohibit harmful products.
   (d) Help the poor.
   (e) Help stabilize the economy.

8. A number of objectives are important in the design of a tax system:
   (a) In general, neutrality is a desirable objective.
   (b) In some cases, however, the government should alter market signals by taxation. For example, a tax can be used to discourage pollution.
   (c) Taxes should be reasonably simple and easily understood.
   (d) Taxes should be fair. There are two ways of judging fairness: the benefit principle and the ability to pay.

9. The burden or "incidence" of taxes (that is, who ultimately pays the taxes) is hard to determine. But the rich don't bear as heavy a burden as the personal income tax rates suggest.

10. A major step toward simplifying the tax system and closing loopholes was taken in the two-stage reform legislation introduced in 1987/88. The first stage involved broadening the base for the personal and corporate income taxes while reducing the tax rates for most taxpayers. In the personal income tax, a number of existing deductions were converted to tax credits. In the second stage of the reform, scheduled to follow in later years, the base of the sales tax will be broadened and the sales tax rates adjusted.

KEY CONCEPTS

regulation

transfer payment

income tax

marginal tax rate

average tax rate

progressive tax

regressive tax

proportional tax

Crown corporation

privatization

federal-provincial transfer

equalization payment

unconditional grant

externality

tax neutrality

merit good

tax loophole

investment tax credit

capital gain

return on home owners' equity

deductions vs. credits

broadening the tax base

tax reform

PROBLEMS

5-1. "That government governs best which governs least." Do you agree? Why or why not? Does the government perform more functions than it should? If so, what activities would you like it to reduce or stop altogether? Are there any additional functions which the government should undertake? If so, which ones? How should they be paid for?

5-2. "Provincial and local governments are closer to the people than the federal government. Therefore, they should be given some of the functions of the federal government." Are there federal functions which might be turned over to the provinces and localities? Do you think they should be turned over? Why or why not? Are there functions which the federal government can do much better than the provinces or localities? If so, which ones?

5-3. The government engages in research. For example, the government has agricultural experimental stations; it also undertakes defence-related research. Why do you think the government engages in these two types of research while leaving most research to private business? Does the government have any major advantages in undertaking research? Any major disadvantages?

5-4. Consider two views of the tax system:

(a) "The government promotes social goals, such as health care research and the arts, through direct payments. It also promotes health care research and the arts by encouraging private giving. This is done by making gifts deductible from taxable income. Tax deductions may be an even more effective way of supporting health care research, the arts, and other desirable causes than direct government grants. Therefore, such deductions do not constitute 'loopholes.' Rather, they represent an efficient way of achieving important social goals."

(b) "The income tax is a mess. Home owners get a tax break, but renters do not. The rich are able to escape taxes by making gifts to universities, the arts, and to charities. The only way to get equity into the system is to eliminate all deductions and make all income subject to tax."

Which of these arguments is stronger? Why?

Part 2

■ ■

High Employment and a Stable Price Level

The five chapters of Part 1 have set the stage for the study of economics, providing analytical and institutional background and outlining the major objectives of high employment, price stability, growth, efficiency, and an equitable distribution of income.

The focus of Parts 2, 3, 4, and 5 will be on the goals of **high employment**, **price stability**, and **growth**. These involve the overall aggregates of the economy. How many workers are employed in the economy as a whole? What is happening to the total quantity of output in the economy? What is happening to the average level of prices? Because they deal with economy-wide magnitudes, these questions are classified under the heading of **macroeconomics**. (*Makros* means ''large'' in Greek.)

As an introduction to Part 2, Chapter 6 describes how economy-wide output (domestic or national) is measured. Chapter 7 provides an overview of macroeconomic performance and problems in recent decades—how output has fluctuated, how unemployment has risen during recessions, and how prices have increased. Chapter 8 introduces the concepts of aggregate demand and aggregate supply; they are at the core of macroeconomic theory just as demand and supply for individual products lie at the centre of microeconomic theory. Chapter 9 describes the Keynesian theory of aggregate expenditures (developed during the 1930s) and its explanation of how high unemployment can exist—and persist—in a market economy.

This will lay the foundation for Part 3, which will address the policy question: If aggregate demand is too low or too high, what can be done about it?

Chapter 6

■ ■

Measuring Domestic and National Product and Income

Never ask of money spent
Where the spender thinks it went
Nobody was ever meant
To remember or invent
What he did with every cent.

Robert Frost
"The Hardship of Accounting"

In our modern economy, we produce a vast array of goods and services: cars, TV sets, houses, clothing, medical care, and food, to name but a few. One way of judging the performance of the economy is to measure the production of all these goods and services. A measure of total production, of course, does not give a complete picture of the welfare of the nation. When we acquire more and more goods, we do not necessarily become happier. Other things are obviously important too; for example, the sense of accomplishment which comes from our everyday work, and the quality of our environment. Nevertheless, the total amount produced is one of the important measures of economic success.

THE MARKET AS A WAY OF MEASURING PRODUCTION

The wide range of products poses a problem: How are we to add them all up into a single measure of total product? How do we add apples and oranges?

Market prices provide an answer. If apples sell for $10 per bushel and oranges for $20 per bushel, the market indicates that 1 bushel of oranges is worth 2 bushels of apples. Thus, when market prices are used, oranges and apples can be compared and added, as shown in the example in Table 6-1. In our complex economy, the total value of output can be found in a similar way. By taking

the quantity times the market price, we find expenditures on a particular product. By adding up the expenditures for the many goods produced — clothing, food, speedboats, etc. — we can get a dollar measure of national product during the year.

National product (or equivalently, *national expenditure*) is the money value of the goods and services produced by a nation during a specific time period, such as a year.

TWO APPROACHES: EXPENDITURES AND INCOME

Before looking in detail at the national product concept or at its close cousin, *domestic* product, we should look

Table 6-1   Using Market Prices to Add Apples and Oranges

	(1) Quantity (bushels)	(2) Price (per bushel)	(3) Market value (3) = (1) × (2)
Apples	3000	$10	$30,000
Orange	2000	$20	$40,000
		Total	$70,000

Market prices provide a way of adding different goods to get a measure of total production.

95

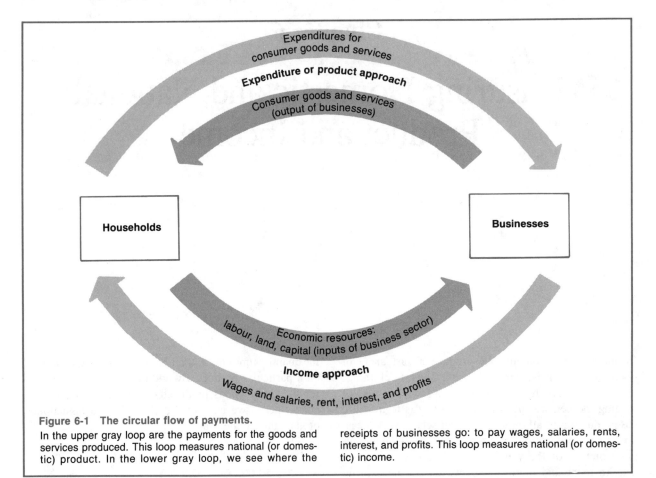

Figure 6-1 The circular flow of payments.
In the upper gray loop are the payments for the goods and services produced. This loop measures national (or domestic) product. In the lower gray loop, we see where the receipts of businesses go: to pay wages, salaries, rents, interest, and profits. This loop measures national (or domestic) income.

at the overall picture. To do so, let's call once more on the circular-flow diagram introduced in Chapter 3, and repeated here as Figure 6-1. This illustrates the simplest of all possible market economies in which the public consumes all the goods and services being produced.

The performance of this simple economy can be measured by looking at the money payments in either the upper gray loop or the lower gray loop. The upper loop shows expenditures by households buying the goods produced by business. Once business has received these payments, where do they go? The lower loop shows that they go to those who have provided the productive inputs: wages and salaries go to the labour force; rents to suppliers of land and buildings; and interest and profits to the suppliers of capital. Profits are what is left over after other payments — wages, salaries, interest, etc. — have been made. Thus, in the very simple economy shown in Figure 6-1, both gray loops give exactly the same total. We may look at the upper loop, which shows

national expenditures or the expenditures for national product. Alternatively, we may look at the lower loop, which measures **national income**.

> *National income* is the sum of all income derived from supplying the factors of production. It includes wages and salaries, rents, interest, and profits.

Domestic vs. *National* Product and Income

As the name suggests, national income is supposed to measure the total income derived by a country's nationals, from supplying the services of the factors of production they own. Similarly, national product measures the value of the goods and services produced through the use of those factors' services.

Normally, national product also can be taken as a reasonably accurate measure of the value of all goods and services produced *within a nation's boundaries*.

However, a problem arises when some of the factors of production used in the economy are owned by *foreign* nationals, rather than by residents of the country itself. For example, some of the revenues derived from the production and sales of goods and services in Canada may accrue as profits to U.S. citizens who own shares in firms that operate in Canada. Conversely, some factors owned by Canadian residents may be used to produce goods and services in other countries. For example, Canadian engineers may earn an income by working on a dam-building project in Pakistan or Canadian investors may earn a profit on firms they own in the United States and other countries. In these cases, the value of a country's **domestic product**—that is, the value of total production within the country — may be considerably different from the value of its *national* product, the value of the goods and services produced by the factors its nationals own.

> *National product* measures the total value of production attributable to the factors of production owned by a country's nationals. *Domestic product* is the total value of output produced within the country's boundaries.
>
> Similarly, *national income* is the total income earned by the factors of production owned by a country's nationals. *Domestic income* is the income earned by the factors of production used within a country, whether owned by nationals or foreigners.

For most countries, it is relatively unimportant whether it is domestic product or national product that is used as the basic measure of aggregate economic activity, because the two concepts are so close. In practice, most countries tend to emphasize the domestic product concept in their statistical publications. However, in some cases, the distinction may be important. For example, in a country such as Turkey, national product is substantially larger than domestic product: The reason is that large number of Turkish nationals are employed as "guest workers" in West Germany and other countries in continental Europe. Conversely, in an economy such as Canada's which employs large amounts of foreign-owned capital, the value of our domestic product typically exceeds the value of national product by a considerable margin. For example, recent national accounts statistics suggest that in 1987, domestic product was some 3% larger than our national product.

In earlier theoretical work on macroeconomics, national product and income were the basic concepts of economy-wide output and income, and the collection of statistics on aggregate economic activity is usually referred to as "national income accounting." However, the current practice in Canada is to put more emphasis on the *domestic* product and income concepts, and the estimates of economic activity that Statistics Canada periodically releases to the media refer to domestic product. Although we will continue to use the terms "national income accounting" and "national accounts," we will otherwise follow Statistics Canada's practice and use domestic product and income as our basic concepts throughout this book.

DOMESTIC PRODUCT: THE EXPENDITURES APPROACH

To calculate domestic product, we look at the upper loop in Figure 6-1, examining expenditures on the goods and services that have been produced. When we calculate what has been produced, it is important to count everything once, but only once. Unless we are careful, we may make a mistake and count some things more than once. The reason is that most products go through a number of stages in the process of production; they are sold a number of times before reaching the hands of the final user. For example, copper wiring and silicon chips are sold to electronics companies that use them to manufacture electronic calulators. In calculating Domestic Product, government statisticians include the calculators sold to consumers. But they do not also count separately the wiring and chips that went into them. Similarly, they count the bread purchased by the consumer. But they do not also count separately the flour that was used in producing the bread. To do so would mean that the flour was counted twice.

The electronic calculators and bread bought by consumers are **final products**; the wheat that went into the bread and the chips that went into the calculators are **intermediate products**. As a first approximation, domestic product is found by adding up just the expenditures on final products. In this way, double counting is avoided.

> A *final product* is a good or service that is purchased by the ultimate user and is not intended for resale or further processing.
>
> An *intermediate product* is one that is intended for resale or further processing.

Note that it is the intended use, rather than the physical characteristics of a product that determines whether it is a final good or not. When gasoline is bought by a service station, it is an intermediate good; it is intended for resale to the public. When it is bought by a farmer or trucker, it is also an intermediate product, since it will be used to harvest grain or produce trucking services. However, when it is purchased by a tourist on vacation, it is a final good. Similarly, when I buy a new car for my family's use, it is a final product. But when a taxi company buys an identical automobile, it is an intermediate product, to be used in the production of taxi rides.

The distinction between final products and intermediate products is illustrated in Table 6-2, which shows a simple productive process with only four stages. The first step in the production of a loaf of bread occurs when the farmer grows 20 cents' worth of wheat. The second stage is the milling of this wheat into flour, which is then worth 45 cents. In other words, 25 cents of value is added to the 20 cents' worth of wheat when it is made into flour. Similarly, the table shows how value is added at the last two stages, when the flour is baked into bread, and when the bread is delivered to the consumer. How much has been produced? The answer: The $1.25 loaf of bread. In calculating domestic product, we use only the $1.25 value of the bread. We must not add up the value of all the transactions in the first column, which would total $2.85.

Value added is the difference between the value of a firm's product and the cost of intermediate products bought from outside suppliers.

In the calculation of domestic product, final products are classified into four categories: (1) personal consumption expenditures, (2) domestic investment, (3) government expenditures for current goods and services, and (4) net exports — that is, exports minus imports. By including government expenditures, investment, and net exports, we are now recognizing that the world is more complicated than the simple one in Figure 6-1, where consumers were assumed to buy all the final goods produced in the economy.

1. Personal Consumption Expenditures (*C*)

Consumption is the ultimate objective of economic activity; we work and produce so that we will have goods and services to consume. Personal consumption expenditures (*C*) constitute the largest component of domestic product. The items in Table 6-3 may be divided into three main components: durable goods, such as cars or washing machines; nondurable goods, such as food or clothing; and services, such as dental care or haircuts.

Note that personal consumption expenditures include only spending by *private individuals*. Government expenditures on various goods and services are divided between the second and third categories below, depending on whether the expenditures are classified as current spending or investment spending.

2. Domestic Investment (*I*)

Each year, we produce not only goods and services for immediate consumption, we also produce capital goods which help in production in future years. Investment may be undertaken by governments — for example, the construction of a power plant. Or it may be undertaken by private businesses — for example, the construction of new factories.

Domestic investment includes three categories: (a) investment in plant and equipment; (b) residential construction; and (c) changes in inventories.

Plant and Equipment

This category includes the construction of factories, power plants, warehouses, stores, and other non-residential structures used by business and government, and the acquisition of machinery and other equipment.

Table 6-2   Final and Intermediate Products

Stage of production	(1) Value of sales	(2) Cost of intermediate products	(3) Value added (1) − (2) = (3)
Intermediate goods:			
Wheat	20 −	0 =	20
Flour	45 −	20 =	25
Bread, at wholesale	95 −	45 =	50
Final good:			
Bread, at retail	$1.25 −	95 =	30
		Total	$1.25

Value is added at the various stages of production. Note that the sum of all the value-added items in the last column (1.25) is equal to the value of the final product.

Table 6-3   The Composition of Personal Consumption Expenditures, 1987

	Billions of dollars	Percent of total
1. Food and non-alcoholic beverages	37.9	12
2. Other non-durable goods	30.7	9
3. Clothing, footwear, and other semi-durable goods	33.8	10
4. Gross rent, electricity, heating	67.2	21
5. Motor vehicles, parts, repairs, fuels, and lubricants	35.2	11
6. Furniture, appliances, and other durable goods	24.4	8
7. Restaurants, hotels, and net expenditures abroad	21.7	7
8. Other services	72.1	22
Total	323.0	100

Source: Compiled from Statistics Canada, *National Income and Expenditure Accounts*, third quarter 1988, table 7.

Residential Construction

The construction of residences is included in the investment segment of domestic product. The reason for including apartment buildings in investment is straightforward. An apartment building, like a factory or machine, is intended to be an income-producing asset. In future years, the apartment building will produce shelter for which the owner will charge rent.

There is a substantial advantage in treating all residential construction similarly in the domestic product accounts. When housing of any kind is built, families have shelter; this is true whether they rent the new housing or own it. For consistency, construction of new owner-occupied housing is included in the investment category. More specifically, domestic product accountants treat owner-occupied housing as if the family had originally invested in the home, and then, in future years, rented the house to itself. Note that houses are treated differently from consumer durables such as refrigerators. Houses are included in investment; refrigerators are part of consumption expenditures.

Changes in Inventories

We have seen that wheat that goes into bread is not counted separately in the domestic product, because its cost is included as part of the total cost of bread and is accounted for in the price of the bread. But how about any wheat we produce above and beyond the amount consumed in bread and pastries? What happens to it? The answer is that it is either exported (a possibility that we will consider in just a moment), or it is used to build up our inventories of wheat. Any such increases in our stocks of wheat represent something we have produced this year. Therefore, they are included in this year's domestic product.

Similarly, increases in inventories of steel are included in domestic product — for example, the additional inventories of steel held by refrigerator manufacturers or the increase in the inventory of unsold steel held by a steel company. But we do not include the steel which went into the production of refrigerators or machines, since it has already been included when we count consumer purchases of refrigerators and investment in equipment.

Earlier, we said that, as a first approximation, domestic product is found by adding up only expenditures on final products. That is an acceptable and commonly used generalization. It is 99% right, and that is not bad. But it is not precisely accurate. Domestic product includes not only final products in the form of consumer goods and services, government purchases, and equipment and buildings. It also includes the intermediate products that have been added to inventories. The precisely correct statement is perhaps worth reiterating: We should measure all goods and services once, but only once.

Changes in inventories can be either positive or negative. In a bad crop year, there may be less wheat on hand at the end of the year than at the beginning. We have taken more out of our stocks than we have put back in. In this case, changes in inventories are negative, and they are subtracted in measuring domestic product.

Finally, note that the domestic investment category (*I*) includes only domestic investment in Canada, since it is Canadian domestic product that is being estimated. If Northern Telecom builds a factory in Brazil, its value is included in Brazil's domestic product, not in Canadian domestic product. On the other hand, if Honda builds an assembly plant in Ontario, that plant is included in Canadian domestic product.

3. Government Expenditures on Current Goods and Services (G)

Government spending includes not only *investment* activities (included in the *I* category) such as the construction of power plants, roads, school buildings, and municipal waste treatment plants, but also the production of goods and services for *current* use, *G*. The government hires workers to keep up the parks; park services are produced for the public to enjoy currently. The government hires teachers and pays the operating costs of hospitals; educational and health care services are produced. Soldiers are paid to provide national defence. Governments at all levels — federal, provincial, and municipal — undertake current expenditures for the public good.[1]

While government expenditures on goods and services (*G*) are included in domestic product, transfer payments are not. When the government buys spare parts for an army truck, the parts are produced. But when the government makes transfer payments — such as Old Age Security benefits to retirees — the recipients are not required to produce anything in return. Therefore, government expenditures on truck parts are included in domestic product, but transfer payments are not.

4. Exports of Goods and Services (X)

Some wheat is exported. Even though this wheat is bought by foreigners, is has been produced in Canada. Therefore, it should be included in Canadian domestic product. Because such wheat does not appear in the first three categories (*C*, *G*, *I*), it is included here—in exports of goods and services (*X*).

It is obvious how we export a good such as wheat: We put it on a ship and send it abroad. But how can we export services, such as haircuts and surgical operations? The answer is this. A tourist from Tokyo visiting Vancouver has all sorts of expenditures: for hotel accommodation, for taxi rides, for haircuts, and perhaps even for medical services. Since these services have been produced in Canada, they must be counted as part of Canada's domestic product. Since they are paid for by the foreigner, they are considered exports of services, even though the hotel, the taxi, the barber shop, and the hospital remain in Canada.

Interest and dividend payments by foreigners to Canadian firms and individuals, and profits of Canadian subsidiaries abroad, are *not* counted as part of the export item in the estimates of Canadian domestic product. True, they represent a source of income for the Canadian nationals who receive these payments (and, therefore, are counted as part of Canadian *national* income). But they do not add to the value of the goods and services produced within Canada's boundaries and, therefore, are excluded from the *domestic* product estimates.[2]

5. A Subtraction: Imports of Goods and Services (M)

When the Japanese buy our wheat, this export is included in our domestic product. What happens, on the other side, when we buy Japanese automobiles? Such purchases of imports are included in the Canadian personal consumption expenditures category. But these cars were not produced in Canada. Therefore, they should not be counted as part of our domestic product. Thus, a subtraction is made for cars imported from Japan (and other countries). Similarly, in calculating domestic product we subtract all other imports (*M*) of goods and services.

Payments of interest and dividends to foreigners for the use of the capital they have invested in Canada are not subtracted in calculating Canadian domestic product.

- - - - -

[1] The inclusion of all government expenditures for goods and services in domestic product is a problem. While some government purchases are for "final" use, other government spending is for intermediate products. A road, for example, can carry both vacation traffic (a "final" or consumption type of use) and trucks loaded with goods (an "intermediate" stage in the productive process). Thus, it might be argued that insofar as roads are used for "intermediate" purposes, this portion of the expenditure for roads should not be included in domestic product. But domestic product accountants have ducked this problem. They simply assume that all goods and services purchased by the government are for "final" use, and they therefore include all such purchases in domestic product.

[2] Logically, the income earned by Canadian nationals who work in foreign countries should also be excluded, for the same reason (and the earnings of foreign nationals working in Canada should be excluded from the import item). In practice, however, it is difficult for Statistics Canada to estimate such earnings, and to distinguish them from exports of services. (For example, how should one treat the earnings of a Canadian truck driver who is paid by an American wholesaler for trucking a load of PEI potatoes to New York City?) Therefore, the only correction that Statistics Canada makes in going from domestic product to national product is to subtract the investment earnings of foreign nationals in Canada, net of the earnings of Canadian nationals with investments abroad.

While they *should* be subtracted when we estimate Canadian *national* income, foreign capital employed in Canada does contribute to the production of goods and services within Canada's borders, just as domestic capital does.

Domestic Product: A Summary Statement

When we measure domestic product using the expenditure approach, we make use of the fact that domestic product is equal to domestic expenditure and, therefore, we estimate domestic product as:

> **Domestic product = personal consumption expenditures (C)**
> **plus   domestic investment (I)**
> **plus   government expenditures for current goods and services (G)**
> **plus   exports of goods and services (X)**
> **minus   imports of goods and services (M)**

In symbols, this is written:

$$\text{\textbf{Domestic product}} = C + I + G + X - M \tag{6-1}$$

(In this chapter, the equations are numbered — starting here with equation 6-1 — because we want to refer back to them at a later point.)

Finally, several details might be noted. Recall that domestic product includes only goods and services produced during the year. Therefore, it does not include expenditures for used goods such as cars or houses. They were produced in a previous year and were included in that year's domestic product. However, renovations of old buildings are included as are repairs to automobiles. They represent current production. Also included in current domestic product are the brokerage fees for selling houses and other buildings. They represent payments for a valuable service — namely, assistance in the transfer of the building to someone who wants it.

Common stocks acquired by an individual or institution are not included in domestic product, since they represent a transfer of ownership rather than production. Of course, if a corporation issues stock and finances the construction of a factory with the proceeds, the factory is part of the domestic product. It has been produced during the current year.

THE COMPLICATION OF DEPRECIATION: GDP AND NDP

The main outline of the domestic product accounts has now been completed, but we still have a number of details to consider. One of the most important is the measurement of investment.

If we count the full value of capital goods such as buildings and equipment produced during this year, domestic product is overestimated. Why? Because existing buildings and equipment have deteriorated — or *depreciated* — during the year from wear and obsolescence. After calculating the total value of all new plant, equipment, and residential buildings produced during the year, we should deduct the amount that plant, equipment, and residences have depreciated during the year. Only if we do this will we get a true measure of how much our total stocks of buildings and equipment have increased during the year (Figure 6-2).

Thus, two concepts of investment should be distinguished:

> *Gross domestic investment* (I_g) is equal to total expenditures for new capital goods such as plant, equipment, and residential buildings plus the change in inventories.
>
> *Net domestic investment* (I_n) is equal to gross domestic investment (I_g) less depreciation. That is,
>
> $$I_n = I_g - \text{depreciation}[3]$$

Corresponding to these two concepts of investment, there are two concepts of domestic product:

Gross domestic product (GDP) =
$$C + I_g + G + X - M \tag{6-2}$$

Net domestic product (NDP) =
$$C + I_n + G + X - M \tag{6-3}$$

From these two equations, it follows that:

$$\text{\textbf{GDP} — depreciation} = \text{\textbf{NDP}} \tag{6-4}$$

This relationship is illustrated in the second and third columns of Figure 6-3.

▪ ▪ ▪ ▪ ▪

[3] More precisely, to go from I_g to I_n, accountants subtract Capital Consumption Allowances (CCA). These allowances include not only depreciation, but also adjustments for the effects of inflation on the measurement of capital. This is a fine point, which we henceforth ignore; we use the simpler concept of depreciation in place of CCA.

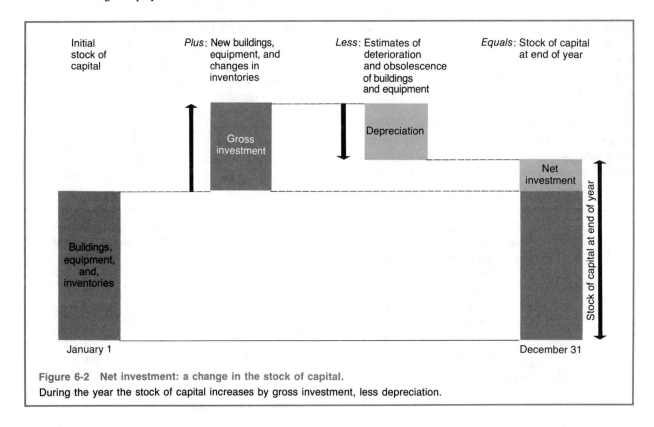

Figure 6-2   **Net investment: a change in the stock of capital.**
During the year the stock of capital increases by gross investment, less depreciation.

In theory, NDP is the measure of domestic product that we should use, because it takes into account the obsolescence and physical deterioration of machinery and buildings during the year. But, in newspapers and statistical publications, NDP is *not* the commonly used measure; much more attention is paid to GDP (or the equivalent measure GDE, gross domestic expenditure). Why is this? The answer is that, while NDP is the best measure conceptually, it is difficult to estimate in practice. Gross investment—the value of new buildings and equipment, plus additions to inventories — is relatively easy to measure. But to estimate net investment, we need to measure depreciation and this raises difficult questions. How rapidly will a machine really wear out? Will it become obsolete before it is physically worn out? If it will be scrapped in 10 years, does its value decline in a "straight line"? by 10% each year? or does it lose most of its productive value in the first few years? Because of such questions, we cannot be confident about estimates of depreciation. In practice, therefore, GDP is used much more commonly than NDP.

FROM NET DOMESTIC PRODUCT TO NATIONAL INCOME: Two Complications

Net Investment Income   As explained earlier, government statisticians distinguish between the total value of the goods and services produced within a country's boundaries (domestic product) and the value of the goods and services produced by the factors owned by its nationals. To get from the domestic product concepts — NDP and GDP — to the corresponding *national* concepts (GNP and NNP), we should *exclude* that part of Canadian domestic product that can be attributed to foreign factors of production—that is, factors such as capital owned by foreign nationals — and *include* earnings of Canadian factors employed in foreign countries. As noted above in footnote 2, because it is difficult to estimate the earnings of Canadians temporarily working abroad or of foreign nationals working temporarily in this country, Statistics Canada uses a simplified method in estimating national product: To get from domestic product to national product or from domestic income to national

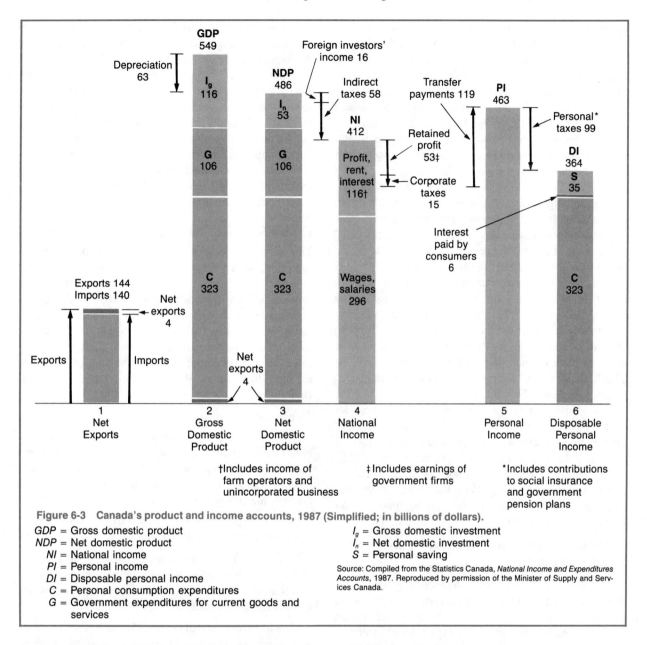

Figure 6-3   Canada's product and income accounts, 1987 (Simplified; in billions of dollars).

†Includes income of farm operators and unincorporated business

‡ Includes earnings of government firms

*Includes contributions to social insurance and government pension plans

GDP = Gross domestic product
NDP = Net domestic product
NI = National income
PI = Personal income
DI = Disposable personal income
C = Personal consumption expenditures
G = Government expenditures for current goods and services

I_g = Gross domestic investment
I_n = Net domestic investment
S = Personal saving

Source: Compiled from the Statistics Canada, *National Income and Expenditures Accounts*, 1987. Reproduced by permission of the Minister of Supply and Services Canada.

income, they simply subtract interest, dividends, and other investment income earned by foreigners on capital they have invested in Canada, and add the interest, dividends, and other investment income of Canadian-owned capital in foreign countries. That is, they subtract the "net payments of investment income to non-residents."

Gross National Product (GNP) =
GDP − net investment income of non-residents.

Similarly,

Net National Product (NNP) =
NDP − net investment income of non-residents.

Indirect Taxes   The next complication refers to the distinction between NNP and national income (NI). At first glance, one might think that they should be exactly the same. After all, NNP is the total value of the goods and services produced by the nationally owned factors of production. NI is the sum of incomes earned by the nationals who supply these factors of production. Similarly, one might think that NDP should be the same as domestic income. How can these measures possibly be different? The answer: They are different because the factors of production do not get all the proceeds from the sale of a good. Instead, part goes to the government in the form of sales taxes (and other similar taxes).[4]

Consider a package of razors priced, say, at $1.99. Most of the $1.99 is divided in the form of wages and salaries, rents, interest, and profits among the various participants who bring the razors to the market. But those who contribute to the production of the blades do not get all of the $1.99: Part of it goes to the government as manufacturer's sales tax. Suppose that this tax is 10 cents. Then it is only the remaining $1.89—that is, the part which goes to wages, salaries, profits, etc.—that is part of national income. Furthermore, when you get to the cash register with your package of razor blades, you will pay more than $1.99 if there is a provincial sales tax (as there is in every province except Alberta). Suppose the provincial sales tax is 7% or 14 cents on the package of razor blades. Then, the total price you pay will be $2.13. Because national product is measured at market prices, it includes the whole $2.13.

This distinction shows up in Figure 6-3, where we subtract sales taxes (and other similar taxes) from NNP in order to get column 4, which shows the national income earned by the suppliers of productive resources.

The tax complication should not obscure a conclusion that is worth emphasizing. With the exception of sales taxes, the proceeds from the sale of the final product become incomes of the factors of production. Thus:

The process of production is also the process of generating income.

In column 4 of Figure 6-3, the income generated on owner-operated farms and unincorporated business is included in the "profits, rent" category rather than being divided into the familiar components of income—wages and salaries, profits, and so on. To understand the

■ ■ ■ ■ ■
[4] These other similar taxes include customs duties on imports, property taxes, and excise taxes on items such as cigarettes. These taxes are sometimes lumped together under the heading of *indirect taxes*. (This term is based on the assumption that these taxes will not be borne by the producer or importer, but will be passed along to the person who buys cigarettes, the imported good, or other item on which a tax is collected.)

reason for this, note that for a large corporation, wages are sharply distinguishable from profits. Wages go to the workers, while profits are the return to the owners of the corporation. However, for some businesses—such as a family farm or a mom and pop store—it is not feasible to separate wages, profits, and other income shares. How much of a farmer's income is the result of the family's labour, and how much a return on its investment in buildings, equipment, and so on? It is not easy to say. Accordingly, no attempt is made to subdivide such income; it is included as a single item in the "profits, rent" category even though it contains some implicit labour income.

OTHER INCOME MEASURES

Thus far, we have seen that GDP includes personal consumption, government expenditures on current goods and services, gross investment, and exports less imports. The difference between GDP and NDP is depreciation, although this is difficult to measure precisely. We also saw that you have to subtract net investment income of foreigners and sales taxes from NDP to get national income, which is the sum of payments for providing factors of production—labour, land, and capital. Now, let's see what happens next.

Personal Income (*PI*)

Although most of *national income* is received by households as their *personal income* (*PI*), national income and personal income are not exactly the same.

One reason is that not all national income flows through the business sector to households:

■ Part of corporate profit is taken by the government in the form of corporate income taxes.

■ Part of profit is retained by corporations to finance expansion. Thus, dividends are the only portion of corporate profits which do flow from corporations to households as personal income.

The other reason that personal income is not the same as national income lies in transfer payments, such as family allowances and Unemployment Insurance benefits. Such transfers are a source of personal income to households. But they are not payments to households for providing factors of production. Therefore, they are not included in national income.

Thus, to find personal income (column 5, Figure 6-3), we begin with national income (column 4), subtract corporation taxes and profits retained by corporations, and then add transfer payments. Personal income is the measure which corresponds most closely to the everyday meaning of "income."

Disposable Personal Income (*DI*)

Not all personal income is available to the individual or family for personal use, however. The government takes a sizable chunk in the form of personal taxes. (These are mainly personal income taxes, but also include compulsory contributions to government pension plans and unemployment insurance, and other miscellaneous items such as inheritance taxes.) After these taxes and contributions are paid, disposable personal income (*DI*) remains. Households can do three things with this income: spend it on consumption, use it to pay interest on consumer debt, or save it.[5] Disposable income is an important concept, because consumers look at this income when they decide how much to spend.

Relative Magnitudes

Before leaving Figure 6-3, observe the relative magnitudes of the major boxes. Consumption is by far the largest component of GDP. In 1987, it amounted to 59% of GDP. Government expenditures for goods and services and gross investment both constituted about 20%. However, more than half of gross investment went to cover depreciation, leaving less than 10% of GDP as net investment.

In the fourth column, we see that wages and salaries were by far the largest component of national income, 72%. In the last column, consumption expenditures were 88% of disposable income.

While most of these items are relatively stable, a few change quite sharply from year to year. Net exports can be either positive or negative; they were usually positive

■ ■ ■ ■ ■
[5] In Canadian national accounting, interest paid by households on consumer debt is not considered part of consumption spending. Instead, it is considered as a transfer (from households which are in debt, to other households which own assets on which they earn interest). Thus, the $6 billion interest payments shown in column 6 are part of the $119 billion in transfer payments in column 5.

in the years prior to 1978, but have been negative in recent years. Net investment has been quite volatile, rising sharply during periods of business prosperity, and falling during recessions. In the quarter century from 1963 to 1988, gross investment ranged from a high of 27% of GDP in the second quarter of 1966 to a low of 19% in the third quarter of 1982. Corporate profits are even more responsive to business conditions—reaching a high of 29% of GDP in the first quarter of 1980, then dropping rapidly to 15% in the third quarter of 1982.

NOMINAL AND REAL GDP

Dollar prices provide a satisfactory basis for calculating national product in any one year; they allow us to add apples and oranges, haircuts and cars. But if we wish to evaluate the performance of the economy over a number of years, we face a major problem. The dollar is a shrinking yardstick. Because of inflation, its value is going down. On average, the dollar in 1988 bought only 51% of what it bought in 1978.

As the years pass, the dollar measure of GDP increases for two quite different reasons. First, there is an increase in the quantity of goods and services produced. This increase is desirable; we have more and more goods and services at our disposal. Second, the prices of goods and services increase. This increase is undesirable; it occurs because we have been unsuccessful in combatting inflation. To judge the performance of the economy, it is essential to separate the desirable increase in the quantity of output from the undesirable increase in prices.

To do this, economists use the concept of *constant dollar GDP*, also known as *real GDP*. This is calculated by valuing GDP at the prices which existed in a beginning or *base year*, not at the prices which actually exist while the GDP is being produced. (Statistics Canada currently uses 1981 as the base year in GDP calculations.) A hypothetical example of an economy producing only two items is given in Table 6-4.

If we looked only at *nominal* or *current dollar GDP* in the first two columns, we might come to the erroneous

Table 6-4 Current-dollar and Constant-dollar GDP

(1) 1981 current-dollar GDP	(2) 1988 current-dollar GDP	(3) 1988 constant-dollar GDP
100 coats @ $60 = $6,000 100 radios @ $40 = $4,000 Total $10,000	120 coats @ $200 = $24,000 120 radios @ $50 = $6,000 Total $30,000	120 coats @ $60 = $7,200 120 radios @ $40 = $4,800 Total $12,000

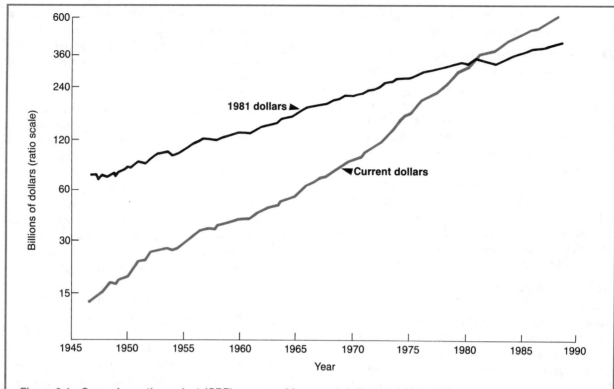

Figure 6-4   Gross domestic product (GDP), measured in current dollars and 1981 dollars.

Much of the increase in current-dollar domestic product has been the result of inflation. Observe that domestic product has grown much more slowly in constant (1981) dollars than in current dollars.

Source: Statistics Canada, *CANSIM Databank*. Reproduced by permission of the Minister of Supply and Services Canada.

conclusion that output had trebled—up from $10,000 in 1981 to $30,000 in 1988. But this clearly misstates the increase in the quantity of goods and services produced. Observe that the quantities of coats and radios have both increased by only 20%. By measuring 1988 output at 1981 prices in the final column, we find constant-dollar GDP to be $12,000. Comparing this with 1981 GDP of $10,000, we come to the correct conclusion: Real output has increased by 20%.

Obviously, this is a very simplified example. Figure 6-4 shows the actual figures for current-dollar and constant-dollar GDP. Observe how much more rapidly the current-dollar series has risen. Most of the increase in nominal GDP between 1971 and 1987 was caused by a rise in prices (Figure 6-5).

Price Indexes

More specifically, we can use current-dollar and constant-dollar GDP to calculate how much the average level of prices has risen since the base year. Returning to the example in Table 6-4, observe that nominal GDP in 1988 is 2.5 times as high as real GDP in that year ($30,000/$12,000 = 2.5). By convention, the average price in the base year is given a value of 100 when calculating a *price index*. Thus, in the example in Table 6-4, the index of prices in 1988 is 250 (that is, 2.5 times the base of 100.)

> An *index* is a number which shows how an average (of prices, or wages, or some other economic measure) has changed over time.

The index calculated from nominal and real GDP figures is known as the *implicit GDP price deflator*, or, more simply, as the *GDP deflator*. In general, it is calculated as:

$$\text{GDP price deflator} = \frac{\text{Nominal GDP} \times 100}{\text{Real GDP}} \quad (6\text{-}5)$$

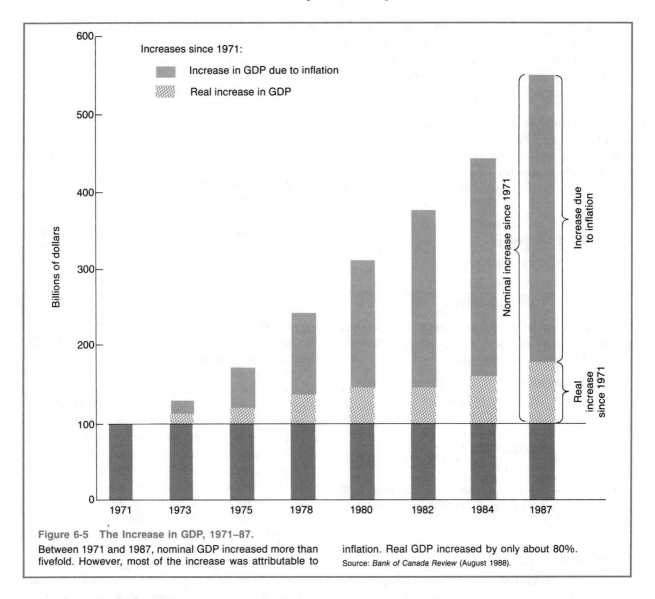

Figure 6-5   The Increase in GDP, 1971–87.

Between 1971 and 1987, nominal GDP increased more than fivefold. However, most of the increase was attributable to inflation. Real GDP increased by only about 80%.

Source: *Bank of Canada Review* (August 1988).

While the GDP deflator measures the change in the average price of the goods and services we have produced, another index—the *consumer price index   PI)*—measures the change in the average price of the goods and services bought by the typical household. Specifically, the CPI measures changes in the cost of a basket of goods and services purchased by the typical urban family — food, automobiles, housing, furniture, repair services, etc.

When the prices of the goods and services that we produce rise, so generally do the prices of what we purchase — for the simple reason that we consume most of

what we produce. Therefore, it's not surprising that the GDP price deflator and the CPI tend to move together. But the two indexes are not identical. For example, much of Canada's production of goods such as wheat, timber, or newsprint is exported to foreign countries. Thus, these products have more important weights in the GDP deflator (which includes all wheat, timber or newsprint produced in Canada) than in the CPI (which includes only the wheat, timber and newsprint consumed in Canada). Partly as a result of this difference, the two indexes moved differently in the early 1970s, when there was a steep rise in the world prices of the raw materials we exported. For example, between 1973 and 1974, the GDP-deflator increased by 15.3%; the CPI increased by a less spectacular 10.9%. (The appendix to this chapter investigates the problem of calculating real GDP when the prices of exported or imported commodities change sharply.)

Short-run movements in the two indexes may also differ because the CPI covers only the goods and services bought by the typical urban household. In contrast, the GDP deflator is calculated from the prices of every item in GDP—that is, the cost of capital goods and government services, as well as consumer goods and services.

Other Real Measures

Equation 6-5 may be rearranged:

$$\textbf{Real GDP} = \frac{\textbf{Nominal GDP}}{\textbf{GDP price deflator}} \times \textbf{100} \qquad (6\text{-}6)$$

This process—dividing by a price index—is known as *deflating*. Similar equations may be used to calculate other real measures. For example:

$$\begin{aligned}\textbf{Real consumption} \\ = \frac{\textbf{Nominal consumption}}{\textbf{CPI}} \times \textbf{100} \qquad (6\text{-}7)\end{aligned}$$

$$\textbf{Real wage} = \frac{\textbf{Nominal wage}}{\textbf{CPI}} \times \textbf{100} \qquad (6\text{-}8)$$

Suppose the nominal or money wage rises from $100 to $107 while the CPI rises by 5%. Then, using Equation 6-8, we find:

$$\begin{aligned}\textbf{Real wage} &= \frac{\textbf{\$107}}{\textbf{105}} \times \textbf{100} \qquad (6\text{-}9)\\ &= \textbf{\$101.90}\end{aligned}$$

The real wage has increased by 1.90%. That is, a worker's wage will buy almost 2% more goods and services. Observe that, in deflating the nominal wage to find the real wage, we use the CPI. This is the most appropriate price index, since it measures changes in the prices of the goods and services that the typical family buys.

While equation 6-9 gives the precise answer, it is cumbersome. A much simpler procedure is often used to find the approximate change:

> **Change in real wage**
> $\cong$ **change in money wage** − **change in CPI**
> = **7% − 5% = 2%** (6-10)

A MEASURE OF ECONOMIC WELFARE

Real GDP is one of the most frequently used measures of economic performance. And large changes in GDP may, in fact, reflect severe problems or impressive gains. When Canada's real GDP fell by 30% between 1929 and 1933, the performance of the economy was very unsatisfactory. On the other hand, the large increase in real GDP in Japan in recent decades has reflected a rapid rise in the Japanese material standard of living.

Yet real GDP cannot be taken as a precise measure of the standard of living. The most obvious difficulty arises because an increase of, say, 10% in real GDP doesn't mean that the average person has 10% more goods and services. The reason is that population is growing. Rather than using total GDP figures, it is appropriate to estimate changes in the standard of living by looking at real GDP *per capita*; that is, real GDP divided by the population.

Other, more subtle problems arise because market sales are taken as the starting point in calculating GDP. When you hire a professional carpenter to build bookcases, the amount you pay appears in GDP. But if *you* build bookcases for your home, only the wood and materials are included in GDP; the value of your time as a carpenter is not. Similarly, a restaurant meal appears in GDP. But when you prepare an even better meal at home, only the ingredients bought from the store are included. Thus, GDP does not include some important items, simply because they do not go through the market.

However, in calculating GDP, government statisticians do not adhere blindly to the idea that GDP should include all market transactions and nothing else. GDP includes some imputed items which do not go through the market. We have already seen that owner-occupied housing is treated as if its owners rent to themselves. Imputed rents on such housing are included in GDP, even though people do not actually pay themselves rent.

On the other hand, some items which actually do go through the market are excluded from GDP, and quite properly so. Since GDP is taken as a measure of the economy's performance, illegal products—such as heroin—are excluded from GDP on the grounds that lawmakers have decided that they are "bads" rather than "goods."

Nevertheless, a number of dubious items remain in GDP. When international relations become more tense, higher expenditures for weapons are included in GDP; however, our situation has scarcely improved. If there is an increase in crime, additional expenditures for police, courts, and prisons are included in GDP. Yet society is certainly no better off than it was before the increase in crime.

Furthermore, some goods are included while the ''bads'' they create are ignored. For example, GDP includes the production of automobiles and electricity, but there is no downward adjustment for the resulting pollution. Indeed, if people need medical attention as a result, GDP will go up, since payments by governments and patients for the services of doctors and hospitals are included in GDP.

Naturally enough, economists are bothered by the shortcomings of GDP as a measure of well-being. During the past two decades, a number of attempts have been made to deal with some of the inadequacies. These attempts fall under two main headings.

1. Emphasis on Additional Social Indicators

The first approach is to downplay GDP as the measure of how the economy and society are performing and to realize that it is only one of a number of important indicators of performance. Rather than focusing on GDP, policy makers can look at a set of indicators that, taken together, provide both a way of judging performance and a set of objectives for policy makers.[6] In addition to real GDP, important indicators of well-being include such things as life expectancy, infant mortality rates, the availability of health care, education and literacy, the amount of leisure, the quality of the environment, and the degree of urban crowding.

2. A Comprehensive Measure of Economic Welfare (MEW)

The second approach is more ambitious: to provide a comprehensive single measure of economic performance, including not only the standard national product, but also additions for the value of leisure and subtractions for pollution and other disadvantages of crowded urban living. Such a measure of economic welfare (MEW) was calculated some years ago for the United

States by two Yale University economists, William Nordhaus and James Tobin.[7]

The difficulties they encountered were formidable. The most interesting implication of their study is that an entirely satisfactory index *can't* be constructed. To see why, consider the problem posed by leisure.

As our ability to produce has increased, the working population has taken only part of the gain in the form of higher wages and other measured incomes; a significant part of the gain has come in the form of a shorter work week. For example, Nordhaus and Tobin calculated that in the United States, the average number of leisure hours had increased by 22% between 1929 and 1965, while real per capita net national product (NNP) had risen by 90%. The question is, What should be made of these facts? Specifically, which of the following conclusions is correct?

1. Production per person went up by 90%, and people had more leisure, too. Therefore, economic welfare improved by more than 90%; it rose *more* than NNP.

2. Production per person went up by 90%. But leisure increased by less than 90%; specifically, by only 22%. So, economic welfare rose by some average of the 90% and the 22%; that is, by *less* than NNP.

The choice between conclusions 1 and 2 is difficult, but it is only the beginning of the problems with evaluating economic welfare in a more comprehensive way. For example, the Nordhaus-Tobin estimates of MEW did not drop during the Great Depression; indeed, they actually rose between 1929 and 1935. The explanation for this quirk, of course, is that Nordhaus and Tobin included leisure as an element of welfare, and leisure certainly increased as people were thrown out of work. But surely there is something wrong here. Leisure after a good day's work may be bliss, but it's not so pleasant to be idle when you've lost your job.

The ultimate test of economic success is the contribution which economic activity makes to the goal of human happiness. But to seek a single, summary measure of this contribution is surely to set out on an impossible task. In the words of the late economist Arthur Okun, the calculation of ''a summary measure of social welfare is a job for a philosopher king.''

■ ■ ■ ■ ■

[6] Examples of lists of such indicators may be found in: Economic Council of Canada, *Eleventh annual review: Economic Targets and Social Indicators* (Ottawa, 1974).

■ ■ ■ ■ ■

[7] William Nordhaus and James Tobin, ''Is Growth Obsolete?'' in *Economic Growth, Fiftieth Anniversary Colloquium* (New York: National Bureau of Economic Research, 1972).

Because it seems impossible to develop a single comprehensive measure of welfare, we are stuck with the national and domestic product accounts. In spite of all their defects and shortcomings, they do provide an important measure of the health of our economy. Downturns in real GDP act as a signal that we have been unable to prevent recessions, while long-run increases in real GDP per capita are an important indicator of economic progress. GDP is a significant and useful social indicator—but we should not view it as the last word.

THE UNDERGROUND ECONOMY: THE CASE OF THE MISSING GDP

The logical question of what GDP statisticians should attempt to measure is, however, not the only controversy surrounding the GDP accounts. Another involves what they are able to measure in practice. In recent years, a number of economists and government officials have expressed concern that many transactions escape the attention of national product accountants, resulting in a substantial underestimate of GDP. The reason is that plumbers, carpenters, and lawyers—to name but a few—have an incentive to perform services without reporting their income, namely to evade taxes. But, when such income is unreported, it not only disappears from Revenue Canada's tax records, it also disappears from the GDP accounts. Moonlighting, and the incomes of illegal aliens, are particularly unlikely to be reported.

Such "subterranean" or "irregular" activities are by no means confined to Canada and the United States: The French have their "travail au noir" (work in the dark); the Italians their "lavorno nero" (same thing); the British their "fiddle"; and the Germans their "Schattenwirtschaft" (shadow economy). The *underground economy* includes not only unreported illegal activities — which, as we have noted, national income accountants intentionally exclude from the GDP—but also such socially desirable services as the work of the moonlighting plumber, whose only illegal aspect is tax evasion. If we want an accurate measure of the goods and services produced in our economy, we should certainly include such socially desirable services.

The problem, of course, is to get information, since those in the underground economy are trying to keep their activities secret. Thus, it is difficult to measure the size of the underground economy directly. Rather, economists have looked for the traces left by irregular activities. What might these traces be?

The most obvious way to keep transactions secret is to use currency rather than cheques. Thus, if the underground economy is growing fast, one would then expect the amount of currency to increase faster than the amount of chequing deposit money. And, as University of Alberta economists Rolf Mirus and Roger Smith have shown, this is exactly what has happened in Canada: The ratio of currency to chequing deposits grew from about 0.33 before World War II to 0.56 in 1980.[8] From this information, Mirus and Smith concluded that a large underground economy has developed, amounting to 14% of GDP. (Using a somewhat different method of calculation suggested by Edgar Feige, they arrived at an even higher estimate, 20% of GDP.)[9]

If, in fact, the underground economy is not only large but also growing relative to reported GDP (as Mirus and Smith found), a number of important conclusions follow: (1) Official statistics understate the growth of the economy. (2) Official statistics overstate the true rate of inflation, because those in the rapidly growing underground sector generally charge lower prices to gain customers. (3) Unemployment statistics overstate the true amount of unemployment. People collecting Unemployment Insurance benefits—but also working "off the record" in the underground economy — are not likely to tell interviewers from Employment and Immigration that they are employed.

In other words, things may be better than they seem from the official statistics. However, we should not take too much comfort from this conclusion. Because estimates of the underground economy are based on circumstantial evidence, they may contain large errors. Without a doubt, many transactions go unreported. But we do not know just how large the irregular economy really is, nor do we know how much of it represents activities which are illegal and which we do not want to count anyway.

■ ■ ■ ■ ■

[8] Rolf Mirus and Roger S. Smith, "Canada's Irregular Economy," *Canadian Public Policy*, Summer 1981, pp. 444–53.

[9] Literature on the underground economy in the United States includes work by Edgar L. Feige, "How Big Is the Irregular Economy?" *Challenge*, November 1979, pp. 5–13; Carl P. Simon and Ann D. Witte, *Beating the System: The Underground Economy* (Boston, 1982); and Vito Tanzi, "The Underground Economy in the United States," *International Monetary Fund Staff Papers*, June 1983, pp. 283–305.

KEY POINTS

1. The market provides a way of adding apples, oranges, automobiles, and the many other goods and services produced during the year. Items are included in domestic product at their market prices.

2. In measuring domestic product, everything should be measured once, and only once. Intermediate products (such as wheat or steel) used in the production of other goods (such as bread or automobiles) should not be counted separately, since they are already included when we count the final products (bread or automobiles).

3. Net investment equals gross investment minus depreciation. If net investment is positive, then more buildings, equipment, and inventories are being produced than are being used up. Thus, the capital stock is rising (Figure 6-1).

4. $GDP = C + I_g + G + X - M$
   $NDP = GDP - depreciation$
   Because depreciation is difficult to measure accurately, statisticians have more confidence in the measure of GDP than NDP and, therefore, GDP is used more commonly.

5. While *domestic* product measures the value of production of goods and services within a country's boundaries, *national* product measures the value of production attributable to all nationally owned factors of production. In practice, Statistics Canada estimates national product from domestic product by subtracting investment income earned in Canada by foreign residents and then adding income earned by Canadians on their investments in foreign countries. Thus, we have:
   $GNP = GDP - $ net investment income of non-residents;
   $NNP = NDP - $ net investment income of non-residents.

6. Receipts from the sale of products are distributed to those who contribute to the productive process by providing labour, capital, or land. In a simple economy, all the proceeds from the sale of goods would be distributed in the form of income payments to the factors of production. Net national product and national income would be the same. However, in a real world economy, national income is less, because some of the proceeds from the sale of goods goes to the government in the form of sales taxes. Thus:
   National income = NNP − sales taxes.

7. Review Figure 6-3 for the relationships among NDP, national income, personal income, and disposable personal income.

8. Market prices provide a good way for adding up the many different goods and services produced in a *single* year. But this would be a misleading way of comparing the domestic product in *different* years. The reason is that the value of the dollar shrinks as a result of inflation. A rise in current-dollar domestic product reflects both an increase in prices and an increase in real production.

9. In order to estimate the increase in real output, constant-dollar figures are used. These are found by measuring GDP at the prices existing in a base year.

10. By "deflating" current data with the appropriate price index, it is possible to get a real measure of other important economic variables, such as the real wage (equation 6-9).

11. Real GDP (or real NDP) per capita is not a good measure of economic welfare. However, attempts to calculate a more comprehensive measure of economic welfare have run into the insoluble problem of how to deal with leisure.

12. The "underground" economy is made up of two components:
    (a) Unreported income of plumbers, carpenters, lawyers, farmers, etc. The failure to report is the only illegal aspect. The services themselves are legal and socially useful; they would be included in GDP if government statisticians knew how large they were.
    (b) Income from illegal activities such as the drug trade. Since the government has decided that these activities represent social "bads," they would not be included in GDP even if statisticians knew how large they were.
    Circumstantial evidence suggests that (a) is growing in proportion to reported GDP. This means that the official GDP statistics understate growth of real GDP.

KEY CONCEPTS

final product
intermediate product
value added
consumption
investment
inventories
government expenditures for
   current goods and services
exports of goods and services
imports of goods and services
net exports

gross domestic product (GDP)
gross national product (GNP)
net domestic product (NDP)
net national product (NNP)
net investment income of
   non-residents
gross investment
net investment
depreciation
national income (NI)
personal income (PI)

disposable personal income (DI)
current-dollar GDP
constant-dollar GDP
price index
base year
deflating with a price index
real wage
measure of economic welfare
underground economy

PROBLEMS

6-1. Consider an economy in which the following quantities are measured (in billions of dollars):

Consumption expenditures	$1,000
Value of common shares purchased	400
Gross domestic investment	300
Net investment income of non-residents	85
Government transfer payments	100
Sales taxes	50
Government expenditures for current goods and services	200
Corporate income taxes	200
Personal income taxes	100
Exports minus imports	10
Depreciation	75
Purchases of second-hand cars	100

(a) Calculate GDP. (Be careful. Not all the items are included.)
(b) Calculate NDP.

6-2. The change in inventories can be negative. Can net investment also be negative? Explain.

6-3. Give an example of an import of a service.

6-4. Which of the following government expenditures are included in GDP?
(a) The purchase of an aircraft for the Air Force
(b) The purchase of a computer for the Department of Finance
(c) The payment of unemployment insurance benefits to those who have lost their jobs
(d) The salary paid to maintenance workers who mow the grass beside the highways.

6-5. Last year a family engaged in the following activities. What items are included in GDP? Explain in each case why the item is, or is not, included.

(a) They purchased a used car from their neighbour.
(b) They deposited $1,000 in a savings deposit at the bank.
(c) They purchased $2,000 worth of groceries.
(d) They flew to London, England for a vacation.

6-6. For 1987 (shown in Figure 6-3):
(a) Which was larger: government expenditures for current goods and services or gross investment?
(b) Approximately what percent of NDP was net investment?
(c) Approximately how large a percentage of national income were wages and salaries?
(d) Approximately what fraction of disposable income was saved?

6-7. Of the two measures of economic welfare of Nordhaus and Tobin, do you think one is better than the other? If so, which one, and why? If not, would it be a satisfactory solution to avoid this problem by excluding leisure when calculating a "measure of economic welfare"?

6-8. For each of the following, state whether you agree or disagree. If you agree, explain why. If you disagree, correct the statement.
(a) When a trucker buys gasoline, the intended use is for the production of trucking services for others, not for pleasure trips. Therefore, this gasoline is an intermediate product, while the trucking service is a final product.
(b) Bread purchased by a household is a final product, but bread purchased by a supermarket or a restaurant is an intermediate product.

(c) If new automobiles were treated like new owner-occupied housing in the domestic product accounts, private domestic investment would be higher, and our living standards would also be higher.

(d) Defence expenditures provide no direct satisfaction to the public. They only protect our freedom to enjoy other goods and services. Therefore, defence expenditures are considered an intermediate product and are not included separately in the calculation of GDP.

(e) A road between two manufacturing centres is an intermediate product, because it is used to transport goods in the process of production. But a road running to a summer resort is a final good, since it is used primarily for pleasure travel.

6-9. Equation 6-10 shows a simplified way of estimating the approximate change in the real wage. To see how close this approximation is, find the true change in the real wage (from equation 6-8), and compare it to the estimate found with equation 6-10 in each of the following cases:

(a) when the money wage increases by 10%, while the CPI increases by 2%

(b) when the money wage increases by 30%, while the CPI increases by 22%

(c) when the money wage increases by 200%, while the CPI increases by 100%.

Do your results from these examples suggest any circumstances under which it would be wise to avoid the use of equation 6-10?

6-10. As we argued in the text, in estimating *national* product, Statistics Canada does not try to correct for the earnings of non-resident labour. Suppose Statistics Canada has decided to improve its estimation procedures in estimating national product by correcting for the net labour earnings of foreign citizens in Canada and the labour earnings of Canadian nationals working abroad. If you were advising Statistics Canada on how this should be done, how would you suggest treating:

(a) the earnings of refugee claimants working in Canada while awaiting a hearing by the Immigration Appeals Board?

(b) the earnings of landed immigrants who intend to become Canadian citizens at a later date?

(c) the income of a U.S. businessman who works part of the year at the Vancouver branch office of a U.S.-owned corporation with a subsidiary in Canada?

(d) the earnings of Wayne Gretzky?

Appendix

■ ■ ■ ■ ■

Exports, Imports, and Real GDP

Nominal or current-dollar GDP is not a very useful measure. If we want to know whether the economy has performed well this year compared to last year, we should look at *real* GDP: Only if the real output of goods and services has been increasing can we say that the economy has done better than last year. Increases in nominal GDP which only reflect price increases don't make Canadians better off; but increases in the real output of goods and services do.

However, there is one component of real GDP where this argument may be misleading: net exports. Real net exports are calculated as follows. First, nominal exports are deflated by the index of export prices to get real

exports, while nominal imports are deflated by the index of import prices to get real imports. Real imports are then subtracted from real exports to get real net exports; the result is then added to the estimates of consumption, investment and government spending to find real GDP.

This procedure seems reasonable enough. But sometimes it gives results that have to be interpreted carefully. Suppose, for example, that the prices of Canada's exports on average rise faster than the prices of the goods we import. (This was what happened during the commodity boom in 1978–80, when the prices of important Canadian export goods such as wheat, metals and minerals, and natural gas, shot up rapidly.)

But consider what can happen when we calculate real GDP. Suppose we begin, in base year 1, with exports (*X*) of $50 billion, and imports (*M*) of $50 billion. Our international transactions are exactly in balance; exports are just large enough to pay for imports.

Now suppose that, by year 2, export prices double, while the quantity of exports remains constant. The *value* of exports now amounts to $100 billion. Suppose, at the same time, that import prices remain constant, while the quantity of imports doubles. Imports now are also $100 billion. Once again, we earn enough from exports to pay for our imports. In the current-dollar GDP accounts, net exports remain zero in year 2.

But now notice what happens when real quantities are calculated. Measured in base year prices (the prices in year 1), exports have remained constant; in constant dollars, they are still $50 billion. But in constant dollars, imports are now $100 billion. Thus our calculation shows a "real" import deficit of $50 billion. But, to say that we have a "real" import deficit is, at the very least, misleading. Remember: Our exports are still large enough to pay for our imports.

Thus, when we want to find out how well we are doing on the international side, we should not look just at constant dollar figures: *We should look also at what has happened to the prices of our exports and imports.* In the preceding example, our real exports did not increase. But because the prices of our exports rose faster than the prices of the goods we imported, our export earnings were still sufficient to buy us a larger amount of real imports.

When the prices of a country's export goods rise faster than the prices of its imports, this is referred to as an improvement in the country's **terms of trade**. Canada's terms of trade improved substantially during the 1970s. Many other countries were less fortunate. In the United States, for example, the import price index rose substantially faster than the export price index. The main reason for this worsening of the U.S. terms of trade was the large increase in the world price of oil, which accounts for a large share of U.S. imports. Japan and most European countries also experienced worsening terms of trade because of rising oil prices.

Canada did not have this problem: While we import large amounts of oil into Eastern Canada, our total energy exports (including natural gas and electricity) are even larger, and prices of all our energy exports rose along with the price of oil. Therefore, while rising world prices for oil and other energy resources *did* raise our import price index, they increased our export price index even more.

In the early 1980s, the recession in the world economy, and the gradual weakening of the OPEC export cartel, combined to produce a rapid fall in the world oil price and falling prices for energy resources in general. As a result, Canada suffered a loss: Our terms of trade worsened once again. The worsening terms of trade, in turn, was one of the factors that contributed to the substantial fall in the international value of the Canadian dollar in the mid-1980s.

Chapter 7

■ ■

Fluctuations in Economic Activity: Unemployment and Inflation

A recession is when your neighbor is out of work.
A depression is when you're out of work.

Harry S. Truman

Economic conditions rarely stand still. Moderate expansions often accelerate into inflationary booms, and inflationary booms give way to recessions.

The most obvious way to measure the ups and downs of the Canadian economy is with real GDP figures, which show how aggregate output has expanded and contracted.[1] Unfortunately, however, detailed GDP data are available for only a fraction of Canadian history; it is only since 1926 that the government has collected national accounting data on a regular basis.

Of all the fluctuations in our history, the largest took place between 1929 and 1944. First came the collapse into the Great Depression, with real GDP falling by more than 30% between 1929 and 1933. This was followed by a long and painful recovery. It was not until the government began spending huge amounts of money for arms, ammunition and military equipment during World War II that the economy recovered fully. After the war, there was a temporary drop in output as factories were converted from weapons to peacetime products. Since that time, there has been a series of recessions: in 1947, 1953/54, 1957, 1960/61, 1970, 1974/75, 1980, and 1982.

Fluctuations in economic activity are irregular; no two recessions are exactly alike. Nor are any two expan-

sions. Some last for years, the 1961–69 expansion, and the expansion that has been going on since 1983, being notable examples. Others are short-lived, such as the expansion of 1980/81, which was interrupted by the 1982 recession after only about a year. The economy is not a pendulum swinging regularly at specific intervals. If it were, the analysis of business fluctuations would be simple: The movement of a pendulum is easily predicted.

THE FOUR PHASES OF THE BUSINESS CYCLE

Because business fluctuations are so irregular, it is perhaps surprising that they are called "cycles." However, they are all similar in the sense that they go through the same four phases (Figure 7-1).

The key to identifying a business cycle is to identify a *recession* — the period when economic activity is declining. This immediately raises a problem of definition. How far down does the economy have to go before we should say that it is in a recession? The answer may have considerable political significance: When the economy is in a recession, people tend to be especially critical of the government in power.

In Canada, government politicians can (and frequently do) try to reduce the extent of the political fall-out from recessions by blaming them on international economic conditions. (As we shall see later, there is a good deal of evidence that they are often justified in doing this.) In the United States, where international trade and capital flows play a less important role than in Canada, recessions are

■ ■ ■ ■ ■

[1] As we discussed in the last chapter, in recent years Statistics Canada has focused on GDP as a measure of aggregate economic activity. In the past the available published data on the Canadian economy usually concentrated on the GNP measure. Since GDP and GNP typically move closely together, we will disregard the distinction in our discussion of the historical experience.

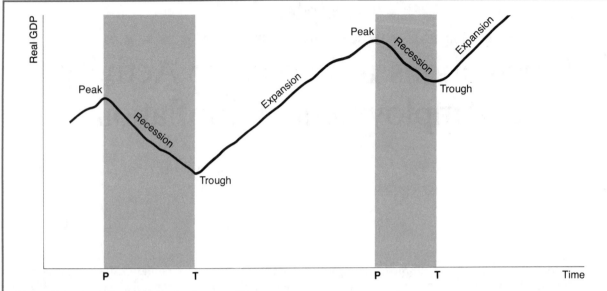

Figure 7-1 Four phases of the business cycle.
Periods of expansion and recession alternate, with peaks and troughs in between. Not every expansion reaches a high degree of prosperity with a low unemployment rate; an expansion sometimes ends prematurely and a new recession begins.

more likely to be considered as having been caused by domestic factors such as government policy. Because of this, the question of whether the economy is in a recession is a more sensitive one in the United States, and much ingenuity has been devoted to come up with a generally acceptable way of answering it.

A private research organization—the National Bureau of Economic Research (NBER)—is the guardian of the keys; it decides what is, and what is not, called a recession. The NBER's major test is historical: Is a downswing as long and severe as declines of the past that have been labelled "recessions"? Prior to 1980, a simple definition was commonly used: A recession occurs when seasonally adjusted real output declines for two or more consecutive quarters. (For an explanation of how GDP and other data are "seasonally adjusted," see Box 7-1.) However, the NBER never actually accepted this definition and, in 1980, it declared a recession which did not meet this test. (Real output fell in only one quarter.)

In Canada, there is no one institution responsible for formally deciding whether or not we are in a recession, nor do we have a universally accepted definition of a recession. Canadian economic commentators sometimes use the term "recession" for periods when the *growth rate* of real GDP slows down markedly, even if there is

no prolonged *decline* in real GDP. The definition offered in Chapter 1 probably comes close to the way most Canadian economists would describe a recession: A general slowdown in economic activity, usually involving a decline in total output, income, and employment, lasting six months or more, and marked by contractions in many sectors of the economy.[2]

A recession ends with the *trough*; that is, the *turning point* where economic activity is at its lowest. This is followed by the *expansion* phase. Output increases, and profits, employment, wages, prices, and interest rates generally rise. Historically, the *peak* or upper turning point was often associated with a financial panic, such as the panic of 1907 or "Black Tuesday" — October 29, 1929, when North American stock markets crashed. Recent peaks have been much less spectacular, with one notable exception. The economic peak in 1973/74 coincided with war in the Middle East, an oil embargo, and skyrocketing oil prices.

■ ■ ■ ■ ■

[2] The definition is a modified version of one suggested in Geoffrey H. Moore, *Business Cycles, Inflation, and Forecasting* (Cambridge, Mass.: Ballinger, 2nd ed., 1983), Chapter 1.

Box 7-1

Seasonal Adjustment of Economic Data

Not all ups and downs in business activity represent the misbehaviour of the economy. Crops grow by the calendar; harvests are gleaned in the summer and autumn months. The month-to-month changes in food production reflect a law of nature with which we learn to live. Retail sales boom during the holiday season in December, only to fall in January.

Such regular month-to-month swings are not our concern. The decline in retail sales in January is the aftermath of the December buying boom; it is not a symptom of an oncoming recession. In order to identify a recession, we must remove the seasonal effects from business activity. That is, we must seasonally adjust our data on production, sales, etc. The following technique is used.

From past information, suppose the statistician discovers that December sales of toys typically run at three times the average monthly rate, only to drop to one-half the average monthly rate in January. The raw data for toy sales can then be seasonally adjusted by dividing December's sales by 3, and multiplying

Courtesy of Cadillac Fairview

January's sales by 2. (In fact, more complicated techniques are used, but this is the general idea.) Similarly, quarterly data for GDP or monthly indexes of industrial production can be adjusted to remove seasonal fluctuations, and help to identify fundamental movements in the economy.

Not only is it difficult to decide when a downturn becomes strong enough to be classified as a recession, it is also difficult to decide when a serious recession should be labelled a *depression*. There is no commonly accepted definition of a depression — except, perhaps, Harry Truman's quip with which we introduced this chapter. Because the Depression of the 1930s was so deep and long-lasting, the reduction in output and employment would have to be exceptionally severe and persistent before we should talk of a depression. In Canada, seasonally adjusted unemployment rates were so high (in the range of 11%–13% of the labour force) for several years in the early 1980s that some commentators wanted to classify this period as a depression. However, even though unemployment rates remained in this very high range, total output grew at healthy rates in 1983/84 (real GDP surpassed its previous peak level at the end of 1983). Therefore, most economists stop short of describing this period as a depression and, instead, refer to the 1982 slump as an exceptionally severe recession.

However, no matter how a depression is defined, there is no doubt that this term should be used to describe the 1930s.

THE GREAT DEPRESSION OF THE 1930s

The Great Depression of more than fifty years ago still haunts us today. Between the peak of 1929 and the depth of the depression in 1933, real GDP declined by more than 1/3. The unemployment rate shot up to almost 20% of the labour force. Prices fell, with the GDP deflator declining about 19%. The combination of falling prices and falling real output meant that current dollar GDP decreased almost 50%. In the United States, the story was much the same.

Nor did the recovery come quickly and strongly. Business revived slowly, with the unemployment rate gradually declining to 9.1% by 1937. In 1938, there was another slowdown with increased unemployment — a recession within the depression. It was not until 1941, after the outbreak of World War II in Europe, that the unemployment rate finally fell below 9%. By 1941, the Canadian economy was on a war footing, rushing to re-arm, with industry working around the clock to produce military equipment and supplies. Between 1938 and 1942, defence spending shot up from less than 1% to more than 30% of GDP. The Great Depression was ended only by an even greater catastrophe—World War II.

The decade of depression was a disaster for many segments of society. Many of those thrown out of work were unable to find other jobs. Nor were the unemployed alone in their misery. Business bankruptcies came thick and fast. Between 1929 and 1932, total corporation profits fell by more than 90%. In the face of slack demand, prices of farm commodities dropped more than 50% between 1929 and 1932. In parts of the country, the plight of farmers was compounded by a natural disaster — a severe and prolonged drought which turned much of the Prairie provinces into a dust bowl. Farmers and the unemployed struggled to get by on the small relief payments of local governments. Offering her engagement ring as collateral, an Alberta housewife wrote to Prime Minister R.B. Bennett asking for a loan:

> We are just one of many on relief and trying to keep our place without being starved out. Have a good 1/2 section not bad buildings and trying to get a start without any money and five children all small. Have been trying to send 3 to school and live on $10.00 a month relief for everything medicine meat flour butter scribblers. Haven't had any milk for 3 months . . .
>
> My husband doesn't know I am writing this letter but I just dont know what to do for money the children come to me about everything its the women & children who suffer in these terrible times . . . [3]

Unemployed single men (who were not eligible for relief payments) roamed the country in search of a job:

> The municipalities steer them off because if they are arrested as vagrants they become a charge on the municipality and it costs a dollar a day to keep them. So their word is 'Keep them moving.' The C.P.R. police advise the men that it is better travelling C.N.R. and the C.N.R. police return the compliment. . . . There is no work, no hope, no place for them.[4]

- - - - -
[3] Quoted in Michiel Horn, ed., *The Dirty Thirties: Canadians in the Great Depression* (Toronto: Copp Clark Publishers, 1972), p. 237.
[4] From a 1932 description by The Rev. Andrew Roddan, quoted in L. Richter, ed., *Canada's Unemployment Problem* (Toronto: Macmillan, 1939), p. 180.

Figure 7-2   Recent business fluctuations. ➤

Areas shaded in gray denote recessionary periods in the Canadian economy, while the areas marked with black bars denote recessions in the United States.

Source: Compiled from data in Statistics Canada, *CANSIM Databank* and *Historical Labour Force Statistics*. Reproduced by permission of the Minister of Supply and Services Canada.

The depression was world-wide; large-scale unemployment was an international phenomenon. There were immeasurable, but perhaps even greater, political consequences. The depression was one of the factors that brought Hitler to power, with his promises of full employment and military conquest. The world in which we live has been shaped by the events of the 1930s.

The Great Depression laid the foundation for modern macroeconomics. ''Never again'' was the determination of the economic scholar, the politician, and the general public. In fact, we have been successful in preventing a repeat of the 1930s. Economic problems in recent decades have been mild compared to those of the thirties.

OUTPUT, UNEMPLOYMENT, AND INFLATION IN RECENT BUSINESS CYCLES

However, in spite of successes, problems have remained. The economy has continued to fluctuate. Furthermore, and perhaps most disconcerting of all, the performance of the economy does not seem to have improved with time. Recessions have not been getting more and more mild: On the contrary, the 1982 recession was the most severe since the Great Depression.

Figure 7-2 shows how output, unemployment, profits, and inflation have changed since 1959. We have identified periods of negative or slow growth as recessions and marked them with shaded gray bars in the diagram.[5] Although recent recessions have caused much less economic dislocation than the collapse of 1929–33, the recent behaviour of the economy is broadly consistent with the 1930s in some important respects. Specifically:

1. During recessions, when production is falling or growing very slowly, the unemployment rate rises.

- - - - -
[5] We have generally defined recessions as periods of slow growth with each period including at least two quarters of negative growth. The 1980 mini-recession does not quite meet this criterion. However, the fall in real GDP in early 1980 was substantial enough so that GDP remained below its previous peak value for two successive quarters; therefore, we include 1980 as a recession anyway.

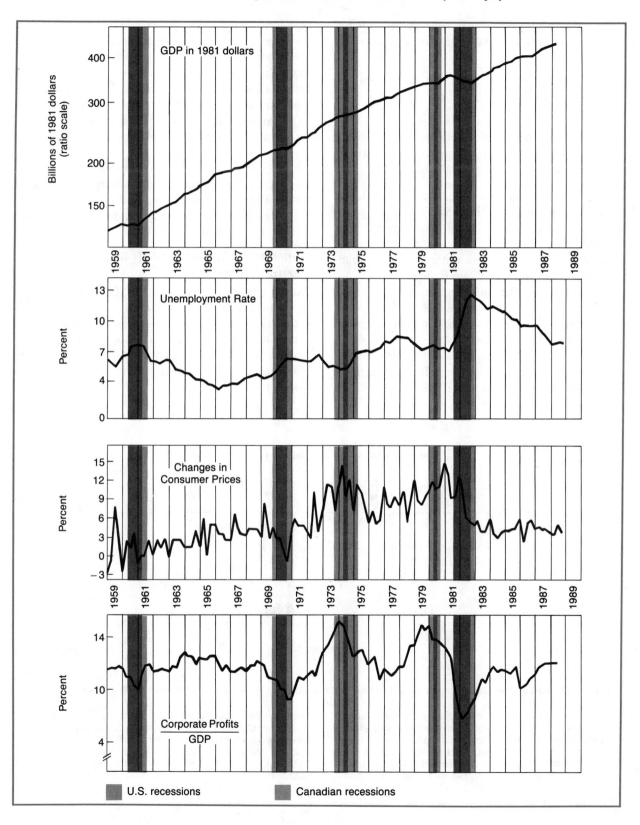

Likewise, when production recovers during an expansion, more workers are needed and the unemployment rate falls.

2. During recessions, profits fall by a much larger percentage than output. They rise rapidly during expansions.

3. During recessions when output is declining, inflation generally declines too. When the economy is expanding, the rate of inflation generally accelerates.

Wages and profits behave quite differently during recessions. While profits fall sharply, money wages remain much more stable. Indeed, recessions have had no readily apparent effect on average wage rates in recent decades. Recessions hit workers primarily in the form of unemployment, not lower wages.

Observe, also, that inflation responds slowly to changing business conditions. During the first half of the long expansion of the 1960s, for example, prices were quite stable. It was only in the latter part of the 1960s that inflation began to accelerate significantly. Similarly, the strong upswings in inflation occurred in the last half of the expansions of 1970–74 and 1975–79.

Furthermore, the upward momentum of inflation may continue into the early part of a recession, as it did in 1974 and 1982. Generally, it is toward the end of recessions that economic slack has its strongest effect in bringing down the rate of inflation. Often, the inflation rate remains low for some time after the economy begins to recover—as in 1971 and 1976, and for a long period during the expansion that followed the deep 1982 recession.

The slowness of prices to respond introduces an important complication into the government's task of stabilizing the economy, as we shall see when we get to the more advanced macroeconomic topics of Parts 4 and 5 (Chapters 15 to 20).

Consumption, Investment, and Net Exports during Recessions

During recessions, some parts of GDP decline much more than others. This is illustrated in Figure 7-3, which shows the changes in various segments of aggregate expenditures between the last quarter of 1979 (which marked the end of the expansion of the 1970s) and the last quarter of 1982 (when the recession reached its trough).

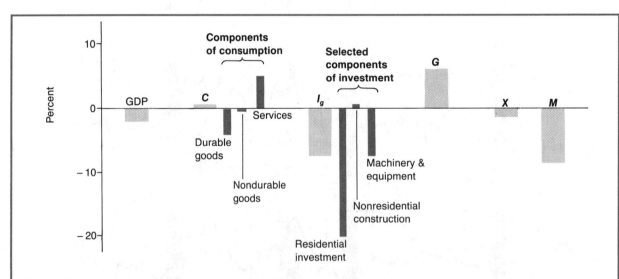

Figure 7-3   Percentage change in real GDP and selected components between last quarter of 1979 and last quarter of 1982.

The economy reached a cyclical peak in the last quarter of 1979. There were then two quick recessions, with the trough of the second occurring in the last quarter of 1982. This figure shows how some components of GDP declined much more than others. In fact, both consumption and government purchases of goods and services increased in real terms, and real exports fell by just a small amount. The recession was concentrated in the investment sector, particularly inventory investment. Real imports fell by a substantial amount. However, because imports are a subtraction from GDP, this fall helped to moderate the severity of the recession.

Source: *Bank of Canada Review* (January 1986).

Consumption

Over this period, real GDP declined by 2.8%. But real consumption expenditures actually rose. Expenditures for services increased by 3% and spending on semi-durables and non-durables also increased. However, consumers cut back their real spending for durable goods by almost 8%.

There is a reason for this different behaviour of durables, on the one hand, and other consumption goods, on the other. Because durables last, people have the option of postponing purchases during hard times, when they are having trouble paying their bills. For example, as incomes decline, people may decide to fix up their old cars or old refrigerators rather than splurging on new ones. They can continue to enjoy the use of durables, even if they are not currently buying them. This obviously does not apply to services such as dental care. Services are consumed as they are produced. Nor does it apply to non-durable goods. Purchases of food represent one of the last things that people will cut back during recessions.

Investment

Much larger fluctuations occur in the investment sector. By the last quarter of 1982, total real investment had fallen by 24% from its level three years earlier. Residential investment decreased by 20%. Other private fixed investment (including machinery and equipment) declined by a less spectacular 4.6%. Inventory accumulation, which had been positive in all but two quarters during 1976–79, was negative for five successive quarters during 1981–82; measured in current dollars, it reached −$12.4 billion (3.4% of GDP) in 1982:4. (1982:4 is an abbreviated way of writing "the fourth quarter of 1982.")

Instability of investment has been a continuing feature of business cycles; fluctuations in investment have accounted for a large fraction of overall fluctuations in the economy. Furthermore, the decline in inventories in 1982 was typical for a period of recession. Inventory investment has become negative in every recession during the last thirty years. In fact, swings in inventory investment have been as large as 70% of the declines in real GDP during the recessions of the past three decades. It is not surprising, therefore, that the business fluctuations in the postwar period have frequently been referred to as *inventory recessions*.[6]

Net Exports

In the 1980–82 period, real exports declined by about 4.4%. Because exports are such a large share of GDP, this decline made a substantial contribution to the overall fall in real GDP. This is a typical pattern in Canadian recessions: Decreases in real exports have contributed to the decline in GDP in five of the six recessions during the last three decades. On average, the fall in exports has accounted for as much as 40% of the overall reductions in GDP.

Since Canadian exports are sold in foreign markets, principally the United States, one would expect that our exports would be sensitive to international economic conditions, and particularly to economic conditions in the United States. Thus, the fact that reductions in our exports usually contribute to the decline in GDP during Canadian recessions suggests that our recessions tend to happen at the same time as those in the United States. Looking back at Figure 7-2 confirms that this is, indeed, what usually happens. The gray shaded areas denote periods of recession in Canada, as explained on p. 119, while areas marked with coloured bars mark off U.S. recessions. As the figure shows, every time there has been a recession in the United States during the past 25 years, there also has been a recession in Canada. Moreover, *every* American recession has resulted in a recessionary period of slow growth in Canada as well.

This should not come as a surprise. Since about 70% of our foreign trade (both on the export and import side) is with the United States, and because most of our international capital flows represent movements between Canada and the United States, it is not strange that our economy is especially sensitive to business fluctuations in that country. As the saying goes: "When the United States sneezes, Canada catches a cold." As the American and Canadian economies become even more interdependent with the gradual implementation of the Canada/United States free trade agreement that came into effect on January 1, 1989, this sensitivity will, if anything, become even more pronounced.

The tendency for business cycles to take place at the same time in different countries is apparent not only when one compares Canada and the United States, but also when one compares the cycles in the North American and European economies. The links between the world's economies (through trade and capital flows)

* * * * *

[6] Sometimes inventory investment does not become negative until after the recession is over. But many of the cutbacks in orders, which ultimately cause the inventory reduction, occur earlier during the recession period.

apparently are strong enough to produce a powerful mechanism for *international transmission of economic fluctuations*. Because this transmission mechanism exists, the policy makers responsible for economic stabilization in the smaller countries of the world are faced with an extra difficulty. Not only will they be responsible for dealing with economic fluctuations that have their origin in domestic disturbances (such as a crop failure, or a strike in a large domestic industry), they will also be called upon to deal with flucuations that originate with disturbances in the large foreign economies. In later chapters, we will consider this issue in more detail.

Figure 7-3 shows that there was a substantial decrease in real imports during the 1980–82 period. This is also typical of recessions: As consumption and investment fall, there is a reduction in the demand for imported consumer goods or imported goods used for investment. Since imports are a *subtraction* from GDP, the fact that imports tend to fall in recessions and rise during expansions has a *stabilizing* effect on the Canadian economy. The fluctuations in imports moderate the effects of fluctuations in consumption and investment demand on the demand for Canadian-produced goods and services. We will discuss this point further in Chapter 10.

UNEMPLOYMENT

The two principal features of a recession are a stagnation or actual decline in output and a rise in the unemployment rate. Changes in output are measured by the domestic product accounts. Changes in unemployment are measured by the unemployment rate.

Calculating the Unemployment Rate

The unemployment rate is estimated each month by Statistics Canada using an obvious, direct approach: It asks people. Because it would be prohibitively expensive and time-consuming to ask everybody, a sample of about 53 000 households is surveyed.[7] Questions are asked about each member of the household who is at least 15 years old, except members of the armed forces and those who are unavailable for work (for example, those who are in prison). Each individual is classified in one of three categories: (1) employed, (2) unemployed, or (3) not in the labour force.

The first category includes all those who have worked in the week of the survey, including part-time employees who have worked as little as one hour. The second category includes people without work who (a) are on temporary layoff but expect to be recalled, (b) are waiting to report to a new job within four weeks, or (c) say they have actively looked for work during the previous four weeks, and are currently available for work. The remainder are "out of the labour force." This group includes retirees, full-time students without paying jobs, and those who stay out of the labour force in order to look after young children. The unemployment rate is calculated as the number of unemployed, as a percentage of the labour force (Table 7-1, line 3).

The method used in calculating the unemployment rate has caused controversy. (1) Some critics think the official unemployment rate overstates the true figure, pointing out that there is no check on those who say they are looking for work; they are simply asked. (2) On the other hand, others observe that, during hard times, workers may become discouraged, and quit looking for work after they have been repeatedly rebuffed. But this means that they will no longer be counted as part of the labour force. Thus, during recessions, the rise in the unemployment rate may not measure the full deterioration in the employment situation. This interpretation is supported by the behaviour of the labour force. During recessions, it generally grows very slowly and sometimes even declines because of the departure of discouraged workers. On the other hand, it grows rapidly during recoveries. When jobs are easier to get, people are more likely to enter the labour force, and less likely to drop out.

Discouraged workers are those who want work but are no longer actively looking for it because they think no jobs are available. When they stop looking for work, they are no longer counted either as part of the labour force or as unemployed.

Finally, during recessions, there is an increase in the number of people who can't get full-time jobs and who are, therefore, involuntarily limited to part-time work. The usual unemployment statistics do not take into account such **underemployment**. However, information is collected on the number of part-time workers who wanted full-time work but were unable to find it (Table 7-1, line 4). Even though underemployment may have less serious consequences than outright unemployment, it nevertheless is a problem for a large fraction of the labour force. Not surprisingly, underemployment becomes larger during recessions when more workers are limited to part-time work.

■ ■ ■ ■ ■
[7] The survey does not include residents of the Yukon and Northwest Territories or people living on Indian reserves.

Table 7-1   The Labour Force and Unemployment, June 1988

		(thousands)
1. Total population		25,950
Less: Those under 15		5,877
Not in Labour Force		6,406
2. *Equals:* Labour Force		13,666
(a) Employed	12,693	
(b) Unemployed	973	

3. Unemployment rate as percent of labour force:

$$\frac{973}{13,666} = 7.1\%$$

4. Underemployment (part-time workers who would like full-time work)   470

As percent of labour force:

$$\frac{470}{13,666} = 3.4\%$$

Addendum: Labour force participation rates
(persons over 14 years of age; percent)

	Male	Female
1953	82.9	23.4
1961	81.1	29.3
1971	77.3	39.4
1981	78.4	51.7
1984	76.6	53.5
1988	78.5	58.2

Source: Statistics Canada, *The Labour Force, 1984, 1988*, and *Bank of Canada Review.*

Underemployment

We have just considered one group of the under-employed: those who can find only part-time work when they want full-time jobs. But underemployment also takes a second form, which results from the way in which businesses respond to falling sales.

During recessions, businesses do not change the number of employees quickly. As the economy begins to weaken, businesses are more likely to cancel overtime than to lay off workers. Thus, employment falls less rapidly than output. And, even after overtime has been substantially eliminated, employers are reluctant to lay off workers. One reason is that a person who has been laid off may take a job somewhere else. When sales revive, the business will then have to go to the bother and expense of hiring and training a replacement. Thus, managers often conclude that it is better to keep workers on the job, even if they are not kept busy. Such workers are underemployed in the sense that they produce significantly less than they could. Thus, as the economy declines into recession, the ***productivity of labour*** generally declines.

Workers are *underemployed* if (1) they can find only part-time work when they want full-time

work or (2) if they are being paid full time, but are not kept busy because of low demand for the firm's products.

The *productivity of labour* is the average amount produced in an hour of work. It is measured as total output divided by the number of hours of labour input.

When the economy finally does recover, labour productivity tends to increase very rapidly. Because many businesses have developed slack during the recession, they have underemployed labour and machinery. Thus, during the early stages of a recovery, businesses can increase their output substantially before they need to add many more workers.

As a result, output fluctuates more than unemployment during the business cycle. A study by University of Toronto economists Peter Dungan and Thomas Wilson[8] suggests that on average, every cyclical change

■ ■ ■ ■ ■

[8] D. Peter Dungan and Thomas A. Wilson, *Potential GNP: Performance and Prospects*, Report No. 10, Institute for Policy Analysis, University of Toronto, 1982.

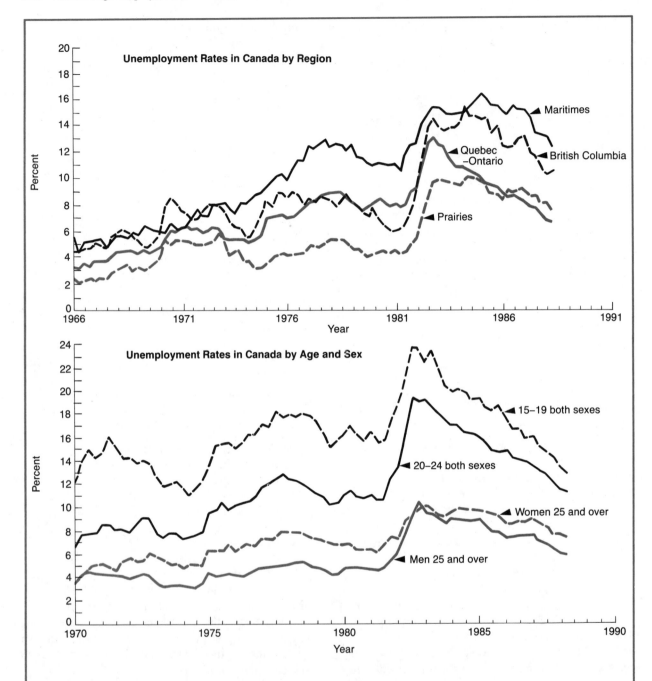

Figure 7-4   Selected unemployment rates.

Unemployment rates vary greatly among different groups in the economy. Unemployment rates in British Columbia and the Maritime provinces are usually higher than rates in other parts of Canada. Historically, women have had higher unemployment rates than men, but the rate for men rose above the women's rate during the recession of 1982. Teenagers have the highest unemployment rate of all. Even during the relatively prosperous years of 1973/74, the teenage unemployment rate was still above 10%. For the recession of 1982, it was more than 20%.

Source: Statistics Canada, *CANSIM Databank*. Reproduced by permission of the Minister of Supply and Services.

in output of 2% leads to a change in the unemployment rate of about 1% in the opposite direction. This tendency for output to fluctuate much more strongly than unemployment was originally found in studies of the U.S. economy in the 1950s and 1960s, and is known as *Okun's Law* after the late American economist Arthur Okun.

Who Are the Unemployed?

Unemployment does not fall equally on all members of society. The unemployment rate for teenagers is much higher than for adults (Figure 7-4). Unemployment rates have consistently been higher in British Columbia and the Maritimes than in the rest of Canada. The unemployment situation is particularly bleak for young people in the Maritimes. For example, teenage unemployment in Newfoundland reached a staggering 40% in the fall of 1982, and it remained in the 30%–40% range well into the mid-1980s, even though the economy was expanding. Historically, the unemployment rate for women has generally been above that for men. However, there is a tendency for the difference to become smaller during recessions, when male-dominated sectors such as construction, heavy manufacturing, and resource industries are hit hard with layoffs. The lower panel in Figure 7-4 confirms this tendency: In the recession of 1982, the rate for men over 25 rose much more than the rate for women in this age category, and the difference between the male and female rate remained small during the recovery in 1983/84. In the expansion since 1984, the gap has again widened: Unemployment for men over age 25 has fallen substantially faster than that for women.

Figure 7-5 illustrates two other important features about the unemployed — how they came to be unemployed, and how long they are unemployed. Not surprisingly, the duration of unemployment increases sharply during recessions, as unemployed workers experience more and more difficulty in finding jobs. At the end of the prosperous year 1979, those who had been out of work for more than 13 weeks made up about 35% of the total number of unemployed. As unemployment peaked in late 1982 and early 1983, the figure had risen to almost 50% This pattern has important implications. Short-term unemployment can be painful, but is scarcely catastrophic. It is long-term unemployment that is so demoralizing. During recessions, this type of unemployment becomes a larger share of the rising overall unemployment rate. Thus, during recessions, the unemployment situation becomes even worse than it appears in the overall unemployment numbers. For example, while the overall number of the unemployed about doubled (from less than 800 thousand toward the end of 1979 to over 1.5 million in early 1983), the number of long-term unemployed (over 13 weeks) nearly tripled, reaching more than 900 thousand in the first quarter of 1983.

During recessions, people are much more likely to lose their jobs, either through layoff or discharge (Figure 7-5, lower panel). However, even during recessions, it is unusual if more than 60% of the unemployed have actually lost their previous jobs. The other 40% are new entrants (young people who are looking, but have not yet found work after leaving school), re-entrants (many of whom are re-entering the labour force after caring for young families), and people who have quit their last jobs to look for something better. Not surprisingly, people are more reluctant to quit during hard times, when other jobs are scarce. But even as unemployment hit its peak of about 1.5 million in early 1983, about 200 thousand of the unemployed were people who had quit their previous jobs (and over 300 thousand were re-entrants into the labour force).

This illustrates something important about the Canadian labour force. It is quite mobile. Many people are ready to quit their jobs to look for something better. This mobility of the labour force is illustrated in Figure 7-6. The arrows show the many ways people move into and out of employment, and into and out of the labour force. Because of this mobility, it is difficult to define precisely what is meant by "full employment." Clearly, we are not striving for an economy in which the unemployment rate is zero. To accomplish such a goal, we would have to forbid people from leaving one job until they already had another lined up.

Types of Unemployment

Before attempting to define the elusive concept of "full employment," let us consider the various types of unemployment. The first is the one we've talked about so far: cyclical unemployment. During recessions, workers are laid off. This is the most important kind of unemployment, and the one on which macroeconomic analysis is focused. But there are also other kinds.

Frictional Unemployment

There will always be some people between jobs, or looking for their first job. Others may be temporarily out of

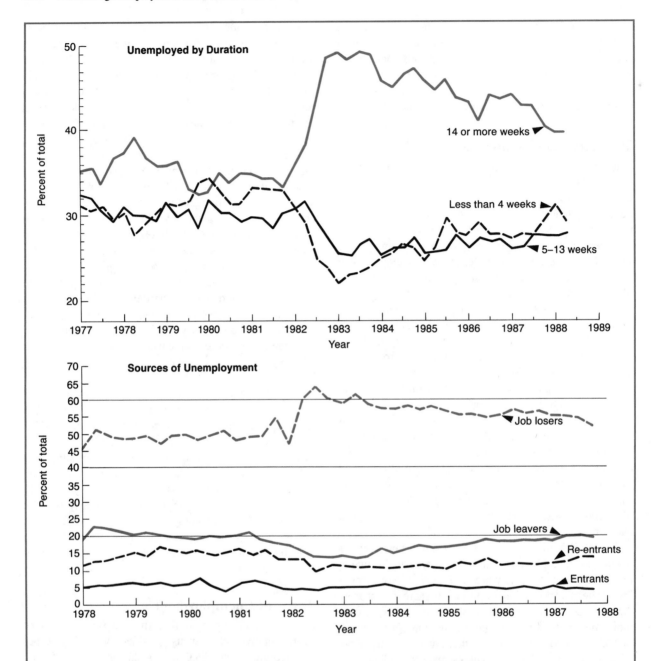

Figure 7-5 Duration of unemployment and its sources.

The upper panel shows how the duration of unemployment increased during the 1982 recession and into the early recovery, when people were still having difficulty finding jobs. The lower panel shows the sources of unemployment. During the relatively prosperous period 1978–81, the share of the unemployed who had lost their jobs through layoff or firing was usually less than half; the rest were people who had quit their jobs and labour-force entrants who had not yet found work. However, during the recession of 1982 more than half the unemployed had lost their jobs—well over 60% in late 1982 and early 1983.

Source: Statistics Canada, *Historical Labour Force Statistics*, 1984, and Statistics Canada, *CANSIM Databank*. Data have been seasonally adjusted by the authors. Reproduced by permission of the Minister of Supply and Services Canada.

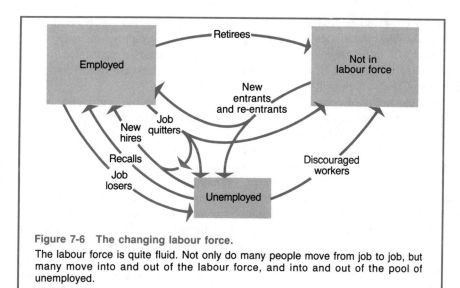

Figure 7-6   The changing labour force.
The labour force is quite fluid. Not only do many people move from job to job, but many move into and out of the labour force, and into and out of the pool of unemployed.

work because of the weather — for example, those employed in construction work or in the fishing industry.

Frictional unemployment is temporary unemployment associated with adjustments in a changing, dynamic economy. It arises for a number of reasons. For example, some new entrants into the labour force take time to find jobs, some workers with jobs quit to look for something better, and some are unemployed by temporary disturbances (for example, bad weather, or a temporary shutdown of an automobile factory to retool for a new model).

Such frictional unemployment is practically inevitable. It is difficult to see how it could be eliminated without a detailed government policy directing people to the first available jobs. And at least some frictional unemployment is desirable. For example, people are often willing to spend some time looking for a job. Such time can be well spent, since the first available job may be quite inappropriate. Having people search for high-paying, high-productivity jobs is not only good for them, it also contributes to the overall efficiency of the economy. Similarly, if we are to have people occupied in building houses, this will inevitably result in some unemployment: Some construction jobs can't be done in bad weather.

In our dynamic, changing economy, some industries gradually decline; others rise. In many cases, when one

firm goes bankrupt, others rise to take its place, and the labour force can move to the new jobs quite quickly and easily. Such transitional unemployment is also classified as frictional; people are temporarily between jobs as they hunt for new ones.

Structural Unemployment

In other cases, the changing pattern of jobs may leave workers stranded. In the Maritimes, many jobs were lost as resource-based industries such as forestry and fishing declined. Many of the unemployed (or underemployed) forestry workers and fishermen have been unable to find local jobs; to find work, they would have had to move hundreds of miles and learn new skills. Similarly, a loss of part of the market to Japanese cars, combined with automation on the assembly line, has permanently reduced the number of jobs in the North American automobile industry. These are illustrations of *structural unemployment*.

Structural unemployment results when the location and/or skills of the labour force do not match the available jobs. It can occur because of declining demand for a product, because of automation or other changes in technology, because industry is moving to a different location, or because new entrants into the labour force do not have the training for the available jobs.

It should be obvious that no sharp distinction can be drawn between frictional and structural unemployment.

If an auto parts factory closes down, and a bicycle factory opens up a mile away, displaced auto workers may quickly and easily find jobs in the bicycle factory. The temporary unemployment is frictional. If the new jobs are 250 kilometres away, the workers will have to move to take them. During the extended period before they actually do move, they may be classified among the structurally unemployed. But what if the new job is 50 kilometres away, near the limit of the commuting range? This case is not so clear. The difference between frictional and structural unemployment is one of degree. Structural unemployment lasts longer because, to get a new job, a greater change in location or a more extensive acquisition of new skills is required.

The Effect of the Canada/United States Free Trade Agreement on Canadian Unemployment

During the 1988 election campaign, one of the most hotly debated issues was the impact that the Canada/United States free trade agreement would have on the labour market in Canada. Opponents claimed that hundreds of thousands of jobs would be lost, as increased competition from U.S. producers would force many firms to close down their plants in Canada. On the other hand, those who favoured the agreement suggested that large numbers of new jobs would open up in Canadian firms that would be able to take advantage of the improved access to the large American market. Who was right?

The answer, most likely, is that both sides were right to some extent. There is little doubt that jobs will be lost in firms that were able to survive in the past only because tariffs or other trade barriers made it difficult for low-cost U.S. producers to penetrate the Canadian market. At the same time, under the terms of the agreement, the United States will also have to reduce tariffs and non-tariff barriers that have hampered the efforts of Canadian companies to compete in the American market. As this happens, new jobs will open up in those firms. Thus, many jobs will be lost; but a large number of new jobs will also be created, as a result of the agreement.

The net effect on the unemployment rate is difficult to predict. However, it is entirely possible that for particular regions and particular groups of workers (such as older employees), the net effect will be a higher probability of unemployment: The new jobs that open up may not be in areas that have experienced plant closings, or the employees that have lost their jobs may not have the kinds of skills that are required for the new jobs. Thus, structural unemployment may well rise, at least for a time, as labour is reallocated from declining industries to industries that are able to compete in the North American market.

In the long run, the reallocation of labour to highly productive internationally competitive firms will also raise the average productivity of Canadian workers. By doing so, it will tend to raise the standard of living of the average Canadian. The process is similar to what happens when a new technology is developed. For example, when the transistor was developed, radios and computers no longer had to have glass vacuum tubes. Although many glass workers lost their jobs as a consequence, it would not have made sense to try to protect these jobs by restricting the use of transistors. In order to take advantage of opportunities to raise productivity and real incomes, we must allow for flexibility in the economy.

But while recognizing this, we should also recognize that increased structural unemployment is a painful thing, and represents a great social problem. There is thus a strong case for government assistance to ease the adjustment process—for example, by subsidized retraining for displaced workers. Thus, the society that benefits from the new transistor technology can help to reduce the burden that falls on a group of glassworkers who have lost their jobs. Similarly, the society that benefits from lower consumer prices and higher real incomes under a free trade agreement has an obligation to assist those who are thrown out of work as plants close under the impact of competition from foreign producers.

HOW MUCH EMPLOYMENT IS "FULL EMPLOYMENT"?

It is impossible—and undesirable—to eliminate all frictional unemployment. Hence, *full employment* must be defined as something less than the employment of 100% of the labour force. Over the past quarter century, there has been a lively debate over the unemployment rate which should be considered "full employment."

In the years following the 1960 recession, the Canadian unemployment rate gradually fell from a high of around 7.5% in 1960/61; by 1965 it had reached a level of 3.5%–4.0%. At that time, the Economic Council of Canada suggested that it should be possible to reach a "target" rate of 3% without unleashing inflationary pressures. Based on past experience, this did not seem unrealistic: The actual unemployment rate had stayed well below 3% for many years during the 1940s and 1950s.

For a time, the 3% target seemed attainable. The unemployment rate was less than 3.5% on the average during 1966, and for a short while actually dipped below 3%. Yet there was little inflationary pressure. However, during the late 1960s, inflationary pressures gathered force. There was a widespread agreement that the expansion of the 1960s had become too strong. Reluctantly, the Economic Council revised its target upward. The Council concluded that the unemployment rate could not be brought below 3.8% without causing inflation.

During the 1970s, the average annual unemployment rate never fell below 5%, yet the government still found itself struggling to control inflation. Consequently, the new target of 3.8% came to be viewed as unrealistic, in the sense that it could be achieved only during temporary periods when the economy was overheating and inflation accelerating. Frictional unemployment seemed to be higher than it had been in previous decades. Several explanations were suggested:

1. Changes in the composition of the labour force. For example, teenagers had become a larger fraction of the labour force, and teenagers are more likely to drift from job to job than are adults with family responsibilities.

2. Increases in the minimum wage, which meant that it was more expensive for employers to hire workers with minimal skills.

3. Reduced pressure on unemployed workers to take the first job available. Family income was being maintained in the face of unemployment by (a) improved unemployment insurance, and (b) increases in the number of families with two or more members in the labour force.

As a result, many economists argued that the "full-employment rate" had to be revised upward again. In 1980, the Economic Council raised its estimate of a realistic target to 6%. In 1983, Ernie Stokes of the Conference Board of Canada published a careful study of the full-employment rate in Canada for the period 1966 to 1981. His results implied that even 6% may have been an underestimate, and he suggested that a realistic full-employment rate for the late 1970s and early 1980s may have been in the 7.0%–7.5% range. More recent work by Andrew Burns for the Economic Council suggests that it may even have been as high as 8.5% in some years.[9]

From mid-1982 through late 1985, the actual unemployment rate remained in the 10%–13% range; during the worst part of the recession, it exceeded 12% for a full year. Since these rates are higher than any reasonable estimate of the full-employment target, the issue of precisely defining the target lost some of its urgency during that period. It was clearly desirable to bring down the unemployment rate substantially. Furthermore, changes in the composition of the labour force during the first half of the 1980s suggested that a realistic target for the mid-1980s should involve a *lower* unemployment rate than in the late 1970s. One reason for this was the changing age structure of the Canadian population: In the late 1980s, the number of teenage entrants into the labour force was much lower than it had been in the 1970s and early 1980s.

In the second half of the 1980s, the average unemployment rate gradually fell; by late 1988, it was below 7.5%. The question of what constituted a realistic full-employment target again became important, and some economists were once more beginning to worry about a building up of inflationary pressures (even though the actual inflation rate in the late 1980s remained well below the rates that had prevailed in the 1970s and early 1980s). One problem that made the issue particularly controversial during this period was that the regional differentials in unemployment rates had widened. While unemployment had fallen substantially in central Canada (especially in Ontario), it remained high in the Atlantic provinces and in the West. Those who advocated a policy that concentrated on fighting inflation were criticized for paying too much attention to conditions in Ontario: In the Maritimes and the West, reducing unemployment still appeared as the more important problem.

ECONOMIC COSTS OF RECESSIONS AND UNEMPLOYMENT

Whenever the economy slips into recession, potential output is lost, never to be recovered. The weeks and months which the unemployed spend in idleness are gone forever. Furthermore, the unemployed are subject to great stress and hardship. Unemployment is costly not

■ ■ ■ ■ ■
[9] Ernie Stokes, *Canada's Output Growth Performance and Potential, 1966–92*, Technical Paper, Conference Board of Canada, April 1983; Andrew Burns, "The Natural Rate of Unemployment: A Regionally Disaggregated Approach," a background paper prepared for the Economic Council of Canada, October 1988.

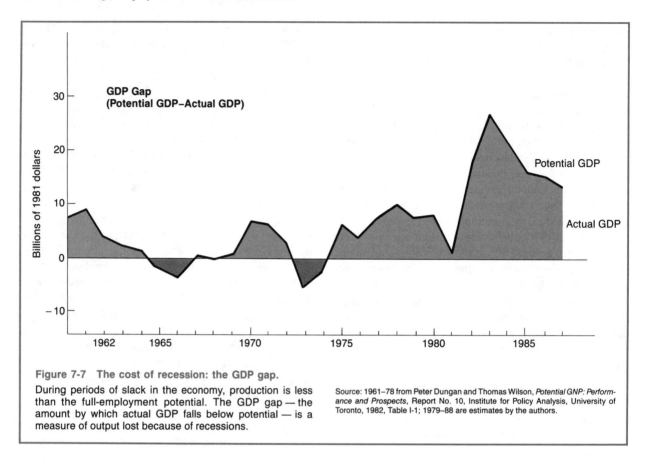

Figure 7-7   The cost of recession: the GDP gap.

During periods of slack in the economy, production is less than the full-employment potential. The GDP gap — the amount by which actual GDP falls below potential — is a measure of output lost because of recessions.

Source: 1961–78 from Peter Dungan and Thomas Wilson, *Potential GNP: Performance and Prospects*, Report No. 10, Institute for Policy Analysis, University of Toronto, 1982, Table I-1; 1979–88 are estimates by the authors.

only in terms of output forgone, but also in terms of demoralization of the population (Box 7-2).

The economic costs of recessions—in terms of output forgone — may be very large. One way of measuring them is based on estimating what GDP *would have been* in the absence of recessions and business cycles; that is, if full employment had been consistently maintained. The resulting hypothetical GDP measure is variously referred to as *full-employment GDP* or *high-employment GDP* or *potential GDP*. Needless to say, it cannot be estimated with a great deal of precision. Most obviously, there is uncertainty — described in the previous section — over just how much employment should be considered "full employment."

Nevertheless, even a rough measure of potential GDP is useful. If we subtract the actually observed GDP from potential GDP, we get an estimate of the amount of output that has been lost when the actual unemployment rate was higher than the full-employment rate of unemployment.

This difference between potential and actual GDP is known as the ***GDP gap***. In Figure 7-7, we show estimates of the GDP gap (measured in billions of 1981 dollars along the vertical axis) since 1960.

> The *GDP gap* is the amount by which actual GDP falls short of potential GDP.

In relative terms, the greatest GDP gap occurred during the Great Depression, before the period shown in Figure 7-7. In recent decades, the greatest gap has occurred during the severe recession of 1982 and the early recovery that followed. The estimated gaps in Figure 7-7 imply that, during 1982–84, over $65 billion in GDP, measured at 1981 prices, was forgone (about 6% of potential output over those three years). In 1988 dollars, this amounts to about $90 billion. To put this in perspective, note that $1 billion represents about $40 for every man, woman, and child in Canada. Thus, the economic slack of 1982–84 meant a loss of approximately

Box 7-2

■ ■ ■ ■ ■ ■ ■ ■ ■ ■ ■ ■ ■ ■ ■ ■ ■ ■ ■

Warning: Recessions Can Be Harmful to Your Health

Harvey Brenner of Johns Hopkins University has found that unemployment and other economic problems have adverse effects on physical and mental health, and shorten life spans. The following excerpts are from his report to the U.S. Congress:[†]

> In addition to a high unemployment rate, three other factors — decline in labor force participation, decline in average weekly hours worked, and an increase in the rate of business failures—are strongly associated with increased mortality. . . .
> Economic inequality is associated with deterioration in mental health and well-being, manifest in increased rates of homicide, crime, and mental hospital admissions.
>   . . . The report presents new evidence on the relationship between pathological [economic] conditions and . . . per capita alcohol consumption; cigarette consumption; illicit drug traffic and use; divorce rates; and the proportion of the population living alone.

Between 1973 and 1974, the U.S. unemployment rate rose from 4.9% to 5.6% of the civilian labor force. The chart below shows Brenner's estimate of the additional stress-related deaths and crimes associated with this increase in unemployment. The statistical relationships found by Brenner do not prove that the recession caused these results. But the evidence is strong enough to provide a warning: Recessions can be harmful to your health.

[†] M. Harvey Brenner, *Estimating the Effects of Economic Change on National Health and Social Well-Being* (Washington: Joint Economic Committee, U.S. Congress, June 1984), pp. 2–3.

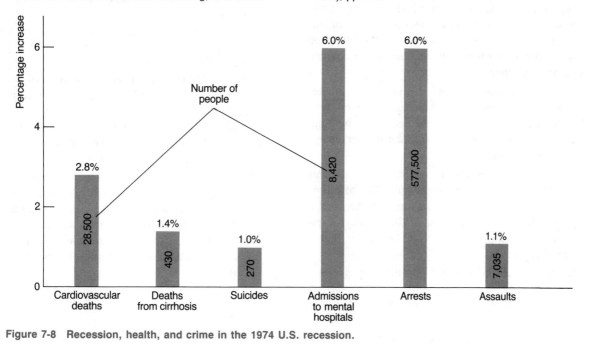

Figure 7-8   Recession, health, and crime in the 1974 U.S. recession.

$3,600 for every person in the nation. (Note: These numbers can change substantially if different estimates are made of potential output. Problems in estimating the potential path will be studied in detail in Chapter 18.)

Observe that according to Figure 7-7, actual GDP *exceeded* the estimate of potential GDP in 1965/66 and in 1973/74. This may seem puzzling: how can the econ-

omy possibly produce more than its potential? The answer is that the economy is capable of short-term bursts of activity which are unsustainable in the long run because of their cumulative adverse effects on the economy. Most notably, the short bursts of activity can cause the overheating of the economy, and an acceleration of inflation.

KEY POINTS

1. The Canadian economy does not expand steadily. From time to time, expansion is interrupted by a recession.

2. During recessions, output declines and the unemployment rate rises. Inflation generally declines. Profits fall sharply.

3. Reductions in investment (especially residential construction and inventories) and in exports have accounted for a large part of the overall decline in GDP in Canadian recessions during the past three decades.

4. Every recession in Canada since World War II has occurred at about the same time as a U.S. recession.

5. During recessions, the increase in the unemployment rate does not reflect all the pressures on the labour force. Some workers are limited to part-time work, when they want full-time employment. Some of the unemployed become discouraged. When they stop looking for work and thus drop out of the labour force, they are no longer counted among the unemployed.

6. During recessions, output declines to a greater extent than employment. Although the unemployment rate rises, the percentage decline in the number of people employed is less than the percentage decline in output.

7. The unemployment rate for young people exceeds that for the labour force as a whole. The Maritime provinces tend to have substantially higher unemployment rates than the rest of the country. Typically, the unemployment rate for women is higher than that for men.

8. Unemployment is classified into three categories:

(a) frictional unemployment
(b) structural unemployment
(c) cyclical unemployment

The first represents the smallest problem: people out of work temporarily as they hunt for jobs. Structural unemployment is more serious. Workers have to move or obtain additional skills in order to find jobs. Cyclical unemployment is attributable to instability in the economy.

9. The causes of structural unemployment include technological progress and intensified foreign competition which force the closing of older plants and firms that become unable to compete. The process of labour reallocation to plants that use a more efficient technology, and to industries that are internationally competitive, helps raise average labour productivity and living standards in the long run. However, because it may cause substantial hardship in the short run, a strong case can be made for government assistance to workers who lose their jobs as part of this process.

10. There is disagreement over the amount of unemployment which should be considered "full employment." While a rate of around 4% was generally considered "full employment" during the 1960s, estimates have been substantially increased in the past 15 years, to 6%, or even 7%.

11. The GDP gap measures how much actual output falls short of the full-employment potential. The gap is an important measure of the cost of recessions; it measures how much potential output has been lost. However, it does not include all the social costs, such as the demoralization of those who are out of work.

KEY CONCEPTS

recession	*underemployment*	*structural unemployment*
trough	*discouraged workers*	*cyclical unemployment*
expansion	*labour force time lost*	*potential or full-employment*
peak	*Okun's Law*	*output*
depression	*frictional unemployment*	*GDP gap*
international transmission		
mechanism		

PROBLEMS

7-1. Why is it difficult to identify a recession? Why can't we simply say that there is a recession whenever real output declines?

7-2. The text notes that inflation may respond slowly to changing economic conditions. For example, the downward pressure on prices may be concentrated in the latter stages of recession, and continue into the early recovery. Why might inflation be slow to respond?

7-3. During business cycles:
   (a) Why do consumer durable purchases fluctuate more than consumer purchases of nondurables and services?
   (b) Why does output fluctuate more than the unemployment rate?

7-4. Part of the reason that U.S. recessions affect the Canadian economy is that they cause a reduction in the demand for Canadian exports. Can you think of any reason why economic conditions in the United States may also indirectly affect the amount of private investment in Canada?

7-5. In 1980, the National Bureau of Economic Research estimated that the downward movement of the American economy lasted six months — February to July, inclusive. Yet real GNP data show only one quarter of decline — the second quarter, from April to June. Can you explain how it is possible for a monthly GNP series to decline from February to July, while GNP measured on a quarterly basis only declines in one quarter?

Chapter 8

■ ■

Explaining Unemployment and Inflation: Aggregate Supply and Aggregate Demand

I believe myself to be writing a book on
economic theory which will largely
revolutionize — not, I suppose, at once but in
the course of the next ten years — the way the
world thinks about economic problems.

John Maynard Keynes

In studying the market for an individual product — such as apples — we illustrated the concepts of demand and supply in a diagram, with the horizontal axis showing the quantity of apples, and the vertical axis showing the price of apples. This diagram was very useful. For example, by shifting the demand and supply curves, we could see how price and quantity respond to changing conditions of demand and supply (Figures 4-5 and 4-6).

In macroeconomics, the concepts of **aggregate demand** and **aggregate supply** are useful in a similar way. Since we are now dealing with the overall magnitudes in the economy, we use the horizontal axis to show the *overall* or *aggregate* quantity of output — that is, real domestic product. (In this and later chapters, we will denote aggregate output and income by the symbol Y.) On the vertical axis, we put the *average* level of prices, as measured by a price index of the type we discussed in Chapter 6.

In drawing the aggregate demand and aggregate supply curves, we must be careful. *We cannot assume that the aggregate demand curve slopes downward to the right simply because the microeconomic demand curve for an*

individual product slopes this way. Nor can we assume that the aggregate supply curve slopes upward to the right, simply because the supply curve for an individual product does.

To see why, reconsider the earlier explanation in Chapter 4, of why the demand curve for apples slopes downward to the right. This curve is drawn on the assumption that the price of apples is the *only* price that changes; when we draw the demand curve for apples, we assume that the prices of all other goods remain stable. Thus, when the price of apples falls, it declines *relative to the prices* of all other goods. With apples becoming a "better buy," people are encouraged to *switch* their purchases away from other goods, and buy more apples instead. Such switching — or *substitution* — is the principal reason the demand curve for an individual product slopes downward to the right.

Now consider what happens when we turn to the macroeconomic demand curve, with total output Y on the horizontal axis and the average level of prices on the vertical. For the economy as a whole, a fall in the level of all prices cannot cause buyers to switch from "other

135

goods.'' There are no such other goods.[1] It is not obvious how the aggregate demand curve should be drawn.

A similar problem arises on the supply side. In drawing the microeconomic supply curve for apples, we assume that the prices of all other goods remain stable. Thus, when the price of apples rises, it increases *relative to the prices* of other goods. Farmers, therefore, have an incentive to *switch* away from the production of other goods and produce more apples instead. When we look at macroeconomics — studying the economy as a whole —producers can't switch away from other goods because there aren't any. We cannot assume that the aggregate supply curve slopes upward to the right just because the supply curve for an individual product does.

How, then, are we to draw aggregate demand and aggregate supply? Historically, there have been two approaches to this problem. The first is the classical approach, which may be traced back several hundred years, to 18th century British philosopher David Hume and beyond. The second is the Keynesian approach, which was introduced during the 1930s as part of an attempt to explain and combat the Great Depression.

THE CLASSICAL APPROACH

Classical theorists argued that the aggregate quantity of goods and services demanded will increase as the average price level falls, as illustrated in Figure 8-1. The reason is this. Suppose that all prices fall by, say, 50% as illustrated by the move from P_1 to P_2. Then, each dollar buys more; the **purchasing power** of money has increased. Finding that they can buy more with their

money, people will step up their purchases. Thus, the aggregate demand curve slopes downward to the right. (But remember: The additional purchases do not come about as a result of *switching* among goods. At a lower average price level, people want to buy more goods *in total*.)

Furthermore, classical economists went beyond this general statement, to be more specific. With prices only half as high at P_2 as at P_1, each dollar will buy twice as much. Therefore, said classical economists, the quantity of goods and services purchased at B will be about twice as great as at A. Alternatively, if prices had doubled, from P_1 to P_3, each dollar would buy only half as much as it did originally, and people would therefore buy only about half as much at C as at A. In other words, classical economists believed that we could be more specific about the shape of the aggregate demand curve than about the demand curve for an individual product. (We cannot generalize in the same way about the demand curve for an individual good. If the price of apples falls by 50%, we may expect people to buy more. But there is no reason to believe that they will buy twice as many. They may buy three of four times as many, if apples are good substitutes for other fruit. On the other hand, if

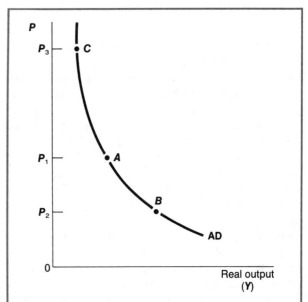

Figure 8-1   The classical aggregate demand function.
According to classical economists, the aggregate demand function slopes downward to the right. As prices fall, the money in the hands of the public will buy more. As a result, the public does buy more goods and services at B than at A.

■ ■ ■ ■ ■
[1] At least, there are no other *domestic* goods. When we take account of trade with foreign countries, things become more complicated, because changes in the overall price level in a country can lead to switching between domestic and foreign goods.

To keep matters simple, the relationship between international transactions and macroeconomic activity is neglected from the discussion of aggregate demand and supply in this chapter. (It is discussed in detail in Chapter 14.) However, the neo-classical economists argued that their analysis applied to an open economy (an economy with substantial international transactions) as well as to the case of a closed economy which we focus on in this chapter. For an exposition of the classical model in an international context, see, for example, M. Parkin, *Modern Macroeconomics* (Scarborough, Ont.: Prentice-Hall Canada, 1982), Chapter 39.

the price of gasoline falls by 50%, people may not drive much more; the quantity of gasoline bought may go up only moderately — say, by 10% or 20%.)

In this theory, classical economists *put money at the centre of aggregate demand*. In their view, the willingness and ability of people to buy goods *depends on the quantity of money in their possession, and on the purchasing power of that money*.

The *purchasing power* of money is the real quantity of goods and services that one dollar will buy. When the price level *rises*, the purchasing power of money *falls*. For example, when the price level doubles, the purchasing power of money falls to half its previous level.

Aggregate Supply: The Classical Approach

Classical economists argued that the aggregate supply function is vertical at the *potential* or *full-employment* quantity of output, as illustrated in Figure 8-2. Why?

To answer this question, consider what happens if the economy is initially at point *F*, with full employment. Now, suppose that all prices double, including the price

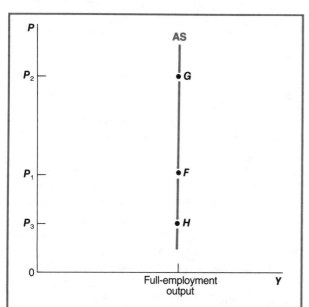

Figure 8-2 The classical aggregate supply function.
According to classical economists, the aggregate supply function is vertical, at the full-employment or potential quantity of domestic product. A general rise or fall in prices and wages does not make producers any more—or less—willing to supply goods and services.

of labour (that is, the wage rate). In other words, there is a *general inflation* with *relative* prices and wages being unaffected. Workers are basically in the same position as before. While their money wages have doubled, so have prices. The real wage — the quantity of goods and services which the wage will buy — is unchanged. Therefore, workers' willingness to work remains the same. Businesses also are in basically the same situation as before. Their productive capacity remains unchanged and the relationship between costs and prices also remains unchanged. As a result, businesses offer the same amount of goods and services for sale. Therefore, point *G* on the aggregate supply curve is directly above point *F*. Similarly, classical economists argued that the quantity of goods and services offered for sale would remain unchanged if all wages and prices fell by 50%, illustrated by the move from P_1 to P_3. Thus, point *H* is directly below point *F*.

Equilibrium at Full Employment

Bringing together the aggregate demand and aggregate supply curves of classical economics, we find the equilibrium at *E* in Figure 8-3. *Classical economists believed that the economy would be in equilibrium only at full employment, at a point like E, and that market forces would lead the economy to full employment.*

To explain this classical view, suppose that the economy is initially at a position of large-scale unemployment, such as point *B* in Figure 8-3. The high unemployment rate occurs because, at the initial price level P_1, the quantity of goods and services demanded (at *B*) is substantially less than the full-employment output (at *A*). What will happen, according to classical economists? At P_1, the quantity of goods and services demanded is less than producers are willing to supply. In order to sell more goods, businesses will cut their prices. At the same time, they will reduce the wage they pay, since the large number of unemployed will be so eager to get jobs that they will be willing to work for less than the prevailing wage. Thus, both prices and money wages will fall. With prices falling below P_1, the purchasing power of the money in the hands of the public will increase, and they will buy more. There will be a move along the aggregate demand curve from *B* to *C* to *D*. This process will continue until the economy gets to equilibrium *E*, with full employment. Once this equilibrium has been reached, there will no longer be downward pressures on prices and wages.

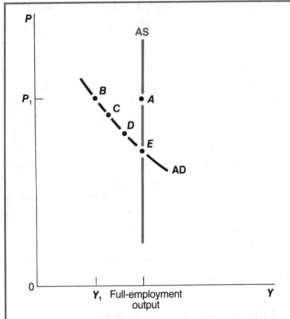

Figure 8-3 Equilibrium in classical economics.
According to classical economists, large-scale unemployment would result in an automatic movement back to full employment. Under the pressure of market forces, prices and wages would fall. The economy would gradually move down the aggregate demand curve toward full-employment equilibrium *E*.

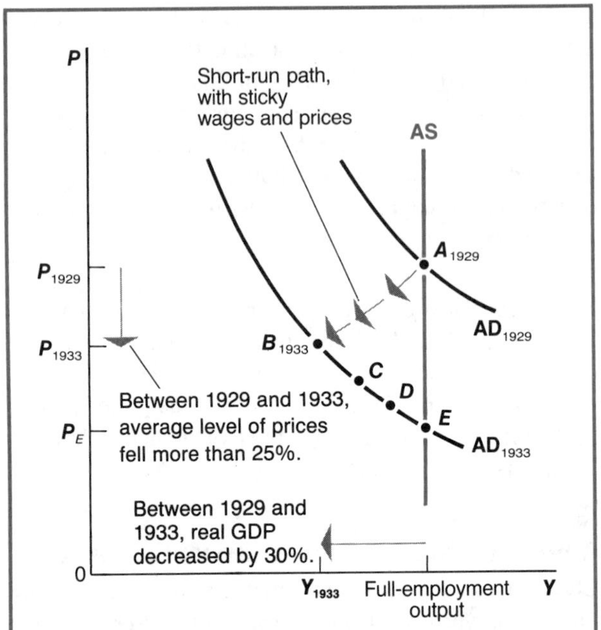

Figure 8-4 The Depression in classical economics.
Classical economists believed that principal cause of the Great Depression was a collapse in demand, caused by a sharp decline in the money stock. Because of wage and price stickiness, the economy did not move directly to its new full-employment equilibrium *E*, but rather to *B*, where output was too low to provide full employment.

The Classical Explanation of the Depression

Since classical economists believed that full employment always exists in equilibrium, how did they explain the Great Depression, when unemployment rates in North America rose to 20% and even higher? Their answer: Large-scale unemployment existed only when the economy was in *disequilibrium*; it was the result of temporary disturbances to the economy.

Most notably, the economy could be disturbed by a *shift* in the aggregate demand curve. As we have already seen, classical economists focused on money and its purchasing power in their analysis of aggregate demand. In drawing any single aggregate demand function (as in Fig. 8-1), classical economists *assumed that the nominal quantity of money was constant*. That is, the number of dollars was fixed. Any changes in the quantity of money would cause a shift in the aggregate demand function. It would shift to the right if the quantity of money increased, or to the left if the quantity of money decreased.

Thus, a classical explanation of the world-wide Depression goes something like this.[2] In 1929, the economy was close to a full-employment equilibrium at *A* in Figure 8-4, with aggregate demand AD$_{1929}$. Then, because of disturbances in the banking and financial system, particularly in the United States, the stock of money declined. (Between 1928/29 and 1933, money in the hands of the public fell by about 15% in Canada, and by as much as 30% in the United States.) As a result, aggregate demand shifted to the left, to AD$_{1933}$.

Even with this fall in demand, classical economists would say, full employment would still have been possible if prices and wages had fallen all the way to *PE*. In this event, full employment would have occurred at new equilibrium *E*. But prices and wages were *sticky* in

■ ■ ■ ■

[2] Details may be found in the very readable chapter on the Depression in Milton Friedman and Anna Schwartz, *A Monetary History of the United States, 1867–1960* (Princeton: Princeton University Press, 1963).

a downward direction; that is, they did not fall quickly in the face of slack demand and high unemployment. One reason for stickiness is that it takes some time for people searching for a job to realize that they will not find the job they want, at the wage they expect. It is only after a frustrating search that they will be willing to settle for a lower wage.[3] Because of stickiness, prices fell only to P_{1933} by 1933. With prices remaining higher than required for the new equilibrium, the amount of goods and services purchased was far less than the economy's full-employment potential. The economy was in a deep depression at point B. Thus, according to the classical view, wage and price stickiness kept the economy from moving directly downward along the aggregate supply function in the face of a collapse in demand. As demand fell, the economy instead moved along the short-run path from A to B. In the absence of any further disturbance to demand, price and wage adjustments could be expected to gradually restore full employment. Although it would take time, the economy would eventually move along the new aggregate demand curve from B to C to D, and finally to the new full-employment equilibrium E. So argued classical economists.

In other words, the classical aggregate supply curve illustrated where the economy would eventually go. Over the **long run**, classical economists were confident that wages and prices would in fact adjust, restoring full employment.

In classical macroeconomics, the *long run* is the period over which prices and wages adjust completely.

This approach led classical economists to suggest two possible solutions for a depression:
1. The initial source of the disturbance might be eliminated. Steps might be taken to prevent a decline in the quantity of money in the first place, or to restore the quantity of money once it had fallen. If the money supply were increased, and aggregate demand restored to AD_{1929}, the economy might be expected to retrace its path from B back toward A in Figure 8-4.

■ ■ ■ ■ ■
[3] Some classical economists argued that distortions among *relative* prices made the depression even more severe. We skip this argument, because it was quite complex. In this section, we consider only the effects of a general, across-the-board inflation or deflation, in which all prices and wages move by the same percentage, and relative prices are accordingly left undisturbed. This allows us to grasp the central points of classical theory.

2. Workers and businesses might be encouraged to accept lower wages and prices quickly, so the economy could move more rapidly to its new full-employment equilibrium E. The more willing workers and businesses were to accept lower wages and prices, the shorter would be the temporary period of unemployment. Note that the classical "long run" is not any fixed number of months or years. It is whatever period is needed for wages and prices to adjust. The faster they adjust, the sooner the economy reaches its long-run equilibrium with full employment.

However, many classical economists were quite skeptical that in practice the government could help much in promoting downward wage and price flexibility. Indeed, many believed that when the government becomes involved in markets, it is likely to keep prices up and increase their stickiness. Thus, many classical economists argued for a policy of laissez-faire. In macroeconomic as in microeconomic questions, they saw little role for the government, apart from providing a stable monetary system. They believed that the operation of market forces would work to restore full employment.

Classical Macroeconomics: A Preliminary Summary

Before proceeding, let us summarize the main points of classical macroeconomics developed thus far:
1. The aggregate demand curve slopes downward to the right. As prices fall, each dollar will buy more, and people accordingly do buy more. A single aggregate demand curve is drawn on the assumption that the nominal quantity of money is constant. If the quantity of money increases, the aggregate demand curve shifts to the right.
2. The aggregate supply curve is vertical at the full-employment output.
3. In the long run, a shift in the aggregate demand curve causes a change in prices, not in output. The reason is that, in the long run, the economy moves back to the vertical aggregate supply curve.
4. However, in the short run — when wages and prices are sticky—a collapse in aggregate demand can cause a depression. Instead of moving from A to E, the economy moves from A to B in Figure 8-4.
5. Although an economy at B will eventually move to E, a better solution is to increase the money stock, thus increasing aggregate demand back up to AD_{1929}. This will move the economy from B back toward A.

THE KEYNESIAN APPROACH

Prior to the Great Depression, most economists considered unemployment to be a relatively minor and temporary problem, associated with short-term fluctuations in the economy. The decade-long depression of the 1930s shattered this confidence and provided the backdrop for a new theory of unemployment put forward by British economist John Maynard Keynes. His major work—*The General Theory of Employment, Interest and Money*—attacked the prevailing classical view. Specifically, Keynes put forward three major propositions concerning unemployment in a market economy:

1. *Unemployment equilibrium.* In contrast to classical economists, Keynes argued that a market economy might have no strong tendency to move to full employment. On the contrary, a market economy might become stuck in an *equilibrium with large-scale unemployment*—often referred to, more briefly, as an **unemployment equilibrium**. Furthermore, even if the economy did temporarily reach full employment, it might be quite unstable, and fall back into depression. In other words, Keynes said that the market economy was defective in two important ways:
   (a) It might lead to a *persistent depression*, such as the Great Depression of the 1930s.
   (b) It might be quite *unstable*, so that even if we did achieve full employment, this happy state of affairs might be short-lived.
2. *The cause of unemployment.* Keynes argued that large-scale unemployment is due to an *insufficiency of aggregate demand*—that is, too little spending for goods and services.
3. *The cure for unemployment.* To cure unemployment, aggregate demand should be increased. The best way to do that, said Keynes, is by an increase in government spending.

This third proposition was the main policy message of the *General Theory*: The goverment has the ability—and the *responsibility* — to *manage aggregate demand*, and thus to ensure continuing prosperity. Cast aside was the classical view, that market forces would solve the unemployment problem, and that the government should strictly limit its interference in the economy. Keynes was particularly impatient with classical economists who were willing to wait for the "long run," when they expected market forces to re-establish full employment. As he put it in a now-famous maxim: "In the long run we are all dead."

Keynes held out the promise that the government could increase aggregate demand, and thus solve the appalling unemployment problem of the 1930s. His book was a spectacular success; it ranks with Adam Smith's *Wealth of Nations* and Karl Marx's *Das Kapital* as one of the most influential economics books ever written. The *General Theory* led to a sharp change in economic thinking. With its appearance in 1936, the *Keynesian Revolution* was underway.

To support his three propositions, Keynes put forward a new theoretical framework, including an approach to aggregate demand and aggregate supply which was quite different from that of classical economists.

The Simple Keynesian Aggregate Supply Function

Classical economists had recognized that prices and wages might be sticky in a downward direction, and had used this stickiness to explain *transitional* periods of large-scale unemployment when aggregate demand decreased. Keynes placed even more emphasis on stickiness. In his view, workers and businesses would *strongly* resist any cut in wages and prices. As a result, wages and prices would remain *rigid* for an *indefinitely* long period in the face of large-scale unemployment.

This idea can be represented by a horizontal section in the Keynesian aggregate supply function, as illustrated by section *BA* in Figure 8-5. Here's why. If, from an initial position of full employment at point *A*, there was an decline in aggregate demand, prices would remain stable. The fall in demand would show up in terms of a decrease in output *Y*, not in prices. This is shown by the movement from *A* to *B*. Furthermore, there would be little tendency, even in the long run, for prices and wages to fall. If aggregate demand remained low, the economy would remain in a depression at *B*.

According to Keynes, the cure was to increase aggregate demand. In response, producers would step up production. Because of the large numbers of unemployed workers and the large quantity of unused machinery, more could be produced at existing prices, that is, without general price inflation. Output would increase, and the economy would move to the right along the horizontal portion of the aggregate supply function back toward *A*. Once the economy got to *A*—to a point of full employment—Keynes had no major objection to the classical approach to aggregate supply. Because the economy was already operating at capacity, any further increase in

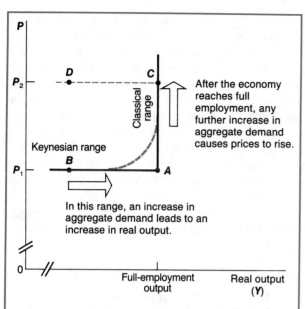

Figure 8-5 The Keynesian aggregate supply function.
There are two main segments of the Keynesian aggregate supply function. In the horizontal section, prices are stable and a change in aggregate demand causes a change in Y, total output, and employment. In the vertical section an increase in demand causes an increase in prices.

aggregate demand would be reflected in higher prices. The economy would move vertically upward toward C. In short, the Keynesian aggregate supply function had two quite different ranges:

1. A *horizontal range*, which was relevant for analysing periods of depression and recession, when inadequate demand resulted in high rates of unemployment. This was the range which most interested Keynes. The major purpose of the *General Theory* was to explain the causes and cures of the Great Depression. Accordingly, this horizontal range of the aggregate supply function is frequently known as the *Keynesian range*.

2. A *vertical range*, which would be reached when aggregate demand was high enough to ensure full employment. Further increases in demand would simply cause inflation. Because Keynes had no quarrel with the classical approach once full employment is reached, this vertical section is sometimes known as the *classical range*.

Together, these two ranges give the aggregate supply function BAC in Figure 8-5, forming a reversed L.

An interesting implication of the approach in Figure 8-5 is that the average level of prices will *ratchet* upward through time. As we have just seen, prices would be downwardly rigid when the economy was at point B. An increase in aggregate demand would first lead to an increase in output, to point A. But any further increase in demand would lead to higher prices. The economy would move up the vertical portion of the aggregate supply curve to point C, with prices rising to P_2. However, once C is reached, any reduction in demand would not lead the economy to retrace its path back toward A because prices and wages would not move down from the new level established at C; businesses and labour would resist such a move. Instead, the response to a fall in aggregate demand would be a decrease in output. The economy would move toward D, along the lightly dashed line. In short, the simple Keynesian aggregate supply function was a reversed L, with the horizontal part of the L shifting upward every time a new, higher price level became established.[4]

A Complication

Unfortunately, the world is more complex than indicated by the simple L-shaped function. From the early days of the Keynesian Revolution, economists recognized that there might be no sharply-defined point at A where the economy suddenly reaches full employment. As the economy expands, not all industries reach capacity at exactly the same time; some reach it before others. In the industries approaching capacity, prices begin to rise. The overall price index begins to creep up. This occurs while other industries are still operating well below capacity, and are still increasing their output as demand increases. Thus, there is a period in which both output and prices are increasing. The economy takes the curved short-cut illustrated in the dashed colour curve in Figure 8-5.

While the horizontal range of aggregate supply was used by Keynesians in their explanation of the Great Depression, the sloping intermediate range is important in more normal times, when the economy is neither in

---

[4] Both Keynesian and classical economists recognized a complication that we avoid here. As time passes, the economy grows, with the full-employment or potential output increasing. Therefore, the vertical section of the aggregate supply function shifts gradually to the right with the passage of time.

an inflationary boom (the vertical section), nor in a depression (the horizontal part).

Aggregate Demand: The Keynesian Approach

As we noted above, the classical economists had a very simple view of the determination of aggregate demand: They saw it as determined by the quantity of money in the economy. Keynes instead proposed that aggregate demand be analysed by studying the demand for the various components of GDP:

1. *Personal consumption expenditures*
2. *Investment demand*; that is, the demand for equipment, plant, housing, and additional inventories
3. *Government purchases of goods and services*
4. *Net exports*

Keynes was intent on explaining the Great Depression, and with finding a way to restore full employment. In his view, the Depression was caused by a collapse in aggregate demand, particularly the private investment component. Keynes stressed the instability of investment demand: Businesses are willing to invest only when they expect the new plant and equipment to add to profits. Expectations are fragile. Once the economy is declining sharply, business executives become pessimistic and, therefore, they cut back on investment. Thus, even though a decline in private investment demand may have been the principal cause of the Depression, it was unrealistic to expect a revival of investment demand to move the economy out of the Depression. Rather, it was up to the government to provide a solution by increasing the component of aggregate demand directly under its control. That is, it was desirable for the government to increase its spending to compensate for the decline in investment demand, and thus restore full employment.

In the coming chapters, we will study the four components of aggregate demand and the forces that cause them to increase or decrease. In these chapters, we will address two of the central questions of Keynesian theory: How large will aggregate demand be? Will it put us near full employment or leave us in a depression?

Before passing on to these topics, we re-emphasize: The four components of aggregate demand highlighted by Keynesian theory correspond to the four major components of domestic or national product studied in Chapter 6. Two major innovations in macroeconomics—the

development of national product accounts and the new Keynesian theory of employment—interacted and reinforced one another during the 1930s and 1940s.

Finally, observe that in Figure 8-5, we have drawn no aggregate demand curve. Thus, something is missing from our introduction to Keynesian theory. We have not shown how the demand for goods and services responds to a change in the average level of prices. The rather complicated Keynesian approach to this issue is deferred to the appendix to this chapter. All we need to note here is the principal conclusion. Except in the special case of a deep depression, Keynesian theory, like the classical theory, suggests that the aggregate demand curve slopes downward to the right.

CLASSICAL ECONOMICS AND KEYNESIAN ECONOMICS: A SUMMARY

In his *General Theory*, Keynes launched an attack on classical economists on the grounds that they had no adequate proposals for dealing with the severe unemployment problem of the 1930s. A heated debate ensued, both over policies and over the proper theoretical framework for studying macroeconomic problems.

Differences between Keynesians and the inheritors of the classical school continue to the present day. These differences attract considerable attention; debates can be interesting. But the fact that differences still exist should not obscure something even more important. On many issues, there is general agreement among macroeconomists, regardless of their intellectual heritage.

Areas of Agreement

Most notably, those in the classical and Keynesian traditions agree on these points:
1. A *sharp decline in aggregate demand* was the principal cause of the collapse into the Great Depression of the 1930s.
2. *Fluctuations in aggregate demand* have been the major cause of fluctuations in real output in recent decades.
3. Accordingly, the *stabilization of aggregate demand* should be an important macroeconomic objective.
4. When the economy is already operating at its full-employment potential, *any large increase in aggregate demand will spill over into inflation.* Both the

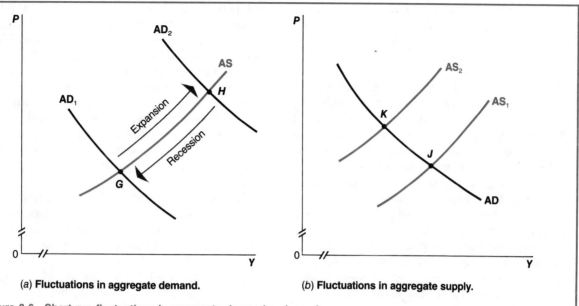

(a) **Fluctuations in aggregate demand.**   (b) **Fluctuations in aggregate supply.**

Figure 8-6   Short-run fluctuations in aggregate demand and supply.

In the left panel, aggregate demand fluctuates. During the expansion, output Y increases and there is upward pressure on prices (the movement from G to H). During recessions, output declines and pressure on prices subsides (H to G). This is the pattern actually observed in most business cycles. In contrast, we do not generally observe the outcome illustrated in the right-hand panel. For example, recessions generally are not accompanied by rising inflation, as they would be if the economy were moving from J to K.

classical and Keynesian aggregate supply functions are vertical once full employment has been reached. Thus, higher demand causes higher prices.

The second point is worth explaining in more detail. Consider Figure 8-6, with a normal, downward-sloping aggregate demand function, AD_1. The aggregate supply function slopes upward to the right; it corresponds to the intermediate range of the Keynesian supply function in Figure 8-5. Panel (*a*), in which aggregate demand shifts, is broadly consistent with the pattern already observed in Chapter 7: During expansions, output increases and inflation generally accelerates. During recession, the opposite happens: Output declines and the rate of inflation generally decreases. If shifts in aggregate supply had been the main cause of business cycles (panel (*b*)), we would expect inflation to rise during recessions (as real output contracts in the move from J to K), and fall during expansions (the move from K to J). But this is not, in fact, what usually happens. Therefore, we may conclude that it is not shifts in aggregate supply, but rather shifts in aggregate demand that are the major cause of business fluctuations. Not surpris-

ingly, then, we will focus on the aggregate demand side in our early study of macroeconomics in Chapters 9 to 14.

Areas of Disagreement

1. We have seen how classical economists attributed the Great Depression to a decline in the money stock and believed that one solution to the Depression lay in the restoration of the money stock (a change in monetary policy). In contrast, Keynes emphasized government spending (fiscal policy) as a way of increasing aggregate demand and restoring full employment.

   There is a continuing difference whether monetary policy or fiscal policy has the stronger and more predictable effect on aggregate demand. Those in the classical tradition focus on *monetary policy*, while those in the Keynesian tradition are most likely to think first of *fiscal policy*. However, it should be emphasized that *most modern macroeconomists believe that both monetary and fiscal policies are important*.

Monetary policy involves a change in the rate of growth of the money stock.

Fiscal policy involves a change in government expenditures or in tax rates.

2. While macroeconomists agree that it would be desirable for aggregate demand to be more stable, they differ sharply over *how* stability is best achieved. Those in the Keynesian tradition emphasize the defects and instabilities of a market economy and believe that the government has the responsibility to *actively manage* aggregate demand in order to reduce the amplitude of business fluctuations.

Those in the classical tradition generally believe that the market economy will be reasonably stable, *if* monetary conditions are kept stable. As a result, many of them have supported a **monetary policy rule**: The authorities should aim for a *steady, moderate increase in the money stock*, at something like 3% or 4% per year. A steady growth is appropriate, since we live in a growing economy. More money is needed to buy the increasing volume of goods and services that can be produced.

Because of their emphasis on money, modern inheritors of the classical tradition are frequently known as **monetarists**. They do not argue that adherence to a monetary rule will create a perfectly stable economy, since aggregate demand will not expand in a perfectly stable way even if money does. But they are very skeptical that the government can make things better by active policy management. Like the earlier classical economists, they fear that the government attempts at stabilizing the economy might, on average, make things worse instead of better. (Some reasons for this fear will be explained in Chapter 18.)

This disagreement—between those who argue for *active management* by government and those who advocate some type of *policy rule*—is probably the most important single dispute among macroeconomists.

3. *The nature of equilibrium.* Those in the classical tradition associate equilibrium with full employment. High rates of unemployment represent a *temporary* problem caused by economic fluctuations and short-run *disequilibrium*. In contrast, Keynesian theory puts forward the possibility that the economy might fall into an unemployment equilibrium, involving an *extended* period of inadequate aggregate demand and high rates of unemployment.

While the possibility of an unemployment equilibrium remains a point of difference between those in the Keynesian and classical traditions, this issue has become less important with the passage of time. A major reason is that half a century has passed since the Great Depression. Keynesians are, therefore, much less worried about a lengthy depression than they used to be.

KEY POINTS

1. Just as demand and supply are useful in microeconomics, so they are also useful in macroeconomics. However, we cannot assume that the macroeconomic demand and supply curves will necessarily have slopes similar to those of microeconomic demand and supply curves.

2. There are two main approaches to aggregate demand and aggregate supply: the classical and the Keynesian approaches.

3. Classical theory stresses the importance of money as a determinant of aggregate demand. In drawing a single aggregate demand curve, we assume that the nominal quantity of money is held constant. When prices fall, the purchasing power of this fixed nominal quantity increases. Therefore, people purchase more goods and services. Accordingly, the classical aggregate demand function slopes downward to the right.

4. According to classical theory, the aggregate supply function is vertical at potential or full-employment output.

5. Consequently, full employment exists in the classical equilibrium where aggregate demand and aggregate supply intersect.

6. According to classical economists, the Great Depression was the result of a leftward shift in the aggregate demand curve which, in turn, resulted from a fall in the money stock. In time—in the "long run"—classical economists believed that wages and prices would fall enough to restore full employment.

7. Keynes emphasized the downward rigidity of wages and prices. In its simplest form, the Keynesian aggregate supply function forms a reversed L, as illustrated in Figure 8-5.

8. According to Keynes, the principal cause of the Great Depression was the collapse of the investment component of aggregate demand. The solution lay in additional government expenditures, whose purpose would be to increase aggregate demand to the full-employment level. Thus, Keynes rejected the laissez-faire conclusions of many classical economists.

9. Keynesian economists often stress fiscal policy as a tool for managing demand, while those in the classical tradition emphasize the importance of money.

However, most modern economists believe that *both* fiscal and monetary policies can have an important effect on demand.

10. A significant debate continues over how actively the authorities should manage aggregate demand. Keynesians generally favour active management, while those in the classical tradition generally favour some type of monetary rule: The authorities should aim for a steady, moderate increase in the quantity of money.

KEY CONCEPTS

aggregate demand
aggregate supply
purchasing power of money
general inflation or deflation
equilibrium at full employment
wage and price stickiness
transitional periods of
  unemployment

long run (classical definition)
Keynesian unemployment
  equilibrium
Reversed-L aggregate supply
  function
Keynesian and classical ranges
  of aggregate supply

monetary policy
fiscal policy
active management of demand
monetary policy rule
monetarist

PROBLEMS

8-1. The demand curve for a specific good, such as wheat, slopes downward to the right. Why can't we simply conclude that, as a result, the aggregate demand curve will have the same general shape?

8-2. Draw a diagram showing the classical aggregate demand function. Why does it have the slope you have shown?

8-3. Why is the classical aggregate supply function vertical?

8-4. If the economy starts at a point of high unem-

ployment, explain two ways in which full employment might be restored in the classical system.

8-5. What is the reason for the horizontal section of the Keynesian aggregate supply function?

8-6. According to Keynes, what was the best way to get out of a depression?

8-7. What evidence suggests that fluctuations in aggregate demand, rather than fluctuations in aggregate supply, have been the principal reason for fluctuations in real output?

Appendix

■ ■ ■ ■ ■

The Aggregate Demand Curve of Keynesian Economics

In order to complete our story about aggregate demand and aggregate supply, we need to look at what Keynes said about the slope of the aggregate demand function in his *General Theory*. Suppose that in the face of a depressed economy at *B* (Figure 8-7), a general deflation did occur with prices and wages all falling by, say, 50%. The horizontal segment of the aggregate supply curve would then be at the new prevailing price level; aggregate supply would have shifted down from AS_1 to AS_2. What would the result be? What would happen to the aggregate quantity of goods and services demanded? To answer this, said Keynes, we have to look at what will happen to the major components of demand, particularly consumption and investment.

1. *Consumption demand.* The amount which people consume depends primarily on their incomes. As wages and incomes fall by the same proportion, people find that they are no better off: Their *real wages* remain unchanged. Accordingly, said Keynes, we would not expect any change in the quantity of goods and services they consume. In other words, if we look only at consumption—the largest single component of aggregate demand — we would expect the aggregate demand function to be *vertical*. If it has any tendency to slope downward to the right or left, it will have to be because of the behaviour of other components of demand, most notably, investment.

2. *Investment demand.* Investment demand depends in part on what is happening to consumer purchases. For example, a rise in the sales of automobiles will encourage auto manufacturers to invest by buying more plant and machinery. However, if consumption is stable in the face of deflation—for reasons explained in point 1—then there is no reason to expect greater investment on this account.

To identify the effects of price changes on investment, we have to look instead at two other forces:

(a) *The interest-rate effect.* As prices and wages fall, the amount of money in the system increases in real terms; that is, in terms of what it will buy. There is the same number of dollars, but each dollar is worth more. Because individuals and businesses have more real money, they are more willing to lend it; interest rates fall as a result. With lower interest rates, businesses find it cheaper to borrow the money with which to buy equipment. Investment should increase on this account.

(b) *The expectations effect.* Investment also depends on people's expectations regarding the future. If prices are expected to rise, for example, businesses have an incentive to buy buildings or equipment quickly in order to avoid the higher prices later. In extreme cases, there can be strong speculation in real estate — there is a rush to get in while the getting is good. On the other hand, expectations of a fall in prices can cause businesses to put off investment in the hopes of buying the plant or equipment even more cheaply in the future. This, said Keynes, is what makes deflation so dangerous. As prices fall, people may come to expect a continuing deflation. This can cause a weakening of investment demand.

Thus, there are two opposite forces at work as prices decline — the interest-rate effect (working toward an increase in investment) and the expectations effect (working toward a decrease).

Keynes was particularly dubious about the interest-rate effect when the economy was suffering substantial slack. During such periods, interest rates may already be very low. For example, the interest rates on long-term government bonds fell below 3% during the Great Depression. No matter what happens, interest rates can't fall much further. Clearly, interest rates can't become

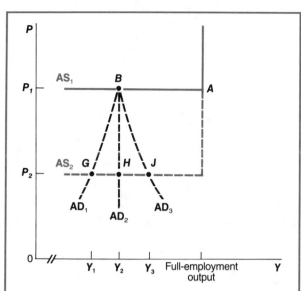

Figure 8-7 Aggregate demand in Keynesian economics.
If prices and wages fall during a depression, the result may be an increase in the quantity of goods and services demanded, as illustrated by the movement from B to J. But we cannot count on this. The quantity demanded may remain stable at H, or decrease to G. In other words, we cannot be sure which way the aggregate demand curve will slope. AD_1, AD_2, and AD_3 are all possible.

In brief, Keynes presented two reasons for rejecting the classical argument that full employment could be restored by a general fall in prices and wages:

1. In the first place, prices and wages *won't* fall much; they are rigid in a downward direction. The downward shift of the aggregate supply curve illustrated in Figure 8-7 won't occur, in fact, according to Keynes.

2. *Even if* prices and wages *did* fall, the market could not be counted on to restore full employment. A more likely outcome would be a movement toward G (Figure 8-7); deflation would worsen the depression.

Market forces would not lead automatically to full employment, even in the long run. Thus, Keynes came to his central policy conclusion. If the economy is at a point like B, the government should not stand idly by while millions remain out of work. It should accept its responsibilities and increase its spending in order to shift aggregate demand to the right and restore full employment at A.

Finally, Keynesian theory suggests that the aggregate demand curve should have a normal slope during a period of prosperity; that is, it should slope downward to the right. During prosperity, interest rates are generally much higher than during a depression; they can fall substantially when the real value of the public's money holdings goes up. Thus, the interest rate effect should be relatively strong, outweighing the expectations effect and giving the aggregate demand function a normal downward slope.

As a result, Keynesian and classical theories become quite similar during prosperity. Both suggest a vertical aggregate supply function. Moreover, both foresee an aggregate demand function sloping downward to the right. The sharp differences in the two theories arise when the unemployment rate is high.

negative; people would simply refuse to buy bonds yielding negative rates and would hold money instead.

Thus, Keynes argued that, during a depression, a weak interest-rate effect is likely to be overpowered by a negative expectations effect. Although it's conceivable that there could be an increase in investment and aggregate demand with aggregate demand going through point J in Figure 8-7, it is much more likely that investment would remain stable or decrease. Therefore, the aggregate demand function is more likely to go through H or G.

PROBLEM

*8-8. As part of Franklin Roosevelt's program to combat the Great Depression of the 1930s, the U.S. National Recovery Act contained provisions to keep prices up. Explain why someone in the classical tradition might consider such legislation a blunder. Explain why a Keynesian would be much more likely to favour such legislation.

Chapter 9

■ ■

Equilibrium with Unemployment: The Keynesian Approach

*The economic system in which we live . . .
seems capable of remaining in a chronic
condition of sub-normal activity for a
considerable period without any marked
tendency either towards recovery or towards
complete collapse. Moreover, . . . full, or
even approximately full employment is of rare
and short-lived occurrence.*

John Maynard Keynes,
*The General Theory of Employment, Interest
and Money*

Of all our economic problems, unemployment is perhaps the most vexing. Unemployment represents an obvious waste: The society forgoes the goods and services which the unemployed might have produced. Unemployed people suffer the demoralization, frustration, and loss of self-respect that come from enforced idleness.

As we saw in Chapter 8, the deep Depression of the 1930s led to a new theory of unemployment, put forward by John Maynard Keynes. This chapter will explain Keynes' major theoretical proposition, that the economy may reach an equilibrium with large-scale unemployment. (The next chapter will outline Keynes' major policy proposals — namely, what the government can do to combat unemployment.)

Equilibrium in an economy is determined by aggregate supply and aggregate demand. To explain Keynesian theory, we begin where Keynes did, focusing on the horizontal section of the aggregate supply function (Figure 8-5), where prices are stable and where changes in spending lead to changes in real output. To determine how large real domestic output will be, we need to know the aggregate quantity of goods and services demanded.

Recall from Chapter 8 that aggregate demand is made up of four components:
1. personal consumption expenditures
2. investment demand
3. government purchases of goods and services
4. net exports

The basic point of Keynesian theory — that the economy may reach an equilibrium with large-scale unemployment — can be illustrated most easily by considering a very simple economy, with only the first two components: consumption and investment. Such a simplified economy is studied in this chapter. Government expenditures and net exports will be considered in Chapter 10.

PERSONAL CONSUMPTION EXPENDITURES

Of all the components of total spending, personal consumption is by far the largest. On what do consumption expenditures depend? An individual's consumption is influenced by many factors. Purchases of clothing depend on the weather. The purchase of an automobile depends in part on the price of gasoline and on the state of the roads. We could easily compile an extensive list of factors affecting consumption. But one stands out as the most important: *Consumption depends on the disposable income that people have left after they pay taxes.*

The behaviour of typical Canadian consumers is illustrated in Figure 9-1. Low-income families on the left confine their spending to little more than the necessities of life—food, clothing, and housing. Even so, they find it hard to make ends meet, and they spend more than their incomes. For example, families at *G* with disposable incomes of $5,000 (measured along the horizontal axis) consume, on average, about $7,000 (measured vertically). But how can low-income families possibly spend more than they have coming in? The answer: by running into debt or by drawing on their past savings. One group of low-income people—those who are retired—are particularly likely to spend more than their current incomes. They draw on the assets, such as their retirement savings plans, that they have accumulated during their working lives.

As the incomes of families rise, they find it easier to live within their current incomes. Thus, the family at *H*, with an income of $14,000, spends $14,000 for consumer goods and services. It *breaks even*, spending all its income. As incomes rise further, consumption also rises, but not as fast as income; at incomes above $14,000, families do not consume their full incomes. For example, families at point *J* with incomes of $40,000 consume considerably less than this amount and save the rest.

Figure 9-1 shows how a family's consumption rises as its disposable income increases. Income of the family is measured along the horizontal axis, and the family's consumption up the vertical axis. For a *nation as a whole*, consumption also rises as disposable income increases. Figure 9-2 provides an illustration with disposable income of the whole nation on the horizontal axis and expenditures of all consumers on the vertical axis. The numbers corresponding to Figure 9-2 are shown in Table 9-1. For example, the first line of Table 9-1 indicates that, if disposable income is $100 billion, consumption is $120 billion. This is shown at point *A* in Figure 9-2, measured 100 units along the horizontal income axis, and 120 units up the vertical consumption axis. Similarly, points *B*, *C*, and *D* in Figure 9-2 can be derived from the corresponding lines in Table 9-1. Because consumer expenditures depend primarily on real incomes, the incomes and expenditures on the axes of Figure 9-2 are measured in real or constant-dollar terms.

The relationship between consumption and disposable income is known as the ***consumption function***.

> The *consumption function* shows how consumption expenditures depend on disposable income.

In Figure 9-2, we may find the ***break-even point*** — at which consumption equals disposable income — with the help of a 45° line drawn from the origin. The 45° line has an important property: *Any point on it is the same distance from the two axes*. Consider, for example, an economy in which disposable income is $400 billion, as shown by the horizontal distance between the origin and point *G* in Figure 9-2. Then the vertical distance from *G* to point *H* on the 45° line is also $400 billion. Thus, this disposable income (*DI*) of $400 billion may be measured either along the horizontal axis from the origin to point *G*, or as the vertical distance from *G* up to the 45° line at *H*.

If disposable income decreases to $200 billion and we move to the left to point *K*, we can once again measure income as the height of the 45° line — in this case, the $200 billion vertical distance from point *K* on the horizontal axis to point *B* on the 45° line. But this vertical distance to point *B* also measures consumption. That is, *B* lies on the consumption function. Therefore, point *B*, *where the consumption function and the 45° line intersect*, is the *break-even point*.

> At the *break-even point*, consumption equals disposable income. That is, every dollar of disposable income is spent on consumer goods and services.

Saving is what is left of disposable income after consumption expenditures:

Saving = disposable income − consumption[1]

$$(9-1)$$

Drawing on this equation, we may derive the ***saving function*** in Figure 9-3 directly from the consumption function. For example: Suppose disposable income is $400 billion at point *G* measured along the horizontal

--

■ ■ ■ ■ ■

[1] More precisely, saving equals disposable income less consumption expenditures less interest paid by consumers, as noted in Chapter 6. However, when explaining the basic Keynesian theory, it is standard practice to ignore the interest complication, and use the simplified equation shown here.

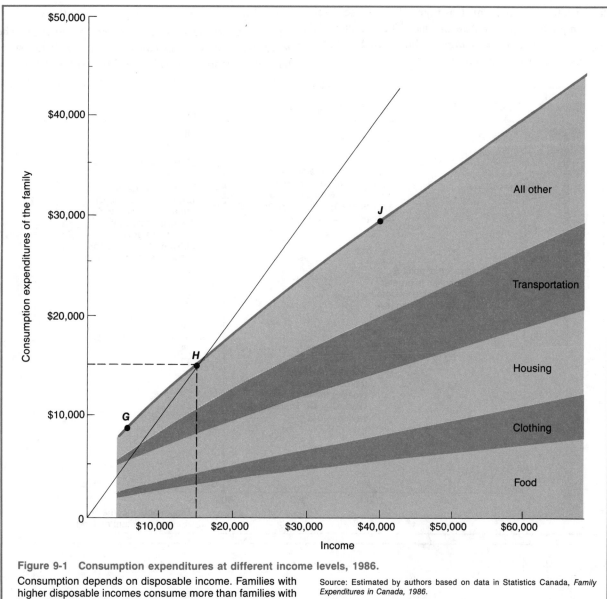

Figure 9-1 Consumption expenditures at different income levels, 1986.

Consumption depends on disposable income. Families with higher disposable incomes consume more than families with lower incomes.

Source: Estimated by authors based on data in Statistics Canada, *Family Expenditures in Canada, 1986.*

axis. Disposable income is also measured by the height of *H* on the 45° line, while consumption is the height of *D* on the consumption function. The difference — distance *HD* — is saving. This distance is used in Figure 9-3 to measure the height of point *D* on the saving function. Similarly, other points on the saving function can be derived by taking the vertical distances between the consumption function and the 45° line in Figure 9-2. Thus, the consumption function (Figure 9-2) and the sav-

ing function (Figure 9-3) are *two alternative ways of illustrating precisely the same information.*

> The *saving function* shows the relationship between disposable income and saving.

Notice that point *B* in Figure 9-3 corresponds to point *B* on the consumption function in Figure 9-2. At this break-even point, where consumption equals income, saving is zero. If we look at points even further to the left, such as point *A* in Figure 9-2, we see that consumption is greater than income. That is, there is negative saving, or *dissaving*, as illustrated by corresponding point *A* in Figure 9-3.

The Marginal Propensity to Consume

As consumers' incomes increase, they spend more. The *marginal propensity to consume*, or MPC, measures how much more. Formally, the MPC is the fraction of

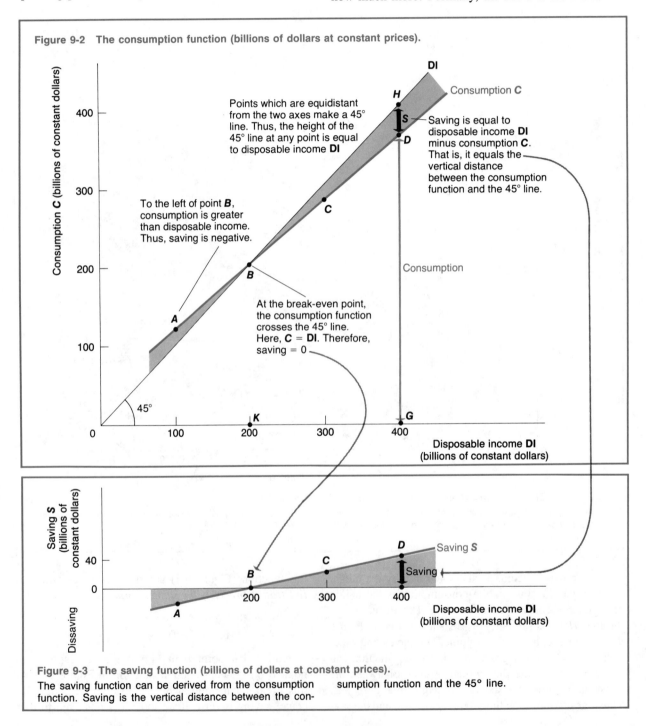

Figure 9-2 The consumption function (billions of dollars at constant prices).

Points which are equidistant from the two axes make a 45° line. Thus, the height of the 45° line at any point is equal to disposable income **DI**

Saving is equal to disposable income **DI** minus consumption **C**. That is, it equals the vertical distance between the consumption function and the 45° line.

To the left of point *B*, consumption is greater than disposable income. Thus, saving is negative.

At the break-even point, the consumption function crosses the 45° line. Here, **C** = **DI**. Therefore, saving = 0

Figure 9-3 The saving function (billions of dollars at constant prices).
The saving function can be derived from the consumption function. Saving is the vertical distance between the con-   sumption function and the 45° line.

Table 9-1   Consumption and Saving
(billions of dollars at constant prices)

	(1) DI Disposable income	(2) C Consumption	(3) Marginal propensity to consume $MPC = \dfrac{\Delta C}{\Delta DI}$	(4) S Saving (4) = (1) − (2)	(5) Marginal propensity to save $MPS = \dfrac{\Delta S}{\Delta DI}$
A	$100	$120		−20	
			$\dfrac{80}{100} = 0.8$		$\dfrac{20}{100} = 0.2$
B	200	200		0	
			$\dfrac{80}{100} = 0.8$		$\dfrac{20}{100} = 0.2$
C	300	280		+20	
			$\dfrac{80}{100} = 0.8$		$\dfrac{20}{100} = 0.2$
D	400	360		+40	

additional disposable income that is consumed:

Marginal propensity to consume =

$$\frac{[\text{change in consumption}]}{[\text{change in disposable income}]} \qquad (9\text{-}2)$$

In abbreviated notation, this is written:

$$MPC = \frac{\Delta C}{\Delta DI} \qquad (9\text{-}3)$$

where the Greek letter Δ means "change in."

If we think of a small $1 increase in disposable income, this formula reduces to:

MPC = the fraction of a $1 increase in
         disposable income that is consumed

This is an obvious restatement of the idea: If your income increases by $1, and your consumption increases by $0.80 as a result, then your MPC is $0.80/$1.00 = 0.80.

Similarly,

Marginal propensity to save (MPS)

$$= \frac{\text{change in saving}}{\text{change in disposable income}}$$

$$= \frac{\Delta S}{\Delta DI} \qquad (9\text{-}4)$$

Or:

MPS = the fraction of a $1 increase in disposable
         income that is saved

In passing, note that economists use the term *marginal* to mean "extra" or "additional." As we shall see in a later chapter, "marginal revenue" means additional revenue, and marginal cost means additional cost.

In Figure 9-4, the MPC is illustrated. It is equal to the vertical change in consumption divided by the horizontal change in disposable income. Thus, the MPC is equal to the slope of the consumption function. Consequently, if the MPC is constant (as it is in our simple numerical example), then the consumption function has a constant slope; it is a straight line. Similarly, the MPS is the slope of the saving function. In our example, the MPC is 0.8 and the MPS is 0.2 (Table 9-1, columns 3 and 5). Observe that

$$MPC + MPS = 1 \qquad (9\text{-}5)$$

This must be the case. If a person gets $1 more in income, whatever is not consumed is saved. For example, if the MPC were only 0.75, an increase of $1 in

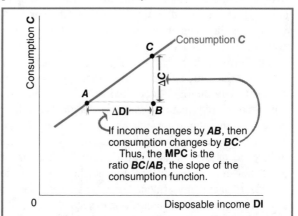

Figure 9-4   The marginal propensity to consume.
Since the slope of the consumption function gives the MPC, the consumption function is a straight line if the MPC is constant.

income would lead to an increase of 75¢ in consumption. The remaining 25¢ would be saved; the MPS would be 0.25.

In our hypothetical example, the MPC of 0.8 is somewhat lower than the long-run MPC in Canada. Over long periods of time, consumers have increased their consumption expenditures by more than 90¢ for every $1.00 increase in disposable income. However, in the short run, the response of consumption is less strong; it takes time for people to adjust to a change in income. An MPC of 0.8 may be taken as an approximation of the MPC during short-run business fluctuations. Appendix 9-A provides further details on the consumption function in the long run and the short.

THE SIMPLEST EQUILIBRIUM: AN ECONOMY WITH NO GOVERNMENT OR INTERNATIONAL TRANSACTIONS

Keynes' objective was to demonstrate that laissez-faire market economies contain a fundamental defect: They may come to rest at a very high rate of unemployment. In order to explain this central proposition as clearly and as quickly as possible, we look at a bare-bones economy, with no international trade, no government spending, no taxes, no depreciation, and no retained corporate profits. We also assume that *domestic* and *national* incomes are the same. Thus, in this very simple economy, GDP = NDP = NNP = national income = disposable income. In other words, all the receipts from domestic product flow through the business sector to become the disposable income of the household sector; there are none of the subtractions explained in detail back in Chapter 6. As in the previous chapter, we use the symbol Y to denote real domestic product.

Furthermore, the absence of government and international transactions means that there are only two groups to buy the final goods and services of the economy—households that buy consumption goods and businesses that invest in plant, machinery, and other types of capital. (We reiterate that, when macroeconomists write of investment, they mean acquisitions of new equipment, plant, housing, and additional inventories. They do not include financial investment, such as the purchase of stocks or bonds, nor the acquisition of second-hand plant, equipment, or housing.)

To make the task even simpler, we initially assume that the quantity of plant, equipment, and other capital demanded by business is a constant $40 billion. We do not claim that this assumption is realistic. Indeed, as we have seen in previous chapters, investment is one of the most volatile components of GDP. However, this simple assumption will allow us to complete the main argument as quickly as possible, and then we will be in a position to consider what happens when investment demand does change.

The $40 billion of investment demand can be added to personal consumption expenditures to get aggregate demand or *aggregate expenditures*, as shown in Table 9-2, column 5, and in Figure 9-5. In this diagram, domestic product Y rather than disposable income DI is shown on the horizontal axis and on the 45° line. We may substitute Y for DI in this diagram, because Y = DI in the simple economy we are considering here.

Equilibrium occurs where aggregate expenditures equal domestic product. Comparing columns 1 and 5 in Table 9-2, we see that this occurs at an output of $400 billion. The same equilibrium of $400 billion is shown in Figure 9-5 at point E, where the aggregate expenditures function cuts the 45° domestic product line.

To see why this is the equilibrium, consider why aggregate demand would not be sufficient to buy a larger quantity of output — say the $500 billion measured from the origin to point L on the horizontal axis, and also vertically from L to point N on the 45° line. The right-hand part of Figure 9-5 shows a magnified view of domestic product LN, which is made up of the dark coloured bar, plus the light coloured bar, plus the gray bar. But aggregate expenditures are less than that. They are just the dark coloured bar (consumer expenditures) plus the light coloured bar (investment demand). Thus, at an output of $500 billion, the amount we produce (domestic product) exceeds the quantity of goods and services demanded (aggregate expenditures).

What happens to the excess production, shown by the gray bar? It remains unsold; it piles up on retailers' shelves and in warehouses. It represents **undesired inventory accumulation**. As unwanted goods accumulate, retailers, wholesalers, and other businesses cut back on their orders. Production falls. Moreover, it continues to contract as long as the aggregate expenditures line remains below the 45° domestic product line. In other words, it continues to fall until the economy reaches equilibrium E, where domestic product Y = aggregate expenditures AE, and there is no further pressure of unsold goods. Therefore, $400 billion is the equilibrium quantity of output.

Table 9-2　Equilibrium Domestic Product
(billions of dollars)

	(1) Domestic product (equals disposable income in this simple economy)	(2) C Consumption demand	(3) S Saving (3) = (1) − (2)	(4) I* Investment demand (assumed constant)	(5) AE Aggregate expenditure = C + I* (5) = (2) + (4)	(6) Relation of aggregate expenditure (5) to domestic product (1)	(7) Economy will:
H	$200	$200	0	$40	$240	Higher	Expand
J	300	280	20	40	320	Higher	Expand
K	**400**	**360**	**40**	**40**	**400**	**Same**	**Stay at equilibrium**
L	500	440	60	40	480	Lower	Contract
M	600	520	80	40	520	Lower	Contract

At a disequilibrium quantity of domestic product, such as $500 billion, it is important to distinguish between *actual investment* and *desired investment*. Actual investment — the quantity which shows up in the official national income accounts studied in Chapter 6—includes all investment in plant, equipment, housing, and inventories, whether that investment is desired or not. Thus, for an economy producing at $500 billion, the investment figure that appears in the national income accounts will be the light coloured bar *plus* the gray bar. (''Gray bar goods'' for which there is no demand, and which therefore pile up as *undesired inventory accumulation*, have clearly been produced during the year, and must therefore be included in the domestic product statistics.) In contrast with actual investment, desired investment — also known as *investment demand*, *planned investment*, or *intended investment* — is the only investment which businesses want, that is, the light coloured bar. In order to keep straight the important distinction between desired investment and actual investment, we use the symbol *I** with an asterisk to represent desired investment. As in Chapter 6, a plain *I* will stand for actual investment — that is, investment as it shows up in the national income accounts.

Actual investment I is the amount of new plant, equipment, and housing acquired during a time period, plus the increase in inventories. All inventory accumulation is included, *whether the inventories were desired or not*.

*Desired investment I** — also known as *investment demand*, *planned investment*, or *intended investment* — is the amount of new plant, equipment, and housing acquired during the period, plus *additions to inventories which businesses wanted to acquire*. It excludes undesired inventory accumulation.

Undesired inventory accumulation is actual investment (*I*) less desired investment (*I**).

Just as an output initially greater than equilibrium results in contraction, so an output initially less than equilibrium generates expansion. Consider an output of $300 billion, at point *J*. Here, the aggregate expenditures line is higher than the 45° domestic product line. Buyers want to purchase more goods than are currently being produced. Retailers and wholesalers find it difficult to keep goods in stock. Inventories are run down below their desired levels; there is an **undesired decrease in inventories**. Because retailers and wholesalers want to meet the large demand and rebuild their inventories, they step up their orders. To fill their larger orders, manufacturers and other producers expand production toward the equilibrium, *E*.

The *undesired decrease in inventories* is equal to desired investment (*I**) minus actual investment (*I*). It exists when undesired inventory accumulation is negative.

Figure 9-5 Equilibrium domestic product.

Point E represents equilibrium, with output of $400 billion. Here, aggregate expenditure equals domestic product Y. A higher rate of production is not stable, as we can see by looking at the magnified version on the right, showing what happens when domestic product is $500 billion. Domestic product equals the vertical distance to the 45° line. For most of this product, there is a market. The quantity of consumer goods demanded is equal to the dark coloured bar. The quantity of investment goods demnded is equal to the light coloured bar. But for the gray bar, there is no demand. Unsold goods pile up in the warehouses. Businesses cut back on production. Output falls to its equilibrium of $400 billion.

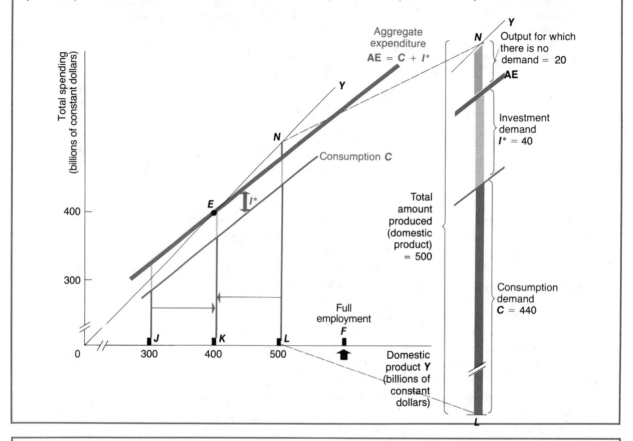

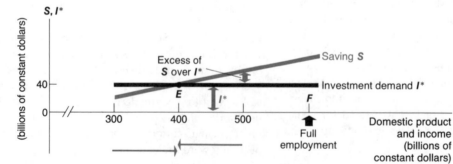

Figure 9-6 The equilibrium of saving and desired investment.

Equilibrium occurs at output of $400 billion, where saving equals desired investment. At a greater domestic product, such as $500 billion, disequilibrium exists. Since the leakages from the spending stream (in the form of saving) are greater than the injections (in the form of investment), domestic product falls toward its equilibrium at $400 billion.

EQUILIBRIUM WITH LARGE-SCALE UNEMPLOYMENT

Now we are in a position to illustrate Keynes' key contention, that the *equilibrium domestic product need not be at the quantity necessary to ensure full employment.* Equilibrium domestic product is determined by aggregate expenditures, as illustrated by point E in Figure 9-5. On the other hand, the full-employment domestic product represents what the economy *can* produce with its current resources of labour, land, and capital; it is shown at domestic product F. The situation which Keynes feared, and which he believed would be a common outcome of a free-market economy, is the one shown in this diagram. Equilibrium domestic product at E is far less than the full-employment quantity at F. (See the quotation from Keynes that introduces this chapter.)

AN ALTERNATIVE APPROACH: SAVING AND INVESTMENT

Figure 9-5 showed how equilibrium domestic product is determined in the simple economy (with no government, etc.) by putting together consumption expenditures C

and desired investment I^*. But we have already seen that the saving function is an alternative way of presenting *exactly the same information* as in the consumption function. It is therefore not surprising that, as an alternative to C plus I^*, we can bring saving S together with desired investment I^* to determine equilibrium domestic product. This is done in Figure 9-6. in the simple economy, *equilibrium occurs when saving equals investment demand* — that is, at point E where domestic product is $400 billion. We may confirm in Table 9-2 that saving (column 3) equals desired investment (column 4) at the same $400 billion equilibrium output at which aggregate expenditures (column 5) equal domestic product (column 1).

The Circular Flow of Expenditure: Leakages and Injections

To explain *why* equilibrium occurs when saving equals investment demand, we call again on the circular flow of payments previously used in Chapters 3 and 6. In Figure 9-7, we see the *extremely* simple economy in which there is no investment demand and in which consumers buy all the goods produced. Suppose that producers sell $400 billion of goods during an initial period.

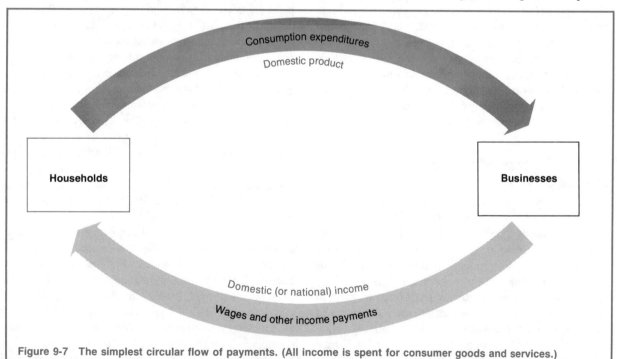

Figure 9-7   The simplest circular flow of payments. (All income is spent for consumer goods and services.)

The simplest economy is one in which people consume all their incomes. Incomes are used to buy consumer goods and services. In turn, the receipts from the sale of consumer goods and services are again paid out as incomes, in the form of wages, salaries, etc. Once more, people use all their incomes to buy consumer goods and services.

In turn, they pay this $400 billion to households in the form of wages, salaries, rents, and other incomes, as shown in the lower loop of the diagram. Suppose, further, that the households turn around and spend all their $400 billion of income on consumer goods in the upper loop. Once more, the producers sell $400 billion in goods and services, and once more they pay out this amount in incomes to the households. Round and round this $400 billion of payments go; domestic product is stable at this level.

Now let us introduce complications, starting with saving. Suppose that instead of consuming all their incomes of $400 billion, people decide that they would like to save $40 billion. They spend only $360 billion on consumer goods. Producers have made $400 billion in goods, but they sell only $360 billion. Unsold goods pile up, and producers cut back on production. When they do so, they pay out less in wages and other incomes. The circular flow of domestic product and income is reduced. Thus, saving represents a leakage from the circular spending stream; it acts as a drag on domestic product and income.

Now, consider investment demand. Suppose that businesses decide to increase their capital stock and that they order $40 billion worth of machinery. In response to the demand, $40 billion in machinery is produced. The machinery companies pay out the $40 billion in wages, salaries, and other incomes. Incomes rise, people consume more, and the circular flow of domestic product and income increases. Investment therefore acts as a stimulus to domestic product and income.

The Equilibrium of Saving and Desired Investment

Thus, in terms of their effect on aggregate expenditures and output, saving and investment have offsetting effects. Saving is a *leakage* from the circular spending stream; an increase in the desire to save leads to a decrease in domestic product. Investment demand represents an *injection* into the circular spending stream; an increase in desired investment leads to an increase in domestic product. Equilibrium exists when the forces of contraction and expansion are in balance, that is, when saving equals desired investment—as it does in Figure 9-6 at point *E*, where domestic product is $400 billion. At any greater domestic income, such as $500 billion, the leakage from the circular flow of spending — in the form of saving — exceeds the injection of investment

spending, and output decreases. If, on the other hand, domestic product is initially at a point to the left of the $400 billion equilibrium, the injection of investment demand exceeds the saving leakage, and domestic product increases. This can be visualized in Figure 9-8: When more is pumped in at the investment end, the income flow becomes greater. This causes more leakages into saving at the other end. The flow stabilizes when the injections and leakages are equal.

Some saving and investment decisions are made by the same people. For example, business executives may decide not to pay dividends. Instead they may save their profits in order to have the funds to buy more equipment. In this case, the decision to save can be closely tied to the decision to invest. But sometimes, saving and investment decisions are made by different groups. Households save to buy a new car, to send the children to university, or for retirement; they save without investing. (Remember: we are talking here about real investment—the purchase of new buildings or equipment—and not about the acquisition of bonds, for example.) Investment decisions are made principally by business executives; they buy additional plant and equipment when their profit prospects are good, even though they may have to borrow to do so. In this case, they invest more than they save. The question therefore arises, what are the forces that tend to bring saving and investment into equilibrium?

Here, there is a sharp difference between Keynesian economics and classical economics. In Keynes' view, the separation of saving and investment decisions meant that *there is no assurance that, if an economy begins at full employment, desired investment will be as great as saving.* If it is not—as illustrated at full-employment output *F* in Figure 9-6 — then domestic product will decrease and unemployment will result. In other words, domestic income will fall by a sufficient amount to make saving equal to desired investment.

[In classical economics, there is an alternative mechanism that can equate saving and desired investment — namely, the *financial market*. For the moment, let us remain a bit mysterious about the financial market. What goes on inside the financial market, according to the classical view, will be explained in Appendix 9-A. For the moment, it suffices to say that, according to Keynes, the operation of financial markets would not ensure full employment. If consumers wanted to save more than business executives wanted to invest, the result would be a contraction in output and in large-scale unemployment, as illustrated in Figure 9-6.]

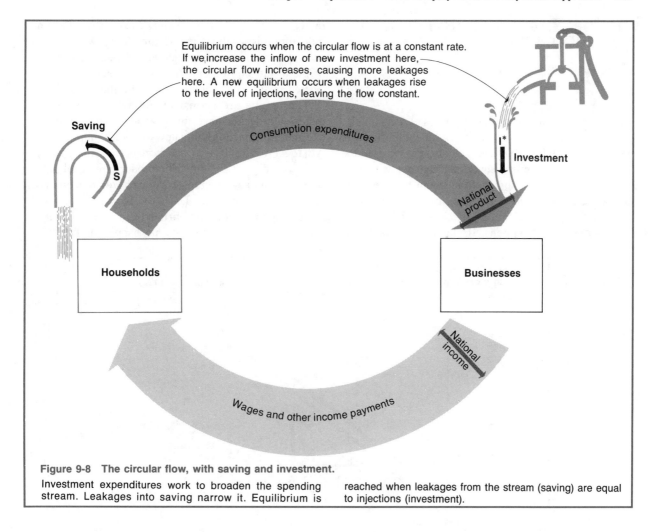

Equilibrium occurs when the circular flow is at a constant rate. If we increase the inflow of new investment here, the circular flow increases, causing more leakages here. A new equilibrium occurs when leakages rise to the level of injections, leaving the flow constant.

Saving

S

Consumption expenditures

I*

Investment

National product

Households

Businesses

National income

Wages and other income payments

Figure 9-8   The circular flow, with saving and investment.
Investment expenditures work to broaden the spending stream. Leakages into saving narrow it. Equilibrium is reached when leakages from the stream (saving) are equal to injections (investment).

The two approaches in Figures 9-5 and 9-6 are exact equivalents; either of those diagrams can be derived from the other. To summarize, we can state the condition for equilibrium in several different ways:

1. Equilibrium exists when domestic output is equal to aggregate expenditures. This is the *output-expenditures approach* to determining equilibrium and is illustrated by point E in Figure 9-5.

2. Equilibrium exists when actual investment I equals desired investment I^* — that is, when inventories are at their desired level and there is no undesired accumulation of inventories such as that shown by the gray bar in Figure 9-5.

3. Equilibrium exists when saving and desired invest-

ment are equal, as illustrated by point E in Figure 9-6. This is the *leakages-injections approach*.

These three statements are different ways of expressing the same basic point.

The reason for unemployment may be stated in two alternative ways. There will be an *unemployment equilibrium if*:

1. Desired aggregate expenditures AE are too low to buy the full-employment quantity of domestic product. For example, at full-employment point F in Figure 9-5, AE are less than NP.

2. The injections of desired investment are less than the leakages into saving when domestic product is at the full-employment quantity. For example, at full-employment point F in Figure 9-6, I^* is below S.

CHANGES IN DESIRED INVESTMENT: THE MULTIPLIER

Investment is a flighty bird.

J.R. Hicks

The basic Keynesian diagrams (Figures 9-5 and 9-6) illustrate how the economy can reach an equilibrium at less than full employment. But they also can be used to illustrate how economic activity can change, with the economy periodically moving from boom to recession and back. During the business cycle, investment is quite unstable.

Consider what happens if desired investment increases. Suppose that business executives become more optimistic about the future. They will plan to expand their operations, undertaking more investment in plant and equipment. Suppose, specifically, that desired investment increases by $20 billion.

The results are shown in Figure 9-9. When the increase in desired investment is added, the aggregate expenditures function shifts upward by $20 billion, from AE_1 to AE_2. Equilibrium once more occurs where aggregate expenditures and domestic product are equal—that is, where the new aggregate expenditures function AE cuts the 45° line at H. Thus, the increase in desired investment moves the equilibrium from E to H. Observe that something very important has happened. The equi-

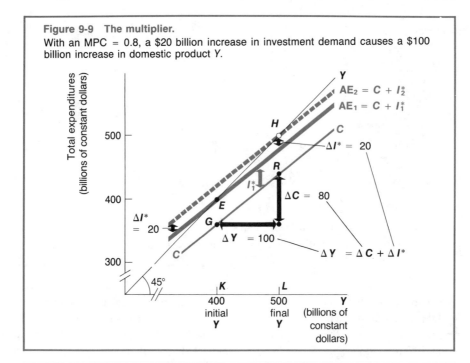

Figure 9-9 The multiplier.
With an MPC = 0.8, a $20 billion increase in investment demand causes a $100 billion increase in domestic product Y.

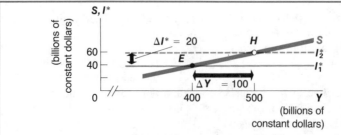

Figure 9-10 The multiplier: saving and investment approach.
With an MPS = 0.2, an increase of $20 billion in desired investment (from I_1^* to I_2^*) causes an increase of $100 billion in domestic product.

librium domestic product has increased *by $100 billion, which is far more than the $20 billion increase in investment demand.*

How can that be? The answer is this. As businesses build more factories and order more equipment, people are put to work producing the factories and equipment. They earn more wages. As their incomes rise, they increase their consumption expenditures. Thus, the nation produces not only more capital goods, such as factories and equipment, but *also* more consumer goods. Domestic product rises by more than investment. Specifically, as the equilibrium moves from E to H, domestic product increases by $100 billion. This includes not only the $20 billion increase in investment spending on capital goods (shown as ∆*I** in Figure 9-9), but also an increase of $80 billion in spending on consumer goods (shown as ∆*C*). These are the additional goods consumers buy as their incomes rise and they accordingly move up the consumption function from G to R.

Thus, the $20 billion increase in desired investment has a *multiplied* effect on domestic product. The relationship between the increase in domestic product and the increase in desired investment is known as the ***investment multiplier*** or, more simply, as the ***multiplier***. Formally, it is defined:

Investment Multiplier =
$$\frac{\text{change in equilibrium domestic product}}{\text{change in desired investment}} \quad (9\text{-}7)$$

In our illustration, equilibrium domestic product rises by $100 billion when desired investment increases by $20 billion. Therefore, the multiplier is 5.

The Multiplier Process: A More Detailed Look

The multiplier process may be better understood by looking in more detail at what happens when there is an additional $20 billion of investment expenditures on capital goods. The *direct impact* is a $20 billion increase in domestic product; more machines and other capital goods are produced. But this is not the end of the story. The $20 billion spent for plant and equipment goes in the form of wages, rents, profits, and other incomes to those who provide the resources used to produce the capital goods. In other words, disposable incomes are $20 billion higher. (Remember, we are dealing with a highly simplified economy in which there is no government to take a tax bite.) Consumers now spend most of

this increase in their disposable income, with the precise amount depending on their marginal propensity to consume (MPC). For example, if the MPC is 0.8, consumers are *induced* to spend $16 billion more, as shown in the "second round" increase in the domestic product in Table 9-3 and Figure 9-11.

But again, this is not the end of the story. When consumers spend $16 billion more for clothing, food and other consumer goods, that $16 billion in spending

Table 9-3   The Multiplier Process: Effect on Domestic Product of an Increase in Investment Expenditure (billions of dollars)

Round	Spending on	Resulting change in aggregate expenditure and domestic product	
First	Investment	20.0	Direct initial effect
Second	Consumption	16.0	Induced increase in consumption = 80.0
Third	Consumption	12.8	
Fourth	Consumption	10.2	
Fifth	Consumption	8.2	
•		•	
•		•	
•		•	
	Total increase in domestic product	100.0	

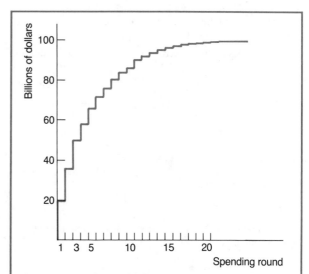

Figure 9-11   The multiplier process: The build-up of domestic product.

This figure portrays the various rounds of spending listed in Table 9-3, which result from an initial increase of $20 billion in investment in round 1. Notice how domestic product builds up toward its equilibrium increase of $100 billion.

becomes income for producers. Thus, the incomes of textile workers, farmers, and others who produce consumer goods rise by $16 billion. With an MPC of 0.8, these people spend $16 billion × 0.8 or $12.8 billion. Once more, domestic product has risen, this time by $12.8 billion. The story goes on and on, with each round of consumer spending giving rise to another, smaller round.

Observe that, with an MPC = 0.8, the total spending resulting from each dollar of initial investment expenditure forms the series $1 × (1 + 0.8 + 0.8² + 0.8³ . . .). It can be shown[2] that the sum of such a series is:

$$\$1\left(\frac{1}{1-0.8}\right) = \$5 \qquad (9\text{-}8)$$

That is:

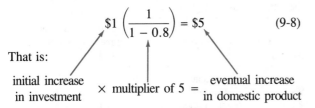

initial increase in investment × multiplier of 5 = eventual increase in domestic product

In this case, because the MPC is 0.8, the multiplier is 5. More generally:

$$\text{Multiplier} = \frac{1}{1 - \text{MPC}} \qquad (9\text{-}9)$$

Thus, the size of the multiplier depends on the size of the MPC, that is, on the slope of the consumption function. The steeper the consumption function—that is, the higher the MPC—the larger is the multiplier.

Observe also how Table 9-3 and Figure 9-11 correspond to Figure 9-9. Each shows that a $20 billion increase in investment causes a $100 billion increase in domestic product. This $100 billion is made up of the original $20 billion increase in investment plus $80 bil-

■ ■ ■ ■ ■
[2] Let c stand for the MPC. As long as c is less than 1 (in our case, 0.8), then the sume of the series

$$1 + c + c^2 + c^3 + c^3 \ldots = \frac{1}{1-c}.$$

This can be shown by actually doing the division on the right side. In other words, divide 1 by $(1 - c)$, as follows:

$$
\begin{array}{r}
1 + c + c^2 \ldots \\
1 - c\overline{)1} \\
\underline{1 - c} \\
c \\
\underline{c - c^2} \\
c^2 \ldots
\end{array}
$$

lion in *induced* consumption that occurs as people spend more when their disposable incomes rise.

The Multiplier Works Both Ways

We have just seen how an increase in investment (of $20 billion) leads to a multiplied increase in domestic product (of $100 billion). A similar multiplied effect occurs when investment decreases. For example, a "first round" reduction of $20 billion in investment causes a direct reduction of $20 billion in domestic product and income. With smaller incomes, consumers will cut their spending by $16 billion in the "second round." They will buy fewer books, shirts, or tickets to baseball games. This in turn will reduce the incomes of authors, textile workers, and baseball teams. As a result, their consumption will fall. Just as in the earlier example, there will be a whole series of "rounds." The sum of all these rounds will be a $100 billion decrease in domestic product.

The Multiplier: The Saving-Investment Approach

Just as the saving-investment diagram may be used to show an unemployment equilibrium, so it may also be used to illustrate the multiplier. This is done in Figure 9-10, which once again provides exactly the same information as the diagram above it. When desired investment increases by $20 billion, from I_1^* to I_2^*, equilibrium moves from E to H. Once again, observe that domestic product increases by more than the initial increase in investment. Indeed, income increases until people are willing to increase their saving by the full $20 billion injected into the spending stream by the new investment. People are not willing to increase their saving by this $20 billion until their incomes have increased by $100 billion. Remember: their marginal propensity to save (MPS) is 1/5; they save only $1 out of every additional $5 they earn. Thus, from this other perspective, we confirm that equilibrium income rises by $100 billion. Appendix 9-B provides a further elaboration of the saving-investment approach.

With the saving-investment approach, the multiplier may be defined in terms of the MPS rather than the MPC. To do so, first note that income is either consumed or saved. Therefore:

$$\text{MPS} = 1 - \text{MPC} \qquad (9\text{-}10, \text{ from } 9\text{-}5)$$

Thus, equation 9-9 can be rewritten:

$$\text{Multiplier} = \frac{1}{\text{MPS}} \qquad (9\text{-}11)$$

However, it should be stressed that output increases by the amount shown in equation 9-11—or in similar equation 9-9—*only if the economy is the very simplifed one we have considered so far.*

In practice, the increase in real domestic product will be smaller than indicated by equations 9-9 and 9-11 because of several complications:

1. Part of the increase in demand may show up in terms of *higher prices*, not in terms of larger real domestic product.

2. *Taxes* and *imports* act as additional leakages from the spending stream. These additional leakages depress the size of the multiplier, even in a world in which prices are stable.

The second point will be explored in Chapter 10. In this chapter, we look at the first.

THE MULTIPLIER WHEN PRICES CHANGE

The Keynesian multiplier model was developed as a way of explaining how output and employment can change as spending changes. In the simple form presented thus far, an increase in spending shows up entirely as an increase in real output. This means that the economy is moving along the horizontal section of the aggregate supply curve, where prices don't change.

When Prices Are Rigid

Figure 9-12 illustrates this fixed-price case, and shows how the aggregate expenditures approach of this chapter is related to the aggregate demand-aggregate supply approach of the previous chapter.

The top panel repeats the idea of the multiplier. A $20 billion increase in investment leads to a $20 billion upward shift of the aggregate expenditure line, and to a $100 billion increase in output as equilibrium moves from E to H.

The lower panel shows the corresponding points of equilibrium in an aggregate demand-aggregate supply diagram. The initial increase of $20 billion in investment spending, plus the induced increase of $80 billion in consumer spending, means that the aggregate demand curve shifts to the right by $100 billion. Domestic product also increases by $100 billion as equilibrium moves from E to H.

Observe that an increase in desired investment leads to an *upward* shift in the aggregate expenditures line AE (top panel), and to a *rightward* shift of the aggregate demand curve AD (lower panel).

Changing Prices: An Upward-Sloping Aggregate Supply

Once the economy enters the range where the aggregate supply function slopes upward, we can no longer ignore price changes. In Figure 9-13, the lower panel—showing what happens to prices—becomes an essential part of the story.

The lower panel again shows how the aggregate demand curve shifts to the right by $100 billion. However, point H can no longer be the equilibrium, because it's not on the aggregate supply curve. Instead, the new equilibrium in Figure 9-13 is at J. The $100 billion increase in aggregate demand shows up as a $60 billion increase in real domestic product, with the remainder showing up in terms of an increase in prices (from P_1 to P_2).

The extent to which spending will be reflected in prices rather than output depends on the slopes of the aggregate supply and aggregate demand curves. For example, if the aggregate supply curve AS were steeper, aggregate demand would generate a smaller increase in output and a larger increase in prices.

Now let's double back to see what's happening in the upper aggregate expenditures diagram. H can no longer be the equilibrium, since part of the additional spending is being dissipated in terms of higher prices. As prices rise, there will be a smaller increase in aggregate real expenditures — the amount of goods and services that consumers and investors are buying. Specifically, the rise in prices will mean that real spending, as measured by the aggregate expenditures line, will rise only to AE_3, rather than AE_2. The result will be an equilibrium at J. Finally, it is possible that all the additional spending will show up entirely in terms of higher prices, not additional output. This will happen if the aggregate supply curve is vertical. In this case, an increase in investment spending will not cause any increase in real output at all. The AE curve won't rise at all, but will remain at AE_1.

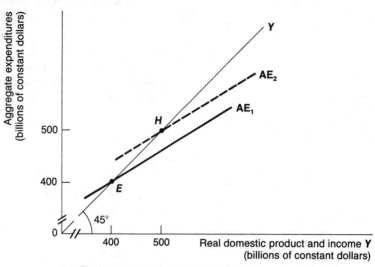

(a) **Real aggregate expenditure when prices are rigid.**

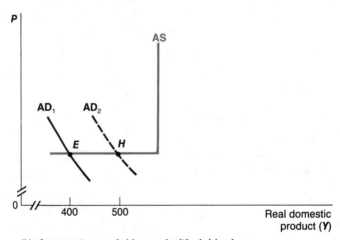

(b) **Aggregate supply/demand with rigid prices.**

Figure 9-12 The economy with rigid prices.

The upper panel repeats the multiplier idea in Figure 9-10. A $20 billion increase in investment spending causes a $100 billion increase in output.

The lower panel shows what's happening with the aggregate demand/aggregate supply approach. As expenditures increase, the aggregate demand function shifts to the right by $100 billion and equilibrium output increases from E to H. The full $100 billion in additional spending shows up as a $100 billion increase in real output.

KEY POINTS

1. During the Great Depression of the 1930s, British economist John Maynard Keynes put forward a new theory of unemployment, arguing that:

   (a) A market economy can come to rest at an equilibrium with large-scale unemployment.

   (b) The cause of unemployment is insufficient aggregate demand.

   (c) The most straightforward cure for unemployment is an increase in government spending. (This point will be deferred until Chapter 10.)

2. The components of aggregate demand are:

   (a) personal consumption expenditures

   (b) investment demand (that is, the demand for

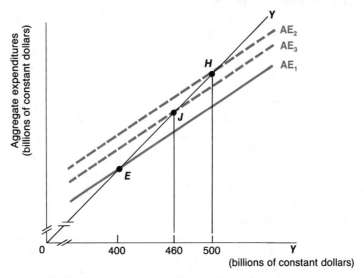

(a) **Real aggregate expenditures when prices rise.**

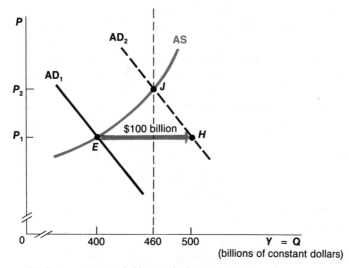

(b) **Aggregate supply/demand when prices rise.**

Figure 9-13   An upward-sloping aggregate supply curve.

If the aggregate supply curve slopes upward, then a rightward shift of $100 billion in the aggregate demand curve will not cause a full $100 billion increase in output. In the lower panel, equilibrium moves to J, not H.

As spending is dissipated in paying higher prices, real expenditures are pushed part of the way back down, from AE_2 to AE_3 in the upper panel. The new equilibrium is at J in both panels.

buildings, equipment, and additional inventories)

(c) government purchases of goods and services

(d) Net exports (that is, exports minus imports)

3. This chapter explains the Keynesian theory of an unemployment equilibrium in a simple economy with only two types of spending for final goods,

namely, consumption and investment.

4. Consumption expenditures depend primarily on disposable personal income. As incomes rise, people consume more. The change in consumption, as a fraction of a change in disposable income, is known as the *marginal propensity to consume* (MPC).

5. Equilibrium domestic product occurs where the aggregate expenditures function cuts the 45° line. A larger domestic product would be unsustainable, since expendiutures would fall short of production and unsold goods would pile up in inventories.

6. In Keynesian theory, equilibrium domestic product may be less than the full-employment quantity.

7. There are several alternative ways of stating the condition for equilibrium. Equilibrium exists when:
   (a) Desired aggregate expenditures and domestic product are equal — that is, where the aggregate expenditures function cuts the 45° domestic product line (Figure 9-5).
   (b) Inventories are at their desired level — that is, when actual investment equals desired investment and there is no undesired buildup or reduction in inventories (Figure 9-5).
   (c) Desired investment and saving are equal (Figure 9-6).

8. An increase in desired investment raises domestic product and income. This induces people to consume more. In the simple economy, domestic product increases by the rise in investment times the multiplier, where the multiplier is:

$$\text{Multiplier} = \frac{1}{1 - \text{MPC}}$$

Because saving equals income minus consumption, Marginal propensity to save $= 1 - \text{MPC}$
Thus, the multiplier in the simple economy may alternatively be expressed as:

$$\text{Multiplier} = \frac{1}{\text{MPS}}$$

9. In practice, the increase in output will be smaller than indicated by these two multiplier equations because of several complications:
   (a) Part of the increase in demand may show up in terms of *higher prices*, not in terms of larger real domestic product.
   (b) *Taxes* and *imports* act as additional leakages from the spending stream. (This point will be explained in Chapter 10.)

10. If the aggregate supply function slopes upward to the right, only part of any increase in aggregate demand shows up in terms of larger output. Part goes to pay higher prices. In such circumstances, the formulas shown in point 8 represent the rightward shift of the aggregate demand function (for example, from *H* to *K* in Figure 9-13). The increase in real output is less than this rightward shift in demand.

KEY CONCEPTS

consumption function
saving function
break-even point at which consumption equals income
45° line
marginal propensity to consume (MPC)
marginal propensity to save (MPS)

aggregate expenditures
desired investment, or investment demand, or planned investment (I*)
actual investment (I)
undesired inventory accumulation
undesired inventory decreases
unemployment equilibrium

saving-investment approach
circular flow of spending
leakage
injection
output-expenditures approach
leakages-injections approach
multiplier

PROBLEMS

9-1. Draw a diagram showing the consumption function, the aggregate expenditures function, and the 45° line. What quantity of output *Y* represents the equilibrium? Explain why a larger *Y* would be unsustainable and would lead to a contraction of production. If domestic product initially is smaller than the equilibrium quantity, explain why it will expand.

9-2. The consumption function and the saving function are two alternative ways of presenting the same information. The text explains how the saving function can be derived from the consumption function. Draw a saving function first, and show how the consumption function can be derived from it.

9-3. Draw a diagram showing desired investment and

the saving function. What is the equilibrium domestic product? Explain why a higher domestic product would be unsustainable. Explain also why domestic product will expand if it initially is smaller than the equilibrium quantity.

9-4. The mathematical formula for the multiplier shows that a high MPC causes a high multiplier. By tracing the effects of $20 billion in additional investment through a number of "rounds" of spending, show that the multiplier is higher with an MPC of 0.9 than with an MPC of 0.8. (Use Table 9-3 on page 161 to start.)

9-5. On a sheet of graph paper, draw a diagram similar to Figure 9-10. (Make the diagram *large* so that you will be able to see what you are doing.) Following Figure 9-10, show the multiplier effects of a $20 billion increase in investment demand when the MPS = 0.2. Now suppose that the MPS increases to 0.5. In colour, draw in a new saving function that goes through the same initial equilibrium E. When investment demand increases by $20 billion, what now is the new equilibrium domestic product? What is the size of the multiplier now?

9-6. What is the difference between actual investment (I) and desired investment (I*)? What happens if desired investment is greater than actual investment? Why?

9-7. Consider an economy with the relationship between consumption and income shown in the accompanying table.
(a) Fill in the blanks in the Saving column.

(b) What is the MPC? The MPS?
(c) Investment demand is originally $40 billion. Fill in the blanks in the Initial aggregate expenditures column.
(d) What is the equilibrium domestic product?
(e) Now assume that desired investment rises to $60 billion. What does this do to aggregate expenditures? (Fill in the Later aggregate expenditures column.) What is equilibrium domestic product now?
(f) Comparing your answers to (d) and (e), find the multiplier.

Disposable income = DP (billions)	Consumption (billions)	Saving (billions)	Initial aggregate expenditures (billions)	Later aggregate expenditures (billions)
$100	$ 90	_____	_____	_____
$110	$ 97.5	_____	_____	_____
$120	$105	_____	_____	_____
$130	$112.5	_____	_____	_____
$140	$120	_____	_____	_____
$150	$127.5	_____	_____	_____
$160	$135	_____	_____	_____
$170	$142.5	_____	_____	_____
$180	$150	_____	_____	_____

9-8. Redraw Figure 9-13 with a vertical, "classical" aggregate supply curve. Now suppose that businesses spend $20 billion more on plant and equipment. What happens to equilibrium real domestic product as a result?

Appendix 9-A

■ ■ ■ ■ ■

Consumption in the Short Run and the Long

Over long periods, consumption responds strongly to increases in disposable income. The consumption function is steep and the marginal propensity to consume (MPC) is more than 0.9. However, during short-run periods when disposable income is fluctuating, consumption responds more weakly; the MPC is smaller.

The distinction between the short-run and long-run consumption function is illustrated in Figure 9-14. During periods when incomes increase slowly and steadily, consumption moves up along the steep long-run consumption function—that is, along path FGH. However, as incomes fall during recessions, consumption does not

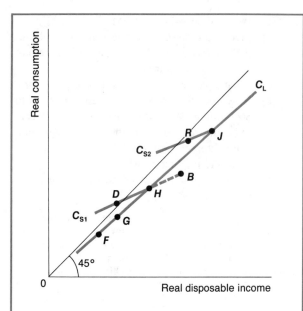

Figure 9-14   The long- and short-run consumption functions.

The short-run consumption function is flatter than the long-run function. During a recession, consumption moves to the left along a short-run consumption function. Over time, the short-run consumption function shifts up.

retreat from H back toward G. Rather, it declines less sharply, following the short-run consumption function C_{S_1} from H toward D. Then, as the economy recovers, consumption again follows the relatively flat consumption function from D back toward H.

If, after an extended period of prosperity, the economy has reached J, a recession will once again result in a movement along a relatively flat short-run consumption function — in this case, along C_{S_2} toward R. In brief:

1. The long-run consumption function is steep, with an MPC of more than 0.9. Over long periods of time, saving is quite small and stable as a fraction of disposable income. The long-run consumption function is a straight line going through the origin.
2. During the business cycle, the consumption function is flatter. (An MPC of 0.75 or 0.8 is a reasonable number to use when talking about an average recession.) As time passes, the short-run consumption function shifts upward from C_{S_1} to C_{S_2}, and so on.

Economists have identified some of the important variables that can affect consumption and explain the upward shift of the short-run consumption function.

Time

One explanation emphasizes that consumers are creatures of habit; it takes time for them to adjust to a new standard of living. This is particularly true in a recession. Consumers have gotten used to the good life. Even though their incomes are decreasing, they try to maintain their standards of consumption; they do not cut back consumption sharply.[3] This explains the relatively flat short-run consumption function. It also explains why the function can shift upward. Over time, people gradually get used to their higher incomes and consume more.

Expectations

Another approach is based on the view that consumers do not look simply at their current disposable incomes when deciding how much to spend. Rather, they take their expected *future* incomes into account, too. Thus, for example, students often dissave — for a very good reason. They will have higher incomes in the future, and it will be easier to save then. A second example occurs during a recession, when people recognize that their current incomes are unusually low. They expect higher incomes in the future and, therefore, they save little or nothing. According to this view, consumption depends not simply on current income, but on expected normal income or *permanent* income, to use the label of Milton Friedman.[4] As time passes, people come to expect higher incomes; the short-run consumption function shifts upward.

Wealth

Wealth also causes an upward shift of the short-run consumption function. Wealth and income are not the same thing. For example, a retired person may have a small income, and yet still own considerable wealth. This person is likely to consume more than current income, running down wealth in the process.

For the economy as a whole, wealth has gradually increased as more capital has been accumulated. This increase in wealth has caused a gradual upward shift of

■ ■ ■ ■ ■

[3] This explanation was suggested by Harvard's James Duesenberry in his early study, *Income, Saving, and the Theory of Consumer Behavior* (Cambridge, Mass.: Harvard University Press, 1949).

[4] Milton Friedman, *A Theory of the Consumption Function* (Princeton University Press, 1957). When he wrote this book, Friedman was a professor at the University of Chicago.

the consumption function. The classical theory explained in Chapter 8 is a variation on this theme. According to the classical view, consumers are strongly influenced by a particular type of wealth—namely, the wealth they hold in the form of real money balances (that is, money holdings adjusted for changes in the average level of prices).

It is now standard practice for economists to use a consumption function that includes both wealth and "permanent income."

Finally, two details might be noted. A recession may be very deep, ending in a depression. In this case, consumers may move a considerable distance to the left along the short-run consumption function. They may reach a point to the left of the 45° line, such as D in Figure 9-14, where consumption exceeds disposable income. This, in fact, happened at the depth of the Depression in 1933.

On the other hand, an upswing may be very strong, ending in a boom. Then the upward momentum may take consumers along short-run consumption function C_{s_1} from D to H and all the way to B, to the right of the long-run consumption function. Here, consumers are saving a large percentage of their incomes. It makes sense for them to do so, because the boom conditions may not last.

Appendix 9-B

■ ■ ■ ■ ■

Classical Economics: Equilibrium with Full Employment

Chapter 8 described the main difference between Keynesian and classical theories. Although classical economists believed that equilibrium occurs at full employment, they conceded that large-scale unemployment could occur temporarily, as a result of disturbances. However, market forces would move the economy back toward its equilibrium with full employment.

This chapter has explained the revolutionary idea in Keynes' *General Theory*, that there could be an equilibrium with large-scale unemployment. The purpose of this appendix is to look in more detail at the contrasting classical argument.

The main point in the classical case was explained in Chapter 8, especially Figure 8-3. In the face of large-scale unemployment, prices fall, increasing the real quantity of money. Because households have more purchasing power at their disposal, they buy more goods and services. Prices continue to fall, and people consequently continue to buy more, until full employment is reached.

SAVING AND INVESTMENT: INSIDE THE CLASSICAL "BLACK BOX"

There also was, however, a second strand to the classical theory of full employment related to the Keynesian theory of saving and investment studied in this chapter. Like Keynes, classical economists recognized that desired investment and saving would have to be equal for the economy to be in equilibrium. But, unlike Keynes (Figure 9-6), they did not believe that real domestic product would have to decrease if desired investment was less than saving.

Rather, classical economists argued that the price mechanism will bring desired investment and saving into equilibrium at full employment. The key "price" that does this is the interest rate. The interest rate is the reward received by savers, and it is also the price corporations and others pay for borrowed funds with which they construct buildings or engage in other investment projects.

Suppose that desired investment falls short of saving when the economy is at full employment. What happens? According to classical economists, savers have large quantities of funds. In their eagerness to acquire bonds and other earning assets, they are willing to settle for a lower interest rate. As the interest rate falls, businesses find it cheaper to borrow. They are encouraged to undertake more investment projects. In other words, desired investment increases. The rate of interest continues to drop until desired investment and saving are brought into equality, as illustrated in Figure 9-15. The full-employment equilibrium (E) occurs at the intersection of the investment demand curve (I^*) and the curve showing saving when the economy is at full employment (S_{FE}). An increase in the desire to save—that is, a rightward shift in S_{FE} causes a fall in the rate of interest which, in turn, causes an increase in the quantity of investment. Full employment is maintained.

In other words, classical economists argued that there was something wrong with Keynes' plumbing. Saving does not simply leak from the economy. Rather, an increase in saving causes a fall in interest rates which, in turn, causes an increase in investment. Thus, the financial markets, where savers supply funds to investors, provide a connection between saving and investment in Figure 9-8; they provide a mechanism that brings saving leakages back into the spending stream in the form of investment demand.

The Keynesian Rebuttal

In response, Keynes said that classical economists were in error in counting on the interest rate to fall enough to equate saving and investment at full employment. In his *General Theory* (p. 182), he argued that there is "no guarantee" that the full-employment saving curve intersects investment demand "anywhere at all" when the interest rate is positive. This possibility is illustrated in Figure 9-16. Here, no full-employment equilibrium exists, since I^* and S_{FE} intersect at a negative interest rate. But it is not possible for interest rates to be negative, since people would be unwilling to lend money; they would simply lock it up in a bank vault instead. In fact, Keynes went one step further, and argued that the minimum interest rate is not zero, but at some positive rate, shown as i_{min} in Figure 9-16. Now, if the economy were temporarily at full employment, saving would exceed desired investment by quantity BA. Being at a minimum, the interest rate cannot fall to bring saving and investment demand into equilibrium. Something has to give. According to Keynes, what will give will be output and employment. As leakages into saving exceed

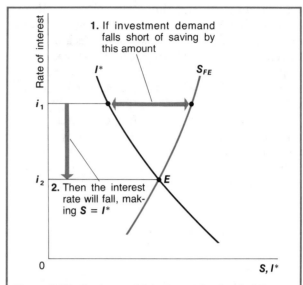

Figure 9-15 Saving and investment in classical theory. The S_{FE} curve shows how much will be saved at various interest rates in a fully employed economy. The I^* curve shows how much businesses will borrow to finance investment projects at various interest rates. Classical economists argued that if saving exceeds investment demand, the interest rate will fall until saving and investment are equalized—without large-scale unemployment.

injections of investment spending, domestic product and employment will decrease. With smaller incomes, people will save less; the saving function in Figure 9-16 will shift to the left, all the way to S_2. Now there is an equilibrium because saving and investment demand are equal. However, there is large scale unemployment at this equilibrium.

Incidentally, Figure 9-16 is based on the only diagram in Keynes' *General Theory* (on p. 180). Clearly, Keynes felt strongly about the errors of classical economists who argued that a change in the interest rate would bring saving and investment into equality at full employment.

The differences between Keynes and the classics may be summarized. Classical economists argued that *an increase in saving*, by depressing interest rates, *causes an increase in investment* and thus stimulates growth. Saving is a benefit to society; it makes us better off in the future. In contrast, Keynes argued that this isn't necessarily so. Saving may be antisocial. It may decrease domestic product and employment, a possibility explored in Appendix 9-C. Furthermore, Keynes believed that it is more correct to argue that *a change in investment demand causes a change in saving* (Figure

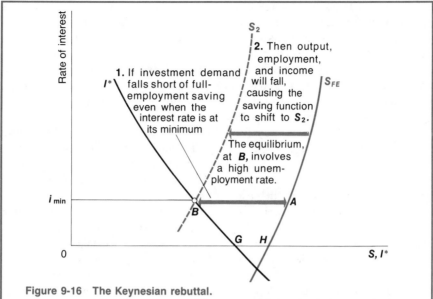

Figure 9-16   The Keynesian rebuttal.

Keynes argued that there was something wrong with the classical approach to saving and investment illustrated in Figure 9-15. Specifically, he said that the full-employment saving curve (S_{FE}) might intersect the investment demand curve I^* at an interest rate below the minimum ($i_{min.}$) which can occur in financial markets. In this case, the gap AB between saving and investment demand cannot be closed by a fall in the interest rate. It is closed by a fall in output, causing the saving function to shift to S_2.

9-10) than to argue that a change in the desire to save causes a change in investment. Thus, said Keynes, classical economists had gotten the relationship between saving and investment backwards. Because of their confusion, they had overlooked the possibility that the economy might reach an equilibrium with a high rate of unemployment.

In rebuttal, classical economists fell back on their general price mechanism to explain why the economy would reach equilibrium at full employment—an argument already explained in Chapter 8. To recapitulate, they said that, in the face of large-scale unemployment, prices would fall. This would increase the purchasing power of money; the real quantity of money would rise. As a result, people would buy a greater quantity of goods and services. This process would continue until full employment was restored. Because this rebuttal was contained in an article by Cambridge professor A.C. Pigou, the idea that an increase in the real quantity of money will cause an increase in purchases is sometimes known as the *Pigou effect.* Alternatively, it is known as the *real balance effect*, because it is the proposition that people will buy more when their real money balances increase.

In summary, classical economists counted on price flexibility to help to restore full employment in *two* ways.
1. *General* price flexibility, illustrated in Chapter 8, Figure 8-3. In the presence of large-scale unemployment, prices would fall, restoring full employment.
2. Flexibility of a *specific* price, namely the interest rate. If saving exceeded desired investment when the economy was at full employment, the interest rate would fall, bringing saving and investment into equality (Figure 9-15).

SAY'S LAW

There was also a third, less precise proposition in classical theory, known as *Say's law*, after nineteenth-century economist J.B. Say.

Say put forward the disarmingly simple idea that *supply creates its own demand.* When people sell a good or service, they do so in order to be able to buy some other good or service. The very act of supplying one good or service thus creates a demand for some other good or service. There can be too much supply for some specific product such as shoes but, if so, there is too much demand and not enough supply of some other product. Surpluses and shortages can exist in an *individual* market. Nevertheless, for the economy as a whole there cannot be an excess of supply over demand.

Keynes put his finger on the problem with Say's simple idea. It is true that, when people create goods and services, they earn income. The income from the production of all the goods and services is sufficient to buy those goods and services. The problem is that people do not spend all their incomes; they save part. Therefore, demand can fall short of production. This shortfall may be offset by investment demand. However, if investment demand is less than full-employment saving, there will be an overall inadequacy of demand, and unemployment will result.

Therefore, Say's simple idea is a weak foundation on which to build the idea that the economy will provide full employment. Say's law simply *assumes* full employment. It provides no mechanism whereby aggregate expenditures can be brought into equality with the full-employment quantity of output.

Furthermore, Say's law is inconsistent with the main body of classical economics. According to Say's law, there can be no excess of supply over demand, *regardless of the general price level*. But, according to the more sensible version of classical theory presented in Chapter 8, supply can exceed demand if the average level of prices is above equilibrium (for example, at P_1 back in Figure 8-3).

Although Say's law has been prominent in economic literature, it should not be considered the main idea in classical macroeconomics. In particular, it does not constitute the central pillar of the classical proposition that full employment will exist in equilibrium. Rather, this proposition depends on the two points explained earlier, namely: (1) the increase in the quantity of goods and services demanded that results when the general level of prices falls (the demand curve in Figure 8-3 slopes downward to the right) and (2) the increase in investment demand, and the decrease in saving, caused by a fall in the interest rate (Figure 9-15).

Appendix 9-C

■ ■ ■ ■ ■

Changes in the Desire to Save: The Paradox of Thrift

Keynesian theory explains how equilibrium domestic product Y changes if there is a change in desired investment — as we saw in Figure 9-10. Now let's consider what happens if the saving function shifts upward — or, what amounts to the same thing, the consumption function shifts downward.

Suppose that people become more thrifty; they save more out of any given income. This causes the saving function to shift upward from S_1 to S_2 in Figure 9-17. Consider what happens at the initial domestic product, A, as a result. The leakage into saving (AG) now exceeds the injections in the form of desired investment (AE_1). Aggregate demand falls short of Y, and unsold goods pile up. Orders are cancelled, and Y decreases to its new equilibrium, B. In this simple case where investment demand is horizontal, an increase in the desire to save has no effect on the equilibrium quantity of saving or

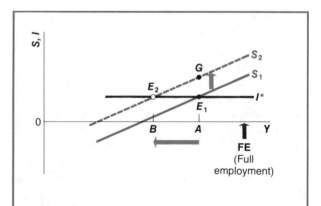

Figure 9-17 An increase in the desire to save.
An increase in the desire to save does not increase equilibrium saving. Instead, it results in a decrease in output.

investment. The amount saved and invested is the same at BE_2 as it was originally at AE_1. The only effect is a decrease in output.

However, that is not the worst of it. In order to make the analysis simple, desired investment so far has been assumed constant. Clearly, that need not be the case. Desired investment can change. Specifically, it may increase as Y increases. As more and more goods are produced, there is a need for more machines and factories. In this case, desired investment is an upward sloping function, as shown in Figure 9-18.

Now a shift in the saving function becomes particularly potent. An increase in the desire to save, moving the saving function from S_1 to S_2, causes a very large decrease in equilibrium domestic product from A to B. Furthermore, the effects on the equilibrium amount of saving and investment are paradoxical. *As a result of the upward shift in the saving function*, observe that *the amount of saving and investment in equilibrium falls*, from distance AE_1 to BE_2. This is the **paradox of thrift**.

> The *paradox of thrift* occurs when an *increase* in the desire to save (a shift from S_1 to S_2) causes a *fall* in actual saving (from AE_1 to BE_2).

What happens is this: Beginning at the initial equilibrium E_1, an increase in the desire to save causes an increase in leakages from the spending stream. Aggregate expenditures and Y fall. As they fall, businesses decide that they need fewer machines and factories. There is a decline in the quantity of investment as the economy moves to the left along the investment function. Equilibrium is restored only when domestic product has fallen enough so that people are content to save an amount which is no more than the diminished quantity of investment, at point E_2. Because the quantity of investment decreases as Y falls, and because domestic product must fall by enough to bring saving into equality with investment, saving declines in the move from E_1 to E_2.

The paradox of thrift is an illustration of one important way in which macroeconomic conclusions — covering the economy as a whole — may be quite different from conclusions for a single individual. If a single individual becomes more thrifty — saving more out of any level of income — then he or she will end up with more saving. But we cannot conclude that, just because this is true for a single individual, it will also be true for the economy as a whole. Such a conclusion would be an illustration of the **fallacy of composition**. Figure 9-18 shows a case in which the results for the society as a

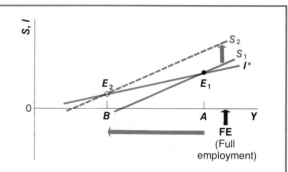

Figure 9-18   The paradox of thrift.
With the investment function sloping upward to the right, an increase in the desire to save results in a movement from E_1 to E_2. In equilibrium, the quantity of saving decreases, since E_2 is not as high as E_1.

whole are exactly the opposite from the results for an individual: For the society, a stronger effort to save means less actual saving.

> The *fallacy of composition* involves the unwarranted conclusion that a proposition which is true of a single individual or single market is necessarily true for the economy as a whole.

The paradox of thrift grows out of Keynesian theory, whose underlying assumptions should be re-emphasized at this point. The Keynesian analysis *deals with the situation in which there is large-scale unemployment and prices are downwardly rigid; changes in aggregate demand lead to changes in output and no change in prices*. In short, changes in aggregate demand cause the economy to move along the horizontal section of the aggregate supply function. If, on the other hand, the economy is experiencing booming demand conditions and is in the inflationary vertical range of the aggregate supply function, then the Keynesian analysis of thrift must be completely reversed. The macroeconomic problem is eased by an increase in the desire to save; that is, by a downward shift in the consumption function. As consumption and aggregate demand fall, inflationary forces are weakened. Furthermore, since the economy is at full employment and, therefore, is fully utilizing its resources, a decrease in consumption releases resources from the production of consumer goods. These resources become available for the production of capital goods. Thus, an increase in the willingness to save indeed adds to the amount of factories and machinery produced; the real saving of society is augmented. *In a world of inflationary excess demand, the paradox of thrift does not hold*.

Part 3

■■■■■■■■■■■■■■■■■■■■■■■■■■■■■■■■■■

The Management of Aggregate Demand

One important message came out of the last two chapters of Part 2. Recessions and depressions are caused by a fall in aggregate demand; inflation is typically caused by too much aggregate demand. In Part 3 we look more closely at several factors that influence aggregate demand and at how these factors can be manipulated by governments in order to combat the problems of inflation and unemployment.

Government spending and *taxation* are two important influences on aggregate demand. **Fiscal policy**—that is, deliberate changes in spending and taxation — thus represents one way in which the government can control aggregate demand. Chapter 10 discusses the basic principles of fiscal policy. It also explains how aggregate demand is influenced by *exports* and *imports*. When foreigners demand more of our export goods, more Canadians are put to work producing these goods. On the other hand, if Canadian consumers import more foreign goods, there is less demand for Canadian-produced goods and domestic income falls.

When individuals and businesses have more money in the form of either cash or balances in their chequing accounts, they are encouraged to spend more. **Monetary** *policy* involves changes in the stock of money held by the public. Because much of our money is held in the form of bank accounts, Chapter 11 explores how the banking system operates; Chapter 12 presents a detailed explanation of the tools that the Bank of Canada can use to influence the banks and control the money stock.

Most economists believe that *both* fiscal policy and monetary policy are important tools for controlling aggregate demand. But there is substantial disagreement over which should be made the centrepiece of aggregate demand policy. As discussed in Chapter 13, those in the Keynesian tradition often emphasize fiscal policy, while those in the classical tradition see money as the key to changes in aggregate demand.

In Chapter 14, the analysis is extended to consider how the choice between monetary and fiscal policy is affected by *international factors*. An important conclusion is that the relative effectiveness of monetary and fiscal policy depends on whether **exchange rates** between Canadian and foreign currencies are pegged by the government (as they were during most of the 1960s) or are allowed to *float*—that is, fluctuate in response to changes in supply and demand factors.

Chapter 10

■ ■

Aggregate Demand: The Effects of Fiscal Policy and Foreign Trade

Fiscal policy has to be put on constant...alert....
The management of prosperity is a full-time job.

Walter W. Heller,
New Dimensions in Political Economy

In Chapter 9, we considered a very simple economy where the only components of aggregate demand were consumption and private investment. In this chapter, we take the analysis closer to reality by bringing into the picture two further determinants of aggregate demand and income: government spending and international trade. Both are important because exports and government spending are large components in the aggregate expenditure on Canadian goods and services. But government finances are also important because the government can use changes in spending and taxation—that is, *fiscal policy* — as tools for stabilizing the economy. By taking steps to increase aggregate spending during a recession or depression, the government can increase the amount of domestic or national product and put the unemployed back to work. By restraining aggregate demand during periods of inflation, it can slow down the rate of increase of prices.

GOVERNMENT FINANCES AND AGGREGATE EXPENDITURES

In order to study fiscal policy in simple steps, we first introduce the effects of government spending and ignore taxes until a later point.

Like investment and consumption expenditures, government purchases of goods and services are a component of aggregate expenditures. Once government spending is added to the bare bones economy of Chapter 9, aggregate expenditures become:

Aggregate expenditures (AE)
= consumption expenditures (C)
  + desired investment (I*)
  + government purchases of goods and services (G)

Government expenditures for goods and services (G) can be added vertically to consumption and desired investment, to get the aggregate expenditures line shown in Figure 10-1. Note that when government purchases of $10 billion are added vertically to consumption expenditures plus desired investment, the equilibrium moves from point D to point E. The increase in domestic product Y, measured by the $50 billion distance AB on the horizontal axis, is a multiple of the $10 billion of government spending. *The multiplier process works on government spending* just as it worked on investment spending. For example, when workers receive income from building roads, a whole series of spending and responding decisions is set in motion. The workers spend most of their wages for consumer goods. For example, they may buy more clothing, and new cars. Additional employees are hired by the clothing and automobile industries, and these employees also spend more as a consequence of their rising incomes. The process is similar to that illustrated earlier for the investment multiplier in Table 9-3.

In spite of government spending, aggregate demand in our economy may nevertheless still fall short of what is needed for full employment. Such was conspicuously

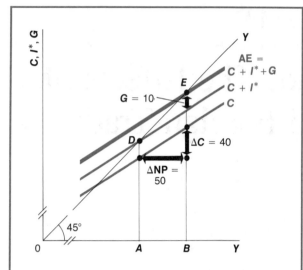

Figure 10-1   The addition of government spending.
Government spending is added vertically to consumption
and investment demand in order to get aggregate expenditures: AE = C + I* + G. Observe that the multiplier process
works on government expenditures. Without government
spending, the equilibrium would be at point D (as we saw in
Chapter 9). With government spending, the equilibrium is at
E. The increase in domestic product (AB = $50 billion) is a
multiple of the $10 billion of government spending. As peo-
ple's incomes rise, they move along the consumption function, consuming $40 billion more.

the case during the Depression of the 1930s. There were
some government expenditures, yet output was nevertheless very low and the unemployment rate very high
—reaching almost 20% of the labour force. This situation
is illustrated in Figure 10-2, where equilibrium *E* is far
to the left of the full-employment domestic product.

If the economy is to reach full employment, the aggregate expenditures function must shift upward. One way
for this to happen is by an increase in government spending. The question is, how much more government spending is needed to restore full employment? Observe that
at the full-employment quantity of domestic product (*F*),
the aggregate expenditures function (AE₁) falls short of
the 45° line by distance *HJ*. This is known as the *recessionary gap*.

> A *recessionary gap* exists when the aggregate
> expenditures function is below the 45° line at the
> full-employment quantity of domestic product.
> The gap is the vertical distance from the aggregate

expenditures line up to the 45° line, measured at
the full-employment quantity of domestic product.

The *output gap* — or *GDP gap* — is the amount
by which domestic product falls short of the full-
employment quantity. It is measured along the horizontal axis.

In order to get to full employment, the aggregate
expenditures function must be shifted up by the amount
of the recessionary gap, *HJ*. Thus, *HJ* is the amount of
additional government purchases needed. Hence, we
come to the first and most important rule of thumb for
fiscal policy:

> **By increasing its purchases of goods and
> services by the amount of the recessionary gap,
> the government can eliminate the gap and move
> the economy to full employment.**

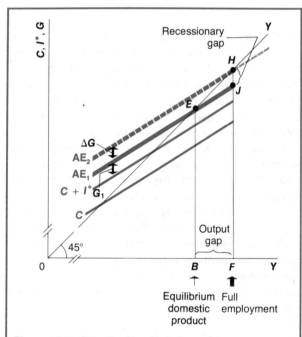

Figure 10-2   Fiscal policy for full employment.
At initial equilibrium *E*, there is large-scale unemployment;
domestic product *B* falls far short of the full-employment
domestic product at *F*. To reach full employment, government spending (G₁) should be increased by *HJ*, the amount
of the recessionary gap. This will shift aggregate expenditures up to AE₂ and move the economy to a full-employment
equilibrium at *H*. Note the *HJ*, the recessionary gap, is the
vertical distance between the aggregate expenditures line
(AE₁) and the 45° line, measured at the full-employment
domestic product.

When the government increases its spending, once again the multiplier process is at work. In Figure 10-2, note that an increase of government spending equal to the recessionary gap (*HJ*) causes output to increase by an even larger amount, *BF*—that is, by enough to eliminate the *output gap* and restore full employment. To put the same point another way: Because the multiplier works whenever the aggregate expenditures function shifts up or down, the output gap (*BF*) is larger than the recessionary gap (the amount by which government spending should increase, *HJ*).

One final point should be emphasized. *For the full impact of the multiplier to occur, it is essential that taxes not be increased to pay for the additional government spending.* As we shall soon see, an increase in taxes would remove purchasing power from the hands of the public, and thus act as a drag on consumption. With consumption discouraged in this way, the increase in aggregate expenditures would be smaller than it would be if tax rates were kept stable.

This, then, is a key policy conclusion of Keynesian economics: During a depression, when a large increase in aggregate expenditures is needed to restore full employment, *government spending should not be limited to the government's tax receipts.* Spending should be increased without increasing taxes. But if taxes are not raised, how is the government to finance its spending? The answer: by borrowing. That is, by adding to the public debt. *Deficit spending is not unsound during a recession or depression.* On the contrary, it is just what is needed to stimulate aggregate expenditures and reduce unemployment.

Restrictive Fiscal Policy: The Suppression of Inflationary Pressures

During the 1930s, aggregate expenditures were too low; the economy was depressed. At other times, spending has been too high — for example, during the Second World War and early postwar period and in the early 1970s, as the government tried to maintain the conditions of low unemployment and high economic growth that marked most of the 1960s. In each case, the very high level of spending caused an increased rate of inflation.

The situation where aggregate expenditures is too high is illustrated in Figure 10-3. At the full-employment domestic product, aggregate expenditures AE₁ are above the 45° line. With existing productive capacity, busi-

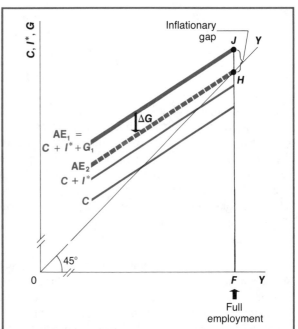

Figure 10-3   The inflationary gap.
At the full-employment quantity of output, aggregate expenditures may exceed the amount that the economy is capable of producing. (*J* is above *H*.) The excess demand will cause inflation. To restrain inflation, aggregate expenditures should be brought down to AE₂. This can be done by a cut in government spending (△*G*) equal to the inflationary gap.

nesses cannot fill all the orders for goods. There is an *inflationary gap* (*HJ*); the excess spending will cause a rise in prices.

An *inflationary gap* exists when the aggregate expenditures line is above the 45° line at the full-employment quantity of domestic product. It is the vertical distance from the 45° line up to the aggregate expenditures line, measured at the full-employment quantity of domestic product.

In such circumstances, the appropriate fiscal policy is a sufficient *reduction* in government spending to bring aggregate expenditures down to AE₂. Specifically, the second rule of thumb for fiscal policy is this:

During a period of inflation, excessive aggregate expenditures can be eliminated by a decrease in government purchases equal to the inflationary gap.

TAXES

There is one difference between a tax collector and a taxidermist—the taxidermist leaves the hide.

Mortimer Caplin, former Commissioner
of the U.S. Internal Revenue Service

Government spending is only one side of fiscal policy; the other is taxation. Although taxes do not show up directly as a component of aggregate expenditures, they do affect aggregate expenditures indirectly. For example, when people pay taxes, they are left with less disposable income and they consequently consume less. Thus, the consumption component of aggregate expenditures is reduced.

A Lump-sum Tax

In order to introduce tax complications one by one, we initially make an unrealistic but very simple assumption —that taxes (*T*) are levied in a *lump sum*. That is, the government collects a fixed amount—say, $10 billion— in taxes *regardless of the size of domestic product*.

How does this tax affect consumption? The answer is shown in Figure 10-4. After the tax, people have 10 billion dollars less in disposable income. As a consequence, their consumption declines. By how much? With a marginal propensity to consume (MPC) of 0.8, they consume $8 billion less. They also save $2 billion less. Thus the $10 billion fall in disposable income is reflected in a $2 billion decline in saving and an 8 billion dollar decline in consumption.

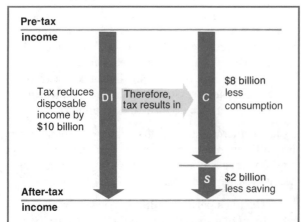

Figure 10-4   A tax depresses consumption.
If the MPC is 0.8, a $10 billion tax reduces consumption by $8 billion, and saving by $2 billion.

This $8 billion decrease in consumption is carried over to Figure 10-5. Point *B* on the after-tax consumption function C_2 is $8 billion below *A*. Similarly, every other point on the original consumption function also shifts down by $8 billion. The new after-tax function is parallel to the original consumption function, but $8 billion lower. In general:

A lump-sum tax causes the consumption function to shift down by the amount of the tax times the MPC.

When taxes are increased and the consumption function shifts downward, the aggregate expenditures line likewise shifts downward. Thus, when aggregate expenditures are too high and prices are rising, an *increase* in taxes is the appropriate policy step. On the other side, a *cut* in taxes represents a *stimulative* policy; the reduction in taxes will increase disposable income and shift the consumption function and aggregate expenditures *upward*.

Note that a change in taxes is almost as powerful a tool for controlling aggregate expenditures as a change in government purchases of goods and services. Almost, but not quite. An increase of $10 billion in government purchases causes aggregate expenditures to shift up by the full $10 billion. However, a decrease in taxes of 10 billion dollars shifts aggregate expenditures up by only $8 billion—that is, $10 billion times the MPC.[1]

Because government purchases of goods and services are more powerful, dollar for dollar, than a change in taxes, there is reason to turn to government purchases when major changes are desired in aggregate demand. During the early Keynesian period, economists did concentrate on government purchases in their fiscal policy recommendations. However, in the 1960s and 1970s, tax changes became a more prominent way to manage aggregate demand. Thus, substantial tax rate reductions were

---

[1] Like taxes, a $10 billion change in transfer payments is less powerful than a $10 billion change in government spending for goods and services. When the government purchases road-building equipment or other goods or services, it provides jobs directly. However, transfer payments — such as Old Age Security benefits—do not provide jobs directly. Like taxes, they affect aggregate expenditure only indirectly, by changing disposable income. Specifically, a $10 billion increase in transfer payments raises disposable income by 10 billion dollars and thus causes an upward shift of the consumption function by $10 billion times the MPC.

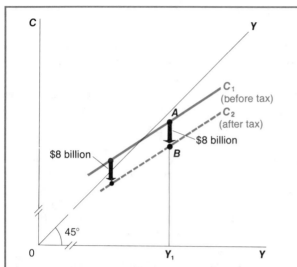

Figure 10-5   Effect of a $10 billion lump-sum tax.
If the MPC is 0.8, a lump-sum tax T of $10 billion causes the consumption function to shift down by $8 billion ($T \times$ MPC).

used to counteract rising unemployment in 1958/59 and, as inflationary pressures grew in 1968/69, tax increases were the main tools used to reduce the size of the inflationary gap. In the 1970s, major tax cuts were employed to combat the 1974/75 recession, and as unemployment again inched upward in 1977/78, further tax cuts were made.

There are three reasons that tax changes have become a more important component of fiscal policy:

1. A tax cut is generally *less controversial* than an increase in government spending as a way of stimulating the economy. This is true in part because of skepticism over the ability of the government to spend money wisely and because of fears that the government will grow bigger and bigger.

2. Tax changes may be put into effect *more quickly* than changes in government spending. For example, an increase in spending for highways, government buildings, dams, or other public works requires considerable planning, and this takes time.

3. Tax changes are *more easily reversed* when conditions change. It is true that the public may be unhappy when a previous tax cut is reversed. However, they may be even more unhappy if new government spending programs are eliminated suddenly. Furthermore, some

government spending—for example, for roads, buildings, or dams—cannot be stopped without considerable waste. A half-finished bridge or dam is no good to anybody.

To summarize our policy conclusions thus far:

1. *To stimulate aggregate demand*, and thus combat unemployment, the appropriate fiscal policy is an increase in government spending and/or a cut in taxes —that is, *steps that increase the government's deficit* or reduce its surplus.

2. *To restrain aggregate demand* and thus combat inflation, the appropriate fiscal policy is a cut in government spending and/or an increase in taxes — that is, *steps that move the government's budget toward surplus.*

A rising government deficit acts as a stimulus to aggregate demand. A reduction in the government's deficit (or an increase in its surplus) acts as a drag.

Adding Realism: A Proportional Tax

These two important policy conclusions have been illustrated by studying a simple lump-sum tax that was 10 billion dollars no matter what domestic product might be. But this tax isn't realistic. In fact, tax collections rise and fall with domestic product. This is obviously true of income taxes. The more people earn, the more taxes they pay. It is also true of sales taxes. If domestic product and total sales rise, government revenues from sales taxes likewise rise.

We may take a giant step toward realism by discarding the lump-sum tax and studying instead a tax that does rise and fall with domestic product. The one we consider is a *proportional* tax — that is, a tax yielding revenues that are a constant percentage of domestic product.

As we saw in Figure 10-5, a lump-sum tax shifts the consumption function down by a constant amount. However, this is not true of a proportional tax. If domestic product doubles, tax collections likewise double, and the depressing effects on the consumption function also double. To illustrate, suppose there is a 20% proportional tax. At domestic product Y_1 in Figure 10-6, this tax depresses consumption from point B to D. But if domestic product is twice as great, at Y_2, this same tax depresses consumption by twice as much—from K to L.

Of course, a 30% tax depresses consumption even more than a 20% tax. Thus, consumption function C_3 lies below C_2. In general, the heavier the tax, the more the

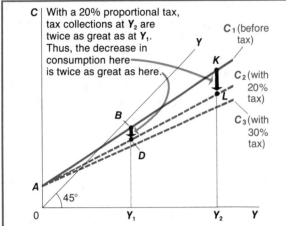

Figure 10-6   A proportional tax: Effect on consumption.
When a proportional tax is imposed, the consumption function rotates clockwise around point *A*. The higher the tax rate, the more the consumption function rotates. As the tax rate rises from 20% to 30%, the consumption function becomes lower and flatter.

consumption function rotates clockwise, as shown in Figure 10-6.[2]

Note two important effects of a proportional tax:
1. The higher the tax rate, the more disposable income is reduced and the more the consumption function is lowered. Thus, an increase in the tax rate lowers the aggregate expenditures function, and a cut in taxes raises the aggregate expenditures function.

On this first point, then, the effects of a proportional tax are similar to those of the lump-sum tax considered earlier. But on the next point, they differ.
2. In an economy with proportional taxes, the consumption function is *flatter* than in a tax-free economy. The higher the tax rate, the flatter the consumption function becomes. However, as we saw in Chapter 9, the flatter the consumption function, the lower the multiplier. Moreover, the effect of a proportional tax in lowering the multiplier can be very substantial. Recall that, with no taxes and an MPC of 0.8, the multiplier was 5. When a 25% proportional tax is introduced, the multiplier drops sharply to only 2.5. (The appendix at the end of this chapter explains why.)

■ ■ ■ ■ ■
[2] Note that the consumption function rotates around point *A*. Why is this so? By assumption, taxes are proportional to domestic product. Therefore, in the limiting case where domestic product is zero, taxes are likewise zero. Consumption is therefore unaffected. Thus, point *A* is on every consumption function, regardless of how high the tax rate is.

EXPORTS AND IMPORTS

Adding government spending and taxes to the bare-bones picture of the economy in Chapter 9 brings us a long way toward a more realistic view of the Canadian economy. But to bring the picture even closer to reality, we must also take account of foreign trade. As we saw in Chapter 6, exports and imports are large in relation to Canada's GDP, and they are important in determining aggregate expenditures.

When exports and imports are taken into account, the expression for the aggregate expenditures on Canadian goods and services becomes

> **Aggregate expenditure (AE)**
> **= consumption expenditures (*C*)**
> **+ desired investment (*I**)**
> **+ government purchases of goods**
> **and services (*G*)**
> **+ export demand (*X*)**
> **− demand for imports (*M*)**

Exports to foreign countries add directly to the aggregate demand for Canadian goods and services. Furthermore, as we export more forest products or subway cars, workers in the forestry or transport equipment industries have larger incomes and, consequently, they step up their consumption expenditures. Thus, an increase in exports sets the multiplier process in motion in the same way as an increase in investment demand or government spending.

Imports, by contrast, are a subtraction from the aggregate expenditures on Canadian goods and services. If part of the consumption expenditures of Canadians is spent on imported goods, such as shirts from Korea, that part of consumption does not become income of Canadian workers or firms. (The value of the shirts is part of Korea's domestic product, not Canadian domestic product.) Or, if a large firm spends $1 million investing in an imported data processing system, that part of investment demand does not become income of Canadians. To account for this, the spending on imports must be *subtracted* from aggregate expenditures.

Notice that there is a similarity between imports and taxes in their effect on aggregate expenditures: A switch by Canadian consumers toward purchases of imported goods will shift the aggregate expenditure schedule downward, just as an increase in taxes would do. Moreover, just like taxes, imports are likely to be large when domestic or national product is large. (When people have high incomes and high expenditures, their spending on imports is also likely to be high.) Therefore, the depressing effect of imports on aggregate expenditures will be larger at higher levels of domestic product.

The combined effect of imports and exports on aggregate expenditures is illustrated in panels (*a*) to (*c*) of Figure 10-7. Panel (*a*) shows how imports increase when domestic product increases. For example, at Y_1 imports are $50 billion; at Y_4 they are $75 billion. However, exports are assumed to remain constant (at $60 billion) for all levels of Canadian domestic product. (The demand for our exports depends on domestic product and income in *foreign* countries, not in Canada.) *Net exports* — that is, exports minus imports — are shown in panel (*b*). When exports are higher than imports, net exports are positive. (For example, at Y_1 net exports are $10 billion and are shown by the black arrow. But as imports grow larger with a higher domestic product, net exports become negative. (At Y_4, net exports are -15 billion dollars, as shown by the coloured arrow.) In panel (*c*), we add net exports to aggregate expenditures. Notice that the aggregate expenditure curve in an ***open economy*** (AE$_2$) is flatter than it would be in an economy with little or no international trade — a ***closed economy*** (AE$_1$). This happens because net exports become smaller and smaller as domestic product rises. Indeed, beyond Y_2 they turn negative; thus AE$_2$ lies *below* AE$_1$ to the right of Y_2.

An *open economy* is an economy where exports and imports are large relative to domestic or national product.

A *closed economy* is an economy where exports and imports are very small relative to domestic or national product.

Because the aggregate expenditure curve becomes flatter as a result of international trade, the multiplier becomes smaller. In the previous section, we saw that introduction of a proportional tax would cause the multiplier to be smaller than in the simple economy with neither taxes nor foreign trade. In an economy with foreign trade, the multiplier becomes smaller yet, as we also show in the appendix to this chapter.

Notice that in panel (*c*) of Figure 10-7, net exports are negative at the equilibrium domestic product Y_3 where the aggregate expenditure curve AE$_2$ crosses the 45° line. As the figure has been drawn, Canada exports less than it imports at the equilibrium domestic product. But there is no reason why that should always be true. For example, if there is an increase in American

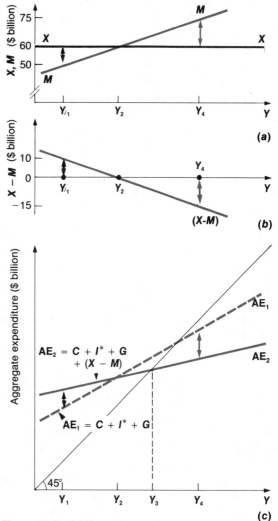

Figure 10-7   Adding net exports to aggregate expenditures.

(*a*) Imports are an increasing function of domestic product: The higher the domestic product, the higher the imports. Exports are assumed to be constant at $60 billion and independent of domestic product.

(*b*) Net exports are found by vertically subtracting imports from exports. Thus, at Y_2 net exports in panel (*b*) are zero: Import spending is equal to export earnings. In panel (*a*) we saw that at a small domestic product such as Y_1, imports are smaller than exports; thus net exports are positive, as shown by the left arrow in panel (*b*). Conversely, at Y_4 imports are greater than exports by an amount shown by the coloured arrow. Net exports are negative.

(*c*) The AE$_1$ line shows the sum of consumption, investment, and government spending. When foreign trade is taken into account, we must add net exports (from panel (*b*)) vertically to AE$_1$, which gives us the AE$_2$ line showing aggregate expenditures in an open economy. Equilibrium domestic product, as usual, occurs when AE$_2$ cuts the 45° line; equilibrium domestic product in this economy is Y_3.

demand for our exports, the horizontal export curve in panel (*a*) would shift upwards, as would the net export curve in panel (*b*) and the aggregate expenditure curve AE$_2$ in panel (*c*). If the increase in exports were large enough, there would be positive net exports at the new equilibrium. As we saw in Figure 6-3, this is in fact what happened in 1987 when our exports exceeded imports by about $4 billion.

INJECTIONS AND LEAKAGES

The previous chapter explained a very simplified economy, with only consumption and investment and no government sector or international transactions. Such an economy *reaches equilibrium when the injections* into the spending stream, in the form of investment spending, *are just equal to the leakages* from the spending stream, in the form of saving.

A similar proposition still holds in a more complex economy, with government spending, taxation, and international transactions. *Equilibrium still exists when injections and leakages are equal.* But now there are several injections and several leakages.

Specifically, *government spending* (*G*) and *exports* (*X*) are *injections* into the spending stream, similar to investment spending. When the government spends more for roads or buildings, the producers of these roads and buildings earn higher incomes and their consumption consequently rises. Similarly, if Canada exports more wheat, our farmers have higher incomes and, accordingly, can increase their purchases of consumer goods. Thus, the circular flow of expenditures broadens when government spending or exports increase.

On the other side, *taxes* (*T*) and *imports* (*M*) are *leakages*, similar to saving. Income taken in taxes cannot be used by the public for consumption expenditures. Imports (*M*) likewise are a leakage from the domestic spending stream; they represent a demand for foreign output, not output at home.

Equilibrium occurs when the injections working to broaden the circular flow of expenditures are equal to the leakages working to narrow it. That is:

> **In an economy with a government and international transactions, equilibrium occurs when:**
> $$I^* + G + X = S + T + M$$

AUTOMATIC STABILIZERS

Because taxes and imports lower the size of the multiplier, they add to the stability of the economy. For example, in an economy with large leakages into taxes and imports, the multiplier is small. Therefore, a fall in investment demand or exports causes only a moderate decline in domestic product. On the other side, a runaway boom is less likely in an economy with large imports and taxes. Much of the increase in income is taxed away before people get a chance to spend it; and part of the extra spending that does occur goes to the purchase of imports and thus leaks out of the domestic economy.

Tax revenues and import spending that vary with domestic product are therefore ***built-in stabilizers*** or ***automatic stabilizers***. As an example, Figure 10-8 illustrates the way that taxes act to stabilize the economy. In this example, taxes (*T*) are just adequate to cover government expenditure (*G*) when the economy is at the initial domestic product Y_1; the budget is balanced (*G* = *T*). Now suppose the economy slips into a recession, with domestic product decreasing to Y_2. Tax collections fall, and the budget automatically moves into deficit. This fall in tax collections helps to keep aggregate expenditures up: Disposable income is left in the hands of the public and consumption, therefore, falls less sharply. Thus, the downward momentum in the economy is reduced. Similarly, the tax system acts as a restraint on an upswing. As domestic product increases, tax collections rise. The government's budget moves toward surplus and the upward movement of the economy is slowed down.

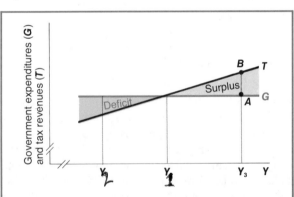

Figure 10-8   Automatic fiscal stabilization.
As domestic product increases from Y_1 toward Y_3, the government's budget automatically moves into surplus. This slows down the increases in disposable income and consumption and thus slows down the expansion. Conversely, the budget automatically moves into deficit during recessions as domestic product decreases from Y_1 toward Y_2. The government deficit helps to keep up disposable income and consumption and thus alleviates the recession.

Similarly, imports help stabilize the economy, as we may see by referring back to Figure 10-7(*a*). Suppose again that the economy is moving into a recession. As domestic product decreases, imports fall. With a smaller leakage into imports, net exports will be larger and the decline in aggregate expenditure and domestic product is moderated. Conversely, when the economy swings upward, imports rise and the upswing is restrained.

> An *automatic stabilizer* is any feature of the economic system that reduces the strength of recessions and/or the strength of upswings in demand, without policy changes being made.
>
> An automatic stabilizer should be distinguished from a *discretionary* policy action, such as a cut in tax rates or the introduction of new government spending programs.

The degree of automatic stabilization depends on how strongly tax collections respond to changes in domestic product. That is, it depends on the *marginal tax rate* for the economy as a whole—the fraction of an increase in domestic product which is paid in taxes. It also depends on the **marginal propensity to import**—the fraction of extra income which is spent on imports.

The marginal propensity to import (MPM)

$$= \frac{\text{Change in imports}}{\text{Change in domestic product}}$$

The greater the marginal propensity to import, the steeper is the import and net export functions in Figure 10-7 and the stronger is the automatic stabilization. Similarly, the greater the marginal tax rate, the steeper is the taxation function (*T*) in Figure 10-8 and the stronger is the stabilizing effect of taxes.

There are also automatic stabilizers on the government expenditures side (not shown in Figure 10-8). As the economy slides into a recession, there is an automatic increase in government spending for Unemployment Insurance benefits and for welfare. The additional government spending sustains disposable income and, therefore, slows the downswing.

Automatic stabilizers reduce the severity of economic fluctuations. But they do not eliminate them. The objective of discretionary fiscal policy is to reduce the fluctuations even more.

TWO COMPLICATIONS

The tendency for the government's budget to swing automatically into deficit during recessions, and into surplus during inflationary booms, helps to stabilize the economy. For this reason, it may be looked on as a plus. But it also introduces two important complications into fiscal policy.

1. A Policy Trap: Attempting to Balance the Budget Every Year

When the budget automatically swings into deficit during hard times, it sets a trap for the unwary policy maker. Suppose that the government tries to balance the budget every year. As the economy enters a recession, tax collections decline, causing deficits. If policy makers are determined to balance the budget, they will have two choices: they can cut government spending or increase tax rates. *Either step will depress aggregate demand and make the recession worse. By raising taxes or cutting expenditures, the government will offset the automatic stabilizers built into the tax system. Trying to balance the budget each year is a policy trap.*

One reason this trap deserves emphasis is that the Canadian government (the Conservatives led by R.B. Bennett) seemed to fall into it during the most serious years of the Great Depression in the 1930s.[3] The government was convinced that deficits had to be avoided so as not to add to the national debt and diminish international confidence in the economic soundness of Canada. Large increases in the rates of sales tax, corporate income tax and personal income tax were introduced in 1932 and 1933—the worst years of the Depression.[4]

The change in fiscal policy was precisely the opposite of what was needed to promote recovery. Rather than the needed stimulus, the country got a large dose of restraint: In attempting to deal with the Depression, the government was making it worse. Ironically, the

- - - - -

[3] For a description of fiscal policy during the Great Depression, see Irving Brecher, *Monetary and Fiscal Thought and Policy in Canada, 1919–1939* (Toronto: University of Toronto Press, 1957), pp. 199–200.

[4] In the United States the story was much the same, with President Hoover recommending, and Congress passing in 1932, one of the largest tax increases in peacetime history.

In the presidential campaign that year, Roosevelt took his strongest stand for fiscal conservatism in a Pittsburgh speech on October 19. This speech became something of an embarrassment as the deficits mounted during his first administration. And it inspired a story which circulated in Washington. When Roosevelt was returning to Pittsburgh several years later, he turned to one of his speech writers for advice on how to explain away his earlier stand for a balanced budget. The reply was, "Deny you were ever in Pittsburgh."

policy of raising taxes did not even succeed in balancing the actual budget. Because of the gradual collapse of the economy, government *revenues* actually fell in spite of the increases in tax rates; the automatic stabilizer was creating a deficit even though the government was trying to raise taxes. In the government's defence, it should be noted that it was only following the accepted wisdom of the day. The Liberal opposition under Mackenzie King, far from urging the government to provide more stimulus, concentrated its criticism on what it regarded as excessive spending: " . . . this vast expenditure and waste."

The accepted wisdom of the day, which led to the government's blunder in recommending a huge tax increase, set the stage for the Keynesian revolution with its important message: Spending and tax policies should be aimed at the goals of full employment and price stability, and not at the goal of balancing the budget. *Fiscal policy should be designed to balance the economy, not the budget.* The government has the ability — *and the responsibility* — to manage aggregate demand and thus ensure continuing prosperity.

2. Measuring Fiscal Policy: The Full-Employment Budget

Because the government's budget swings *automatically* toward deficit during recessions and toward surplus during booms, the state of the budget cannot be taken as a measure of how fiscal *policy* has changed. For example, the federal deficits of the early 1930s did not mean that the government was following an expansive fiscal policy; in fact, it was doing the opposite.

In order to determine whether fiscal *policy* is moving in an expansive or restrictive direction, some measure other than the actual budgetary deficit or surplus is therefore needed. What might that measure be?

To answer this question, economists break down the government's deficit into two components:

1. The part of the deficit that is attributable to cyclical downturns in the economy. As the economy moves into recession, tax receipts are automatically depressed, and the deficit is thereby pushed up. This part of the deficit is called the *cyclical* component.

2. The deficit that would occur *even if* there were no business cycles, and the economy were always at full employment. This deficit is due to the structure of the tax and spending programs of the government. It is accordingly known as the *structural* deficit, the *full-employment* deficit, or the *cyclically adjusted*

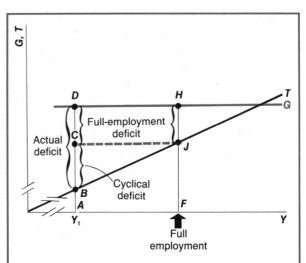

Figure 10-9 The full-employment deficit and the cyclical deficit.

This figure illustrates how the actual budget deficit *BD* can be broken down into its structural component *CD* and its cyclical component *BC*. The economy is in a recession; domestic product Y_1 is less than the full-employment quantity. The actual budget deficit is *BD* — that is, government spending *AD* less tax revenues *AB*. The full-employment deficit, however, is only *CD*. The cyclical component of the deficit is the difference between the actual deficit and the full-employment deficit.

Whenever tax rates are cut, the line *T* becomes flatter. As a result, both the full-employment deficit and the actual budget deficit will become larger. Similarly, a rise in government expenditures *G* will raise both deficits.

deficit. Figure 10-9 illustrates how the full-employment deficit *HJ* is less than the actual deficit *BD* when the economy is in a recession.

The *full-employment budget* or *structural budget* measures what the government's deficit or surplus would be with existing tax rates and spending programs *if* the economy were at full employment.

The full-employment budget provides an answer to the question posed earlier. *It provides a measure of what is happening to fiscal policy* because it changes only in response to changes in tax rates and spending programs and not in response to business cycles. Specifically:

When the full-employment budget is moving toward a larger deficit (or smaller surplus) fiscal policy is expansive. When the full-employment budget is moving toward a larger surplus (or smaller deficit), fiscal policy is restrictive.

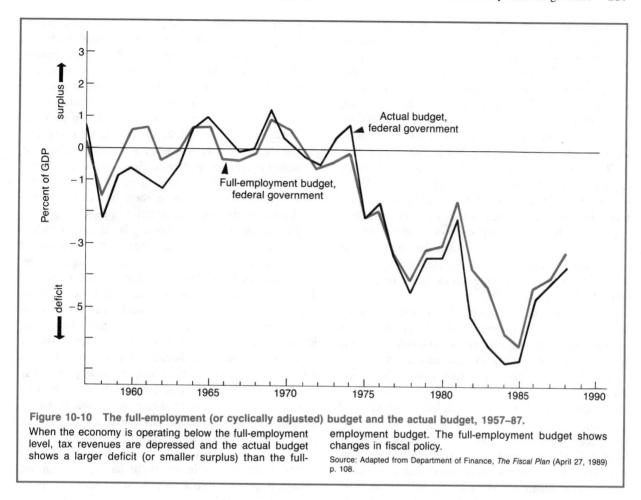

Figure 10-10   The full-employment (or cyclically adjusted) budget and the actual budget, 1957–87.

When the economy is operating below the full-employment level, tax revenues are depressed and the actual budget shows a larger deficit (or smaller surplus) than the full-employment budget. The full-employment budget shows changes in fiscal policy.

Source: Adapted from Department of Finance, *The Fiscal Plan* (April 27, 1989) p. 108.

The Full Employment Budget, 1957–87

The comparison between the federal government's actual budget and its estimated full-employment budget in Figure 10-10 gives several illustrations of how misleading the actual budget can be as a measure of fiscal policy. For example, the actual budget shows an increase in the deficit during the 1959–61 period. However, the full-employment budget shows a move from a deficit to a surplus during the same period; the deficits in 1960 and 1961 were due to the economy's weak performance, rather than to an expansionary policy. The change in the full-employment budget shows that policy was actually becoming tighter, not more expansionary. During 1972–74, the actual budget shows a large change from a deficit to a surplus. But, according to the full-employment budget (which remained in deficit throughout), there was little change in policy. The large surplus in 1974 was primarily due to the 1973/74 inflationary export boom. Finally, both the actual and full-employment budgets show increased deficits in 1982 and 1983. However, the full-employment budget shows that to a large extent, the huge deficits in those years were caused by the recession.

The estimated full-employment budget also shows how fiscal policy has been used on several occasions to try to counteract economic fluctuations. As the U.S. economy slid into a deep recession in 1974/75, Ottawa enacted large tax reductions and spending increases which provided needed stimulus. (Partly as a result of this policy, the recession in Canada was much less severe than in the United States.) The full-employment budget also shows how the government was willing to try to fight the 1982 recession by moving the federal budget toward more stimulus, even though the deficit was already very large.

At the same time, Figure 10-10 shows some disquieting aspects of our recent fiscal history. Consider first the 1970–73 period. Between 1970 and 1971, the full-employment budget indicates that fiscal policy was changed (somewhat belatedly, since the recession occurred in 1970) from restraint to stimulus. However, during 1970–73 the economy was recovering nicely, and unemployment gradually fell; by 1974, severe inflationary pressures were developing. Yet according to Figure 10-10, the government continued to change fiscal policy in the direction of more stimulus throughout the 1970–73 period: While the actual deficit turned into a surplus under the influence of the buoyant economy, the full-employment budget showed a growing deficit. In retrospect, the expansionary fiscal policy during this period contributed substantially to the inflationary spiral that started in the early 1970s and led to double-digit inflation rates in the mid-1970s.

Again, following the end of the 1974/75 recession, the economy gradually recovered through 1979. The recovery was slow, however, and the unemployment rate did not come down significantly. In an attempt to accelerate the recovery, the government moved the budget toward more stimulus, even though it was starting from a large deficit in 1975. As a result, both the actual and full-employment budgets showed growing deficits throughout. Then when recessions occurred in 1980 and again in 1982, the government was caught on the horns of a dilemma. On the one hand, the deficit was already very large, and there was considerable political pressure on the government to reduce it. On the other hand, there were calls for tax reductions and increased expenditures to fight the recessions.

Why wasn't fiscal policy used in a more precise way to combat recessions and inflations, in line with the theory of this chapter? There are two major reasons why fiscal policy has not been strongly stabilizing in practice:

1. At any particular time, there will always be some disagreement over what the thrust of fiscal policy should be. In part, this is because there is disagreement on what should constitute a realistic full-employment target to aim for. As we saw in Chapter 7, most economists now agree that it was not realistic to expect unemployment rates in the 1970s to go as low as they had been in the 1950s and 1960s without causing strong inflationary pressures. But this may not have been clear to the politicians who were making the decisions concerning fiscal policy at that time.

2. Even if agreement can be reached about the direction in which fiscal policy should be changed, there are often sharp disagreements about *how* the change should be accomplished. For example, suppose it is agreed that government should move fiscal policy in a more restrictive direction, reducing the budget deficit. Those politicians who think that the government is already too big and the tax burden on Canadians too high will insist that the proper way to reduce the deficit is to cut expenditures. However, once it comes down to actually specifying particular programs where cuts are to be made, there will be vociferous opposition from the beneficiaries of those programs.

The persistence of exceptionally large federal budget deficits through the 1980s provides a good example of this problem. During the 1984 election campaign, the Conservatives had promised decisive action to reduce the large deficit they had inherited from the previous Liberal government. However, the Conservatives were initially reluctant to raise taxes, and their attempts at reducing spending by such measures as reduced inflation protection for old-age pensioners produced a public outcry. The result was that very little in the way of deficit reduction was accomplished during their first years in office. The reduction that did take place could be partly explained by the automatic increase in tax receipts as the economy rebounded through the 1984–88 period.

The federal government's difficulty in bringing the deficit under control in the 1980s has revived an old debate. Aren't we passing a crushing burden of debt to future generations?

THE BURDEN OF THE PUBLIC DEBT

Surprisingly, there is no simple "yes" or "no" answer to this question. One reason is that government debt is quite different from an individual's debt.

An individual can use debt to make the time pattern of consumption much different than the pattern of income. For example, a student goes into debt, keeping up consumption even though no current income is being earned. Then, during middle age, this debt is paid off and additional assets acquired. At this time, the individual produces more than he or she is consuming. Finally, in retirement, the assets from a lifetime's saving can be called upon. The individual can continue to consume, but no longer has to work.

For the society as a whole, it is not as easy to separate the timing of production and the timing of consumption.

Clearly, services must be produced when they are consumed; haircuts or medical services can't be "put in the bank." Most of the food we eat is produced in the year in which it is consumed. In this sense, society as a whole cannot borrow from the future: It cannot consume goods that have not yet been produced. In a fundamental sense, then, the costs of current government expenditures are borne at the time, even though they are financed by borrowing.

As an illustration, consider the question of who bore the burden of the enormous government deficit during World War II, when Canada's public debt expanded at its fastest rate ever. To fight the war, Canada needed warships, ammunition, and thousands of troops in the field. This required enormous resources which were no longer available for other uses. Military production in 1943, say, came *at the opportunity cost of giving up consumer goods in 1943*. For example, when a firm like Canadian General Electric was making navigational equipment for warships, it couldn't make refrigerators at the same time. It was the people of 1943 — and not their children—who had to do without new refrigerators. They were the ones who suffered, not only in terms of lives lost, but also in terms of consumer goods forgone.

It is, of course, true that only part of the spending for the war was paid through taxes and that the government ran up a large debt to pay for the rest. This was passed on to future generations; debt from World War II has never been repaid. But when we pay interest on this debt in 1990, we obviously are not paying the people who lived in 1943. Rather, interest payments are made by some people in 1990 to other people in 1990. Specifically, the government collects taxes from the general public and uses some of the taxes to pay interest to bondholders. Thus, government debt — indeed, any debt — transfers funds from one group *now* to another group *now*. It does not transfer funds from people in one time period to people in an earlier period.

The Burden of Deficits and the Debt

Nevertheless, large government debts undertaken now can be a burden on future generations in several ways:
1. Even though a society cannot separate the timing of production and consumption to the extent that an individual can, *some* separation is possible. Indeed, *investment* (in roads, machines, and other productive equipment) is a way of giving up consumption now in order to have even more consumption in the future. The standard of living of our children and grandchildren will depend on how much real capital we bequeath them.

When the government engages in deficit spending, it may depress investment; the resources used by the government in its spending programs could have gone into investment instead. In this case, deficit spending *will* impose a burden on future generations; they will *inherit a smaller capital stock than they otherwise would have*.

Not all deficit spending comes at the expense of investment, however. It depends on how close the economy is to full employment. If the economy is in a depression or major recession, then producing goods for the government does not require a reduction in consumption or investment. We are operating *within* the production possibilities curve, and can produce more across the board. When the government runs deficits, consumer spending will be stimulated through the operation of the multiplier. As more consumer goods are produced, investment demand is encouraged: To produce more cars and refrigerators, businesses need more machines and factories. Thus, deficit spending *during a period of high unemployment* generates benefits rather than burdens for future generations. It stimulates the production of consumer goods for the present generation, and more capital stock for future generations.

2. To finance its deficits, the federal government has not only borrowed from Canadian residents during the 1980s; it has also *borrowed substantial amounts from foreigners to finance its deficits*. As a nation, we were going into debt to foreigners — debt on which we will *have to make interest payments in the future*. When Canadian government debt is held by foreigners, some of the foreign money that we earn through exports must be used to pay interest to foreign bondholders. As a result, there is less left to pay for imports of goods and services in the future. The reduction in the amounts we will be able to import is part of the real burden of the debt that we are passing on to future generations.

3. When the government collects taxes to pay interest on the debt — whether held at home or abroad — there is another cost: the **excess burden** of taxation. When taxes are imposed, the public has an incentive to alter its behaviour to avoid paying taxes. For example, people have an incentive to hire lawyers to search for tax loopholes, and to divert their savings into tax sheltered investments — that is, investments on which

little or no tax is paid. As a result, the efficiency of the economy is reduced.

The *excess burden of taxes* is the decrease in the efficiency of the economy that results when people change their behaviour to avoid paying taxes. It should be distinguished from the *primary burden*, which is measured by the amount of taxes people actually pay.

When the Reagan administration in the United States made large tax cuts in the early 1980s, one of the main reasons was the belief that these tax cuts would stimulate aggregate supply by making the economy more efficient — that is, by reducing the excess burden of taxation. But in the long run, this "supply-side" strategy may turn out to have been self-defeating. By creating large deficits, the supply-side tax cuts will lead to higher taxes in the future to pay interest on the increased debt: They, therefore, will cause a higher excess burden and a less efficient economy in the future.

4. The need for the government to pay interest may lead to an *undesirable redistribution of income*. This depends on who has to pay the taxes and who holds the bonds and receives the interest. (It also depends on what we consider a "desirable" distribution of income.)

5. The need to pay interest payments on a large debt may also contribute to *inflation*. For example, inflation may result if the government decides to finance interest payments, not by collecting taxes but, instead, by borrowing and thus running up its deficit. The rising deficits stimulate aggregate demand and add to inflationary pressures. The inflationary effects are particularly strong if the Bank of Canada (our central bank) creates new money and lends it to the government in order to help the government make its interest payments.

6. The national debt can *feed on itself*. As the debt rises, the government's interest payments also rise. But, as these interest payments are part of the government's expenditures, they make it more difficult to get the expenditures under control in the future.

This sixth problem has caused concern in the mid-1980s, as deficits mounted and the debt grew rapidly. (See Table 10-1.) These deficits were very different from the large deficits of the early 1940s, which were caused by a temporary wartime crisis. When the war ended, military spending plunged, automatically eliminating the deficits. In contrast, recent deficits have arisen because the government has committed itself to long-run spending programs that substantially exceed its tax revenues. If the government can't get rid of its deficit now, how will it be able to do so in the future, when it must make much larger interest payments?

7. The danger of the debt "feeding on itself" has become so severe that some economists fear that *we may have lost our ability to use fiscal policy to combat future recessions*. If we run large deficits even in prosperous years, what will happen if we use fiscal policy vigorously to combat the next recession? With even larger deficits, won't we generate an unstoppable tide of debt and even greater interest payments and deficits in the future?

Could the Government "Go Broke"?

If it gets more and more deeply into debt, could the federal government, like a business corporation, go bankrupt? The answer is no, but the reason it won't "go broke" should be carefully stated.

First, consider one common, but inaccurate, argument. It is frequently asserted that the government cannot go bankrupt because it has the authority to tax. Thus, it has the power to extract from the public whatever amounts are necessary to service the debt. But surely there is something wrong with this argument. Provincial and local governments also have the power to tax, yet they can, theoretically, go broke. In a democracy, the government must face elections. Even dictatorships depend on public support. As a result, there are political and practical limits to taxes. The holder of a government bond does not have a guarantee of repayment merely because the government has the right to tax.

The federal government cannot go bankrupt for quite a different reason. It has a power even more potent than the power to tax. Bonds are repayable in money. The government has the *power to print money* to pay interest or principal — either directly or, more subtly, by pressuring or coercing the central bank (the Bank of Canada) to create money and lend it to the government to avoid default. In other words, a national government does not go bankrupt because bonds are repayable in something — money — which national governments can create.

However, if large quantities of money are created to help make payments on the public debt, the consequence will be a rise in prices. (Recall what happened in the

Table 10-1   Federal Government Debt and Interest Payments, 1929–87
(billions of current dollars)

1 Year	2 Government Debt	3 Interest Payments on Government Debt	4 Government Debt as Percent of GDP	5 Interest Payments as Percent of GDP
1929	2.28	0.12	37	2.0
1940	5.15	0.14	77	2.0
1946	16.00	0.44	135	3.7
1954	14.26	0.48	55	1.9
1960	16.88	0.75	44	2.0
1966	20.26	1.15	33	1.9
1969	22.87	1.59	29	2.0
1973	29.13	2.52	24	2.0
1975	37.18	3.71	22	2.2
1978	59.66	6.41	26	2.8
1980	79.49	9.90	27	3.3
1981	91.96	13.74	27	4.0
1982	110.60	16.68	31	4.7
1983	136.68	17.41	35	4.5
1984	162.24	21.32	39	5.1
1985	193.89	24.62	42	5.3
1986	214.61	26.11	44	5.3
1987	237.73	27.74	45	5.2

Source: Compiled by authors from data in F.H. Leacy, M.C. Urquhart, and K.A.H. Buckley, eds., *Historical Statistics of Canada*, 2nd ed. (Ottawa: Statistics Canada, 1982), *Bank of Canada Review*, and Statistics Canada, *CANSIM Databank*. Statistics Canada figures reproduced by permission of the Minister of Supply and Services Canada.

prisoner-of-war camp when large quantities of cigarette ''money'' suddenly came on the scene.) Thus, an excessive national debt has quite different consequences from an excessive corporate debt: It causes excess demand and inflation, not bankruptcy.

Nevertheless, there is one situation in which even a national government may be forced to default on its debts — namely, if it has borrowed in terms of a foreign currency. If the Canadian government issues bonds repayable in Canadian dollars, it can, in an extreme case, print the dollars to repay the debt. But suppose that it borrows large amounts in a foreign currency, such as U.S. dollars, German marks, or Japanese yen. In such circumstances, default would be possible. No matter how desperate our situation might become, the government of Canada could not print foreign currency. Similarly, other national governments that borrow large amounts of U.S. dollars may run the risk of default. Indeed, during the past decade, a number of governments that have borrowed heavily in U.S. dollars were in danger of default — for example, Argentina, Brazil, Mexico, and Poland. (We will discuss these international debt problems in more detail in Chapter 20.)

THE ISSUE OF RESTRAINT

Modern economics throws into question the old rule that the government should try to balance its budget every year. But if there is no rule, what will prevent the government from careless increases in expenditures, or from cutting taxes without corresponding restraint on spending? We may warn of the dangers of excess, but can we really expect restraint? With the large deficits of the 1980s, these old questions are posed again.

A number of alternative guidelines have been suggested to provide restraint, while avoiding the destabilizing fiscal policies which can occur if the government tries to balance the actual budget every year.

1. Balance the Full-employment Budget Every Year

Remember why the old balanced-budget rule was destabilizing: As the economy moves into recession and a budget deficit automatically appears, the balanced-budget rule requires an increase in tax rates or cuts in government spending. These can make the recession worse. Such destabilizing actions can be avoided if the government aims at balancing the *full-employment* budget. Since this budget does not automatically swing into deficit during recessions, it does not give a false signal that a tax increase or spending cut is needed. Thus, the full-employment budget has two major uses: as a *way of measuring* fiscal policy and as a *guide* to fiscal policy.

However, in a severe recession, balancing the full-employment budget may be inadequate. All it does is allow the automatic stabilizers to combat the recession. It does not allow the government to go one step further and actively fight the recession by introducing fiscal stimulus. (Such stimulus—for example, a cut in tax rates — would violate the rule, since it would put the full-employment budget into deficit.) Thus, this first rule represents an unambitious strategy. Its aim is to avoid destabilizing actions, not to actively stabilize the economy. It therefore is reminiscent of the doctor's motto: *Primo non nocere*, or "First, do no harm."

2. Balance the Full-employment Budget, But Only When the Economy Achieves Full Employment

This alternative approach is more ambitious. It allows a government to take the initiative in managing the economy. During a recession, tax rates *can* be cut or spending increased in order to speed the return to full employment. In other words, the full-employment budget can be shifted into deficit during recessions. But the government is still subject to restraint. It has to return to a balanced budget when the economy reaches full employment.

3. The Cyclically Balanced Budget

Either of the first two guidelines permits the government to have an *actual* budget which is in deficit on the average. The reason is that, whenever the economy falls short of full employment, either guideline allows a deficit in the actual budget. There is no need for offsetting surpluses during periods of full employment.

More long-term restraint can be provided by *balancing the actual budget over the business cycle*. According to this approach, there should be sufficient surpluses during good times to cover the deficits of the recessions. But, unlike the annually balanced budget, the cyclically balanced budget is consistent with active fiscal management. Tax rates can be cut and spending increased to combat recessions.

4. Built-in Spending Restraints

Experience in Canada and elsewhere, especially since the mid-1970s, has led a number of observers to wonder whether any of these principles can be used as a realistic guideline for fiscal policy. In practice, while it appears to be relatively easy to increase spending during a recession, governments seem to have found it difficult to reduce their deficits even when they have announced that this has been their objective.

Therefore, more attention has been given to attacking the problem on the expenditure side by building *direct restraints* into the administrative process where spending decisions are made.

In its early budgets, the Mulroney government outlined several new approaches to the problem of giving incentives to government officials to restrict spending and improve management efficiency. They included:

- Abolition of the past practice of automatically increasing departmental budgets to compensate for inflation;

- A commitment to gradual reduction in the number of federal public service employees according to a fixed schedule (starting with a 2% reduction in 1985/86);

- A substantial reduction in the contingency funds usually included in departmental budgets.

In addition, plans were outlined for more extensive use of the user-pay principle under which private firms pay the government for special services it provides. For example, firms may, for a fee, contract to have Statistics Canada provide them with unpublished data.

In the United States, there have been a number of more radical proposals to pressure governments into reducing their spending. Both President Carter, in the late 1970s, and President Reagan set explicit goals that would have limited U.S. federal government spending to a specific percentage of GNP. Moreover, during his first term in office, Reagan proposed an amendment to the U.S. constitution that would have forced the administration and Congress to balance the budget every year. Not surprisingly, Congress was unenthusiastic, since a balanced-budget amendment would limit its powers. It, therefore, declined Reagan's invitation to initiate the constitutional process by drafting a balanced-budget amendment for the states to ratify. However, the debate and procedural wrangling about this issue continued, and a somewhat weaker balanced-budget law was actually passed in the mid-1980s (see Box 10-1).

Box 10-1

■ ■ ■ ■ ■ ■ ■ ■ ■ ■ ■ ■ ■ ■ ■ ■ ■ ■ ■ ■

Outlawing Budget Deficits in the United States: The Gramm-Rudman Act

When the U.S. Congress refused to support President Reagan's proposals for a balanced-budget amendment, those who supported it tried to bypass Congress by having a special constitutional convention called. This can happen if two-thirds (34) of the American states petition for a convention. By 1984, 32 states had submitted such petitions, and proponents of the amendment were hoping that two more would be added. However, they were disappointed. In 1988, several states rescinded their petitions. The balanced-budget amendment was dead.

However, although Congress rejected the idea of a balanced-budget amendment to the constitution, it provided a weaker version in the Balanced Budget Act of Dec. 1985, commonly known as Gramm-Rudman after its sponsors. This act set a strict numerical timetable for reducing the budget deficit of the federal government. The deficit, which had ballooned to $212 billion, was to be reduced to zero by 1991. (Congress was, however, mindful of the sad history of the 1930s and, therefore, permitted higher deficits in the event of recession.)

Gramm-Rudman also avoided the rigidity of a constitutional amendment. Because it was a law passed by Congress, it could also be changed by Congress. Its history indicated that, just like the administration, Congress could be schizophrenic over deficits. The same Congress that passed the Balanced Budget Act also passed the appropriations that resulted in the $212 billion deficit in fiscal 1986.

It was a classic case of wanting to have your cake and eat it, too. Congress wanted lower deficits. But it was loath to raise taxes, particularly after 1984. In the presidential election of that year, Mr. Mondale promised higher taxes. Not much has been heard of him since. Congress was likewise hesitant to cut spending.

The fundamental problem is that there are only two decisions, and Congress wants to make three. If it sets taxes and authorizes spending, then the deficit is determined. If it sets taxes and the deficit, then it cannot be free on the spending side. Gramm-Rudman was designed to put spending at the end of the line in the decision process, and thus exert restraint at that point. If the Gramm-Rudman deficit ceilings are exceeded, expenditures are to be cut automatically, more or less across-the-board, with Social Security and interest payments exempted.

KEY POINTS

1. An increase in government spending causes an increase in equilibrium domestic product. An increase in taxes causes a decrease in equilibrium domestic product.

2. Net exports (that is, exports minus imports) are added to consumption, investment and government spending in determining aggregate expenditure. An increase in our exports to foreign countries increases Canada's domestic product. An increase in Canadian imports from foreign countries decreases domestic product.

3. When aggregate expenditures are low and the rate of unemployment is high, fiscal policy should be expansionary; that is, the government should increase spending and/or cut tax rates. These steps tend to increase the government's deficit.

4. When excess aggregate expenditures are causing inflation, fiscal policy should be restrictive; the government should cut spending and/or increase tax rates. These steps will move the government's budget toward surplus.

5. Tax collections automatically rise as domestic product increases, and fall as domestic product falls. Thus, the government budget *automatically* tends to move into deficit during a recession, and into surplus during expansions. This tendency helps to reduce the amplitude of cyclical swings, and thus provides *built-in stability* to the economy.

6. Because the government's budget automatically responds to changes in domestic product, the actual budget cannot be taken as a *measure* of fiscal policy actions. The appropriate measure is

the *full-employment budget*, which indicates what the surplus or deficit would be, with current tax and spending legislation, if the economy were at full employment.

7. Imports also tend to change automatically in the same direction as domestic product. Imports are a leakage from the circular flow of income just as taxes are. Therefore, this tendency for imports to rise and fall as domestic product flucuates also helps to reduce the swings in aggregate expenditures and to stabilize the economy.

8. If the government attempts to balance the actual budget every year, it will fall into a *policy trap* and take destabilizing actions. During a downturn in economic activity, when the budget automatically moves toward deficit, the government will cut expenditures or raise taxes in an effort to balance the budget, thereby making the downturn worse. The Bennett government fell into this policy trap in 1932 when it initiated legislation for a large tax increase.

9. This trap can be avoided if the full-employment budget — rather than the actual budget — is used as a policy guide. The full-employment budget has no tendency to swing automatically into deficit during recessions and, therefore, it does not erroneously suggest that taxes should be raised. Thus, the full-employment budget has two major functions: (1) as a *measure* of fiscal policy; and (2) as a *guide* for fiscal policy.

10. Most goods and services must be produced at or near the time that they are consumed or used. A society as a whole has much less ability than an individual to separate the timing of production and consumption. Wars must be fought with the resources available at the time. In a fundamental sense, then, the burden of a war — or other deficit spending by the government — must be borne at the time the expenditures are made. Nevertheless, future generations may be adversely affected. Insofar as deficit spending shifts resources away from investment, future generations will inherit a smaller capital stock. If deficit spending in Canada is financed through *foreign* borrowing, future generations of Canadians will bear the burden of a larger foreign debt.

11. A large government debt involves transfers from one group (taxpayers who finance the interest payments) to another group (bondholders who collect interest). The interest payments on a large government debt can cause a number of problems:
    (a) They may cause an undesirable redistribution of income within a country.
    (b) Insofar as the debt is held abroad, people at home will be taxed to pay interest to foreigners.
    (c) When taxes are imposed to pay the interest, there will be a loss of economic efficiency as people look for ways to avoid taxes. This loss of efficiency is called the "excess burden of taxes."
    (d) If the government pays interest by borrowing rather than taxing, it can add to inflationary pressures.
    (e) The debt can "feed on itself." A large debt requires large interest payments. This makes it difficult to avoid future deficits that add to the size of the debt.
    (f) Since a large debt requires large interest payments, it can cause such large deficits that the government feels that it has lost the ability to fight recessions with additional deficit spending.

KEY CONCEPTS

management of aggregate
    demand
recessionary gap
output gap or GDP gap
inflationary gap
lump-sum tax
proportional tax
open economy

closed economy
taxes as a leakage
imports as a leakage
marginal propensity to import
government spending as an
    injection
exports as an injection
deficit spending

automatic stabilizers
discretionary policy action
actual budget
full-employment budget
annually balanced budget
cyclically balanced budget
public debt
excess burden of taxes

PROBLEMS

10-1. Using a diagram, explain the difference between the recessionary gap and the output gap. Which is larger? How are these two measures related to the multiplier?

10-2. During the Great Depression, Keynes argued that it would be better for the government to build pyramids than to do nothing. Do you agree? Why or why not? Are there any policies better than pyramid building? That is, can you think of any policies which would give all the advantages of pyramid building, plus additional advantages? Explain.

10-3. During the Great Depression, the following argument was frequently made:

A market economy tends to generate large scale unemployment. Military spending can reduce unemployment. Therefore, capitalism requires wars and the threat of wars if it is to survive.

What part or parts of this argument are correct? Which are wrong? Explain what is wrong with the incorrect part(s). Rewrite the statement, correcting whatever is incorrect.

10-4. (a) When the United States experiences an upswing in economic activity, American demand for Canadian exports generally rises. Explain why this increase in the demand for our exports is likely to increase Canada's domestic product.

(b) If price inflation in Canada is higher than in the United States, Canadian goods will begin to be more and more expensive compared with U.S. goods. What effect do you think this would have on the import function in panel (a) of Figure 10-7? On the net export function in panel (b) of the same figure? How would it affect aggregate expenditures and the equilibrium domestic product in Canada?

10-5. In 1965 and 1974, when the government wanted to stimulate aggregate demand, it cut tax rates. What are the advantages of cutting tax rates, rather than increasing government spending? What are the disadvantages? When restraint is needed, would you favour increases in taxes, cuts in government spending, or a combination of the two? Why?

10-6. Assume that full employment initially exists and that the actual budget is in balance.
(a) If the economy then slips down into a recession and there are no policy changes, will the actual budget and the full-employment budget behave the same? Explain why or why not. (For help with this question, refer to Figures 10-8 and 10-9.)

(b) Suppose, as an alternative, that the government takes strong fiscal policy steps to combat the recession. Will there be a difference in the behaviour of the actual budget and the full-employment budget? Explain.

10-7. Attempting to balance the budget every year can set a trap for policy makers. It leads to incorrect policies during a depression. Does such a balanced-budget rule also lead to incorrect policies during an inflationary boom? Why or why not?

10-8. (a) Explain why a large increase in the government debt may impose a burden on future generations even if it is entirely held by Canadian nationals, and even if the total amount of productive capital in the future is the same as it would have been without the government debt. (Hint: Consider the possible role of foreign ownership of private-sector capital.)

(b) Suppose the government prohibited all foreign ownership of capital in the Canadian economy. Would this change your answer to the question in (a) above?

Appendix

■ ■ ■ ■ ■

The Multiplier in an Economy with Taxes and Imports

Taxes have a substantial effect on the multiplier process. Consider an economy with a marginal propensity to consume (MPC) of 0.8 and a tax rate of 25%. Each $1 change in planned investment or in government spending will then have the following effect on aggregate expenditures.

	Change in aggregate expenditures for each $1 increase in planned investment
1. First round Increase in investment of $1	$1
2. Second round (a) Producers of investment goods have earned $1 more in first round (b) Government takes 25¢ in taxes, leaving disposable income of 75¢ (c) With MPC = 0.8, consumption as a consequence is 0.8 x $0.75. Thus, in the "second round" of spending, there is an increase in consumption of 0.8 x $0.75 = $0.60 =	$1(0.6)
3. Third round (a) Producers of consumer goods have earned 60¢ more in first round (b) Government takes 25% (or 15¢) in taxes, leaving disposable income of 45¢ (c) With MPC = 0.8, consumption as a consequence is 0.8 x 45¢ = $0.36 =	$1(0.6)^2
4. Fourth round Consumption is	$1(0.6)^3$ ⋮

We find the sum of all rounds in a manner similar to equation 9-8:

$$\text{Sum} = \$1(1 + 0.6 + 0.6^2 + 0.6^3 + \ldots)$$

$$= \$1 \times \frac{1}{1 - 0.6} =$$

$2.50

Therefore, the multiplier is 2.5.

More advanced texts derive the general formula for the multiplier in an economy with taxes:

$$\text{Multiplier} = \frac{1}{s + t - st}$$

where s is the marginal propensity to save, and t is the marginal tax rate; that is, the change in tax collections as a fraction of the change in domestic product.

This formula is not derived here in order to avoid a preoccupation with algebra.

Once we consider international transactions, the multiplier process is even more complicated. Consider what happens if The Great Canadian Shakes and Shingles Corporation exports a truckload of shingles to the United States. The value of the shipment is the initial injection. In the "first round," domestic product goes up by the full amount of the shingles. What is the "second round" effect?

Because the government takes a slice in taxes — of, say, 20% — only 80¢ of each dollar of shingles sales gets into the hands of consumers as disposable income. Of this 80¢, consumers save, say, one-eighth (10¢), leaving only 70¢ in consumption. But not all of this is spent on Canadian goods and services. A portion — say, 20¢ — goes to purchase imported goods. As a result, the "sec-

ond round" increase in domestic product is only 50¢ for each initial injection of $1.

At this second round, one-half of each $1 in income leaks out into taxes, saving, and imports; only 50¢ is spent by consumers for domestically produced goods. Similarly, one-half is consumed, and one-half leaks out of the domestic spending stream in each later round. For each $1 in initial injection, this gives a sum of all rounds equal to:

$$\$1(1 + 0.5 + 0.5^2 + 0.5^3 + \ldots)$$

Using equation 9-8, we find:

$$\text{Sum} = \$1 \left(\frac{1}{1 - 0.5} \right) = \$2.00$$

Therefore, the multiplier is 2.

In this more complicated economy with international transactions:

1. The multiplier is smaller because of the additional leakage into imports.
2. Equilibrium occurs when total injections (investment plus government spending plus exports) equal total leakages (saving plus taxation plus imports).

Chapter 11

■ ■

Money and the Banking System

You can't appreciate home till you've left it,
[nor] money till it's spent.

O. Henry

Fiscal policy is the first major tool for managing aggregate demand. Monetary policy is the second. Monetary policy involves control over the quantity of money in our economy. If the quantity of money is increased, spending is encouraged; aggregate demand tends to rise. Similarly, if the quantity of money decreases, aggregate demand tends to fall. By adjusting the quantity of money, the authorities can affect aggregate demand.

However, there is also another reason why money is an important topic in macroeconomics. Money not only provides a way to stabilize the economy; it can also represent a source of problems. Indeed, monetary disturbances have been associated with some of the most spectacularly unstable episodes in economic history. Two examples stand out. One occurred in the years following the First World War, when Germany went through a period of hyperinflation. In December 1919, there were about 50 billion marks in circulation. Four years later, this figure had risen to almost 500,000,000,000 billion marks — an increase of 10,000,000,000 times! Because money was so plentiful, it became practically worthless; prices skyrocketed. Indeed, money lost its value so quickly that people were anxious to spend whatever money they had as soon as possible, while they still could buy something with it. (For a more recent case of hyperinflation, see Box 11-1.)

The second illustration involves the North American experience in the Great Depression of the 1930s. Economists are still debating how important monetary disturbances were as a cause of the Depression. But there is little doubt that the misbehaviour of the monetary and banking system played some role, particularly in the United States.[1] As the U.S. economy slid down into the Depression, the quantity of money fell from $26.2 billion in mid-1929 to $19.2 billion in mid-1933 — that is, by 27%. By the time Roosevelt became U.S. President in 1933, many banks had closed their doors, and many people with large deposits had been wiped out. In Canada, there were no major bank failures during the Depression, but the quantity of money fell in this country, too; it declined about 15% between 1928 and 1932.

In the mid-1980s, many institutions in the North American financial system were once more in difficulties; in Canada, several trust companies went under, and in 1985 two small chartered banks went bankrupt. But in the 1980s, the money stock continued to increase in spite of these problems in the financial system, and we avoided the sort of economic collapse that occurred in the 1930s.

In the coming chapters, we will investigate the *problems* and *opportunities* which the monetary system

■ ■ ■ ■ ■

[1] As we saw earlier in Chapter 8 (especially in Figure 8-4), those in the classical tradition argue that a fall in the quantity of money was a major cause of the collapse into the Depression. For details, see Milton Friedman and Anna Schwartz, *A Monetary History of the United States, 1867–1960* (Princeton, N.J.: Princeton University Press, 1963), Ch. 7. Keynesians tend to be more skeptical. See, for example, Peter Temin, *Did Monetary Forces Cause the Great Depression?* (New York: W. W. Norton, 1976). The disagreements between Keynesians and classical economists over the importance of money will be explained in more detail in Chapter 13.

Box 11-1

■ ■ ■ ■ ■ ■ ■ ■ ■ ■ ■ ■ ■ ■ ■ ■ ■ ■ ■

When the Inflation Rate Is 116,000%, Prices Change by the Hour*

In Bolivia, the Pesos Paid Out Can Outweigh the Purchases;
No. 3 Import: More Pesos

LA PAZ, Bolivia, Feb. 6, 1985 — A courier stumbles into Banco Boliviano Americano, struggling under the weight of a huge bag of money he is carrying on his back. He announces that the sack contains 32 million pesos, and a teller slaps on a notation to that effect. The courier pitches the bag into a corner.

"We don't bother counting the money any more," explains a loan officer standing nearby. "We take the client's word for what's in the bag." Pointing to the courier's load, he says, "That's a small deposit."

At that moment the 32 million pesos were worth only $500. Today, less than two weeks later, they are worth at least $180 less.

Bolivia's inflation rate is the highest in the world. In 1984, prices zoomed 2,700%, compared with a mere 329% the year before. Experts are predicting the inflation rate could soar as high as 40,000% this year. Even those estimates could prove conservative. The central bank last week announced January inflation of 80%; if that pace continued all year, it would mean annual inflation of 116,000%.

Prices go up by the day, the hour, or the customer. Julia Blanco Sirba, a vendor on this capital city's main street, sells a bar of chocolate for 35,000 pesos. Five minutes later, the next bar goes for 50,000 pesos. The two-inch stack of money needed to buy it far outweighs the chocolate.

Bolivians aren't yet lugging their money about in wheelbarrows, as the Germans did during the legendary hyperinflation of the Weimar Republic in the 1920's. But Bolivia seems headed in that direction.

Tons of paper money are printed. Planeloads of money arrive twice a week from printers in West Germany and Britain. Purchases of money cost Bolivia more than $20 million last year, making it the third largest import, after wheat and mining equipment.

The 1,000 peso bill, the most commonly used, costs more to print than it purchases. It buys one bag of tea. To purchase an average size television set with 1,000 peso bills, customers have to haul money weighing more than 68 pounds into the showroom. (The inflation makes use of credit cards impossible here, and merchants generally don't take checks, either.)

Courtesy of *Plain Truth* magazine. Two-million mark banknote, later overprinted to read 60,000,000,000 marks, from the German hyperinflation of 1923.

"When it comes to inflation, we're the international champs," says Jorge von Bergen, an executive with a paper-products company, who lugs his money around in a small suitcase. His wife has to take the maid along to the market to help carry the bales of cash needed for her shopping. But all that money buys so little that Mrs. von Bergen easily carries her purchases back home on her own.

Because pesos are practically worthless, dollars now are being demanded for big-ticket purchases. People get their dollars from the 800 or so street-side money vendors who line Avenida Camacho, long La Paz's Wall Street. Banking, in effect, has moved outside.

*Abridged, from the *Wall Street Journal*, Feb. 7, 1985, p. 1.

presents. Specifically, we will explore the following questions:

1. What are the forces that cause disturbances within the monetary system? What has been done in the past, and what can be done in the future, to reduce the disturbances, and make the monetary system more stable?
2. How can money be managed to stabilize aggregate demand and reduce fluctuations in economic activity?

In this chapter, we explain how the monetary system works, and begin to answer question 1. Future chapters (especially 12, 13, 14, 18, and 20) will provide greater detail on the first point (the problems) and explain the second (the opportunities).

THE FUNCTIONS OF MONEY

Without money, specialized producers would have to resort to barter. Because barter is so cumbersome, a monetary system will naturally evolve, even in the absence of a government—as the development of a cigarette money in the prisoner-of-war camp so clearly illustrated (Chapter 3).

Money has three interrelated functions:

1. First, money acts as the *medium of exchange*. That is, it is used to buy goods and services.
2. When money is used as a medium of exchange, it also becomes the basis for quoting prices. For example, a car is priced at $10,000 and a pair of shoes at $50. Thus, money acts as the *standard of value*.
3. Finally, money serves as a *store of value*. Because it can be used to buy goods or services whenever the need arises, money is a convenient way of holding wealth.

Of course, money is not a perfect store of value, because its purchasing power can change. As we saw in Chapter 1 (Figure 1-4), prices of goods and services have risen, and the purchasing power of money has consequently declined.

MONEY IN THE CANADIAN ECONOMY

If it waddles like a duck,
And quacks like a duck,
Then it is a duck.

Anonymous

Money is what money does. To define money, we should begin by looking at *what is actually used* to buy goods and services. What is used by the householder paying the electric bill? By the customer at the supermarket? By the child buying candy? By the employer paying wages?

Coins and paper currency (pennies, quarters, $2 bills, $20 bills, etc.), which together are known as *currency*, are used in many transactions—but certainly not in all. Indeed, most payments are made by cheque. When you write a cheque, it is an order to your bank to make payment out of the balance in your account.

Until the mid-1970s, most of the money held in bank accounts that were used for writing cheques was held in the form of *demand deposits*—that is, deposits which the owner has the legal right to withdraw without prior notice, and on which the banks usually pay little or no interest. Consequently, until a few years ago, economists usually defined money as currency plus demand deposits in the chartered banks.[2]

This concept of money—which is denoted by *M1*—continues to be used by analysts as one of the indicators of monetary and financial conditions and, in the 1970s, it was the M1 measure that the Bank of Canada used when it followed policies of setting specific targets for the rate of growth of the money stock.

M1 = currency + demand deposits in chartered banks

Over the past decade, there have been a number of developments in the financial system that have led economists to question whether the M1 concept is not an overly restrictive definition of money. For some years, banks have been offering several other kinds of deposits which are close substitutes for demand deposits. For example, they issue "daily interest chequable savings accounts" on which interest is calculated on the actual balance each day, and which can be used for writing cheques. (Technically, savings deposits are referred to as *notice deposits*, because the chartered banks have the

■ ■ ■ ■ ■
[2] Here and elsewhere in the discussion of money definitions, we skip over some of the details. For example, M1 also includes an item referred to as "net float," consisting mainly of Bank of Canada cheques issued to the public (but not yet deposited in a chartered bank), net of outstanding cheques drawn on chartered banks for deposit in the government account with the Bank of Canada. For an excellent and readable account of this and other technical issues relating to monetary statistics, see Peter Martin, *Inside the Bank of Canada's Weekly Financial Statistics: A Technical Guide* (Vancouver: The Fraser Institute, 1985).

formal right to demand a few days' notice before the funds can be withdrawn; however, in practice they routinely waive this right.) Further, notice deposits held by large corporations (''non-personal'' notice deposits) can effectively be used for making payments, since the chartered banks will automatically transfer funds from these accounts to the demand deposits on which the corporations' cheques are drawn.

Since many individuals and corporations have switched from demand deposits to chequable daily interest savings accounts or notice deposits, a case can be made for broadening the definition of money to include such deposits as well. For some time in the early 1980s, economists at the Bank of Canada focused on a money supply concept — referred to as M1A — that included daily interest chequable savings deposits and non-personal notice deposits as well as currency and demand deposits.

In going from the M1 to the M1A definition of money, we include an item such as chequable savings accounts because they can be used directly in transactions. This makes sense: The most important function of money is to be used as a medium of exchange. By making the exchange of goods and services work more smoothly, it makes the economy work more efficiently than a barter system. But for those who are in charge of economic policy, money is also important for a different reason: The amount of money in the economy can influence aggregate demand. When people have more money, they are likely to spend more.

Once we concentrate on the effect of money on spending, it is even less clear precisely how we should define money. For example, the line between M1A and other similar assets is a fine one. Consider savings deposits against which cheques cannot be written. It is true that such deposits cannot be used directly to make payments. But they can be switched easily into chequable deposits that, in turn, can be spent. The spending patterns of someone with $10,000 in a non-chequable savings account may not be very different from the spending of a person with $10,000 in a demand deposit account, or a daily interest chequable savings account. Thus, when economists are investigating the effects of the banking system on aggregate demand, they sometimes broaden their horizons further—beyond the narrowly defined M1 or M1A. Specifically, they often use an even broader definition of ''money,'' *M2*, which includes non-chequable notice deposits and other close substitutes for M1A:

M2 = currency + all chequable, notice, and personal term deposits

In this definition, *non-chequable* personal savings accounts are included in ''notice deposits.'' A *term deposit* is similar to a notice deposit, except that it has a specific time to maturity. For example, if you have a term deposit that matures in three months, your asset is tied up until that date. If you want to withdraw it sooner, you must pay a penalty.

Notice in Figure 11-1 that at the end of 1987, the narrowly defined money concept M1 had become small relative to the broader M2 definition: M2 was some five times as large as M1. This ratio has been changing rapidly. Twenty years ago, M2 was less than three times as large as M1.

Several complications should be noted about the M1 and M2 definitions of money. Even though they include currency and bank deposits that can be used to make payments, or that can easily be converted into means of payment, something seems to have been left out: When shopping, people often use credit cards rather than either currency or cheques. Yet, there is no mention of credit cards in either definition of money. There are two related reasons.

First, in a fundamental sense, people don't ''pay'' with credit cards. They simply defer the payment for a few weeks or months. When the credit card bill comes, it must be paid with a cheque (or, conceivably, with currency). Thus, it is the final payment with a cheque, rather than the initial charging with a credit card, that represents the fundamental payment. It is the balance in the bank account which is money, not the credit card. Second, people *own* currency and bank accounts. Credit cards, on the other hand, represent an easy way to run up debt. If, as the result of a sudden windfall, I acquire an extra $1,000 which I deposit in my bank account, I will be very much aware of the fact, and will clearly be better off as a result. On the other hand, if the credit card issuer informs me that I can charge an extra $1,000, I will not necessarily be better off. Indeed, I may scarcely notice. When we are calculating the quantity of money, we should not mix together *assets*—such as currency and bank deposits—with the **lines of credit** available to holders of credit cards.

A *line of credit* is a commitment by a lender to lend up to a specific amount to a borrower. For example, if I have a $2,000 line of credit with a credit card company, the company is committed to letting me charge up to $2,000.

The second complication is a technical point regarding the currency item in Figure 11-1. Coins are issued by the federal government through the Royal Canadian Mint. Paper currency is issued by the **Bank of Canada**, our government-owned central bank. (Look at a 20-dollar bill and you will see the Bank's name written across the top.) The bank deposits shown in the M1 and M2 data in Figure 11-1 are liabilities (debts) of the chartered banks. When the quantity of money is calculated, currency and deposits are counted only when they are held by the public; that is, by individuals and non-bank institutions. Holdings by the federal government, the Bank of Canada, and chartered banks are not included in the money stock, since these are the institutions that create money. This exclusion makes sense. For example, if the Bank of Canada has a million $5 bills printed up and stored in its vaults, it makes little sense to say that the money stock has gone up by $5 million. That currency gains significance and becomes "money" only when it passes out of the hands of the Bank of Canada and into the hands of the public.

M2 + , M3, and Liquid Assets

In the late 1980s, the Bank of Canada appeared to be moving toward the use of M2 as the fundamental indicator of monetary conditions. But this raised a new question: If the basic money definition is to include items such as daily interest savings deposits and personal term deposits issued by chartered banks (that is, banks that have received a "charter" permitting them to do business under the provisions of the federal Bank Act), should we not also include the notice and personal term deposits issued by trust and mortgage loan companies, credit unions, and similar institutions? After all, many small firms and individuals today do not use the services of the chartered banks: They may do all their "banking" at an institution such as a trust company.

Part of the explanation for the growing role of these institutions in Canada's financial system is changes in regulation. Some years ago, financial institutions were not allowed to offer interest-bearing chequable deposit accounts. Moreover, only chartered banks were allowed to offer demand deposit accounts against which cheques could be written. At present, however, regulations are different, and not only banks but also trust companies and similar institutions are allowed to issue interest-bearing chequable deposits. Thus, some of the deposits issued by non-bank financial institutions are in fact used to make payments by cheque, and non-chequable deposits at these institutions can be converted into deposits

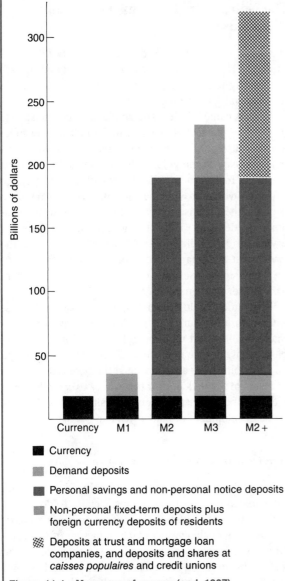

Figure 11-1 Measures of money (end–1987).
Deposits with the chartered banks constitute the largest component of "money," whether "money" is defined as M1 or M2. The still more broadly defined concepts of money M2+ and M3 (explained later in the text) are much larger than M1.

Source: *Bank of Canada Review* (August 1988).

Legend:
- ■ Currency
- ▨ Demand deposits
- ■ Personal savings and non-personal notice deposits
- ▨ Non-personal fixed-term deposits plus foreign currency deposits of residents
- ▨ Deposits at trust and mortgage loan companies, and deposits and shares at *caisses populaires* and credit unions

that can be used to make payments almost as easily as at a chartered bank.

Because deposits at trust and mortgage loan companies and credit unions (as well as at Quebec's *caisses populaires* which are similar to credit unions) are very close substitutes for assets that are included in M2, many analysts favour the use of an extended money concept, *M2 +* which includes such deposits:

> M2+ = M2+ deposits at trust and mortgage loan companies, and deposits and shares at *caisses populaires* and credit unions

Finally, even broader concepts of money are sometimes used. For example, *M3* is defined as currency plus all privately held deposits in chartered banks. M3 differs from M2 by including large term deposits (over $100,000), generally held by businesses. Such deposits are often held in the form of "Certificates of Deposit" (CDs). CDs can be sold by the depositor on financial markets at any time prior to maturity, so that even though they are issued for a fixed term, depositors can effectively "withdraw" their funds at any time. M3 also incorporates foreign currency deposits (mostly in U.S. dollars) held by Canadian residents in the chartered banks.

In studying what determines spending, one can go even further and consider other *liquid assets* or "near monies" — such as Canada Savings Bonds, short-term marketable securities issued by government or large nonbank corporations, etc.

> A *liquid asset* is an asset that can be converted quickly into money (M1 or M2, say) with little fuss and cost, and at a stable dollar value.

(An example of an asset which is generally not liquid is real estate. It may be very difficult to sell, and its price may be quite uncertain, particularly if the owner is eager to sell quickly.)

BANKING AS A BUSINESS

Because chequable deposits in chartered banks constitute a large share of the money used in everyday purchases, banks occupy a strategic position in the economy. But, in addition, they also have a particular significance to a small fraction of the population: the stockholders of banks. Like manufacturing corporations or retail stores, banks are privately owned, and one of their major objectives is to make profits for their stockholders. Therefore,

two questions are relevant in an analysis of banking operations: (1) How do banks earn profits? and (2) How can banks be used by the authorities to stabilize the economy?

The Goldsmith: The Embryonic Bank as a Warehouse

The quest for profits led to the development of the modern bank. How this happened can be illustrated by dipping briefly into the history of the ancestors of banks—the medieval goldsmiths.

As their name implies, goldsmiths worked and shaped the precious metal. But they also undertook another function. Because gold wares were extremely valuable, customers looked to the goldsmith for safe storage of their treasures. In return for the deposit of a valuable, the goldsmith would provide the customer with a warehouse receipt — the promise to return the valuable to the customer on demand. Thus, the goldsmiths performed a service for a rich élite that was basically similar to the service that a baggage checkroom performs for you or me. They stored packages for a fee, and returned them to the owner on demand.

When unique gold ornaments were deposited, the customer naturally wanted to get back precisely the item which had been left with the goldsmith. But goldsmiths held not only unique items for their customers; gold bars and gold coins were also deposited. In these cases, it was not essential to the depositor to get back *exactly* the same gold bars or coins that had been deposited. Thus the basis for the development of banks was laid.

Fractional-Reserve Banking

To see how the banking business developed, let us look at the goldsmith's business in more detail. To do so, we need to look at the *balance sheet* of the goldsmith's business. A firm's balance sheet gives a picture of its financial status at a given point in time; for example, at the close of business on December 31 last year. It shows (1) the *assets* that the firm *owns*; (2) the *liabilities* that it *owes*; and (3) the firm's *net worth*—that is, the value that the ownership of the firm represents to the person (or persons) who owns it. To use a simple illustration: If you have a car worth $7000 (an asset), for which you still owe $4000 to the bank (your debt or liability), then $3000 is the value of your ownership of the car.

The same fundamental equation also holds for a firm (whether owned by a single person — such as the goldsmith — or by several persons, such as the shareholders in a corporation):

Assets = *liabilities* (what is owed) + *net worth*
(the value of ownership)

Assets are listed on the left side of the balance sheet, while liabilites and net worth are listed on the right. Because of the fundamental equation, the two sides must add to the same total. The balance sheet must balance.

Consider now an early goldsmith who had 10,000 "dollars" of his own funds invested in a building. This investment showed up as a building on the left-hand asset side of the goldsmith's balance sheet, and as net worth on the right-hand side (Table 11-1). Now, suppose the goldsmith accepted $100,000 in gold coins for safekeeping. As the coins were in his possession, they appeared on the asset side. But the owners of the gold had the right to withdraw them at any time upon demand. The goldsmith had **demand deposit liabilities** of $100,000; he had to be prepared to provide the depositors with this much gold whenever they requested it. Thus, the early goldsmith had the balance sheet shown in Table 11-1.

At this stage, a fundamental question arose regarding the goldsmith's business. If it operated simply as a warehouse, holding the $100,000 in gold coins which the customers had deposited, it would not be very profitable. Its sole source of profits would be the small amount charged for safeguarding gold.

After some years of experience holding gold for many different depositors, the goldsmith might have noticed something interesting. Although he was committed to repay the gold of the depositors on demand, he did not actually repay them all at once in the normal course of events. Each week some of the depositors

Table 11-1 Balance Sheet of the Early Goldsmith

Assets		Liabilities	
Gold coins	$100,000	Demand deposit	
Building	$ 10,000	liabilities	$100,000
		Net worth	$ 10,000
Total	$110,000	Total	$110,000

The early goldsmith operated a warehouse, holding $1 in gold for every $1 in deposits.

made withdrawals, but others added to their balances. There was a flow of gold out of the warehouse, but there was also an inflow. While there was some fluctuation in the goldsmith's total holdings of gold, a sizable quantity remained on deposit at all times.

Sooner or later, therefore, a question occurred to the goldsmith. Why not *lend out* some of this gold that was just sitting in the vaults, "collecting dust"? Since the depositors did not all try to withdraw their gold simultaneously, he did not need to have all the gold on hand. Some could be put to work earning interest. We can therefore imagine the goldsmith beginning to experiment by making loans. Undoubtedly, he started cautiously, keeping a relatively large quantity of gold in his vaults. Specifically, suppose that he kept a large reserve of $40,000 in gold to pay off depositors in the event that a group of them suddenly demanded their gold back. He lent the remaining $60,000 in gold, with the borrowers giving him promissory notes stating their commitment to pay interest and repay the principal after a period of time. Then the goldsmith's balance sheet changed to the one shown in Table 11-2. The only difference was on the asset side: The goldsmith had exchanged $60,000 of gold for $60,000 in promissory notes (shown simply as "Loans").

In making loans, the goldsmith went beyond warehousing and entered the **fractional-reserve banking** business. That is, *he held gold reserves that were only*

Table 11-2 The Goldsmith Becomes a Banker

Assets		Liabilities and net worth	
Reserve of		Demand deposits	$100,000
gold coins	$ 40,000	Net worth	$ 10,000
Loans	$ 60,000		
Building	$ 10,000		
Total	$110,000	Total	$110,000

When loans are made . . .
. . . reserves decline . . .
. . . and are now only a fraction of deposit liabilities.

Once the goldsmith had begun to lend the deposited gold and kept gold reserves equal to only a fraction of demand deposit liabilities, the business ceased to be a simple warehouse and became a bank.

a fraction of his demand deposit liabilities. In normal times, everything worked out well. He kept enough gold to pay off all depositors who wanted to make withdrawals. And he earned interest on the loans he had made.

As time passed and goldsmiths gained confidence in the banking business, they experimented by keeping gold reserves that were lower and lower fractions of their deposit liabilities. Sometimes they had only 20% in reserve, or even less. They had an incentive to reduce reserves, because each additional dollar taken out of reserves and lent out meant that additional interest could be earned. But, while the entry into fractional-reserve banking allowed goldsmiths to prosper, they faced two major risks in their new banking business:

1. Their loans might go sour. That is, goldsmiths might lend to businesses or individuals who became unable to repay. Clearly, then, the evaluation of *credit risks* (the estimation of the chances that borrowers would be unable to repay) became an important part of goldsmithing—and of modern banking.
2. Because they kept reserves equal to only a fraction of their demand deposit liabilities, the goldsmith-bankers were counting on a reasonably stable flow of deposits and withdrawals. In normal times, these flows were indeed likely to be stable. But the goldsmith-banker could not count on times being normal. If for some reason depositors became frightened, they would appear in droves to make withdrawals; in other words, there would be a *run* on the bank.

Bank Runs and Panics

During business downturns, people were particularly likely to become frightened, and look for safety. What could be safer than holding gold? In crises, then, the public tended to switch into gold—that is, they withdrew gold from their banks. But the banks, operating with gold reserves equal to only a fraction of their deposits, did not have enough gold to pay off all their depositors. A panic, with a run on the banks, was the result. Since banks could not possibly pay off all their deposit liabilities, every individual depositor had an incentive to withdraw his or her deposit before the bank ran out of gold and was forced to close. For all depositors as a group, this was self-destructive behaviour: The run could push banks into bankruptcy, with some depositors losing their money forever. But individual depositors could not be expected to commit financial suicide for the common good; they could not be expected to stay out of a line-up of those

making withdrawals. Indeed, each depositor had a personal interest to be *first* in line to get back his or her gold.

THE MODERN CANADIAN BANKING SYSTEM

This account obviously has been an extremely simplified version of the history of banks. But it does help to explain the crises that occurred in the Canadian and U.S. banking systems during the nineteenth century, and why monetary problems contributed to the Great Depression in both Canada and the United States.

In the United States, following a crisis in 1907, a National Monetary Commission was set up to study monetary and banking problems. As a result of the Commission's recommendations, the *Federal Reserve System* was established in 1914, giving the United States a central bank. In Canada, a Royal Commission on Banking and Finance was appointed during the Great Depression; it concluded that the authorities needed more powers to resolve the monetary problems that had arisen during the Depression. Following the Commission's recommendations, the **Bank of Canada** was founded in 1935.

The Bank of Canada

The Bank of Canada is our central bank. It is the Canadian equivalent of foreign central banks such as the Bank of England, the Deutsche Bundesbank of Germany, and the U.S. Federal Reserve (sometimes known only as "the Fed"). As our central bank, the Bank of Canada:

1. Has the responsibility to *control the quantity of money* in Canada.
2. *Issues paper currency* (2-dollar bills, 5-dollar bills, etc.).
3. *Acts as a "bankers' bank."* (While you and I may keep our bank deposits in the chartered banks, the chartered banks in turn keep deposits in the Bank of Canada. While you and I—and business corporations—can go to the chartered banks for loans, chartered banks in turn can borrow from the Bank of Canada. The Bank of Canada also helps the chartered banks make the system of payments by cheque work smoothly and inexpensively.)
4. *Supervises the chartered banks* and collects detailed data on all aspects of their operation. (The formal responsibility for ensuring that the chartered banks comply with the provisions of the Bank Act, however, rests with the Inspector General of Banks, who is appointed by the federal government and is an official

in the Department of Finance, not the Bank of Canada.)

5. *Acts as the federal government's bank.* The government keeps some of its deposits in the Bank of Canada, and the Bank administers the sale of government bonds and their repayment when they come due. The Bank also acts on behalf of the government in buying and selling foreign currencies, such as U.S. dollars or German marks.

How the Bank of Canada carries out these responsibilities will be a major topic in future chapters.

The Chartered Banks

Currency issued by the Bank of Canada is a significant component of the money stock in Canada. However, as we have seen, deposits held by individuals and firms in financial institutions are much larger than the currency component, no matter which concept of money we look at. Most of these deposits are held in Canada's *chartered banks*. (Even though institutions such as trust companies and credit unions have become increasingly important in recent years, the chartered banks continue to be the dominant deposit-taking institutions. They are also the institutions that are most directly influenced by the policies of the Bank of Canada.)

In contrast to the banking system in the United States, where there are about 15 000 separate banks, Canada has a highly concentrated banking system. If we exclude foreign banks operating here through subsidiaries, Canada has no more than a dozen chartered banks. The five largest ones (the Royal Bank, Canadian Imperial Bank of Commerce, Bank of Montreal, Bank of Nova Scotia, and Toronto Dominion Bank) account for about 90% of the total assets of chartered banks. Each of these banks operates a large number of branches throughout the country. (A branch is a building, other than the head office, where the bank accepts deposits.) This contrasts with the situation in the United States, where some states confine each bank to a single building, and interstate branching has not been permitted. (In the formative years of U.S. banking, politicians feared that large banks might become too powerful, and set up regulations that hindered their expansion across the country. However, the regulations against banking in more than one state are gradually being relaxed.)

The two functions at the heart of banking show up clearly in the combined balance sheet of the Canadian chartered banks in Table 11-3: accepting deposits (items 7 and 8), and making loans to businesses and individuals (item 2). As we have already seen, chartered bank deposit liabilities constitute the largest component of the money stock in Canada.

Table 11-3   Combined Balanced Sheet, Chartered Banks, December 1987 (billions of dollars)

Assets			Liabilities	
1. Reserves (Currency and deposits in Bank of Canada)		6.7	7. Demand deposits	22.5
2. Loans		210.0	8. Notice and term deposits	192.5
Short-term	(1.8)		9. Foreign currency liabilities	200.9
Mortages	(66.8)		10. Shareholders' equity	21.5
Other loans	(141.4)		11. All other liabilities	48.7
3. Securities		28.1	12. Total liabilities and net worth	486.10
Treasury bills	(11.4)			
Government bonds	(3.8)			
Canadian securities	(12.9)			
4. Foreign currency assets		191.5		
5. All other assets		49.8		
6. Total assets		486.1		

Source: *Bank of Canada Review.*

A number of other items on the chartered banks' balance sheet are also worthy of note, beginning with the first entry — reserves. Unlike the goldsmiths and the early banks, modern banks do not hold gold as reserves; gold is no longer the basic money of Canada or of other countries. Instead, banks hold two kinds of *cash reserves*: deposits in the Bank of Canada and currency. Banks are *required by law* to keep cash reserves equal to certain percentages of their deposits. (In 1987, the Bank Act stipulated that the chartered banks had to hold reserves equal to 10% of demand deposit liabilities, and an additional amount equal to 3% of notice deposit liabilities.) Note that reserves, which appear on the *asset* side of the balance sheet, must meet the required percentages of the deposits (items 7 and 8) on the *liabilities* side of the banks' balance sheet. (For example, if the required reserve ratio were set at 10% of all deposits, a bank with $50 million in deposit *liabilities* would have to hold $5 million of its *assets* in the form of reserves.)

> *Required reserves* are reserves that chartered banks are required to hold in order to meet their legal obligations. These reserves are specified as percentages of deposits. Required reserves are held in the form of currency or deposits in the Bank of Canada.

Continuing down the asset side of the balance sheet, note that $210.0 billion of assets are *loans* that banks have extended to businesses and individuals (item 2). The banks also hold substantial amounts of *securities* issued by the federal and provincial governments or by corporations (item 3). An individual bank may also hold *deposits in foreign banks*, or other foreign currency assets (item 4). It may also have borrowed money from foreign banks or have accepted deposits denominated in U.S. dollars (rather than in Canadian dollars). These foreign liabilities are shown in item 9. Finally, "other assets" of banks (item 5) include the value of bank buildings, computers, and other equipment.

Excess Reserves and Secondary Reserves

Even though bankers may generally count on a reasonably steady inflow and outflow of deposits, they must still protect themselves against temporary surges of withdrawals. The reserves that banks hold to meet the reserve requirements laid down by the Bank Act do not provide an adequate cushion against such withdrawals. Suppose, for example, that the required reserve ratio is 20%, and that a bank holds just barely enough reserves to meet this requirement. Then assume that owners of deposits withdraw $100,000 in currency. With a required reserve ratio of 20%, required reserves fall by $20,000 as a result of the $100,000 withdrawal. But the bank's *actual* reserves fall by a full $100,000 when it pays out the currency, since currency is counted as part of total reserves. Thus, with actual reserves declining by $100,000, and required reserves declining by only $20,000, the bank's reserves are now $80,000 short of the legal requirement.

There are three ways in which a bank can protect itself against this danger. First, it may regularly hold **excess reserves** of currency and Bank of Canada deposits. For example, if the bank initially held $90,000 in excess reserves, this sudden withdrawal would create no problem. The holding of excess reserves is, however, expensive: currency earns no interest, nor is interest paid on reserve deposits in the Bank of Canada. As a result, banks generally hold only small amounts of excess reserves. (Typically, excess reserves are less than 1% of total reserves.)

> *Excess reserves* are reserves, in the form of currency or deposits in the Bank of Canada, that are in excess of those required by law.
>
> Excess reserves
> = total reserves − required reserves

Another way for the bank to protect itself is to hold other kinds of **secondary reserves**; that is, assets that do not count as part of required reserves, but that can be liquidated (converted into cash) on short notice. If the bank needs cash to deal with a surge in withdrawals by its depositors, it can quickly get it by selling off secondary reserves. The Canadian chartered banks usually maintain relatively large amounts of secondary reserves, not only as a protection against sudden deposit withdrawals but also because they are forced to. Under the Bank Act, the Bank of Canada can require the chartered banks to hold secondary reserves (defined as short-term Treasury bills, day-to-day loans to investment dealers, and any excess cash reserves) equal to a specific minimum percentage of their deposit liabilities.

As a precautionary measure, the banks usually maintain a cushion of secondary reserves over and above the legal minimum: Because they earn interest on their secondary reserves, it is not as expensive to maintain excess secondary reserves as it would be to have large excess cash reserves.

The third protection against a shortfall in cash reserves is the banks' *ability to borrow*. In difficulty, a bank may replenish its reserves by borrowing from the Bank of Canada. Or, it may turn to the **short-term money market**; that is, a market for short-term loans in which banks with inadequate reserves can borrow some from other institutions.[3]

BANKS AND THE CREATION OF MONEY

The public's use of bank deposits as money would be reason enough to look carefully at the operation of banks. But banks require attention for an additional reason—and one of great economic importance. In the normal course of their operations, they create money.

Most people have heard of this power in a vague and imprecise way. Banks are consequently looked on with a mixture of awe and resentment. How did they acquire this magical ability, and why should they have such extraordinary power? These attitudes reflect a lack of understanding of banking. There is, in fact, nothing magical in the process whereby money is created. Your local bank branch does not have a magical fountain pen with which it can create unlimited amounts of money out of thin air.

The operations of banks, and how they create money, can be understood most easily by looking at the balance sheets of individual banks. An individual chartered bank, like the aggregate of chartered banks shown in Table 11-3, has a list of assets and liabilities. To avoid being burdened with detail, we simplify the following tables by showing only the *changes* in the balance sheet of a bank. (Like the whole balance sheet, changes in the balance sheet must balance.) To avoid untidy fractions, we assume that the required reserves of banks are a nice round figure—20% of their deposit liabilities—even though requirements are not, in fact, this high. To simplify further, we assume that all deposits are chequable demand deposits in chartered banks, and that banks initially have just enough reserves to meet the legal reserve requirement.

■ ■ ■ ■ ■

[3] The chartered banks are not the only firms that are allowed to borrow from the Bank of Canada: The *authorized investment dealers* also may do so. Thus, when the banks need cash reserves, they may call in the loans they have made to investment dealers. If the dealers pay off these loans by borrowing from the Bank of Canada, the chartered banks' cash reserves will increase. (The dealers' cheques drawn on the Bank of Canada will be credited to the chartered banks' accounts with the Bank of Canada.) Investment dealers will be discussed further in Chapter 12.

Now, suppose that you find $100,000 left in a shoe box by your eccentric old uncle when he died. In a state of bliss, you rush to the nearest branch office of your bank to put the $100,000 into your chequing account. As a result, your bank—call it bank A—has $100,000 more in currency on the asset side of its balance sheet (Table 11-4). It also has $100,000 more in liabilities, since you have a $100,000 claim on the bank in the form of a chequing deposit. (This $100,000 deposit represents an *asset* to you; it is something you own. However, this same $100,000 deposit is a *liability* to the bank; the bank must be prepared to pay you $100,000 in currency if you ask.)

As a result of this deposit, what has happened to the quantity of money in the economy? The answer is: nothing. You initially held the $100,000 in currency; you exchanged the currency for $100,000 in deposit money. Once the deposit is made, the $100,000 in dollar bills ceases to be counted as part of the money stock, since it is held by the bank. (Remember the technical point regarding the data in Figure 11-1: Currency and deposits are included in the money stock only when they are held by the public, but not when they are held by the Bank of Canada, the federal government, or the chartered banks themselves.) The *composition* of the money stock has changed—there is now $100,000 more in deposits and $100,000 less in currency in the hands of the public. But, the total amount has not changed.

However, this is not the end of the story, because the bank now has excess reserves. Its deposit liabilities have gone up by your $100,000. Therefore, its required reserves have risen by $20,000 (that is, $100,000 times the required reserve ratio of 20%). But its total reserves have risen by the $100,000 in currency that you deposited. Therefore, it now has $80,000 in excess reserves. Like the goldsmith of old, it is in a position to make loans to businesses and other customers.

Suppose that a local shoe store wants to expand its operations, and approaches bank A for a loan of $80,000—an amount that just happens to equal the excess reserves of the bank. The bank agrees. Mechanically, what happens? The bank could, presumably, hand over $80,000 in dollar bills to the store owner, in exchange for the promissory note that commits the store to repay the loan. However, the bank does not normally operate this way. Instead, when it makes the loan, it simply adds $80,000 to the deposit account of the borrower. This is entirely satisfactory to the borrower, who can write cheques against the account. As a result of this loan, the balance sheet of the chartered bank is modified; see Table 11-5.

Table 11-4   Changes in Assets and Liabilities when Chartered Bank A Receives a Deposit

Chartered bank A

Assets		Liabilities	
Reserves of currency	+ $100,000	Chequing deposits	+ $100,000
Required $20,000 Excess $80,000			
Total	$100,000	Total	$100,000

When you deposit $100,000 in currency . . .

. . . bank reserves also rise by $100,000.

Your balance sheet

Assets		Liabilities	
Currency	– $100,000	No change	
Chequing deposit	+ $100,000		
Total	0	Total	0

When chartered bank A receives your $100,000 deposit, its assets and liabilities both rise by $100,000. But your holdings of money do not change. You have merely switched from one type of money (currency) to another (a chequing deposit).

Now, what has happened to the money supply? Observe that when *the bank makes a loan, the stock of money in the hands of the public increases.* Specifically, there now is $80,000 more in chequing deposit money. But what has the bank done? Nothing extraordinary. It has merely lent its excess reserves. That is, it has lent less than was placed in its safekeeping when you made your original deposit.

How a Cheque Is Cleared

So far, so good. However, our story has just nicely begun. The shoe store borrowed from the bank in order to buy inventory, not to leave its money sitting idly in a chequing account. Suppose that the shoe store orders shoes from a Montreal manufacturer, sending a cheque for $80,000 in payment. The shoe company in Montreal deposits the cheque in its bank (bank B). This sets in motion the process of **cheque clearing**—which straightens out accounts between bank A in your home town and bank B in Montreal (Figure 11-2). Bank B sends the cheque along to the Bank of Canada, receiving in exchange a reserve deposit of $80,000. Bank B's accounts balance, since its assets in the form of reserves have gone up by the same amount ($80,000) as its chequing deposit liabilities to the shoe manufacturer. (The $80,000 reserve deposit represents an *asset* to bank B and a *liability* to the Bank of Canada.)

The Bank of Canada, in turn, sends the cheque along to bank A, subtracting the $80,000 from bank A's reserve deposit. Bank A balances its accounts by subtracting the $80,000 from the deposit of the shoe store that wrote the cheque in the first place.

Table 11-5   Bank A Makes a Loan

Assets		Liabilities	
Reserves of currency	$100,000	Chequing deposits: yours	$100,000
Loan†	+ $ 80,000	shoe store's†	+ $ 80,000
Total	$180,000	Total	$180,000

When a bank makes a loan . . .

. . . chequing deposits increase.

When the bank lends $80,000, chequing deposits increase by $80,000. This represents a net increase in the money stock.

†Items resulting from the loan.

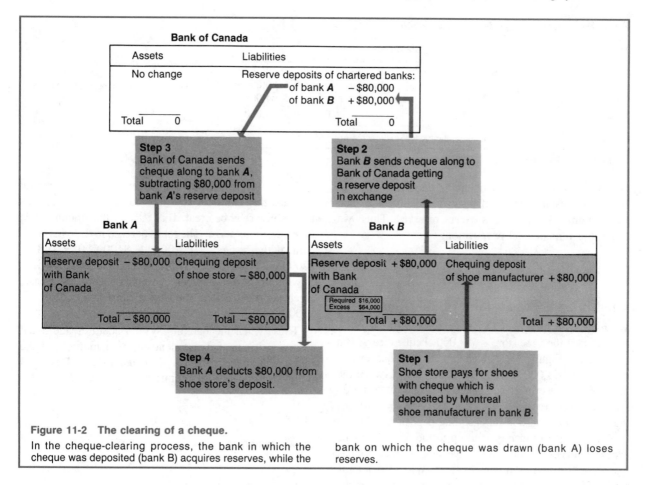

Figure 11-2 The clearing of a cheque.

In the cheque-clearing process, the bank in which the cheque was deposited (bank B) acquires reserves, while the bank on which the cheque was drawn (bank A) loses reserves.

Why a Bank Can Safely Lend No More Than Its Excess Reserves

When the effects of the cheque clearing (in Figure 11-2) are added to bank A's earlier transactions (shown in Table 11-5), the net effects on bank A's balance sheet may be summarized in Table 11-6. Observe that, as a result of the cheque clearing, bank A's excess reserves have completely disappeared. (Its currency reserves rose by $100,000 when you deposited the original $100,000. Its reserve deposit in the Bank of Canada fell by $80,000 when the shoe store's cheque cleared. Thus, its net change in reserves is $20,000, just the amount required

**Table 11-6   Net Effects on Bank A
(cheque clearing combined with earlier transactions)**

Assets		Liabilities	
Reserves	+$ 20,000	Chequing deposits:	
Required $20,000 Excess 0		yours	+$100,000
Loan	$ 80,000		
Total	$100,000	Total	$100,000

This table gives the combined effect on bank A of cheque clearing (Figure 11-2) and earlier transactions (Table 11-5). After the cheque is cleared, bank A has no excess reserves.

Table 11-7   Bank B Lends to Camera Store

Assets		Liabilities		
Reserve deposit	$ 80,000	Chequing deposits:		
		shoe manufacturer's	$ 80,000	
Loan†	+$ 64,000	camera store's†	+$ 64,000	
Total	$144,000	Total	$144,000	

When bank B lends $64,000 . . .

. . . chequing deposits increase by $64,000.

As a result of the second round of lending, the money stock increases by $64,000.

†Items resulting from the loan.

as a result of its $100,000 chequing deposit liability to you.) This was the result of bank A's lending the shoe store an amount equal to its excess reserves. Thus, we come to a fundamental proposition:

A bank may prudently lend an amount up to, but no greater than, its excess reserves.

The Multiple Expansion of Bank Deposits

We have seen how bank A's excess reserves are eliminated when the shoe store's $80,000 cheque clears. But observe (in Figure 11-2) that bank B now has excess reserves of $64,000; that is, the difference between the $80,000 increase in its actual reserves and the $16,000 increase in its required reserves. ($16,000 = 20% of the $80,000 increase in its chequing deposit liabilities.)

Bank B may prudently lend up to the $64,000 of its excess reserves. In Table 11-7, we suppose that it lends this amount to the local camera store. When the loan is made, $64,000 is added to the chequing deposit of the camera store. Because the amount of chequing deposits held by the public goes up by $64,000, *the money stock increases by this amount.*

Suppose that the camera store has borrowed the $64,000 to buy film, cameras, and equipment from Kodak. To pay for its purchases, it writes a cheque to Kodak. Kodak deposits the cheque in its Toronto bank — bank C. Once again, the cheque-clearing mechanism is set in operation. When bank C sends the cheque to the Bank of Canada, it receives a reserve deposit of $64,000 (Table 11-8). But when the cheque is sent along to bank B (the camera store's bank), that bank loses $64,000 in reserves, and no longer has any excess reserves.

Observe, however, that bank C now has excess reserves of $51,200, which it can lend out. When it does so, it will create a new chequing deposit of $51,200, thus increasing the money stock once again. And so the process continues. As a result of your initial deposit of $100,000, there can be a chain reaction of loans, as shown

in Figure 11-3 and Table 11-9. At each stage, the amount of loans that can be made (and the amount of deposits that can thereby be created) is 80% of the amount made in the previous stage. The total increase in deposits is the sum of the series: $100,000 + $100,000 \times 0.8 + $100,000 \times 0.8^2$. . . . If this series is taken to its limit — with an infinite number of rounds — then, by a basic algebraic proposition,[4] the sum is equal to: $100,000/(1 - 0.8) = $500,000.

Thus, when the banking system acquires additional reserves, it can increase deposits by a multiple of the initial reserve increase. The *deposit multiplier D* is equal to the reciprocal of the required reserve ratio R:

$$D = \frac{1}{R}$$

In our example:

$$D = \frac{1}{20\%} = 5$$

The initial acquisition of $100,000 in reserves made possible an increase in chequing deposits of $500,000 (that is, $100,000/0.2). Alternatively, if the required reserve ratio were only 10%, the banking system would have been capable of creating up to $1,000,000 (that is, $100,000/0.1) in deposit money on the basis of $100,000 in reserves. Thus, *when there is a change in the required reserve ratio, there is a powerful effect on the amount of loans which the banks can make, and on the amount of deposit money which they can create.*

A few pages earlier, we emphasized that required reserves provide a bank with little cushion in the event

■ ■ ■ ■ ■

[4] Mathematically, this is the same theorem used in the derivation of the multiplier in Chapter 9 (footnote 2). But the economic issues are quite different in the two cases. In the multiplier, the total effects of various rounds of spending are derived. Here, changes in the stock of money are calculated.

Table 11-8   The Creation of Money: After the Second Round

Bank B

Assets			Liabilities		
Reserves		$16,000	Chequing deposits of shoe manufacturer		$80,000
Required $16,000 Excess 0					
Loans		$64,000			
	Total	$80,000		Total	$80,000

Bank C

Assets			Liabilities		
Reserves		$64,000	Chequing deposits of Kodak		$64,000
Required $12,800 Excess $51,200					
	Total	$64,000		Total	$64,000

When bank C receives deposits and reserves of $64,000, it can prudently lend $51,200. And so the process continues.

of a withdrawal of deposits. That is not their primary purpose. Rather, the requirement that banks hold reserves is a way of *controlling the amount of loans they can make and the amount of money they can create*. (In the late 1980s, a proposal to abolish legal reserve requirements for the chartered banks was being actively considered. The main concern of those who opposed this proposal was precisely that, with no legal reserve requirements, it would be very difficult for the Bank of Canada to prevent the chartered banks from expanding their loans and creating large amounts of new money. We will discuss this issue further in Chapter 12.)

During the multiple expansion of deposits, *the banking system as a whole does something which no single bank can do*. The banking system as a whole can create deposits equal to a multiple of the reserves which it acquires. But any single bank can create deposits (by lending its excess reserves) by an amount equal to only a fraction (80% in our illustration) of the reserves which it acquires.

Banks' Securities Holdings and the Deposit Multiplier

Thus far we have assumed that a chartered bank with excess reserves lends these excess reserves to its cus-

tomers in order to earn interest. But as we saw in Table 11-3, the chartered banks' asset portfolios include substantial amounts of securities, such as Treasury bills and bonds issued by federal, provincial, and local governments or by private corporations. Thus, in reality, a bank with excess reserves does not always use them to make more loans; it may use them instead to buy securities. How does this affect the deposit multiplier process?

The answer is that it does not make much difference: The effect on the money stock is similar, whether the banks use their excess reserves to make loans or purchase securities.

To illustrate this point, suppose that, in the *n*th round in the monetary expansion chain, bank N acquires $10,000 in chequing deposits and reserves. If the required reserve ratio is 20%, it then has $8,000 in excess reserves. Suppose that it uses these reserves to purchase $8,000 in government bonds owned by the XYZ Corporation. Bank N pays for the bonds by writing a cheque, which the XYZ Corporation deposits in bank O. Then the money stock as a consequence rises by $8,000; that is, by the $8,000 chequing deposit which the XYZ Corporation now owns. The change in the money stock is thus exactly the same as it would have been if bank N had used these excess reserves to make

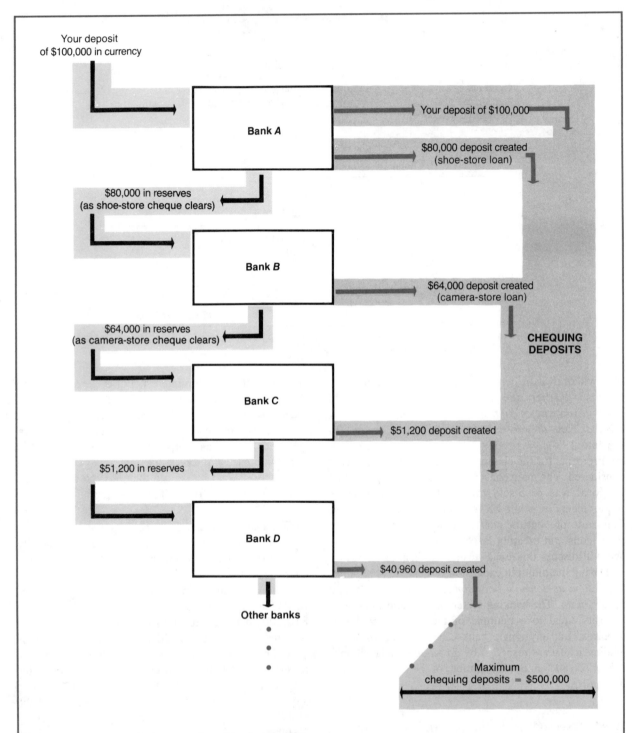

Figure 11-3   The multiple expansion of bank deposits.
The banking system as a whole can do what no single bank can do. It can transform the original deposit of $100,000 currency into as much as $500,000 in chequing deposit money.

Table 11-9 **The Multiple Expansion of Bank Deposits**

A. The chain reaction

Bank	(1) Acquired reserves and chequing deposits	(2) Required reserves (2) = (1) × 0.20	(3) Excess reserves = loans that banks can make (3) = (1) − (2)	(4) Changes in money stock (4) = (3)
A	$100,000 (yours)	$20,000	$80,000	$80,000
B	$800,000 (shoe manufacturer's)	$16,000	$64,000	$64,000
C	$64,000 (Kodak's)	$12,800	$51,200	$51,200
D	$51,200	$10,240	$40,960	$40,960
•	•	•	•	•
•	•	•	•	•
•	•	•	•	•
Maximum sum	$500,000	$100,000	$400,000	$400,000

B. Effects on consolidated balance sheet of all chartered banks (with maximum permissible expansion)

Reserves	$100,000	Chequing deposits	$500,000
Required $100,000 Excess 0			
Loans	$400,000		
Total	$500,000	Total	$500,000

The banking system as a whole can do what no single bank can do. It can transform the original deposit of $100,000 in currency into as much as $500,000 in chequing deposit money.

a loan rather than to buy a bond. Moreover, as a result of this transaction, bank N loses its $8,000 of excess reserves, while bank O gains $8,000 of reserves. It is now bank O that finds itself with excess reserves ($6,400, to be precise). When it uses these reserves to make a loan or buy securities, the process of money creation continues.

Two Complications

With a required reserve ratio of 20%, $500,000 is the *maximum* increase in chequing deposits following a $100,000 acquisition of reserves by the banking system. In practice, the actual increase in deposits is likely to be considerably less, because of two complications: (1) In some circumstances, banks may voluntarily decide to continue holding reserves in excess of those they are legally required to hold. (2) When more deposit money is created, the public may want to increase its holdings of currency as well.

Excess Reserves in a Depression

If banks choose to use only *part* of their excess reserves

to make loans or buy securities, the amount of deposits created by an initial acquisition of reserves will be less than the maximum amount that could be legally created. During prosperous times, this is not an important complication. Because reserve holdings don't earn interest, banks have a strong incentive to make loans or buy interest-bearing securities: They prefer to hold only small amounts of excess reserves.

But, during a depression, bankers may become panicky. They may be afraid to make loans because they doubt the ability of borrowers to repay. They may decide to keep their funds secure by holding them as excess reserves. Thus, during the Great Depression, Canadian banks held large excess reserves. (So did U.S. banks.) This unwillingness of the banks to lend tended to keep down the amount of money in the hands of the public and thereby slowed the recovery from the Depression.

Increased Public Currency Holdings

As loans are made and people get more deposit money, they may want to hold more currency, too. In other words, they may withdraw currency from their deposits.

Insofar as this happens, the reserves of the chartered banks are reduced; the initial deposit of currency that started off the expansion is partially reversed. As a consequence, the total amount of monetary expansion is reduced.

When currency is held by the public, it is, in a sense, just ordinary money. The dollar coin I hold in my pocket is only a dollar. On the other hand, when currency is deposited in a bank, it becomes "high-powered." Although the dollar ceases to count directly in the money stock (since chartered bank holdings of currency are excluded from the definition of money), that dollar is a bank reserve. On this reserve base, the banking system can build a superstructure of as much as $5 of chequing deposit money if the required reserve ratio is 20%. The large amount of chequing deposit money, built on a much smaller base of reserves, can be represented graphically by an inverted pyramid (Figure 11-4).

DEPOSITS IN NON-BANK FINANCIAL INSTITUTIONS

When chartered banks make loans, some of the funds they lend may end up being deposited in a trust company, for example, rather than in a chartered bank. How does this affect the process of bank deposit creation?

The answer is that, typically, it doesn't. Like other firms, trust companies have deposit accounts in the chartered banks. Therefore, a trust company that receives a deposit from the public may simply use the funds to increase the balance in its deposit account with a chartered bank. This chartered bank will now have excess reserves, and the deposit creation process can continue just as before.

Like chartered banks, however, trust companies and similar institutions also try to increase their earnings by making loans or buying securities when they receive an inflow of funds. But, like chartered banks, they will not lend out all the funds they receive. Even though trust companies and other non-bank institutions are not subject to the legal reserve requirements specified in the Bank Act, they must still hold some of their assets as reserves for meeting any sudden withdrawals of funds by their depositors. Like the chartered banks, they hold some of their reserves in the form of currency. But unlike chartered banks, trust companies and other non-bank institutions do not hold balances with the Bank of Canada. Instead, they use their deposits in the chartered banks as reserves. Thus, some of the currency and chartered bank deposits that are included in the various definitions of money (such as M1 or M2) are, in fact, held

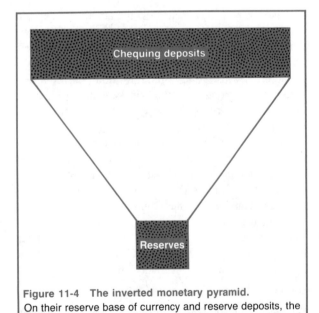

Figure 11-4 The inverted monetary pyramid.
On their reserve base of currency and reserve deposits, the chartered banking system can build a superstructure of chequing deposits—of as much as $1/R$ times the base.

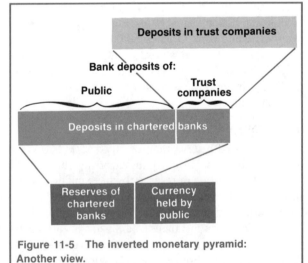

Figure 11-5 The inverted monetary pyramid: Another view.
Part of the chartered bank deposits is held by trust companies and similar institutions as reserves against *their* deposit liabilities. Like the chartered banks, they build a relatively large superstructure of deposits on a narrow reserve base.

by institutions such as trust companies or credit unions as part of their reserves.

But if trust companies, for example, hold assets equivalent to 10% (say) of their deposit liabilities as reserves, their balance sheet will show deposit liabilities that are 10 times as large as their reserves. Thus, just as chartered banks can "create money" (deposit liabilities) by lending out any excess reserves, trust companies can also increase the amount of deposit liabilities in the financial system by increasing their lending whenever they receive an inflow of deposits. Indeed, if we use the M2 + definition of money (which includes deposits held in trust and mortgage loan companies, credit unions, etc.), then we could properly say that trust companies can "create money" as well.

In Figure 11-5, we show a version of the inverted monetary pyramid of Figure 11-4 that takes account of deposits in trust companies and similar institutions as well as of chartered bank deposits. As in Figure 11-4, the chartered banks have used a relatively small reserve base to build a superstructure of deposits. Trust companies and credit unions, in turn, hold some of the chartered bank deposits as reserves against *their* deposits from the public, which again are much larger than their reserve holdings. If we use a broad definition of money — such as M2 + — both the chartered bank deposits and the deposits of trust companies and similar institutions in Figure 11-5 are counted as part of Canada's money supply.

KEY POINTS

1. Money is important in the study of macroeconomics because:
   (a) The authorities can take steps to alter the quantity of money and thus affect aggregate demand. *Monetary policy* is the second great tool, along with fiscal policy, that can be used to manage aggregate demand. The details of monetary policy will be explained in Chapter 12.
   (b) At times, strong disturbances have occurred in the monetary system; for example, during the Depression of the 1930s. Such disturbances can make the economy unstable.

2. Money has three interrelated functions. It acts as:
   (a) the medium of exchange
   (b) the standard of value
   (c) a store of value

3. The traditional, narrow definition of money, M1, includes only currency in the hands of the public and demand deposits in the chartered banks. In recent years, economists at the Bank of Canada and elsewhere have increasingly focused on a broader concept of money, M2, as the main indicator of monetary policy. M2 is defined to include currency plus all chequable, notice, and term deposits in chartered banks.

4. An even broader concept of money is M3, which includes all privately held deposits in the chartered banks (those denoted in foreign currency as well

as in Canadian dollars). Because deposits in trust companies and similar institutions are close substitutes for deposits in chartered banks, some economists favour the use of another extended money concept, M2 + . The M2 + definition consists of the same items as in M2, plus all deposits in trust and mortgage loan companies, credit unions, and Quebec's *caisses populaires*.

5. The Bank of Canada is our central bank. As such—
   (a) it has the responsibility to control the quantity of money;
   (b) it issues paper currency;
   (c) it acts as the "bankers' bank";
   (d) it supervises and inspects the chartered banks;
   (e) it acts as the federal government's bank.

6. Banks have two principal functions: to accept deposits and to make loans. When a bank makes a loan or purchases a bond, it increases the stock of money.

7. Chartered banks are required to hold reserves in the form of currency or reserve deposits in the Bank of Canada. These reserves must meet required percentages of the chartered banks' deposit liabilities. The purpose of required reserves is to control the quantity of money that banks can create.

8. When a *single* bank acquires additional deposits and reserves, it can safely lend out only a fraction

of these reserves—specifically, its excess reserves. However, the banking *system* (all chartered banks taken together) can create deposits that are a multiple of any new reserves that it acquires.

9. The maximum increase in deposit money that can be created by the banking system is:

$$\frac{1}{R} \times \text{the acquisition of reserves}$$

where R is the required reserve ratio.

10. In practice, the actual increase is likely to be less than the maximum, for two reasons:

   (a) Banks sometimes hold substantial excess reserves, expecially during a depression. During the 1930s, the unwillingness of banks to lend their excess reserves kept down the quantity of money in the hands of the public and slowed the recovery from the Great Depression.

   (b) As people get more deposit money, they are likely to want to hold more currency, too. When they withdraw currency from their deposits, the reserves held by the banks are reduced.

11. Trust companies and similar institutions hold reserves in the form of currency and deposits in the chartered banks. Like chartered banks, trust companies have an incentive to make more loans and buy more securities when they receive an inflow of reserves. As a result, like the chartered banks they will build a relatively large superstructure of deposits on a small base of reserves.

KEY CONCEPTS

monetary policy	*M1*	*Bank of Canada*
medium of exchange	*M2*	*central bank*
standard of value	*M2 +*	*chartered bank*
store of value	*M3*	*trust company*
purchasing power	*liquid assets*	*required reserve ratio*
currency	*credit card*	*required reserves*
Bank of Canada note	*line of credit*	*excess reserves*
demand deposit	*fractional-reserve banking*	*secondary reserves*
notice deposit	*balance sheet*	*cheque clearing*
daily interest chequable notice	*deposit liability*	*multiple expansion of bank*
* deposit*	*promissory note*	* deposits*
term deposit	*loan*	*deposit multiplier*
certificate of deposit (CD)	*bank run*	*"high-powered" reserves*
		monetary pyramid

PROBLEMS

11-1. (a) Suppose that a corporation that previously paid its workers in cash decides to pay them by cheque instead. As a result, it decides to deposit $10,000 that it previously has held in currency in its safe. Show how this deposit will affect the balance sheets of (1) the corporation and (2) its bank (the Bank of Nova Scotia).

   (b) Does this deposit of $10,000 affect the money stock? Why or why not?

   (c) How much can the Bank of Nova Scotia now lend, if there is a required reserve ratio of 10%? If it lends this amount to a farmer to buy machinery, show the direct effect of the loan on the bank's balance sheet. Then show the Bank of Nova Scotia's balance sheet after the farmer spends the loan to buy machinery and the farmer's cheque is cleared.

   (d) As a result of the original deposit (in part (a) of this problem), what is the maximum increase in chequing deposits that can occur if the required reserve ratio is 10%? The maximum amount of bank lending? The maximum increase in the money stock?

11-2. Suppose that a bank receives a deposit of $100,000 and decides to lend the full $100,000. Explain how this decision can get the bank into difficulty.

11-3. If all banks are required to keep reserves equal to 100% of their chequing deposits, what will be the consequences of a deposit of $100,000 of currency in bank A?

11-4. During the 1930s, banks held large excess reserves. Now they hold practically none. Why? If you were a banker, would you hold excess reserves? How much? Does your answer depend on the size of individual deposits in your bank? On interest rates? On other things?

11-5. Suppose that there is a single huge chartered bank that holds a monopoly on all banking in Canada. If this bank receives $100,000 in deposits and the required reserve ratio is 20%, how much can the bank safely lend? Explain. (Hints: (1) Study Table 11-9, Part B. (2) In Figure 11-2, bank A lost reserves to bank B. If there is only one bank, will it lose reserves in this way?)

11-6. During the 1930s, the banking systems in Canada and the United States did not work well. Banking disturbances contributed to the depth and duration of the Great Depression.

(a) Explain how, during a financial crisis, individual bank depositors have an incentive to behave in a manner that makes the crisis worse. Do you think that an educational campaign to teach depositors the dangers of such actions would help to solve this problem? If so, explain how. If not, explain why not.

(b) Explain how, during a depression, individual banks have an incentive to behave in a manner that makes the depression deeper and longer-lasting. Do you think that an educational campaign to teach bankers the dangers of such actions would help to solve this problem? If so, explain how. If not, explain why not.

Chapter 12

■■■■■■■■■■■■■■■■■■■■■■■■■■■■■■■■■

The Bank of Canada and the Tools of Monetary Policy

There have been three great inventions since
the beginning of time: fire, the wheel, and
central banking.

Will Rogers

The Bank of Canada is our central bank, acting as the federal government's bank and the bankers' bank. As the central bank, it has one responsibility of prime importance: to see that monetary conditions are consistent with the achievement of the goals of high employment and stable prices. If business is getting worse and the economy is sliding into a recession, the job of the Bank of Canada is to expand the money stock, and thus support aggregate demand. And when business is booming and inflation threatens, the job of the Bank is to exercise restraint, to prevent an excessive monetary growth from fueling the fires of inflation.

The principal purpose of this chapter is to explain:

1. *Open market operations*, that is, purchases or sales of government securities by the Bank of Canada. Through open market operations, the Bank of Canada can control the quantity of reserves held by the chartered banks, and thereby control the quantity of deposit money that the chartered banks can create.

Open market operations constitute the main policy tool in the hands of the Bank of Canada. In this chapter, we also will look at other actions which influence chartered bank reserves, namely:

2. *Purchases or sales of foreign currencies* by the Bank of Canada, and

3. *Transfers of federal government deposits* between the Bank of Canada and chartered banks.

We also will study other monetary policy tools that the Bank of Canada has used at various times in the past; specifically, we will discuss:

4. *Changes in the Bank Rate*, that is, the interest rate at which the Bank of Canada lends to chartered banks.

5. *Changes in required reserve ratios* that specify the reserves that banks must hold as percentages of their demand and other deposit liabilities.

But, before turning to these topics, let us look briefly at the origins of the Bank of Canada.

ORIGINS AND ORGANIZATION OF THE BANK OF CANADA

The establishment of a Canadian central bank was a controversial step. While the need for some form of central control and regulation of banking was recognized by many economists and political leaders long before the Great Depression, there was also strong opposition, in part based on the fear of centralized financial power. And there was opposition from the existing private banks: they feared that a central bank would become an instrument for political manipulation of the banks. There was still another reason for the banks' lack of enthusiasm: Until the 1930s, the Canadian chartered banks were allowed to issue their own bank notes. (These notes circulated in the economy as currency, side by side with the government-issued ''Dominion notes.'') Since the note issue was a profitable part of their business, the banks were opposed to a central bank which would get a monopoly on the issue of currency.

The fact that the banking system was dominated by a small number of well-organized large-scale banking institutions made it less susceptible to crises than the U.S. system. (In the United States, many banks went under during the Great Depression, and bank failures have continued to be fairly common. In contrast, no Canadian bank failed during the Depression, and the only bank failures since the 1920s involved two relatively small western institutions, the Canadian Commercial Bank and the Northland Bank, both of which went bankrupt in 1985.) The smaller number of banks in Canada also made it easier for the authorities to influence banking conditions without using a formal system of regulation through a central bank. As a consequence, there was no central bank in Canada until 1935, more than twenty years after the Federal Reserve was set up in the United States. By 1935, however, the government had come to recognize that it had to take more complete responsibility for the control of banking conditions, and the Bank of Canada was set up. At the beginning of its life, the Bank was privately owned, but the government bought out the last private shareholders in 1938. Since that time, the Bank of Canada has been wholly owned by the federal government.

The affairs of the Bank of Canada are managed by a board of directors, appointed by the government; the directors then appoint the governor and the deputy governor of the Bank, but these appointments also have to be approved by Cabinet.

The division of responsibility for monetary conditions between the government and the Bank of Canada has on occasion given rise to conflicts, most notably in 1959/60 when the Bank stuck to a tight monetary policy in spite of a high rate of unemployment and slow economic growth. The government objected to the tight policy and asked the Bank of Canada's governor, James Coyne, to resign when he rejected suggestions that the policy be changed. At first, Coyne refused. However, after considerable government pressure, he finally did resign in June 1961. Partly as a result of this affair, however, the Bank Act has been clarified and now explicitly states the duty of the governor is to resign in case of a fundamental conflict with the government. The principle of the government's ultimate responsibility was described by Governor Louis Rasminsky (who replaced Governor Coyne in 1961) in the following way:

> If there should develop a serious and persistent conflict between the views of the government and the views of the central bank . . . , the government should be able formally to instruct the Bank what monetary policy it wishes carried out and the Bank should have the duty to comply.

In the United States, economic policy is much less centralized than in Canada. For example, both the executive and legislative branches have responsibility for taxation and other policies. In addition, the Federal Reserve has a considerable degree of independence from the U.S. administration; it does not have to follow suggestions of the president. The Federal Reserve also has a somewhat complex and untidy organizational structure, in part because of the opposition to the idea of a central bank when the Fed was established. Technically, there is not a single central bank in the United States, but twelve regional Federal Reserve banks and a board of governors in Washington. The important policy decisions, however, are made by committees acting for the Federal Reserve System as a whole.

We now turn to a discussion of the Bank of Canada's principal policy tools; the most important one is open market operations.

OPEN MARKET OPERATIONS

The Bank of Canada can increase the quantity of chartered bank reserves — and thereby increase the quantity of deposit money which the banks can create — by purchasing government securities on the *open market*. That is, it puts in a bid on the securities market; the seller may be any bank or any member of the general public who holds government securities and is willing to sell. Who the actual seller will be, the Bank does not know. But whether the government security is sold by a chartered bank or by the public, the results are similar.

Suppose the Bank of Canada puts in a bid for a $100,000 Treasury bill (a short-term form of government debt, usually issued with a maturity of 90 days) and that Algoma Steel Ltd. is the seller. Algoma Steel delivers the Treasury bill and gets a cheque for $100,000 in return. It deposits this cheque in its chartered bank (bank A). In turn, bank A sends the cheque along to the Bank of Canada, and has its deposit with the Bank of Canada increased by this amount. In other words, bank A's reserves increase by $100,000. The changes in the balance sheets of the Bank of Canada and chartered bank A are shown in Table 12-1.

At this initial step, the money supply has gone up by $100,000; Algoma Steel's chequing deposit is counted as part of the money stock. And the stage is set for a further expansion because of the new reserves held by bank A. Specifically, bank A now has $80,000 in excess reserves that can be lent. And a whole series of loans, similar to those already described in Chapter 11, can take

Table 12-1   An Open Market Purchase: Initial Effects
(thousands of dollars)

Bank of Canada

Assets		Liabilities	
Government securities	+ 100	Reserve deposits of bank A	+ 100
Total	100	Total	100

Chartered Bank A

Assets		Liabilities	
Reserve deposit with Bank of Canada	+ 100 + 100	Chequing deposits of Algoma Steel	+ 100
Required 20 Excess 80			
Total	100	Total	100

The open market purchase increases A's reserves by $100,000. At this stage the money supply has also increased by $100,000, because Algoma Steel has a chequing deposit of that amount.

Chartered bank A has excess reserves, and therefore a further expansion of the money supply can take place.

place. Thus, with a 20% required reserve ratio, the $100,000 open market purchase makes possible a maximum increase of $500,000 in chequing deposits—that is, an increase of $500,000 in the money stock. (Again, as explained in Chapter 11, this is a maximum. In practice, the actual increase will be less, insofar as the public decides to hold more currency along with its higher chequing deposits, and insofar as chartered banks hold excess reserves.)

This, then, is the power of the Bank of Canada open market operations. The Bank carries out the simple transaction of buying a government bond or Treasury bill, and the reserves of the banking system increase as a result. Thus, the Bank makes possible a multiple increase in the nation's money supply.

Now suppose that the Bank of Canada buys the $100,000 Treasury bill from a chartered bank rather than from Algoma Steel. The result is the same: The maximum increase in the money stock is once again $500,000, although the mechanics are slightly different. Table 12-2 shows the initial effects of an open market operation if the Bank of Canada buys the Treasury bill from the Canadian Imperial Bank of Commerce. The CIBC sends the Treasury bill to the Bank

of Canada and gets a reserve deposit in the Bank of Canada in exchange. At this initial stage, no change has yet taken place in the money stock. But note that the CIBC now has a full $100,000 in excess reserves, since its total reserves have gone up by $100,000 while its deposit liabilities — and therefore its required reserves—have not changed. The CIBC can safely lend out the full $100,000 in excess reserves, creating a $100,000 chequing deposit when it does so. Once again, the maximum deposit expansion is the series

$100,000 + $80,000 + $64,000 + . . .

giving a total of $500,000.

In both examples of an open market purchase (Tables 12-1 and 12-2), note that when the Bank of Canada acquires an asset (the government security), its liabilities also go up. This is scarcely surprising, since the balance sheet must balance. The increase in the Bank's liabilities takes the form of chartered bank deposits, which act as the reserves of the chartered banks. Thus, we have a fundamental rule:

When the Bank of Canada wants to increase chartered bank reserves and thus make possible an expansion of the money supply, it acquires assets.

Table 12-2   An Open Market Purchase: When a Chartered Bank Is the Seller
(initial effects, in thousands of dollars)

Bank of Canada

Assets		Liabilities	
Government securities	+ 100	Reserve deposits of CIBC	+ 100
Total	100	Total	100

CIBC

Assets		Liabilities	
Government securities	− 100	No Change	
Reserve deposit	+ 100		
Required 0 Excess 100			
Total	0	Total	0

If the Bank of Canada buys the government security from a chartered bank (say, The Canadian Imperial Bank of Commerce), no change takes place in the money stock at this initial stage. However, the CIBC now has a full $100,000 in excess reserves, which it can lend out.

Restrictive Open Market Operations

Just as the Bank of Canada *purchases* securities when it wants to increase the money supply, so it *sells* securities when it wants to decrease the money supply. The numbers on the balance sheets are the same as in Tables 12-1 and 12-2, but the signs are the opposite.

However, an actual open market sale might lead to very tight monetary conditions. We live in a growing economy, in which productive capacity increases. It is appropriate that the money stock grow through time in order to encourage aggregate demand to grow and keep the economy at full employment. Thus, restrictive policies by the Bank of Canada normally do not involve actual sales of securities. Rather, a *reduction in the rate of purchases of securities* aimed at reducing *the rate of growth* of the money stock generally provides monetary conditions that are as tight as the Bank wishes in its fight against inflation.

OPEN MARKET OPERATIONS AND INTEREST RATES

When the Bank of Canada goes on the market to buy government bonds or shorter term securities, it increases the demand for these securities. As a result, it puts upward pressure on their prices.

There is an important relationship between security prices and interest rates, which may be clarified by looking at Treasury bills more closely. Unlike a government bond, which provides semiannual interest payments, a Treasury bill involves no such explicit interest payment. It simply represents a promise by the government to pay, say, $100,000 on a specific date, usually three months after the date of issue. The purchaser obtains a yield by purchasing the bill at a discount; that is, for less than the full $100,000 face value. For example, a buyer who pays $97,000 for a three-month bill gets back $3,000 more than the purchase price when the bill reaches maturity. Thus, the interest, or *yield*, on that bill is approximately 3% for the three-month period — that is, 12% per annum. (By convention, interest is quoted at an annual rate, even for securities with less than one year to maturity.)

Now, suppose that the Bank of Canada enters the market, bidding for bills and pushing up their price to $98,000. What is the gain of a purchaser who buys a bill at this price? Only $2,000, or about 2% for the three months; that is, 8% per annum. Thus, we see that:

Security prices and interest rates move *in opposite directions*. A "rise in the price of Treasury bills" is just another way of saying "a fall in

the interest rate on Treasury bills." Similarly, a fall in the price of securities involves a rise in the interest rate.

Thus, when the Bank of Canada purchases government securities on the open market and bids up their prices, it is thereby bidding down interest rates. The proposition that a rise in security prices means a fall in interest yields also holds for long-term bonds. (See Box 12-1.)

Secondary Effects

The secondary effects of the open market purchase also work toward a reduction of interest rates. As chartered bank reserves rise, the banks will purchase securities and step up their lending activities. The purchase of securities once again tends to push up security prices and push down interest rates. And, in their eagerness to make additional loans, banks may reduce the interest rate they charge. Specifically, they may shave their *prime rate*.

> The *prime rate* is the interest rate charged by banks on their least risky loans.

Thus, an open market purchase by the Bank of Canada has three important, interrelated effects: (1) it increases the money stock; (2) it makes more funds available for the chartered banks to lend; and (3) it lowers interest rates. The way in which these three forces can stimulate aggregate demand are considered in detail in Chapter 13.

SALES AND PURCHASES OF FOREIGN CURRENCIES BY THE BANK OF CANADA

According to the Bank of Canada Act, one of the responsibilities of the Bank is to "control and protect the external value of the national monetary unit." (By the "external value" is meant the price of the Canadian dollar in terms of foreign monetary units such as the U.S. dollar or the Japanese yen. Such a price—of one currency in terms of another — is known as an *exchange rate*. For example, Can.$1.00 = U.S. $0.82 is an exchange rate.)

In order to carry out this responsibility, the Bank of Canada buys or sells foreign currencies (particularly U.S. dollars) in the markets for foreign currencies. In Chapter 14, we will discuss in detail how exchange rates are determined and how they are affected by the foreign exchange transactions of the Bank of Canada. However,

the important point to be made here is that Bank purchases and sales of foreign currencies will influence chartered bank reserves and therefore the stock of money in Canada.

Suppose as an example that the Bank of Canada buys U.S. $100,000 at a price of Can. $1.20 per U.S. dollar, and that the seller is Abitibi Paper Ltd. (Abitibi may have earned the U.S. dollars by exporting paper products to the United States.) The Bank pays for the U.S. currency by issuing a cheque for Can. $120,000 to Abitibi; this cheque is then deposited in Abitibi's chartered bank account with, say, the Royal Bank. The Royal Bank sends the cheque back to the Bank of Canada and its reserve deposit is increased by $120,000. If the reserve requirement is 20%, the Royal now has excess reserves of $96,000 (0.8 × $120,000), and it can expand its lending. When it does this, it will create new chequing deposits and the money stock will expand through the process described in the previous section.

The effects of this transaction on the Canadian money stock are similar to the effects of a purchase by the Bank of Canada of $120,000 worth of Treasury bills (rather than foreign currency) from Abitibi: In either case, Abitibi's Canadian dollar deposits increase by $120,000 and Abitibi's bank has $96,000 in excess reserves. In either case, there can be an increase in chartered bank lending, and the money supply can expand by a multiple of $120,000. Conversely, if the Bank of Canada were to *sell* foreign currency, the chartered banks would lose reserves and the money supply would be reduced in the same way as when the Bank of Canada sells Treasury bills. We may therefore conclude:

When the Bank of Canada buys foreign currencies, the stock of money in Canada will increase in precisely the same way as it does when the Bank buys an equivalent amount of government securities. When the Bank sells foreign currencies, the money stock contracts in the same way as it does with an open market sale of government securities.

As we shall see in detail in Chapter 14, the effects on the money supply of Bank of Canada sales and purchases of foreign currencies sometimes creates a problem. The foreign currency transactions may be undertaken for the purpose of stabilizing exchange rates — that is, the external value of the Canadian dollar. But the resulting effects on the Canadian money supply may destabilize the domestic economy.

Box 12-1

■ ■

Bond Prices and Interest Rates

The relationship between bond prices and interest rates can be seen most easily by considering a perpetuity—that is, a bond that has no maturity date and is never paid off. It represents a commitment by the government of the issuing nation to pay, say, $80 per year forever. (Several governments have, in fact, issued such bonds, for example, the famous British "consols"—the common abbreviation for their formal name, Consolidated Fund Annuities, the *rentes perpetuelles* of France, and the "perps" issued by the Canadian government.) Just as the semiannual interest or coupon payments on an ordinary bond remain fixed regardless of what happens to market interest rates after the bond has been issued, so the commitment of the government to pay $80 per year forever to the holder of the perpetuity remains in force regardless of what happens to current interest rates in the financial markets.

Like other bonds, perpetuities may be sold by their initial owners. A buyer willing to pay $1,000 for such a perpetuity would obtain an interest rate or yield of 8%; that is, $80 per year on the purchase price of $1,000. But if the price fell, and the buyer could get the perpetuity for $800, the annual $80 payment would provide a yield of 10%. Again, we see that a fall in the price of a security means a rise in the interest rate or yield that the security offers.

A bond with a specific maturity of, say, 10 years involves a much more complex calculation. As a background, note that if $100 is deposited in an account paying 10% per annum, the deposit will be worth $110 at the end of the first year. During the second year, 10% interest will be paid on this $110. That is, $11 interest will be added, raising the deposit to a total of $121 by the end of the second year.

This can be expressed:

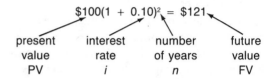

$$\$100(1 + 0.10)^2 = \$121$$

present value PV	interest rate i	number of years n	future value FV

In general, this can be rewritten:

$$PV (1 + i)^n = FV$$

This relationship is often written in the alternative form:

$$PV = \frac{FV}{(1 + i)^n}$$

In our example:

$$\$100 = \frac{\$121}{(1 + 0.10)^2}$$

This tells us that, if the interest rate is 10%, an asset that has a future value or payoff of $121 is worth $100 today.

---

*A Bookkeeping Complication: The Exchange Fund Account

Even though the Bank of Canada sometimes buys and sells large amounts of foreign currencies, the Bank's balance sheet rarely shows any substantial sums of foreign currency assets. The reason for this is that Canada's foreign currency reserves are not held by the Bank of Canada, but by the federal government in the **Exchange Fund Account** (EFA). When the Bank of Canada buys and sells foreign currency in order to stabilize exchange rates, it technically does so on behalf of the federal government: When it buys foreign currency, the Bank immediately resells it to the EFA, and when the Bank sells foreign currency, the foreign funds come from the government's EFA reserves.

When the government is acquiring foreign currency reserves that have been bought for it by the Bank of Canada, how does it pay for these reserves? The answer is that *it generally pays by issuing an equivalent amount of government securities to the Bank*. Thus, when $100 million worth of foreign currency is bought by the Bank of Canada for the EFA, we can think of it as a transaction involving two steps:

1. The Bank of Canada buys $100 million worth of foreign currency. The $100 million in foreign currency is added to the asset side of the Bank's balance sheet; on the liability side of the balance sheet, the transaction results in an increase of chartered bank deposits with the Bank of Canada by $100 million, as shown in Table 12-3 (top panel). As chartered banks now have increased reserves, the money stock can expand.

CANADIAN BOND QUOTATIONS

As supplied to FRI by Canadian Bond Rating Service.

Data compiled on July 14.

Quote is estimate of price at current interest rate levels. On extendibles and retractibles, yield on bond trading over par is calculated to long date, yield on bond under par is based on earliest maturity.

Canadas

Issuer	Maturity	Coupon	Quote	Yield
Canada	1 Aug 89	13.75	100.00	13.75
Canada	6 Sep 89	9.75	99.60	12.11
Canada	1 Oct 89	10.00	99.50	12.03
Canada	1 Oct 89	10.50	99.60	12.04
Canada	1 Nov 89	10.75	99.55	12.05
Canada	1 Nov 89	12.25	99.95	12.12
Canada	6 Dec 89	9.25	99.10	11.51
Canada	15 Dec 89	11.25	99.80	11.64
Canada	1 Feb 90	12.00	100.25	11.49
Canada	1 Feb 90	13.25	100.90	11.48
Canada	26 Feb 90	10.00	99.25	11.25
Canada	6 Mar 90	8.75	98.45	11.26
Canada	15 Mar 90	13.75	101.45	11.38
Canada	1 May 90	5.25	95.88	10.75
Canada	1 May 90	13.00	101.45	11.00
Canada	1 Jun 90	11.75	100.63	10.95
Canada	1 Jul 90	8.00	97.50	10.79
Canada	1 Aug 90	7.50	96.90	10.69
Canada	1 Aug 90	9.00	98.35	10.69
Canada	1 Sep 90	10.75	100.25	10.48
Canada	5 Sep 90	10.25	99.85	10.37
Canada	1 Oct 90	10.50	100.10	10.38
Canada	1 Oct 90	12.50	102.13	10.56
Canada	5 Dec 90	10.25	100.10	10.15
Canada	15 Dec 90	10.25	100.10	10.16
Canada	1 Feb 91	12.50	103.10	10.28
Canada	1 Mar 91	9.25	98.95	9.95
Canada	5 Mar 91	11.00	101.70	9.84
Canada	1 May 91	9.75	99.85	9.83
Canada	1 May 91	14.50	106.88	10.19
Canada	6 Jun 91	10.50	101.50	9.60
Canada	1 Jun 91	11.00	101.65	10.00
Canada	1 Jul 91	8.50	97.70	9,81
Canada	1 Sep 91	9.00	98.55	9.76
Canada	1 Oct 91	18.00	115.00	10.23
Canada	15 Dec 91	8.75	97.90	9.74
Canada	15 Dec 91	11.50	103.25	9.95
Canada	1 Feb 92	15.50	111.63	10.20
Canada	1 Mar 92	8.50	97.50	9.59
Canada	1 Apr 92	7.75	95.75	9.55
Canada	1 Jun 92	10.25	101.90	9.47
Canada	1 Jun 92	15.00	112.12	10.04
Canada	1 Jul 92	9.25	99.40	9.48
Canada	1 Jul 92	15.00	112.37	10.06
Canada	1 Sep 92	5.75	90.00	9.51
Canada	1 Sep 92	14.25	111.25	9.97
Canada	15 Oct 92	13.50	109.75	9.91
Canada	15 Nov 92	12.75	108.13	9.82
Canada	15 Dec 92	11.75	105.90	9.68
Canada	1 Feb 93	11.25	104.70	9.65
Canada	1 May 93	10.75	103.60	9.59
Canada	1 Jun 93	15.25	116.75	9.93
Canada	1 Jul 93	8.75	97.55	9.50
Canada	1 Jul 93	14.75	115.50	9.92
Canada	1 Sep 93	9.50	100.00	9.50
Canada	15 Oct 93	11.75	107.25	9.62
Canada	15 Dec 93	11.50	106.60	9.63
Canada	1 Feb 94	8.75	97.63	9.40
Canada	1 Feb 94	10.25	103.20	9.37
Canada	1 Mar 94	8.25	95.60	9.44
Canada	1 Mar 94	12.00	108.65	9.63
Canada	1 Apr 94	13.00	112.05	9.74
Canada	15 May 94	13.75	115.12	9.74
Canada	15 Jun 94	9.50	100.50	9.37
Canada	15 Jul 94	7.75	93.63	9.38
Canada	15 Jul 94	13.50	114.62	9.74
Canada	1 Oct 94	9.25	99.80	9.29
Canada	1 Oct 94	12.75	112.25	9.69
Canada	15 Dec 94	12.50	111.65	9.68
Canada	1 Feb 95	11.50	108.25	9.55
Canada	1 Feb 95	12.25	111.25	9.59
Canada	1 Mar 95	10.00	102.80	9.34
Canada	1 Mar 95	11.75	109.30	9.57
Canada	1 Apr 95	11.25	107.45	9.52
Canada	1 Jun 95	10.50	104.60	9.46
Canada	1 Oct 95	6.50	88.13	9.03
Canada	1 Oct 95	10.00	102.80	9.39
Canada	15 Dec 95	10.75	106.15	9.45
Canada	1 Mar 96	10.25	104.15	9.39
Canada	1 May 96	9.25	99.40	9.37
Canada	1 Jun 96	8.75	96.95	9.36
Canada	15 Sep 96	3.00	72.75	8.08
Canada	1 Mar 97	8.25	93.90	9.38
Canada	15 May 97	9.25	99.20	9.39
Canada	15 Mar 98	3.75	72.50	8.25
Canada	15 Mar 98	10.75	107.60	9.44
Canada	1 Oct 98	9.50	101.00	9.33
Canada	1 Dec 98	10.25	105.75	9.31
Canada	15 Oct 99	9.00	97.50	9.38
Canada	1 Dec 99	13.50	124.75	9.67
Canada	15 Mar 00	13.75	126.62	9.69
Canada	1 Jul 00	15.00	135.12	9.72
Canada	15 Dec 00	9.75	102.25	9.42
Canada	1 Feb 01	15.75	141.75	9.67
Canada	1 May 01	13.00	123.00	9.68
Canada	1 Oct 01	9.50	100.38	9.44
Canada	1 Feb 02	8.75	94.63	9.49
Canada	15 Mar 02	15.50	141.12	9.77
Canada	1 May 02	10.00	103.88	9.47
Canada	15 Dec 02	11.25	112.00	9.64
Canada	1 Feb 03	11.75	115.62	9.66
Canada	1 Oct 03	9.50	99.63	9.55
Canada	1 Feb 04	10.25	106.13	9.46
Canada	1 Jun 04	13.50	128.25	9.84
Canada	1 Oct 04	10.50	107.35	9.57
Canada	1 Mar 05	12.00	117.62	9.77
Canada	1 Sep 05	12.25	119.62	9.80
Canada	1 Mar 06	12.50	122.00	9.79
Canada	1 Oct 06	14.00	133.50	9.90
Canada	1 Mar 07	13.75	132.12	9.87
Canada	1 Oct 07	13.00	125.87	9.90
Canada	1 Mar 08	12.75	125.00	9.80
Canada	1 Jun 08	10.00	105.50	9.37
Canada	1 Oct 08	11.75	117.62	9.71
Canada	1 Mar 09	11.50	115.75	9.69
Canada	1 Jun 09	11.00	112.00	9.63
Canada	1 Oct 09	10.75	110.25	9.59
Canada	1 Mar 10	9.75	102.30	9.49
Canada	1 Jun 10	9.50	100.75	9.42
Canada	1 Oct 10	8.75	93.55	9.46
Canada	1 Mar 11	9.00	96.80	9.35
Canada	1 Jun 11	8.50	91.63	9.41
Canada	15 Mar 14	10.25	107.25	9.48
Intl Bank	14 Aug 09	11.00	105.00	10.40

Provincials

Issuer	Maturity	Coupon	Quote	Yield
Alberta	15 Apr 90	8.88	98.38	11.14
Alberta	15 Jun 91	8.13	96.75	10.02
Alta Gov Tel	1 Mar 90	9.00	98.63	11.27
Alta Gov Tel	15 Dec 91	7.50	95.38	9.68
Alta Gov Tel	31 May 03	11.50	107.88	10.41
Alta Mun Fc	15 Aug 89	13.50	100.00	13.50
Alta Mun Fc	15 Mar 93	7.25	92.25	9.81
Alta Mun Fc	15 Dec 02	12.25	113.12	10.41
BC Hyd & Pwr	15 Dec 93	5.25	84.75	9.56
BC Hyd & Pwr	15 Oct 00	10.00	98.88	10.17
BC Hyd & Pwr	14 Apr 06	14.50	128.50	10.78
BC Hyd & Pwr	15 Jan 11	13.50	124.50	10.59
Br Columbia	1 Oct 89	12.75	100.13	11.73
Br Columbia	6 Feb 90	10.75	99.75	11.19
Br Columbia	20 Oct 93	12.00	106.75	10.00
Man Hydro	1 Apr 90	9.00	98.50	11.19
Man Hydro	15 Sep 91	8.50	96.88	10.13
Man Hydro	31 Aug 92	8.25	95.63	9.90
Man Hydro	10 Jun 94	10.00	100.88	9.77
Man Hydro	1 Aug 98	8.38	91.25	9.86
Man Tel	15 Nov 91	7.88	95.50	10.07
Man Tel	1 Mar 99	8.75	92.88	9.91
Manitoba	15 Mar 93	11.75	105.25	10.00
Manitoba	1 Oct 93	8.75	96.13	9.89
Manitoba	15 May 95	11.50	106.88	9.91
Manitoba	5 Dec 99	10.00	100.50	9.92
N Bruns Elec	15 May 90	13.75	101.75	11.44
N Bruns Elec	8 Feb 93	11.75	104.63	10.17
N Bruns Elec	15 May 95	10.38	101.63	10.00
N Bruns Elec	15 Nov 96	7.88	89.75	9.87
N Bruns Elec	15 Oct 97	8.38	90.75	10.05
N Bruns Elec	15 Nov 98	8.50	90.75	10.05
N Bruns Elec	1 Oct 99	11.00	104.75	10.23
N Bruns Elec	1 Mar 00	10.00	98.38	10.25
N Bruns Elec	21 Dec 03	10.25	99.63	10.30
N Bruns Elec	1 Nov 04	13.25	117.87	10.83
N Brunswick	30 Jun 92	15.50	112.00	10.66
N Brunswick	10 May 94	11.00	103.75	10.00
N Brunswick	2 Mar 90	9.50	98.00	12.83
N Brunswick	2 Jul 94	9.00	96.88	9.81
N Brunswick	17 Jul 98	9.88	99.50	9.96
NB Mun Fin	27 Nov 89	10.00	99.50	11.26
NB Mun Fin	27 Nov 90	10.25	99.00	11.04
NB Mun Fin	29 May 93	11.50	104.25	10.14
NB Mun Fin	29 May 94	11.50	105.13	10.13
NB Mun Fin	12 Jun 94	13.75	113.62	10.15
NB Mun Fin	15 Dec 96	12.25	109.88	10.31
NB Mun Fin	15 Dec 97	12.25	110.63	10.33
NB Mun Fin	15 Dec 98	12.25	111.38	10.33
Nfld	15 Aug 90	9.75	98.00	11.74
Nfld	15 Sep 94	8.88	95.25	10.07
Nfld	15 May 95	10.38	101.25	10.08
Nfld	1 Dec 95	10.50	101.88	10.09
Nfld	17 Feb 96	10.00	99.38	10.13
Nfld	29 Jun 97	10.75	103.25	10.14
Nfld	5 Jan 99	10.00	99.25	10.12
Nfld	19 Oct 02	14.75	129.00	10.62
Nfld	6 Apr 03	12.88	116.00	10.63
Nfld	15 Oct 04	13.50	121.37	10.63
Nfld Mun Fin	15 Aug 99/89	10.75	103.63	10.16
Nfld Mun Fin	15 Nov 03	13.00	116.37	10.73
Nfld-Lab Hyd	15 Dec 95	10.75	102.63	10.18
Nfld-Lab Hyd	15 Oct 01	10.25	99.13	10.37
Nfld-Lab Hyd	28 Sep 02	10.00	97.63	10.33
Nfld-Lab Hyd	27 Jun 03	10.00	97.50	10.34
Nova Scotia	15 Jul 90	9.25	97.38	12.11
Nova Scotia	1 Dec 91	7.63	94.50	10.28
Nova Scotia	1 Nov 93	12.00	106.38	10.12
Nova Scotia	1 Dec 96	7.63	88.00	9.96
Nova Scotia	15 Apr 97	15.50	127.12	10.32
Nova Scotia	3 Mar 00	9.25	93.13	10.33
Nova Scotia	18 Dec 04	12.63	115.62	10.55
Nova Scotia	3 Jul 09	11.25	104.25	10.73
Nova Scotia	12 Dec 09	10.88	104.25	10.37
NS L&P	15 Apr 91	8.50	97.13	10.32
NS Mun Finc	22 Dec 96	15.00	122.75	10.51
NS Power	10 Aug 92	16.75	115.62	10.65
NS Power	15 Dec 91	15.50	110.38	10.52
NS Power	15 Nov 92	8.13	94.75	10.00
NS Power	1 Mar 01	10.00	98.38	10.24
NS Power	21 Jul 02	9.25	92.88	10.25
NS Power	1 Dec 02	13.50	120.62	10.58
NS Power	20 Dec 03	12.50	114.75	10.49
NS Power	14 Feb 05	12.13	112.12	10.52
NS Power	15 Jul 05	11.50	107.63	10.51
Ont Hydro	14 Aug 89	13.75	100.00	13.75
Ont Hydro	14 Feb 90	10.75	99.75	11.17
Ont Hydro	6 May 90	11.25	100.00	11.25
Ont Hydro	4 Mar 91	10.50	100.63	10.06
Ont Hydro	15 Sep 93	12.00	107.00	9.90
Ont Hydro	18 Oct 93	11.75	106.25	9.91
Ont Hydro	22 Feb 94	12.00	107.63	9.89
Ont Hydro	1 Apr 94	9.00	97.38	9.70
Ont Hydro	28 Aug 94	13.00	112.12	9.92
Ont Hydro	30 Jun 95	9.00	96.38	9.82
Ont Hydro	14 Jan 96	10.00	100.88	9.81
Ont Hydro	1 Apr 96	7.63	89.63	9.76
Ont Hydro	21 Jul 96	8.25	92.00	9.86
Ont Hydro	15 Sep 97	8.25	91.63	9.76
Ont Hydro	30 Nov 98	8.50	92.13	9.80
Ont Hydro	1 Mar 99	8.50	91.88	9.82
Ont Hydro	14 Jun 99	9.75	99.50	9.83
Ont Hydro	15 Aug 99	10.25	100.88	10.11
Ont Hydro	15 Nov 99	10.00	99.13	10.13
Ont Hydro	21 May 00	10.25	101.13	10.07
Ont Hydro	30 Oct 00	10.75	104.50	10.07
Ont Hydro	29 Jan 01	10.25	101.25	10.06
Ont Hydro	18 May 01	10.00	100.00	10.00

Courtesy of Canadian Bond Rating Service. Printed from *The Globe and Mail*.

For many assets, the payoff is strung out over many years. In other words, there are many terms on the right-hand side of the present value equation. For example, a bond with a 10 year maturity and coupon payments of \$8 per year will have a payoff of \$8 each year until the tenth year, when the owner receives a final payoff of \$8 plus the face value of \$100. If the market interest rate is, say, 9%, the present value of this bond (the price at which it can be bought or sold today) is calculated as follows:

$$PV = \frac{\$8}{1.09} + \frac{\$8}{(1.09)^2} + \frac{\$8}{(1.09)^3} + \ldots + \frac{\$8 + \$100}{(1.09)^{10}} = \$93.58$$

Or, in general,

$$\text{Price (PV) of bond} = \frac{C}{1+i} + \frac{C}{(1+i)^2} + \ldots + \frac{C + \$100}{(1+i)^n}$$

where C is the coupon payment.

From this equation, we can calculate the price if we know the rate of interest (i), or we can calculate the interest rate if we know the price of the bond. The higher the one, the lower the other. Thus, once again we see that the higher the price of bonds, the lower the interest rate.

Table 12-3 The EFA Acquires Foreign Currency Reserves (millions of dollars)

Bank of Canada			
Assets		**Liabilities**	
Government securities	+100	Deposit of chartered banks	+100
Federal Government (EFA)			
Assets		**Liabilities**	
Foreign currencies	+100	Government securities	+100

When the Bank of Canada has bought \$100 million in foreign currency, it immediately resells it to the EFA. The foreign currency disappears from the Bank's assets but is replaced by \$100 million in new government securities.

2. The Bank of Canada then sells the foreign currency to the EFA, in return for $100 million in securities issued by the government. The Bank's foreign currency assets are decreased by $100 million, but $100 million in government securities is added to the Bank's assets (Table 12-3, bottom panel). The Bank's liabilities are not affected in this step: Thus, step 2 does not affect chartered bank reserves or the money stock.

Notice that the effect on chartered bank reserves and, therefore, on the money stock would have been the same even if step 2 had not taken place. The transaction between the Bank and the government is purely a matter of bookkeeping, and has no effect on the money stock or the rest of the economy. The effects on the economy of Bank of Canada sales and purchases of foreign currency would be exactly the same even if the EFA didn't exist and Canada's foreign exchange reserves were held by the Bank as part of its assets.

*TRANSFERS OF GOVERNMENT DEPOSITS

As we noted in Chapter 11, the Bank of Canada acts as the federal government's banker: the government maintains a deposit account with the Bank, and public revenues and expenditures are channelled through the government's account with the Bank of Canada.

The government also maintains deposits in the chartered banks. In its role as the government's principal bank, the Bank of Canada *can transfer government funds into or out of chartered banks*. It thereby has another powerful tool for influencing chartered bank reserves and the money stock. Suppose, for example, that the Bank of Canada wants to increase chartered bank reserves. It can do this by buying government securities in the open market, as explained earlier. As an alternative, the Bank may instead transfer part of the government's deposits with the Bank of Canada to the chartered banks. When the Bank of Canada transfers, say, $10 million in government funds to the chartered banks, the banks receive $10 million in reserves, as shown in Table 12-4.

The transfer of government deposits does not directly increase the money supply: Remember that deposits owned by the government are not counted as part of the money supply, whether they are held with the Bank of Canada or the chartered banks. But it does create excess reserves in the chartered banks. (For example, if the required reserve ratio is 20%, the chartered banks in Table 12-4 now have excess reserves of $8 million.) As a result, the chartered banks can expand their lending, and create new deposits in exactly the same way as described in the section on open market operations. Thus, by transferring government deposits to the chartered banks, the Bank of Canada can cause the money

Table 12-4 The Bank of Canada Transfers Government Deposits to the Chartered Banks (millions of dollars)

Bank of Canada		
Assets	**Liabilities**	
(No change)	Deposits of the federal government	− 10
	Deposits of chartered banks	+ 10

Chartered Banks		
Assets	**Liabilities**	
Deposits with Bank of Canada + 10	Deposits of the federal government	+ 10

As the Bank of Canada transfers $10 million of government deposits to the chartered banks, chartered bank reserves increase by $10 million. They now have excess reserves and can expand their loans.

Table 12-5   The Bank of Canada Grants a Loan
(thousands of dollars)

Assets		Liabilities	
Chartered bank borrowing	+ 100	Reserve deposits of chartered bank	+ 100
Total	100	Total	100

When the Bank of Canada lends to a chartered bank, bank reserves are increased.

stock to increase. Conversely, if the Bank wants to decrease the money stock, it can do so by transferring government deposits from the chartered banks to the government's account with the Bank of Canada. This will reduce chartered bank reserves, forcing them to reduce their lending and thereby reduce the stock of deposit money.[1]

While deposit transfers *can* be used to control the money stock, it could equally well be controlled by open market operations. Why, then, does the Bank sometimes use government deposit transfers rather than open market operations? The answer may be that the Bank may want to influence the money stock without bringing about sharp changes in securities prices and interest rates. Suppose, for example, that the Bank wants to *reduce* the money stock. If it tries to do this by selling government securities, the prices of securities will fall and interest rates rise, as we discussed above. But if the Bank instead reduces the money stock by transferring government deposits from the chartered banks, it will not directly affect the market for securities: There will be no direct impact on securities prices or interest rates.

However, most economists believe that, in the end, the effects of the deposit-transfer method will be similar to the effects of open market operations. While the deposit transfers do not directly influence securities prices and interest rates, they will do so indirectly: As chartered banks lose reserves, for example, they will begin to sell securities, thereby depressing their prices and raising interest rates. And the banks may increase the interest rates they charge on loans, in order to cut back on lending. In other words, the *indirect* effects of controlling the money stock through deposit transfers

will be similar to the secondary effects of open market operations which we described in the previous section.

CHANGES IN THE BANK RATE

The Bank of Canada acts not only as the government's bank, but also as the banker of the chartered banks. Just as chartered banks lend to the general public, so the Bank of Canada may lend to chartered banks. In exchange for such a loan (or "advance") from the Bank of Canada, the chartered bank gives the Bank of Canada its promissory note. The interest rate on these advances is known as the *Bank Rate*.

> The *Bank Rate* is the interest rate charged by the Bank of Canada on its loans to chartered banks.

In Chapter 11, we saw how a chartered bank provides its customer with a chequing deposit when it makes a loan. The transaction between the Bank of Canada and a chartered bank is similar. When the Bank of Canada grants an advance to a chartered bank, it increases that bank's reserve deposit in the Bank of Canada, as shown in Table 12-5. Thus, *such loans add to the total reserves of the banking system.*

Unlike open market operations, Bank of Canada lending is at the initiative of the chartered banks rather than the Bank of Canada. However, the Bank of Canada is able to influence the amount which the chartered banks borrow. For example, if it increases the Bank Rate, borrowing will become more expensive for the chartered banks. Thus, they will try to avoid borrowing; rather, they will try to meet their required reserve ratios in other ways, such as selling securities or calling in loans. Unlike borrowing from the central bank, these alternative ways do not increase the total reserves of the chartered banking system. Therefore, an increase in the Bank Rate is a restrictive move: It discourages borrowing, holds down total chartered bank reserves, and restricts the total quantity of money in the system.

■ ■ ■ ■ ■
[1] A comprehensive discussion of government deposit transfers and other tools of monetary policy can be found in Thomas J. Courchene, *Money, Inflation and the Bank of Canada: An Analysis of Canadian Monetary Policy from 1970 to Early 1975* (Montreal: C. D. Howe Research Institute, 1976).

From time to time, the Bank of Canada has adjusted the Bank Rate as one of its tools of monetary policy—for example, in the decade following World War II and, again, in the period from 1962 to 1980. Particularly in the earlier period, Bank Rate changes took place infrequently and, when they were announced, they were interpreted as strong indicators of Bank policy. (That is, an increase was important not only because of its direct effect in discouraging chartered bank borrowing, but also as a signal of the Bank of Canada's intention of following a tighter policy.)

At other times, however, the Bank of Canada has not used Bank Rate changes as an active tool of monetary policy. Between 1956 and 1962, the Bank of Canada had a *floating Bank Rate*. That is, it continuously adjusted the Bank Rate to keep it at a fixed margin (1/4 of 1%) above the market rate of interest on Treasury bills. Since 1980, the Bank of Canada has again used a floating rate. Thus, even though the weekly changes in the Bank Rate are prominently announced in newspapers and on television, they do not in themselves reflect changes in the Bank of Canada's policy. Rather, they reflect an adjustment of the Bank Rate to what has already happened in the market for Treasury bills. (Of course, what happens in this market may depend on Bank of Canada sales and purchases of Treasury bills—that is, on the Bank of Canada's open market operations.)

Because the Bank Rate is kept at a *penalty rate*—that is, it is kept above market interest rates—chartered banks have an incentive not to borrow. In practice, Bank of Canada loans to the chartered banks usually have been very small and of short duration. Thus, a penalty Bank Rate is a way for the Bank of Canada to back up the constraints it sets on chartered bank reserves through its open market policies: The chartered banks do not escape discipline by borrowing from the Bank of Canada.

Loans to Investment Dealers

In addition to the chartered banks, there is also another group of firms with access to credit from the Bank of Canada: the *authorized investment dealers*. These are firms which buy and sell short term money market securities, and finance a large part of their securities holdings with *call loans* from the chartered banks. Since the chartered banks can demand repayment of these loans ("call" the loans) at very short notice (usually one day), the banks will normally lend out any excess reserves they have to the dealers. As soon as they need more reserves to meet legal reserve requirements, they can

simply call the loans. The dealers will then have two options: They can either sell some of their securities in order to get the funds to repay their loans from the banks or they can borrow from the Bank of Canada. If they borrow from the Bank of Canada to repay the chartered banks, the reserves of the chartered banks will increase (just as they increase when the chartered banks themselves borrow from the Bank of Canada): The dealers will repay their chartered bank loans with cheques drawn on the Bank of Canada. However, the rate charged by the Bank of Canada on loans to investment dealers is usually very close to the Bank Rate and has always been held above the Treasury bill rate. This means that if the dealers hold Treasury bills or other assets with similar rates of interest, they have an incentive to repay their loans to the Bank of Canada as quickly as possible.

Bank of Canada lending to chartered banks and investment dealers has sometimes been criticized. For example, it has been argued that it reduces the effectiveness of open market operations. Suppose, for example, that the Bank wants to restrain the growth of the money stock. To do this it may sell securities in the open market, causing chartered banks to lose reserves. However, by borrowing from the Bank of Canada, the chartered banks may replenish their reserves. Thus, the Bank of Canada with its left hand (loans to chartered banks) may pump back the reserves which it is extracting with its right hand (open market operations). Bank of Canada loans to investment dealers have a similar effect.

In response, it is argued that advances to chartered banks act as a safety valve, allowing the Bank of Canada to follow tighter policies than it would otherwise dare. If there were no lending of this kind, the Bank would have to tread lightly in restrictive open market operations, taking care not to put too much pressure on the chartered banks. Even though Bank of Canada lending involves some slippage, it may nevertheless be possible to get even tighter policies than in the absence of such lending: The Bank can safely push harder on the open market lever.[2]

■ ■ ■ ■ ■

[2] In the United States, where loans by the Federal Reserve are known as "discounting" and the "Bank Rate" is known as the "discount rate," the discount rate has from time to time been below market rates of interest. This has led to the criticism that discounting involves hidden subsidies to the "commercial banks" (that is, the U.S. equivalent of chartered banks).

CHANGES IN RESERVE REQUIREMENTS

The quantity of deposits that the chartered banks can create depends on the size of their reserves and on the required reserve ratio. In the last chapter, we saw, specifically, that deposits can be created up to a theoretical maximum equal to the amount of total reserves times $1/R$. Thus, an *increase* in R (the required reserve ratio) will *decrease* the maximum amount of deposits that can be created.

Before 1967, the Bank of Canada had the legal power to change the required reserve ratio within certain limits. Clearly this was a very powerful tool. With total reserves of, say, $100 million, an increase in the required reserve ratio from 10% to 12.5% would reduce the maximum quantity of chequing deposits from $1000 million to $800 million.

Because this tool would have a very strong impact on financial markets and because other tools (such as open market operations or transfers of government deposits) already give the Bank a high degree of control over the stock of money, the power to change the reserve ratio was never used by the Bank. When the Bank Act was revised in 1967, the power was therefore abolished and, between 1967 and 1980, required reserves were fixed at 12% of demand deposits and 4% on notice and term deposits. However, the 1980 Bank Act revision provided for a gradual reduction in the required ratios to 10% and 3%. (Note that reduced reserve ratios work to increase chartered bank profits: The banks can hold less reserves—on which they earn no interest—and more loans and other assets on which they do earn interest.) And, as we discuss below, by the late 1980s it was proposed that legal reserve requirements should be abolished altogether.

Secondary Reserve Ratios

Since 1967, the Bank of Canada has had the additional power to require the chartered banks to hold a specified portion (between 0 and 12% of their Canadian-dollar deposit liabilities) in the form of *secondary reserves*. Secondary reserves are defined as the sum of their holdings of Treasury bills, loans to investment dealers, and cash reserves in excess of required reserves. The Bank of Canada made use of this tool on several occasions in the 1970s. (Because the banks earn interest on most secondary reserves, they find this tool less objectionable than the primary reserve requirement.)

What happens to the stock of money when the Bank of Canada increases the secondary reserve ratio? The answer is that nothing much is likely to happen. The chartered banks may be forced to buy more Treasury bills, thus increasing their secondary reserves, and sell long-term securities which do not qualify as a secondary reserve asset. Such transactions don't affect the public's deposit holdings. Thus, there will be no effect on the stock of money.

Most economists now believe that the most important way in which the Bank of Canada can influence the economy is by controlling the stock of money. Thus, they tend to be skeptical about the usefulness of changes in the secondary reserve ratio as a tool of monetary policy: Changes in the ratio may force the chartered banks to rearrange their assets, but they do not affect the stock of money.

OTHER MONETARY TOOLS: MORAL SUASION

The Bank of Canada may reinforce its control over the monetary and financial system with *moral suasion* — that is, requests to chartered banks and other financial institutions that they take certain actions or refrain from others.

The Bank of Canada has exerted moral suasion on many occasions. At various times, there have been requests to the chartered banks to increase their lending to specific groups of customers, such as small businesses or borrowers in the less prosperous areas of Canada (for example, the Maritime provinces). At other times, the Bank of Canada and the government have tried to use moral suasion as a way of dealing with temporary disturbances in the financial system, especially when fast action has been needed to prevent a problem from developing into a major crisis. A recent example was the government's attempt to persuade the major chartered banks to contribute to the effort to save the Canadian Commercial Bank from bankruptcy in March 1985. On that occasion, the strategy was not succesful: the CCB did go under in September that year (see Box 12-2).

In this and other episodes, moral suasion was used to persuade chartered banks to do certain things that they would otherwise have preferred not to do, such as increasing their lending for house building, limiting their loans to large firms, or lending money to a bank that was expected to go bankrupt. But, as the critics of moral suasion point out, there is no reason to expect that all

Box 12-2

■■■■■■■■■■■■■■■■■■■■■

Double Flips and Loan Workouts: Are the Regulators Keeping Up?

In the United States, government regulation of financial institutions is an issue that has always been high on the political agenda. Many have called for more regulation, to reduce the frequency of failures among banks and other financial institutions.

In Canada, there were no bank failures between the 1920s and the mid-1980s. (The last time a bank failed before 1985 was in 1923 when the Toronto-based Home Bank went under following large losses on bad loans.) Thus, few people saw any need for strengthening the existing regulatory legislation or for tightening the relatively loose and informal system of enforcement that had evolved over the years. In comparison with the U.S. context, some economists have argued that, if anything, the existing regulatory framework is too restrictive, discouraging entry of new firms and competition in the financial system.

In reply, however, the defenders of the existing system could point to several signs that competition was alive and well in the Canadian financial system. In Alberta, for example, the dominant position of the big Eastern banks was being challenged in the mid-1970s

by two newly founded chartered banks, the Canadian Commercial Bank and the Northland Bank. In Toronto, entrepreneur Leonard Rosenberg was aggressively expanding his Greymac Trust Company; ultimately, his aim was to merge several trust companies and a bank, to form a giant new financial institution that would be able to compete head to head with the dominant chartered banks.

Starting in the early 1980s, it gradually became clear that there might be severe weaknesses in the regulatory system. In late 1982, both the federal and provincial governments began looking more closely at Rosenberg's affairs. The federal government was concerned about the attempts of Rosenberg and his associates to take control of the Canadian Commercial Bank, in violation of "the spirit" of Bank Act provisions intended to prevent an individual or firm from controlling more than one financial institution. The provincial government became involved after Rosenberg arranged a $500 million real estate transaction (that he estimated yielded him a $43 million profit): It appeared that the deal might have violated a regulatory provision that limits the amount that a trust company is allowed to lend for financing any one transaction. The province was interested in the deal for another reason as well: It involved a "double flip," that is, a sale and subsequent repurchase at a higher price, of a large apartment complex, undertaken primarily for the purpose of making it possible to get regulatory approval to raise rents for the apartments.

After examining the books, an investigator appointed by the Ontario government concluded that the

---

banks will respond with equal willingness to the persuasion of the Bank of Canada or the government. The result may then be that only some banks will, for example, reduce their loans to large firms. This may mean that the large firms will switch their business to the other banks. Thus, those chartered banks that try to "act responsibly" and obey the instructions of the Bank of Canada may end up with less business and lower profits. Or, again, those chartered banks that agreed to participate in the 1985 attempt to rescue the CCB ended up with a potential loss of $60 million; those that did not participate lost nothing.

For these sorts of reasons, some people argue that moral suasion often is ineffective, or unfair, or both. Thus, they believe that the Bank of Canada should concentrate its efforts on achieving effective control over the money stock through its general tools (most notably, open market operations). Moral suasion should be used only

temporarily as a device to deal with short-term disturbances in financial markets and not to do the job of the general policy instruments. Furthermore, other objectives such as stimulating the housing industry or the small business sector are political ones and, therefore, are more appropriately dealt with by the government and Parliament. The conduct of monetary policy is a difficult enough task as it is and should not be complicated by asking the Bank of Canada to perform other quite different functions, such as controlling how credit will be allocated among different sectors of the economy.

SHOULD WE ABOLISH STATUTORY RESERVE REQUIREMENTS?

Legal reserve requirements is a key factor in the mechanism that the Bank of Canada uses to influence mon-

money of the depositors in Rosenberg's trust companies was in danger and, in January 1983, the provincial government simply took over Greymac and two other trust companies controlled by Rosenberg and his associates. The lawsuits resulting from this action had not yet been settled in the late 1980s.

That there were problems at the Canadian Commercial Bank was known to the federal government as early as 1982, when the inspector general of banks became worried about the extent to which the CCB had concentrated its lending in the risky real estate business and in the energy sector, which was being severely hurt by the weakening international market for oil. In early 1985, the CCB was faced with a loss of around $90 million on assets it was holding in the United States, and it was clear that it was going to have trouble with many of its Canadian loans as well. (Some of the potential losses were being concealed by giving loans a "workout": lending more money to a borrower in trouble so as to avoid having to explicitly write off the original loans.)

In an attempt to stave off bankruptcy, the CCB turned to Ottawa for help. In March 1985, on the recommendation of the inspector general, the federal government persuaded the six largest chartered banks, as well as the governments of Alberta and British Columbia, to contribute to a $255 million effort to rescue the CCB. The effort failed.

In early September, after nervous depositors had withdrawn more than $1.5 billion from the CCB, the federal government ordered its liquidation. Later in 1985, a second Alberta bank, the Northland Bank, was also liquidated; it had faced problems similar to the CCB's.

In an interview with *Maclean's* magazine, William Kennett, the inspector general of banks, defended the actions of his officials in the CCB/Northland affairs. In this interview, Kennett referred to the "limited powers" of his department, and the fact that it has "traditionally relied on 'moral suasion' (rather than compulsion) to convince companies to change what it thinks are unsafe business practices."

In the wake of the Rosenberg affair and the CCB/Northland failures, there were many calls for strengthened regulation of banks and trust companies. Ironically, however, the actions of the federal government were also criticized for being too interventionist. By raising the limit on insured deposits to $60,000 in the middle of the Rosenberg affair, and by unilaterally offering to protect uninsured depositors in the CCB and the Northland Bank, the government reduced the incentive on depositors to check the reputation of an institution which is trying to attract funds by paying higher interest rates than others, as the CCB and Northland were doing. In the words of Toronto Dominion's president, Robert Korthals, this action "says that people who have taken imprudent risks are smart and those who have taken lower rates are the fools." As a result, the government may also have reduced the incentive on managers of financial institutions to be conservative in their lending practices. The consequence of this, the critics charge, may be more non-performing loans and more instability in the financial system.

etary conditions in Canada. Most of the tools that the Bank of Canada can use to control the money supply work through their effect on the total quantity of reserves available to the chartered banks. Given the quantity of reserves, the total amount of money that the banking system can create then depends on the required reserve ratios.

It may seem surprising, therefore, that by the late 1980s there was active discussion of proposals to eliminate the legal reserve requirements from the Bank Act. The chartered banks argued in favour of the proposal. They pointed out that the existing requirements put them at a competitive disadvantage relative to non-bank institutions such as trust companies. Because such institutions are not legally required to hold reserves, they can hold a larger percentage of their portfolio in the form of interest-earning assets. As a result, they are able to offer higher interest rates to their depositors and this enables them to expand their market share at the expense of the chartered banks. (Moreover, regulatory restrictions that earlier made it difficult for non-bank institutions to compete for deposits—such as the regulation that prohibited them from offering chequable deposits—have been gradually relaxed, further strengthening their competitive position.)

Abolishing legal reserve requirements is not, of course, the only way to reduce the competitive disadvantage of the chartered banks. Another possibility would be to require trust companies, credit unions, and similar institutions, to hold minimum amounts of reserves as well. (A problem with this solution, however, is that non-bank financial institutions are regulated by the *provincial* governments, while regulation of the chartered banks is the responsibility of the federal government.) Yet another way of reducing the competitive disadvantage of the chartered banks would be for the Bank of Canada to pay interest on the reserve deposits of the chartered banks; this proposal has also been seriously considered in Canada at various times. But the simplest way of enabling chartered banks to compete on equal terms is to abolish legal reserve requirements altogether; this was the alternative that was receiving most attention in the late 1980s.

However, this proposal raises an obvious concern: Would it not reduce or even eliminate the Bank of Canada's ability to control the money supply? After all, the required reserve ratio sets the limit to the maximum amount of money that the banking system can create on the basis of a given quantity of reserves. If the required reserve ratio is zero, wouldn't the chartered banks be able to create an infinite amount of deposits, with uncontrolled inflation as a consequence?

The answer is that even if there are no *legal* reserve requirements, the Bank of Canada can still retain ultimate control over the total money supply. The reason is that even if they are not legally *obliged* to hold particular quantities of reserves, banks would still *voluntarily* choose to hold a certain amount of reserves.

One reason is convenience. As we discussed in the previous chapter, the Bank of Canada is responsible for running Canada's system of cheque clearing. This gives the chartered banks a reason for maintaining some reserve deposits with the Bank of Canada: Such deposits can be used to settle temporary imbalances in a bank's transactions with other banks.

Moreover, chartered banks will want to hold some reserves in the form of currency. Even though most of the money stock in Canada is in the form of bank deposits, the public does want to hold some portion of its assets as currency; therefore, banks and other deposit-taking institutions must hold some currency reserves in order to enable the public to withdraw currency on demand. But the Bank of Canada is the institution that controls the amount of currency in the economy. (Like chartered bank reserves, currency is an item on the liability side of the Bank of Canada's balance sheet, and total Bank of Canada liabilities can only increase when the Bank increases its assets.) Indirectly, the Bank can therefore control the total amount of deposit money that the banking system can create as well, since (even without a legal reserve requirement) the chartered banks would hold some fraction of their assets in the form of currency and Bank of Canada deposits.

To sum up, there is no doubt that the Bank of Canada will continue to be able to exercise ultimate control over the money supply in Canada even if legal reserve requirements are abolished. (After all, trust companies and similar institutions have not created infinite amounts of deposits even though they have not been subject to legal reserve requirements.) Nevertheless, some analysts are concerned that abolition of reserve requirements may make precise control of the money supply more difficult. Even *with* legal reserve requirements, the Bank has sometimes had trouble keeping the rate of monetary growth close to preassigned targets. If reserve requirements are abolished, there may be even more variability in the relation between the money stock and the amount of reserves that the Bank of Canada makes available to the system. The result, say the critics, is likely to be increased instability in the rate of monetary growth.

THE BALANCE SHEET OF THE BANK OF CANADA

Some actions of the Bank of Canada do not show up directly on its balance sheet (for example, moral suasion, or changes in secondary reserve requirements). But other actions do — for example, its open market operations. Thus, the balance sheet of the Bank of Canada can provide important insights into some of the Bank's activities.

The balance sheet of the Bank of Canada is shown in Table 12-6. Two entries on the right side are particularly worth noting. First is the large amount of Bank of Canada notes outstanding. This is the result of the desire of the public to hold more currency as its overall holdings of money have increased.

The second noteworthy item on the right side is the small net worth of the Bank of Canada. If the Bank were a private corporation, this would be cause for alarm. The slightest reversal in its fortunes might cause the value of its assets to dip below the amount of its liabilities, wiping out its net worth and threatening bankruptcy. But the Bank is no ordinary corporation. It is a part of the government, and a very special part, as it has the power to issue currency. Because of this special power, the Bank has an assured high flow of profits, and need not worry about building up its net worth. (The Bank of Canada is very profitable because it earns interest on the large holdings of government securities on the asset side, while it pays no interest on most of its liabilities, in particular, chartered bank reserve deposits and Bank of Canada notes.) Instead of building up a large net worth, the Bank simply turns over its profits to the federal government.

Table 12-6   Balance Sheet of the Bank of Canada, December 1987
(billions of dollars)

Assets		Liabilities		
1. Government of Canada securities	20.2	5. Notes outstanding		19.4
2. Loans to chartered banks		6. Deposits		3.3
and investment dealers	0.8	Chartered banks	(2.6)	
3. All other assets	2.0	Government	(0.02)	
4. Total assets	23.0	Foreign and other	(0.7)	
		7. All other liabilities		
		and net worth		0.3
		8. Total liabilities		23.0

Source: *Bank of Canada Review* (August 1988).

On the asset side of the Bank of Canada's balance sheet, Government of Canada securities are by far the largest entry; these securities have been accumulated through past open market operations. Chartered bank borrowings and loans to investment dealers were 0.8 billion dollars at the end of 1987. Normally, these items are very small, although they occasionally shoot up when the chartered banking system as a whole is short on reserves. At the end of 1985, they were as large as 3.5 billion dollars, as the Bank of Canada lent large amounts to the chartered banking system as part of its efforts to avert failure of the CCB and Northland Banks (Box 12-2).

WHAT BACKS OUR MONEY?

Money is debt. The largest component of the money stock (namely, bank deposits) is debt of the chartered banks. And Bank of Canada notes — the currency of everyday use — are liabilities of the Bank of Canada.

In a sense, the money supply is backed by the assets of the banking system. Bank deposits are backed by the loans, bonds, and reserves held by the chartered banks. And Bank of Canada notes are backed by the assets of the Bank, mainly Canadian government securities. What, in turn, backs the government securities? The government's promise to pay, based in the first instance on its ability to tax, but in the final analysis on its ability to borrow newly created money from the Bank of Canada or to print money directly. (Recall the section in Chapter 10 entitled: "Could the Government Go Broke?")

Clearly, we have gone in a circle. Currency is backed with government debt; and government debt is ultimately backed by the ability of the federal authorities to print more currency. In a sense, the whole game is played with mirrors; money is money because the government says it is. Until a few years ago, Bank of Canada notes boldly proclaimed that "the Bank of Canada will pay to the bearer on demand" the face value of the note. And what would happen if an individual submitted a $5 bill and demanded payment? He or she would receive another $5 bill in exchange. This does not make much sense, and the bold proclamation has been eliminated from Bank of Canada notes. Now, we can say simply: A dollar is a dollar is a dollar.

What, then, determines the value of Bank of Canada notes? Currency notes have value because of (1) their relative scarcity compared to the demand for them, and (2) their general acceptability. As long as the Bank of Canada keeps the supply of money in reasonable balance with the demand for it, money retains its value even though it has no explicit backing with precious metal or any other tangible commodity.

Paper currency such as $5 bills, $20 bills, etc., are generally acceptable by such diverse people as the taxi driver, the house painter, and the dentist. They all know they can turn around and buy other goods and services with the bills. In part, general acceptability is a matter of convention (as in the case of cigarettes in the POW camp). But convention and habit are reinforced by the status of currency as *legal tender*. Creditors *must* accept currency notes in payment of a debt. (Coins are also legal tender, but only up to reasonable limits. The electric utility company is not obliged to accept 4,562 pennies if a customer offers them in payment for a bill of $45.62.)

Legal tender is the item or items that creditors must accept in payment of debts.

The Canada Deposit Insurance Corporation

But how about bank deposits? What protects their role as part of the money stock? Unlike currency, bank deposits are not legal tender. A gas station is not obliged to accept a personal cheque and usually won't do so.

People are willing to hold money in the form of bank deposits because of the convenience of paying many types of bills by cheque and because they are confident that they can get currency for the deposits when they want it. But what assurance do depositors have of actually being able to get $100 in currency for every $100 they hold in bank deposits?

The first assurance lies in the assets of the banks — their reserves and earning assets of loans and securities. If a bank finds that people are withdrawing more than they are depositing, it may cover the difference by selling securities on the financial markets or using the proceeds of its loans or bonds as they come due. But bank assets may not always be enough; in the United States, for example, they proved to be woefully inadequate during the Depression of the 1930s. As the economy collapsed, many businesses could not repay their loans, and the value of bank assets shrank. As their assets fell to less than their deposit liabilities, the banks were driven into bankruptcy, and many depositors suffered heavy losses.

This situation clearly was dangerous because bank runs are contagious. In early 1933, the contagion spread like wildfire and the U.S. banking system collapsed. In order to prevent a repetition of the 1930s, an important additional backing was therefore provided for bank depositors. The U.S. government set up the Federal Deposit Insurance Corporation (FDIC) to insure bank deposits up to a sizeable limit.

Even though the Canadian banking system has generally been much more stable than the U.S. system throughout most of this century, Canada nevertheless followed the U.S. example and, since 1967, deposits in Canadian chartered banks and trust companies have been insured through the **Canada Deposit Insurance Corporation** (CDIC). The maximum amount covered per deposit has been changed several times; in the late 1980s the limit was $60,000 per deposit.

In return for the insurance coverage that it provides, banks and trust companies pay premiums to the CDIC, and part of the backing for the deposit insurance consists in the premium reserves that the CDIC has accumulated over the years. In addition, however, the CDIC is authorized to borrow as much as it needs from the federal government so that, indirectly, the insurance is, in fact, backed by the government.

In the mid-1980s, the system of deposit insurance came under renewed debate. As Box 12-2 explains in more detail, some critics of the system argued that the existence of insurance had made it easier for institutions like the Ontario trust companies controlled by Leonard Rosenberg, or the Canadian Commercial Bank and the Northland Bank in Alberta, to attract deposits with which to finance the kind of speculative real estate deals that ultimately got them into trouble. According to this view, putting stricter limits on the extent to which deposits are insured would reduce the flow of deposits to institutions engaged in these sorts of practices, and thus reduce the amount of funds wasted on speculative ventures that ultimately fail. Therefore, while everyone agrees that some type of deposit insurance is needed (to help prevent the kind of financial instability that contributed to the Depression in the 1930s), the events of the mid-1980s brought attention to the problems that may arise if *too much* insurance is provided and if reform of the system of deposit insurance is moved higher on the political agenda.

Why Not Gold?

There is an obvious problem with *fiat money* — that is, money that is money solely because the government says it is. The government or central bank can create such money at will. What, then, is to restrain the authorities from creating and spending money recklessly, generating a runaway inflation?

It is this question that provided a rationale for the *gold standard* to which many countries adhered prior to World War I, and which was briefly resurrected during the interwar period. If the currency issued by the government and the central bank is convertible into gold, the authorities will not be able to create money recklessly. Like the goldsmith of old, they will have to keep a gold backing equal to a reasonable fraction of their currency liabilities.

> A country is on the *gold standard* when its currency is convertible into gold; that is, when the government and/or central bank stands ready to buy or sell gold at a fixed price (for example, 1 ounce of gold = $20.00). When a country is on the gold standard, gold coins may circulate as part of the money stock.

How did the monetary system function under the gold standard? The system formed a large inverted pyramid built on a base of gold. On the base of its gold holdings, a central bank could build a structure of deposits and currency, the maximum size of which depended on the gold reserves that the central bank kept. This structure, in turn, formed the base for an even larger superstructure of chartered bank deposits, the maximum size of

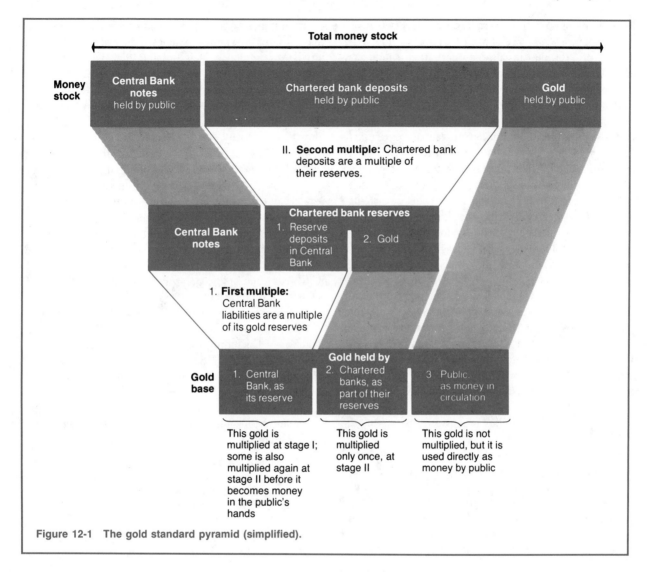

Figure 12-1   **The gold standard pyramid (simplified).**

which depended on the required reserve ratio of banks (Figure 12-1).

While the gold standard fulfils its objective of restraining reckless money creation, it has two serious flaws.

First, the quantity of money tends to fluctuate as a result of changes in the quantity of gold. When the central bank buys gold flowing into the country from abroad —or from domestic gold mines—the effects are similar to those of an open market operation: Chartered bank reserves increase. Moreover, the gold improves the reserve position of the central bank itself. Therefore, the central bank is able to lend more to the chartered banks

or buy more government securities on the open market. Thus, chartered bank reserves can be increased in this indirect way as well. Consequently, a gold inflow can lead to a large increase in the money stock. Similarly, a gold outflow can have a very powerful contractionary effect. There is no assurance that a monetary system that responds to gold flows in this manner will provide the quantity of money needed for a full-employment, non-inflationary economy.

The second difficulty is even more severe. Because of the fractional-reserve system applying to both the chartered banks and the central bank under the gold standard, any tendency for the public to demand items lower in the pyramid has a powerful contractionary effect on the size of the money stock. We saw in Chapter 11 how your deposit of $100,000 in currency permitted a monetary expansion; a withdrawal of currency by the public likewise has a contractionary effect. But if the public withdraws gold (for example, during a depression), it is withdrawing the item at the base of the whole pyramid. In this case, the contractionary effect is particularly severe: Reserves have been removed from the central bank itself, and the bank must take restrictive steps (such as reducing its loans to chartered banks) in order to meet its own required reserve ratios. In short, the money supply shrinks as part of the gold base is withdrawn.

During the Great Depression, people became frightened as unemployment and business bankruptcies shot upward. Being frightened, they tried to get their assets in the safest form possible. In the United States, they withdrew currency from banks and switched from paper currency into gold. (Canada had effectively left the gold standard already in 1928, but the United States stayed on the gold standard even while their economy collapsed.) The U.S. monetary system thus came under strong contractionary pressures when the economy was already headed downward. When things became bad enough, the rules of the game were changed: The U.S. government suspended the convertibility of currency into gold in 1933.

The problem with the gold standard, then, is that it does not provide a *steady* and *measured* restraint. Rather, it exerts restraint in the form of a *threat of disaster*: If too much money is issued, there will be a crisis of confidence, a switch by the public away from paper money and into gold, and a collapse of the monetary structure. As long as the authorities are lucky (with gold flowing

in from mines or from foreign countries) and as long as they follow far-sighted policies aimed at avoiding any crisis of confidence, it is possible that the system will work reasonably well. But in the period between the two world wars, the authorities were neither far-sighted nor lucky. The gold standard added to the disaster of the 1930s. Any system which "kicks an economy when it is down" is basically destructive and should be discarded.

The history of the gold standard and, in particular, the role of gold in the Great Depression in the United States and Europe have been debated vigorously in the last several years. With the apparent unwillingness or inability of present-day governments and central banks to exercise enough restraint to control inflation, some observers, especially in the United States, have concluded that the only way to restore a sound monetary system is to re-establish some link to gold, and thus impose an external constraint on monetary policy.

While we grapple with the problem of inflation, we should be aware of the problems in some of the proposed solutions — including the suggestion of a return to the gold standard. In particular, we should remember how the gold standard contributed to the Depression of the 1930s. And we might remember the words of British economist D.H. Robertson, who, looking back at the economic wreckage of the period between the two world wars, wrote:[3]

> The value of a yellow metal, originally chosen as money because it tickled the fancy of savages, is clearly a chancy and irrelevant thing on which to base the value of our money and the stability of our industrial system.

■ ■ ■ ■ ■

[3] D. H. Robertson, *Money*, rev. ed. (Cambridge: Cambridge University Press, 1948), p. 144.

KEY POINTS

1. The Bank of Canada is responsible for controlling the quantity of money in the Canadian economy. It has several major quantitative tools at its command:
   (a) open market operations
   (b) transfers of government deposits
   (c) changes in the Bank Rate

2. While the Bank of Canada is owned by the government, it has been organized in such a way that it has considerable freedom from political influence in its day-to-day operations. However, the government retains ultimate responsibility for the

   Bank's policy: If there were a fundamental disagreement between the government and the governor of the Bank of Canada, the governor would be obliged to resign.

3. When the Bank of Canada purchases securities on the open market, it creates chartered bank reserves; when it sells securities, it eliminates reserves. Changes in reserves affect the amount of deposit money that chartered banks can create.

4. A purchase of securities by the Bank of Canada tends to bid up security prices. When this happens,

the yields (interest rates) on securities are bid down.

5. Purchases and sales of foreign currencies are sometimes made by the Bank of Canada in order to stabilize the exchange rates between the Canadian dollar and foreign currencies. Foreign currency sales and purchases by the Bank of Canada affect the money stock in the same way as sales and purchases of government securities.

6. The Bank of Canada can also influence the money stock by transferring federal government deposits between itself and the chartered banks. Such transfers create or eliminate chartered bank reserves and thereby affect the money stock.

7. An increase in the Bank Rate discourages borrowing by the chartered banks and investment dealers from the Bank of Canada. Such a decrease in borrowing reduces chartered bank reserves. In recent years, the Bank Rate has been floating: It has been tied to the Treasury bill rate and has not been used actively as an instrument of Bank policy.

8. Less important tools of the Bank of Canada include *moral suasion*. For example, the Bank may try to persuade chartered banks to restrict certain types of lending or increase credit to particular groups of borrowers.

9. The legal reserve requirements imposed by the Bank Act on chartered banks tends to put the banks at a competitive disadvantage relative to other deposit-taking institutions, such as trust companies, that are not subject to such requirements. In the late 1980s, there was active consideration of proposals to abolish legal reserve requirements in order to enable chartered banks to compete on equal terms.

10. Even if there were no *legal* reserve requirements, chartered banks and other institutions such as trust companies still want to hold some fraction of their deposits as currency or balances with the Bank of Canada in order to facilitate cheque clearing and to be able to meet their depositors' demands for currency. Since the Bank of Canada would continue to control the total amount of currency and reserves in the system, it would retain effective control over the money supply even without legal reserve requirements.

11. In the last analysis, there is nothing backing our currency: "A dollar is a dollar." Money retains its value because it is scarce. Even though it doesn't cost the Bank of Canada anything to create reserve deposits, and the costs of printing currency are small, the Bank does not create money recklessly. If it did so, there would be a wild inflation.

12. Under the old gold standard, there was a restraint on irresponsible money creation. But the gold standard had two enormous defects. First, the amount of money that could be created on the available gold base was not necessarily the quantity needed for full employment with stable prices. The second defect was even worse. In a crisis of confidence, people exchanged other forms of money for gold. This caused a sharp contraction of the money supply. Because of its defects, the gold standard was abolished.

KEY CONCEPTS

open market operation
foreign currencies
exchange rate
transfers of government deposits
Bank Rate
required reserve ratio
Bank of Canada board of
directors

governor of the Bank of
Canada
Treasury bill
prime rate
penalty rate
authorized investment dealer
moral suasion

legal tender
acceptability
fiat money
legal reserve requirements
voluntary reserve holdings
gold standard
monetary pyramid

PROBLEMS

12-1. What are the major tools of the Bank of Canada for controlling the quantity of money? Which of these tools affect the quantity of reserves of the chartered banks?

12-2. Suppose that the Bank of Canada purchases $100,000 in Treasury bills from chartered bank A. Explain how the balance sheets of the Bank of Canada and chartered bank A are affected. How much can chartered bank A now safely lend? (Assume that bank A's reserves were just adequate prior to the purchase by the Bank of Canada.)

12-3. Suppose that the price of a three-month, $100,000 Treasury bill is $96,000. What is the yield on this bill? (Following the conventional practice, quote the yield at an annual rate.) Now suppose that the price of three-month bills falls to $95,000. What happens to the yield?

12-4. The Bank of Canada makes loans at the initiative of the chartered banks and investment dealers. In what way do such loans reduce the control of the Bank of Canada over the money supply? In what way might the power of the Bank to change the Bank Rate increase its control over the money stock?

12-5. "Counterfeiting is generally an antisocial act. But when there is a depression, all counterfeiters should be let out of jail." Do you agree or disagree? Explain why.

12-6. What backing do Bank of Canada notes have? Why are these notes valuable?

12-7. A problem with the old gold standard was that it tended to be unstable, because so much money was built on a relatively small base of gold. Explain why this issue may or may not be relevant in assessing the proposals in the 1980s for abolishing legal reserve requirements for chartered banks in Canada.

Chapter 13

■ ■

Monetary Policy and Fiscal Policy: Which Is the Key to Aggregate Demand?

Nothing in excess.

Ancient Greek adage (Diogenes)

In Chapters 10 to 12, we have dealt with the two major tools with which aggregate demand can be controlled: fiscal policy and monetary policy. When we have two tools, the question naturally arises: "On which one should we rely?"

Views on that question have changed considerably in recent decades. The Keynesian revolution not only emphasized the responsibility of government to manage aggregate demand, it also identified fiscal policy as the primary tool to do so. Monetary policy was considered much less important. Keynes and his followers argued that, in the deepest pit of a depression, expansive monetary policies might be completely useless as a means of stimulating aggregate demand. An increase in the money stock might have no effect on spending. In more normal times, Keynes was less skeptical regarding the effects of monetary policy. In fact, he emphasized the importance of money in his earlier works, especially *Monetary Reform* (1924) and *A Treatise on Money* (1930). Nevertheless, his work in the *General Theory* left a strong legacy in favour of fiscal policy as the primary tool to control aggregate demand.

In the two decades between 1945 and 1965, when Keynesian theory dominated macroeconomic analysis in North America, fiscal policy was at the centre of attention with monetary policy being considered much less important. Some Keynesians went so far as to dismiss

the control of aggregate demand through monetary policy as "a mirage and delusion."[1]

During the 1960s, there was a resurgence of interest in monetary policy and in the classical theory which had identified money as *the* determinant of aggregate demand. The most prominent role in this revival of classical economics was played by Milton Friedman, then a professor at the University of Chicago (now retired). Friedman summarized his position: "Money is extremely important for nominal magnitudes, for nominal income, for the level of income in dollars. . . . " Furthermore, Friedman was skeptical about the effectiveness of fiscal policy as a tool for controlling aggregate demand. He recognized, of course, that the government budget has an important influence on the allocation of resources: The budget determines how much of domestic and national product is spent by the government, and how much is left for the private sector. But Friedman doubted that fiscal policy has an important

■ ■ ■ ■ ■

[1] Warren Smith, in *Staff Report on Employment, Growth, and Price Levels* (Washington: Joint Economic Committee, U.S. Congress, 1959), p. 401. Smith was writing about general monetary controls, such as open market operations, that affect the quantity of money. He was less skeptical of the effectiveness of selective controls, such as those on consumer instalment credit.

effect on aggregate demand: "In my opinion, the state of the budget by itself has no significant effect on the course of nominal income, on inflation, on deflation, or on cyclical fluctuations."[2]

While Friedman and other monetarists have had a profound effect, neoclassical theory has not attained the predominant position enjoyed by Keynesian theory in the decades following the Second World War. Most macroeconomists are eclectic, agreeing with some parts of Keynesian analysis and with some parts of classical economics. In response to the question posed back in the first paragraph, most present-day macroeconomists would answer: "Both monetary and fiscal policies are important. It would be a mistake to rely exclusively on either one or the other."

To understand current thinking on monetary and fiscal policies, it is important to study both Keynesian and classical theories. Each theory provides a sensible framework for the orderly investigation of macroeconomic developments. Each can heighten our understanding of how the economy works. Chapter 10 explained the Keynesian view of how fiscal policy can affect aggregate demand. To complete our discussion of fiscal and monetary policies, this chapter will explain:

1. The Keynesian view of how monetary policy can affect aggregate demand and the circumstances in which the effect may not be very strong.
2. The classical view on how monetary policy can affect aggregate demand and why those in the classical tradition expect the effects of monetary policy to be both strong and predictable.
3. The reasons some of those in the classical tradition have doubts about fiscal policy; specifically, why they doubt that fiscal policy has the strong and predictable effect on aggregate demand suggested by the Keynesian theory outlined in Chapter 10.
4. The advantages of using a *combination* of monetary and fiscal policies as part of an overall strategy of stabilizing aggregate demand.
5. Why monetary policy has in fact been the predominant demand-management tool since the late 1970s, in spite of the widely recognized advantages of using a balanced combination of monetary and fiscal policies.

■ ■ ■ ■ ■
[2] Milton Friedman and Walter Heller, *Monetary vs. Fiscal Policy: A Dialogue* (New York: W. W. Norton, 1969), pp. 46, 51.

In order to keep the discussion from becoming too complicated, we will concentrate in this chapter on the *domestic* effects of monetary policy. But, in doing so, we should recognize that, from the viewpoint of a Canadian policy maker, the analysis will be seriously incomplete. In an economy such as ours where international trade and capital flows play such an important role, the effectiveness of both monetary and fiscal policies depend a great deal on how they influence our transactions with foreign countries. A detailed discussion of these issues is postponed until the next chapter. In the meantime, it is important to keep in mind that as we lay the groundwork for understanding monetary policy in this chapter, we are telling only half the story of how monetary policy works in Canada.

THE EFFECTS OF MONETARY POLICY: THE KEYNESIAN VIEW

Keynes identified a three-step process by which an expansive monetary policy could increase aggregate demand (Figure 13-1):

1. An open market purchase generally causes a *lower interest rate*.
2. A lower interest rate encourages businesses to *invest more*. It is cheaper for them to borrow money to finance the purchase of new machines or building of new factories.
3. Higher investment demand will have a *multiplied effect* on aggregate expenditure and domestic product.

The third step involves the familiar multiplier explained in Chapter 9. Here, we will look at steps 1 and 2.

Step 1: Monetary Policy and the Interest Rate: The Stock of Money, and the Demand for It

The first step in the process—how an open market purchase can lower interest rates—was discussed briefly in Chapter 12. Because this step is important in the Keynesian evaluation of monetary policy, we consider it in more detail here.

In Keynes' theory, the interest rate reaches equilibrium when the quantity of money demanded is equal to the quantity in existence—that is, *when people are willing to hold the amount of money that exists in the economy*.

People hold money in order to buy goods and services. As a result, the demand for money *depends on aggregate*

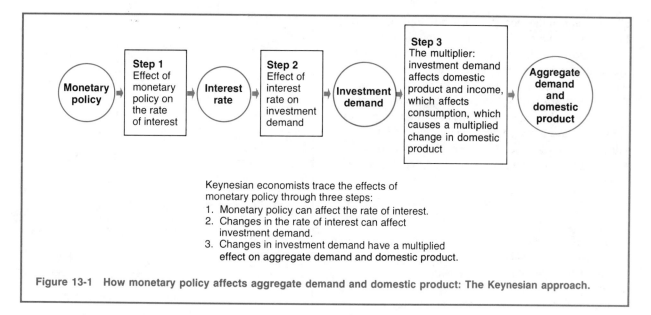

Keynesian economists trace the effects of monetary policy through three steps:
1. Monetary policy can affect the rate of interest.
2. Changes in the rate of interest can affect investment demand.
3. Changes in investment demand have a multiplied effect on aggregate demand and domestic product.

Figure 13-1　How monetary policy affects aggregate demand and domestic product: The Keynesian approach.

domestic income. The reason is straightforward. The higher income is, the more purchases people will plan to make and, consequently, the larger the money balances they will want to hold on average.

The demand for money also *depends on the interest rate.* Whenever money is held, rather than used to buy a bond or other interest-bearing security, the holder of money gives up the interest that could have been earned on the security. Suppose that interest rates are high. The treasurers of corporations will try to keep as little money on hand as is conveniently possible, putting the rest into interest-bearing securities. At an interest rate of 10% per annum, for example, $10 million earns almost $20,000 in interest per week—a tidy sum. On the other hand, if interest rates are low, people do not need to be so careful about cash management; they do not forgo so much interest by holding money rather than securities. It is convenient for people to hold more money and not very costly for them to do so.

The willingness of people to hold more money at a lower rate of interest is illustrated by the downward-sloping demand curve in Figure 13-2. Now, suppose that $20 billion of money has been created by the banking system. S_1 illustrates this money supply. The equilibrium interest rate is 8% at the intersection of the demand and supply curves. Note that the demand curve in Figure 13-2 has been drawn for a given aggregate nominal income. If nominal income rises, the demand

curve shifts out: At any given interest rate, there is a larger demand for money balances.

Consider next what happens if the Bank of Canada purchases securities on the open market, thereby causing

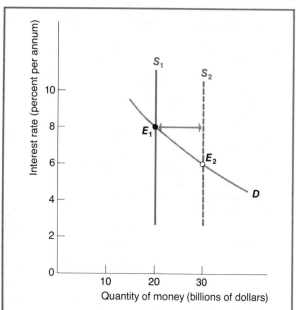

Figure 13-2　The stock of money, and the demand for it. There is an increase in the quantity of money demanded when the interest rate falls. The equilibrium interest rate occurs when the quantity of money demanded is equal to the stock in existence.

an expansion of the money stock to $30 billion, as shown by S_2. At the old 8% interest rate, there is a surplus of money shown by the arrow; people have more than they are willing to hold at this interest rate. What do they do with the excess? They buy interest-bearing securities. Bond prices are bid up — that is, interest rates are bid down. The interest rate falls to its new equilibrium, 6%.

An increase in the stock of money can thus lead to a fall in the interest rate. Now consider the second step: How a fall in the interest rate can lead to an increase in investment.

Step 2. The Interest Rate and the Demand for Investment

Businesses undertake new investment in the expectation that it will increase their profits. The expected profitability of new investment depends on:

1. Expected sales and prices of the goods produced with the investment. Expectations can change quite rapidly when business conditions are changing. For example, fears of a recession can cause business executives to scale back their expectations of future sales, and thus postpone or cancel investment projects. Changes in expectations are the major reason investment fluctuates so much during business cycles.
2. The technology that determines how productive the new capital will be. For example, a new generation of larger, fuel-efficient aircraft can encourage airlines to re-equip their fleets.
3. The costs of other inputs. For example, the cost of steel and labour can influence the willingness of auto companies to buy new machines.
4. The cost of the new investment, which has two major components:
   (a) The price of the capital—for example, the price of the machine or new factory.
   (b) The cost of *financing* the new investment — that is, the interest rate.

Monetary policy affects investment primarily through item 4(b). To concentrate on this variable, we assume for

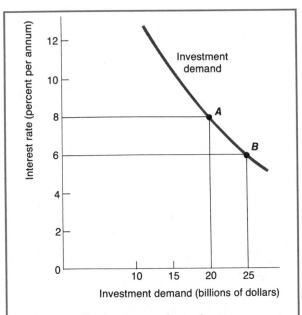

Figure 13-3   The investment demand curve.
The investment demand curve slopes downward to the right. At a lower interest rate, it is cheaper for businesses to finance their investment projects. More projects are therefore undertaken.

the moment that all the other determinants of investment (items 1 through 4(a)) remain unchanged.

The effect of the interest rate on the quantity of investment demanded is illustrated in Figure 13-3. As the interest rate falls from, say, 8% to 6%, it is cheaper to finance investment projects and business executives are therefore encouraged to undertake new ones. The desired quantity of investment (I^*) increases from $20 billion to $25 billion.

Problems with Monetary Policy

We may now summarize in Table 13-1 and Figure 13-4 the Keynesian view as to how monetary policy works. By this three-step process, open market operations can affect aggregate demand. Why, then, were early

Table 13-1   How Monetary Policy Works: The Keynesian Approach

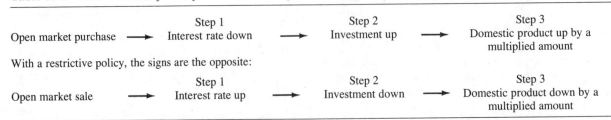

	Step 1		Step 2		Step 3
Open market purchase →	Interest rate down	→	Investment up	→	Domestic product up by a multiplied amount

With a restrictive policy, the signs are the opposite:

	Step 1		Step 2		Step 3
Open market sale →	Interest rate up	→	Investment down	→	Domestic product down by a multiplied amount

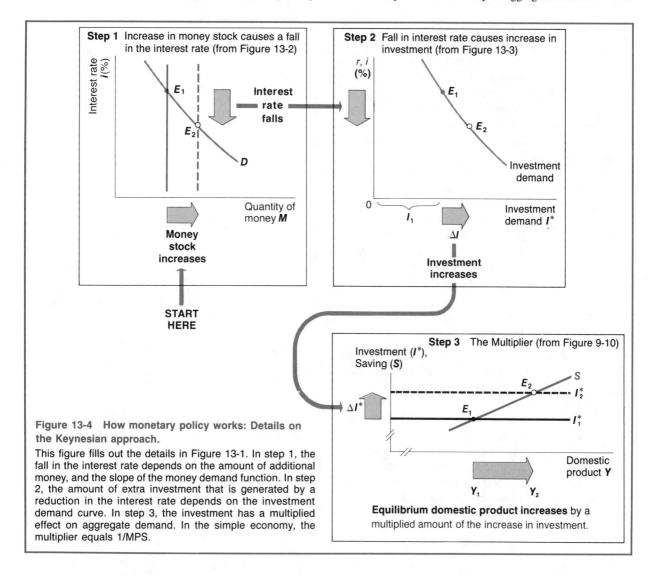

Figure 13-4   How monetary policy works: Details on the Keynesian approach.

This figure fills out the details in Figure 13-1. In step 1, the fall in the interest rate depends on the amount of additional money, and the slope of the money demand function. In step 2, the amount of extra investment that is generated by a reduction in the interest rate depends on the investment demand curve. In step 3, the investment has a multiplied effect on aggregate demand. In the simple economy, the multiplier equals 1/MPS.

Keynesians skeptical regarding the possible effectiveness of monetary policy as a tool for managing demand? The answer is: We cannot be certain that the effects at either of the first two steps will be very strong.

Step 1

Keynes himself was particularly concerned that an expansive monetary policy might be ineffective at the very first step, and therefore could not be counted on as a way of getting out of the deep depression that existed when the *General Theory* was written. During a deep depression, interest rates may be very low—for example, in the 2% to 3% range that prevailed during much of the Depression of the 1930s. In such circumstances, the ability of the Bank of Canada to push the rates down even further is not very great. Clearly, interest rates cannot be pushed all the way down to zero. (At a zero interest rate, nobody would be willing to hold bonds. They would be giving up the use of their money and getting nothing in return. It would be better to hold money in the bank instead.) Thus, when interest rates are already very low, it may become impossible for the Bank of Canada to move them much lower. Expansive monetary policy cannot have much effect on interest rates; it fails at step 1.

In more normal times, open market operations can significantly affect the interest rate, and the second step becomes the principal concern in the operation of monetary policy.

Step 2

As Figure 13-3 is drawn, investment is quite responsive to a change in the rate of interest. For example, a fall in the interest rate from 8% to 6% will cause a 25% increase in investment demand from $20 billion to $25 billion. An alternative possibility is illustrated in Figure 13-5. Here, the investment demand curve falls much more steeply than it did in Figure 13-3. Now, even with a sharp drop in the interest rate from 8% to 6%, investment does not increase very much—only by $1 billion. This, then, is the second reason why monetary policy may be ineffective.

This view—that investment would not respond very strongly to changes in the interest rate—was widely held during the 1940s and 1950s, and contributed to the prevailing skepticism regarding the effectiveness of monetary policy as a demand-management tool.

MONETARY POLICY: THE CLASSICAL VIEW

During the 1960s, there was a major revival in the old classical school, which made money the centerpiece of aggregate demand theory.

In contrast to Keynes, who started his analysis of aggregate demand and aggregate expenditures by looking at its components (consumption, investment, government purchases of goods and services, and net exports), classical economists began from quite a different starting point. Their analysis was based on the concept of the *income velocity of money* and the *equation of exchange*:

$$MV = PQ \qquad (13\text{-}1)$$

where
M = quantity of money in the hands of the public
P = average level of prices
Q = quantity of output — that is, real domestic product or real income[3]
Thus,
PQ = domestic product, measured in nominal (dollar) terms and
V = *income velocity of money*—that is, the average number of times that the money stock (M) is spent

■ ■ ■ ■ ■
[3] Earlier, we used the symbol Y to denote domestic product. However, the classical economists used the symbol Q instead, and we follow this convention here.

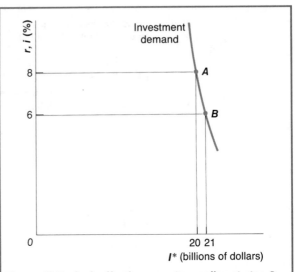

Figure 13-5 An ineffective monetary policy at step 2.
If the investment demand curve is steep, investment will not increase much when the interest rate falls. Therefore, the effect of monetary policy on aggregate demand is not very powerful.

to buy final output during a year. Specifically, V is defined as being equal to PQ/M.

Suppose that the money stock is $80 billion. Assume that, in the course of a year, the average currency note and the average chequing deposit are spent six times to purchase final goods and services. In other words, V is 6. Then, total spending for final output is $80 billion times 6, or $480 billion. In turn, this total spending (MV) equals the total quantity of goods and services (Q) times the average price (P) at which they were sold.

But how can the same dollars be used over and over to purchase final goods? Very simply. When you purchase groceries at the store, the $50 you pay does not disappear. Rather, it goes into the cash register. From there, it is used to pay the farmer for fresh vegetables, the canning factory for canned goods, or the clerk's wages. The farmer or the clerk or the employee of the canning factory will, in turn, use the money to purchase goods. Once more, the money is used for final purchases. The same $5 bills or bank deposits can circulate round and round.

The Quantity Theory of Money

The equation of exchange, by itself, does not get us very far, because it is a *tautology* or *truism*. That is, it *must* be true because of the way the terms are defined. Note that velocity is defined as $V = PQ/M$. Thus, by definition, $MV = PQ$. (Just multiply both sides of the first equation by M.)

However, in the hands of classical economists, the equation of exchange became more than a tautology; it became the basis of an important theory. This theory — the **quantity theory of money** — was based on the proposition that *velocity (V) is stable*.

> The *quantity theory of money* is the proposition that velocity (V) is stable. Therefore, a change in the quantity of money (M) will cause nominal domestic product (PQ) to change by approximately the same percentage.

If, for example, the money stock (M) increases by 20%, then as a consequence, nominal domestic product (PQ) will also rise by about 20%. In other words, the old classical economists and their modern monetarist followers put forward the following central proposition:

1. A change in the quantity of money (M) is the key to changes in aggregate demand. When people have more M, they spend more on the nation's output. Specifically, an increase in M will cause an approximately proportional increase in nominal domestic product (PQ). The aggregate demand curve shifts when the money stock changes, as already illustrated back in Figure 8-4.

In Chapter 8, we encountered several other important classical propositions:

2. *In the long run*, real output (Q) moves to the full-employment, capacity level. The long-run aggregate supply curve is vertical. Therefore, the long-run effect of a change in M is on P, not on Q. Most notably, a rapid increase in the quantity of money causes a rapid inflation.

3. *In the short run* (over periods of months or quarters), a change in M can have a substantial effect on both P and Q. For example, a decline in the quantity of money can cause a decline in output (Q) and the onset of a recession. During a recession, growth of M can cause a short-run increase in Q, moving the economy back toward full employment.

4. Monetary disturbances are a major cause of unstable aggregate demand and of business cycles. If M is kept stable, a market economy will be quite stable.

5. Thus, the major macroeconomic responsibility of the authorities is to provide a stable money supply. Specifically, the money supply should be steadily increased at a rate that is adequate to buy the full-employment output of the economy at stable prices. As the capacity of the economy grows gradually, economists in the classical tradition argue that the authorities should adhere to a *policy rule*, increasing the money stock at a slow, steady rate of 3% or 4% per year.

Why Should Velocity Be Stable? The Demand for Money

The quantity theory may be traced back over 200 years, at least as far back as the writings of the English philosopher David Hume in the eighteenth century. The early quantity theorists attributed the inflation of the time to the inflow of gold and silver from the New World. The exact mechanism by which money affected aggregate demand and prices was not spelled out in detail by these early theorists. They believed that it was self-evident that, when people have more money, they spend more. When they spend more — with more money chasing a relatively fixed quantity of goods — prices rise.

More recently, particularly in response to the criticisms by Keynesians, neoclassical economists have been more explicit about their theory. Velocity is stable, they argue, because *the demand for money is stable*. The demand for money arises because of the usefulness of money in purchasing goods and services. Money is held only temporarily, from the time people receive income until they spend it to purchase goods and services. The higher people's incomes, the more money they will need to make purchases. Therefore, the quantity of money demanded depends on the size of domestic income. And it is domestic income in current dollars (that is, PQ rather than simply Q) that is important in determining the demand for money: If prices rise, people will need more money to pay for the more expensive goods and services. Thus, neoclassical economists focus on nominal domestic income as the principal determinant of the demand for money.

Figure 13-6 illustrates this relationship. The higher the current dollar or nominal domestic product (measured up the vertical axis), the greater the quantity of money demanded (measured along the horizontal axis). Suppose that the actual amount of money in the economy is initially at S_1, and the current-dollar domestic product is at A_1. Then, the supply S_1 and demand for money will be in equilibrium at point E_1. The quantity of money demanded, measured by the distance A_1E_1, will be equal to the quantity of money S_1 actually in existence.

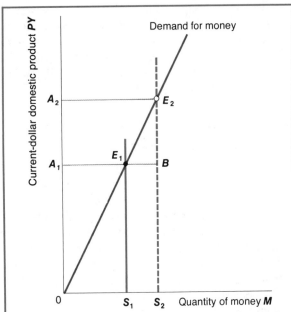

Figure 13-6 **The demand for money: A classical view.**
Those in the classical tradition believe that the demand for money is stable and depends primarily on current-dollar domestic product. If the stock of money which people hold exceeds the demand for money, then people will increase their spending.

Now, suppose that an expansive monetary policy is followed, with the money supply increasing to S_2. At the existing domestic product A_1, the stock of money that people have A_1B is greater than the amount they want to hold A_1E_1; there is a temporary surplus of money of E_1B. With more money than they want, people spend it to buy more goods and services. In other words, aggregate demand goes up.

If the economy is initially in a depression, with large amounts of excess capacity, output Q will respond strongly to the increase in money. But, if the economy is already at or near full employment, then Q can't increase substantially, and higher aggregate demand will cause a rise in prices P. In either case, current-dollar domestic product PQ will increase. As this happens, people become willing to hold more money. The process continues until current-dollar domestic product rises to A_2, where the quantity of money and the demand for it are again in equilibrium at E_2. In this way, a change in the quantity of money causes an approximately proportional change in domestic product PQ. But this in turn means that V is stable. (If a 10% increase in PQ occurs whenever there is a 10% increase in M, then the ratio PQ/M is constant. That is, V is constant.)

Thus, the theoretical underpinning of the quantity theory of money—the proposition that V is stable—is this: There is a stable demand for money, similar to the straight line shown in Figure 13-6.

In conclusion, note that when there is an excess supply of money, Keynesian and classical economists present quite different ideas as to what will happen. According to Keynes' theory, people with excess money think of buying bonds. If interest rates are already very low, they will skip bonds, and simply hold the money instead. An expansive monetary policy will have little or no effect on aggregate demand. Not so, said classical economists. If people have excess quantities of money, they have a very straightforward option: They can spend it. This they will do. The connection between money and spending is very tight and very short; it is not the complicated three-step Keynesian process explained at the beginning of this chapter.

CLASSICAL DOUBTS ABOUT FISCAL POLICY: CROWDING OUT

Classical economists were united in emphasizing the importance of money as a determinant of aggregate demand. However, their views on fiscal policy were much less unanimous. In fact, classical views on fiscal policy have ranged over a wide spectrum.

During the Great Depression of the 1930s, some of them recommended deficit spending as a way of increasing demand, output, and employment. For example, at the depth of the Depression in 1933, Jacob Viner (a Canadian-born economist who taught at the University of Chicago) wrote:

> The outstanding though unintentional achievement of the [U.S. federal government] in counteracting the depression has in fact been its deficits of the last two years. . . . Had the government and the business magnates retained their mental balance, there would have been less cause to fear net ill effects during a depression than during the war from even a ten billion dollar deficit.[4]

- - - - -

[4] Jacob Viner, *Balanced Deflation, Inflation, or More Depression* (Minneapolis: University of Minnesota Press, Day and Hour Series, 1933), pp. 18–19. At that time, a $10 billion deficit would have been more than 10% of U.S. full-employment GNP.

In spite of his approval of fiscal stimulus in 1933, Viner was very skeptical of the theoretical analysis of Keynes' *General Theory* when it appeared three years later.

Keynesian theory was thus not necessary to reach Keynes' main policy proposal in favour of deficit spending during the Great Depression. Some classical economists also supported this proposal.

At the other end of the spectrum, other classical writers were very skeptical about the effects of fiscal policy on aggregate demand, output, and employment. For example, the British Treasury opposed additional government spending during the Great Depression on the ground that it would do no good, since it would merely displace — or **crowd out** — an equivalent amount of private investment demand. (One of Keynes' principal objectives in writing the *General Theory* was to combat this view of the British Treasury.) Most monetarists — the modern inheritors of the classical tradition—are also skeptical about the effects of fiscal policy on aggregate demand.

Expansive fiscal policies may crowd out investment demand in the following way. When the government increases its expenditures or cuts taxes, its deficit rises. To finance its deficit spending, the government sells new bonds or shorter-term securities. That is, it borrows from the financial markets. The additional borrowing pushes up interest rates. Higher interest rates, in turn, cause a decrease in desired investment as businesses move along the investment demand curve (Figure 13-7).

> *Crowding out* occurs when an expansive fiscal policy causes higher interest rates, and these higher interest rates in turn depress investment demand.

There is little doubt that some crowding out takes place. The question is, how much? Keynesian economists — and particularly early Keynesians — have often argued that investment is not very responsive to interest rates. This view was illustrated back in Figure 13-5, where investment decreases only a little in a move from *B* to *A*. As a result, not much crowding out of investment takes place. Consequently, fiscal policy is a powerful tool for controlling aggregate demand (and monetary policy is weak). Monetarists, on the other hand, generally believe that the MEI curve is quite flat, as shown in Figure 13-7, and that deficit spending by the government tends to crowd out a relatively large amount of private investment.

In casting doubt on the effectiveness of fiscal policies, monetarists make one important qualification. If the central bank buys any of the additional bonds being issued by the government, it will be engaging in an expansive open market operation. New money will be created and

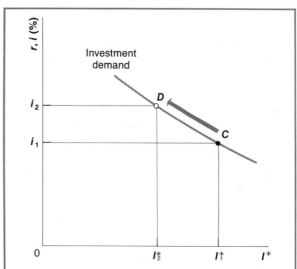

Figure 13-7   Crowding out: The monetarist view. Government deficits may push up the interest rate—from i_1 to i_2, for example. This causes a movement along the investment demand curve from *C* to *D*, and investment demand decreases from I_1^* to I_2^*.

this will have a powerful expansive effect on aggregate demand. But monetarists attribute the higher demand to a change in the money stock, not to the government deficit itself. They see **pure fiscal policy** as having little effect on aggregate demand.

> *Pure fiscal policy* involves a change in government spending or tax rates, unaccompanied by any change in the rate of growth of the money stock.

FISCAL POLICY AND NET EXPORTS

There is a second reason fiscal policy may sometimes become ineffective: Its effect on aggregate demand may be partially offset by opposite changes in net exports. Consider again the case in which the government is increasing the budget deficit as a way of stimulating the economy. As we explained above, when the government has to increase its borrowing in the capital market to finance the larger deficit, there will be a tendency for interest rates to rise. As we have just seen, it is this tendency for interest rates to rise that leads to a reduction in private investment (that is, causes some crowding out of investment). But higher Canadian interest rates also make Canadian financial assets (such as government bonds) more attractive to foreign investors.

As we will explain in more detail in the next chapter, when foreigners increase their demand for Canadian assets, there is a tendency for the value of the Canadian dollar to rise in international markets. But as the Canadian dollar becomes more expensive in terms of foreign currencies, foreign buyers will find Canadian export goods more expensive. When Canadian goods become more expensive in terms of foreign currencies, foreign buyers will buy fewer of them. That is, our exports will decrease. A change in the international value of the Canadian dollar also affects imports into Canada. If the Canadian dollar rises in value, imports will appear relatively cheaper to Canadian buyers. Consequently, imports into Canada will rise.

With rising Canadian imports and declining exports, the net export component of aggregate expenditure decreases. This partially cancels out the stimulative effects of budgetary deficits.

Even though foreign trade and capital flows usually play a much less important role in the United States than in Canada, the relation between the budget deficit and net exports became an issue of considerable concern in the United States in the mid-1980s. Because of the very large U.S. government deficit under the Reagan administration, federal borrowing became very large and interest rates in the United States reached unprecedented highs in the early 1980s. In response, there was a large capital inflow into the United States, and the value of the U.S. dollar increased substantially in terms of currencies such as the German mark and the Japanese yen, especially in 1983 and 1984. As a result, there was a large reduction in U.S. net exports. In fact, the reduction in net exports was considerably greater than the reduction in investment: Even though interest rates were high, capital investment recovered strongly after the 1982 recession. Thus, in those years, the main effect of the large U.S. federal deficits was to crowd out net exports. (The relationship between the U.S. federal budget and trade deficits will be discussed in more detail in Chapter 20.)

THE UNCERTAIN LESSON OF RECENT HISTORY

To summarize the major debate in this chapter: Monetarists argue that velocity is stable. Money is the key to changes in aggregate demand. An increase in the quantity of money causes an increase in domestic product, measured in dollars. Many monetarists are skeptical about pure fiscal policy, arguing that it will have little effect on aggregate demand. In contrast, Keynesians believe that fiscal policy has a powerful impact on aggregate demand. Early Keynesians argued that monetary policy is not very effective.

It would seem easy to settle this dispute—simply look at the facts and see which theory is more in line with the observations of the real world. Unfortunately, this is easier said than done. The history of recent decades does not give clear, unambiguous support to either position.

The Rise of Monetarism

The revival of classical economics was given a boost in the late 1960s and early 1970s, when events tended to confirm the quantity theory and cast doubts on the Keynesian view. In Canada, the recession of 1970 occurred at the same time as a sharp reduction in the rate of monetary growth: The growth rate of M1 in 1970 (at about 2%) was the lowest in ten years. Fiscal policy, on the other hand, appeared to be shifting in an expansionary direction. (Even though the combined federal and provincial budgets showed a surplus in 1970, the surplus was considerably smaller than in 1969.) Moreover, in the 1972–74 period, while fiscal policy was basically neutral, nominal income grew at very high rates. Monetarists were not surprised: The Bank of Canada was pursuing an expansionary policy, with very high growth rates in the money supply, during those years.

The evidence from 1968/69 in the United States also appeared to support the monetarists. In mid-1968, Congress imposed an income tax surcharge and placed a limitation on federal government spending in order to cool down the inflation generated by the Vietnam conflict. Economists using the Keynesian approach expected a powerful restrictive effect on aggregate demand. In fact, they expressed fears that Congress had engaged in "fiscal overkill," and that a recession would be caused by the sharp shift toward fiscal restraint. In order to soften the expected recession, the Federal Reserve eased monetary policy, allowing a rapid rate of growth of the money stock. Thus, monetary and fiscal policies were pulling in opposite directions: Monetary policy was expansive, while fiscal policy was restrictive.

What happened? Aggregate demand followed the path set by monetary policy and continued to expand vigorously throughout late 1968. Indeed, the boom continued until after monetary policy was shifted sharply toward restraint in early 1969. Monetarists seemed vindicated, and Keynesians were shaken in their beliefs. In the words of contemporary commentators, Keynesian economic advisers were sent "scurrying back to their universities with their doctrinal tales (*sic*) between their legs.''[5]

In 1974, monetarism was given a further boost. Tight monetary policies in the United States were followed by the worst recession in decades, confirming the view that money has a powerful effect on aggregate demand. Furthermore, the U.S. Federal Reserve apparently blundered, falling into the trap against which monetarists warned. In setting monetary policy, they focused primarily on interest rates rather than on the quantity of money. But this may lead to a problem when the economy is moving into a recession, as it was doing in 1974. The weakening economy meant that business demand for loans was falling. To stabilize interest rates in the face of falling loan demand, the Federal Reserve had to sharply restrict the growth rate of the money stock. But, in hindsight, the reduction of the rate of money growth made the recession worse.

In Canada, the 1974/75 recession was much less severe than in the United States. Keynesians have argued that this can be explained by the stimulative effect of the easy fiscal policy in 1975, when the government budget showed a large deficit. Monetarists agree that this shift in fiscal policy may have helped the economy *recover* from the recession (though the recovery can also be explained by the stimulative monetary policy in 1975). However, they argue that fiscal policy cannot explain why the recession was relatively mild (in comparison with the U.S. recession) in the first place. To explain this, one must look at fiscal and monetary policies in 1974, when the recession was in its early stages. And in 1974, fiscal policy was clearly contractionary with the federal budget moving into surplus. Monetary policy, on the other hand, was relatively easy (at least in comparison with that of the United States): While the rate of growth of M1 in 1974 was somewhat lower than in the preceding two years, it was much higher than in the United States and considerably higher than in the 1960s. Thus, monetarists argue, the relatively good performance of the Canadian economy in 1974/75 supports their position that monetary policy is the most important factor in determining aggregate demand.

■ ■ ■ ■ ■
[5] Alan Blinder and Robert Solow, ''Analytical Foundations of Fiscal Policy,'' in Blinder, Solow, et al., *The Economics of Public Finance* (Washington, D.C.: The Brookings Institution, 1974), p. 10.

Monetarism in Practice: Canada, 1975–80

The empirical support for the monetarist doctrines in the early 1970s led to a change in the thinking of economic policy makers. If aggregate demand could be closely controlled by controlling the rate of monetary growth, as the evidence seemed to suggest, it would make sense, according to the monetarists, to stabilize aggregate demand by following a policy of stable monetary growth. In the mid-1970s, many people agreed with this argument and attention was focused on monetary policy.

Particularly notable was the policy announced by the Bank of Canada in late 1975. The new policy involved a significant step in the direction of the monetarist policy prescriptions: From November 1975, the Bank would follow a policy of letting M1 grow at a rate that would lie somewhere in a pre-announced ''target range.'' The target range would be revised from time to time, but the Bank made clear its intention of gradually lowering the target growth rate in order to reduce inflationary pressures. The announcement was particularly significant in that it implied a change in the Bank's earlier policy of using interest rates and credit availability as the criteria by which to judge monetary tightness or ease: The new policy put the money supply, and the rate of growth of money, at centre stage.

There are several explanations why the Bank made this decision in 1975. The velocity of M1 had remained relatively stable for several years. Furthermore, the decision seemed an appropriate response to the policy problem facing the government and the Bank of Canada at the time. Inflation had been accelerating rapidly, from about 3% in 1970/71 to well over 10% in 1974/75. People were wondering how far the inflationary spiral would go. Fears of even higher inflation in the future were themselves contributing to inflation. For example, unions were demanding higher wages in the expectation that prices would continue to rise. In turn, businesses were raising prices further in order to cover their higher wage costs. When compared with the United States, Canada had escaped the 1974/75 recession relatively lightly, and cooling inflation and breaking inflationary expectations seemed the highest priority of economic policy. The federal government had just announced a program of wage and price controls as a short-run response to high inflation, and the time seemed ripe for making it clear that monetary policy could provide effective support in bringing inflation down.

Monetarism, with its focus on price stability as a policy goal, provided an appropriate framework for this campaign. By declaring its intention to lower the rate of growth of the money stock, the Bank of Canada hoped to convince the public that it meant business. Furthermore, emphasis on the supply of money could reduce the Bank's political problem. An anti-inflationary tight monetary policy would lead to an increase in interest rates, at least in the short run. By emphasizing its responsibility for controlling the money supply, the Bank hoped to reduce the political pressures on it to keep interest rates down.

The Early 1980s: Abandoning the Monetarist Experiment

From 1975 to 1980, the Bank of Canada did stick fairly close to its announced targets for monetary growth. The growth rate of M1 was steadily reduced. However, the results were disappointing. Even though the money stock was growing more slowly, aggregate expenditure continued to grow at a high rate and the inflation rate did not come down. Instead, it accelerated: In each year during 1977–81, the rate of price inflation was higher than it had been in the previous year.

In the early 1980s, interest rates rose dramatically in the United States in response to very tight monetary policies in that country. In response, the Bank of Canada reduced the growth rate of M1 even more than it had announced it would; during 1982, M1 actually *fell* below its 1981 level. (As we will explain in more detail in Chapter 14, the Bank was concerned that the high interest rates in the United States would drive down the value of our dollar in the foreign exchange markets unless interest rates were raised in Canada as well.) But even so, inflation continued at a high rate: The increase in the consumer price index in 1982 was well above 10%. What went wrong?

Figure 13-8 shows the main reason that inflation in Canada did not come down even though M1 grew relatively slowly: The velocity of M1 kept rising. In particular, it rose substantially during the period of monetary contraction in 1981/82. In other words, if we use M1 to represent the money stock in the equation of exchange, the increase in PQ was largely attributable to an increase in V, not an increase in M. The data did not support the monetarist view that V is stable.

In the United States, velocity also fluctuated in the early 1980s. But while the velocity of M1 *rose* in Canada, in the United States it *fell* substantially. That is,

growth in U.S. aggregate demand was much weaker than the growth in the money stock. In contrast to the recession of 1974, the 1982 recession in the United States could not be interpreted as primarily a monetary phenomenon; something other than changes in the money stock was a major cause of weakness in aggregate demand. Thus the U.S. data are also inconsistent with a strict monetarist hypothesis, though in a different way than the Canadian data.

As we noted in Chapter 11, some analysts have suggested that part of the reason that the velocity of M1 has been unstable is that M1 is too narrowly defined. According to this view, if "money" were to be more broadly defined, one would find that velocity would have been more stable.

In response to this suggestion, economists at the Bank of Canada paid considerable attention to a somewhat broader definition of money, M1A, as an indicator of monetary policy during the early 1980s. (As we noted in Chapter 11, M1A was defined as M1 plus daily interest chequable and non-personal notice deposits.) But as Figure 13-8 shows, the velocity of M1A fluctuated even more than the velocity of M1 in the first half of the 1980s.

On the other hand, the velocity of even more broadly defined concepts of money (such as M2 and M2 +) did remain considerably more stable. Thus, if one uses one of these broader definitions of money, the data look much more consistent with the monetarist hypothesis. Accordingly, a monetarist could argue that the high rate of inflation in the early 1980s *was*, in fact, due to a high rate of growth of the money supply M2 or M2 +.

But if monetarists have to switch back and forth from one definition of money to another in order to defend their position, their defence leaves a nagging question: If there is uncertainty about whether it is M1, M2, or M2 + that explains aggregate demand, which one is the policy maker supposed to increase slowly and steadily?

The history of the past two decades has not been kind to doctrinaire economists, whether monetarist or Keynesian.

The Recent Reliance on Monetary Policy

Changes in velocity have weakened the case for monetarism in the past decade. Nevertheless, the emphasis on monetary policy has been substantially greater in the past decade than in previous years.

Indeed, problems with fiscal policy left monetary policy at centre stage from the mid-1970s to the late 1980s.

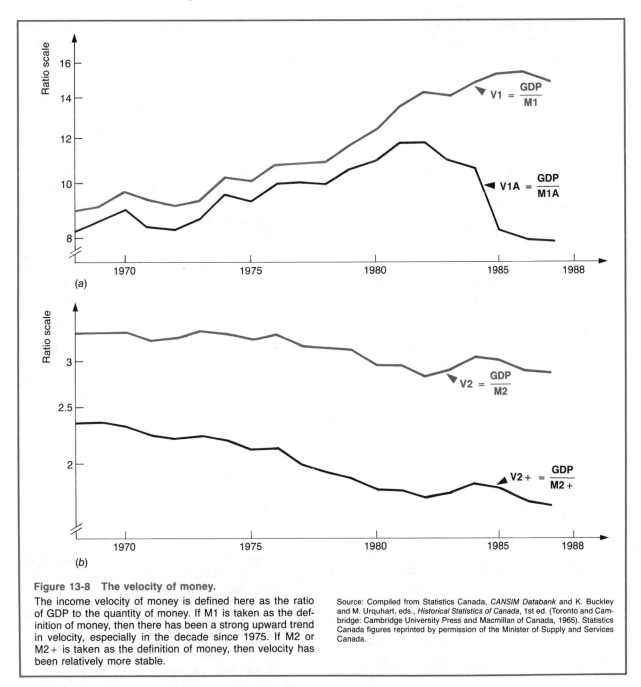

Figure 13-8 The velocity of money.

The income velocity of money is defined here as the ratio of GDP to the quantity of money. If M1 is taken as the definition of money, then there has been a strong upward trend in velocity, especially in the decade since 1975. If M2 or M2+ is taken as the definition of money, then velocity has been relatively more stable.

Source: Compiled from Statistics Canada, *CANSIM Databank* and K. Buckley and M. Urquhart, eds., *Historical Statistics of Canada*, 1st ed. (Toronto and Cambridge: Cambridge University Press and Macmillan of Canada, 1965). Statistics Canada figures reprinted by permission of the Minister of Supply and Services Canada.

Tax cuts and increases in transfer payments resulted in very large deficits in the federal budget. Although many political leaders believed that it was important to reduce deficits, there was little agreement on how to do so. Each spending program had its supporters and tax increases were unpalatable. Fiscal policy was caught in a political gridlock: Conflicting pressures made it very difficult to cut spending or raise taxes substantially. Because major adjustments in fiscal policy seemed out of the question, monetary policies were the only macroeconomic "game in town." Monetary policy became the principal demand-management tool by default.

THE CASE FOR USING MONETARY AND FISCAL POLICIES TOGETHER

This concentration on monetary policy has not, however, been a desirable outcome. A substantial case can be made that the best macroeconomic policy includes both fiscal and monetary policies, used cooperatively.

The controversy covered in this chapter provides the first reason. Although the profession has moved away from the extremes and toward the centre, there is still a difference of opinion over the relative strengths of monetary and fiscal policies. Historical evidence does not provide a sharp, clean resolution to this dispute. Continuing uncertainties over the relative effectiveness of monetary and fiscal policies provide a case for using both. It's unwise to put all our eggs in one basket, particularly when we're not sure which basket it should be.

Furthermore, there are other reasons for favouring a combined monetary-fiscal strategy. During a boom in aggregate demand, restrictive steps are desirable. Such steps are painful. Cuts in government spending hurt various groups in the economy. Nobody wants an increase in their taxes. A tighter monetary policy and higher interest rates can put a squeeze on housing construction and other types of investment. If a combination of policies is used, the effects of each may be kept moderate and the adverse impacts diffused. Thus, it may be possible to avoid placing a very heavy burden on any single segment of the economy.

Since 1986, the Mulroney government has made some progress in reducing Canada's federal deficit. In part, the reduction was the result of the long economic expansion 1983–89, which led to decreased expenditures on unemployment insurance benefits and to automatic increases in tax revenue. But the government also implemented expenditure restraints (such as the 1989 decision to cancel the plans to acquire a fleet of nuclear submarines), and imposed an income tax surcharge. Moreover, the new federal sales tax described in the 1989 budget (the Goods and Services Tax) will provide a ready source of additional revenue if it is introduced as planned in the early 1990s. Thus, by 1989, the prospects for getting the deficit under control appeared somewhat brighter than before, and there was reason to expect that fiscal policy might once again become a tool that could be effectively used for economic stabilization. For those who believe that successful aggregate demand management requires that monetary and fiscal policy be used together, this would be welcome news indeed.

KEY POINTS

1. Most present-day economists take a central position, believing that both fiscal and monetary policies have substantial effects on aggregate demand. However, some economists have taken polar positions. Early Keynesians not only focused on fiscal policy, but some also believed that monetary policy might have little effect on aggregate demand. On the other side is the monetarist view that money is the predominant force determining aggregate demand and that fiscal policy has little effect.

2. Keynes proposed that the effects of monetary policy be analysed by looking at three steps:
   (a) the effect of monetary policy on the rate of interest
   (b) the effect of the interest rate on investment
   (c) the effect of a change in investment on aggregate expenditures (the multiplier)

3. Keynes himself believed that expansive monetary policies could not be counted on to get the economy out of the Depression of the 1930s because of a problem at the very first step. Interest rates were already very low and could not be pushed down much further by an expansive monetary policy.

4. Some early followers of Keynes had more general doubts about the effectiveness of monetary policies —not just in a depression, but also in more normal times. Specifically, they argued that a problem would arise at step 2 because investment is not very responsive to changes in the rate of interest. That is, the investment demand schedule is steep, as illustrated in Figure 13-5.

5. Classical macroeconomics was based on the equation of exchange ($MV = PQ$) and on the proposition that velocity V is stable (the quantity theory). If velocity is stable, a change in money M will cause current-dollar domestic product PQ to change by approximately the same percentage.

6. Classical economists believed that, in the long run, the principal effect of a change in the rate of growth

of M would be a change in the price level P. In the short run, however, changes in the growth of M could also affect real domestic product Q.

7. Indeed, those in the classical tradition believe that monetary disturbances are one of the principal causes of fluctuations in real output.

8. The view that velocity is stable is based on the belief that there is a stable demand for money. If, after a period of equilibrium, people get more money, their holdings of money will exceed their demand for it (Figure 13-6). They will use the surplus to buy goods and services, thus increasing current-dollar domestic product PQ.

9. Some of those in the classical tradition doubt that fiscal policy has a substantial effect on aggregate demand, unless the fiscal policy is accompanied by changes in M. That is, they have doubts about the effectiveness of *pure* fiscal policy. These doubts are based on the belief that an increase in deficit spending will push up interest rates and therefore *crowd out* private investment.

10. The crowding-out effect is powerful and fiscal policy is, therefore, weak if investment is very responsive to changes in interest rates (the investment demand function is flat). Strong monetarists believe the investment demand function is quite flat. Some years ago, strong Keynesians believed it was quite steep and, therefore, monetary policy was weak.

11. In addition to crowding out of investment, there is a second way in which the expansive effects of an increase in deficit spending may be partially offset. Higher interest rates may encourage foreigners to buy Canadian financial assets (such as bonds), thus raising the price of the Canadian dollar in terms of foreign currencies and, consequently, depressing net exports.

12. Recent history does not give a clear, unambiguous confirmation of either the strong Keynesian or the strong classical view. At times—in the early 1970s, for example—the evidence supports the quantity theory and, at other times—the second half of the 1970s and the early 1980s—the evidence tends to contradict it.

13. Because of this—and for other reasons, too—it is undesirable to place exclusive reliance on either monetary or fiscal policy. Instead, it is wiser to use a combined monetary-fiscal strategy.

14. Nevertheless, there has been a very heavy reliance on monetary policy from the mid-1970s until the late 1980s. One reason has been the desire of the Bank of Canada to control the rapidly accelerating inflation of the late 1970s. Another reason has been the great difficulty in changing fiscal policy during the 1980s.

KEY CONCEPTS

demand for money
responsiveness of investment to
    a change in the interest rate
equation of exchange

income velocity of money (V)
quantity theory of money
monetary rule
crowding out

pure fiscal policy
trade deficit

PROBLEMS

13-1. In the Keynesian framework, there are three separate steps in the process by which monetary policy affects aggregate demand.
   (a) What are these three steps?
   (b) Keynes argued that expansive monetary policy would be ineffective in getting the economy out of the Depression of the 1930s because of a problem at one of these three steps. Which step? What was the nature of the problem?
   (c) Some of the followers of Keynes argued that monetary policy is generally a weak and ineffective tool for controlling aggregate demand. They foresaw a problem at another one of the steps. Which step? What was the nature of the problem?

13-2. The Keynesian theory of the demand for money (shown in Figure 13-2) was developed at a time when no interest was paid on chequing deposits. There was an obvious cost in holding money: namely, the interest which could otherwise have been earned by buying a security. Now banks and other institutions are permitted to pay interest on chequing deposits, as we saw in Chapter 11. When banks pay interest on such deposits, how would you expect the demand for money to be affected as a result?

13-3. The investment demand curve shows how investment responds to changes in interest rates. What other things does investment demand depend upon? Explain how the investment demand curve would shift if one of these other things changed.

13-4. How do strong Keynesians and strong monetarists disagree on the way in which the investment demand curve should be drawn? How does the way a strong Keynesian draws the investment

demand curve cast doubt on the effectiveness of monetary policy? How does the way a strong monetarist draws the investment demand curve cast doubt on the effectiveness of fiscal policy in controlling aggregate demand?

13-5. "I accept the equation of exchange as valid. But I do not accept the quantity theory of money." Is it consistent for an economist to hold such a position? Why or why not?

13-6. Suppose that the demand for money is initially equal to the quantity of money in existence. Then suppose that the quantity of money is doubled because of action by the central bank. According to a Keynesian economist, what will happen? According to a classical economist, what will happen?

13-7. Explain how a budget deficit might cause a trade deficit. (A trade deficit is an excess of imports over exports.)

Appendix

■ ■ ■ ■ ■

Doubts About Fiscal Policy: How Do Consumers Respond?

The 1960s began with high hopes that fiscal policy could be used to manage aggregate demand. By the end of the decade, doubts were widespread. One reason was the experience in the United States in 1968. To restrain the high level of aggregate demand at that time, the administration imposed a substantial tax increase in the form of a "temporary tax surcharge." However, contrary to the predictions made at the time, this tax increase did not slow down aggregate demand. Part of the reason was that the predictions were based on a simple consumption function, similar to that presented in Chapter 9. That consumption function was a good place to begin a study of macroeconomics; consumption does depend primarily on income. But reality is somewhat more complicated.

To see why, consider why people save. Presumably, they do so in order to be able to consume more at a later

date. Saving is a way of rearranging consumption through time. If their current income is abnormally low — less than they can reasonably expect in the future — they have an incentive to dissave. Thus, students often borrow in order to consume more than their current income. They expect to repay in the future when their incomes will be higher. On the other hand, when incomes are abnormally high — during the peak earning years of middle age, in particular — people have an incentive to save for their future when they expect lower incomes.

Thus, consumption depends not simply on *current* income. Rather, it depends on the income that people consider to be normal — or, in the jargon of economists, on their **permanent income**.

Now, consider again the U.S. income tax surcharge of 1968. This was a *temporary* extra tax, intended to cool the overheating economy. Suppose that you have to pay $400 extra to the government as a result of such a surcharge. What is your reaction likely to be? While your present disposable income is down by $400, the government has already said that this is temporary. Your permanent income — what you consider normal — will be changed little, if at all. Why should you cut back your consumption in the face of this temporary disturbance? You are likely to respond by reducing your consumption only a little, and simply save less. In this way, you will spread the effects of the tax over a number of years. Thus, a *temporary* tax change has only a weak effect on consumption. It is only when a tax change is expected to be *permanent* that consumers will respond strongly.

This throws into question the whole idea of changing tax rates in an attempt to reduce fluctuations in aggregate demand. Such changes by their very nature are for the short run, and are likely to be reversed when conditions change. Because the public recognizes that they are temporary, they won't have much effect on consumption or on aggregate demand.

Barro-Ricardo

Some economists go much further, and question whether even a longer-run, fundamental change in the tax code will have much effect on consumption. The most prominent proponent of this view is Robert Barro of Harvard University, who traces his argument back to David Ricardo (1772–1823).

Barro observes that a tax cut, unaccompanied by any change in government spending, has implications for the future. The resulting deficit means that the government will have to borrow. Therefore, it will have to raise taxes in the future to pay interest on the additional debt. People recognize this: They realize that they will have to pay higher taxes in the future. How can they protect themselves? The answer is, by saving more. Suppose the government cuts taxes by $100 and issues $100 in debt. The only way the public can protect itself completely is by saving the whole $100 current tax cut; this will provide a future flow of interest just sufficient to cover the additional future taxes. This, says Barro, is what people will do. A $100 tax cut will lead to a $100

increase in saving. There will be *no* effect on consumption or aggregate demand.[6]

The Barro conclusion is based on a number of very strong assumptions. One is that people see *very* far into the future — past their own lifetimes, to the lifetimes of their children and grandchildren. If their grandchildren are going to be burdened with $100 more in debt, people will save $100 more now to enable them to bear that burden. If we depart from Barro's theory and assume that people do not look beyond their own lifetimes in this way, a $100 tax cut *will* have an effect on consumption. For example, a 60-year-old whose tax is cut will spend part of the tax cut. There is no need to save the full amount, since the burden of the debt can be left to future generations.

Most economists are skeptical of Barro's conclusion; they are skeptical that people are farsighted enough to increase their saving by $100 for every $100 cut in taxes. If they are correct, a fundamental tax cut — not aimed at temporary demand-management objectives — *will* affect consumption expenditures; people will not save the whole tax cut. Evidence from a number of countries appears to support this conclusion and undercuts Barro's argument.[7] For example, the major cuts in tax rates in the United States in 1981–84 were clearly intended to be long run. When people found their taxes falling, they spent more; they did not save the whole amount.

In summary, we have a paradoxical conclusion: Short-run changes in taxes, intended to manage aggregate demand, have little effect on permanent income. Therefore, they have little effect on consumption or aggregate demand. Most of a tax cut is saved. On the other hand, if fundamental, long-run changes are made in tax rates, consumption and aggregate demand will be affected. Thus, paradoxically, the policies that have the greatest effect on aggregate demand are those not intended to affect demand!

■ ■ ■ ■ ■

[6] This is sometimes known as the *Ricardian equivalence theorem*. The effects will be equivalent whether the government finances its spending by taxes or by issuing debt.

[7] B. Douglas Bernheim, "Ricardian Equivalence: An Evaluation of Theory and Evidence," in Stanley Fischer, ed., *NBER Macroeconomics Annual, 1987* (Cambridge, Mass.: MIT Press, 1987), p. 299.

Chapter 14

■ ■

Stabilization Policy with International Transactions

Cecily, you will read your Political Economy
in my absence. The chapter on the Fall of the
Rupee you may omit. It is somewhat too
sensational. Even these metallic problems
have their melodramatic side.

Miss Prism, in Oscar Wilde's
The Importance of Being Ernest

Economic efficiency requires specialization. It is efficient to grow wheat on the Prairies and potatoes in Prince Edward Island. The scope for specialization goes far beyond the boundaries of any single country. Even such a large nation as the United States can gain by international specialization. It is efficient for the United States to export wheat and import oil and bananas. For the smaller and resource-rich Canadian economy, the gains from specialization are even more important. While the United States exports less than one-tenth of its domestic product, over 25% of the goods and services produced in Canada are exported to foreign markets — products such as wheat, softwood lumber, automobiles, and various other manufactured goods. In return, we import such things as coffee, fresh fruits and vegetables, automobiles, computers, and other manufactured goods.

The way in which international specialization can contribute to a high standard of living fits into the study of economic efficiency in Part 8; we therefore defer the detailed consideration of international trade and efficiency to Part 8. In this chapter (and in Chapter 20 which deals with the international monetary system), we study the relationship between macroeconomic policy and international transactions.

We begin by explaining the role of the foreign exchange market in facilitating international trade and capital flows, and the balance-of-payments accounts that summarize these transactions. We then go on to the chapter's main topic: the way in which international transactions affect economic stability, and the opportunities for stabilization policy, in the Canadian economy. The chapter raises a number of questions: How can we use monetary and fiscal policies to reduce the effects of international business cycles on the Canadian economy? If there are large government deficits and high interest rates in the United States, must interest rates rise in Canada too? Does the relative effectiveness of monetary and fiscal policy depend on the way these policies influence foreign trade and capital flows? Is it better for Canada to have fixed or flexible exchange rates? Since international transactions play such a large part in Canada's economy, the answers to these questions are of great importance to our policy makers.

EXCHANGE RATES

In many ways, international trade is like domestic trade; it adds to economic efficiency because of comparative advantage and economies of scale. But there are two major complications that make international transactions different from domestic trade:

1. Domestic trade involves a single currency. For example, when a Manitoban buys a bottle of British Columbia wine, both the consumer and the producer want the payment to be made in the same currency; namely, Canadian dollars. But consider a British importer of Canadian wheat, who has British pounds

to pay for the wheat. The Canadian exporter wants to receive payment in Canadian dollars, not in pounds. Therefore, the British importer will go to the *foreign exchange market* in order to sell pounds and buy the dollars needed to pay for the wheat, as illustrated in Figure 14-1. (Foreign exchange markets are located in financial centres such as London, New York, Montreal, and Toronto.)

Foreign exchange is the currency of another country. For example, U.S. dollars, British pounds, and Japanese yen are foreign exchange to a Canadian. Canadian dollars are foreign exchange to a Briton, a German, or an American.

A *foreign exchange market* is a market in which one national currency (such as the Canadian dollar) is bought in exchange for another national currency (such as the British pound). An *exchange rate* is the price of one national currency in terms of another national currency. For example, the price £1 = $2 is an exchange rate, and so is $1 = 120 Japanese yen.

2. International trade is complicated by *barriers* that do not exist in trade between regions, provinces, or cities within the same country. Most notably, *tariffs* (also called *duties*) protect domestic producers of

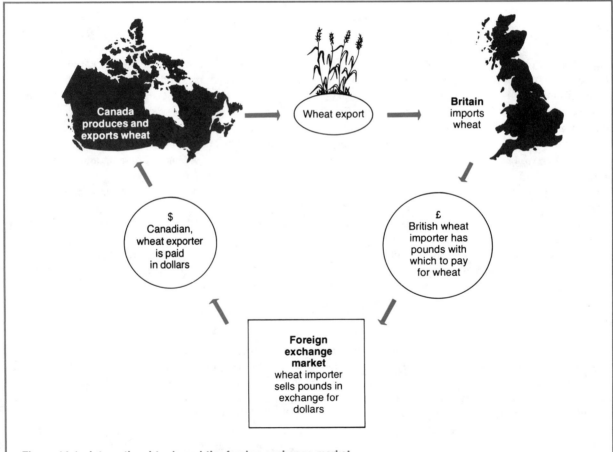

Figure 14-1 International trade and the foreign exchange market.
International trade normally involves more than one national currency. The British importer wants to pay in pounds; the Canadian exporter wants to receive payment in dollars. Con- sequently, the British import results in a transaction on the foreign exchange market, with pounds being sold for dollars.

many goods by giving them an advantage over foreign competitors.

A *tariff* is a tax imposed on a foreign good as it enters the country.

Other barriers also impede international trade. For example, the Canadian government has sometimes imposed a *quota* on the amount of beef that can be imported, in order to protect domestic beef producers.

A *quota* is a limit on the quantity of a good that can be imported.

Tariffs and other trade barriers will be studied in Chapter 34. Here, we concentrate on the first point — foreign exchange transactions and the complications they raise for domestic stabilization policies.

THE FOREIGN EXCHANGE MARKET

Because there are more than a hundred countries in the world, the foreign exchange markets involve many currencies, and transactions can be complicated. In order to keep the discussion simple, let us first concentrate on transactions between only two countries, Canada and the United States. Just as the price of wheat is determined in the market where wheat is bought and sold in exchange for money, so the exchange rate between the Canadian dollar and the U.S. dollar is determined in the foreign exchange market where Canadian dollars are bought and sold in exchange for U.S. dollars. And just like the market for wheat, the foreign exchange market can be studied by looking at demand and supply. The demand for Canadian dollars (C$) by those originally holding U.S. dollars (U.S.$) arises from three types of transactions:

1. *American imports of Canadian goods*; that is, Canadian exports of goods to the United States. For example, when an American firm buys Canadian newsprint, a demand for Canadian dollars is created. (The American firm has U.S. dollars, but the Canadian firm wants Canadian dollars. Thus, either the American or the Canadian firm has to buy Canadian dollars in exchange for U.S. dollars to complete the transaction.)
2. *American imports of Canadian services*. For example, an American tourist may stay in a Canadian hotel, or travel on a Canadian airline. When the Canadian hotel or airline receives payment in U.S.

dollars, it sells these dollars in order to obtain the Canadian dollars it wants. In other words, spending by the tourist creates a demand for Canadian dollars in exchange for U.S. dollars.

(What is the difference between trade of a good and trade of a service? When an American imports a good such as newsprint from Canada, the good physically leaves Canada and enters the United States; the newsprint is unloaded at an American railroad terminal. In the case of most services, there is no such physical transfer of a good; obviously, the hotel room stays in Canada. But in either case, a demand for Canadian dollars is created.)

3. *American acquisitions of Canadian assets*. For example, if an American corporation wants to invest in Canada by building a new factory here, it will need Canadian dollars to pay the firm that constructs the factory.

The demand for Canadian dollars, like the demand for wheat, depends on the price. Suppose, for example, that the price of the Canadian dollar rises in terms of U.S. dollars, from U.S.$0.80 to U.S.$1.10. What would this mean? Because the Canadian dollar has become more expensive to Americans, Canadian goods and services also become more expensive to Americans. To illustrate, suppose a Canadian hotel room costs C$50 per day. When the price of the Canadian dollar was U.S.$0.80, that room would cost $40 in U.S. money. But when the price of the Canadian dollar rises to U.S.$1.10, that same room would cost an American $55 in U.S. money. Therefore, with a more expensive Canadian dollar, American tourists would be less likely to go to Canada, and American firms would be less likely to buy Canadian goods. Thus, when the Canadian dollar costs U.S.$1.10, the quantity of Canadian dollars demanded is less than when a Canadian dollar costs U.S.$0.80, as illustrated by the demand curve (*D*) in Figure 14-2. Notice that the price an American pays for a Canadian hotel room depends on two things: (1) The Canadian price for the room (C$50 in the example); and (2) the exchange rate between the U.S. dollar and the Canadian dollar.

Now consider the other side of the market, the supply of Canadian dollars to be exchanged for U.S. dollars. Whenever Canadians want to buy something that has to be paid for in U.S. dollars, a supply of Canadian dollars is created: The firms and individuals who want to buy American goods and services, or American assets, have to offer Canadian dollars in the foreign exchange market

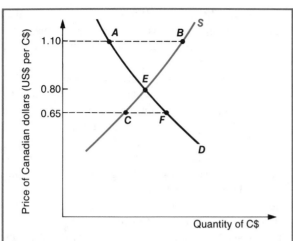

Figure 14-2 The demand and supply of Canadian dollars in the foreign exchange market.

The equilibrium exchange rate is determined by the intersection of demand and supply. The demand for Canadian dollars in terms of U.S. dollars depends on (1) U.S. imports of Canadian goods; (2) purchases of Canadian services by Americans; and (3) purchases of Canadian assets by Americans. The supply of Canadian dollars depends on (1) Canadian imports of United States goods; (2) Canadian purchases of U.S. services; and (3) Canadian purchases of U.S. assets.

in order to get U.S. dollars. Thus, the supply of Canadian dollars depends on:

1. Canadian imports of U.S. goods
2. Canadian imports of U.S. services
3. Canadian acquisitions of U.S. assets; that is, Canadian investment in the United States.

The supply of Canadian dollars to the foreign exchange market also depends on price. If the price of the Canadian dollar falls, that is another way of saying that the price of the U.S. dollar rises. Thus, American goods and services become more expensive to Canadians. (For example, suppose the price of the Canadian dollar falls from C$1.00 = U.S.$1.00 to C$1.00 = U.S.$0.80. This means that Canadians now will have to pay C$1.25 for one U.S. dollar. Thus, a Canadian car dealer now would have to pay C$12,500 for an American car costing U.S.$10,000. But before the fall in the price of the Canadian dollar, the dealer would have had to pay only C$10,000.)

When the price of the Canadian dollar falls on the exchange markets, Canadians will therefore reduce their purchases of American goods and services, and this will tend to reduce the amount of Canadian dollars supplied to the foreign exchange market. A rise in the price of

the Canadian dollar has the opposite effect: It will make American goods and services cheaper in terms of Canadian money. As a result, Canadian buyers will increase their imports from the United States, and this tends to increase the quantity of Canadian dollars supplied to the foreign exchange market, as the supply curve (*S*) in Figure 14-2 illustrates.[1]

The preceding example deals with the market where Canadian dollars are exchanged for U.S. dollars. There are also markets where Canadian dollars are exchanged for German marks, Swiss francs, Japanese yen, British pounds, and so forth. Clearly, some of these markets are more important than others, because they involve countries with which Canada has large transactions. Specifically, the largest volume of foreign exchange transactions by far takes place in the market in which Canadian dollars are exchanged for U.S. dollars. The main reason for this, of course, is that the largest part of our international transactions is with the United States.

However, another reason is that many transactions between Canada and other foreign countries (Mexico, for example) take place using U.S. dollars (rather than Mexican pesos or Canadian dollars). Consider, for example, a Mexican firm that imports lumber from a Canadian sawmill and pays for the lumber in U.S. dollars, or a Canadian tourist who pays for hotel expenses in Acapulco with a U.S.-dollar traveller's cheque bought in Canada. Note that although these transactions are with

■ ■ ■ ■ ■
[1] Actually, the quantity of Canadian dollars supplied to the foreign exchange market will not *necessarily* increase when the price rises. Suppose that, when C$1.00 = U.S.$1.00, Canadians buy one million units of U.S. goods, each worth U.S.$1.00. Then to buy these goods worth U.S.$1 million, Canadians must supply C$1 million. Now, suppose that the price of the Canadian dollar rises to C$1.00 = U.S.$1.11; that is, the U.S. dollar falls to U.S.$1.00 = C$0.90. Suppose that, as a result of the fall in the prices of U.S. goods as measured in Canadian dollars, Canadians now buy only slightly more U.S. goods — 1,050,000 units, worth U.S.$1,050,000. Then the cost in Canadian dollars is only C$945,000 (that is, 1,050,000 x 0.90 = 945,000). In this example, the increase in the quantity of Canadian imports is not enough to outweigh the lower value of the U.S. dollar; Canadian expenditures on imports fall, measured in Canadian dollars. That is, the quantity of Canadian dollars supplied to the foreign exchange market *decreases*. Normally, however, a rise in the exchange value of the Canadian dollar will increase imports by a sufficiently large amount so that there is an increase in the quantity of Canadian dollars supplied to the foreign exchange market.

Mexico rather than with the United States, they still involve the market where Canadian dollars are exchanged for U.S. dollars.

Thus, demand and supply in the market where Canadian dollars are exchanged for U.S. dollars depend not only on our transactions with the United States but also on our transactions with other foreign countries. To keep the discussion simple, we can let the supply and demand for Canadian dollars in exchange for U.S. dollars represent our total transactions with *all* foreign countries. Using this simplification, we can interpret Figure 14-2 as saying that a fall in the value of the Canadian dollar in terms of the U.S. dollar will increase the quantity of Canadian dollars demanded throughout the world because it will make our goods less expensive in world markets, and thus induce foreigners to increase their purchases of our exports. Similarly, a fall in the exchange value of the Canadian dollar will make foreign goods and services more expensive in Canada. Accordingly, the quantity of Canadian dollars supplied to the foreign exchange market will tend to fall.

CANADA'S BALANCE-OF-PAYMENTS ACCOUNTS

Canada's **balance-of-payments** accounts provide a record of transactions between residents of Canada and those of other countries. The accounts are constructed with a positive or "credit" side, and a negative or "debit" side. The credit side corresponds to the *demand* for the Canadian dollar on the foreign exchange market, and the debit side to the *supply*. Thus, on the credit side, one records transactions that give rise to a foreign demand for Canadian dollars; for example, Canadian exports of goods and services to foreign countries, and acquisitions of Canadian assets by foreigners. On the debit side, we find transactions which represent a *supply* of Canadian dollars to the foreign exchange market: Canadian imports of goods and services, and Canadian acquisitions of foreign assets.

Canada's balance of payments is divided into two main accounts. In one of these — the **capital account** — statisticians enter changes in foreign ownership of assets in Canada, and changes in Canadian ownership of foreign assets. That is, *international investment* is entered in the capital accounts. All other items — that is, those that do not represent changes in the ownership of foreign assets — are put in the **current account**, shown at the top of Table 14-1.

The Current Account

The current account is subdivided into two main categories. First are the figures for *merchandise trade*: Exports and imports of goods from and into Canada (category I). Observe that in 1988, Canadian exports of merchandise ($137.1 billion) were larger than imports of merchandise ($127.5 billion). Thus, Canada had a **merchandise trade surplus** of $9.6 billion.

> A country has a *surplus on merchandise trade* (or, more simply, a *merchandise surplus*) when its exports of goods exceed its imports of goods. When imports of goods exceed exports of goods, a country has a *deficit on merchandise trade*.

Category II is made up principally of exports and imports of *services*. In addition to services mentioned earlier — expenditures by foreign tourists for hotels or airline tickets — the service category includes interest and dividends; they represent payments for the services rendered by capital. Note that *returns* from investments (in the form of interest and dividends) appear in the current account, even though investments themselves appear in the capital accounts. The reason is this: If Dominion Textiles of Montreal acquires a subsidiary in Germany, Canadian-owned assets abroad rise. Therefore, this investment belongs in the capital accounts. But when Domtex receives dividends from this foreign subsidiary, there is no change in ownership. Domtex receives the dividends, but still owns the foreign subsidiary. Thus, the dividends go in the current account (Item II.1.b). Similarly, interest from a foreign bond appears in the current account. (But, if the foreign bond were paid off, that would represent a change in asset holdings, and would appear in the capital accounts.) In addition to services, category II also includes **unilateral transfers** — items such as remittances by Canadian immigrants to foreign relatives and Canadian aid to less developed countries on the debit side; and inheritances by Canadian citizens from relatives abroad on the credit side.

While Canada had a substantial merchandise surplus in 1988, the services and transfers categories together showed a deficit ($20.9 billion). This pattern, which has been typical in the Canadian balance-of-payments accounts in recent years, is explained partly by the large income earned by foreigners on their past investments in Canada — earnings that appear on the debit side of the services account. Taken together, the merchandise surplus and the deficit on services and transfers produced a *current account deficit* of $11.3 billion in 1988.

Table 14-1 Canada's Balance of Payments, 1988
(in billions of dollars)

Credits (+)		Debits (−)	
A. CURRENT ACCOUNT			
I. Merchandise Trade			
1. Exports of Goods	137.1	1. Imports of Goods	127.5
II. Other Current Accounts			
1. Exports of Services	30.6	1. Imports of Services	55.8
(a) Travel	6.9	(a) Travel	9.7
(b) Interest and dividend receipts	10.9	(b) Interest and dividend payments	29.3
(c) Other service receipts	12.8	(c) Other service payments	16.8
2. Unilateral transfers (receipts)	8.0	2. Unilateral transfers (payments)	3.7
B. CAPITAL ACCOUNT			
III. Capital Flows, Excluding Changes in Official Reserves			
1. Long-term capital inflows	18.7	1. Long-term capital outflows	9.0
(a) Foreign direct investment in Canada	4.9	(a) Canadian direct investment abroad	7.9
(b) Long-term portfolio investment in Canada	13.8	(b) Long-term portfolio investment abroad	1.1
2. Short-term capital inflow	15.0	2. Short-term capital outflow	2.9
		3. Net errors and omissions	0.5
IV. Change in Official Reserve Assets			
		1. Net increase in Canada's foreign exchange reserves	10.0

Source: *Bank of Canada Review.*

The Capital Account

On the credit side of the capital account are shown foreign acquisitions of Canadian assets, also referred to as *capital inflows* into Canada. On the debit side, we find Canadian acquisitions of foreign assets — also referred to as *capital outflows.*

> Acquisitions of Canadian assets by foreign residents are referred to as *capital inflows.*
>
> A *capital outflow* occurs when Canadians acquire foreign assets.[2]

------

[2] Capital inflows are also sometimes called *capital imports.* But be wary of this terminology. Note that a capital *import* appears on the same side of the balance of payments as an *export* of goods. Why is this? Because both result in a demand for Canadian dollars.

The capital account is divided into two main groups: Category IV, "change in official reserve assets" (explained below), and Category III, which includes all other capital flows. Category III is subdivided into *long-term* capital flows and *short-term* capital flows, depending on whether the asset acquired has a maturity of more or less than one year. (A bond and common stock are examples of long-term assets; bank deposits and Treasury bills are short-term assets.) In turn, long-term capital flows are subdivided into **direct investment** and **portfolio investment**.

On the credit side, *direct investment* occurs when a foreign firm or individual acquires a controlling interest in a Canadian firm or invests additional funds in a firm that is already foreign-controlled. As an example, when Honda of Japan establishes a Canadian subsidiary and constructs an assembly plant in Canada, this appears as a direct investment (part of the $4.9 billion figure shown in Table 14-1).[3] Other kinds of capital inflow are referred to as *portfolio investment*. In other words, while direct investment increases the extent of foreign control of Canadian business, portfolio investment occurs when foreigners simply provide financing for Canadian-controlled businesses or for other Canadian borrowers (such as provincial governments). Both direct and portfolio investment by foreigners in Canada appear on the credit side, because they add to the *demand* for Canadian currency: Foreign investors buy Canadian dollars when they want to acquire assets here.

If Canada's Northern Telecom builds a plant in the United States, this appears on the debit side as a direct investment. And if you or I were to buy a British government bond, this would appear on the debit side as a portfolio investment. In either case, the Canadian investment in a foreign country adds to the *supply* of Canadian dollars in the exchange market.

The final category (IV), "change in official reserve assets" or "net official monetary movements," reflects purchases and sales of *foreign exchange reserves* by Canadian monetary authorities—that is, by the Bank of Canada and the Exchange Fund Account. These reserves include foreign currencies—mainly U.S. dollars—plus two other assets which are readily exchanged for foreign currencies—namely, gold and Canada's balance held in the *International Monetary Fund* (IMF). (We will discuss the IMF in Chapter 20.)

> *Foreign exchange reserves* are foreign currencies, gold, and balances in the IMF which are held by the government or central bank.

Acquisitions of foreign exchange reserves by the Canadian monetary authorities appear on the debit side of the accounts: When the Bank of Canada adds to its reserves by *buying* foreign currencies in the exchange market, it adds to the *supply* of *Canadian* dollars in that market.

■ ■ ■ ■ ■
[3] When *Canadian* residents purchase a controlling interest in firms which operate in Canada under foreign control, this is recorded as a negative direct investment on the credit side of the capital account. For example, in the second quarter of 1981, following the introduction of the government's National Energy Program, there were takeovers by Canadian investors of some large Canadian subsidiaries of foreign oil companies. For that quarter, the balance of payments statistics show a foreign direct investment of −$3.5 billion.

Theoretically, this should be the end of our story; we should now have finished with the complete balance-of-payments accounts. To see why, note that the credit side provides a record of all transactions in which foreigners bought Canadian dollars in exchange for foreign currencies. Thus, the sum of all the credit items measures the total amount of foreign currencies that Canadian residents *received* (through sales of goods, services, or assets). The debit side, on the other hand, records all transactions in which Canadian residents *paid out* foreign currencies in exchange for Canadian dollars. Thus, the debits tell us what the foreign currencies *were used for*. Some were used to pay for imports of goods and services into Canada, while others were used by Canadian firms or individuals to increase their holdings of foreign assets. Whatever was left over must have ended up as part of our official foreign exchange reserves. When changes in our official reserves are included, the balance-of-payments accounts *should* balance; that is, the two sides should add to the same total.

And the accounts would, in fact, balance if government statisticians had perfect information. But they do not. For example, government officials do not tag along with tourists to see just how much they spend, nor do they have perfect information on how many foreign assets are acquired. To compensate for such measurement inaccuracies, government statisticians calculate "errors and omissions." This item—which is whatever number is needed to make the two sides of the balance of payments add to the same total — is entered in the capital accounts (item 3 on the debit side), because it is believed that this is where the greatest problems of measurement occur.

The Concept of the Balance of Payments

But if the two sides of the balance-of-payments accounts *must* be equal (because of the way the accounts are constructed), what do we mean when we talk of the balance of payments being in "deficit" or "surplus"? The answer is that a deficit or surplus can exist only when certain items in the accounts are excluded. The standard concept of the balance of payments is the difference between the credits and debits in categories I, II, and III; that is, the balance of payments is calculated by *excluding* the changes in reserves shown in category IV. If the credits in the first three categories exceed the debits, we have a *balance-of-payments surplus*. In this case, the total amount of foreign currency received from foreigners who demand Canadian dollars to buy Canadian goods, services, and assets exceeds the amount of foreign currency used by Canadians to pay for foreign goods, services, and assets. The difference ends up in our official reserves. Thus, the Canadian-dollar value of the changes in foreign exchange reserves (category IV) is a balancing item in the balance-of-payments accounts. As the authorities add to their stock of foreign exchange reserves by buying foreign currencies, they are supplying the amount of Canadian dollars by which foreign demand exceeds the quantity supplied by other firms and individuals. Thus, when Canada has a balance-of-payments surplus, we are acquiring reserves. Conversely, when we have a deficit, we are losing reserves.

> A country has a *balance-of-payments surplus* when it is acquiring foreign exchange reserves; that is, when the sum of its credits in categories I, II, and III exceed the sum of the debits.
>
> It has a balance-of-payments *deficit* when it is losing reserves.

When studying demand and supply curves on the foreign exchange market, economists generally omit the balancing item provided by the monetary authorities (item IV). That is, they look at the demand and supply that would exist if the Bank of Canada was not buying or selling in the foreign exchange market, so that there was no "change in official reserve assets." In this chapter we follow this convention; that is, we exclude the authorities' purchases or sales of Canadian dollars in exchange for foreign reserves when we write of the demand or supply of the Canadian dollar in the exchange market. Thus, at the exchange rate C$1 = U.S.$1.10 in Figure 14-2, the amount *AB* by which the supply of C$ exceeds the demand is equal to the balance-of-payments deficit and loss of reserves expressed in Canadian dollars. Similarly, at an exchange rate of C$1 = U.S.$0.65, the demand for C$ would exceed the supply, and the amount *CF* of excess demand would measure the surplus in the balance of payments and the gain of reserves by the monetary authorities.

FLUCTUATIONS IN THE EXCHANGE MARKET: Pegged vs. Flexible Exchange Rates

Suppose we start with an exchange rate of, say, C$1.00 = U.S.$0.80. It is possible that at this exchange rate, the quantity of Canadian dollars demanded in the foreign

exchange market exactly equals the quantity supplied by everyone except the monetary authorities. Thus, the demand and supply curves would intersect when the price of the Canadian dollar equals U.S. $0.80, as shown at the intitial equilibrium *E* in Figure 14-3.

But we live in a changing world. Even if the demand and supply are initially in equilibrium at the price C$1.00 = U.S.$0.80, one or both curves may shift as time passes. Suppose that the demand for Canadian dollars decreases from D_1 to D_2. It might do so for any number of reasons; anything that decreases foreign demand for Canadian goods, services, or assets will cause a leftward shift of the demand curve.

As a result of the leftward shift, the initial price of C$1.00 = U.S.$0.80 is no longer an equilibrium. In the face of this change, the Canadian government has the option of taking any one (or a combination) of the following steps:

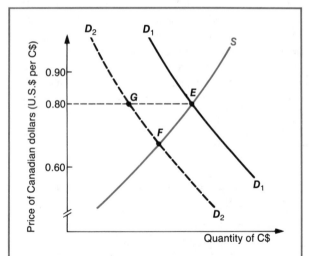

Figure 14-3   Disequilibrium in the foreign exchange market.

If the demand for Canadian dollars shifts to the left from D_1 to D_2, there will be an oversupply (*GE*) at the old exchange rate. The Canadian government can eliminate this oversupply by one of, or a combination of, the following steps: (1) The purchase of Canadian dollars in exchange for U.S. dollars by the Canadian authorities. (This will work only temporarily, however, because Canadian reserves of U.S. dollars are limited.) (2) A change in the exchange rate to its new equilibrium *F*. (3) A reduction in the supply of Canadian dollars by Canadian restrictions on imports and other international transactions. (4) Restrictive aggregate demand policies in Canada, which also reduce Canadian imports and capital outflows, and hence the supply of Canadian dollars to the exchange market.

1. Intervention in the Foreign Exchange Market

In the example in Figure 14-3, the Canadian authorities can keep the price of the Canadian dollar stable by selling foreign exchange reserves in order to buy up the surplus GE of Canadian dollars. (As noted earlier, GE would then show up as a deficit in the balance-of-payments accounts. For example, if the distance GE were $500 million per year, this would be the loss of reserves that would show up in the accounts.)

The initial disturbance may be only temporary. The U.S. demand for our goods and services may pick up, or foreign investors may decide to acquire more Canadian assets; demand will then shift back from D_2 to D_1, and E again becomes the equilibrium. In this event, official intervention in the foreign exchange market is no longer necessary; the temporary intervention has successfully smoothed out the aberration. But not all shifts in supply and demand are temporary. For example, the U.S. demand for Canadian goods may be permanently lower. In this case, the Canadian authorities cannot maintain the original exchange rate of C$1.00 = U.S.$0.80 indefinitely by selling reserves of U.S. dollars on the foreign exchange market. Why? Because our holdings of U.S. dollars and other reserve assets are limited; sooner or later we will face the prospect of running out of reserves.

Thus, in the face of a permanently reduced foreign demand for Canadian dollars, the Canadian government must move to one of its other options.

2. Imposing Direct Restrictions on International Transactions

In order to maintain the initial exchange rate, the Canadian government may reduce the supply of Canadian dollars by taking direct action affecting international transactions. That is, it may shift curve S to the left so that it passes through G, and thus again make $0.80 the equilibrium price. For example, the government can do this by limiting the amount of foreign assets that Canadians are legally permitted to acquire (as it did during World War II). Or it may limit Canadian imports of foreign goods by the imposition of additional tariffs or quotas.

3. Altering Domestic Monetary and Fiscal Policies

The Canadian government may try to reduce indirectly the supply of Canadian dollars coming onto the foreign exchange market (that is, shift S to the left) by adopting *restrictive monetary and fiscal policies*. For example,

tighter monetary or fiscal policies will slow down economic activity and reduce incomes. As a result, consumption will fall, including the consumption of imported goods. Furthermore, the tighter policies will reduce Canadian inflation. And, as our goods become more competitive in price, Canadian consumers will be encouraged to buy domestic goods instead of imports. (Moreover, tight economic policies also tend to increase exports: More competitively priced Canadian goods may capture a larger share of U.S. and other foreign markets. As foreigners buy more Canadian goods, the demand for Canadian dollars will increase, helping to eliminate the gap GE between the demand and supply for Canadian dollars at the exchange rate C$1.00 = U.S.$0.80.)

4. Allowing the Exchange Rate to Adjust

The Canadian government may allow the exchange rate to move to the new equilibrium F, where the price of the Canadian dollar is lower, at U.S.$0.70.

Since the end of World War II in 1945, the central debate in international finance has been over which of these four options should be used by countries facing disequilibrium in their exchange markets. In the early postwar period, most countries leaned toward the second option (direct restrictions). This tool, however, has a grave defect: By interfering with international trade and investment flows, it reduces the efficiency of the world economy.

Thus, most of the discussion in recent decades has focused on the other three options. In particular, there has been a debate whether countries should try to maintain a system of *fixed* or *pegged* exchange rates through use of a *combination of options 1 and 3*—official intervention in the exchange markets and supporting monetary and fiscal policies—or allow exchange rates to fluctuate in response to changing supply/demand conditions, option 4.

Exchange Rates Since World War II

Since 1973, most of the world's industrialized countries have followed a policy of *flexible* (or *floating*) exchange rates, allowing rates to respond to changes in market conditions. Historically, however, many countries tried to maintain a system of fixed or pegged exchange rates. Before World War I, the major industrialized nations adhered to the **gold standard**. Under the gold standard, the values of different currencies were kept stable in terms of gold; but this meant that the exchange rates between the currencies were kept stable as well. Between 1945 and 1973, most countries tried to maintain a system of pegged exchange rates, supervised by the IMF. We will discuss the gold standard and the IMF system, as well as the problems of the floating-rate system since 1973, in Chapter 20.

For part of the postwar period, Canada also belonged to the pegged-rate system. Thus, between 1946 and 1949, the Bank of Canada intervened to keep the value of the Canadian dollar fixed at C$1 = US$1. However, in 1950 Canada decided to allow exchange rates to float. During the following twelve years the value of the Canadian dollar showed substantial short-term variation. For most of the period, however, its value stayed reasonably close to C$1 = US$1, as Figure 14-4 shows.

In 1962, there was a sudden large fall in the value of the Canadian dollar in terms of U.S. dollars. That is, the Canadian dollar *depreciated*.

> A flexible or floating currency *depreciates* when its price falls in terms of other currencies.
>
> A floating currency *appreciates* when its price rises in terms of other currencies.

Following the 1962 crisis, the government announced that it would henceforth stabilize the dollar at an exchange rate of C$1 = US$0.925. Thus, Canada had effectively re-joined the international system of pegged exchange rates, and for the next eight years the exchange rate between the Canadian and U.S. dollars was kept fixed at that level. However, as we will discuss in Chapter 20, in the early 1970s the international pegged-rate system came under severe stress, and in 1970 the Canadian dollar was again allowed to float. In the early 1970s, it appreciated against the U.S. dollar but, during 1975–85, its value depreciated substantially, reaching a low point of about 70 U.S. cents in 1985; by 1988, it had rebounded again to more than 80 U.S. cents.

Arguments for Pegged Exchange Rates

The main argument that has been used in favour of a system of fixed or pegged exchange rates is that it eliminates (or at least greatly reduces) the *exchange risk* in international transactions. Exchange risk is important for international trade and investment because trade and investment decisions are influenced by expectations about the future values of foreign currencies. For example, suppose a Canadian firm contracts to sell equipment to a Mexican mining company at a price of U.S.$1 million, with payment to be made six months hence. With a fixed exchange rate, the exporting firm in Canada knows how many Canadian dollars it will eventually get

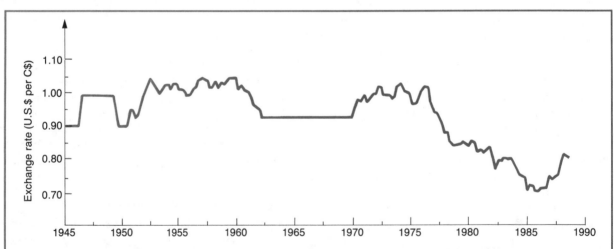

Figure 14-4   The exchange rate between the Canadian and U.S. dollars, 1945–88 (U.S.$ per C$).

At the end of World War II, the Canadian dollar was pegged at a value of U.S. $0.909. In 1946, the pegged value was changed to C$1 = U.S.$1.00; however, it was changed back again in 1949. During 1950–62, Canada allowed the exchange rate to float; during most of the period, the dollar remained fairly stable in value at around C$1 = U.S.$1.00. However, the Canadian dollar began to fall in 1960 and,

following an exchange crisis in 1962, the government decided to peg the exchange rate at C$1 = U.S. $0.925. In 1970, the dollar was again allowed to float. In the mid-1980s, it reached its modern-era low value of around C$1 = U.S.$0.70.

Source: Computed from data in Statistics Canada, *CANSIM Databank*. Reprinted by permission of the Minister of Supply and Services Canada.

in exchange for the U.S.$1 million. But if rates are flexible, the exporter is taking a risk: The price of the U.S. dollar in terms of Canadian dollars may fall, which means the firm will get a smaller amount of Canadian dollars than anticipated. The Canadian exporter may try to avoid this risk by making the Mexican firm agree that payment will be in Canadian funds. But that does not really solve the problem: If payment is in Canadian dollars, the Mexican *importing* firm runs the risk that the value of the Canadian dollar will *rise*, forcing it to pay a larger amount in U.S. funds than it originally expected.

In a situation where business firms expect substantial fluctuations in exchange rates, they may try to avoid the exchange risks by doing more business with domestic firms rather than foreign firms. As a result, there is less international trade and specialization, and the efficiency of the world economy suffers.

The Conflict between Fixed Exchange Rates and Domestic Stablization

Thus, the fact that fixed exchange rates help reduce exchange risk is one major argument in their favour. On the other hand, maintaining fixed rates may involve an important cost to the economy: It puts constraints on the government's ability to use monetary and fiscal policies to stabilize the economy. In the very short run, exchange rates may be stabilized through purchases and sales from a country's international currency reserves. But since reserves are limited, factors that give rise to substantial fluctuations in the supply and demand for a country's currency in the international markets have to be counteracted by changes in monetary and fiscal policies (option 3 above). The problem is that, sometimes, *the policies that are needed to stabilize exchange rates are in conflict with the policies that are needed to stabilize the economy.* (Some aspects of this problem are discussed further in the appendix to this chapter.)

The conflict between the objectives of domestic stabilization and exchange rate stabilization contributed to the breakdown of the international system of pegged exchange rates in the mid-1970s, as we shall see in Chapter 20. Specifically, pegged exchange rates greatly reduced the authorities' ability to use monetary policy as an effective tool for stabilizing the economy: As the next section shows, the effectiveness of monetary policy is likely to be much greater under a system of flexible exchange rates than under pegged rates.

HOW MONETARY AND FISCAL POLICY INFLUENCE THE BALANCE OF PAYMENTS

In Chapter 13, we raised the question: Which of the two main macroeconomic policy instruments — monetary policy or fiscal policy — is likely to be more effective in stabilizing aggregate demand and domestic or national income? The discussion above suggests that in answering this question, one must consider not only the impact of monetary and fiscal policies on domestic conditions, but also their impact on international transactions. Moreover, the answer may depend on whether exchange rates are pegged or flexible.

The question of how the relative effectiveness of monetary policy and fiscal policy is influenced by international transactions obviously is very important for a country like Canada where international trade and capital flows play such a large role in the economy. In answering it, we first consider the effect of monetary and fiscal policy on Canada's foreign trade (the current account); then we examine the effect of each policy on capital flows (the capital account).

Monetary and Fiscal Policies and the Current Account

Any *restrictive* policy (monetary or fiscal) that reduces aggregate demand and income will tend to move the current account toward a *surplus*. There are two reasons for this:

1. As we saw in Chapter 10, there is a high *marginal propensity to import* (MPM) in Canada: Whenever there is an increase in domestic income, a substantial proportion of this increase goes into additional purchases of imported goods and services; similarly, a decrease in aggregate demand and domestic income causes a substantial decrease in imports. Therefore, a restrictive policy that *reduces* aggregate demand and income will reduce imports and therefore move the current account toward a surplus.

2. A restrictive monetary or fiscal policy reduces Canadian inflation. This will tend to make Canadian-produced goods more attractive relative to imported goods; it will also make Canadian export goods more competitive in foreign markets. These effects on the prices of Canadian goods will reinforce the tendency for the current account to move into surplus.

Similarly, any *expansive* monetary or fiscal policy will move the current account toward a *deficit*.

Monetary and Fiscal Policies and the Capital Account

The inflows and outflows of capital which appear in the balance-of-payments accounts represent purchases and sales by foreigners of Canadian assets, or transactions by Canadians in foreign assets. The main determinant of these purchases and sales of assets is the difference in the rate of return which an investor can expect to get by buying Canadian rather than foreign assets. Financial institutions and other corporations are constantly trying to invest their short-term assets where they yield the highest return, and will quickly move their funds into Canada if interest rates here rise above foreign interest rates — and move them out again as quickly if Canadian rates fall below world levels.

To see what happens to capital flows under a restrictive *monetary* policy, note that this policy will make interest rates in Canada rise relative to U.S. rates. This encourages both Canadian and American investors to sell U.S. assets in order to buy the Canadian assets that are now yielding a higher return. Thus, the result of this tight monetary policy is a capital inflow into Canada — that is, a movement in the capital account toward a surplus. Sim-

ilarly, an easy money policy that lowers Canadian interest rates will move the capital account toward a deficit.

Fiscal policy also has an impact on the capital account. The reason is that fiscal policy affects interest rates. For example, if the government moves toward a tighter fiscal policy by decreasing expenditure or raising taxes, the result is a smaller government budget deficit (or even a budget surplus). Hence, there is a reduction in the amount that the government has to borrow in the bond market. But as we saw in Chapter 13, decreased government borrowing will tend to push down Canadian interest rates; and this will cause a capital *outflow* from Canada.

To sum up:

Whereas a tight monetary policy and a tight fiscal policy have the *same* effect on the current account (they move it toward a surplus), they have *different* effects on Canadian interest rates and therefore on the capital account. A tight monetary policy *raises* interest rates and therefore results in a capital *inflow,* whereas a tight fiscal policy *lowers* interest rates and results in a capital *outflow.* Figures 14-5 and 14-6 illustrate these effects.

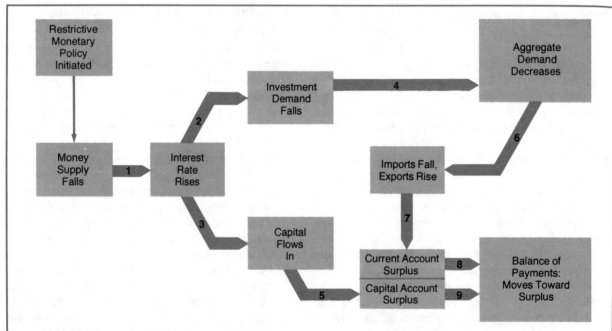

Figure 14-5 Effects of restrictive monetary policy on the balance of payments.
A restrictive monetary policy raises domestic interest rates (arrow 1). This affects the balance-of-payments accounts in two ways: (a) Because investment and aggregate demand decrease (arrows 2 and 4), there is a tendency for imports to decrease and exports to increase (arrow 6). Thus, the current account moves toward a surplus (arrow 7). (b) A higher domestic interest rate causes a capital inflow (arrow 3), and the capital account moves toward a surplus (arrow 5).

Thus, the overall balance of payments moves toward a surplus (arrows 8 and 9).

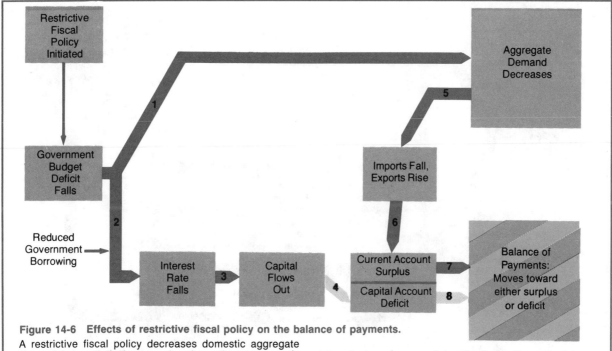

Figure 14-6   Effects of restrictive fiscal policy on the balance of payments.

A restrictive fiscal policy decreases domestic aggregate demand (arrow 1); furthermore, it reduces the government's need to borrow, and therefore tends to lower domestic interest rates (arrow 2). There are two kinds of effect on the balance of payments: (a) The reduced aggregate demand causes imports to decrease and exports to increase (arrow 5), moving the current accounts toward a surplus (arrow 6). (b) The lower interest rate causes a capital outflow (arrow 3), moving the capital account toward a deficit (arrow 4).

Because the current and capital accounts move in opposite directions, we cannot tell whether the overall effect (arrows 7 and 8) will be to move the balance of payments toward a surplus or a deficit.

With the preceding discussion as a background we can now return to the important policy issue: How does the relative effectiveness of monetary and fiscal policy depend on whether Canada has a fixed exchange rate or a flexible exchange rate?

EXCHANGE RATES AND THE EFFECTIVENESS OF MONETARY POLICY

(a) *With a fixed exchange rate.* Figure 14-5 showed a restrictive monetary policy having a favourable effect on both the current account (arrow 7) and on the capital account (arrow 5). The resulting move toward a surplus in the balance of payments is shown as arrow 2 in Figure 14-7. Under a fixed exchange rate, the Bank of Canada must buy foreign currencies in order to prevent the Canadian dollar from rising (arrow 3). But as we have seen, this expands chartered bank reserves and therefore the money supply (arrow 5). This *tends to offset the original restrictive monetary policy.* In other words, Figure 14-7 confirms one of the major criticisms against a fixed

exchange rate system. With fixed exchange rates, international complications make it difficult for the authorities to use monetary policy effectively, as shown by the "inner loop" of arrows 3, 5 and 7 in Figure 14-7.

(b) *With a floating exchange rate.* Again assume a restrictive monetary policy with a resulting balance-of-payments surplus. With a floating exchange rate, the Bank of Canada simply lets the Canadian dollar rise in value (arrow 4 in Figure 14-7). Because the Bank makes no attempt to hold the Canadian dollar down by buying foreign exchange, there is no complication in the form of an expansion of the money supply. But a rise in the Canadian dollar *does* affect our exports and imports: The higher-priced Canadian dollar makes our goods more expensive relative to foreign goods, and thus reduces our exports and increases our imports (arrow 6). The resulting reductions in Canadian output—in both our export and import-competing industries — *augment* the restrictive effects of the initial tight money policy. Thus, the "outer loop" of Figure 14-7 (arrows 4, 6, and 8) shows how a floating exchange rate *strengthens* the traditional domestic impact of a tight monetary policy.

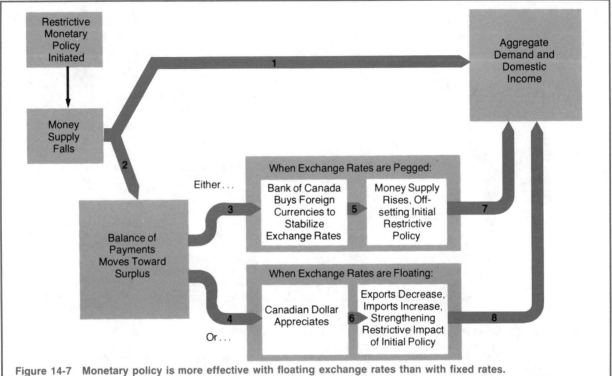

Figure 14-7 **Monetary policy is more effective with floating exchange rates than with fixed rates.**
Arrows 1 and 2 summarize the effects of a restrictive monetary policy from Figure 14-5. With fixed exchange rates (arrow 3), Bank of Canada purchases of foreign currencies tend to increase the Canadian money supply (arrow 5); this increase in the money supply tends to offset the initial restrictive policy (arrow 7). With floating exchange rates (arrow 4), the balance-of-payments surplus causes an appreciation of the Canadian dollar. As a result (arrow 6), Canadian net exports tend to decrease, which further reduces aggregate demand (arrow 8).

Fixed exchange rates make it difficult for a country to use monetary policy effectively. Flexible exchange rates *reinforce* the effectiveness of monetary policy.

(As an exercise, recast Figures 14-5 and 14-6 to show the effects on the balance of payments of easy monetary policies; then change Figure 14-7 to show that the conclusion in boldface above still holds.)

In Chapter 13 we saw that much of the early debate in Britain and the United States about the potential effectiveness of monetary policy focused on the lack of responsiveness of investment to changes in the rate of interest. However, in an open economy with interest-sensitive capital flows, monetary policy may potentially be very powerful *even if* investment is not very interest-sensitive: If exchange rates are flexible, monetary policy may have a very strong effect on aggregate demand because it influences net exports as well as investment. As we will discuss in more detail in Chapter 18, the

Bank of Canada appears to consider the link between monetary policy and the exchange rate as a very important part of the mechanism through which money affects aggregate demand. During the early 1980s the Bank appeared to use exchange rate movements as the most important indicator in making monetary policy decisions.

Finally, recall that exchange-rate flexibility adds to the *freedom* of the monetary authorities to follow an expansive policy when they consider it desirable: They do not have to worry about running out of reserves, and therefore do not have to tighten monetary policy on that account. However, this conclusion — that a flexible exchange rate adds to the freedom of the central bank to pursue domestic objectives — should not be overstated. Freedom is a matter of degree; there is no absolute policy freedom in a world of close international economic relationships. To illustrate: Although the Bank of Canada can pursue an easy monetary policy without fear of running out of exchange reserves (it lets the Canadian dollar fall instead), its freedom may be constrained by the fear of the inflation that will be generated by a falling dollar.

EXCHANGE RATES AND THE EFFECTIVENESS OF FISCAL POLICY

As shown in Figure 14-6, a restrictive fiscal policy results in a positive move in the current account (arrows 1, 5,and 6) and a negative move in the capital account (arrows 2, 3,and 4). Because of these conflicting pressures, we cannot be certain of the overall effects on the balance of payments. However, in a country where capital is very mobile, even small changes in the rate of interest lead to large capital flows. In such a country the capital account effect may well dominate; in this case, the balance of payments will move in a deficit direction in response to a restrictive fiscal policy. If this happens, we get the following effects of fiscal policy under each exchange rate regime:

(a) *With a fixed exchange rate.* Because of the balance-of-payments deficit, the authorities will lose foreign exchange reserves, thus reducing the chartered banks' reserves and the money supply. In other words, the original restrictive fiscal policy will induce monetary restrictiveness, and will thereby be strengthened. Similarly, an expansionary fiscal policy indirectly induces monetary expansion, which reinforces the fiscal policy. Thus, under a fixed exchange rate, the effectiveness of fiscal policy is *increased*.

Notice that this conclusion can be related to the discussion of "crowding out" in Chapter 13. Crowding out potentially reduces the effectiveness of an expansionary fiscal policy, say, because an expansionary policy increases the government's need to borrow, and this tends to drive up interest rates which, in turn, reduces private investment. Thus, the initial stimulating effect of a larger fiscal deficit is partially offset by reduced investment demand. However, with fixed exchange rates, there will be less of a tendency for interest rates to rise: As the extra government borrowing begins to put upward pressure on interest rates, foreign capital will begin to flow in, forcing the central bank to buy foreign exchange, thereby expanding the reserves of chartered banks and thus the money supply; this induced expansion in the money supply will limit the increase in interest rates, so that there will be less crowding out of private investment.

(b) *With a flexible exchange rate.* In this case, the balance-of-payments deficit that results from a restric-tive fiscal policy does not result in a loss of foreign exchange reserves, but instead causes a depreciation of the country's currency. As noted earlier, this depreciation tends to raise aggregate demand for the country's goods and services, and therefore offsets some of the restrictive effects of the tighter fiscal policy. Thus, fiscal policy is *weakened* under a flexible exchange rate.

The overall conclusions in the last two sections may be summarized thus:

> **Monetary policy is weakened by a fixed exchange rate, but strengthened by a flexible exchange rate.**
>
> **When international capital is sufficiently mobile, the reverse is true for fiscal policy: Fiscal policy is strengthened by a fixed exchange rate, but weakened by a flexible rate.**

EXCHANGE RATES, MONETARY POLICY, AND INFLATION, 1970–88

In Chapter 13, we discussed some reasons why monetary policy has been more important than fiscal policy as a tool for economic stabilization during the late 1970s and 1980s. The fact that the Canadian dollar has been allowed to float since 1970 is another reason: As we have just seen, with floating exchange rates monetary policy becomes a relatively more effective tool for managing aggregate demand. Canadian experience during the last two decades provides an interesting illustration of the complex interactions between monetary policy, inflation, and exchange rate movements in an open economy with interest-sensitive capital flows.

The 1970s

As the 1960s drew to a close, Canada (along with most other countries) was maintaining fixed exchange rates. Our dollar had been pegged at a value of U.S.$0.925 per C$ since 1962 (see Figure 14-4 on page 268). In 1968/69, inflationary pressures were building up in the United States, partly as a result of the heavy American spending on the war in Vietnam. With the exchange rate being fixed, the inflationary pressure began spilling over into Canada. To prevent this from happening, the Canadian authorities decided in 1970 to abandon the pegged rate system, even though most other industrialized countries continued to maintain pegged exchange rates until 1973.

In response to U.S. inflation, the Canadian dollar began to appreciate rapidly as soon as it was allowed to float (again, see Figure 14-4). Soon, however, the Bank of Canada became concerned that the appreciation was too fast: The rising value of the Canadian dollar was making Canadian goods more expensive on world markets, and was thus creating difficulties for our export and import-competing industries. Accordingly, the Bank bought up large amounts of foreign exchange (sold large amounts of Canadian dollars) in order to limit the rise in the Canadian dollar. We therefore had a *managed float* or *dirty float*: The Canadian dollar wasn't floating completely freely since the authorities were intervening in the exchange market.

> A currency is *freely flexible* or *freely floating* if there is no official intervention in the foreign exchange markets. A *free float* is also sometimes spoken of as a *clean float*.
>
> A float is *managed* (or *dirty*) if the government intervenes in the foreign exchange markets, buying or selling foreign exchange in order to influence the exchange rate.

The accumulation of foreign exchange reserves by the Bank of Canada continued in 1971 and 1972 and resulted in a high rate of growth in the Canadian money supply. This monetary expansion set the stage for the rapid increase in inflation which took place in 1973–75.

Thus, the floating of the dollar in 1970 provided the *opportunity* to insulate Canada from the world inflationary trend of the 1970s. But it was an opportunity that was missed, because the authorities intervened to stabilize the exchange rate, thereby getting a result partway between a pegged and freely flexible rate. By the mid-1970s, it became clear that we had indeed missed the opportunity: Canada's inflation rate had risen to the inflation rate in the United States.

The deep recession in 1974/75 led to a substantial reduction in the inflationary pressure in the U.S. economy. In Canada, both monetary and fiscal policies were set to provide a strong stimulus to aggregate demand, and our recession was much less severe than in the United States. However, inflationary pressures in Canada also remained strong: We had double-digit inflation (that is, the rate of inflation exceeded 10%) both in 1974 and 1975, and the Canadian dollar depreciated sharply in relation to the U.S. dollar (by more than 7% between March of 1974 and September 1975). By late 1975, reducing inflation became the government's top priority.

The Bank of Canada announced that it would begin a policy of gradually decreasing the rate of growth of the money supply, and the Trudeau government created the Anti-Inflation Board to supervise the wage and price controls that were applied in October 1975. Following these measures, the Canadian dollar appreciated substantially between 1975 and 1976, and inflationary pressures moderated somewhat. However, the Canadian inflation rate continued to remain well above the U.S. rate throughout the rest of the decade. Beginning in late 1976, the Canadian dollar started to fall; by mid-1979 it had fallen from $1.04 (in November of 1976) to as low as U.S.$0.83. The resulting steady increase in import prices helped fuel the inflationary spiral, offsetting much of the Bank of Canada's efforts at reducing inflation by gradually decreasing the growth rate of M1.

The 1980s

In 1979, the U.S. Federal Reserve Bank moved its monetary policy sharply toward restraint, driving up U.S. interest rates to record levels. The Bank of Canada was now faced with a dilemma. If it decided to stick with its previous policy of reducing the growth rate of the money supply only gradually, the high interest rates in the United States would almost certainly cause a large outflow of capital from Canada, and the Canadian dollar would depreciate even further. With inflationary pressures already high, adding further to these pressures by allowing a continued fall in the dollar was the last thing the Bank of Canada wanted to do. But the alternative was not very attractive either: The very high interest rates in the United States were coming under criticism for the hardships they created for farmers, small businesses, and home owners whose mortgages were coming up for renewal. If the Bank of Canada decided to follow the policy of the Federal Reserve and move to a highly restrictive policy, the same problems would arise in Canada.

In the final outcome, the Bank of Canada decided that the battle against inflation would take precedence. It put on the monetary brakes sharply in 1979, sending short-term interest rates above 16%. In 1981, U.S. interest rates again rose substantially as the economy recovered from the mini-recession in 1980. In Canada, the Bank again refused to allow our dollar to depreciate; it continued tightening monetary policy until short-term interest rates at one point went above 20%, even higher than

U.S. rates. Criticism of the Bank became louder, and many observers feel that the extreme restrictiveness of monetary policy in 1981 contributed to the severity of the 1981/82 recession; while Canada had escaped the 1974/75 recession much better than the United States, the 1981/82 recession was, if anything, *more* severe in Canada than south of the border. And while the Bank succeeded in its objective of preventing the Canadian dollar from depreciating, this did not seem to be enough: The rate of inflation remained high well into the recession.

Starting toward the end of 1982, however, Canada's inflation rate finally began coming down. By 1984, it was less than 5%. The Bank of Canada had finally proved its point: It had showed that with a sufficiently restrictive monetary policy, inflation can be beaten. But the price had been very high, with punishing interest rates and a degree of monetary restriction that aggravated and prolonged the deepest Canadian recession since the Great Depression.

Many observers have been highly critical of the Bank's policies during this period. While they recognize that the sharp monetary restraint and the stabilization of the exchange rate certainly helped beat inflation, they argue that the policy of gradual reduction in monetary growth that the Bank was following before 1979 would in the end have accomplished the same thing, and at a substantially lower cost in terms of the depth of the recession. Also, while allowing some depreciation of the Canadian dollar in 1982 would have added somewhat to inflationary pressure in Canada in that year, the addition would not have been large: The rate of increase in the Canadian prices of goods imported from the United States depends *both* on the depreciation of the exchange rate *and* on the rate of increase in the U.S. prices of these goods, and U.S. prices in 1982 were relatively stable.

As the inflationary pressure abated, the Bank of Canada began moving in the direction of a less restrictive policy. In spite of Canada's relatively low rate of inflation, the easier monetary policy led to a substantial depreciation of the dollar in terms of U.S. funds. One reason why the Bank was prepared to allow this depreciation was the fact that the *American* dollar had *appreciated* very substantially against other currencies such as the Deutschmark and the British pound. This meant that even though the Canadian dollar was falling relative to the U.S. dollar, it actually *rose* in terms of these other currencies. In early 1986, however, the Canadian dollar briefly reached a historic low of less than U.S.$0.70. At this point, the Bank of Canada produced a sharp tightening of monetary conditions, driving short-term Canadian interest rates as much as three percentage points above U.S. rates; the Canadian dollar stabilized in the range of U.S.$0.70-0.73. In 1987/88, the Bank continued to keep Canadian short-term rates well above U.S. rates, and the dollar gradually appreciated. By mid-1988, it had climbed to well above U.S.$0.80.

KEY POINTS

1. International trade is different from domestic trade because:
    (a) Imports are often subjected to special taxes (tariffs).
    (b) International trade involves more than one national currency.
2. A foreign exchange market is a market where the currency of one nation (for example, the Canadian dollar) is exchanged for the currencies of other nations. The supply of a nation's currency to the world's foreign exchange markets depends on:
    (a) The nation's imports of goods
    (b) Its imports of services
    (c) Its acquisitions of foreign assets
    Similarly, the demand for a national currency in the world's foreign exchange markets depend on:
    (a) The nation's exports of goods
    (b) Its exports of services
    (c) Foreign acquisitions of assets from the nation
3. A country's balance-of-payments accounts provide a record of transactions in the foreign exchange market between residents of that country and residents of foreign countries. For example, the debit side of Canada's balance-of-payments accounts shows the transactions which give rise to a supply of Canadian dollars in exchange for foreign currencies (imports of goods and services and capital outflows); the credit side shows the transactions which cause a demand for Canadian dollars in the foreign exchange markets (Canadian exports of goods and services and capital inflows into Canada).
4. Exports and imports of goods and services are shown in the current account. Capital inflows and

outflows are recorded in the capital account, which shows Bank of Canada transactions in official reserve assets as well as private transactions in non-reserve assets. The surplus or deficit in the balance of payments is calculated by taking the net amount of all credits and debits in both the current and capital accounts, but excluding transactions in official foreign exchange reserves.

5. Suppose that after a period of equilibrium, Canada's balance of payments begins to move toward a deficit—that is, the demand and supply curves in the foreign exchange market shift so that the demand for Canadian dollars decreases relative to the supply. The Canadian government can deal with this change in the relationship between supply and demand by one of, or a combination of, the following steps:

   (a) By intervention in the foreign exchange market; that is, by selling foreign currencies (from its foreign exchange reserves) for Canadian dollars;

   (b) By allowing the Canadian dollar to depreciate in response to market forces, if exchange rates are floating;

   (c) By reducing the supply of Canadian dollars through restrictions on imports or other international transactions;

   (d) By restricting aggregate demand in Canada, and thus reducing Canadian imports and the supply of our dollars to the foreign exchange market.

6. When a country belongs to a system of fixed or pegged exchange rates, the authorities are committed to buying and selling the country's currency in exchange for foreign currencies in order to maintain stable exchange rates. With flexible or floating exchange rates, the authorities do not have to intervene in the foreign exchange market: Instead, they can simply let the country's currency appreciate or depreciate in response to changing supply and demand factors.

7. Before the Great Depression, and later on between 1945 and the early 1970s, most countries of the world tried to maintain systems of fixed exchange rates. However, Canada allowed exchange rates to float between 1950 and 1962, and, like most other countries, has been following a policy of floating rates since the early 1970s.

8. The main advantage of a system of fixed exchange rates is that it reduces the exchange risks in international transactions. By encouraging international trade and specialization, it promotes efficiency in the world economy.

9. The main disadvantage with a system of fixed exchange rates is that it places constraints on domestic policy makers: The policies needed to stabilize exchange rates may sometimes conflict with the policies needed to stabilize the economy.

10. The effectiveness of monetary and fiscal policy as tools for stabilizing a country's domestic economy depends on whether the country is on a fixed or flexible exchange rate. With a fixed exchange rate, monetary policy may be relatively ineffective, particularly if capital is highly mobile across borders. A floating rate, on the other hand, tends to increase the effectiveness of monetary policy. When capital is very mobile, the reverse conclusion holds for fiscal policy: It tends to be more effective under a fixed than under a flexible rate.

KEY CONCEPTS

exchange rate
foreign exchange market
imports of goods and services
tariff
acquisition of foreign assets
   (that is, investment in foreign countries)
long-term capital inflow/outflow
direct investment
foreign exchange reserves

official intervention in the
   exchange market
current account deficit/surplus
balance-of-payments deficit/
   surplus
changes in official reserve
   assets
appreciation/depreciation of a
   currency
flexible or floating exchange rate

fixed or pegged exchange rate
clean/dirty float
international mobility of capital
exchange risk
monetary policy under fixed/
   floating exchange rates
exchange rates and foreign
   inflation
fiscal policy under fixed/float-
   ing exchange rates

PROBLEMS

14-1. Suppose that, after a period of equilibrium, there is a fall in the demand for Canadian dollars in the foreign exchange market. What alternatives does the Canadian government have for dealing with this change?

14-2. With fixed exchange rates, why does a balance-of-payments surplus usually cause an increase in a country's money supply?

14-3. Because the balance-of-payments accounts must always balance, each international transaction gives rise to two entries, one on the credit side and one on the debit side. As an example, consider a single transaction—namely, the sale of a de Havilland airplane to a U.S. buyer. The effects on Canada's balance of payments are shown in Table 14-2.

 Since each international transaction affects both sides of the balance of payments equally, the two sides of the balance of payments always sum to the same total.

 For each of the following transactions, construct a simple balance of payments like the one shown in Table 14-2, showing how each transaction results in the same dollar entry on each side of the balance sheet:

(a) Canada imports $100 million in goods, and pays for these goods with $100 million of exports.

(b) Northern Telecom buys a factory from a foreign cable manufacturer, and the foreign company deposits the proceeds in a Montreal bank.

(c) A Canadian company pays a U.S. resident dividends of $500. The U.S. resident deposits the dividends in a Canadian bank.

(d) Later, the U.S. resident makes a trip to Canada, spending the $500 previously deposited for motels, meals, and other similar expenses.

(e) A Canadian manufacturer exports a $100,000 machine. The importer does not pay now, but promises to pay in 3 months.

14-4. The purpose of Problem 14-3 was to help you keep straight which side of the balance of payments various items are entered on. Now go back to Problem 14-3, and identify which of the items are included in the capital account, and which in the current account.

14-5. Explain why monetary policy is a more powerful policy instrument under floating exchange rates than under fixed exchange rates.

*14-6. Suppose Canadian capital is very mobile internationally. Try to draw a diagram similar to Figure 14-7 to illustrate why fiscal policy is relatively more effective under fixed exchange rates than under floating exchange rates.

*14-7. Consider a country where capital is very immobile, so that the capital-account effects of a tight fiscal policy are dominated by the current-account effects. Would a restrictive fiscal policy be more effective under a fixed or floating exchange rate?

*14-8. Some observers have suggested that, in 1981/82, the Bank of Canada was engaged in a "managed float" of the Canadian dollar because it was influencing its value not so much by intervention in the foreign exchange market (although it did some of this) as by raising interest rates in Canada to attract and hold international capital. Explain why you agree or disagree.

Table 14-2   An International Transaction

Positive Items (Credits)	Negative Items (Debits)
Export of Canadian-made airplane $1 million	Increase in Canadian-owned bank account in the United States $1 million

Appendix

■ ■ ■ ■ ■

Domestic Stabilization Policy and Pegged Exchange Rates: Some Further Considerations

A commitment to a pegged exchange rate may sometimes force a country to undertake policies that exacerbate a recession. Consider, for example, a case where the Canadian economy is in a slump and unemployment is high. Suppose now that there is a fall in the demand for Canadian exports. As a result, there is a reduced international demand for Canadian dollars, and the Bank of Canada will be losing international reserves as it buys Canadian dollars in exchange for foreign currencies. To stem the loss of reserves, the government *must* follow policies that reduce inflationary pressures in Canada. In other words, the government must use contractionary monetary and fiscal policies. But these contractionary policies are precisely the opposite of what is needed to fight the high unemployment rate.

The classic case of a conflict between the policies needed to maintain fixed exchange rates and those that were needed to stabilize the domestic economy occurred during the Great Depression. The attempts by countries such as Britain and the United States to maintain fixed exchange rates and preserve the gold standard led them to tighten policies in the early 1930s even though unemployment was rising. By doing so, they made the Depression worse.

As another example of how a commitment to fixed exchange rates constrains domestic policy makers, consider a situation where there is an increase in inflationary pressures in the Canadian economy. Suppose the Bank of Canada decides to fight inflation through restrictive monetary policies.

To decrease the money supply, the Bank proceeds to reduce chartered bank reserves by selling government bonds in the open market. But open market sales will raise interest rates in Canada. To take advantage of the higher Canadian interest rates, investors in the United States and other countries will increase their holdings of Canadian assets: That is, there will be a *capital inflow* into Canada. As a result, there will be a tendency toward a balance-of-payments surplus and an increased demand for Canadian dollars in the foreign exchange market. If Canada is on fixed exchange rates, the Bank *has to* increase the supply of Canadian dollars in the foreign exchange market—that is, buy foreign currencies. But, as we saw in Chapter 12, Bank of Canada purchases of foreign currencies *increase* chartered bank reserves. Thus, the Bank of Canada's open market sales of government bonds and its induced purchases of foreign reserves tend to offset each other: There may be little or no net effect on chartered bank reserves and the money supply.

Exchange Rates and Foreign Inflation

As the previous example illustrates, a commitment to a fixed exchange rate limits the ability of the authorities to use monetary policy as a tool to stabilize the domestic economy because the money supply becomes partially controlled by balances-of-payments pressures. During the late 1960s and early 1970s, when many of the world's industrialized nations began to experience rapid inflation, this raised an important question: Is it possible for a small country (like Canada, or Sweden) to insulate its own economy from a world inflationary trend while still maintaining fixed exchange rates?

The answer, most economists now agree, is no: A commitment to fixed exchange rates effectively ties a small country to world inflation rates. To see why, suppose, for example, that there is a sudden increase in U.S. inflation. Some of this inflation is quickly imported into Canada because of the higher prices we must pay for U.S. goods. As U.S. goods are priced out of the Canadian market, Canadian imports will fall and the Canadian balance of payments will move into surplus. But this will tend to increase Canada's money supply as the Bank of Canada buys U.S. dollars to keep the exchange rate stable. To counteract the inflationary pressures, the Bank may try to cancel out the monetary effects of the purchase of foreign reserves through open-market sales of government bonds: It may try to *sterilize* the increase in Canada's reserves of U.S. dollars (that is, try to offset the effect of this increase on the money stock). However, the open market sales will increase Canadian interest rates, which will attract U.S. capital; this will further increase the balance-of-payments surplus, forcing the Bank to add even more to its foreign reserves. As long as exchange rates remain fixed, the balance-of-payments surplus will persist until the Canadian inflation rate has risen to roughly the world rate. Therefore, with a fixed exchange rate, a small country such as Canada cannot protect itself from international inflation. In the long run, Canada would have about the same inflation rate as the countries with which it trades.

Fixed Exchange Rates as a Disciplinary Device

According to the preceding discussion, one of the main arguments against fixed exchange rates is that they place a constraint on domestic policy makers: With fixed rates, they are less able to manipulate fiscal and monetary policies to stabilize the domestic economy.

Paradoxically, however, some of those who *favour* fixed exchange rates do so precisely *because* a system of fixed rates places constraints on domestic policy makers. In particular, an argument often used by the proponents of fixed exchange rates is that they may exert an important *anti-inflationary discipline* on those in charge of monetary and fiscal policies. With fixed exchange rates, a country that follows inflationary policies will find that its goods are being priced out of world markets. Its balance of payments will move in a negative direction, and it will lose reserves. The fear of further reserve losses will act as a restraint; unless it is prepared to allow exchange rates to change, the country will have to follow less inflationary domestic policies. In the view of those who argue this way, the independence from foreign inflation that a floating rate gives a country represents a *disadvantage*: A floating rate allows the authorities to follow policies that result in a higher rate of inflation than elsewhere. If the government is prepared to accept a continuing depreciation of the exchange rate, inflationary policies can be continued.

Both those who favour fixed exchange rates and those who oppose them agree that a commitment to fixed rates puts constraints on the use of monetary and fiscal policies to achieve domestic objectives. What they disagree on is whether such constraints are good or bad. Those who believe that the government has a tendency to pursue policies that on average are too inflationary sometimes argue that the constraints imposed by fixed exchange rates will indirectly lead to lower inflation. However, as we have just seen, there also may be times when fixed exchange rates lead to higher inflation: They make it difficult or impossible for Canadian policy makers to prevent inflation in foreign countries from spreading into Canada.

Part 4

■ ■

Aggregate Supply: Theory and Policy Issues

Part 3 focused on the issue of how aggregate demand is determined and how monetary and fiscal policies can be used to stabilize it. In Part 4, we turn our attention to *aggregate supply*.

Chapter 8 in Part 3 introduced several simple aggregate supply functions. However, none of them is adequate to explain a problem that was particularly severe in the late 1970s and early 1980s: How can a high rate of price inflation and a high rate of unemployment exist *together*? This question is considered in Chapter 15.

The principal effect of a *deficiency* of aggregate demand in the economy is unemployment. On the other hand, when aggregate demand is too high, the result tends to be a high rate of price inflation. We study some of the economic problems caused by rapid inflation in Chapter 16. Although the problems with rapid inflation are not as obvious as those with unemployment, public resentment of inflation became very strong in the late 1970s and early 1980s, and North American governments took a strong anti-inflationary stance.

In the short run, real output rises and falls because of cyclical fluctuations in aggregate demand. But the long-run trend in real output depends on supply factors. For example, as the economy's stock of capital increases, or as new technologies are invented, the economy's productive capacity rises and the aggregate supply curve shifts to the right. One reason that macroeconomic analysis has put more emphasis on the supply side in recent years has been the relatively slow *productivity growth* in the North American and European economies. Productivity growth is also a crucial issue for the less developed countries (LDCs), where much of the population continues to live in abject poverty. The problem of productivity growth, both in advanced and less developed countries, is discussed in Chapter 17.

Chapter 15

■ ■

Aggregate Supply: The Inflation and Unemployment Problems

*The first panacea for a mismanaged nation is
inflation of the currency; the second is war.
Both bring a temporary prosperity; both bring
a permanent ruin. But both are the refuge of
political and economic opportunists.*

Ernest Hemingway

In the three decades following the Great Depression, macroeconomists were preoccupied with aggregate demand. How could we prevent a repeat of the Depression, with its decade-long inadequacy of demand? How, and to what extent, could we hope to manage aggregate demand in order to reduce short-run fluctuations in the economy? Then, beginning in the 1960s, macroeconomists also began to pay close attention to aggregate supply. Any study of macroeconomics is now incomplete without an investigation of *both* demand and supply.

The last five chapters have dealt in detail with the demand side and, in particular, with the use of monetary and fiscal policies to affect aggregate demand. In this chapter, we turn to aggregate supply.

Chapter 8 introduced the aggregate supply function of Keynesian theory, repeated here as Figure 15-1. According to this view, if there initially is a deep depression at *A*, with output falling far short of the economy's full-employment potential, then an increase in aggregate demand will cause the economy to move toward *B*. In the horizontal range *AB*, the increase in demand will be reflected entirely in an increase in output, and prices will remain stable. At the other end, if an economy begins on the vertical section at *F*, an increase in demand will be reflected entirely in terms of higher prices as the economy moves upward from *F*. Finally, there is an

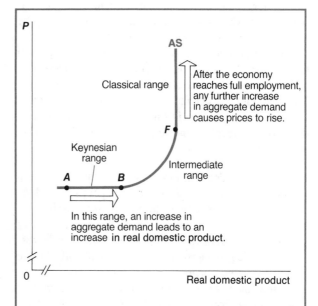

Figure 15-1   The Keynesian aggregate supply function.
This figure repeats the aggregate supply function of earlier chapters. If the economy begins at a point of depression, such as *A*, an increase in demand will increase real output. The economy will move from *A* toward *B*, with prices remaining stable. Once full employment has been reached at point *F*, a further increase in aggregate demand will cause inflation, with the economy moving upward from *F*.

intermediate range, between *B* and *F*. As the economy approaches full employment, an increase in demand will be reflected partly in terms of higher output, and partly in terms of higher prices.

In passing, we re-emphasize a point already encountered several times. A change in *demand* causes a movement *along* a *supply* curve. For example, an increase in aggregate demand causes a movement along the aggregate supply curve from *B* to *F* in Figure 15-1.

In all probability, the reader has become increasingly uncomfortable with the view of the world represented by Figure 15-1. It doesn't seem to fit the facts very well. In particular, it suggests that, whenever inflation rates are high, the economy should be at full employment, at *F* or above. On the other hand, prices should be stable whenever the unemployment rate is high, to the left of *B*. Yet there have been times when *both* the unemployment rate and inflation have been high. In 1980, for example, the inflation rate exceeded 10% at a time when unemployment averaged 7.5%. In 1982, both unemployment and inflation had risen to about 11%. While Figure 15-1 has been useful as an introduction to the idea of aggregate supply, it is too simple. It is not consistent with what has happened in recent decades. The time has come to look closely at the facts.

To do so, economists use a slightly different approach from Figure 15-1. Instead of looking at how prices and output change, they use a diagram with the two central macroeconomic problems—inflation and unemployment—on the axes, as shown in Figure 15-2. In this diagram, the three general ideas behind Figure 15-1 can be illustrated:

1. First is the idea that prices will be stable in a deep depression. This is illustrated by points *A* and *B*. When *prices* are *stable*, the *rate of inflation* is zero. Thus, points *A* and *B* are on the horizontal axis of Figure 15-2. If, starting from a point of severe depression at *A*, aggregate demand rises, output will increase and the rate of unemployment will fall. The decrease in the unemployment rate shows up as a *leftward* movement from *A* to *B* in Figure 15-2. This corresponds to the *rightward* movement when output increases in Figure 15-1.
2. The second idea from Figure 15-1 is this: Whenever there is rapid inflation, the economy is at full employment. This idea is illustrated by the vertical range above *F* in Figure 15-2. Because of frictional unemployment, there is some unemployment—something

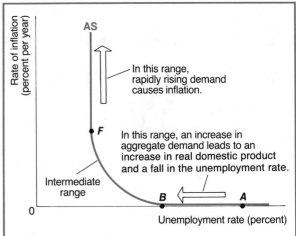

Figure 15-2   An alternative presentation: Inflation and unemployment.

The major ideas in Figure 15-1 are repeated in this diagram. Starting from a point of depression, such as *A*, an increase in demand will leave prices stable. The rate of inflation will be zero. Output will increase. Unemployment will fall, as illustrated by the leftward movement to *B*. In the intermediate range from *B* to *F*, an increase in aggregate demand is reflected partly in inflation, and partly in output and employment. Once full employment has been established at *F*, a more rapid growth in aggregate demand is reflected entirely in terms of inflation, with no change in the unemployment rate.

like 5% or 6%—even at points of "full employment." In the range above *F*, a faster growth in aggregate demand will mean more inflation with no change in output or employment.
3. Third is the intermediate range, between *B* and *F*. An increase in demand is reflected partly in higher prices, and partly in terms of rising output and falling unemployment.

However, just as Figure 15-1 was too simple, so too is the curve in Figure 15-2. Many of the facts do not fit this figure.

THE FACTS

Historical observations are plotted in Figure 15-3, where each point shows the inflation rate and the unemployment rate in every one of the years since 1960. Two major points stand out:

1. During most of the 1960s, the data form a smooth curve, similar to the intermediate range of the aggregate supply function in Figure 15-2. Such a curve is known as a *Phillips curve*, after British economist

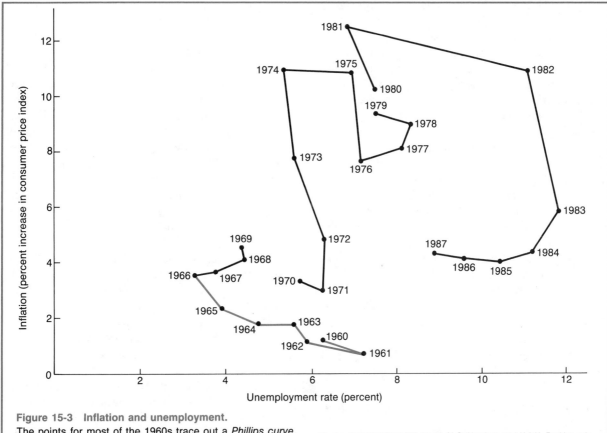

Figure 15-3   Inflation and unemployment.
The points for most of the 1960s trace out a *Phillips curve.*
Points for the 1970s and 1980s are highers and further to the
right, reflecting higher inflation *and* more unemployment.

Source: Compiled from F.H. Leacy, M.C. Urquhart, and K.A.H. Buckley, eds.,
Historical Statistics of Canada, 2nd ed. (Ottawa: Statistics Canada, 1982), and
Bank of Canada Review (August 1988), Table A1.

A. W. Phillips, who found that British data for 1861-1957 fitted a similar curve.[1]

When the rate of inflation (or the rate of change of money wages)[2] is put on the vertical axis and the rate of unemployment on the horizontal axis,

historical data sometimes trace out a smooth curve bending upward to the left — namely, a *Phillips curve.*

2. The observations since 1968 are above and to the right of the Phillips curve traced out earlier in the 1960s. In the 1970s and 1980s, we frequently suffered from high rates of both inflation and unemployment. To use an inelegant but common term, we suffered from **stagflation**.

Stagflation exists when a high rate of unemployment (stagnation) and a high rate of inflation occur at the same time.

In the rest of this chapter, we will look closely at these two points. First, we will look at why the economy might move along a Phillips curve, as it did during the 1960s. Second, we will look at the puzzle presented by

■ ■ ■ ■ ■
[1] A. W. Phillips, "The Relation between Unemployment and the Rate of Change of Money Wages in the United Kingdom," *Economica*, November 1958, pp. 282–99. For a readable account of the controversies over the Phillips curve (on which this chapter concentrates), see Robert M. Solow, "Down the Phillips Curve with Gun and Camera," in David A. Belsley, et al., eds., *Inflation, Trade and Taxes* (Columbus: Ohio State University Press, 1976), pp. 3–32.
[2] The original Phillips curve showed the rate of change of money wages — rather than inflation — on the vertical axis. Since money wages rise rapidly during periods of high inflation, a similar curve is traced out in either case.

the 1970s and 1980s. Why did things get worse after the 1960s, with higher inflation *and* higher unemployment?

The importance of answering the second question can scarcely be exaggerated. Suppose we cannot figure out what is happening. Suppose the economy does not behave in a predictable manner—it does not move along a predictable aggregate supply curve or Phillips curve in response to a change in aggregate demand. Then the basis for the demand management policies discussed in earlier chapters is undercut. If expansive fiscal and monetary policies are introduced during a recession, can we count on an increase in output? Or will we get more inflation instead? On the other hand, if we apply restraint during an inflationary boom, can we count on a reduction in the rate of inflation? Or will we merely get less output? In other words, demand management policies require *both* a knowledge of how monetary and fiscal policies affect aggregate demand *and* a knowledge of how the economy responds to changes in aggregate demand. Making sense of what has happened since 1970 is, therefore, one of the major tasks of macroeconomic theorists. But, before turning to this central question, we lay the background by looking at the Phillips curve traced out in the 1960s.

THE PHILLIPS CURVE OF THE 1960s

During the 1960s, available empirical evidence — particularly from the United States and Britain — pointed strongly toward the conclusion that increases in aggregate demand move the economy along a smooth, stable Phillips curve. Increases in aggregate demand had an effect partly on output and employment, and partly on prices. And, as the economy moved further and further to the left up the Phillips curve, this curve became steeper and steeper. In other words, each additional increase in demand caused more and more inflation, and a smaller and smaller decline in the unemployment rate. Why might the economy move along such a curve in response to changes in demand?

The Phillips Curve: Theoretical Underpinnings

Consider, first, the position of businesses. When there is large-scale unemployment of the labour force, plant and equipment are also likely to be used at much less than capacity. If demand increases in these circumstances, the primary response of businesses is to increase output rather than prices. An increase in output will allow the fuller utilization of plant and equipment and

result in rising profits. Furthermore, businesses may be skeptical about their ability to make price increases stick. If they raise prices rapidly, their competitors — who also have excess capacity — will be only too eager to capture a larger share of the market.

As the expansion continues and plant and equipment are used more fully, businesses respond differently to an increase in demand. They have less excess capacity. Therefore, as demand increases, they have less opportunity to raise profits by increasing output rapidly. At the same time, they are increasingly in a position to raise prices. Higher prices involve less risk of a loss of markets to competitors, since the competitors are also approaching capacity and are in no position to expand output rapidly to capture additional sales. Furthermore, as the unemployment rate falls, businesses find it harder to hire and keep workers. As the labour market tightens, businesses become increasingly aggressive in their bidding for workers, offering higher wages. As wage rates move upward, the costs of production rise. Businesses respond by raising the prices of their products.

Similarly, labour responds differently to increases in aggregate demand as employment increases. When the unemployment rate is high, the first concern of workers is with jobs. If they are offered work, they are generally quick to take it without too much quibbling over pay. However, as economic expansion continues, the situation gradually changes. Workers become less concerned with getting and keeping a job, and more aggressive in demanding higher pay.

These changing conditions, which affect both business and labour, do not come about suddenly at some well-defined point of full employment. On the contrary, they occur gradually. When demand increases, the economy may consequently move smoothly up a Phillips curve like the colour curve in Figure 15-3, with successive increases in demand being reflected more in terms of inflation, and less in terms of output and employment.

Thus, there were two reasons for policy makers to believe that they faced a well-defined, stable Phillips curve during the 1960s. (1) It seemed plausible from a theoretical viewpoint. (2) It conformed to the facts — most notably, Phillips' historical study, and the unfolding situation in the United States.

The Phillips Curve in Canada

In Canada, the evidence of a well-defined Phillips curve was not as clear-cut as in the United States and Britain. This should not be surprising. With the very important role of international trade in our economy, Canada's rate of price inflation is not influenced only by the prices set by Canadian firms or by the cost of labour in Canada: In addition, our inflation rate also depends on price changes in foreign countries. For example, if Canada is on fixed exchange rates, foreign inflation would quickly lead to rising prices here because the prices of our imports would rise — and this could happen even if Canada had a high rate of unemployment. (The fact that the observations for 1968 and 1969 in Figure 15-3 lie to the right of the other observations during the 1960s can be explained in this way. During 1968/69, Canada was on fixed exchange rates, and inflation in the United States was relatively high.) Nevertheless, as Figure 15-3 shows, the data for *most* of the 1960s pointed to a fairly stable Phillips curve in Canada as well. Statistical studies confirmed this: After allowing for the influence of foreign price increases on Canadian inflation, there was still a strong tendency for low unemployment rates to go with high rates of price inflation.

The Policy Dilemma of the 1960s: The Trade-off between Inflation and Unemployment

This belief by policy makers — that they faced a well-defined Phillips curve — presented them with a *policy dilemma*. By adjusting aggregate demand policies, they could move the economy along the Phillips curve. But what point should they try to pick? A point like *G* in Figure 15-4, with low inflation and a high rate of unemployment? Or a point like *H*, with low unemployment but a somewhat higher rate of inflation? Or some point in between? Facing a *trade-off* between the goals of high unemployment and price stability, what relative importance should they attach to the two objectives?

Faced with this dilemma, the response of both the Canadian and U.S. governments was to emphasize the objective of high employment. After all, unemployment represents a clear and unambiguous loss to the economy, whereas the costs of inflation are much more difficult to identify. In the United States, the decision was gradually made to pursue an expansionary policy. The policy was successful — in the latter half of the 1960s, U.S. unemployment averaged well below 4%.

In Canada, during the first half of the 1960s, the unemployment rate also fell rapidly to less than 4%. One important reason for this was the decision in 1962 to peg the Canadian dollar at the relatively low value of U.S.$0.925; this action increased aggregate demand by stimulating exports and discouraging imports. Another

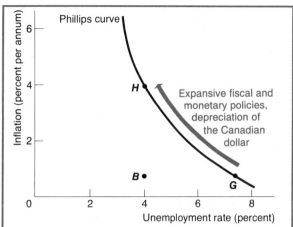

Figure 15-4   The problem of the sixties: The inflation-unemployment trade-off.
The Phillips curve presents policy makers with a dilemma. By adjusting aggregate demand, they can choose a point on the Phillips curve. But what point should they choose? *G* provides a low rate of inflation but high unemployment. *H* provides high employment but at the cost of substantial inflation.

important factor was the sizeable government deficits during the early 1960s.

As the data in Figure 15-3 show, the reduction in unemployment was accompanied by an increase in the inflation rate: The economy moved from a point such as *G* in Figure 15-4 in 1961, to a point like *H*, with 4% unemployment *and* 4% inflation by 1966. But, by the standards of the 1970s and 1980, 4% is not a very high rate of inflation. By and large, it still seemed possible to attain a fairly low rate of unemployment without much inflation.

However, by 1968/69, there were signs that trouble was ahead. In those years, under the restrictive influence of a rising government budget surplus and sluggish monetary expansion, unemployment rose considerably. But, in spite of this, the rate of inflation did not come down. Thus, as the 1970s began, the prospect of avoiding inflation without a high cost in the form of unemployment suddenly appeared much less bright.

THE RECORD SINCE 1970: HIGHER INFLATION AND HIGHER UNEMPLOYMENT

In comparison with the 1960s, the performance of the economy during the 15 or so years after 1970 was extremely disappointing. During that period, we had the worst of both worlds. High rates of unemployment and inflation occurred simultaneously. What went wrong? Two principal explanations have been offered.

Cost-push vs. Demand-pull Inflation

> The age of Keynesian economics is over; the macroeconomic revolution in fiscal and monetary management we owe to Keynes has run afoul of the microeconomic revolution in trade union and corporate power.
>
> John Kenneth Galbraith

The first explanation involves the distinction between *demand-pull* and *cost-push* inflation. This distinction can be illustrated most easily with the simple aggregate demand and aggregate supply curves in Figure 15-5. The left panel shows what happens when aggregate demand increases — that is, when the aggregate demand curve shifts to the right. Output increases, and unemployment declines. But the rising demand also pulls up prices. The economy moves upward to the right, from *G* to *H*. This is the typical inflation — rising prices are accompanied by rising output. (It can also be illustrated with a Phillips curve diagram. Rising demand causes a movement upward to the left along a Phillips curve. The increase in demand causes a decrease in the unemployment rate, but a rise in inflation.)

Demand-pull inflation occurs when demand is rising rapidly. Buyers bid eagerly for goods and services, "pulling up" their prices.

Now suppose that strong labour unions and monopolistic companies have the power to influence wages and prices. Even during a period of slack in the economy, when the demand for labour is low and the unemployment rate is high, a strong union may be able to use the threat of a strike to negotiate higher wages. Furthermore, a firm with few competitors may raise its prices even though demand is sluggish. If this firm is producing basic materials, parts, or other intermediate goods, its higher prices will push up the costs of other companies using its products. Businesses with higher costs of labour and material inputs may pass them along to the consumer in the form of higher prices. In other words, there is *cost-push* inflation.

Cost-push or *supply-side* inflation occurs when wages or other costs rise and these costs are passed along in the form of higher prices. Prices are "pushed up" by rising costs. Cost-push inflation is sometimes known as *market power* inflation.

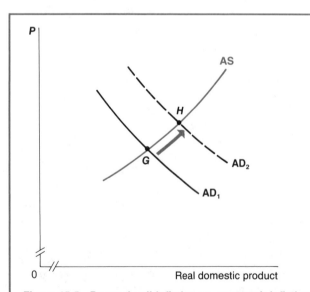

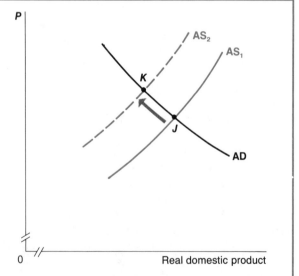

Figure 15-5   Demand-pull inflation vs. cost-push inflation.
(a) Demand-pull inflation. When the demand curve shifts upward, higher prices are accompanied by an increase in output.

(b) Cost-push inflation. When the supply curve shifts upward, higher prices are accompanied by a decrease in output.

This possibility is illustrated in the right-hand panel of Figure 15-5. As costs rise, the aggregate supply curve shifts upward, from AS₁ to AS₂. As the economy moves from *J* to *K*, rising prices are accompanied by a *decline* in output and a rise in the unemployment rate.

As far back as the late 1950s, cost push was used to explain why inflation and unemployment were both increasing. This early round in the cost-push debate was heated. In particular, it invited a search for culprits. Business executives blamed inflation on the aggressive and "irresponsible" bargaining of labour unions for higher wages that had forced businesses — so they claimed—to pass along their higher labour costs in terms of higher prices. On the other hand, labour blamed powerful corporations for pushing up prices in their greed for "fantastic profits."

Oil

While labour and management blamed each other for cost-push inflation during the late 1950s, one cost-push culprit stood out in the 1970s: the Organization of Petroleum Exporting Countries (OPEC). In a brief period during 1973 and 1974, OPEC doubled and then redoubled the prices which importers had to pay for oil. In 1979/80, oil prices more than doubled again.

Because of the importance of oil as a source of power for industry, as a fuel for our transportation system, and as a source of heat for our homes and factories, the skyrocketing price of oil had a powerful effect on all oil-importing countries — including the United States which still had to import roughly half the oil used. (Japan was perhaps the hardest hit of all, because practically all of its oil must be imported.)

Canada was not as badly hurt as the large oil importers. Although we had to pay more in the world market for the oil we import into the Eastern provinces, we also received higher prices for the oil, natural gas, and electricity we exported. Furthermore, the government's policy in 1973/74 was to keep the domestic Canadian oil price well below the world price.

However, indirectly the cost-push pressure of higher oil prices spilled over into Canada as well. Because prices rose in countries such as the United States and Japan, the prices of goods imported into Canada from these countries rose rapidly. Rising prices of imported goods contributes to inflation both directly (as people have to pay more for imported consumer goods) and indirectly (as businesses pass on the higher cost of imported inputs in

the form of higher prices for the goods they produce).[3] In response to this international *supply shock*, inflation soared into the "double digit" range—that is, above 10% per year—in 1974, 1975, and again in 1980–82.

> A *supply shock* is a sudden, unexpected change in the price or availability of inputs that can push up costs and shift the aggregate supply curve upward.

The cost-push idea can be illustrated by an upward shift of the aggregate supply curve in Figure 15-5(*b*), or, alternatively, by an upward shift of the Phillips curve from PC₁ to PC₂ in Figure 15-6. Earlier, we saw that even a stable Phillips curve—such as PC₁ in Figure 15-6 — presents the authorities with a dilemma. They can choose low inflation, but this will mean high unemployment (at point *G*). Alternatively, they can choose low

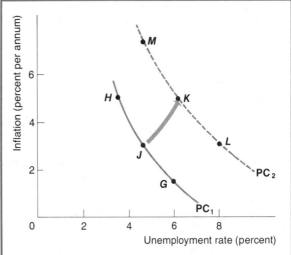

Figure 15-6   Cost-push inflation: The policy problem.
Cost-push shifts the Phillips curve upward, from PC₁ to PC₂. If demand is restrained in order to fight inflation, the unemployment rate will increase from *J* to *L*. If demand is expanded in order to keep the unemployment rate from rising, the rate of inflation will increase from *J* to *M*.

■ ■ ■ ■ ■
[3] As we saw in Chapter 14, rising prices of foreign goods need not cause inflationary pressure in Canada if the Canadian dollar is allowed to appreciate. However, while there was some appreciation of the Canadian dollar relative to the U.S. dollar in 1974, it was not nearly enough to offset the effects of the increasing world price levels. During 1979 to 1981, the effects of rising world prices were reinforced by a *depreciation* of the Canadian dollar.

unemployment, but this will mean high inflation (at point *H*). Or they can pick an intermediate point, such as *J*. Observe how much more difficult the situation becomes when cost-push forces are strong, and the Phillips curve shifts upward. If the authorities keep aggregate demand stable, both unemployment and inflation will increase, as illustrated by the move from *J* to *K*. If they decide to prevent any increase in inflation, regardless of the cost, they will have to restrain aggregate demand. The result will be a move from *J* to *L*. While inflation will be no higher at *L* than it was at *J*, there will be a large increase in unemployment. On the other hand, if the authorities aim at preventing any increase in unemployment, they will stimulate aggregate demand, and the rate of inflation will go even higher as the economy moves to *M*.

In Canada, the international cost-push pressures in 1973/74 and 1979/80 showed up primarily in terms of inflation. On the first occasion, there was some increase in the unemployment rate—from 5.5% in 1973 to 6.9% in 1975—but the increase in the inflation rate was substantially larger, from 7.7% in 1973 to 10.8% in 1975. During 1979–81, unemployment stayed almost constant at about 7.5%, and the cost-push forces were reflected almost exclusively in prices—inflation rose from 9.2% in 1979 to 12.5% in 1981.

In summary, this first explanation of stagflation depends on disturbances from the cost side. The Phillips curve can be shifted up by aggressive wage and pricing activities by unions and businesses, or by shocks from abroad, such as increases in the prices of imported goods. When such a shift occurs, the economy is likely to suffer an increase in inflation (the move from *J* to *M*) and perhaps also in unemployment (*J* to *K*).

PRICE EXPECTATIONS AND THE WAGE-PRICE SPIRAL: THE ACCELERATIONIST ARGUMENT

The second explanation of simultaneous high rates of inflation and unemployment goes further, throwing into question the whole concept of a permanent curve such as the one discovered by Phillips. According to this line of argument, the Phillips curve is inherently unstable. *It shifts whenever people's expectations of inflation change.* In particular, it shifts upward as inflation gathers momentum. If the managers of monetary and fiscal policies aim for a low rate of unemployment, inflation will accelerate to higher and higher rates. Hence, this is known as the *accelerationist* argument.

The easiest way to explain this argument is to assume initially that prices have been stable for a long period of time. On the basis of past experience, they are expected to remain stable into the indefinite future. The economy rests at a stable equilibrium at *G* on the initial Phillips curve (Figure 15-7), where the inflation rate is zero.

Now suppose that the government decides that the unemployment rate at *G* is unacceptable. Expansive fiscal and monetary policies are introduced in order to increase aggregate demand and reduce the unemployment rate to a target of U_T.

What happens? To meet the higher demand, producers need more workers. Job vacancies increase, and those looking for jobs get them easily and quickly. Production increases and unemployment falls. In the face

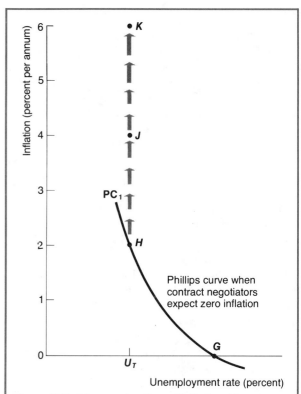

Figure 15-7   The acceleration of inflation: The wage-price spiral.

If demand is continuously increased by whatever amount is necessary to maintain the low target rate of unemployment U_T, the result is an ever-increasing rate of inflation. The economy moves successively to points *H*, *J*, *K*, and higher. The original Phillips curve PC₁ shows how the economy responds to changes in aggregate demand during the short-run period *when the initial wage contracts remain in force.*

of higher demand, producers gradually begin to raise prices. But in the early stages of inflation, little change takes place in money wages. Most collective bargaining contracts are for three years, and union wages change only slowly as a result. Non-union wages are also sticky. People may work on individual contracts that run for one year or more. Even where there is no written contract, it is customary to review wages only periodically — say, once a year. Thus, the initial reaction to the increase in demand is a relatively large increase in output, only a moderate increase in prices, and an even smaller increase in wages. The economy moves along the Phillips curve to point *H* (Figure 15-7).

However, *point H is not stable*. The initial Phillips curve (PC$_1$) reflects wage contracts *that were negotiated on the assumption of stable prices*. But prices are no longer stable, and the contracts do not last forever. As new contract negotiations begin, workers observe that their real wages — the amount of goods and services their wages will buy — have been eroded by inflation. They demand a cost-of-living catch-up. So long as aggregate demand rises rapidly enough to keep the economy operating at full blast, the unions are in a good position to get their demands. With booming markets, employers capitulate to strike threats. Non-union employees are likewise granted raises to keep them from quitting to look for more highly paid work.

Because demand is high and rising, businesses can easily pass along the higher wages in the form of higher prices, and they do so. The rate of inflation accelerates; the economy moves to point *J*, above the original Phillips curve. But, with a higher rate of inflation, workers find that once again they have been cheated by inflation; once again their real wages are less than expected. At the next round of wage negotiations, they demand a larger cost-of-living catch up. The **wage-price spiral** gathers momentum. So long as demand is expanded enough to keep unemployment at the low target rate of *U$_T$*, inflation will *continue to accelerate*, from *H* to *J* to *K*, and so on.

Thus, the Phillips curve gives the wrong impression. It creates the illusion that there is a simple trade-off between inflation and unemployment, that a low rate of unemployment can be "bought" with a moderate, steady rate of inflation. But, in fact, the cost of trying to achieve a low rate of unemployment is much more serious: *an ever-accelerating rate of inflation*. Wages and prices spiral upward, with higher prices leading to higher and higher wage demands, and higher wages being passed along in the form of higher and higher prices.

Limiting the Rate of Inflation

An ever-accelerating rate of inflation is intolerable. If prices rise faster and faster, sooner or later the whole monetary system will break down and the economy will revert to an inefficient barter system. (The rate required for a complete breakdown is very high indeed — thousands of percent per annum. Nevertheless, severe disruptions may be caused even by rates of inflation of 10% or 20%.) At some time, therefore, the monetary and fiscal policy makers will decide to draw the line; they will refuse to increase aggregate demand without limit.

To keep this illustration simple, assume that (1) the monetary and fiscal line is drawn sooner rather than later, and (2) aggregate demand policies can be adjusted quickly and precisely. As soon as the economy gets to point *H*, the government recognizes the danger of an ever-accelerating inflation. It therefore switches aggregate demand policies. Instead of increasing aggregate demand by whatever amount is necessary to maintain a low target rate of unemployment, the authorities limit aggregate demand to whatever degree is necessary to prevent inflation from rising above the 2% reached at *H*. In other words, the authorities *change the policy target*. Their objective is no longer to keep the unemployment rate low at *U$_T$*, but instead to keep inflation from rising above the 2% target level *I$_T$* (Figure 15-8).

What happens? Workers still push for higher wages because the 2% rate of inflation is still eroding their

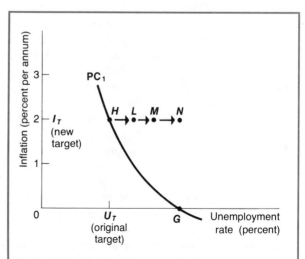

Figure 15-8 Limiting the rate of inflation.
If the policy makers switch targets, limiting demand to prevent inflation greater than *I$_T$*, then the economy will begin to move to the right.

purchasing power. But employers are now in a bind. They cannot easily pass along higher wages because of the restraint on demand. Furthermore, the restraint on demand means that output begins to fall and unemployment rises. The economy moves to the right. The question is: How far?

The Vertical Long-run Phillips Curve

If demand is restrained to keep inflation permanently at a rate of 2%, where will the ultimate equilibrium be in Figure 15-8? At *L*? At *M*? Further to the right? There are reasons to believe that the economy will stop at *N*, directly above the original equilibrium *G*.

To see why, let us go back to the initial point, *G*. This represented a stable equilibrium. It was the result of an extended experience with a zero rate of inflation. Both businesses and labour had a chance to adjust completely to the stable price level. If they now get a chance to adjust completely to a 2% rate of inflation—and this may take some time — then the new equilibrium should be at *N*, where both labour and business are in the same *real* position as at *G*. At *G*, prices were stable. Now, at *N*, prices are rising by 2%. However, workers are just as well off as at *G* because they are receiving enough additional money income to compensate for the inflation. Their *real* wage is unaffected by the inflation. Consequently, they should be neither more nor less eager to work. Businesses are also in the same real situation at *N* as at *G*. They pay 2% more for labour and for material inputs each year than they would have paid at *G*, but they are compensated by the average increase of 2% in their prices. Their profits are the same in real terms. Therefore, they should hire the same number of workers at *N* as they did at *G*. Thus, *N* lies directly above *G*, and the unemployment rate is the same at *N* as at *G*.

With a steady 2% rate of inflation, the economy moves eventually to *N*, where the unemployment rate, real wages, and real profits are the same as at *G*. Alternatively, if the rate of inflation rises to 4% before monetary and fiscal policy makers draw the line to prevent more rapid inflation, the economy eventually moves to *R* (Figure 15-9); or with a steady 6% rate of inflation, to *T*. All these are points of stable equilibrium. In each case, people have adjusted completely to the prevailing rate of inflation. (In contrast, point *H* was unstable because workers had not yet had a chance to renegotiate their wages to reflect the new inflation.)

In other words, the points of long-run equilibrium trace out a vertical line; the ***long-run Phillips curve*** (*PC$_L$*)

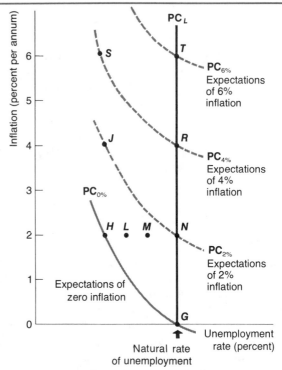

Figure 15-9   The vertical long-run Phillips curve.
The economy gravitates toward the vertical long-run Phillips curve (PC$_L$) as the negotiators of wages and other contracts adjust to the prevailing rate of inflation. There is no long-run trade-off between unemployment and inflation.

However, the short-run Phillips curve is *not* vertical. For example, once contracts have adjusted completely to a 4% rate of inflation at *R*, then an unexpected disturbance in aggregate demand will cause the economy to move along the short-run Phillips curve (PC$_{4\%}$) running through *R*. Thus, a spurt in demand will cause an increase in output, a fall in unemployment, and an increase in inflation as the economy moves from *R* to *S*.

is *perfectly vertical. In the long run, there is no trade-off* between inflation and unemployment. By accepting more inflation, we cannot *permanently* achieve a lower rate of unemployment. Expansive demand policies cause a lower rate of unemployment *only during a temporary period of disequilibrium* — at *H*, for example. During the temporary disequilibrium, workers and others are committed to contracts they would not have accepted if they had correctly anticipated the rate of inflation. As people have time to adjust, unemployment gravitates toward the equilibrium or ***natural rate***.

The *long-run Phillips curve* is the curve (or line) traced out by the possible points of long-run equilibrium; that is, the points where people have adjusted completely to the prevailing rate of inflation. At such points, actual inflation is the same as expected inflation.

The *natural rate of unemployment* is the equilibrium rate that exists when people have adjusted completely to the prevailing rate of inflation. Alternatively, it may be defined as the equilibrium rate that exists when the public gets the inflation rate it expects.

Through each of the long-run equilibrium points — such as *N, R,* or *T* in Figure 15-9 — there is a *short-run Phillips curve*, each reflecting contracts based on the prevailing rate of inflation. For example, the short-run Phillips curve ($PC_{4\%}$) running through *R* is based on the expectation by contract negotiators that there will be a continuing rate of inflation of 4% per year. Suppose that after a number of years at *R*, the authorities adjust monetary and fiscal policies to make aggregate demand grow more rapidly. Faced with a high demand, businesses increase output, hire more workers, and begin to raise prices by more than 4% per annum. Their profits temporarily shoot up because workers are committed to the old labour contracts based on expectations of 4% inflation. The economy moves along the short-run Phillips curve $PC_{4\%}$ to a point such as *S*, with a low rate of unemployment.

But *S* is unstable for the same reason that *H* was unstable. Point *S* results from wage contracts that were agreed to when inflation was expected to be 4%. But actual inflation is 6%. Therefore, contracts will be adjusted during the next round of negotiations. When wage contracts are adjusted upward, an accelerating wage-price spiral will result if the authorities continue to follow expansive aggregate demand policies. Alternatively, if demand managers take steps to prevent any further increase in inflation, the economy will move to the right, back toward the long-run Phillips curve and the natural rate of unemployment at *T*.

The *accelerationist* theory includes the following propositions:
1. The long-run Phillips curve is vertical. There is an equilibrium or "natural" rate of unemployment which is independent of the rate of inflation.
2. If demand is stimulated by however much is needed to keep the unemployment rate below the natural rate, the result will be a continuous acceleration of inflation.

Because of point 1, the accelerationist theory is also known as the *natural rate hypothesis*.

Note that there is a similarity between this accelerationist or natural rate theory and the earlier explanation of inflation based on cost push. In each case, the Phillips curve shifts upward and, in each case, higher wage contracts can play an important role in the shift. But here the similarity stops. While cost-push theorists see higher wages as a major *cause* of inflation, accelerationists believe that wage and price increases are *both* the result of a *single* underlying cause: excess demand. The government should not go looking for culprits in the form of powerful unions or powerful businesses or OPEC. Rather, the culprit is right in Ottawa: the government itself (including the Bank of Canada), which has generated the inflationary demand in the first place with excessively expansionary policies.

The vertical long-run Phillips curve brings us back to the view of classical quantity theorists. *In the long run*, changes in aggregate demand affect prices (*P*) and not the quantity of output (*Q*) or employment. Thus, the vertical long-run Phillips curve turns out to be the same as the vertical aggregate supply curve of classical economics (originally shown in Figure 8-2), but in another guise.

Because we are brought back to the classical view, it is not surprising that the case for the vertical long-run Phillips curve — together with other aspects of the accelerationist argument — came from the pen of one of the leading monetarists, Milton Friedman. (Another early proponent was Edmund Phelps of Columbia University.)[4] Friedman wrote, "There is *always* a *temporary tradeoff* between inflation and unemployment; there is *no permanent tradeoff.*" The short-run Phillips curve slopes downward to the right; the long-run Phillips curve is vertical. A steady long-run increase in aggregate demand will lead to the same rate of unemployment — namely, the natural rate — whether demand is being increased by 4% per year or 14%. The only difference will be in the rate of inflation, not in output and employment.

During the 1970s, the idea of a vertical long-run Phillips curve became widely accepted by those in the

■ ■ ■ ■ ■
4 Milton Friedman, "The Role of Monetary Policy," *American Economic Review*, March 1968, pp. 1-17; and Edmund S. Phelps, "Phillips Curves, Expectations of Inflation and Optimal Unemployment over Time," *Economica*, August 1967, pp. 254–81.

Keynesian and classical traditions alike. Now, it would be difficult to find any economist who believes that the original, curved Phillips curve represents a stable, long-run relationship. By 1975, economist Arthur Okun was willing to concede on behalf of the original Phillips curve school: ''We are all accelerationists now.''[5]

THE PROBLEM OF UNWINDING INFLATIONARY EXPECTATIONS

The short-run Phillips curve represents another trap for policy makers. Those who decide on monetary and fiscal policies may think that they can achieve low rates of unemployment to the left of the long-run Phillips curve by expansive demand policies. In fact, they will be able to maintain such a low rate of unemployment only if they allow inflation to spiral higher and higher.

Furthermore, the problem is even worse than that. Once inflation becomes engrained in negotiators' expectations, it can be eliminated with demand-management policies only at the cost of a high rate of unemployment, to the right of the long-run Phillips curve.

This is illustrated in Figure 15-10. Suppose that the economy has reached point T, with inflation consistently running at 6% year after year. This point is stable; inflation will neither rise nor fall, and the unemployment rate will remain steady. Now, suppose that policy makers decide that an inflation rate of 6% is too high. They are determined to reduce it by restrictive monetary and fiscal policies.

As aggregate demand is restrained, businesses find their sales falling. Production is cut back and workers are laid off. The unemployment rate rises. Because of intensifying competitive pressures as businesses scramble to make sales, businesses no longer insist on such high price increases and the rate of inflation begins to slacken off. However, this does not happen quickly.

■ ■ ■ ■ ■

[5] Okun, ''Inflation: Its Mechanics and Welfare Costs,'' *Brookings Papers on Economic Activity* 2:1975, p. 356. Okun was paraphrasing an earlier concession of Friedman: ''In one sense, we are all Keynesians now.'' (Friedman had, however, tacked on the qualification that ''in another [sense] no one is a Keynesian any longer.'' From Milton Friedman, *Dollars and Deficits* (Englewood Cliffs, N. J.: Prentice Hall, 1968), p. 15.)
   Okun pointed out that the data fit a Phillips curve ''like a glove'' during the 1960s. However, he observed that, since 1970, ''the Phillips curve has become an unidentified flying object.''

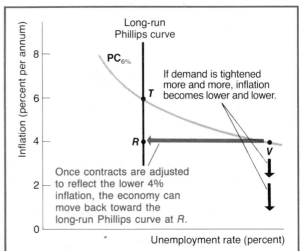

Figure 15-10   High unemployment while inflation is being unwound.

Once inflation becomes built into contracts, it is painful to unwind. The short-run Phillips curve shown here reflects contracts based on the expectation of 6% inflation. It takes a period of high unemployment at V before wage contracts are adjusted downward.

Businesses are still committed to pay the hefty wage increases under the old labour contracts; their costs continue to rise even though demand is slack. As a result, the short-run effect of the restrained demand shows up most strongly in a fall in output and a rise in unemployment, and only to a limited extent in lower inflation. The economy moves to point V.

Because point V is off the long-run Phillips curve, it is unstable. It is on the short-run Phillips curve running through point T, reflecting wage contracts negotiated on the expectation that inflation would continue at 6% per year. But actual inflation is now only 4%. Because of the lower inflation rate, workers are willing to settle for more moderate wage increases at the next round of wage negotiations. This willingness is reinforced by their desire to protect their jobs during a period of high unemployment. Furthermore, employers take a strong bargaining stance because of disappointing sales and low profits.

When wage settlements become more moderate, the economy moves from point V. If monetary and fiscal policies are kept tight, the rate of inflation will continue to drop. The economy will move down from V to progressively lower points. The argument here is similar to that in Figure 15-7, except that everything is operating in the opposite direction. (A complication is explained in Box 15-1.)

Box 15-1

■ ■

The Natural Rate Theory and the Great Depression

The accelerationist or natural rate theory is accepted by most economists as a framework for explaining changes in inflation and unemployment during the past four decades. But an important warning is necessary. Not all available evidence supports the natural rate theory. In particular, the behaviour of the economy during the Great Depression is flatly inconsistent with it.

To see why, consider Figure 15-10 in more detail. If demand remains weak once the economy reaches point *V*, then inflation will be lower and lower each succeeding period. Facing slack demand, firms will be in a poor position to raise prices, and workers will agree to smaller increases in nominal wages. The rate of inflation will fall from 4% to 2% to zero. But that should not be the end of it. If demand remains weak, prices should begin to *fall*; firms are under pressure to cut prices to increase their lagging sales. The result should be an accelerating *deflation* — with prices falling at 2%, then 4%, and so on, for as long as demand remains depressed and unemployment remains greater than the natural rate. Whenever the rate of inflation or deflation stabilizes, unemployment should move back toward the equilibrium or natural rate. So says the theory.

However, things didn't happen that way in the 1930s. It is true that prices did fall during the early

Courtesy of Miller Comstock Inc.

years of the Depression, between 1930 and 1933. But the deflation didn't accelerate, as predicted by the theory. Rather, prices rose at a moderate, stable rate between 1934 and 1937 even though unemployment rates remained between 10% and 20% — far greater than any reasonable estimate of the natural rate.

Thus, the natural rate theory that is useful in explaining periods of inflation was apparently not valid during the Great Depression, when prices fell. Let us hope that this point will be of historical interest only; let us hope that there will be no future depression to test the validity of the natural rate theory during a period of deflation.

On the other hand, if monetary and fiscal restraint is eased as the economy reaches 4% inflation, sales will begin to revive, the unemployment rate will fall, and the economy will move back toward the long-run Phillips curve at point *R*. This argument corresponds to the earlier one in Figure 15-8, again operating in the opposite direction.

This theory provides another possible explanation for the simultaneous high rates of unemployment and inflation in the period from 1974 to 1981 (as an alternative to the explanation based on the cost-push forces arising in the international oil market). During the late 1960s and early 1970s, aggregate demand was overstimulated, and inflation was allowed to gather steam. Then, as inflation became more and more of a concern to the

government and the Bank of Canada, the Bank followed the example of the U.S. Federal Reserve and in 1980 moved to a very tight monetary policy. The result of the sharp contraction in aggregate demand was the deep recession in 1981/82. By 1984, inflation had finally been "wrestled to the ground" (in the words of former Prime Minister Pierre Trudeau), but at a very high cost: an unemployment rate that remained above 10% for over three years.

Because the unemployment cost can be so high if inflation is hammered out of the economy in this way, governments have searched for other policies to supplement tight aggregate demand, and thus make the transition to a lower rate of inflation less painful. These policies are the subject matter of Chapter 19.

KEY POINTS

1. Data for most of the 1960s trace out a *Phillips curve*. Observations since 1968/69 are above and to the right of this curve.

2. Since 1970, a high rate of unemployment and a high rate of inflation have sometimes occurred at the same time. This means that the economy is no longer on the Phillips curve of the 1960s; the (short-run) Phillips curve has shifted upward.

3. There are two major explanations for the upward shift of the short-run Phillips curve:
   (a) higher oil prices have created cost-push pressures.
   (b) people have responded to a higher rate of inflation by negotiating higher wages, causing the short-run Phillips curve to shift upward.

4. The short-run Phillips curve is unstable. There is a different curve for every expected rate of inflation.

5. In the short run, there is a *trade-off* between inflation and unemployment. Expansive aggregate demand policies lead to less unemployment but more inflation. Restrictive aggregate demand policies lead to less inflation but more unemployment.

6. Natural rate theorists argue that people adjust completely to a steady, expected rate of inflation. As they adjust, unemployment moves to its equilibrium or *natural* rate.

7. As a consequence, the long-run Phillips curve is a vertical straight line. There is *no long-run trade-off* between inflation and unemployment. Even if policy makers are willing to accept inflation, they cannot permanently keep the unemployment rate below its natural rate.

KEY CONCEPTS

Phillips curve
stagflation
policy dilemma
*the trade-off between inflation
    and unemployment*

demand-pull inflation
cost-push inflation
*exchange rates and the Phillips
    curve*
supply shock

accelerationist theory
wage-price spiral
long-run Phillips curve
*natural, or equilibrium, rate of
    unemployment*

PROBLEMS

15-1. Why might expansive demand policies aimed at a low rate of unemployment cause a wage-price spiral, with an ever-accelerating rate of inflation?

15-2. For each of the following statements, state whether you agree or disagree, and explain why. If the statement is incorrect, fix it.
   (a) On each short-run Phillips curve, there is one and only one stable point, namely, the point at which the short-run Phillips curve intersects the long-run Phillips curve.
   (b) According to accelerationist or natural-rate theory, the rate of unemployment will be less than the natural rate whenever inflation is less than the expected rate, and it will be greater than the natural rate whenever inflation is greater than the expected rate.
   (c) According to accelerationist or natural-rate

theory, there is no trade-off between the objectives of high employment and stable prices in the short run. Such a trade-off occurs only in the long run, after the economy has had a chance to adjust to the prevailing rate of inflation.
   (d) Short-run fluctuations in aggregate demand can affect prices, output, and employment. But long-run trends in aggregate demand are unimportant; they do not affect prices, output, or employment.

15-3. When prices rise more than wages, what generally happens to profits? What is likely to happen to output and unemployment as a result?

15-4. Now, suppose that prices rise more than wages as a result of a rise in the price of imported oil. How would your answers to question 15-3 be modified?

*15-5. If the Phillips curve—such as that shown in colour in Figure 15-3—is stable only in the short run, how was it possible for Phillips to find a curve for Britain that was stable for almost a full century?

*15-6. In the text it was explained how a depreciation of the Canadian dollar would make it hard to control inflation because it would tend to make import prices rise.

A depreciation of the Canadian dollar also tends to increase the prices received by Canadian *exporters* for the goods they sell in foreign markets. Explain what effect (if any) that this tendency might have on Canadian inflation.

Chapter 16

■ ■

How Does Inflation Cause Problems?

*Inflation is the time when those who have
saved for a rainy day get soaked.*

Inflation ranks with unemployment as one of the two major macroeconomic diseases. Every trip to the car dealer or the department store is a nagging reminder of how much the value of the dollar has shrunk.

Only a few decades ago, inflation was considered a problem of secondary importance — and with good reason. It is true that there had been an inflationary burst in the 1940s and early 1950s, associated with the Second World War and the conflict in Korea. But, following the end of the Korean war in 1953, the price level remained quite stable for more than a decade. In 1965, prices on average were only 18% higher than in 1953, reflecting an average rate of inflation of less than 2% per year.

Furthermore, from a longer historical viewpoint, rapid inflation had been an exceptional disease associated with war, as Figure 16-1 illustrates. During wars, the governments typically resort to the printing press, creating money to help finance their military expenditures. As a consequence, prices shoot upward. (During the U.S. Revolutionary War, the quip ''not worth a continental'' reflected the sharp decline in the value of the currency issued by the new ''continental'' government of the United States.) During peacetime periods, in contrast, there had been no strong upward trend of prices. In 1914, the average level of prices in Canada was no higher than at the turn of the century. On the eve of the Second World

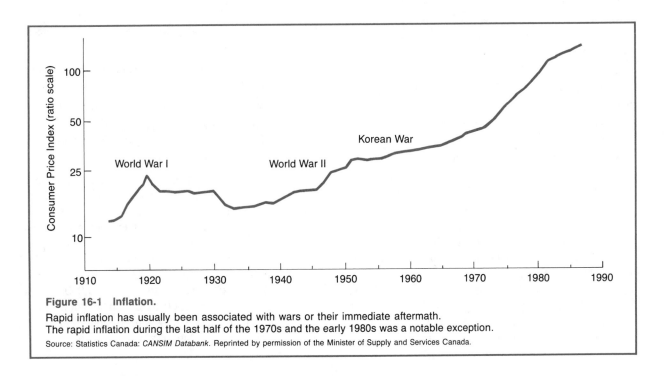

Figure 16-1   Inflation.
Rapid inflation has usually been associated with wars or their immediate aftermath.
The rapid inflation during the last half of the 1970s and the early 1980s was a notable exception.
Source: Statistics Canada: *CANSIM Databank*. Reprinted by permission of the Minister of Supply and Services Canada.

War in the late 1930s, the average level of prices was *below* the peak of 1920.

In the 1970s, a fundamental change took place. The rapid inflation of the period from 1973 to 1981 was new; it cannot be attributed to military spending. Like Canada, a number of other industrialized countries—such as Britain and the United States — also suffered high rates of inflation in spite of extended peace. It is true that since 1982, inflation has been lower—in the 4% to 6% range. But our willingness to look on this rate of inflation as a success shows just how much our attitudes have changed. A few decades ago, inflation of 4% would have been considered very high indeed. In the late 1960s and early 1970s, the government became so concerned with an inflation rate of about 5% that it considered following the U.S. example by imposing wage and price controls.

In this chapter, we will study the problems created by inflation. Specifically, we will:

■ See how *unexpected* inflation can cause capricious shifts in income and wealth among various segments of the population.

■ See how losers can take steps to protect themselves when inflation is *expected*. Thus, we will confirm the conclusion of Chapter 7, that *expected* or *anticipated* inflation has smaller effects than does *unexpected* or *unanticipated* inflation.

■ See why inflation can nevertheless have substantial, continuing effects even when it is anticipated. Taxes are one reason.

■ See that *when inflation is rapid*, it tends to be *highly variable* from year to year. Consequently, it is hard to anticipate what the inflation rate will be when it is rapid. As a result, a rapid inflation can have serious consequences.

■ Study the effects of high inflation on the government's budget, and see why it becomes so *difficult to figure out the best macroeconomic policies* during periods of rapid and changing inflation.

In this chapter, a recurring theme will be the effects of inflation on the cost of buying a home. The importance of housing scarcely needs to be emphasized. In the late 1980s, the average household spent close to 20% of its income on housing. The largest asset that the typical family acquires is its home, and paying off the mortgage rivals the pension fund as the most important way to save. The housing market is particularly significant for university students; many will be buying their first homes in the next decade. Because of inflation, it will be more difficult to do so, for reasons that will be explained in this chapter.

UNEXPECTED INFLATION: WHO LOSES AND WHO GAINS?

Inflation gives people a feeling that they have no basis for planning, no sense of fairness and justice.
                                                    Arthur Okun

The costs of inflation are much less clear than the costs of unemployment. That may seem surprising, as people are almost unanimous in expressing dislike of inflation. But, in any transaction, there is a buyer and a seller. When a price rises, the buyer loses but the seller gains. Thus, the analysis of inflation is quite different from the study of unemployment. Unemployment represents an obvious loss; fewer goods and services are produced. However, inflation creates both losers *and* gainers.

Losers

During inflation, money loses its value. Thus, the losers are those whose income or receipts are stable in money terms. These include:

■ people who are working for a wage or salary that is fixed in dollar terms

■ any business that has undertaken to deliver goods or services in the future at fixed prices

■ retirees who receive pensions fixed in dollar terms

■ those who have bought bonds or have loaned money in other ways. (They eventually will be paid back in dollars that are worth less.)

Consider the individual who purchased in 1965 a $10,000 government bond that came due in 1990. In addition to interest of 5% per annum, the bond purchaser expected to get $10,000 back when the bond reached maturity. In a formal sense, that expectation was fulfilled: The government did pay the bondholder $10,000 in 1990. But that $10,000 represented a pale shadow of its original value. In 1990, $10,000 bought no more goods and services than $2,200 bought in 1965. In 25 years, money had lost 78% of its value. For bondholders, unexpected inflation is bad news.

Some people might say that this doesn't matter much because only wealthy people own bonds. But this is not so. Many elderly people of moderate means hold bonds or savings accounts, whose purchasing power also declines as a result of inflation. (During the rapid inflation in 1979/1980, many elderly people with bonds became angry as they saw the real value of their assets diminish rapidly. In the United States, an organization [the Gray Panthers] that represents the elderly became incensed when the government continued to advertise U.S. savings bonds as ''the one sure way to make your dreams come true.'' Instead, said the Panthers, savings bonds should be advertised as a ''way to save dough that runs right through your fingers.'')

The elderly are also hard-hit by unexpected inflation in another way: They have saved through private pension funds which, in turn, hold bonds. With inflation, pensions financed by these bonds provide less real income for retirees. For the private pension system, the unexpected acceleration of inflation during the 1970s was a calamity. (However, Old Age Security benefits and other *government* pensions have been adjusted upward to compensate for inflation.)

Winners

While almost everyone understands that some people lose from unexpected inflation, it is not as well understood that other people win. Businesses that employ workers at stable wages will win if the prices of what they sell rise more rapidly than their costs.

Just as bondholders and other lenders lose from unanticipated inflation, so bond issuers and other borrowers win. When $10,000 is repaid after a period of rapid inflation, we have seen how the lender is worse off. He or she is repaid in dollars whose value has declined. For exactly the same reason, the borrower is better off. He or she repays the debt with dollars that have decreased in value.

Among the big winners are people who borrowed money to buy homes in the early 1960s, when inflation was expected to remain at low levels. The rapid, *unexpected* inflation of the last three decades wiped out much of their debt; they had an easy time paying off their mortgages. (However, as we shall soon see, the *expected* inflation of recent years makes it more difficult for their children to buy homes now.)

Because *unexpected inflation* can lead to a capricious reshuffling of wealth — away from lenders and toward debtors — it makes the economic system *less fair*.

ADJUSTING TO EXPECTED INFLATION: THE REAL RATE OF INTEREST

When inflation is anticipated, those who are hurt can take steps to protect themselves. We have already seen in Chapter 15 how the labour market may adjust: wage contracts may include compensation for inflation. Financial markets may also adjust, with changes in interest rates providing compensation for inflation.

Because inflation has such a strong effect on borrowers and lenders, it affects the interest rates that lenders charge and that borrowers pay. We have already seen how inflation can harm lenders; they are repaid in money whose value has declined. Consequently, inflation makes them reluctant to make loans. The quantity of funds that lenders are willing to supply to the financial markets decreases, as illustrated by the move from S_1 to S_2 in Figure 16-2. At the same time, inflation benefits borrowers. Therefore, the demand for loanable funds by businesses, home buyers, and others increases from D_1 to D_2. Equilibrium moves from E_1 to E_2. There is an increase in the price of loans (the interest rate).

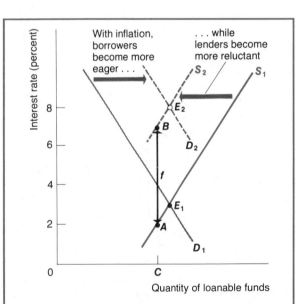

Figure 16-2 Inflation and the demand and supply of loanable funds.

As a result of inflation, people are eager to borrow; the demand for funds increases to D_2. Lenders are reluctant, causing the supply of loanable funds to decrease to S_2. As a result, the rate of interest rises.

The question is, how much does the interest rate rise? One common argument—traced back a half century to the work of Irving Fisher of Yale University—is that the interest rate will rise by the amount of inflation, thus leaving borrowers and lenders in the same real position as before. That is, borrowers and lenders will face the same **real rate of interest** as before, with this real rate calculated in a manner similar to that used for the real wage in Chapter 6. Specifically:

> The real rate of interest = the nominal rate of interest − the expected rate of inflation.[1]   (16-1)

Figure 16-2 illustrates the reason for believing that the nominal rate of interest will include full compensation for inflation, bringing the real interest back to its original level. The non-inflationary equilibrium is at E_1, with a nominal rate of interest of 3%. With zero inflation, the real rate of interest is likewise 3%.

With a steady, expected inflation of 5% per year, how much does the supply of loanable funds (S_1) shift? Point A on supply curve S_1 shows us that, *before inflation*, lenders had to receive 2% interest to induce them to provide C units of loanable funds. This suggests that, once there is an inflation of 5%, those lenders will be willing to lend the same C units only if they receive an interest rate of 7% at point B. This provides them with a 5% compensation for inflation—shown by arrow f—and the same 2% real rate of interest as before. No matter what point we consider on S_1, the corresponding point on S_2 is 5% higher. Thus, the entire supply curve shifts up by the amount of the inflation arrow f.

A similar argument applies to borrowers. With inflation, their enthusiasm for borrowing increases, since they will repay with money whose value has declined. Their demand for loans shifts up by 5%. No matter how much they borrow, they will be willing to pay 5% more for it, because this is the benefit they get from inflation.

With both curves shifting up by the same 5%, new equilibrium E_2 is 5% above original equilibrium E_1. In this simple case of a stable, predictable inflation, the nominal rate of interest therefore should rise to 8% to compensate for the 5% inflation, leaving the real interest rate unaffected at 3%. Of the 8% total, 3% can be looked on as a net payment to lenders, while the other 5% compensates them for the decline in the value of the money they have loaned (Figure 16-3).

■ ■ ■ ■ ■

[1] This is only an approximation. As in the case of the real wage (Equation 6-10), a precise calculation requires division.

THE REAL INTEREST RATE IN CANADA

The previous section suggests that, as inflation was increasing during the late 1960s and 1970s, nominal rates of interest should have been rising. Figure 16-4 confirms that this did, in fact, happen. Moreover, as inflation fell during the 1980s, nominal interest rates fell as predicted by the theory.

Unfortunately, it is difficult to go further and determine whether the nominal rate of interest includes a full compensation for inflation. One major problem is that people look to the *future* when they borrow or lend; the theory says that nominal interest rates should include compensation for *expected* inflation. The difficulty is that we do not live in the simple world we have assumed so far, where the rate of inflation is perfectly stable and predictable. In the real world, we don't know the expected rate of inflation with any degree of precision and, therefore, we have no straightforward way to calculate the real rates of interest that bond buyers and other lenders expect to receive.

The situation is not hopeless, however. Expected future inflation surely depends in part on what is hap-

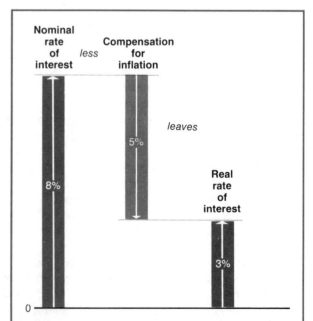

Figure 16-3   Nominal and real rates of interest, with 5% inflation.

On a $100 loan, $5 is required to compensate the lender for the yearly loss of value of the $100 loaned. With a nominal payment of $8, this leaves the lender ahead by $3. Thus, the real rate of interest is 3%.

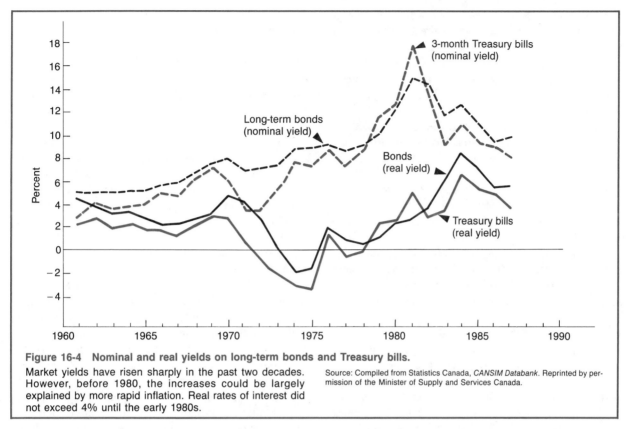

Figure 16-4   Nominal and real yields on long-term bonds and Treasury bills.

Market yields have risen sharply in the past two decades. However, before 1980, the increases could be largely explained by more rapid inflation. Real rates of interest did not exceed 4% until the early 1980s.

Source: Compiled from Statistics Canada, *CANSIM Databank*. Reprinted by permission of the Minister of Supply and Services Canada.

pening currently. One very simple approach is to assume that people expect the current rate of inflation to continue into the future. This rate of inflation can then be used in equation 16-1 to estimate the real rate of interest. In Figure 16-4 we have used this method to calculate real interest rates (or *real yields*) on short-term and long-term federal government securities (Treasury bills and long-term bonds).

Three broad conclusions may be drawn from this figure:

1. During the 1960s, the estimated real interest rates on both short-term and long-term assets were quite stable, averaging about 1.5%-3.5%. The evidence thus suggests that, until the 1970s, nominal rates of interest did contain full compensation for expected inflation.

2. In the mid-1970s, nominal interest rates responded to higher inflation, but they did not compensate fully. As a result, as the inflation rate soared, real rates of interest were depressed, falling below zero between 1973 and 1975. In the words of Lawrence Summers of Harvard University (commenting on similar findings for the United States), the data for the 1970s

"suggest some tendency for interest rates to adjust to inflation, but far less than predicted by the theory."[2] To the degree that nominal interest rates failed to adjust fully, inflation helped borrowers and harmed lenders.

3. Finally, the very large swings in nominal interest rates in the 1980s cannot be explained by changes in expected inflation. In particular, nominal rates of interest in 1980/81 were much higher than could reasonably be accounted for by inflationary expectations; if anything, most people probably expected inflation to decrease, not to increase, at that time. Moreover, while nominal rates fell as inflation subsided after 1983, they did not fall by nearly enough to compensate for the reduction in inflation, and estimated real rates rose to very high levels.

Of course, these conclusions follow from calculations where we have simply *assumed* that people expect the current rate of inflation to continue, and this assumption

■ ■ ■ ■ ■
[2] Summers, "The Nonadjustment of Nominal Interest Rates," in James Tobin, ed., *Macroeconomics, Prices and Quantities* (Washington: Brookings Institution, 1983), p. 232.

may be wrong. Thus, our estimates of the real rate of interest may be biased. However, estimates of real interest rates in the United States have shown a similar pattern even though they were based on a more accurate method of measuring inflationary expectations: Financial experts were simply asked what they thought inflation was going to be.

Thus, the evidence strongly suggests that something other than inflation expectations have been influencing nominal interest rates in the 1980s. What could this something else be?

In one sense, the answer is easy: Real interest rates were high in Canada in 1981 and in 1984/85 because real interest rates were high in the United States in these years. When nominal rates in the United States rise sharply, investment in American assets will appear more attractive than investment in Canadian assets unless interest rates rise in Canada, too. Of course, the relative attractiveness of U.S. assets may be reduced if investors expect the U.S. dollar to depreciate (that is, if they expect the value of the American dollar to fall in terms of Canadian funds). But if investors expect inflation in the United States to decline, they have little reason to expect the U.S. dollar to depreciate. On the contrary, if inflation in the United States is expected to fall, one would expect the American dollar to *appreciate* against the Canadian dollar, making investment in U.S. assets even more attractive.

Thus, when nominal interest rates skyrocketed in the United States in late 1981, they rose rapidly in Canada as well. As we saw in Chapters 13 and 14, the increase was reinforced by contractionary monetary policies by the Bank of Canada. The growth rate of M1 in 1981 was substantially below the Bank's earlier target rate, and in 1984 (when the Bank was no longer following explicit monetary targets), the growth rate of the money stock (whether measured by M1 or a broader aggregate) was also very low.

The Bank of Canada has been criticized by some observers for allowing interest rates in Canada to closely follow rates in the United States, even when U.S. rates fluctuate wildly as they did in 1981 and 1984/85. However, to some extent this criticism may be unfair. Suppose that the Bank had not put on the monetary brakes in 1981. With sharply rising rates in the United States, this would most likely have led the Canadian dollar to depreciate. But as we discussed in Chapter 14, a depreciation of the Canadian dollar contributes to inflation because it makes imported goods more expensive. If these inflationary pressures lead to an increase in

expected inflation as well, nominal interest rates in Canada will rise in any event.

The tendency for real interest rates in Canada to follow U.S. real rates is clearly evident in Figure 16-5. But if the high real interest rates in Canada in the early 1980s are to be explained by high real rates in the United States, the next question is: What caused the high real rates in the American economy?

Major changes in monetary and fiscal policies provide the most obvious answer. In 1980/81, the U.S. Federal Reserve was determined to stop inflation; its tight monetary policy pushed nominal and real interest rates upward. On the fiscal side, the Reagan administration and Congress were working on a major cut in tax rates by 1981. This was expected to cause larger budget deficits and more borrowing by the government, and this put further upward pressure on interest rates. Similarly, as the U.S. economy gathered steam in 1984/85 following the recovery from the 1982 recession, the Federal Reserve again tightened monetary policy in order to prevent renewed inflationary pressures and to stabilize the American dollar in international currency markets.

To summarize, even though there is a strong tendency for nominal interest rates to change when there are changes in inflation rates, the response is incomplete. In particular, as inflation increases, nominal interest rates do not always compensate fully for inflation. Thus, inflation can depress real interest rates, thereby helping borrowers and harming lenders.

This is not the only unfortunate effect of inflation. Even if inflation has *no* effect on *real* interest rates, it can still have real effects—as we shall see in the following sections.

INFLATION AND THE TAX SYSTEM

Inflation can introduce major complications into the tax system. Here we concentrate on two. (1) In the past, inflation has pushed people into higher tax brackets. (2) Inflation greatly complicates the taxation of interest.

1. Tax Bracket Creep: Inflation and the Increasing Burden of Taxes

Until 1974, inflation meant that, as dollar incomes rose, taxpayers were pushed up into higher and higher tax brackets. The general idea may be illustrated by referring to the 1987 tax schedule for Ontario residents. A low-income couple with taxable income of $27,500 would have an income tax liability around $4,060 or 15% of their income. Suppose that the average level of prices doubles, and so does the couple's taxable income.

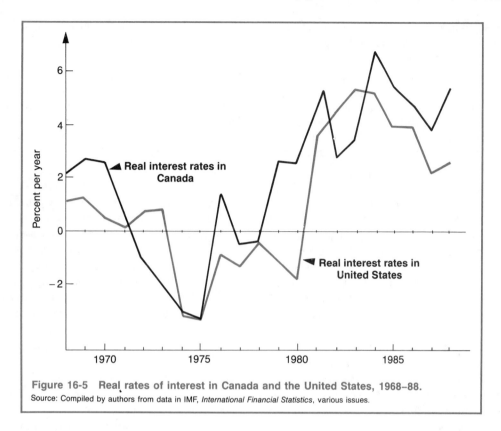

Figure 16-5   Real rates of interest in Canada and the United States, 1968–88.
Source: Compiled by authors from data in IMF, *International Financial Statistics*, various issues.

It is now $55,000, which barely keeps up with inflation. If the tax schedule were to remain unchanged, taxes would now take about $15,070 or 27% of their income. Although they are earning no more in real terms, taxes take a larger share. Similarly, inflation can cause taxes to rise for other families, both rich and poor, whose incomes barely keep up with inflation. While all are affected, the problem is most severe for the middle class. The poor do not pay much income tax. The rich are already in the highest marginal tax bracket. It is the middle class whose taxes rise the most if the tax schedule is not adjusted for inflation.

In order to eliminate this effect, the federal government introduced provisions for the income tax to be ***indexed*** beginning in 1974. Indexation means that tax brackets and exemptions rise with inflation. If prices double, so does the nominal income at which the various tax brackets begin. For example, the tax bracket with a 26% marginal rate of federal income tax begins at $55,000 instead of $27,500. Thus, if your money income doubles when prices double, you stay in the same place in the tax table. Your income remains the same in real terms, and so does your tax.

If the income tax is *indexed*, the law provides for exemptions, credits, tax brackets, and other dollar measures in the tax code to increase automatically, in the same proportion as the increase in the price index.

The 1974 indexation reform meant that the federal government's share of GDP no longer increases automatically when there is inflation. In addition, because individuals' provincial income tax liabilities are generally specified as a percentage of the federal tax liability, provincial income taxes have also in effect become indexed. (For example, if the provincial income tax payable is specified as 50% of federal tax payable, then when the federal tax is reduced by indexation so is the provincial tax liability. Other federal and provincial taxes — such as the proposed federal sales tax, or the provincial sales taxes — are specified in constant percentages which are unaffected by inflation.)

In the United States, the federal income tax remained un-indexed through the high-inflation period in the 1970s and early 1980s. While indexation was not part of President Reagan's early tax proposals, he ultimately came to strongly support it. When opposing suggestions in

1983 and 1984 that indexing be deferred or eliminated as a way to reduce the large U.S. budget deficits, he summarized the case for indexing:

> Let's not kid ourselves. Government has found inflation a very handy method for getting additional revenues without having to face the public and demand a tax increase. It is a tax. Government gets a profit from inflation. And I would like to see indexing put in place to permanently take away from government the incentive to create inflation in order to get more money.

In Canada, the *principle* of indexing is by now firmly established. Recently, however, the principle has been partially compromised as the government has been trying hard to increase revenues and reduce the federal deficit. In 1982, Finance Minister McEachen put a "cap" on indexing as part of his "6 and 5" restraint program: The maximum increase in tax brackets and exemption levels would be 6% even if the rate of price inflation turned out to be more than this. And, in the 1985 budget of the Mulroney government, the indexing provisions were substantially modified: Brackets and exemptions were raised by *three percentage points less* than the rate of inflation in the 1986 taxation year. (For example, an inflation rate of 5% would only cause the brackets and exemptions to rise by 2%.) By the late 1980s, this limit on indexation still remained in force.

Thus, with an indexing system that adjusts only partially for price changes, inflation has a real effect on the economy since it increases the percentage of Canadian income that is paid in taxes. (As a further move to reduce the deficit, the Conservatives also proposed at one time to abandon the principle of raising transfer payments such as Old Age Security benefits and family allowances to compensate for inflation. However, these proposals ran into strong opposition and were subsequently modified.)

2. Inflation and the Taxation of Interest

Inflation increases the tax burden on bondholders and gives a tax break to many borrowers. To illustrate, consider a non-inflationary situation where the interest rate is 3% in both nominal and real terms. A bondholder in the 50% tax bracket pays one-half (that is, 1.5%) of the interest in taxes, leaving an after-tax return of 1.5% in both nominal and real terms.

Now suppose that there is a continuing inflation of 5%, which gets built into the interest rate. The results are shown in Figure 16-6. The nominal interest rate rises to 8%, leaving a constant pre-tax real rate of interest of 3%. The bondholder in the 50% tax bracket pays one-half of the 8% interest in taxes, leaving 4% after taxes. Note what has happened to the *real after-tax return*. Subtracting the 5% inflation, we find that the real after-tax return has not only disappeared—it has become *negative*! The reason is that the tax is collected, not only on the 3% real rate of interest that represents the bondholders' real income, but also on the 5% that is simply offsetting inflation and is not real income at all.

While the tax system adds to the woes of bondholders and other lenders, it lessens the interest burden on borrowers. The reason is that interest payments reduce the taxable incomes of many borrowers. For example, interest payments represent a business expense; they reduce profits and therefore the taxes that corporations pay. Similarly, farmers and small businessmen may deduct interest payments on borrowed money in calculating their taxable income, thereby reducing the tax that they pay. Just as lenders must add the full 8% of nominal interest to their taxable income, so too these borrowers can subtract the full 8% of nominal interest from their income, thus lowering their tax. (The calculations of Figure 16-6 also apply to a borrower in the 50% tax bracket. The tax advantage more than compensates for the real interest paid; the real after-tax interest payment is negative.)

Thus, the combination of taxes and inflation penalizes those who hold bonds or other interest-bearing assets, while it encourages businesses and others to borrow.

For people in high tax brackets, it may sometimes pay to use a loophole in the tax law which is particularly effective in reducing taxes when there is a high rate of inflation. As we discussed in Chapter 5, a substantial portion of any *capital gains* they make are exempted from tax. Thus, instead of buying a bond which yields taxable income, people in the upper income brackets may be better off buying an asset (such as an expensive home) that does not yield a taxable income, but that may yield them a non-taxable capital gain as its value rises. For this reason, people with high incomes may come to view housing "primarily as an investment rather than as necessary shelter."[3] Thus, the inflation-taxation combination can distort the housing market. Builders may construct too many oversized houses to provide tax advantages to the wealthy, and not enough housing for lower-income people. When this happens, inflation has a real impact on the economy.

■ ■ ■ ■ ■

[3] Anthony Downs, *Rental Housing in the 1980s* (Washington: Brookings, 1983), p. 33.

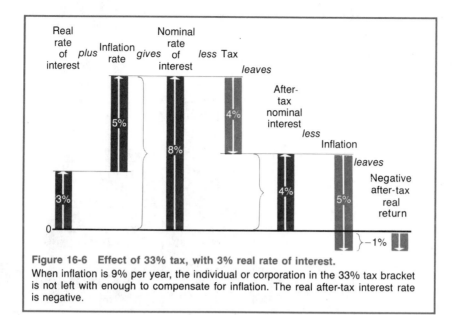

Figure 16-6   Effect of 33% tax, with 3% real rate of interest.
When inflation is 9% per year, the individual or corporation in the 33% tax bracket is not left with enough to compensate for inflation. The real after-tax interest rate is negative.

Inflation introduces many quirks and inequities into the tax system, which was developed on the assumption that the average level of prices would remain reasonably stable. It would be *very* complicated to rewrite the tax laws to remove all effects of inflation. One of the best ways to limit tax inequities is to keep the rate of inflation down.

INFLATION CAUSES UNCERTAINTY

The chief evil of an unstable dollar is uncertainty.

Irving Fisher

When the average rate of inflation is high, it generally is *erratic* and *unpredictable*. A country with a very rapid inflation may, for example, find that inflation bounces from 100% one year to 50% the next, and to 90% the next. On the other hand, a country with a low average rate of inflation will find that the inflation rate is quite stable from year to year. Observe in Figure 16-7 that the year-to-year change in Canada's rate of inflation was quite small in the 1960s and early 1970s, when the average rate was low. Between 1972 and 1982, inflation in Canada was more rapid *and* more erratic. After 1982, it once more became lower and less erratic.

When inflation is erratic and unpredictable, it causes the shifts in income and wealth noted at the beginning of this chapter. An unexpected increase in inflation creates a windfall for borrowers and inflicts a penalty on lenders. An unexpected decrease in inflation creates a windfall for lenders and inflicts a penalty on borrowers.

Erratic Inflation Makes the Bond Market Shrink

Bonds are generally bought by people interested in a stable income; those who are willing to take risks are more likely to go into the stock market. While increases in nominal interest rates help compensate bond buyers for *predictable* inflation, an unpredictable inflation makes the real return on bonds very uncertain. If the rate of inflation shoots up above the nominal interest rate, the bondholder will be ''soaked;'' the interest won't even cover the dollar's loss of value through inflation. On the other hand, if the inflation rate unexpectedly comes down, the bondholder will receive a windfall.

Because of the risks, potential buyers of bonds may be frightened away if inflation becomes erratic. Similarly, potential borrowers become reluctant to issue bonds; they also are uncertain whether erratic inflation will make them winners or losers. Thus, erratic inflation can make the long-term bond market shrink. For example, in 1982/83 there was great uncertainty whether inflation would come down and, if so, by how much. For this reason (and also because of the recession), the number of new bonds issued in Canada fell sharply. Businesses had difficulty issuing bonds to finance long-term projects. Thus, erratic inflation imposed a real cost on the economy.

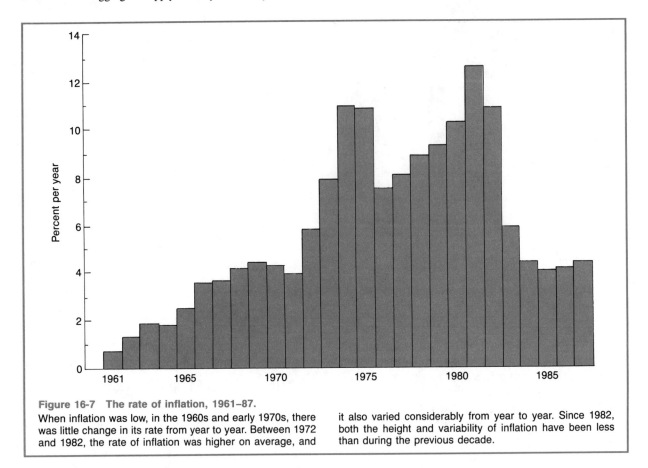

Figure 16-7 The rate of inflation, 1961–87.

When inflation was low, in the 1960s and early 1970s, there was little change in its rate from year to year. Between 1972 and 1982, the rate of inflation was higher on average, and it also varied considerably from year to year. Since 1982, both the height and variability of inflation have been less than during the previous decade.

Innovations in the Mortgage Market

Like the bond market, the market for residential mortgages may also be severely affected by uncertainty about the inflation rate. Because buying a home represents a very large investment for most people, they need a mortgage to cover a large proportion of the purchase price, and most people will want to pay back the mortgage over a long period, perhaps twenty or even thirty years. But with uncertainty about inflation, the borrower and the lender may be reluctant to commit themselves to a constant interest rate for such a long time.

Because of this problem, most lending institutions in Canada currently issue mortgages which provide for renegotiation of the interest rate periodically, say, every one to five years. If the inflation rate and the interest rate on other debt instruments change, the interest rate on the mortgage will be adjusted correspondingly. Therefore, with such *renegotiable* mortgages, real interest payments can be stabilized in the face of changing conditions.

Other adjustments to uncertainty about inflation are possible. In Britain, the building societies (which are similar to our trust companies) have used *variable-rate mortgages* since the end of World War II. Such mortgages have added to the financial stability of the building societies: During periods of high inflation and high market rates of interest, they automatically receive high nominal interest on the mortgages they own. Since the early 1980s, Canadian banks and trust companies have also begun offering variable-rate mortgages.

> A *variable-rate mortgage* has an interest rate that is adjusted periodically in response to changes in the market interest rate.

Variable-rate mortgages are similar to wage contracts in which it is agreed in advance that the employee's pay increases during the life of the contract will depend on the rate of inflation. (Such contracts are referred to as *indexed wage contracts*, and will be discussed further in Chapter 19.) In each case, the objective is to protect people from capricious shifts in income when the rate of inflation unexpectedly changes during the life of a contract.

INFLATION CAUSES FRONT-LOADING OF DEBT

Now let us return to the simple case where inflation is steady and predictable, and where the nominal interest rate adjusts to keep the real rate constant. Even in this case, we have seen that inflation can have arbitrary effects: Taxes are increased for bondholders and reduced for borrowers.

Such steady, predictable inflation can also have a second important effect. Here, however, it is the *borrower* who faces a major problem. To see how the borrower can be hurt, suppose a family buys a home. They take out a mortgage of $100,000, to be repaid over a 30-year period.

First, consider their situation in a non-inflationary world, with nominal and real interest rates at 4%. Their payments are approximately $475 per month for 30 years. This monthly payment covers both interest and the repayment of the $100,000 loan. Because there is no inflation, the burden of the debt is spread evenly over the 30-year period. The $475 they pay in the last month has the same purchasing power as the $475 paid in the first month.

Now, consider what happens with an expected inflation of 10%. If the real interest rate remains at 4%, the nominal rate will be 14%. With a traditional mortgage — requiring the same dollar payment each month over a 30-year period — the payments will be approximately $1,500 per month. This $1,500 represents a *huge* burden at first, since prices have not yet risen very much. However, by the final year, the $1,500 will be trivial. It will represent less purchasing power than $100 in the first year. To restate this point: If *nominal* payments are constant every month, then *real* payments decline through time as prices rise and the value of money falls.

Thus, inflation and high nominal rates of interest result in the burden of mortgages being shifted forward to the early years. The mortgages are ***front-loaded***.

A debt is *front-loaded* if the payments, measured in real terms, are greater at the beginning than at the end of the repayment period.

Many people who could buy a home in a non-inflationary situation find they cannot do so if inflation is rapid. The burdens of the early years may be impossibly heavy; people may simply be unable to afford the early payments, even though they would be compensated by very light real payments in future years. This is an important real effect of inflation — *even if the real interest rate is unchanged*.

In the early 1980s, young families faced great difficulties in financing their first homes:

- Real interest rates were high (as seen in Figure 16-4;

- Nominal interest rates were even higher, causing a front loading of mortgages;

- Most houses were expensive. One reason was the eagerness of high-income people to buy homes for the tax advantages; their demand created upward pressures on home prices.

These three factors combined to discourage home purchases by young middle-income families.

Inflation presents an interesting paradox. People who bought houses in the early 1960s — while inflation was still low — gained from the *unexpected* inflation in the following years. They paid their low-interest mortgages off with dollars whose value had declined. More recently, however, *expected* inflation and the resulting high nominal rates of interest have created difficulties for home buyers. Home buyers now face front-loaded mortgages, with very high real payments in the early years. The older generation benefitted from unexpected inflation. The younger generation suffers from expected inflation.

Graduated-payment Mortgages

Why not remove front loading by starting with low dollar payments, increasing them gradually as prices rise? In our example in which prices rise steadily at 10% per annum, home buyers would have an initial payment of approximately $480 at the end of the first month. The monthly payment would then rise gradually, in line with inflation, to reach $8,400 by the time the final payment was made at the end of the thirtieth year. In this way, the real burden would be the same every month — *provided that inflation continued at a steady 10% per year*. (The figures are correct. With 10% inflation, $8,400 at the end of thirty years has the same purchasing power as $480 at the beginning; see Box 16-1.)

However, a family with such a ***graduated-payment mortgage*** would be in trouble if inflation slowed down. To see why, consider the extreme case where inflation fell to zero. The monthly payment would continue to

BOX 16-1

■ ■

The Rule of 70: How Long Does It Take for Prices to Double?

Consider the effects of a steady inflation at 10%. During an initial base year, the index of prices is 100; in the second year, it becomes 110. During the third year, the index rises again by 10%. That is, it rises to 110% of the previous year's height, or to 121 (= 110 x 110%). Because the index grows at a compound rate, it increases by a larger number each year. As a result, the index reaches 200 in less than 10 years. But how long does it take? The answer is: about 7 years.

This answer is found by using the **rule of 70**:

Approximate number of years required to double

$$= \frac{70}{\text{percentage rate of growth per year}}$$

In our example, where the rate of growth was 10% per year:

Approximate number of years required to double

$$= \frac{70}{10} = 7$$

Because it is a general formula, the rule of 70 has broad applicability. Not only can it be used to estimate how long prices take to double, but also how long your interest-bearing bank account takes to double, or how long a GDP growing at a constant real rate takes to double. For example, if GDP grows at 3.5% per year, it will double in about 70/3.5 = 20 years.

The rule of 70—reflecting the underlying phenomenon of compounding — would lead to spectacular results in the event of persistent inflation of 7% per year, the average rate since 1970. Between 1990 and 2000, prices would double, then redouble by year 2010. By 2020, they would be eight times their 1990 level; by 2030, sixteen times. If you wanted to earn $31,000 in 1990 dollars just before the time of your retirement in 2040, you would have to bargain for a million bucks a year. But that would be just a hint of things to come. If all prices were to rise at the same average rate, by 2070 your grandchildren would be paying $166 for a cup of coffee. If they were to go to university, they might have to pay some $50,000 per month to rent a room during the school year!

---

increase by 10% per year in dollar terms. But now the *real* payment would also increase by 10% per year. Similar, but less dramatic, increases in real payments would occur if inflation only slows down.

> A *graduated-payment mortgage* is one whose money payments rise as time passes. A *fully graduated* mortgage is one whose money payments will rise enough to keep real payments constant if the present rate of inflation continues. (In reality, there are no fully graduated mortgages.)

To ease the burden on young home buyers, the Canadian government, through the Canadian Housing and Mortgage Corporation (CMHC), began to experiment with graduated-payment mortgages in the high-inflation years in the late 1970s. However, the experiment was not particularly successful; even though the CMHC guaranteed repayment, mortgage lending institutions such as banks and trust companies were reluctant to issue mortgages of this type. Furthermore, a mortgage which was graduated according to the schedule sug-

gested by the CMHC fell *far* short of the degree of graduation that would have been needed to level out the real burden, and thus leave the pattern of real payments unaffected by inflation.

To sum up: Full graduation of mortgages does not occur. Therefore, inflation continues to result in the front loading of mortgages. Even after inflation has continued for some time and has been built into people's expectations, it continues to have an effect on real aspects of the economy. Most notably, it increases the real burden faced by home owners in the early years. In this important way, our financial institutions have not adjusted to an inflationary environment.

Graduated-payment Mortgages and Variable-rate Mortgages: A Comparison

Note that the graduated-payment mortgage and the variable-rate mortgage are designed to deal with different problems. The variable-rate mortgage is designed to deal with the problem of *variable* inflation and interest rates. It does not solve the problem of front loading. (If inflation is high and stable, nominal interest rates will be high and stable. The interest-rate adjustments on a variable-rate mortgage will be small and the nominal interest rate will remain high and stable. The mortgage will be front loaded.) Graduated-payment mortgages, in contrast, *are* designed to reduce the problem of front loading. As we have seen, they are appropriate when interest rates are high and stable, but are not appropriate when inflation and interest rates are erratic.

Variable-rate mortgages have become common, while graduated-rate mortgages remain rare. Thus, the mortgage market has dealt with the problem of *variable* inflation and interest rates much more effectively than with the problem of *high* rates and front loading. *Front loading remains a major problem for home buyers.*

MACROECONOMIC POLICY IN AN INFLATIONARY ENVIRONMENT

Inflation not only creates uncertainties for borrowers and lenders. It also means that policy makers have difficulty in figuring out what is going on and what policies are most appropriate. In particular, inflation changes the value of outstanding government debt and, therefore, complicates the measurement and evaluation of fiscal policy.

To see why, we will have to begin with the fundamental relationship between deficits and debt. Recall that, when the government runs a deficit of $1 billion, it is spending $1 billion more than its revenues. It must borrow the $1 billion. Therefore, its debt increases by $1 billion. Thus, the *deficit* equals the *increase in debt*.

With this background, let us reconsider some of the major facts about the federal government's finances in a recent year. (The numbers we are using are approximations only, so that we can work with nice round figures.) At the beginning of 1988, the government's total outstanding debt was about $240 billion. During that year, government expenditures were $130 billion, receipts were $110 billion, and the deficit was accordingly $20 billion. The deficit necessitated additional government borrowing, which raised the national debt to $260 billion by the end of the year. That is, the debt rose by the amount of the deficit. Of the government's expenditures, $25 billion were interest payments on the national debt. The inflation rate was approximately 5%.

Calculating the "Real" Deficit

Here's one possible interpretation of these facts. With 5% inflation, the beginning debt of $240 billion could

grow by a similar 5% — or by $12 billion — without its real size changing at all. Thus, the first $12 billion of the deficit is not really a deficit. It does not add to the government's obligations in real terms; it simply offsets the effects of inflation. Thus, the true deficit was not the $20 billion difference between expenditure and revenue. Rather, it was $12 billion less, or only $8 billion. That is, the real deficit was only the amount by which the real debt of the government rose. According to this line of argument, the standard figures greatly overstate the real deficit and, therefore, greatly overstate the stimulus coming from the fiscal side.

> The *real deficit* of the government is measured by the increase in the real debt of the government. If the debt falls in real terms, then the government has a *real surplus*.

Proponents of this view include Professors John Bossons and Peter Dungan of the Institute for Policy Analysis at the University of Toronto. When they recalculated the total deficit of all governments (federal, provincial and local) as the increase in the real value of government debt, Bossons and Dungan found that this greatly altered the picture of fiscal policy. For example, the standard estimates of the impact of fiscal policy in 1979 and 1980 show sizeable deficits in those years. But if the budget is corrected for inflation, the deficit disappears: The real budget of the total government sector was in approximate balance in 1979 and 1980.

Even more striking are their calculations for 1983. According to the Department of Finance estimate, the full-employment deficit of the overall government sector in 1983 was about $7.5 billion; that is, fiscal policy was providing a substantial stimulus to aid the recovery from the 1982 recession. The Bossons-Dungan picture of the fiscal policy stance is quite different. Their estimates imply that the *real* full-employment budget was in *surplus* by about $1 billion. They concluded that when correctly measured, fiscal policy was actually *restrictive*, and that this had "contributed to the magnitude of the current economic depression."[4]

An Alternative View

An alternative view is that it is a great mistake to measure fiscal policy in real terms, even though it is, of

------
[4] John Bossons and D. P. Dungan, "The Government Deficit: Too High or Too Low?", *Canadian Tax Journal* (January/February 1983), pp. 1–29. (The quote is from p. 23.)

course, perfectly correct that inflation lowers the real value of outstanding government debt.[5]

According to this alternative view, it is reasonable and desirable for individuals and corporations to recalculate their debt and other liabilities and assets in real terms, to get a better idea of how they are doing. Individuals and corporations may *adjust* and *respond* to inflation in this way. However, the government is fundamentally different. The government should not simply respond to inflation. Through its monetary and fiscal policies it is primarily *responsible* for inflation. If it keeps its accounts in real terms, it is likely to make inflation worse and *destabilize the economy*.

To see why, consider what happens if the economy enters a period of inflation. As a result, the real value of the debt falls. If we make an inflation correction along the lines of Bossons and Dungan, we will see the real budget automatically swinging into surplus. Measured in this way, fiscal policy is becoming more restrictive. To offset this unexpected restraint, we might suggest that the government cut taxes or increase spending. But something is wrong here: Cutting taxes or increasing spending will make the inflation worse!

Similarly, if the government focuses on the real deficit or surplus, it may destabilize the economy during a deflationary period such as the early 1930s. Between 1929 and 1933, prices fell approximately 20%. As a result, the real value of the goverment debt rose. In real terms, the government's budget was moving even more deeply into deficit. If the government focused on this real deficit, it might erroneously assume that it was already providing a large stimulus, and fail to make the needed shift toward expansion. It might even cut expenditures to limit the increase in the real debt. But such cuts would make the depression worse.

Monetary Policy in an Inflationary Environment

Similar issues arise with respect to monetary policy. The *real quantity of money* in the economy is important; it helps to determine the quantity of goods and services that people will buy. What would happen if the Bank of Canada were to concentrate on the real quantity of money? To make things simple, suppose that the Bank follows a policy of slowly increasing the real money stock, in line with the slow increase of the productive capacity of the economy.

Again, the focus on *real* magnitudes could have destabilizing results. Consider again an economy entering a period of inflation. The nominal quantity of money has undoubtedly been rising. However, when we adjust it for inflation, we may find that the real amount of money has not been rising much. It may even have been falling.[6] If the central bank is focusing on the real quantity, it may conclude that monetary policy is too tight, and create more money. This is precisely the wrong way to respond to inflation.

Similarly, concentrating on the real quantity of money can be the wrong thing to do during a period of deflation. Again, consider what happened between 1929 and 1933. Prices fell approximately 20%, while the nominal quantity of money also fell by about the same percentage. Thus, in real terms, there was little or no change in the quantity of money. A central bank focusing on the real quantity might conclude that there was no problem with monetary policy. But, in fact, the large decline in the nominal quantity of money was having catastrophic effects. The central bank should not focus on the real quantity of money. Furthermore, outside observers should not use changes in the real quantity of money as the primary way of judging the tightnesss or looseness of monetary policy.

In brief, real accounting — which makes sense for individuals and corporations — does not make nearly so much sense for the government and central bank, since they are responsible for the overall operation of the economy. Real accounting can lead to destabilizing actions.

It is going too far to argue that real magnitudes are not important. They are. But the use of real magnitudes as guides for macroeconomic policy is problematic, to say the least. Even in the best of times, policy makers face difficulties in determining the best macroeconomic policies. When inflation is rapid, it greatly adds to their difficulties.

■ ■ ■ ■ ■

[5] The authors of this book take the alternative view. Paul Wonnacott, ''The Nominal Deficit Really Matters,'' *Challenge* (Sept. 1986), pp. 48–51.

*[6] Indeed, if the inflation is rapid, the real quantity of money is likely to decline. Suppose, for example, that the nominal quantity of money doubles during a year and prices rise rapidly. Because money is quickly losing its value, people have an incentive to spend it quickly. Thus, a 100% increase in the money stock may cause aggregate demand and prices to rise by more than 100%. If prices rise by a greater percentage than the nominal quantity of money, the real quantity of money declines.

In conclusion, we now have found a total of *three policy traps*—apparently plausible policy guides that can cause destabilizing actions:

■ the annually-balanced-budget rule (Chapter 10)

■ the use of a real, inflation-adjusted budget as a guide for fiscal policy (this chapter)

■ an attempt by the Bank of Canada to stabilize the real quantity of money (this chapter)

A fourth policy trap will be discussed in Chapter 18:

■ Setting a target of stabilizing the exchange rate between the Canadian and American dollars.

KEY POINTS

1. Unexpected inflation causes a capricious redistribution of wealth, away from bondholders and toward debtors.

2. During periods of high expected inflation, people are eager to borrow and reluctant to lend. This causes nominal rates of interest to rise.

3. The real rate of interest is (approximately) the nominal rate less the expected rate of inflation.

4. The real rate of interest has been much more stable than the nominal rate. However, real interest rates have not remained perfectly stable. They were low in the middle 1970s and high during most of the 1980s.

5. Without tax indexing, inflation causes people to move into higher income tax brackets, even if their real incomes are stable. To eliminate this effect of inflation, the Canadian income tax code has been indexed since 1974. However, since the mid-1980s the government has reduced the extent of indexing to help reduce the federal budget deficit.

6. The combination of high inflation, high nominal interest rates, and taxation means that lenders in high tax brackets end up with low or even negative after-tax returns. Borrowers in high tax brackets end up gaining in real terms. Thus, during periods of rapid inflation, well-to-do people are discouraged from lending, and encouraged instead to borrow — for example, by purchasing large houses with big mortgages.

7. High inflation is usually erratic inflation.

8. One way to limit the redistribution of wealth from erratic, unexpected changes in inflation is through variable-rate mortgages.

9. When inflation pushes up nominal rates of interest, the effect is that borrowers have to repay loans more quickly. For example, the normal mortgage, with the same dollar payment each month, becomes ''front-loaded.'' People have difficulty buying homes, since higher real payments are required in the early years.

10. One way to deal with this problem would be with graduated-payment mortgages, whose money payments rise over the life of the mortgage, thus lessening the front loading. However, graduated-payment mortgages are very rare. As a result, the front loading of mortgages remains a major problem for home buyers.

11. If the government's deficit or surplus is measured as the increase or decrease in the real value of government debt, then the government has been running surpluses, not deficits, in some years when both the actual and full-employment budgets showed nominal deficits.

12. It is, however, questionable whether fiscal policy should be measured in this way, as the change in the real debt. In particular, governments that focus on this real measure may engage in destabilizing fiscal actions. Similarly, a central bank may destabilize the economy if it focuses on what is happening to the real quantity of money.

KEY CONCEPTS

nominal rate of interest	*real after-tax return on saving*	*real deficit of the government*
real interest rate	*variable-rate mortgage*	*real debt of the government*
tax bracket creep	*front-loaded mortgage*	*real quantity of money*
indexing of the tax system	*graduated-payment mortgage*	

PROBLEMS

16-1. Which of the following would gain from unexpected inflation and which would lose? In each case, explain why.

(a) The person who has put $10,000 in a savings account and intends to use it as a down payment on a house.

(b) The person who has used $10,000 as a down payment on a house just before the unexpected inflation occurred.

(c) An airline that has borrowed large amounts to buy 50 new airplanes.

16-2. How would your answers to problem 16-1 change if the inflation were expected?

16-3. How does inflation make it difficult for people to acquire their first homes, even if they have assurance that their future incomes will rise with the general price level? Why are the problems less severe for those who already own a home, but are selling it to move into a larger one?

16-4. Suppose that, after a period of stable prices, inflation rises gradually to a rate of 10% per annum. At 10%, it hits a peak, and then gradually disappears.

(a) How will this affect home owners who acquired their homes before the inflation began?

(b) How will those who acquire homes when inflation peaks at 10% be affected as inflation decreases?

16-5. Do you favour indexation of the income tax code? Why or why not? What is the best case to be made on the other side?

*16-6. Would full indexation make the income tax a more or less powerful "automatic stabilizer"? (Refer back to the section on automatic stabilizers in Chapter 10. And be careful: In answering this question you should consider both what happens during a strong upswing and during a recession.)

16-7. What problem can be reduced with graduated-payment mortgages? What problem with variable rate mortgages?

16-8. In the early 1970s, the maximum marginal tax rate on "unearned" income (including interest) was 98% in Britain. (Top marginal rates have since been reduced.) During that period, the rate of inflation in Britain rose to more than 20% per annum.

(a) With 20% inflation and 98% tax rates, what would the nominal interest rate have to be to leave the high-income bondholder with a zero real after-tax return? With a 3% real after-tax return?

(b) Without looking up the facts, can you make an educated guess whether nominal interest rates in Britain rose by enough to leave high-income individuals with a positive after-tax real return? If you looked at the list of holders of bonds of a British corporation, would you expect to find many high-income individuals?

16-9. How did Bossons and Dungan measure the real deficit of the government? Consider an alternative. Suppose the real deficit is calculated as the nominal deficit, deflated by a price index (similar to the way real GDP can be calculated from nominal GDP back in Equation 6-7). Would the two approaches lead to the same estimate of the real deficit? Why or why not? (Hint: Consider the case where the nominal deficit is zero during a period of inflation.)

16-10. What difficulties arise if the government's real deficit or surplus is used as a guide in the making of fiscal policies? Does the same problem arise if the real stock of money is used as a guide by the central bank? Why or why not?

Chapter 17

■ ■

Productivity and Growth: An International Perspective

Not to go back, is somewhat to advance,
And men must walk, at least, before they dance.

Alexander Pope

In previous chapters we have focused on the goals of high employment and price stability. In this chapter we turn to a major macroeconomic objective that is especially important in the long run: economic growth.

As we saw in Chapter 1, the growth performance of the Canadian economy since the turn of the century has been very impressive. The average Canadian in the mid-1980s produces some five times as much as his or her counterpart in 1900, with less effort. Similarly, the economies of the United States, the United Kingdom, the Scandinavian countries, and the industrialized nations in continental Europe have also been growing steadily during this century, and have reached living standards comparable to Canada's. An even more remarkable case is Japan. As recently as 1960, Japanese per capita income was only about 40% of per capita income in Canada, and 55% of that in the United Kingdom. Estimates by the World Bank for 1986 show that by that time, Japan's per capita income had grown to within 10% of Canada's, and was 45% higher than per capita income in the United Kingdom. In many countries in Africa, Asia, and Latin America, in contrast, long-term economic growth has been much slower, and living standards in the mid-1980s remained painfully low for the vast majority of their populations.

This chapter considers the question: What are the sources of economic growth? Why have some countries been so successful at achieving economic growth, while others remain so poor? What policies can the government pursue to promote economic growth?

PRODUCTIVITY AND ECONOMIC GROWTH IN CANADA

The key to economic growth is an increase in productivity. Total output and average living standards in Canada and other countries have risen secularly because there has been an increase in the amount that a typical worker can produce in an hour, that is, in the *average productivity of labour*. If we concentrate on the growth of total output, we can use the following basic relationship:

Total output (Q) = labour hours (L) × average productivity of labour (Q/L)   (17-1)

In other words, total output depends on:
1. the total number of hours worked
2. the average productivity of labour. This is often known as "labour productivity" or, even more simply, as "productivity."

In Figure 17-1, we apply equation 17-1 to Canadian data. The three curves show the average annual rates of change of the three items in the equation, namely, the quantity of output (Q), labour hours (L), and labour productivity (Q/L). (The dates on the horizontal axis indicate the beginning and end of the periods. Thus, the leftmost point of the black curve in Figure 17-1 shows that total output rose at an average annual rate of 2.6% during the period from 1926 to 1940.)

During the 15 years before World War II, labour productivity grew by less than 2% per year, as the coloured curve shows. (This relatively slow growth is

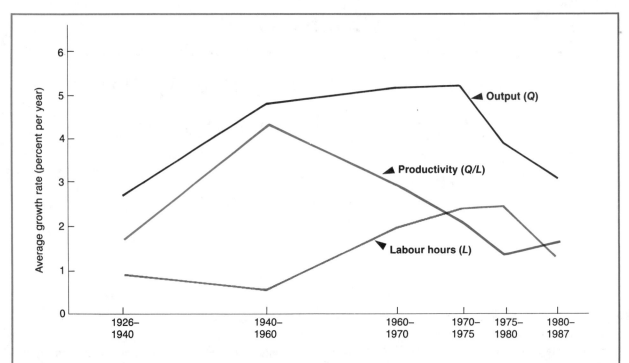

Figure 17-1   Average annual rates of change of output, labour hours, and productivity, Canada 1926–87.

Between 1926 and 1960, there was a strong upward trend in the rate of growth of labour productivity (Q/L). This trend coincided with a downward trend in the rate of growth of total labour hours worked (L). But, since the 1960s, the rate of productivity growth has been falling, while labour hours have been increasing more rapidly. Note also the sudden slowdown in productivity growth in the second half of the 1970s.

Source: Based on data from Statistics Canada's *CANSIM Databank*. Reprinted by permission of the Minister of Supply and Services Canada.

not surprising, since the period includes the Great Depression during the 1930s.) During the next 20 years, productivity grew very fast (at over 4% per annum). However, in the 1970s the rate of productivity growth declined. It was especially slow during the second half of the 1970s: In particular, between 1975 and 1980, labour productivity increased by less than 1.5% per year, compared to the annual increase of more than 3% in the peak periods in the 1950s and 1960s. During the 1980s there was some improvement. On average, productivity rose by 1.7% per year between 1980 and 1987. While this was an improvement over the late 1970s, it was still well below the average for the postwar period.

These big changes in the rate of productivity improvement raise three major issues:

1. Why did productivity increase so rapidly in the period following World War II?

2. Why was the productivity performance so poor in the second half of the 1970s?

3. What are the prospects for the 1990s? Can we expect a return to the high rates of growth of the 1950s and 1960s, or are there factors that will cause productivity growth to remain permanently lower for the foreseeable future?

In later sections, we will consider several possible explanations for the variability in the economy's productivity performance. To start with, however, a look at Figure 17-1 suggests that one factor may simply be variations in the rate of change of labour hours.

Increases in Labour Hours and Productivity

Observe in Figure 17-1 how the increase in labour productivity generally has moved in the opposite direction to the increase in labour hours. When the input of labour hours has risen slowly, productivity has generally increased rapidly. In particular, the most rapid increase in productivity (1940-60) coincided with the slowest rate of increase in labour hours. Moreover, the somewhat improved productivity performance in 1980-87 (in comparison with 1975-80) was accompanied by a substantial decrease in the growth rate of labour hours.

There is a good reason for this inverse relationship. The fewer workers entering the labour force, the more capital each one has to work with. With more capital, each worker can produce more.

Therefore, one of the explanations for the relatively slow increase in productivity in the 1970s is straightforward: The labour force grew rapidly. As a result, there was only a slow increase in the amount of capital at the disposal of the average worker, and productivity likewise increased slowly.

The two reasons for the rapid growth in the labour force during the 1970s were:

1. The "baby boom" after World War II. Following a long depression and war, many people felt free for the first time to have children. By the late 1960s, these children were reaching working age.
2. The increasing participation of women in the labour force. In 1966, no more than 35% of women over 15 were in the labour force (that is, were either employed or looking for work). By 1980, the figure had risen to more than 50%. As a result, *employment increased rapidly during the 1970s*. The number of civilians with jobs rose from less than 8 million in 1970 to over 10.5 million in 1980.

Thus, the slower increase in productivity in the 1970s was partly attributable to the normal working of the economy. More people wanted jobs. On the whole, the economy was successful in providing these jobs. The result was less capital for each worker than there otherwise would have been and, consequently, a less rapid increase in productivity.

However, a rapid growth in employment was *only partly* responsible for the disappointing productivity performance in the 1970s. There were other, less reassuring, forces that depressed productivity growth, as we shall soon see.

THE SOURCES OF PRODUCTIVITY CHANGE

The question what makes productivity grow has preoccupied economists for a long time. Much of the empirical work has used the framework developed by Edward F. Denison in his study of the sources of growth in the American economy between 1929 and 1957. Studies of productivity growth by economists at the Economic Council of Canada and elsewhere owe a great deal to

the methods developed by Denison for trying to sort out the contributions of various factors to economic growth.[1]

In a comparative study of productivity growth in various countries, J.W. Kendrick has used methods similar to Denison's to analyse the sources of Canadian growth for the periods 1960–73 and 1973–78. As Figure 17-1 shows, there was an exceptionally large change in the rate of productivity growth between these two time periods. Looking at the way in which various factors contributed to this change may therefore help suggest an answer to an important question: Is it possible to find a single factor (or a few factors) that explain most of the variability in the rate of productivity growth?

Between 1960 and 1973, real income and output in Canada grew on average by about 5.8% per annum. Out of this increase, Kendrick attributed 1.6 percentage points to an increase in the number of hours worked. (The increase in the number of persons employed would have contributed 2.3 percentage points. However, there was another factor which *reduced* labour's contribution to growth — a decrease in the number of hours worked each week by the typical worker. This acted as a drag on growth. The effect of shorter hours was large by historical standards: It reduced growth by 0.7 percentage points.) The difference of 4.2 percentage points between the growth rates of output and labour input (5.8 − 1.6 = 4.2) represents growth which was due to increased labour productivity during the period.

In 1973–78, real output growth fell by 2.5 percentage points to an average of 3.3% per year. This happened in spite of a more rapid increase in the number of hours worked: During 1973–78 the number of persons employed increased by as much as 2.8% per year, and the number of hours worked by 1.8% annually. Thus, the annual increase in labour productivity during 1973-78 was only 1.5% (3.3 − 1.8 = 1.5), less than half the rate of increase during the earlier period. Kendrick's study shows that a similar slowdown occurred in most industrialized countries, including the United States where productivity growth fell from an annual rate of 2.9% in 1960–73 to 1.2% in 1973–78. What went wrong?

Part of the answer lies in cyclical factors. In 1973, aggregate demand and capacity utilization were high; in

■ ■ ■ ■ ■

[1] The original study by Denison was *The Sources of Economic Growth in the United States and the Alternatives Before Us* (New York: Committee for Economic Development, 1962). Denison has subsequently updated his study several times.

Table 17-1 Sources of Growth in Real Income, Canada 1960-73 and 1973-78 (percent per year)

		Col. 1 1960-73		Col. 2 1973-78		Col. 3 Difference (2-1)
Growth of real income		5.8		3.3		−2.5
Contribution to growth by: Increase in labour hours		1.6		1.8		0.2
Increase in persons employed	(2.3)		(2.8)		(0.5)	
Decrease in average hours worked	(−0.7)		(−1.0)		(−0.3)	
Increase in labour productivity		4.2		1.5		−2.7
Improvement in quality of labour force		0.0		0.3		0.3
Education	(0.5)		(0.6)		(0.1)	
Age-sex composition	(−0.5)		(−0.3)		(0.2)	
Increase in capital		1.5		1.5		0.0
Improved resource allocation		0.2		−0.1		−0.3
More economies of scale		0.6		0.3		−0.3
Change in capacity utilization		0.2		−0.8		−1.0
Advances in knowledge; residual		1.7		0.3		−1.4

Source: Adapted from John W. Kendrick, "International Comparisons of Recent Productivity Trends," in Sam H. Schurr, Sidney Sonenblum, and David O. Wood, eds., *Energy, Productivity, and Economic Growth* (Cambridge, Massachusetts: Oelgeschlager, Gunn & Hain Publishers, 1983), pp. 86-87.

1978 they remained weak following the world-wide recession in 1975. As we shall see in more detail shortly, there is a tendency for productivity to vary systematically over the cycle. It tends to rise rapidly as the economy begins to move toward a cyclical peak, and then to fall (or at least rise less rapidly) before and during recessionary periods. This kind of cyclical effect shows up in the "capacity utilization" item in Table 17-1: While rising capacity utilization contributed 0.2 percentage points to productivity growth during 1960–73, Kendrick estimates that *falling* capacity utilization *reduced* productivity growth by 0.8 percentage points during 1973–78.

The cyclical effect explains why *actual* productivity will fall when demand is weak, but it does not explain why *potential* productivity (after correcting for short-term cyclical factors) changes. What are the factors that cause variations in potential productivity?

Capital Accumulation and the Quality of the Labour Force

As we noted earlier, an obvious factor that leads to rising labour productivity is capital accumulation. As the amount of capital in the economy increases, each worker has more machinery and equipment to work with. As a result, labour productivity grows.

Another potentially important factor that may raise labour productivity has been emphasized in recent years: Improvements in the quality of labour. These improvements may come from two kinds of sources.

First, workers may become more productive because they have more education. Over the years, the amount of education of a representative Canadian worker has increased: Young people, on average, have received more education when they enter the labour force than older workers had when they entered. As a result, the average amount of education in the labour force has been rising. Second, workers may become more productive over time because they receive training on the job.

The increase in productivity as workers have more education or experience is often seen as analogous to the increased productivity that results from capital accumulation. The skills that make workers more productive can be thought of as a form of "human capital" (as distinct from machinery and equipment which is "physical capital"), and acquiring them requires investment of resources (for education and training) just as acquiring physical capital requires that resources be invested in the production of machinery and equipment.

Physical capital accumulation was a major contributor to labour productivity in both 1960–73 and 1973–78. But while it is an important factor, it *can't* be used to explain the decreased productivity growth between the periods: It added some 1.5 percentage points to the productivity growth rate in both periods. Human capital accumulation through education was estimated as having added about half a percentage point to the growth of productivity during both periods. However, there was an increase in the proportion of young people and women in the labour force during the 1970s. Because both women and younger workers tend to have shorter periods of continuous on-the-job experience, their productivity tends to be lower than that of older males. The change in the age-sex composition of the labour force, therefore, was estimated as having made a negative contribution to productivity growth: −0.5 percentage points during 1960–73, and −0.3 points during 1973–78.

Structural Shifts

Thus, while capital accumulation and changes in the quality of the labour force may be important determinants of variations in the productivity growth rate, their contributions remained relatively stable through the 1960s and 1970s: They cannot be used to explain why productivity growth fell in the 1970s. One factor that *can* be used to explain part of the change, on the other hand, is the efficiency of resource allocation. According to Table 17-1, it appears that during 1973–78 we were less able than in earlier periods to increase productivity by reallocating resources from low-productivity industries to others in which their productivity was higher.

Productivity-increasing changes in resource allocation may come about for several reasons. For example,

over the last few decades there has been a gradual lowering of the barriers against international trade, both in Canada and in other countries. As a result, both imports and exports have increased. This has led to a transfer of resources out of Canadian industries where domestic production has been displaced by imports, and into industries that produce goods for exports. But this process tends to increase productivity: Industries that lose ground to imports tend to be industries where Canadian labour productivity is relatively low, while labour productivity tends to be high in our export industries. Furthermore, during earlier decades, there was a steady transfer of labour from low-productivity agriculture to other higher-productivity sectors. As a consequence, the nation's overall productivity has improved. But by the 1970s, the structural shift of resources out of agriculture had become much less important (in part because agriculture already was a relatively small part of the economy). A more significant trend in the 1970s was the transfer of labour into the service industries; but in these industries, labour productivity tends to be *lower* than elsewhere in the economy.

Economies of scale is another factor that can contribute to productivity growth. (Recall from Chapter 2 that economies of scale means that if labour and other inputs grow by 4%, say, output will grow by more than 4%.) The gains in real income from larger-scale production can come about in several ways. There may be a larger Canadian demand for an industry's products, so that each existing plant produces a larger volume of output. Or there may be a consolidation of production for the Canadian market in a smaller number of large-scale plants. Or again, the gains may come about as more and more Canadian firms try to take advantage of economies of scale by producing for the world market, rather than for the smaller Canadian market only.

Increased scale economies raised labour productivity an estimated 0.6% during 1960–73, but only 0.3% during the 1973–78 period, according to Kendrick's estimates. The reduction in the contribution of this factor thus accounts for 0.3 percentage points of the reduction in productivity growth during the 1970s.

The Mysterious Residual

Between 1960–73 and 1973–78, productivity growth decreased by 2.7 percentage points. Out of this decrease, cyclical variation in capacity utilization accounted for 1 percentage point. Together, the other factors discussed above explain another 0.3 percentage points. The remaining decline of 1.4 percentage points is just a decline in the residual item "advances in knowledge." During 1960–73, this factor was estimated as having contributed as much as 1.7% to overall productivity growth; in 1973–78, on the other hand, it only contributed 0.3%.

"Advances in knowledge" is usually thought of as reflecting productivity increases through **improvements in technology**; that is, new inventions, better designs of machinery, and better methods of production. However, it is important to recognize that there are no independent estimates of the contribution of these factors. The contribution is simply measured as a residual: It is what is left over after we have estimated the contributions of all other factors to the rate of productivity growth.

Thus, the most striking aspect of the estimates in Table 17-1 is that *they leave a large part of the slowdown in productivity growth unexplained*. In a similar study of the productivity slowdown in the United States, Edward Denison was able to explain no more than 30% of the decline by looking at the traditional factors discussed above; over 70% of the slowdown was left unexplained.[2]

Perhaps the most important conclusion from Kendrick's study is that growth resulted from a *combination* of causes. *No single determinant held the key to growth*, nor could any simple strategy — such as increasing investment in plant and equipment — hold out hope for a major acceleration of growth. Commenting on similar findings in a study of productivity in the United States, Denison observed: "The tale of the kingdom lost for want of a nail appears in poetry, not in history."

SOME OTHER EXPLANATIONS

Because the traditional factors considered by Kendrick and Denison do not explain much of the slowdown in productivity growth since the mid-1970s, a number of alternatives have been suggested. One is a possible *decline in the rate of technological improvement* in the world economy. Another relates to the impact of the *rise in world energy prices* in the 1970s.

■ ■ ■ ■ ■

[2] Denison's analysis was based on *potential* output (with the cyclical effects removed), while the estimates in Table 17-1 are based on *actual* output which includes cyclical effects. If cyclical effects are excluded, the factors shown in Table 17-1 would have explained less than 20% of the Canadian productivity slowdown.

Research and Development

In the United States, the suggestion that a decline in the rate of technological improvement may be to blame for slower productivity growth has been largely motivated by an observed decline in the rate of spending on research and development (R&D). However, Denison, in a study of the U.S. productivity slowdown in the 1970s is skeptical that smaller R&D explains much of the disappointing U.S. performance. As a percentage of U.S. GDP, R&D expenditures did decline, from a peak of 3.0% in 1964 to 2.3% in 1977. But this decline was gradual, and it is hard to see how it could account for the abrupt deterioration in the growth of output per U.S. worker from 1973/74. Furthermore, the decline in R&D was concentrated in the government category, mostly for weapons and space research. Private R&D expenditures — that is, expenditures by industries and universities which make the greatest contribution to higher output — remained relatively stable from 1970 to 1977 as a percentage of GDP.

Canada also had a decline in R&D expenditures relative to GDP: From a peak of almost 1.3% R&D expenditures had fallen to less than 1% of GDP by 1980. But again, it seems unlikely that this decrease was a major explanation of the sharp drop in Canada's productivity growth during the 1970s, partly because the decrease was so gradual, and partly because R&D spending is less important relative to GDP in Canada than in the United States.

The Increase in Energy Prices

The rise in energy prices is perhaps the most interesting of the remaining possible explanations for slower productivity growth in the 1970s. Energy prices are an obvious scapegoat, since they could explain the timing of the sharp deterioration after 1973/74 when the price of oil skyrocketed. Moreover, the higher oil price might explain why the growth rate declined abruptly in *many* countries at about this time.

In a study of productivity in the 1970s, the Economic Council of Canada did indeed find that in the middle of the decade, following the oil price increases, the amount of energy per unit of output declined in a majority of industries. But the Council was skeptical of the suggestion that this was a major cause of the overall productivity slowdown. The principal reason was that the amount of energy per unit of output did not decrease by very much. (If it had fallen sharply, this would have indicated the adoption of different and probably less productive methods of doing business. But, since oil use did not fall much, it is difficult to explain the productivity deterioration in this way.)

In spite of the Council's findings, many economists continue to believe that the energy price increases must have been at least part of the explanation for the disappointing productivity performance in Canada and elsewhere in the 1970s and early 1980s. After all, not only did productivity growth slow down sharply in 1974; it also fell dramatically again in 1979/80, following the second sharp increase in OPEC's oil prices. The coincidence is too strong to ignore.

PRODUCTIVITY GROWTH: PROSPECTS FOR THE 1990s

If we had a more precise idea of the causes of the poor productivity performance in the 1970s, we would be in a better position to interpret the fluctuations that have occurred during the 1980s, as shown in Figure 17-2. For example, if we knew that spiralling oil prices really were the major culprit in the earlier productivity slowdown, we would have expected productivity to rebound in the late 1980s with the falling oil prices in 1986/87.

However, it is not just our uncertainty about what happened as productivity growth slowed down in the 1970s that makes it hard to interpret the fluctuations in the 1980s. Year-to-year changes in productivity can be strongly affected by the business cycle, and Canada's economic performance in the 1980s has been strongly affected by cyclical fluctuations.

Cyclical Swings in Productivity: A Reprise

During cyclical recoveries, productivity generally increases very rapidly. During recessions, it generally increases very slowly, or even declines. Why?

A major reason is that employment is sticky in the face of fluctuating demand. Many white-collar workers are on annual salaries, and cannot be laid off easily during recessions. Nor is it costless to lay off production-line workers. They may get jobs elsewhere and be unavailable when the company wants to expand. Because of the costs of hiring and training, a company's labour force represents an investment which may be lost if workers are laid off. As the economy slides into a recession, firms therefore reduce their employment less than their output. Because underemployed workers are

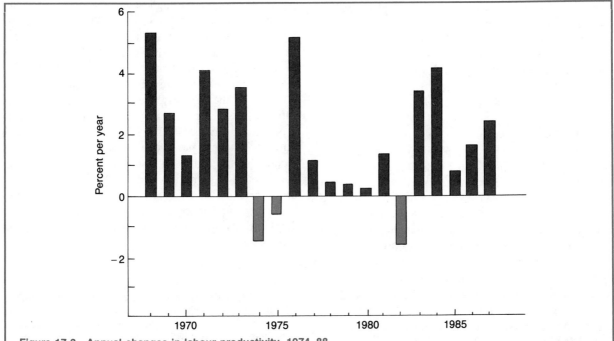

Figure 17-2 Annual changes in labour productivity, 1974–88.
During recessions, productivity is weak. Notice how productivity actually declined during the recessions of 1974–75 and 1982. On the other hand, productivity expands rapidly during cyclical expansions, as in 1976 and in the mid-1980s.

Source: Based on data from Statistics Canada's *CANSIM Databank*. Reprinted by permission of the Minister of Supply and Services Canada.

retained, productivity suffers. Then, as economic conditions improve and output recovers, the slack is picked up. Firms can increase their output rapidly without adding many new workers. As a result, productivity rises rapidly during the recovery from a recession.

Figure 17-2 shows how productivity declined during the recessions of 1974/75 and 1982. And while 1977-80 were not recession years, the weak productivity performance in these years can be partly explained by the fact that they were years of weak demand and slow growth of real output.

Productivity growth during 1983-87 has averaged around 2.4%, somewhat better than the performance during the second half of the 1970s. However, as Figure 17-2 shows, the average mostly reflects the substantial increases of 1983 and 1984. While total output grew relatively rapidly during 1985-87, employment and labour hours also increased substantially, and productivity growth was modest. In predicting productivity growth for the 1990s, should we focus on the slow growth in 1985-87 (attributing the productivity growth in 1983 and 1984 to the economy's cyclical recovery) or should we treat the stagnation in 1985-87 as an effect of the unusually high rates of labour force growth during those years, and predict a return to the higher productivity growth rates of the past?

While it may still be too early to tell, some observers are arguing that there are a number of factors that point toward relatively high productivity growth rates over the next decade. For one thing, there is likely to be relatively slow growth in the labour force. Moreover, energy prices have been falling; there is a tendency toward reduced regulation; and, in many sectors in the economy, productivity will rise rapidly as there is increasing use of computerized technology. In addition, productivity may increase as firms take advantage of economies of scale by increasing exports in response to better access to the U.S. market under the Canada-United States Free Trade Agreement that came into effect in 1989. On the other hand, there is also great uncertainty about the effects on productivity of the increasingly stringent measures that may be necessary to safeguard the environment during the 1990s. If there is one thing that recent history has taught us, it is that predictions concerning economic growth should be interpreted cautiously: Our track record in predicting growth and productivity performance has not been outstanding.

INTERNATIONAL COMPARISONS

The countries of the world are often classified into three groups:

1. *High-income industrialized countries* with market economies: Western European nations, the United States, Canada, Japan, Australia, and New Zealand.

2. *Centrally planned economies:* the Soviet Union and Eastern Europe. Because of the central role of the government in these economies, they are considered separately in Chapter 40.

3. *Less-developed countries* (LDCs): mainly in Africa, Asia, and Latin America. They are also often known as the *developing nations* or *Third World nations*. (The high-income countries are the First World, and the centrally planned countries are the Second World. China, Vietnam, and Cuba are sometimes classified in the Second World, sometimes in the Third.)

Oil-exporting countries are sometimes classified as a separate group because their experience has been so different from that of other countries. For a few countries with low populations, oil has been a quick and easy path to riches. During the first half of the 1980s, when oil prices were high, the highest income countries in the world were not the United States, Switzerland, or Japan, but the United Arab Emirates. The fortunes of the oil-exporting countries can, however, change very rapidly as the price of oil fluctuates.

There are major differences within groups, particularly among the less-developed countries. For example, Ethiopia, in 1986 the poorest country in the world with a per capita income of U.S.$120, was far poorer than Singapore, where per capita income was $7,410.[3] In fact, Singapore and Hong Kong, which are classified as members of the Third World for geographic and historical reasons, have higher per capita incomes than Ireland or Spain. The most important generalization about the Third World is this: One should be careful about generalizations.

■ ■ ■ ■ ■

[3] Such comparisons are not very precise. There are major difficulties in comparing output per person in various countries. See Irving B. Kravis *et al.*, *A System of International Comparisons of Gross Products and Purchasing Power* (Baltimore: Johns Hopkins University Press, 1975). The numbers cited here are from the World Bank, *World Development Report* (Washington, D.C.: 1988), pp. 223-24.

Figure 17-3 illustrates how much growth in per capita income differs among countries. Since 1965, per capita GDP has increased at an annual average of more than 4% in Japan and more than 6% in Singapore and South Korea. Unfortunately, some of the poor countries have made little or no progress in improving their incomes — for example, Ethiopia and Bangladesh: Since 1965, GDP per capita has not increased at all in Ethiopia and only by 0.4% per year in Bangladesh.

PROBLEMS OF THE LEAST DEVELOPED COUNTRIES: THE VICIOUS CIRCLE OF POVERTY

Why is it so difficult for people in the poorest countries to improve their lot? Figure 17-4 illustrates some of the reasons that countries can be caught in a *vicious circle of poverty*.

1. Low saving and investment

When incomes are very low, people are preoccupied with survival; when they are hungry, they may be unwilling and unable to save and invest. As a result, they have difficulty accumulating the capital that is so important for growth. The outside loop in Figure 17-4 illustrates this point. Low incomes mean low saving; low saving means low investment; and low investment means a slow rate of increase in productivity and per capita incomes. Low saving is a *result* of poverty. It is also a *cause* of continuing poverty.

2. Slow technological progress

Low investment not only limits the amount of capital, but also retards technological progress (Figure 17-4, box 2). The reason is that technology is often embodied in physical capital equipment. To adopt new ways of doing things, it is often necessary to acquire new machinery

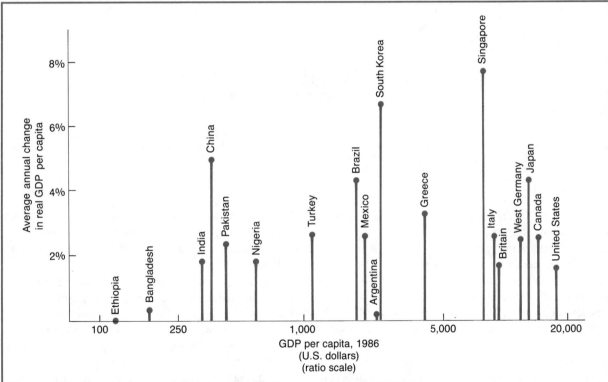

Figure 17-3   Increases in per capita output: International comparisons, 1965–86.

Growth in real GDP per capita has varied considerably among countries. A number of countries have enjoyed very rapid increases — for example, Singapore and South Korea. A wide range of countries at quite different levels of development have been at or near the world average of 2.5% — for example, Pakistan, Turkey, Mexico, Italy, West Germany, and Canada. Particularly disappointing has been the nonexistent or very small improvement in two countries with very low per capita incomes, Ethiopia and Bangladesh.

Source: World Bank, *World Development Report 1988*, pp. 222–23.

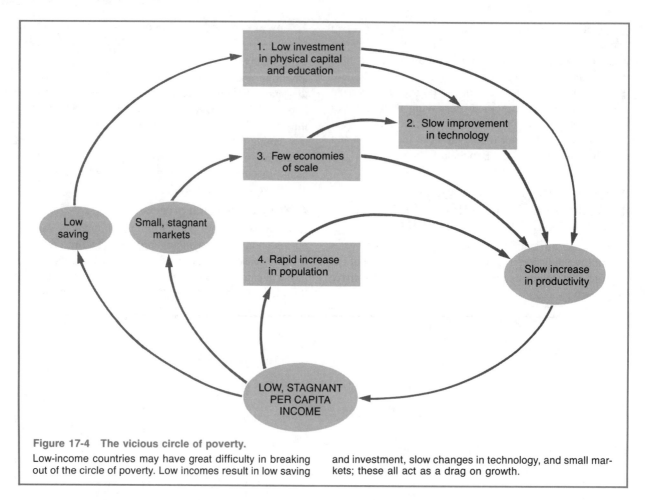

Figure 17-4   The vicious circle of poverty.
Low-income countries may have great difficulty in breaking out of the circle of poverty. Low incomes result in low saving and investment, slow changes in technology, and small markets; these all act as a drag on growth.

or equipment. Therefore, low investment can mean slow technological advance.

3. Small, stagnant markets

In many sectors of the economy, particularly manufacturing, firms have to produce in high volume to gain economies of scale and produce efficiently. If a country has low and stagnant incomes, businesses will not be able to sell in large quantities. Productivity will suffer as a result (Figure 17-4, box 3).

4. Rapid increase in population

Many low-income countries have a rapid growth in population. As a result, the already low quantities of capital and other resources must be spread even more thinly. Once again, this can act as a drag on output per person (Figure 17-4, box 4).

Paradoxically, a high rate of infant mortality has been one reason for the rapid growth of population in some

LDCs. In these regions people need children for economic support in their old age. If infant mortality is high, couples may have many children to be sure some will survive.

There is, however, hope for the future. Improvements in sanitation and public health almost always accompany the early stages of economic development. These improvements not only make a direct contribution to the quality of life but, in the long run, they can also contribute to lower birth rates and a stabilization of population. Fertility rates have already fallen from an average of 6.5 per woman in 1965 to 3.9 in 1985 in the very low-income countries (with per capita incomes of less than $500 per year). However, it will be many years before the rate of population growth shows a corresponding decrease. In the short run, better sanitation and public health programs lead to lower death rates and a more rapid rate of growth of population. In the short run, they add urgency to the development process.

One important caution is necessary regarding population. The oft-heard term, *overpopulation*, is fuzzy and imprecise. A high and growing population can put pressure on resources and slow the development process. But we cannot identify any particular population as "too high." Hong Kong and Singapore are two of the most densely populated areas on earth. Yet their per capita incomes have grown very rapidly. (For an important early view on the population question, see Box 17-1.)

In addition to the barriers to development shown in Figure 17-4, several others may be noted:

5. Social and cultural barriers

For economic development to take place, individuals and social groups must want it badly enough to change their old ways of doing things; they must be willing to bear the costs. The process of development can cause profound changes in social and political relationships. A political élite may be indifferent or even hostile to economic development; a growing merchant and manufacturing class may challenge their power. In some developing countries, *entrepreneurship* may be the critical missing ingredient. New industries do not take root and grow by themselves; they need vigorous entrepreneurs.

Negative attitudes toward business do not always raise an insuperable barrier to development. During the eighteenth and nineteenth centuries, British industry and commerce developed rapidly in spite of the view of the upper class that gentlemen do not pursue business careers. Other groups in society were quite ready to step forward and take a lead in the new industries.

6. Lack of social capital

To develop, countries need more capital. A particularly strategic role is played by **social capital** or **infrastructure**, such as roads, electric power, and telephone systems. If these are lacking, even the most talented and ambitious entrepreneur may fail. Most machinery requires an assured, steady source of electricity. A smoothly running telephone system can contribute to business efficiency in many ways—in particular, by permitting close contact with suppliers and markets.

In all countries, roadbuilding is the responsibility of the government. In almost all countries, so are railroads and electric power. In most countries, the government has responsibility for telephones and other forms of communication.

The central role of government provides one huge advantage: The government may be able to raise the large amounts of financing necessary for a new power plant or for a telephone system. Private entrepreneurs might be unable to do so because most LDCs have poorly developed markets for bonds and other financial capital. But heavy government involvement can have disadvantages, too. Government ownership can lead to cronyism and poor management. If government enterprises receive large subsidies, they may lack a strong incentive to cut costs and increase efficiency.

7. War

Finally, peace and a reasonably stable society are prerequisites for vigorous economic growth. The success stories—South Korea, Hong Kong, Singapore, and Taiwan—have enjoyed 30 or more years of uninterrupted peace. The most depressing story comes from Ethiopia. Its already low income fell during the long civil war of the 1980s. (Figure 17-3 shows an average increase of zero, but this includes both the prewar years of growth and the wartime years of decline.) Fragmentary information suggests that per capita income also declined in Iran and Iraq during their war in the 1980s.

BREAKING THE VICIOUS CIRCLE

One path out of the vicious circle of poverty lies in saving, hard work, and vigorous entrepreneurship. Although progress may be very slow and difficult at first, it becomes easier as the economy grows. As incomes rise, it is easier to save: Saving may be taken out of the increase in income, with no actual fall in consumption.

Development and the International Economy

Contacts with the international economy provide another path out of the vicious circle. The rest of the world can help in a number of ways, by providing a number of critical inputs.

1. Financial capital

Financial capital can be used to pay for imported machinery, equipment, and other inputs. When foreign funds are available, investment is no longer limited to the level of domestic saving.

Foreign capital comes in various forms and from various sources. It can come in the form of *grants*, *loans*, or *direct investment*. It can come from foreign governments, from international organizations such as the

Box 17-1

■ ■ ■ ■ ■ ■ ■ ■ ■ ■ ■ ■ ■ ■ ■ ■ ■ ■ ■

Will Population Explode? The Malthusian Problem

There is a wide variation among the less-developed countries. In some, per capita output has risen rapidly in the past two decades; in others, it has remained relatively stagnant. The very poorest are haunted by the grim prospect described by the young English clergyman Thomas Malthus in his *Essay on the Principle of Population* (1798). Malthus emphasized the scarcity of natural resources — particularly land — which limits the production of food. Specifically, he argued that the output of food increases at best at an arithmetic rate (1, 2, 3, 4, 5, 6, and so on). However, the "passion between the sexes" means that population tends to increase at a geometric rate (1, 2, 4, 8, 16, 32, and so on):

> It may safely be pronounced that population, when unchecked, goes on doubling itself every twenty-five years, or increases in a geometrical ratio. The rate according to which the productions of the earth may be supposed to increase, will not be so easy to determine. Of this, however, we may be perfectly certain, that the ratio of their increase in a limited territory must be of a totally different nature from the ratio of the increase in population. A thousand millions are

just as easily doubled every twenty-five years by the power of population as a thousand. But the food to support the increase from the greater number will by no means be obtained with the same facility....

> It may be fairly pronounced, therefore, that considering the present average state of the earth, the means of subsistence, under circumstances the most favourable to human industry, could not possibly be made to increase faster than in an arithmetic ratio... The ultimate check to population appears then to be a want of food, arising necessarily from the different ratios according to which population and food increase.*

Because of the tendency of population to outstrip food production, the per capita income of the working class will be driven down to the subsistence level. During the nineteenth century, this proposition came to be known as the **iron law of wages**.

After the wage reaches the subsistence level, population growth cannot continue at the same rate; there isn't enough food. Famine, pestilence, or war will keep the population in check. Malthus' theory pointed to a cruel conclusion. Public relief for the poor would do nothing in the long run to improve their condition. It would simply result in an upsurge in population; there would be more people to starve in the future.

As a general forecast, Malthus' theory proved inaccurate. The standard of living in most countries has

*Thomas Malthus, *An Essay on the Principle of Population* (London: 1798).

World Bank, or from foreign corporations and other private sources.

Needless to say, grants provide one clear advantage over loans: They don't have to be repaid. For borrowing to be advantageous in the long run, the funds must be invested in projects that will generate future payoffs sufficient to pay interest and retire the loan. If loans are used simply to finance consumption, they will make matters worse: The nation will face a future burden of interest and repayment, without any corresponding increase in productive capacity. (We will consider some of the problems that foreign debt can create in Chapter 20.)

As noted in Chapter 14, direct investment occurs when a business in one country establishes operation in another. Direct investment often carries major advantages for low-income host countries since it comes as a package, together with management and technology. Direct investment is nevertheless quite controversial, since host countries often fear that the foreign company will extract excessive profits and possibly delay the

development of domestic entrepreneurship and management.

2. Technology

Other nations can likewise be a source of technology. It is not necessary for every country to reinvent the wheel — or the computer, or advanced methods of production.

In this respect, the developing nations have an advantage. Because much of their technology is outmoded, they have a great opportunity to borrow foreign technology. Borrowed technology is one of the secrets of success in Taiwan, Korea, and a number of other rapidly growing economies. However, as countries catch up, the technological gap closes. Because there is less foreign technology still to be borrowed, growth may slow down.

3. Markets

By exporting into the world market, firms may be able to achieve *economies of scale* in spite of limited domestic markets. Thus, for example, the fledgling Korean automobile industry is exporting much of its output in order to bring its per-unit costs down.

Courtesy of Canapress Photo Service/Camera Press

risen markedly in the past 200 years. Birth control has been a much greater constraint on population growth than Malthus anticipated. Food production has increased beyond Malthus' expectation, because of the technological revolution that has extended to agriculture as well as manufacturing. Nevertheless, Malthus' theory — that there can be a race between population growth and the ability to produce—is worth remembering in a world that is becoming more crowded.

Canada and other industrialized countries have contributed in each of the above ways to the growth of the developing nations. They have provided grants, loans, direct investment, technology, and markets. Each of these is helpful to the developing countries, but they certainly do not all fall under the category of "aid." Many loans, most trade, and practically all direct investment are motivated by commercial considerations, with both sides expecting to gain.

LIVING IN A GLOBAL ECONOMY: THE "FOUR TIGERS" OF EAST ASIA

Development can be a slow and painful process. What can be learned from economies that have broken out of the vicious circle and grown very rapidly? Specifically, what can be learned from the group of four new industrializing economies of East Asia—Hong Kong, Singapore, South Korea, and Taiwan—whose output per capita has grown by more than 6% per year over the past two decades?

The first message is that an economy does not have to be richly endowed with natural resources to grow rapidly. None of the four has plentiful mineral resources, and two — Hong Kong and Singapore — have only minimal amounts of land.

Their secret lies in the two paths out of the vicious circle noted in the previous section: (1) saving, hard work, and vigorous entrepreneurship; and (2) contacts with the world economy.

In each of the four economies, high saving rates provide the resources for high investment. For the four as a group, gross saving averages almost 30% of GDP. In one year, 1985, saving in Singapore reached an astonishing 42% of GDP! Furthermore, the work ethic is deeply engrained and constantly reinforced. Koreans awake to hear the radio announcers urge them to "work harder to make our nation better." They work an average of 2700 hours a year — 25% more than the Japanese and some 40% more than North Americans. Furthermore, each of the four has a vigorous group of entrepreneurs. In some respects, however, they are dissimilar. Large conglomerates (*chaebol*)—such as Daewoo and Hyundai—dominate the Korean economy, and have been actively encouraged by the government. In contrast, Taiwanese firms are mostly small and medium-sized.

International Economic Relations

Each of the four is strongly *export oriented*. Korea exports 40% of GDP, and the others, even more. (In contrast, Japan exports no more than 13% of its GDP, and the United States 6%.) Indeed, the exports of Singapore and Hong Kong are *greater* than GDP; Singapore and Hong Kong export more goods than they produce. How can that be? These two ports operate as major transshipment centres, re-exporting many goods they have previously imported. Hong Kong plays a particularly important role as a transshipment port for many of China's exports and imports.

All four tigers are voracious users of *foreign technology* and *foreign equipment*. In the late 1980s, the most modern fleet of aircraft in the world was owned by Singapore Airlines. Korea produces video cassette recorders (VCRs); the United States doesn't, even though the VCR was invented there. The Daewoo group of Korea is in the process of hiring 1000 Ph.D.s by 1990, many of them trained in North American universities. The fledgling Korean auto industry has close contacts with Japan and North America (Hyundai already has a Canadian assembly plant) as sources of both technology and markets.

Although foreign markets and foreign technology have made substantial contributions to the rapid growth of these four economies, access to foreign *financial capital* has on average not been very important. In fact, these four export much more than they import, meaning that they have a net capital *outflow* to the rest of the world (they use their merchandise trade surplus to acquire assets from foreign nations). During the 1980s, the trade surpluses of Taiwan and Korea became so large as to cause frictions with their trading partners, especially the United States. In 1986, Taiwan's trade surplus amounted to almost 10% of its GDP, one of the highest ratios ever recorded in any country.

This is not to say that foreign capital can be completely ignored as a contributor to growth. At an early stage, both Korea and Taiwan were major recipients of U.S. aid. During the 1960s and 1970s, Korea was a sizable borrower in international capital markets; by 1985, its foreign debt amounted to almost $50 billion.

Since that time, however, Korea has repaid some of this debt with the proceeds from its trade surpluses.

Why have the four been so successful in exporting? One important reason is that they have kept their products highly competitive through their exchange rate policies. That is, they have used policies that have kept the prices of their currencies low in international markets.

In this respect, the experience of the four East Asian economies is the opposite of a number of other developing countries that have kept their currencies *overvalued* (priced too high in terms of other currencies). This overvaluation has resulted in a chronic tendency for their exports to fall short of their imports, and an excess demand for foreign currencies by domestic residents. To cope with this excess demand, they have often restricted import demand through licencing arrangements; but this has sometimes added to the woes of their domestic industries. For example, Indian manufacturers sometimes face great difficulty in obtaining licences to import needed spare parts for their machines. It is obviously inefficient when the government delays imports of spare parts with the result that expensive machinery is left idle.

The Role of Government

In addition to keeping their exports competitively priced through their exchange rate policies, what role have the governments played in the four rapidly developing economies in East Asia?

In each, the government has provided excellent social capital and extensive services to the public in the form of free education, subsidized health services, and large programs of subsidized housing. In other areas of the economy, their attitudes toward government regulation and intervention, however, are quite different. Singapore follows a policy of free trade. Korea and Taiwan still maintain significant barriers to imports, although they have been reducing these barriers in recent years. With regard to domestic industries, Hong Kong has followed a policy close to laissez-faire. The Korean government has been much more interventionist, fostering large-scale industry, promoting government-business cooperation along Japanese lines, and setting export targets for individual firms. Even in Korea, however, the government has taken some steps away from regulation. Regulations on capital markets—including interest rate ceilings—have been relaxed, thereby stimulating domestic saving and investment.

In conclusion, what lessons can be learned from the experience of these four? We should be careful; what works in one time or place will not necessarily work in another. In particular, the emphasis on exports will work only if other countries are willing to take the exports; it will not work if foreign nations are highly protectionist. Nevertheless, the experience of the four economies suggest the following lessons:

1. Domestic *saving* can be a major engine of growth.
2. Access to *foreign technology* and *foreign markets* can similarly contribute to growth.
3. An *export-oriented* strategy can be very effective. Exports provide a quick way to capture economies of scale. Each of the four governments has sent a clear message to businesses: It is your responsibility to get out and compete on world markets. In contrast, less success has been achieved by countries that have followed an *import-substitution* strategy—that is, a strategy of restricting imports in order to stimulate domestic production of goods previously bought abroad. Import-substitution policies generally result in a high-cost, inefficient industrial sector—for example, the Indian firm that sometimes can't run its machines because it can't get spare parts.
4. An *undervalued currency* can promote exports. However, there is a danger if export-promotion policies are pursued too vigorously. In the face of large trade imbalances, trading partners may raise their barriers to imports in order to protect their own domestic industries.
5. Rapid growth is *consistent with a variety of approaches by government*. Government may intervene extensively; on the other hand, it may lean in the direction of laissez-faire. However, in each of the four cases, government provides high-quality social capital and extensive programs in education, health, and housing. The governments that do intervene most heavily—most notably, in Korea—do so in order to spur business to greater achievements; few of their regulations are anti-business. Indeed, each of the four governments takes a strongly pro-business stance.

Finally, the picture is not completely rosy. Not everybody shares fully in the rising incomes. Strains are especially apparent in South Korea. The nation has a somewhat more equal distribution of income than most countries, but the rapid changes of recent decades have provided special advantages to those with jobs in the export industries. It is true that people in those industries generally work very hard, but they have also earned incomes far above those of their compatriots. Particularly in the late 1980s, their incomes rose very rapidly. Employers were willing to pay higher wages because their exports were selling so well in foreign countries; they were eager to avoid strikes that would interrupt their lucrative business. Rapid wage increases seem likely to continue. If Korean cars sell in world markets, why should Korean auto workers not hope for wage rates approaching those in the auto industries of Japan, North America, or Europe? As the incomes of auto workers rise, however, other Koreans feel left behind.

GROWTH IN THE DEVELOPED COUNTRIES: Two Important Issues

In the poor nations of the world, the low average standard of living means that a high rate of growth of productivity and income is the major objective of economic policy. In richer nations too, the desire for a higher material standard of living remains a strong argument in favour of economic growth. Even if most of us are well off in comparison with the average person in developing countries, we still may want more comfortable cars, less crowded housing, and better health care, education, and entertainment.

In recent years, however, there has been increasing concern over the potential conflict between growth and the environment. If we continue to produce more and more goods and services, won't we end up destroying our natural environment?

Unsustainable Development?

No one disputes that one of the most important costs of economic growth in this century has been the degradation of the environment. The dangers of water and air pollution from radioactive materials, toxic wastes, and acid rain have been known for some years. Recently, we have become increasingly aware of the threats of the "greenhouse effect" and the depletion of the ozone layer in the atmosphere. In many poor countries, overly intensive use of forests, farmland, and water is causing drought and a disastrous reduction in agricultural productivity.

While our present-day material standard is important, so is an environment that is tolerably clean and capable of sustaining development in the long run. As E. J. Mishan, formerly of the London School of Economics, has pointed out, if we really wanted to construct an accurate measure of growth in people's standard of living, we should treat environmental degradation as a negative contribution to growth.[4] If we did that, Mishan argues, we would find that in many countries living standards haven't really been rising, even though there has been economic growth as conventionally measured by the change in per capita GDP. Moreover, as the 1987 report of the World Commission on Environment and Development (usually referred to as the Brundtland Commission after its chairperson, the Prime Minister of Norway, Gro Harlem Brundtland) has argued forcefully, we may not have much choice in the matter: A policy which does *not* take the environment into account cannot be sustained in the long run, because environmental deterioration will ultimately threaten human survival.

There is little doubt that environmental preservation will become an increasingly prominent goal of government policy in the 1990s and beyond. *Productivity* will still be an important objective. But we will have to recognize that in the future, improving productivity will not just refer to our ability to produce larger amounts of goods and services; it will also refer to our ability to do so in a way that doesn't despoil the natural environment.

Growth in North America: The Role of Government

We have already seen that an important issue for growth and development in poor nations is the role of government in promoting economic growth. This obviously is a very significant question in the industrialized countries as well.

There is a considerable difference between the views on this issue in Canada and the United States. In the United States, the government's role in stimulating growth has typically been seen as fairly limited; the government's main function is seen as that of providing a favourable milieu in which private enterprise will bring about growth. In Canada, on the other hand, the government has always been more active in promoting growth.

During our early history, the common attitude was that the government should assist in the opening of the new land. The Dominion Land Act of 1879 reflected this view. It gave the right to any settler to claim 160 acres of Crown land for farming purposes, and the set-

tler was given permanent title to the land if he could show that he had been using at least part of it for food production. And, during the nineteenth century, the government granted extensive subsidies and substantial blocks of land to the Canadian Pacific Railroad, providing not only the right-of-way needed for its lines, but also additional lands whose value would rise as new Western territories were opened up.[5]

In modern times, government in Canada has continued to take an active role in growth promotion, by subsidizing private projects, or by investing public money in specific enterprises considered beneficial to growth. The federal involvement in rail and air transportation, through Crown corporations such as the CNR and Air Canada, or the provincial governments' investment in industries such as hydro-electric power generation or telephone services, are examples of this more active role. (In the United States, these industries are generally in private hands.)

In the last several years, the debate over the appropriate extent of government involvement in the growth process has become more intense. In the business community, it is a widely held belief that one of the major obstacles to faster productivity growth is the increasing cost and effort that has to be devoted by business to dealing with various levels of government. A common attitude is that business could be much more productive if only government would leave it in peace. One major source of aggravation has been regulation. While most businessmen, both in large corporations and small firms, understand and sympathize with the need for health, safety, and environmental regulation, they are upset at the complications and delays that arise because of confusion in the regulatory process.

Partly in response to these concerns, significant steps toward regulatory reform have been taken in the 1980s. However, deregulation is not a simple matter. One problem is how to streamline the regulatory process and eliminate excessively detailed and inconsistent regulation, while still giving appropriate weight to other social goals such as safety and cleaner air. Another major issue is how to protect the interest of various groups in society (such as farmers) through regulation, without reducing

------

[4] E.J. Mishan, *Technology and Growth* (New York: Praeger, 1969).

[5] For a fascinating history of the CPR, see Pierre Berton, *The National Dream: The Great Railway, 1871-1881* (Toronto: McClelland and Stewart, 1970) and Pierre Berton, *The Last Spike: The Great Railway, 1881-1885* (Toronto: McClelland and Stewart, 1971).

the productive efficiency of the industries in which they work. These issues are discussed more fully in Part 8.

An Industrial Strategy?

Some proponents of growth want to achieve even closer cooperation between business and government, and do more than simply reduce tension between them. One common suggestion is for Canada to develop an *industrial strategy*. An attempt would be made to identify the most promising products for future development. Research grants or other government programs could then be used to encourage resources to move into the future "winners," and out of declining industries. Part of the motivation for these suggestions is provided by the example of Japan and nations such as Korea where government-business cooperation in research and marketing has played a major role in the growth of their export-based manufacturing industry.

Although the proposal to "pick winners" seems attractive, such a policy runs substantial risks. It may be as difficult for governments as for racetrack bettors to pick winners. Governments may, in fact, be less able than capital markets to pick winners. Before investing in a company, private individuals or firms have a great incentive to investigate it carefully, until they are convinced that it is a likely winner. But, in deciding how

to invest the public's money, a politician has two separate objectives: to "pick winners" with a high economic payoff and to "pick winners" which gain votes. Thus, rather than picking the economic winners (as the Japanese sometimes — but not always — do), the Canadian government might end up picking losers, as the British and Italian governments sometimes do. The government might come to the aid of corporations in danger of collapse. Consequently, an industrial strategy might lead to "lemon socialism" — that is, government ownership and support of dying companies.

CONCLUSION: Uncertainties about Productivity and Growth

If one thing stands out in this chapter, it should be this: Growth and productivity are complex phenomena. There is great uncertainty about the best policies to pursue in the struggle to raise incomes in the world's poor countries, and in the task of ensuring that our desire for a rising material standard does not lead to disastrous environmental consequences. These questions are difficult. But because they are so important, finding some answers ranks among the most important tasks that economists and politicians will be facing in the coming decades.

KEY POINTS

1. The growth of output depends on the combined effect of increases in (1) the number of hours worked, and (2) labour productivity.

2. Productivity in Canada grew most rapidly in the 1940-60 period. This corresponded to the slowest rate of growth of labour hours. Productivity growth has been slow since the second half of the 1970s, especially when labour hours were increasing rapidly.

3. Studies of productivity growth have shown that a number of factors contributed to rapid productivity increase before the mid-1970s. No single cause was the "key" to rapid growth.

4. A large part of the deterioration in Canada's productivity performance since 1973 cannot be accounted for by traditional factors. However, those who have analysed this problem may have underestimated the effects of declining R&D and the increase in the world price of energy in the 1970s.

5. A number of the lowest income countries have grown very slowly; some seem caught in a vicious circle. Saving is low because incomes are low, and incomes remain low because saving and investment are low.

6. There are two sets of factors that seem to have helped some nations break out of the vicious circle of poverty: on the one hand, a combination of hard work, saving, and investment; on the other, policies that increase a country's ties with the world economy.

7. The world economy can be a source of financial capital, permitting countries to invest more than they save. Foreign technology may be copied. Foreign markets can permit a new industry to gain economies of scale even if the domestic market is small.

8. Hard work, high rates of domestic saving, access to foreign technology, and an emphasis on exports have contributed to the rapid development of the

''four tigers'' of East Asia — Hong Kong, Singapore, South Korea, and Taiwan.

9. We should not simply assume that the faster the growth rate, the better. If we single-mindedly pursue the growth objective, we may give insufficient attention to other goals, such as preservation of the environment.

10. A proposal for stimulating industrial growth in Canada is for government to adopt an industrial strategy to help ''winners.'' One risk in this policy is that the government might in practice slip into ''lemon socialism,'' that is, helping losers and keeping resources in low-productivity industries.

KEY CONCEPTS

average productivity of labour
sources of growth
human capital vs. physical capital
resource re-allocation and productivity

technological improvement
cyclical productivity changes
export-based growth
borrowed technology

the vicious circle of poverty
social capital or infrastructure
industrial strategy
lemon socialism

PROBLEMS

17-1. Why might a rapid increase in population cause a drag on productivity? Are there any circumstances in which a rapid increase in population might *encourage* a rapid increase in productivity?

17-2. Observe in Figure 17-1 that the rate of growth of labour hours in the 1926-40 period was almost as slow as in 1940-60. But the rate of growth of productivity was substantially less rapid. That is, productivity did not grow as rapidly between 1926 and 1940 as we might expect simply by looking at the low rate of growth of labour hours. Were there any events during this period that acted as a drag on productivity? Explain how they acted to keep productivity from increasing more rapidly.

17-3. During recessions, productivity generally expands very slowly, or even declines. On the other hand, it generally expands very rapidly as the economy recovers from recession. Explain why.

17-4. What is the ''vicious circle of poverty?'' How can nations get out of it?

17-5. What are the advantages of an ''export-oriented'' growth strategy? What can governments do to encourage exports?

17-6. Keeping the value of a country's currency low in terms of foreign currencies will promote exports. Can you think of any disadvantages of such an approach?

17-7. How might an increase in energy prices cause a slowdown in productivity? Which of your explanations will show up in a reduction in the quantity of oil used? In 1985/86, oil prices *fell* rapidly. Do you think that this caused productivity growth to increase? Why or why not?

17-8. Opponents of an industrial strategy fear that government aid to specific industries would end up by helping the ''losers.'' Can you think of possible examples of this danger in recent Canadian history? Can you think of any ways an industrial strategy might be designed to reduce this danger?

Part 5

■■■■■■■■■■■■■■■■■■■■■■■■■■■■■■■■■■■

Three Great Macroeconomic Controversies

Following the review of aggregate demand and aggregate supply in Parts 3 and 4, we turn in Part 5 to three great macroeconomic controversies.

First, in Chapter 18, we discuss the issue of **policy rules**. Because of such things as time lags in the government's information about economic conditions and in the effects of fiscal and monetary policy on the economy, an "activist" strategy where the settings of monetary and fiscal policies are changed in response to economic conditions may, paradoxically, have the unintended effect of destabilizing the economy. Consequently, it is possible that the economy would be *more* stable if the policy makers were instructed to conduct monetary and fiscal policies according to some type of fixed *rule* that did not depend on the way the economy was behaving. The controversy between those who favour policy rules and those who advocate a more activist, discretionary policy is perhaps the most important single macroeconomic debate of our time.

Chapter 19 discusses several policy questions related to the unemployment/inflation trade-off introduced in Chapter 15. First, what determines the natural unemployment rate and what policies can we use to reduce it? Second, could we not sidestep the unemployment/inflation trade-off (at least temporarily) by using *wage and price controls* to directly suppress inflationary pressures? After these issues are discussed, we then also consider the conclusion of the "rational expectations" school that what matters more than anything else in macroeconomic policy is *credibility*: If the public believes that the government will stick with an anti-inflationary policy, say, then inflation will come down quickly, at a relatively low cost in terms of increased unemployment.

In Chapter 20 we consider the question of how the **international monetary system** should be organized. A system of *fixed* exchange rates facilitates international trade and payments, but it also puts restraints on the ability of policy makers to use monetary policy to stabilize the domestic economy. The postwar IMF system of pegged exchange rates was somewhat more flexible than the fixed-rate system implied by the old gold standard, but in the end it, too, broke down. The floating-rate system in use since the early 1970s also has been subject to problems. There have been large fluctuations in exchange rates between major world currencies, partly in response to large international capital flows, and the growing indebtedness of a number of LDCs has threatened to destabilize the system.

Chapter 18

■ ■

Fine Tuning or Stable Policy Settings?

If something works,
don't fix it.
American proverb

In the study of macroeconomics, better policies are the ultimate goal. No matter how elaborate our theories, and no matter how much progress we make in understanding detailed macroeconomic relationships, our work has not succeeded if it cannot be translated into better policies. And the ultimate test of macroeconomic policies is the degree to which they help in the achievement of high employment and stable prices.

It is not clear whether we should judge the policies of the past 25 years as a success or a failure. In part, the answer depends on the question: Successful compared to what? Certainly, compared to the depressed decade of the 1930s, the economy has performed well during the past quarter-century. The unemployment rate has never come anywhere close to the levels it reached during the 1930s. However, we have not been doing better and better as time passes. The recession of 1981/82 was much more severe than any during the preceding 30 years, with the unemployment rate rising to 12.8%, the highest rate since the Great Depression. With respect to inflation, the experience of the past two decades has also been worse than that of the preceding period. Bursts of inflation occurred during the mid-1970s and the early 1980s, with inflation hitting a peak of 12.7% in 1981. Although inflation was brought under much better control in the mid-1980s, it still remained in the range of 4%-5% per year during 1983 to 1988, substantially above the average annual rate of 1.8% between 1955 and 1966.

The mediocre performance of the economy in the past two decades has revitalized an old debate that goes back to the early days of the Keynesian-classical controversy in the 1930s. On the one side are those in the Keynesian tradition, who argue that aggregate demand policies should be *actively managed* in pursuit of the goals of high employment and stable prices. As the economy heads toward recession, expansive policies should be adopted. As the economy heads toward an inflationary boom, restraint should be exercised.

On the other side are the monetarists, who argue that activist, *discretionary* policies are more likely to do harm than good, no matter how well-intentioned policy makers might be. Consequently, they argue that discretionary policies should be avoided. Instead, permanent policy settings should be chosen and maintained regardless of the short-term fluctuations in economic activity. That is, a *policy rule* should be followed. It is, of course, important that the rule be chosen carefully and, in particular, that it be consistent with economic stability. For example, it would be a mistake to adhere to the rules of the old gold standard. Because banks under that system kept fractional reserves in the form of gold, a large superstructure of money could be built on a relatively small base of gold reserves. This made the banking system vulnerable to runs.

However, monetarists suggest that there is a policy rule that *is* consistent with a high degree of economic stability. Specifically, they suggest that the Bank of Canada should aim at a slow, steady increase in the money supply, at something like 5% or less per year. This increase would provide the money needed to purchase the expanding total output at stable prices.

Discretionary fiscal and monetary policies are policies that the government and the central bank adjust periodically in order to deal with changing conditions in the economy.

The sharp contrast between Keynesians and monetarists may be illustrated by comparing the statements of Keynesian Warren Smith and monetarist Milton Friedman. The flavour of the activist, hands-on-the-helm Keynesian view was given by Smith:[1]

> The only good rule is that the budget should never be balanced—except for an instant when a surplus to curb inflation is being altered to a deficit to fight deflation.

Friedman explicitly criticized the activist policy of attempting to "fine-tune" the economy:[2]

> Is fiscal policy being oversold? Is monetary policy being oversold? . . . My answer is yes to both of those questions. . . . Monetary policy is being oversold. . . . Fiscal policy is being oversold. . . . Fine tuning has been oversold.

We introduce this debate over the active management of demand by looking more closely at the Keynesian approach, in which aggregate demand policies are adjusted in pursuit of the goals of high employment and stable prices. In later sections of this chapter, we will explain criticisms of that policy, and problems with the alternative of following a monetary rule.

AIMING FOR A STABLE, HIGH-EMPLOYMENT ECONOMY: THE ACTIVE KEYNESIAN APPROACH

As we have seen — especially in Chapter 9 — Keynes believed that a market economy would suffer from two major diseases. The economy would move toward an equilibrium where there probably would be inadequate aggregate demand and high unemployment. And, even if the economy did get to a position of full employment, it would be unlikely to stay there primarily because of the instability of investment demand. In short, demand would tend to be both *inadequate* and *unstable*.

In the early days of the Keynesian revolution, inadequate aggregate demand was considered a more important problem than instability. This was scarcely surprising, because of the depth and persistence of the Great Depression. However, since the late 1940s, the emphasis of Keynesian thinking has shifted away from the problem of stagnation and toward the problem of instability. The economy did not lapse back into depression in the period after World War II as many economists

feared it would. In the past four decades, it has gone through bouts of inflation, as well as periodic recessions. There has been no long-run lack of aggregate demand, although demand has been unstable.

Nevertheless, concern continued over both the adequacy and the stability of aggregate demand. Therefore, the policy problem, as seen by Keynesian economists, was (1) to stimulate aggregate demand to the full-employment level, and then (2) to adjust or *fine-tune* it whenever needed to combat business fluctuations.

This Keynesian strategy is illustrated in Figure 18-1. Suppose that the economy in year 1 begins at a position of high unemployment. The actual production of the economy, at *A*, is well below the potential at full employment (*B*). Of course, the potential output of the economy does not remain constant. As time passes, the labour force grows, the capital stock increases, and technology improves. Thus, the path of full-employment or potential GDP has an upward trend. The objective of policy in year 1 should be to aim the economy toward the full-employment path. However, full employment cannot be achieved immediately; there are lags in the implementation and effect of policy. Thus, policy in year 1 should be aimed at stimulating the economy so that it approaches full employment at some time in the reasonably near future, as shown by the arrows in Figure 18-1.

An Example

By going back to the early 1960s, we can find a very clear and explicit illustration of this Keynesian strategy.

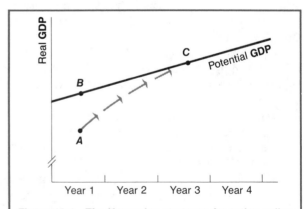

Figure 18-1 The Keynesian strategy: An active policy.
The activist Keynesian strategy is to move to the potential GDP path. Fiscal and monetary policies should then be fine-tuned to combat instability and keep the economy as close as possible to potential GDP.

■ ■ ■ ■ ■
[1] Warren Smith, statement to a meeting of U.S. Treasury consultants, as quoted by Paul A. Samuelson, *Economics*, 11th ed. (New York: McGraw-Hill, 1976), p. 222.
[2] Milton Friedman and Walter Heller, *Monetary vs. Fiscal Policy* (New York: W. W. Norton, 1969), p. 47.

By early 1961, the recession which started in 1960 had produced an unemployment rate in excess of 7%, the highest rate in Canada since the Second World War. As a consequence, a large GDP gap estimated at more than 6% of potential GDP had emerged, as shown in Figure 18-2. The policy problem was to try to eliminate the GDP gap fairly quickly, by making actual GDP follow a path like the thin line *A*. On the other hand, if the policy makers failed to stimulate the economy, it might follow a path like *B*: Along this path, the GDP gap would remain as wide in 1963/64 as it was in 1961.

The policies actually pursued in 1962/63 were intended to stimulate demand: The federal and provincial governments together ran substantial deficits, and the Canadian dollar was devalued. (Recall that a reduction in the international value of the Canadian dollar stimulates Canadian exports and reduces imports; it therefore stimulates aggregate demand for Canadian goods.) The results of the policy are shown by the coloured curve in Figure 18-2. Although the GDP gap was not eliminated very quickly, it was eliminated within four years; by 1964, the economy was pretty much on target. What remained now was to fine-tune the economy, keeping it as close as possible to the potential growth path.

There were, of course, problems. One was the well-

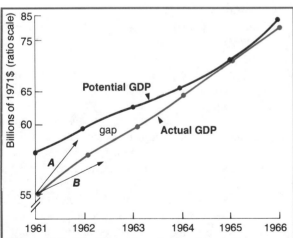

Figure 18-2   The Keynesian strategy in practice, 1961–66.

The diagram shows the estimated paths of potential and actual GDP during the first half of the 1960s, and illustrates how different policies might have affected the large GDP gap existing in 1961. Path *A* would have eliminated the gap quickly, but would have called for very expansionary policies. If policies had not been expansionary enough, the economy might have followed path *B*: Along this path, a large GDP gap would have persisted for a long time.

recognized problem of lags: How do you adjust policies when the actions taken today do not affect the economy until some future time when they may no longer be appropriate? Keynesians believed that they had an adequate—although far from perfect—answer. By forecasting, policy makers can get a fairly good idea of where the economy is headed. Thus, they should be able to "lead" their moving target. Details of economic forecasting are deferred until a later section in this chapter. Here, we turn to the way in which lags are used as an argument against an active demand-management policy.

THE CASE AGAINST ACTIVISM: LAGS

The core of the case against activism is the argument that active policies are more likely to destabilize than to stabilize the economy. Often, they are badly timed; they are designed to fight the battles of last year and are inappropriate to deal with the problems of the present and, more important, those of the future.

There are *three lags* between the time that aggregate demand should be changed and the time when the change actually occurs. To illustrate, suppose that the economy begins to slide down into a recession. This fact may not be recognized for some time. It takes time to gather statistics on what is happening. Initial signs of weakness may be dismissed as temporary disturbances; not every little jiggle in economic activity grows into a recession or boom. Thus, the first lag is the *recognition lag*, which occurs between the time the weakness in the economy begins and the time when it is recognized. Furthermore, even after the decline is recognized, policy makers take some time to act; this is the *action lag*. For example, spending programs must be designed before they can be implemented. Finally, after action is taken, there is some delay before the major *impact* on the economy is felt. For example, when government spending is finally increased, the various rounds of consumer spending in the multiplier process take time. For monetary policy, there is a lag between the open market purchase that pushes down interest rates and the actual investment that is stimulated as a consequence. These, then, are the lags that occur before aggregate demand actually changes: the *recognition lag*, the *action lag*, and the *impact lag*.

Consider how these lags can lead to incorrect policies and add to the instability of the economy. Suppose, for example, that the ideal path of aggregate demand is shown by the solid line in Figure 18-3. But actual demand follows the dashed curve. Starting at point *A*, aggregate demand starts to slip below the desired level;

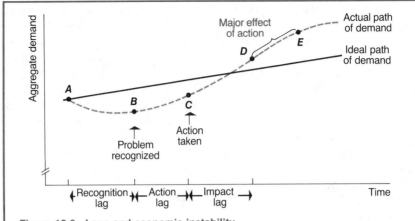

Figure 18-3 Lags and economic instability.
Because of the recognition, action, and impact lags, it is possible that policy changes will make things worse. Expansive steps aimed at fighting the recession at point C may add to a later inflationary boom at E. Similarly, policies aimed at restraining on inflationary boom may make the next recession worse.

the economy begins to move into a recession. However, this problem is not recognized for some time—not until point B. Even then, taxes are not cut immediately; action does not take place until point C. By this time, it may be too late. There is a further lag before the action affects demand (between points D and E); by then the economy has already recovered. Fuel is added to the inflationary fire. Then, as the severity of inflation is recognized, policies are shifted in a restrictive direction. But once again there are lags; the policies can come too late, making the next recession worse. Rather than trying to adjust to changing conditions, it might be better to follow a stable set of policies. Thus it is argued by those in the classical tradition.

The Helmsman's Dilemma

The slowness of the economy to respond, and the momentum that can accumulate in the downswing or upswing, mean that the problem of the policy maker can be compared with that of the helmsman of an ocean-going ship. The helmsman may turn the wheel, but a large ship does not respond immediately. Suppose a ship heads out of Halifax harbour, with plans to go due south past the eastern tip of Cuba on the way to the Panama Canal. If the helmsman finds his course drifting to the east, he can correct it by turning the wheel to starboard.

The problem is, how much? If he turns the wheel just slightly, the ship will continue on its easterly course for some time; it does not respond quickly. In his anxiety, he may then turn the wheel more sharply. Clearly, the

more sharply the wheel is turned, the more quickly the ship will return to its course. But, if the wheel is swung hard to starboard, a new problem will arise. Once the ship points in the right direction, it will be turning with considerable momentum; the ship will move in a westerly direction. In his panic, the helmsman may be tempted to swing the wheel back hard to port. We can imagine the voyage of the anxious mariner—zigzagging down the Atlantic Ocean.

Of course, ships do not zigzag all over the ocean. With some practice, the helmsman learns not to lean too hard on the wheel. He learns to move the wheel back to the centre *before* the ship gets back to its intended course; the ship's momentum will complete the turn. Policy makers face the same type of problem. They must try to switch toward restraint *before* an economic expansion turns into an inflationary boom. As a former chairman of the U.S. Federal Reserve once sadly observed, central bankers have an unpopular task: to take away the punch bowl just when the party really gets going.

Not only do policy makers have the helmsman's problem; they also face a few more which provide extra excitement. One of the additional complications is that the helm and the rudder of the economic ship are connected by elastic bands and baling twine. Unlike the mechanism connecting the ship's wheel to the rudder, the mechanism connecting monetary and fiscal policies to aggregate demand does not work in a precise, highly predictable manner. Furthermore, the economic policy maker may have to chart a course across turbulent and stormy seas. Between 1965 and 1988, there were large shocks to the Canadian economy: first, a sustained export boom in 1966-68 (caused partly by the high level of economic activity in the United States as a result of the Vietnam War); then the inflationary pressures in food prices stemming from Soviet crop failures and large-scale North American grain exports during 1972-1974, and also stemming from the effects of the quadrupling of world oil prices in 1973 and 1974; then the second big jump in oil prices in 1979/80; and, finally, exceptionally high world interest rates since the early 1980s and the deep recession in 1981/82. If the ship is being guided across placid seas, the policy maker has the luxury of turning the wheel meekly and slowly so as not to over-correct. But in stormy waters, this is not good enough. Gentle, cautious policies will be overwhelmed by other forces. This, then, is the helmsman's dilemma: How hard should the wheel be swung, and how soon should it be moved back toward centre?

THE CASE AGAINST ACTIVISM: THE OVERESTIMATION OF POTENTIAL

The danger of overreaction is increased by a fourth type of lag. The three lags in the previous section represented delays *before* aggregate demand changes. The fourth lag occurs *after* aggregate demand changes. It involves the differing speeds with which real GDP and prices respond to changes in demand. Specifically, when aggregate demand rises, the short-run effect on real output is generally powerful. Unless producers are already straining hard against their capacity limitations, they respond to an increase in demand by producing more. However, as time passes, the higher demand is reflected more and more in terms of higher prices, and less and less in terms of real output. Thus, *when aggregate demand is stimulated, the favourable output effects come quickly; the unfavourable price effects are delayed.* This creates a temptation to stick with expansive fiscal and monetary policies too long in order to gain their short-term benefits in terms of higher output.

Figure 18-4 illustrates this lag. Note that the response of prices in the lower panel comes after the change in output shown in the top panel. Figure 18-4 also illustrates some of the criticisms directed at the activist Keynesian approach. The first step in the Keynesian approach is to estimate potential GDP. Policy makers tend to be optimistic, overestimating potential GDP and the amount by which unemployment can be reduced by

expansive demand policies. Such an overly optimistic estimate is shown by the black potential GDP line in Figure 18-4. The coloured line shows the true potential path which can be followed without causing an over-heating of the economy and an acceleration of inflation.

Now let us see what the critics fear if activists are in charge. Beginning at *A*, the economy is recovering from a recession. Monetary and fiscal policies are set for the expansion of aggregate demand. Real output is rising briskly, the unemployment rate is falling, and inflation — with its delayed response — is still slowing down because of the previous period of slack. Everything seems to be going well. The expansive policy settings are retained. But, without anyone noticing, the economy moves past *B*, crossing the true potential path. The error in estimating the potential path means that policy makers incorrectly believe that aggregate demand is still too low. (GDP is still below the optimistic black estimate of potential.) As a result, expansive policies are continued. In reality, however, aggregate demand is too high, since the economy is above the true potential path shown in colour. Therefore, a less expansive policy is appropriate.

As the economy crosses the true potential path, the seeds of a more rapid inflation are being sown, although the inflationary result does not appear for some time. As the curve in the lower diagram illustrates, inflation does not begin to accelerate until time *C*.

If the error in estimating the black potential GDP path has been large, the economy may never actually reach it. The expanding demand shows up increasingly in terms of inflation, and less and less in terms of real output. The expansive fiscal and monetary policies cause an increase in aggregate demand, but they do not control the extent to which the higher demand will cause higher output or show up in the form of higher prices.

Between *C* and *D*, a sharp policy debate is likely. Those focusing on the optimistic black path argue that to reach it, aggregate demand should be increased even more. But, as inflation is by now accelerating (to the right of point *C* in the lower part of the diagram), others urge caution. As time passes and inflation gets worse and worse, those urging restraint eventually win the debate. With inflation by now rising rapidly, the policy adjustment may be abrupt.

As a result, the economy may fall into a sharp recession. But, as always, inflation responds with a lag. *It remains serious even though tight policies have been introduced. As a consequence, everything seems to be*

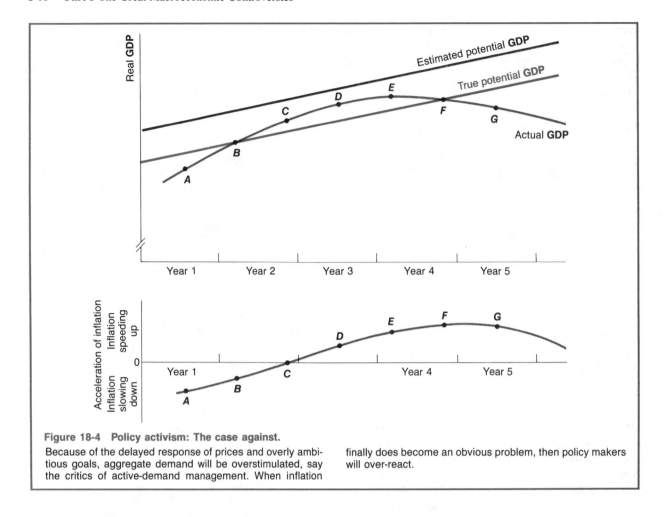

Figure 18-4 Policy activism: The case against.

Because of the delayed response of prices and overly ambitious goals, aggregate demand will be overstimulated, say the critics of active-demand management. When inflation finally does become an obvious problem, then policy makers will over-react.

going wrong during the period between E and G—just as everything went right during the expansion between *A* and *B*. The economy is headed into a recession and unemployment is rising, yet inflation is still getting worse. As the unemployment rate rises higher and higher while inflation continues stubbornly, more and more people argue that demand restraint simply won't stop inflation. Inflation has become "built in," and skeptics charge that nothing much can be done about it with monetary and fiscal policies. Aggregate demand policies, therefore, are turned in an expansive direction quite quickly, in order to increase output and reduce unemployment. A new upswing begins. But inflation has accelerated more as a result of the extended period of excess demand than it has fallen as a result of the shorter period of slack. Thus, each upswing begins with a higher rate of inflation than the previous one. This, then, is the case against activism.

Just as the case in favour of activism can be supported with real-world evidence (most notably from the early 1960s, as shown in Figure 18-2), so the critics can point to evidence of failures of discretionary policies. First, they note that in fact most recent recoveries have begun with higher and higher rates of inflation. The inflation rate was less than 1% in the early recovery year of 1961; between 4% and 5% in the recovery of 1972; about 10% in the early recovery of 1975; and well over 10% as the economy came out of the mini-recession in 1980. (The recovery from the 1981/82 recession was a notable exception: In 1983/84 inflation fell to about 4% and remained below 5% for the next several years. But even if the recession of 1981/82 broke the inflationary spiral, it can hardly be taken as an example of successful discretionary policy.)

Second, the 1970s and early 1980s provide a real-

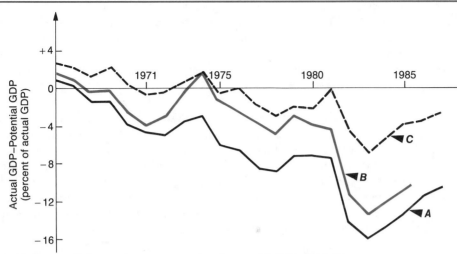

Figure 18-5   Estimates of the gap between actual and potential GDP, 1966–87.

With a full-employment target of 3.8% (the target used by the Economic Council of Canada in the mid-1970s), the estimated gap between actual and potential GDP remained large throughout the 1970–73 period (the solid black curve). Accordingly, expansionary policy settings were followed in order to close the gap. Later estimates (coloured curve and broken black curve) based on more realistic full-employment targets show that the gap decreased during 1970–73 and that, in 1973, actual GDP was *above* potential. Hence, restrictive policies to contain the inflationary pressure would have been the appropriate policy stance.

In the late 1970s, estimates of the gap between actual and potential GDP based on the relatively optimistic full-employment targets of Dungan and Wilson (the coloured curve) indicate that GDP in those years was well below potential. However, the gap estimated on the basis of Andrew Burns' full-employment target indicate that GDP was quite close to potential during those years, and that policy may have been too expansionary.

Source: Estimates by authors.

world illustration of the principal point of Figure 18-4; that is, how an overestimation of potential GDP can lead to policy problems. With the benefit of hindsight, it seems clear that Canadian policy makers in the 1970s substantially overestimated potential GDP because they were using an unrealistically high full-employment target. The target used by the Economic Council of Canada at that time was an unemployment rate of no more than 3.8%. But later studies show that a realistic target in the 1972–75 period would have been between 5% and 6% unemployment.[3] Nor is there a consensus concerning what a realistic full-employment target should have been in the 1980s. A study carried out by Peter Dungan and Thomas Wilson of the University of Toronto shows the full-employment rate *declining* from about 6% in the mid-

1970s to 5% in the mid-1980s. In contrast, a study by Andrew Burns for the Economic Council suggests that the attainable full-employment target was well over 8% for most of the 1980-85 period.[4]

In Figure 18-5 we show several simplified estimates of the gap between actual and potential GDP based on alternative full-employment targets. Curve *A* traces the gap if one takes the Economic Council's 3.8% unemployment as a target. Curves *B* and *C* show the estimated gaps between actual and potential GDP if one uses the more realistic estimates of Dungan/Wilson (curve *B*) or Andrew Burns (curve *C*).

Consider now the situation in the early 1970s. The estimates actually used by the policy makers at that time would have been close to those shown by curve *A*.

■ ■ ■ ■ ■

[3] The reasons given for these changes in the full-employment rate include the increase in the share of young workers and women workers in the labour force during those years. Because these groups traditionally have higher unemployment rates than other groups, the studies argue that the unemployment target has to be raised when this share increases.

■ ■ ■ ■ ■

[4] D. Peter Dungan and Thomas A. Wilson, *Potential GDP: Performance and Prospects* (Toronto: Institute for Policy Analysis, University of Toronto, 1982), and Andrew Burns, ''Unemployment in Canada: Frictional, Structural, and Cyclical Aspects,'' a background paper prepared for the Economic Council of Canada, March 1988.

According to these estimates, the gap between actual and potential GDP remained almost as large through 1973 as it had been during the recession year 1970. To close the gap, the policy makers moved toward expansionary monetary and fiscal policy settings; monetary policy especially was expansionary, with M1 growing at nearly 15% per year in both 1972 and 1973.

But in retrospect, GDP was *not* substantially below its potential in 1973. Using later estimates of a realistic full-employment target, the unemployment rate in 1973 had fallen well below the full-employment target. In other words, actual GDP was *above* potential GDP. As a result, the stage was set for the outburst of double-digit inflation in the second half of the 1970s.

In the early 1970s, potential GDP was overestimated mainly because the policy makers had an unrealistically low target for the unemployment rate. In the late 1970s and early 1980s, it was overestimated for another reason as well: the economy's declining productivity performance. For reasons that were discussed in Chapter 17, the rate of productivity growth fell sharply in the mid-1970s. Once again, the policy makers were slow to recognize that potential GDP was growing less rapidly than expected; consequently, the gap between actual and potential GDP was overestimated. Partly because of this, the policy makers did not adequately restrain aggregate demand, even though inflation was running at a high level. Fiscal policy, in particular, was highly expansionary from 1975 to 1978; had it been recognized that the gap was far smaller than most economists thought, policy might have been more restrictive and inflationary pressures less severe.

In the United States, a number of policy errors were made in the 1970s, for similar reasons as in Canada. The 1980 *Annual Report* of the Council of Economic Advisors summarizes the problem: ''Projecting potential GDP growth into the future is subject to large errors.'' But this conclusion throws into question the whole strategy of active aggregate demand management which is based on the assumption that potential GDP can be accurately forecast and taken as a target at which aggregate demand policy should be aimed.

THE CASE FOR A MONETARY RULE

There are many doubts about how well discretionary demand-management policies have worked. However, discretionary policies cannot be considered in a vacuum. It is also necessary to compare them to the alternative suggested by monetarists, namely, that the quantity of money be increased at a steady, moderate rate. There are several elements in this monetarist case:

1. The desirable path of aggregate demand is one of steady, moderate growth, which will make possible the purchase of the growing output of the economy at approximately stable prices.

2. The best way to ensure a steady, moderate increase in aggregate demand is with a steady, moderate increase in the money stock. Velocity is, of course, not perfectly constant, and therefore even a perfectly stable growth of money would not lead to a perfectly stable growth in demand. But, say the advocates of a monetary rule, the amount of instability would be less than the instability caused by discretionary policies. Furthermore, a rule involving a slow growth of the money stock would avoid the strong inflationary tendencies which have resulted from discretionary policies during the past quarter-century. Thus, monetarists have two objectives: to reduce the *instability* of aggregate demand, and to avoid an inflationary *trend* in demand.

3. Some of the proponents of a policy rule base their case on political as well as economic considerations. They believe that a policy rule will result in less interference by government officials in the free enterprise system. Several decades ago, Henry C. Simons of the University of Chicago made rules a cornerstone of his *Economic Policy for a Free Society*:[5]

> In a free enterprise system we obviously need highly definite and stable rules of the game, especially as to money. The monetary rules must be compatible with the reasonably smooth working of the system. Once established, however, they should work mechanically, with the chips falling where they may. To put our present problem as a paradox—we need to design and establish with the greatest intelligence a monetary system good enough so that, hereafter, we may hold to it unrationally —on faith—as a religion, if you please.

Moving Toward a Rule: Canadian Monetary Policy in the 1970s

In the mid-1970s, support for the monetarist position grew in Canada. Our experience with fine tuning during the first half of the 1970s had not been encouraging:

■ ■ ■ ■ ■

[5] Henry C. Simons, *Economic Policy for a Free Society* (Chicago: University of Chicago Press, 1948), p. 169.

The contractionary monetary and fiscal policies initiated in 1968/69 to counteract the threat of inflation almost certainly contributed to the high unemployment rates in the 1970 recession. The attempt at fighting the persistently high unemployment during 1971–73 through a very expansionary monetary policy resulted mainly in accelerated inflation without accomplishing any significant reduction in unemployment rates. Similarly, although the expansionary fiscal policy in 1975 may have reduced the severity of the 1975 recession, it also created a huge government deficit which turned out to be very difficult to reduce. In retrospect, it seems fairly clear that smaller and more gradual changes in the settings of both monetary and fiscal policy would have lessened the severity of the subsequent inflation problem without necessarily aggravating the unemployment problem at the time.

Thus, it did not come as a surprise when the Bank of Canada moved decisively in the direction of a monetarist rule in November 1975. The Bank announced that it would follow a policy of establishing given *target ranges* for the growth of the money supply (narrowly defined as M1). When a target range was first adopted, it allowed for relatively high rates of monetary growth; the Bank announced that M1 would grow no faster than an annual rate of 15%, but no slower than 10%. But the Bank also made it clear that it intended to reduce the target rates gradually, so that there would be a gradual reduction of the inflationary pressures in the Canadian economy. The first decrease in the target growth rate came in less than a year: In August 1976, the Bank announced that M1 would be growing between 8% and 12% per year. Subsequent decreases brought the target growth down to a range of 4% to 8% by early 1981.

But while the disappointing experience with discretionary policies in the early 1970s set the stage for a move toward a monetary rule in 1975, the experience in the late 1970s and early 1980s was also disappointing, as we shall soon see.

THE CASE AGAINST A MONETARY RULE

On behalf of discretionary policy making, we will examine several major criticisms of a fixed monetary rule.

1. In practice, it is not possible to have a policy rule that will be followed *regardless of the consequences*. No government will continue to stick blindly to a policy rule if it turns out that the effects of the rule are very different from what was originally expected, or if adherence to the rule makes it impossible to attain important policy objectives other than those that the rule was intended to serve. (For example, as we shall see, part of the reason the Bank of Canada departed from its anti-inflationary monetary targets in 1979/80 was to prevent sharp changes in the exchange rate.)

2. The proponents of a monetary rule generally aim for a slow rate of increase in aggregate demand to ensure price stability. The critics argue that, in practice, the result may be an unnecessarily high rate of unemployment. That is, *the trend of demand may be too low* if the monetarist proposal is followed.

3. Even though there is much to be said for a stable rate of growth of aggregate demand, a monetary policy rule will not provide it. *Velocity is not stable.* In other words, there are substantial non-monetary sources of disturbance in the economy. In reality, policies must be changed from time to time to combat these disturbances and to smooth aggregate demand. (One major non-monetary source of instability is studied in the appendix to this chapter.)

Let us consider each of these points in more detail.

1. No Rule Can Be Followed Regardless of the Consequences

Monetarists argue for a policy rule that should be followed regardless of current conditions. In Simons' view, it should be followed regardless of how the chips fall. However, this rigid position can scarcely be taken literally. After all, evidence regarding economic institutions and economic behaviour should be taken into account in establishing any rule; not to do so would be foolish. Yet these institutions and patterns of behaviour change. When they do, any rule based on them should be reconsidered—not held to steadfastly, like a religion. There used to be a monetary "religion" based on the gold standard. However, it contributed to the disaster of the 1930s. As Simons himself observed: "The utter inadequacy of the old gold standard, either as a definite system of rules or as the basis of a monetary religion, seems beyond intelligent dispute."[6] But that is exactly the point —the evidence indicated that the gold standard was a bad rule. Rules should not be maintained regardless of the evidence, regardless of how the chips fall.

■ ■ ■ ■ ■

[6] Simons, *Economic Policy for a Free Society*, p. 169.

The difficulties that may arise in following a rule were well illustrated by Canadian monetary policy in the early 1980s. During the 1975–79 period, the policy followed by the Bank of Canada was reasonably consistent with the intentions announced in 1975. M1 remained close to the predetermined target ranges and grew at a reasonably steady rate. (During the postal strikes in late 1975 and in 1978, the Bank allowed M1 to grow very rapidly for short periods. But these episodes can be seen as deliberate exceptions to the main thrust of the Bank's policy: They were temporary measures taken to make it easier for businesses to borrow money in order to cover the strike-induced shortfall in their cash flow.)

However, following the sharp increase in U.S. interest rates in 1979 and early 1980 (in response to the tighter policy being followed by the Federal Reserve), the Bank began departing from its announced rule. It tightened monetary policy by sharply restraining the growth of M1. By mid-1980, M1 was substantially lower than it would have had to be in order to stay within the target range that the Bank had announced. Then, as U.S. interest rates fell during the 1980 recession, the Bank sharply reversed itself and allowed a very high rate of growth in M1 during the second half of 1980; in late 1980 M1 was *above* the Bank's target range. By the end of 1981, it looked as though the Bank had all but abandoned its policy rule: M1 was sharply reduced and fell some 10% below the lower end of the target range. It remained well below the target range throughout the 1982 recession. And, in November 1982, the Bank confirmed what by then had become obvious: It announced that it was no longer controlling M1 according to specific targets. Thus ended the Canadian experiment with a monetarist rule.

In retrospect, it is not difficult to find the main reason the Bank departed from its earlier policy beginning in 1979. With the record-high interest rates in the United States, there would have been a large capital outflow from Canada if the Bank had not driven up Canadian interest rates as well. Such an outflow would have led to a depreciation in the Canadian dollar, which would have added to our inflation rate. It was precisely in order to prevent this that the Bank started following a policy of trying to keep Canadian interest rates relatively close to U.S. rates.

Not surprisingly, the supporters of the monetarist position were critical of the Bank. While they agreed that the Bank's policy may have reduced capital outflows and, therefore, stablized the exchange rate, they noted that it also resulted in Canadian interest rates following the wild gyrations of U.S. rates during 1980-82. Critics believe that a better policy would have been for the Bank to stick more closely to its original monetary growth target, even if this would have meant a bit more fluctuation in the exchange rate. In the words of Tom Courchene (then of the University of Western Ontario):[7]

> This [policy] is not [a monetary rule. It] is pegging the exchange rate, or essentially equivalently, following U.S. monetary policy. The Bank of Canada may express concern that U.S. policy is forcing some unattractive options on Canada. The fact is that this is the Bank's own doing, since it has effectively tied Canada's fortunes to U.S. monetary policy.

The Bank's policy, its critics argued, gave monetarism a bad name. The record high interest rates in 1981/82 gave rise to a public outcry against monetarist policies. But, say the Bank's critics, those interest rates were not the result of the Bank's long-run strategy of following a monetary rule; instead, they resulted from the Bank's *departure* from a rule as it tried to stabilize the exchange rate.

2. Insufficient Aggregate Demand?

Monetarists generally propose a monetary rule designed to allow aggregate demand to rise no more rapidly than the productive capacity of the economy. If successful, the rule would result in long-run price stability.

However, not everyone agrees that it is desirable to have a trend in aggregate demand which is just barely adequate to buy the growing output of the nation at stable prices. Critics of a monetary rule fear that monetarists would keep the trend of aggregate demand too low, creating extended periods of high unemployment. On the other hand, monetarists believe that this danger is not very severe, because the economy has a strong tendency to return to equilibrium at full employment (or more precisely, to an unemployment rate that represents a realistic full-employment target). Furthermore, monetarists believe that discretionary policy makers will take the path of least resistance, creating too much demand and persistent inflation.

■ ■ ■ ■ ■

[7] Thomas J. Courchene, *Money, Inflation and the Bank of Canada, Volume II: An Analysis of Monetary Gradualism, 1975-80* (Montreal and Calgary: The C.D. Howe Institute, 1981), p. 194.

3. Would a Monetary Rule Make the Growth of Aggregate Demand More Stable?

In 1982 when the Bank of Canada announced that it was no longer keeping M1 within a specific target range, it also referred to another important reason that a stable rate of monetary expansion could no longer be considered the best policy: the instability of velocity. Clearly, a stable rate of monetary expansion makes most sense if velocity is stable: It will then lead to a stable rate of expansion of aggregate demand as well. But as we already saw in Chapter 13, the velocity of M1 (the narrowly defined money stock that the Bank was controlling during 1975–80) was highly unstable during the late 1970s and early 1980s. And while the velocity of M2 appears to have been more stable during those years, the critics of monetarism rightly observe that we cannot be sure how long it (or any other velocity) will *remain* stable.

However, although the recent changes in velocity in Canada (and also in the United States) have weakened the monetarist case, the debate over a "rule vs. discretion" cannot be settled simply by looking at one of the options. The issue is not whether a monetary rule would work well in some absolute sense. The question is, which works *better*: a discretionary policy or a monetary rule? To rephrase the question: Do discretionary policies on average stabilize or destabilize the economy when compared to a rule?

Most of the recent debate on this issue has focused on monetary policy, particularly in the past decade when fiscal policy in North America has been influenced by "supply-side" objectives, and large and persistent government deficits have reduced its effectiveness as a demand-management tool. Both sides in the debate find some support for their position in the empirical evidence on monetary growth and the economy's performance.

Those who favour discretionary policies point to the instability of velocity in the late 1970s and early 1980s, and attribute part of the *economy's* instability during 1979-82 to the stubbornness of both the Bank of Canada and the United States Federal Reserve Bank in sticking to their monetary targets for too long. Moreover, they point to the relatively successful performance of both economies since 1982, when monetary growth has been far from stable. (In Canada, the narrowly defined M1 grew at a 10% annual rate in 1983, and at almost 13% in 1987. In the United States, M1 grew more rapidly between 1982 and 1986 than between 1968 and 1978 when high rates of monetary growth were roundly criticized as the cause of accelerating inflation.) Yet during 1983 to 1988, the inflation rate in both countries remained fairly stable at less than 5% per year, and unemployment fell gradually. If the Bank of Canada and the Federal Reserve had followed the monetarist prescription and held the increase in the money stock to a slow, stable rate, would this not have led to insufficient aggregate demand and slowed the expansion out of the deep 1981/82 recession? Yes, it would, say those who favour discretionary policy, and the Bank of Canada should be applauded for its decision to abandon its restrictive monetary targets in 1982.

On the other hand, those who continue to favour a strict monetary rule point to the historical evidence. They note that a fall in the rate of monetary growth has preceded almost all recent recessions in North America. Presumably, recessions would have been less severe if the rate of growth of money had been more stable. Milton Friedman, the most prominent of the monetarists, has been blunt in his condemnation of the discretionary policies of the U.S. Federal Reserve: "No major institution in the United States has so poor a record of performance over so long a period yet so high a public reputation."[8]

The weakest point in the monetarist position is the evidence that velocity has been unstable, whether measured using M1 or M2, the most commonly used money definitions. To overcome this problem, some monetarists suggest a rule which focuses not on M1 or M2, but on an alternative target: GDP itself.

An Alternative Target?

When using a monetary rule or monetary target, the objective is to achieve a steady rate of growth in aggregate demand and in nominal GDP. But if a steady growth in nominal GDP is the objective, why not target it directly? For example, why not pick the following rule?: Whenever nominal GDP grows at a rate of more than 5%, tighten policy; whenever it grows more slowly, switch to a more expansive policy.

The answer lies in lags. A change in monetary or fiscal policy today will have its major effect some

■ ■ ■ ■ ■

[8] Milton Friedman, "The Case for Overhauling the Federal Reserve." *Challenge* (July–August 1985), p. 5.

months in the future. If the Bank of Canada targets nominal GDP, it risks over-reactions and may end up following the zigzag path of the anxious helmsman. In other words, the case for a monetary target depends on a basic idea: A monetary target will result in a more stable growth of nominal GDP than would a direct targeting of nominal GDP.

For this idea to be valid, there must be a stable relationship between the targeted item and nominal GDP *6 or 12 months in the future*. This suggests an answer to the question: What should be targeted? The target should be the item with the most stable relationship to nominal GDP.

Because of the instability of the velocity of M1 in the 1980s, it has lost favour: The Bank of Canada no longer declares a target for M1. It is not clear that targeting M1 is superior to targeting nominal GDP itself. With the benefit of hindsight, one might say that this is not altogether surprising. The major financial innovations of the past 15 years — most notably, the introduction of interest-bearing chequable deposits — have reduced the need for non-interest-bearing demand deposits and have, therefore, made the velocity of M1 less stable.

The problem is that the velocity of the other common money definition, M2, has sometimes been unstable too. Thus, monetarists have continued to search for yet other money definitions (such as M2+ or M3) or some even broader asset measure, such as liquid assets (*L*) or total debt (*D*) that would bear a more stable relationship to GDP. But the problem that we referred to above still remains: Even if we find some variable that has had a close statistical relationship with GDP in the past, there is no assurance that such a relationship will remain stable in the future.

Table 18-1 summarizes the main points of difference between economists in the Keynesian and classical traditions, as explained in Chapters 8, 13, and 15.

The Outcome of the Debate

While monetarist rule makers remain in the minority, significant changes in attitude have occurred since the 1960s and early 1970s as a consequence of their criticisms of activist policies and as a consequence of the disappointing results with aggregate-demand management:

1. There has been increased awareness that demand management itself may be a cause of economic instability. Overly ambitious demand management may cause accelerating inflation. Furthermore, substan-

tial lags may result in actions that are too late and that add to the magnitude of cyclical swings.
2. There is more widespread recognition of the importance of paying attention to the long-term consequences of policies. In particular, because aggregate demand has a lagged effect on prices, there is a general recognition that anti-inflation policies should be made with the long run in mind.

FORECASTING

If a little knowledge is dangerous, where is the man who has so much as to be out of danger?

Thomas Huxley

The advocates of a fixed monetary rule did not win the debate: In the end, no country abandoned discretionary policy. Moreover, since 1982, the money stock has played a much less important rule as a policy target than it did before that time, both in Canada and the United States.

However, the debate over rules vs. discretion has been very useful: It has highlighted the dangers that may arise if the authorities try to use activist discretionary policies in managing aggregate demand.

In particular, long time lags mean that policies adopted today will not have their full effect until some months in the future. The problem is, will the effects of the policy be appropriate at that time? In deciding whether to change policy, the Bank of Canada and fiscal policy makers have *no alternative but to forecast*. The question is not *whether* to forecast or not, but *how*. Anyone who thinks that forecasting can be avoided is, in fact, forecasting in a naive way. By implying that policy be designed for the needs of the moment, a person is making the simple forecast that the problems of the future will be the same as those of today. Even the proponents of a monetary rule are forecasting in a sense. Their case is based on the forecast that velocity will be stable in the future.

Forecasting with a Model

In developing a forecast for the coming months, economists in and out of government use a number of techniques, most of them involving computers. Typically, past information on consumption, income, etc., is used to estimate how the economy behaves. For example, how is consumption related to income? Based on past

Table 18-1   Classical and Keynesian Views: A Contrast

Issue	Classical/ Monetarist View	Keynesian View
Nature of market economy	Quite stable, *if* quantity of money M is stable	Contains major flaws: 1. Quite unstable 2. May reach equilibrium with large-scale unemployment
Nature of equilibrium	Only at full employment	Maybe at full employment, maybe with large-scale unemployment
Aggregate supply	Vertical in long run, sloped in short run (long- and short-run Phillips curves)	Reversed *L* (prices downwardly rigid)
If aggregate demand is less than aggregate supply	Prices sticky in short run; will adjust in long run	Prices are rigid in downward direction; depression will persist until demand recovers
Key to changes in aggregate demand	Changes in quantity of money M	Fluctuations in investment demand I^*
Cause of Great Depression	Collapse in aggregate demand, caused by collapse of money stock M	Collapse in aggregate demand, collapse of investment demand I^*
Key macroeconomic equation	$MV = PQ$	Aggregate Expenditures $= C + I^* + G + X - M$
Best tool to control aggregate demand	Monetary policy	Fiscal policy, especially changes in government spending *G*
Best policy	Monetary rule	Discretionary fiscal policy, to make aggregate demand: 1. high enough 2. more stable
If people have surplus holdings of money, they will:	Spend it	Buy bonds
Responsiveness of investment to changes in interest rate	Very strong (therefore, crowding out is strong, and fiscal policy is weak)	Very weak (and therefore monetary policy and crowding out are both weak)

relationships, future consumption is estimated. Typically, forecasters also estimate future investment, government expenditures, and net exports. The path of investment is forecast on the basis of current and expected future interest rates and other important influences. The budget is used to estimate the probable course of government spending.

Exports are estimated on the basis of expected economic activity abroad; the more prosperous foreign economies are, the more likely they are to buy our exports. Such pieces are fitted together to make a statistical — or *econometric* — model of the economy. With such a model, it is possible to make a projection of GDP.

A simple example will give a general idea of how this is done. We begin with the fundamental equation of an earlier chapter:

$$GDP = C + I_g + G + X - M$$

(18-1, repeat of 6-2)

Suppose that statistical evidence indicates that consumers in the past have spent 90% of their disposable incomes, and that two-thirds of GDP flows through to consumers in the form of disposable income. That means that consumption is 60% of GDP (that is, 90% × 2/3):

$$C = 0.6 \; GDP \tag{18-2}$$

Suppose, also, businesses are expected to invest $90 billion in the coming period:

$$I_g = \$90 \tag{18-3}$$

The budgets of the federal, provincial, and local governments commit them to $120 billion in purchases of goods and services:

$$G = \$120 \tag{18-4}$$

Exports are expected to amount to $100 billion:

$$X = \$100 \tag{18-5}$$

Finally, past experience indicates that imports are about 25% of GDP:

$$M = 0.25 \; GDP \tag{18-6}$$

Substituting the last five equations into equation 18-1, we can solve for GDP:

$$GDP = 0.6 \; GDP + \$90 + \$120 +$$
$$\$100 - 0.25 \; GDP$$
$$GDP = 0.35 \; GDP + \$310$$

That is:

$$GDP = \$476.92 \tag{18-7}$$

We thus forecast GDP to be $477 billion.

In practice, of course, economists use substantially more complicated equations. For example, consumption expenditures depend not only on consumers' disposable income, but also on their wealth (such as stocks and bonds). When forecasting, economists pay particular attention to the time element, for example, *how quickly* consumption responds to changing levels of disposable income. Taking these two complications into account, we get a more sophisticated consumption function:

$$C_t = 0.5 \; DI_t + 0.2 \; DI_{t-1} + 0.05 \; W_t \tag{18-8}$$

where DI stands for disposable income, W stands for wealth, and the subscripts stand for time periods; specifically, $t-1$ is the quarter before t. In plain English, equation 18-8 says that consumption expenditures in any quarter (C_t) depend on disposable income in that quarter (DI_t) and in the previous quarter (DI_{t-1}), and also on wealth in that quarter (W_t).

Although equation 18-8 is still relatively simple, it is beginning to resemble the consumption function used in actual econometric models. The appendix to this chapter will introduce some of the basic ideas used to explain investment in such models.

Over the years, economists have developed a number of econometric models of the Canadian economy.[9] Several of them are used primarily for short-term forecasting. Well-known models in this category include the Data Resources of Canada Model, The Informetrica Model (TIM), and the Medium Term Forecasting Model (MTFM) of the Conference Board of Canada. Because of the close links of the Canadian and U.S. economies, several of these models are linked with similar forecasting models for the United States, so that the effects of changing U.S. economic conditions can be directly incorporated into the Canadian forecasts. (Other models, such as the Economic Council of Canada's CANDIDE model, the Bank of Canada's RDX2, or the FOCUS model of the Institute for Policy Analysis at the University of Toronto, are used primarily to investigate the medium-term effects of policy changes, rather than for short-term forecasting of the business cycle.)

These models provide a useful starting point for forecasts, and are particularly helpful in cross-checking the various components of aggregate demand (consumption, investment, government spending, and net exports) to make sure that they are consistent. However, models have a major limitation. Essentially, they project the future on the basis of relationships which have held in the past, but which may change. The future of the economy depends on many forces, some of which are not easy to incorporate into formal econometric models. Thus, forecasters

■ ■ ■ ■ ■

[9] A useful summary of Canadian econometric models is provided in Ronald G. Bodkin, Lawrence R. Klein, and Kanta Marwah, ''Canadian Macroeconometric Modelling, 1947–1979 and Beyond,'' Research Paper #8502, University of Ottawa, July 1985.

generally adjust the initial results of their econometric models to allow for additional factors that they consider important. The final result is a "judgemental" forecast —using the results of models, but with modifications.

In adjusting the raw output of econometric models, forecasters use the results of various surveys of future intentions, for example, the Conference Board's questionnaires regarding business investment intentions and surveys of consumer attitudes.

Turning Points

One of the hardest problems in forecasting is to tell when a turning point will take place—when an expansion will reach a peak and a decline will begin, or when a recession will hit the trough and a recovery begin. One of the weakest features of econometric models is that they do not forecast turning points very accurately. But turning points are very important. If an upswing will end in the next several months, now is the time to consider more expansive policies.

What is needed, then, is something that will signal a coming turn. To fill this need, economists have tried to construct indexes of *leading indicators*. Since the 1970s, such indexes have been published on a regular basis by several chartered banks and, since 1981, by Statistics Canada. While each of the indexes is somewhat different, they are all computed on the basis of economic variables that tend to turn up or down well in advance of turning points for GDP. Variables which usually behave in this way include stock prices, new orders for durable goods, and the number of job vacancies in business firms.

> A *leading indicator* is an economic variable that reaches a turning point (peak or trough) before the economy as a whole changes direction. (New orders for durable goods is an example.)

As we saw in Chapter 7, business fluctuations in Canada often occur simultaneously with fluctuations in the United States. For this reason, several of the leading indicator indexes used in Canada take account of the U.S. Department of Commerce leading indicator index as well, so that our indexes include both the leading indicators in the domestic economy and information on variables that will affect future demand by foreigners for Canadian goods and services.

As Figure 18-6 shows, leading indicators may be helpful. The Trendicator index published by the Royal Bank of Canada correctly forecast the recessions in 1970, 1974, and 1980, as well as earlier slumps. But the figure also shows that leading indicators may sometimes give confusing signals. In 1966, the index predicted a recession that failed to materialize. In late 1983, it again indicated a coming downturn, but the economy grew at a healthy rate through 1984 and 1985. Moreover, even when leading indicators correctly signal a future recession, they may not tell very precisely *when* it will occur; they don't provide the same period of advance warning each time. For example, the Trendicator usually predicts a downturn with a lead time of about two quarters. But the 1980 recession did not occur until about a year after the index first indicated a downturn was coming and, more seriously, the deep 1981/82 recession occurred with almost no lead time at all.

The record: How well can we forecast?

To evaluate the accuracy of various forecasting methods, economists have compared a number of forecasts with actual outcomes. In a 1979 study, a group of economists at the University of Ottawa found that during the 1970s, the quarterly changes in GDP predicted by several forecasting models were much more accurate than the changes that would have been predicted on the basis of some "naïve" procedure, such as extrapolating from recent trends or assuming that the increase over the next year will be the same as the average increase for the past few years.[10] More recent studies in the United States have found a similar result. These conclusions are reassuring. Businesses and governments pay millions for forecasts. They are not wasting their money.

Less reassuring, however, is the record of forecasters during the recession of 1981/82. Forecasters in the United States largely failed to predict this recession, even though it was the most severe one in decades. Partly as a result, there was little or no advance warning of the recession in Canadian forecasts as well.

In defence of the forecasters, one can argue that forecasting was particularly difficult during 1981/82 both in the United States and Canada because, in both countries, fiscal policy was set for expansion while monetary policy was contractionary. This reinforces the point made

■ ■ ■ ■ ■
[10] Ronald G. Bodkin, Victoria Cano-Lamy, Edward Chow, Jean Fortin, Leslie Gunaratne, John Kuiper, and Christine Serrurier, "*Ex ante* Forecasting with Several Econometric Models of the Canadian Economy," *Journal of Post-Keynesian Economics*, Spring 1979, pp. 18-40.

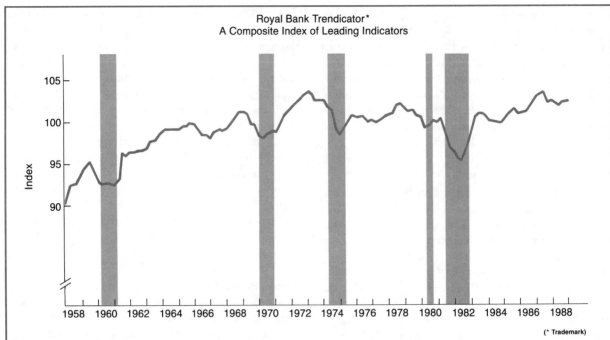

Figure 18-6 Index of leading indicators.

The curve shows the behaviour of the Royal Bank Trendicator index since 1956. Note that the index correctly predicted the downturns in 1970, 1974, and 1980. But it has not always been reliable. In 1966 it turned down sharply, but there was not a recession at that time. Similarly, in late 1983 the index predicted a coming recession, yet the economy continued to expand through 1984 and 1985. And even though the index turned down sharply *during* the 1981/82 recession, it provided no advance warning: The downturn of the index did not come until mid-1981 when the recession had already started.

Source: Adapted from *Royal Bank Trendicator* Report*, February, 1989. (*Trademark)

at the end of Chapter 13. When monetary policy is pushed in one direction, and fiscal policy in another, the path of the economy becomes particularly uncertain.

Nevertheless, it is worrisome that forecasters are not able to anticipate recessions better. If discretionary policies are to be successful, it is particularly important that policy be moved in an expansive direction as the economy is approaching a recession. But this can only be done if we can rely on forecasts to give us advance warning of coming recessions.

KEY POINTS

1. The mediocre record of monetary and fiscal policies in recent years has enlivened an old debate: Should aggregate demand policies be actively adjusted in the quest for high employment and stable prices? Or should monetary and fiscal rules be followed?

2. The activist Keynesian approach involves several steps. First, the full-employment or potential path of GDP is estimated. Second, if actual GDP is significantly below potential GDP, aggregate demand should be expanded until the potential path is approached. Thereafter, fiscal and monetary pol-

icies should be adjusted as needed to combat fluctuations.

3. This strategy was followed with success during the first half of the 1960s. However, aggregate demand became too high and inflation accelerated in the last half of the decade.

4. The existence of time lags makes it difficult to design countercyclical policies. Actions taken today may not be appropriate to the economy of tomorrow when they will have their major effect.

5. There are *three lags* between the time that aggregate demand should be changed and the time when the change actually occurs. The *recognition lag* is the interval before changes in economic conditions are recognized. The *action lag* is the interval between the time a problem is recognized and the time when fiscal and monetary policies are adjusted. The *impact lag* is the interval between the time when policies are changed and the time when the major effects of the policies occur. Because of lags, policies implemented today will have their effects some time in the future, but by then it may be too late.

6. There is also another important lag. When aggregate demand changes, the effects on prices lag behind the effect on output. That is, when aggregate demand increases, output generally responds quickly, with inflation increasing only after a lag. When aggregate demand falls, output generally falls quickly, with the economy sliding into a recession. Inflation begins to fall only after a lag.

7. Monetarists believe that discretionary policies are likely to do more harm than good. They recommend a *policy rule* — that the money stock be increased by a fixed percentage, year after year, regardless of current economic conditions. Monetarists believe that discretionary adjustments in aggregate demand policies are likely to do more harm than good because:
(a) There are lags before aggregate demand can be adjusted, and between changes in demand and the effect on prices.
(b) People tend to be overly optimistic in estimating the potential path of real GDP (Figure 18-5).
(c) Because of the lags and overoptimism, expansive policies are generally continued too long. Then, when inflation becomes a clear and present danger, policy makers generally over-

react, causing a fall in aggregate demand and a recession. However, inflation does not respond quickly to the lower aggregate demand. The restrictive policies are, therefore, deemed a failure and another round of expansive policies is begun. Consequently, discretionary policies are likely to cause instability and an inflationary bias in the economy. Each recovery tends to begin with a higher rate of inflation than the previous one. (However, this did not happen after the 1981/82 recession.)
(d) Policy rules will result in less interference by the government, and therefore in more economic freedom.

8. A number of arguments can be made against a monetary rule and in favour of discretionary policies:
(a) In practice, no government will follow a policy rule regardless of the short-run consequences (how the chips fall) and competing objectives (such as wartime finance).
(b) Rule makers tend to propose a rule that will keep the trend of aggregate demand too low. An unnecessarily high rate of unemployment will be the result. (Compare this with key point 7(c), the monetarist view that activist policies will give the economy an inflationary bias.)
(c) A monetary rule does not ensure a stable increase in aggregate demand.

9. In spite of these counterarguments, important changes in attitudes have occurred as a consequence of the monetarist criticisms of fine-tuning and the disappointing results with aggregate demand management:
(a) The problem of lags is more clearly recognized.
(b) The importance of keeping long-term objectives in mind is more widely recognized.

10. Because policies have their major effect on aggregate demand some months in the future, a forecast of future conditions must be made — explicitly or implicitly — whenever policy is changed. To forecast, economists use econometric models, supplemented with survey data and ''judgemental'' adjustments. The experience of recent years suggests that it is particularly difficult to forecast recessions.

KEY CONCEPTS

policy activism
discretionary policy
policy rule
fine-tuning
potential GDP

GDP gap
recognition lag
action lag
impact lag

lag between output changes and
  price changes
econometric model
turning point
leading indicator

PROBLEMS

18-1. Explain the various steps in the activist Keynesian strategy.

18-2. If discretionary policies are followed, what are the consequences of overestimating potential GDP growth? Use the Canadian experience since 1970 in your answer.

18-3. What case can be made against a monetary policy rule?

18-4. In 1981, as interest rates rose to record highs in the United States, the Bank of Canada reduced the growth rate of M1 well below the target range that it had previously announced. As a result, interest rates in Canada rose rapidly as well.

   Some critics of the Bank argued that by not sticking to its own target range, the Bank *destabilized* the economy. In defence of the Bank, others argued that if the Bank had stuck to its target range, the economy would have been even less stable than it was. Try to explain the possible reasons underlying these conflicting views.

18-5. In the section describing the possible overestimation of potential GDP, we observed that output and prices do not respond at the same rate to changes in aggregate demand. In such circumstances, why do the statistics sometimes give policy makers conflicting signals about the appropriate way to adjust aggregate demand? How do the conflicting signals add to the "recognition lag"?

18-6. Why must future economic conditions be forecast when monetary or fiscal policies are changed? If policy makers do not believe they are forecasting, why may we conclude that they are in fact using implicit forecasts? If someone argues for no change in monetary and fiscal policies, is he or she making any forecast about the future? Why is it particularly important to forecast turning points? Can you think of any reason why it is difficult to forecast turning points accurately?

*18-7. The Bank of Canada may focus on any of the following targets in developing monetary policies. For each of the following, explain the advantages and disadvantages of the target:

(a) a low unemployment rate of, say, 4% or 5%

(b) a steady growth in real GDP of, say, 4% per year

(c) a steady growth in nominal GDP of, say, 6% per year

(d) a low inflation rate of, say, 1% or 2% per year

(e) a stable exchange rate between the Canadian and the U.S. dollar.

Appendix

■ ■ ■ ■ ■

The Accelerator: A Non-Monetary Explanation of Business Fluctuations

If business cycles were primarily the result of monetary disturbances, a smooth growth in the money stock would make the economy more stable. However, the stronger non-monetary disturbances are, the less the economy can be smoothed by a monetary policy rule, and the stronger is the case for discretionary policies to offset the disturbances — provided that the authorities can act quickly enough in the presence of lags. Separating monetary from non-monetary disturbances is not a simple matter. "Non-monetary" theories of business cycles generally focus on the investment component of aggregate demand, since this is the most unstable. The theory of investment presented in this appendix will be "non-monetary" in the sense that money is not an integral part of the theory. However, we cannot demonstrate that it is completely "non-monetary." In fact, we will see later that monetary issues are lurking in the background.

INVESTMENT DEMAND: THE SIMPLE ACCELERATOR

Suppose we put ourselves in the business executive's shoes. Why should we want to invest? Why, for example, should we want to acquire more machines?

The simplest answer is that businesses want more machines because they want to produce more goods. *The desired stock of capital depends on the amount of production.* This fundamental proposition lies behind the **acceleration principle**, illustrated in Table 18-2 and Figure 18-7. In the first two years of this example, a bicycle manufacturer sells 200 000 bicycles per year. Suppose that one machine is needed for every 10 000 bicycles produced. Assume also that the manufacturer initially has the 20 machines needed to produce the 200 000 bicycles. As long as the demand for bicycles remains stable (as shown in Table 18-2, Phase I, years 1 and 2), there is no need for additional machines; there is no net investment.

That does not mean, however, that machine production is zero. Suppose that a machine lasts for 10 years, with two of the original 20 machines wearing out each year. As long as the demand for bicycles remains constant at 200 000 per year, gross investment will continue to be two machines per year. (That is, two machines will be purchased to replace the two that wear out each year.)

Now, suppose that the demand for bicycles starts to grow in Phase II. In the third year, sales increase by 10%, from 200 000 to 220 000. As a consequence, the manufacturer needs 22 machines; two additional machines must be acquired. Gross investment therefore rises to four machines — two replacements plus two net additions. An increase in sales of only 10% has had an *accelerated* or magnified effect on investment. Gross investment has risen from two to four machines, or by no less than 100%. (This magnified effect on investment provides an important clue as to why investment fluctuates so much more than GDP.) Then, in the fourth year, with the growth of sales remaining constant at 20 000 units, gross investment remains constant at four machines per year.

Next, let's see what happens in Phase III. In the fifth year, demand begins to level out. As growth slows to 10 000 bicycles, only one additional machine is needed. Both net and gross investment *decline* as a result of *slowing* of the growth of bicycle sales. We emphasize: *An actual decline in sales is not necessary to cause a decline in investment.* (Sales did not decline in the fifth year; they merely grew more slowly than in the fourth year.) Then, when the demand for bicycles levels out in the sixth year, there is no longer a need for any additional machines; net investment drops to zero, and gross investment falls back to two. Then, if bicycle sales begin to decline in Phase IV (year 7), the number of machines the manufacturer needs will decline; the machines that are wearing out will not be replaced. Net investment becomes negative, and gross investment can fall to zero.

This example of the acceleration principle (or "accelerator") illustrates a number of important points:

Table 18-2   The Acceleration Principle

Time	(1) Yearly sales of bicycles (in thousands)	(2) Desired number of machines (column 1 ÷ 10 000)	(3) Net investment (change in column 2)	(4) Gross investment (column 3 + replacement of 2 machines)
Phase I: Steady sales				
First Year	200	20	0	2
Second year	200	20	0	2
Phase II: Rising sales				
Third year	220	22	2	4
Fourth year	240	24	2	4
Phase III: A levelling off				
Fifth year	250	25	1	3
Sixth year	250	25	0	2
Phase IV: Declining sales				
Seventh year	230	23	−2	0
Eighth year	210	21	−2	0
Phase V: A levelling off				
Ninth year	200	20	−1	1
Tenth year	200	20	0	2

Investment fluctuates much more than consumption. Net investment depends on the *change* in consumption.

1. Investment (in machines) fluctuates by a much greater percentage than output of the goods for which capital is used (bicycles).
2. Net investment depends on the *change* in the production of the goods for which capital is used.
3. Once output begins to rise, it must continue to grow by the same amount if investment is to remain constant. A reduction in the growth of output will cause a *decline* in investment (year 5). But a very rapid growth of sales may be unsustainable. Therefore, a rapid upswing in economic activity contains the seeds of its own destruction. As the growth of consumption slows down, investment will fall.
4. It is possible for gross investment to collapse, even though there is only a mild decline in sales (year 7).
5. For investment to recover, it is not necessary for sales to rise. A smaller decline in sales is sufficient (year 9). Thus, a decline in economic activity contains the seeds of recovery.

This illustration is simplified, but the validity of its major points may be shown in a few examples. If business slackens off and fewer goods are shipped, the amount of trucking declines. Consequently, the demand for new trucks will decline sharply. Or consider what happens when the birthrate declines. Construction of schools is cut back. (New schools are needed primarily to accommodate an increase in the student population.) Note how the accelerator applies not only to machines, but also to other forms of investment such as school buildings and factories.

The accelerator can also apply to inventory investment, and this can add to the instability of the economy. Merchants may attempt to keep their inventories in proportion to sales. Thus, if sales increase by 10%, orders to the factory may be increased by perhaps 20% in order to bring inventories up into line with the higher sales. Nevertheless, inventory investment does not always act as a destabilizing force. There is no need for retailers to keep any rigid relationship between their sales and inventories. On the contrary, the effects of temporary spurts in sales may be cushioned by the existence of inventories: Retailers may meet the increased sales by running down their inventories.

MODIFICATION OF THE SIMPLE ACCELERATOR: LAGS IN INVESTMENT

Even in the case of a manufacturing operation, it is an oversimplification to assume that a rigid relationship exists between sales and the number of machines. In practice, the firm does not need exactly one machine for every 10 000 bicycles produced. Instead of acquiring new machines, a firm can run its factories overtime when demand increases. In this way, it can change its

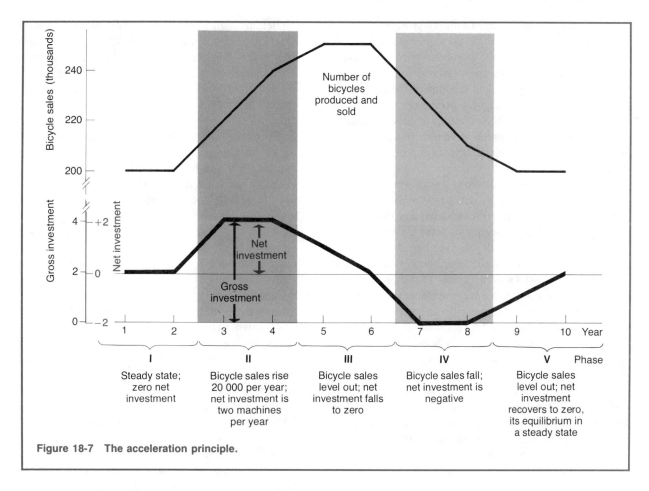

Figure 18-7   The acceleration principle.

capital/output ratio. Furthermore, at the end of 10 years, an old machine does not suddenly disintegrate; it wears out gradually. During a boom, older machines can be kept in use beyond their normal retirement age.

> The *capital/output ratio* is the value of capital (machines, factories, etc.) divided by the value of annual output.

What should be taken into account by businesses in deciding whether to buy new machinery or to "make do" by patching up old machinery or scheduling overtime? One important consideration is how long an increase in sales is expected to last. If it is just a temporary spurt and will quickly subside, expensive new machines should not be ordered. They may not be received quickly enough to meet the bulge in demand, and may add to idle capacity during the next downturn. Thus, the immediate response to increases in sales may be to schedule overtime, and to wait and see before

ordering new machines. As a result, there are significant delays in the response of investment to changes in sales.

In the short run, these delays add to stability. Businesses do not rush out to buy new machines with every little increase in sales. However, over longer periods, lags can add to the force of an upswing or a downswing. If high sales continue for some time, businesses conclude that prosperity is permanent. Orders for new machines are placed. Once this happens, competitors may become concerned. If they don't jump on the bandwagon, they may lose their place in a growing market. A boom psychology can develop. Although investment demand is initially slow to respond, it can gain momentum.

INTERACTIONS BETWEEN THE ACCELERATOR AND THE MULTIPLIER

Interactions between consumption and investment add to the momentum of the economy. As more machines are ordered, incomes rise in the machinery-producing industries. As incomes rise, people consume more. As they buy more consumer goods, business optimism is confirmed — the rising sales are "for real." As a consequence, orders for plant and equipment increase even more. Once again, the higher incomes resulting from higher investment stimulate consumption; the multiplier process makes the expansion stronger. Thus, increases in investment demand and increases in consumer demand reinforce one another.

Eventually, however, a strong expansion must slow down. Economic resources—land, labour, and capital— are limited, and total output cannot expand indefinitely at a rapid pace. Output begins to increase more slowly. Because of the accelerator principle, investment turns down. Because of the multiplier, domestic product declines by several times as much as the decrease in investment. A recession is underway. Thus, the interaction of the accelerator and multiplier helps to explain not only (1) the *strength* of cycles, but also (2) *why turning points occur*—why, for example, a boom does not continue indefinitely, but instead reaches a peak and then turns into a recession.

However, an expansion does not *inevitably* turn into a recession. If the increase in demand and output can be kept moderate and steady, the natural rebound into recession may be avoided. For this reason, *moderate growth can be more healthy and lasting* than a business boom.

The Downswing and Lower Turning Point

When the lessons of the simple accelerator model (listed earlier as points 1 through 5) are modified to take account of time lags and the interaction between the multiplier and accelerator, the following sequence occurs as a result of a reduction in the growth of sales:

1. In the short run of a few weeks or months, there is little if any decline in investment in plant and equipment. This is because investment in plant and equipment is cushioned from the effects of changing sales in a number of ways:
   (a) Inventories are temporarily allowed to increase, with the result that factory orders hold up better than final sales.
   (b) Overtime is reduced.
   (c) The opportunity is taken to retire machines that have been kept in service past their normal lifetimes.
2. If sales continue to be weak, business executives begin to fear the worst. Rather than accumulate

higher and higher inventories, firms cut back sharply on their orders. As production falls, factories slash new orders for machines. (These are the effects of the accelerator.) Momentum is added to the downswing as laid-off workers reduce their consumption (the multiplier).

3. However, consumption demand does not continue to decline indefinitely. While some purchases may easily be postponed, consumers try to maintain their expenditures for food and other necessities. Furthermore, as automobiles and other consumer durables wear out, consumers become increasingly anxious to replace them. As the decline in consumer spending moderates, investment in machinery and buildings begins to recover. (However, the recovery may be delayed by the desire of retailers, wholesalers, and manufacturers to work off excessive inventories.)

Each of these three stages is important, and each contains its own valuable lesson. These lessons are, respectively:

1. Investment is not volatile in the face of small and temporary reductions in the rate of growth of sales.
2. If sales remain weak for some time, investment falls. The downswing gathers momentum because of feedbacks between falling investment and falling consumer demand—that is, because of the interaction of the multiplier and the accelerator.
3. However, the downward movement does not continue forever. Even in the worst depressions, economic activity does not collapse toward zero. The accelerator process generates natural forces of recovery even before consumption bottoms out.

In deciding whether or not to invest, business executives compare the advantages of new machinery with the alternative of "making do" by scheduling overtime and keeping old machines in production. In this decision, a relevant consideration is the cost of new machines. There are two important costs: (1) the price of the machine itself and (2) the price of the financing — that is, the interest rate. Here is an important place where money comes into the picture. For example, open market purchases can be used to push down interest rates, and thereby lower the cost of acquiring new machines, buildings, and inventories. Thus, the Bank of Canada or the Federal Reserve can encourage the recovery from a recession. Similarly, open market sales (or less-than-normal purchases) and higher interest rates discourage investment, and thus can help prevent a healthy expansion from turning into an unhealthy boom.

KEY POINTS

11. Investment fluctuates more widely than other components of GDP. The accelerator principle illustrates why. Investment depends on the change in output, and investment demand can change by a large percentage in the face of relatively small percentage changes in sales. The accelerator also helps to explain why turning points occur in the business cycle. Investment can fall even in a growing economy, if the *growth* of sales slows down. An actual decline in sales is not necessary. During a recession, investment can recover when sales decline at a slower rate. An actual upturn in sales is not necessary.

12. While the acceleration principle illustrates important forces that help to determine investment demand, it represents a simplification. In practice, there may be delays in the response of investment to changes in sales. These delays contribute to the stability of the economy in the face of small disturbances. However, they mean that, once an expansion or contraction gets going, it can gather momentum.

13. The interaction between the accelerator and the multiplier also adds to the momentum of an upswing or downswing. When investment demand falls, incomes and consumption demand also fall, causing a further decline in output (the multiplier). This decline in output, in turn, depresses investment (the accelerator).

PROBLEMS

18-8. Complete the table below illustrating the acceleration principle. Assume that one machine is needed to produce every 1000 automobiles. Assume that a machine lasts 10 years. Assume also that one-tenth of the initial number of machines is scheduled for retirement in each of the next 10 years.

Year	(1) Yearly sales of autos	(2) Desired number of machines	(3) Net investment	(4) Gross investment
1	100 000			
2	100 000			
3	90 000			
4	80 000			
5	80 000			
6	80 000			
7	90 000			
8	100 000			
9	100 000			

18-9. Suppose, alternatively, that there is a lag in investment. The number of machines desired in any year is calculated by taking the average number of autos produced in that year and the previous year. In other respects, follow the assumptions of Problem 18-8. Then recalculate the table in Problem 18-8. Does this change in the assumption make investment demand more stable or less stable?

18-10. Suppose you are in business, and demand for your product has recently increased. You now have to choose among (1) turning away some of your new customers, (2) scheduling overtime, (3) adding a new shift, or (4) expanding your factory and the number of your machines. Explain the important considerations in choosing among these four options.

Chapter 19

■■■■■■■■■■■■■■■■■■■■■■■■■■■■■■■■■■■■

How Do We Deal with the Unemployment-Inflation Dilemma?

The connection between [unemployment and inflation] . . . is the principal domestic burden of presidents and prime ministers, and the major area of controversy and ignorance in macroeconomics.

James Tobin

The coexistence of unemployment and inflation has created a painful dilemma for monetary and fiscal policy makers. No matter what they do, their decisions may seem wrong in the short run. If they expand aggregate demand in order to reduce unemployment, the result can be higher inflation. If they tighten policy to fight inflation, they may depress the economy and make unemployment worse.

Nevertheless, they must do something. Even standing pat—continuing past policies—is a policy. What are policy makers to do? This chapter describes several suggestions for easing the unemployment-inflation dilemma:

■ Reduce the natural rate of unemployment by policies to improve the labour market;

■ Restrain inflation directly with wage and price controls or other policies;

■ If inflation has already gained momentum, do not try to stop it by relying exclusively on tight demand policies, which can cause an extended period of high unemployment. Look for ways to add flexibility to the economy in order to achieve a quicker adjustment to stable prices, with a shorter period of high unemployment.

In the final sections of the chapter, we will look in detail at the way in which people's *expectations* of inflation can change. We shall see that, if expectations change rapidly, it may be possible to unwind inflation in a relatively painless way, with relatively little unemployment.

WHAT CAN BE DONE TO REDUCE THE NATURAL RATE OF UNEMPLOYMENT?

No matter how successful policy makers may be in stabilizing aggregate demand to remove cyclical unemployment, there will still be a sizeable amount of unemployment due to frictional and structural causes. Not all of this represents voluntary unemployment while people search for appropriate jobs. Some workers—particularly teenagers—have trouble finding jobs no matter how hard they look. Accordingly, it is appropriate to study ways of reducing the natural rate of unemployment —that is, ways of *shifting the long-run Phillips curve to the left*.

Increases in the Natural Rate of Unemployment

First, however, we must consider an unfortunate fact. The long-run Phillips curve shifted in the opposite direction during the late 1960s and 1970s; there was an increase in the natural rate of unemployment, below which inflation will accelerate.

In the mid-1960s, the Economic Council of Canada suggested that it should be possible to achieve an unemployment rate as low as 3% without unleashing inflationary pressures. In the mid-1970s, the Council revised their "target rate" of unemployment upward, to just under 4%; it concluded that trying to drive unemployment below 4% would lead to an acceleration of inflation. For the second half of the 1970s, studies have suggested that the natural rate was even higher—above 7%. For the early 1980s, the evidence indicates that it was higher still: A recent study for the Economic Council suggests that it might have been as high as 8%-9% in 1981-85.[1] However, the same study also suggests that by the late 1980s the natural rate had fallen somewhat again. Specifically, the actual unemployment rate in 1988 was below 8%, and inflation did not seem to be accelerating significantly in that year.

Such changes in the natural rate of unemployment do not conflict with the accelerationist theory that the long-run Phillips curve is vertical. According to that theory (presented in Chapter 15), there is no long-run trade-off between inflation and unemployment; the equilibrium or natural rate of unemployment is not affected by changes in aggregate demand. However, it *can* change if conditions in the labour market change. In this case, the whole long-run Phillips curve can shift to the right or left.

Several explanations have been offered for the increase in the natural rate of unemployment during the late 1960s and 1970s, and for its decline in the 1980s.

1. The Changing Composition of the Labour Force

In 1960, teenagers (that is, 15- to 19-year-olds) were less than 10% of the civilian labour force; by 1974, the number had increased to over 12%. Teenagers have higher unemployment rates than adults; they are more likely to move from job to job, trying various options before settling down to a life's work. This is not necessarily bad. A period of experimentation may pay off, in terms of long-term satisfaction with the jobs they finally choose. But it does mean that frictional unemployment is relatively high among teenagers. As teenagers became a larger proportion of the labour force in the 1970s and early 1980s, the natural rate of unemployment rose.

However, because of changes in the birthrate, the percentage of teenagers in the labour force has been fall-

ing in the 1980s. By 1988, it was down to 8%. This decline in the number of teenagers is part of the reason that the natural rate of unemployment appears to have fallen in the 1980s. Indeed, this downward pressure on the natural rate will continue for the next few years, as the percentage of teenagers in the population will continue to decline. (Good statistics are available on this; those who will be teenagers in the 1990s have obviously been born already.)

2. The Minimum Wage

During the 1960s and 1970s, the level of federal and provincial minimum wages were increased periodically, and more workers were covered. This increased the natural rate of unemployment because it discouraged employers from hiring low-productivity workers. They become particularly reluctant to hire teenagers with limited training and work experience.

While minimum wages have continued to increase in the 1980s, they have not increased very fast. Recent research suggests that the effect of minimum wage laws in raising the unemployment rate has, if anything, declined in the 1980s.

3. Unemployment Insurance and Welfare

Improvements in unemployment insurance and welfare provide a third possible explanation for the increase in the natural rate of unemployment during the 1960s and 1970s. These programs help to maintain the incomes of the unemployed. As a consequence, they are less desperate to take the first jobs available. Frictional unemployment may rise when those out of work engage in a more leisurely search for jobs.

There is some evidence to support this conclusion. According to several studies, the substantial increase in benefits under the government's Unemployment Insurance program in 1971 may have added anywhere between 0.5 and 1.3 percentage points to the unemployment rates in the 1970s. University of Toronto economists Peter Dungan and Tom Wilson have attributed more than half of the increase in the natural rate of unemployment between the late 1960s and late 1970s to this factor.[2] Moreover, international comparisons indi-

■ ■ ■ ■ ■
[1] These estimates were made by Andrew Burns, "Unemployment in Canada: Frictional, Structural, and Cyclical Aspects", a background paper prepared for the Economic Council of Canada, March 1988.

■ ■ ■ ■ ■
[2] D. Peter Dungan and Thomas A. Wilson, *Potential GNP; Performance and Prospects* (Toronto: Institute for Policy Analysis, University of Toronto, Report No. 10, 1982). See also Ronald G. Bodkin and André Cournoyer, "Legislation and the Labour Market: A Selective Review of Canadian Studies," in H.G. Grubel and M. Walker, eds., *Unemployment Insurance: Global Evidence of Its Effects on Unemployment* (Vancouver: The Fraser Institute, 1978).

cate that in countries where unemployment insurance benefits continue to be paid for a relatively long time (a year or more) after a job loss, each spell of unemployment tends to last longer than in a country such as the United States where benefits for unemployed workers generally last no more than six months. But if long-lasting benefits make unemployment last longer, they contribute to a higher unemployment rate.

The sharp increase in unemployment insurance benefits in the early 1970s may have contributed substantially to the increase in the natural unemployment rate in Canada during those years, as the results of Dungan and Wilson suggest. However, in 1976 and 1979, further revisions to the Unemployment Insurance Act made benefits *less* generous, by decreasing both the benefit rate and the duration of the benefit period, and by lengthening the period of time that a worker has to be employed before qualifying for benefits. Thus, the contribution of unemployment insurance to the natural unemployment rate has probably *decreased* since the 1970s. Proposals announced in 1989 will continue this process, if they are implemented: There will be further restrictions in eligibility for benefits and reductions in the benefit period.

In deciding on eligibility criteria and benefit rates in unemployment insurance, there is a conflict of objectives. It is desirable to reduce the hardship of the unemployed by providing unemployment insurance. But their incentive to take unattractive jobs is thereby lessened, and this makes it more difficult to achieve the goal of lower unemployment. However, one thing is clear. Government programs should be designed, insofar as possible, to maintain incentives to get a job. In particular, care should be taken to avoid programs that allow people to be better off not working.

Steps to Reduce the Natural Rate of Unemployment

A number of steps have been suggested to make labour markets work more smoothly and to reduce the natural rate of unemployment.

1. Abolish the Minimum Wage?

Some economists, particularly in the United States, have suggested that the minimum wage be abolished because it can cause unemployment. Sometimes this suggestion is combined with a proposal for more comprehensive government grants to low-income families.

In Canada, where there are both federal and provincial minimum wage laws covering different categories of workers, there is little political support for the idea of simply doing away with minimum wages. Instead, the debate focuses on the question of what the *level* of minimum wages should be. Since minimum wages are set in dollar terms, this issue becomes especially important in inflationary times: When prices rise, the value of the minimum wage in real terms will be gradually eroded unless it is raised in step with inflation.

Proponents of the minimum wage recommend that it be raised at least enough to compensate for inflation. They argue that the minimum wage has little effect on unemployment. They believe that, whatever the small unemployment effect may be, it is more than outweighed by the need to provide a living wage to the unskilled.

In rejoinder, opponents of a minimum wage point out that many of those working at the minimum wage do not have families to support; many are teenagers, and some of them come from families whose incomes are well above the poverty line. At the same time, the minimum wage may prevent a second breadwinner in a poor family from getting a job: Thus, in some cases, the minimum wage can *contribute* to the poverty problem rather than solve it.

2. A Two-tiered Minimum Wage

The minimum wage is most likely to push up the unemployment rate of teenagers; many have little experience and limited skills. For this reason, some Canadian provinces have a lower minimum for teenagers than for adults. Such a two-tiered minimum wage is sometimes criticized because it gives employers an incentive to replace adults with lower-wage teenagers.

3. Training Programs

A lack of skills is one reason that some workers have difficulty finding jobs. Thus, government training programs may be a useful way to help the chronically unemployed prepare themselves for productive work. The *Adult Occupational Training Act* of 1967 was intended to speed up the retraining of unemployed workers, to provide them with the skills needed for new jobs. (In 1989, the government announced plans to make more funds available for such retraining.) The services provided by Canada Manpower assist in the process of matching prople looking for jobs and firms looking for workers. By filling vacancies more quickly, Canada Manpower helps reduce unemployment. Furthermore, the Department of Regional Economic Expansion (DREE) was set up in 1969, with the purpose of creating jobs in those areas of Canada where unemployment traditionally is high. By moving the jobs to the unemployed, it was hoped to reduce the unemployment rate faster than by waiting for the unemployed to move to where the jobs are.

Some economists have criticized these programs because they are so expensive. The alternative solution of assisting people to move to where the jobs are involves only a once-and-for-all relocation cost. But moving the jobs to the unemployed may mean a continuing cost. For example, inducing an industry into an unfavourable location that is far distant from its markets may mean it continues to face high transportation costs. Thus, unless it is provided with a continuing subsidy, it may eventually leave or collapse.

The Government as the Employer of Last Resort?

Government programs which provide jobs for the unemployed might be made more ambitious. The government might act as the *employer of last resort*. That is, the government might stand ready to provide jobs to all those who want work but are unable to find it in the private sector.

Proposals to make the government the employer of last resort are very controversial. On the positive side, government projects might give the unemployed something useful to do. For example, the unemployed might do maintenance jobs in the cities, or carry out conservation and public works projects such as reforestation.

If people are unemployed, it might seem obviously worthwhile for the government to hire them for, say, $4 per hour even if they can produce only $3 worth of output. Society at least gets the $3 in output, which is better than the zero output that the unemployed produce. However, critics argue that this reasoning misses an important point: Without last-resort jobs, people might look harder for work in the private sector. Thus, over time, public employment could come to include people who would otherwise have found jobs in the private sector where workers typically produce at least as much as they earn. Consequently, public employment could be a drag on the economy.

There seems to be no simple, painless, and uncontroversial way to lower the high natural rate of unemployment.

DIRECT RESTRAINTS ON WAGES AND PRICES: INCOMES POLICIES

Governments sometimes attempt to restrain inflation with direct controls or guideposts, and thus improve the trade-off between unemployment and inflation. Direct restraints on money wages and prices are sometimes known as *incomes policies*. Wage restraints affect the money incomes of workers. Price restraints affect other incomes, such as profits and rent.

Price and wage controls have often been introduced during wartime to suppress the inflationary pressures unleashed by excess demand. For example, they were used during World War II, when aggregate demand rose rapidly because of huge increases in military spending. In the four and a half decades since the war, controls have also been used from time to time, in North America and elsewhere.

International Experience with Incomes Policy

Experiments with different kinds of incomes policy were especially common during the 1960s and 1970s. During the 1980s, incomes policy became less popular and more emphasis was put on aggregate demand management, not only in North America but also in a number of European countries. In the 1960s and 1970s, for example, the United Kingdom used incomes policies extensively but, since Margaret Thatcher came to power in 1979, they have not been used. In the Scandinavian countries, incomes policy is made easier because of the highly centralized organization of the trade union movement, which means that a small group of union representatives can negotiate with the government on behalf of very large numbers of organized workers. This is one reason that incomes policy continues to be used in Scandinavia even after they have become less important in a number of other countries.

In the United States, incomes policy has not been used during the Reagan-Bush administrations in the 1980s, in line with their objective of reducing the role of government in the economy. During earlier administrations, however, there were attempts at using incomes policy. For example, in the early 1960s the Kennedy administration tried to control inflation by announcing two basic "guideposts":

1. On average, prices should not rise.
2. In general, money wages should not rise by more than the increase in labour productivity in the economy as a whole, estimated at 3.2% per year in the early 1960s.

These two guideposts are consistent. If wages increase by no more than productivity, no inflation need result. Labour can be paid more because labour produces more. Employers can afford to pay the higher wages and still keep prices constant on average.

The guideposts came under severe strain in the mid-1960s, when the rapid expansion of aggregate demand began to pull prices up strongly. In these circumstances, workers could scarcely be expected to stick to a 3.2% wage increase. If they did so, their real wages would fall; they would not get a share of the rising total product. After 1965, less and less attention was paid to the guideposts. They became irrelevant.

A second major attempt at using incomes policy in the United States was made in 1971, when the Nixon administration imposed a 90-day freeze on wages, prices and rents, followed by less rigid controls which lasted through 1972. These wage and price controls were accompanied by expansionary monetary and fiscal policies aimed at reducing the rate of unemployment.

In one way, the controls in the early 1970s seemed to work very well—the inflation rate dropped sharply in late 1971 and 1972, and the unemployment rate declined slightly. But inflation quickly spiralled up again after the controls were relaxed. Consequently, there are two conflicting views of this episode:

1. The wage-price controls worked, breaking the inflationary momentum and laying the basis for stable prices without going through the costs of an extended period with high unemployment. But the initial success was wiped out when monetary and fiscal policy became too ambitious.

2. The controls were not really a success at all, but merely a short-run illusion. They temporarily suppressed price increases but did not improve underlying trends. When the freeze was ended, prices quickly regained lost ground.

Canadian Incomes Policy in the 1960s and 1970s

Unlike the Kennedy-Johnson administration, the Canadian government stayed away from incomes policies until the late 1960s. While there was a "suggestion" that wage increases should not exceed a specific figure (6% per year) as early as 1966, the first real attempt to intervene in wage negotiations did not come until 1969 when the federal government created a *Prices and Incomes Commission* headed by British Columbia economist John Young. The mandate of the Commission was to push for *voluntary* agreements by unions and firms to limit wage and price increases. In the early discussions with labour representatives, however, it quickly became clear that there was little support from labour for voluntary restraints and, in the end, no attempt was made to impose specific guideposts such as those in the

United States. The Prices and Incomes Commission continued in existence as a government advisory body until 1972; in its final report it concluded that, despite the problems involved, Canadians should consider an incomes policy on a temporary basis if inflationary forces became strongly entrenched.

By the mid-1970s, inflation in Canada had reached double-digit figures (more than 10% annually). In October 1975, the Trudeau government instituted a program of wage and price controls, under which the allowable increases in most wages, salaries, and professional fees were limited to 10% per year. This figure was to be gradually reduced: The program was to last for three years, and goals were set which would provide for a step-by-step reduction in the rate of inflation.

Because of the difficulty in predicting trends in labour productivity and in the prices of imported goods and services, no specific figures were given for the allowable rates of price increases by firms. But the general rule was to be that price increases would be subject to approval by a new *Anti-inflation Board* (AIB), which would allow firms to raise prices only at a rate that depended on the increase in their cost of production.

It remains a matter of controversy whether the 1975–78 controls program had any appreciable effect on inflation in Canada. Initially, there seemed to be some grounds for optimism: Most wage settlements in 1976 were not very far out of line with the target set by the AIB, and the rate of inflation in 1976 was considerably below the 1975 figure. But difficulties also began to appear as the AIB approved a number of wage settlements well above the guidelines for the allowable wage increases, causing bitterness among those labour unions that had complied with the guidelines. Thus, as the program wore on, fewer unions were willing to go along with it. And following the initial success in reducing the inflation rate in 1976, the rate went higher again in 1977 and 1978—rather than lower as foreseen in the program. In 1978, inflation was back up to about 9% per year (rather than down to 4% as planned). Since wage increases were no higher than 6%-7% on average, real wages were falling, and it is clear that labour unions could not be expected to go along with continued controls in these circumstances.

What was perhaps even more disappointing was that the main objective of the controls program—to shift the Phillips curve back toward the origin—was not realized. Indeed, in 1977/78 the inflation rate was rising *and* Canada's unemployment rate had increased to a level that was higher than at any time since World War II. As an attempt to get rid of the problem of "stagflation," the AIB was a clear failure.

Thus, the conclusions of those who have studied Canada's experience under the AIB are similar to the assessments of the Nixon wage-price freeze in the United States. On the positive side, the advocates of the program point to the initial success of the AIB in moderating the very strong inflationary forces that had appeared in 1974/75. The critics, by contrast, point to its failure to achieve the gradual reduction in the inflation rate that was hoped for at the outset. They also point out that whatever reduction in the inflation rate *did* take place in the mid-1970s can equally well be explained by the relatively restrictive monetary policy of the Bank of Canada, by the high rate of unemployment that prevailed in those years, and by conditions in the world economy.

TIP and 6-and-5

Toward the end of the 1970s, American and Canadian experience with formal incomes policies led a number of economists to look for alternative types of incomes policy that might be less rigid and less complicated than earlier programs, but that would still contribute to reducing inflationary pressures.

One proposal was for some type of **Tax-based Incomes Policy** (TIP). According to this concept, the government would use tax incentives to encourage businesses and unions to comply with wage and price guidelines. Government might offer "carrots" in the form of tax rebates to firms and workers who complied with the guidelines. Alternatively, it might use a "stick"—a tax surcharge on violators.

The TIP approach originated among academic economists in the United States, where it attracted considerable attention during the Carter administration in the late 1970s. But it was never tried out: Critics doubted that TIP would be effective enough to justify the complications it would introduce into the administration of the tax system. Nevertheless, in a book published in 1979, Toronto economists Arthur Donner and Douglas Peters argued that Canada should also seriously consider using some form of TIP.[3] In their view, the strategy of monetary restraints had been a failure. It had produced rising unem-

ployment rates, but had not brought much of a reduction in the inflation rate. Therefore, Donner and Peters argued, Canada should once again try an incomes policy, but it should use a TIP, instead of a traditional approach, in order to avoid the rigidities and enforcement problems that the AIB had experienced.

The Donner-Peters proposal was widely discussed at the time, and was said to be under serious consideration by the Liberal government in 1981. Even some economists who are generally opposed to wage and price controls gave TIP some support. In the words of University of Ottawa's Ronald Bodkin, " . . . one might regard as the strongest feature of tax-based incomes policies their role in taking the place of an even more objectionable set of policies."[4] But many observers, including some former AIB officials, remained unimpressed: Even if a TIP is more flexible than other kinds of incomes policies, it still has many of the same disadvantages and might, in reality, be even more difficult to administer than other kinds of programs.

In the end, the Liberal government decided against a TIP. Instead, the June 1982 budget introduced a *partial* controls program which was essentially limited to the public sector. Under this program (which became known as the "6-and-5" policy), the government committed itself to limiting the wage settlements in the federal public sector to a maximum of 6% in 1982/83 and 5% in 1983/84; it also announced that prices of goods and services subject to government regulation (such as transportation, many agricultural commodities, and so on) would not be allowed to rise by more than these same percentages. The federal government appealed to the provinces to follow similar guidelines for that part of the public sector subject to provincial jurisdiction. However, there was no attempt at formally regulating wages and prices in the private sector, though the government tried to put some pressure on private-sector unions and firms to comply voluntarily with the guidelines.

Like other control programs, 6-and-5 was also controversial. In particular, labour unions in the federal and provincial public sectors complained that they were being unfairly singled out, since the program effectively nullified their right to collective bargaining while other unions were not affected.

■ ■ ■ ■ ■
[3] Arthur W. Donner and Douglas D. Peters, *The Monetarist Counter-revolution: A Critique of Canadian Monetary Policy 1975–1979* (Toronto: James Lorimer and Company in association with the Canadian Institute for Economic Policy, 1979), pp. 45–50.

■ ■ ■ ■ ■
[4] Ronald G. Bodkin, "The Challenge of Inflation and Unemployment in Canada during the 1980s: Would a Tax-Based Incomes Policy Help?," *Canadian Public Policy*, supplement to vol. VII, April 1981, p. 213.

But many other observers were sympathetic to 6-and-5. Because it was limited to the public sector, the difficulties of enforcement were far less severe than they would have been with a comprehensive program. And, in one sense, the program was successful: By 1984, the actual inflation rate in Canada was less than 5%, down from more than 10% per year in 1982 and early 1983.

However, those who are skeptical about incomes policy are quick to point out that with the severe 1982 recession and an unemployment rate exceeding 10% for almost two years, inflation probably would have come down anyway. In support of this view, the critics point out that in the United States, the inflation rate came down even faster, even though American unemployment rates were lower than in Canada and there were no wage and price controls in the United States during this period.

INCOMES POLICY: CONTROVERSIAL ISSUES

The desirability of guideposts or more formal controls on wages and prices has been the subject of continuing and heated debate. Several points are at issue.

1. *Workability*. Perhaps the most important criticism against comprehensive wage-price controls is the empirical evidence that suggests that they simply are not capable of keeping inflation down *for a significant length of time*. As we already noted, the attempts by the AIB in Canada to limit inflation during 1975–78 initially appeared successful but, by 1978, inflation was once again accelerating and, after the controls were lifted in 1978, inflation quickly reached double digits. In the United States, the skeptics point to the breakdown of the Kennedy-Johnson guideposts and the inflation that followed President Nixon's price freeze in 1971. In European countries, too, there have been a number of disappointing experiences with incomes policy. Indeed, in the United Kingdom, the United States, and a number of other countries, there was a move away from incomes policy in the 1980s, and since the end of the 6-and-5 program there has been little discussion of such policies in Canada as well.

2. *The problem of import prices*. As we saw in Chapter 6, imported goods and services play a very large role in Canada's economy: The value of imports in 1988 amounted to 25% of GDP. Because imports are so large, the prices of imported goods have a large weight in Canadian price indexes such as the CPI.

But the prices of goods imported into Canada cannot be controlled by a Canadian government agency such as the AIB: The AIB could not control the prices charged by California producers for fresh vegetables imported into Canada, or the prices set by Japanese manufacturers for their cars, nor could it control the value of the Canadian dollar in the foreign exchange market. Because imported commodities have such a large weight in our CPI, it is difficult for the agency in charge of enforcing an incomes policy to set a specific target for the overall inflation rate. And if the agency cannot control the overall rate of price inflation, it is difficult to ask workers to accepts firm limits on maximum permissible wage increases, since labour will be reluctant to go along voluntarily with a program which may result in a reduction in workers' real wages.

3. *Allocative efficiency*. Opponents of guideposts and controls point out that they interfere with the function of the price system in allocating production. As explained in Chapter 4, prices provide information and incentives to producers. When goods are scarce, prices rise, thus encouraging producers to make more. If prices are controlled, they no longer can perform this important role.

A particular problem arises because controls or guideposts may be enforced erratically. Responding to political pressures, the government may enforce price restraints most vigorously for essential goods. As a result of the low prices, businesses will switch to the production of more profitable items. Thus, *price controls may end up creating shortages of the very goods the society considers most essential*. For example, rent controls are the most common form of price control, since housing is so important. But, in cities with rent controls, it is generally extremely difficult to find an apartment for rent.

Proponents of incomes policies recognize this danger but believe that it can be dealt with. Advocates of guideposts or controls generally propose that a government agency be given the authority to grant exemptions, permitting higher wages and prices in industries where there are shortages.

4. *Economic freedom*. Because of the need for flexibility, any kind of incomes policy requires a government agency (such as the AIB) with authority to approve exceptions to the price or wage guidelines. The need for such an agency is viewed with alarm by the opponents of incomes policies, because of the

economic power it places in the hands of government officials. If officials are allowed to decide whether a firm will be able to raise its prices, they may gain the power to decide whether the firm will survive or not. Price and wage controls restrict the freedom of businesses and labour.

Proponents of controls point out that these dangers must be kept in perspective. In the absence of incomes policies, the government will have to restrain aggregate demand and generate high rates of unemployment if it wants to suppress inflation. The unemployed will be used as cannon fodder in the war against inflation. Thus, the freedom of business executives and labour leaders to do as they please must be weighed against the need for workers to have jobs.

Incomes Policies: A Final Word

A discussion of incomes policies would be incomplete without noting that governments also follow policies that raise prices. For example, government-sanctioned agricultural marketing boards keep farm prices up, while restraints on imports reduce competition and raise the Canadian price of products such as textiles from India and cars from Japan. In the face of political lobbies, it is easy for the government to take the line of least resistance and extend such price-raising policies. But to do so is to sabotage its fight against inflation. Thus, in evaluating a government's anti-inflationary policies, several related questions should be kept in mind: What policies have been followed to benefit specific industries or specific groups of workers? To what extent have these policies raised prices and wages? By adding to inflationary pressures, do such policies signal the need for monetary and fiscal restraint, and thus make it more difficult to achieve high employment in the economy as a whole?

OTHER PROPOSALS TO EASE THE TRANSITION TO LOWER INFLATION

Inflation is like toothpaste. Once it's out, you can hardly get it back in again.
Karl-Otto Pohl, President of the West German Central Bank

If tight aggregate-demand policies are used to wring inflation out of the economy, the result can be a long period of high unemployment. Incomes policies are sometimes used in an attempt to short-cut this painful process (for example, in 1975–78). Two other suggestions have also been made to ease the transition to lower inflation.

Indexation of Wages

In the face of inflation, workers can protect themselves in several ways. One way, discussed in Chapter 16, is for workers to negotiate an adjustment for inflation in their wage contracts. For example, during a period when inflation is running at 6%, they might negotiate a wage increase of 7.5% — a 6% adjustment for the inflation, plus a 1.5% real increase.

For workers, this approach has a major defect. It protects them only from *expected* inflation, not from *unexpected* inflation. If, for example, the inflation rate unexpectedly rises to 8%, they will find that their 7.5% nominal wage increase means a reduction in the real wage.

One way to deal with this problem is through **wage indexation**, which adjusts nominal wages during the life of the contract to compensate for inflation. For example, a contract might include a 1.5% basic increase in wages, with an **escalator clause** providing automatic adjustment for inflation. Thus, workers would be protected from inflation, even though they could not tell ahead of time what it might be.

During the 1970s, when the rate of inflation was accelerating rapidly and unpredictably, indexed contracts became quite common — although they generally were *capped* and therefore provided only a limited adjustment for inflation.

An *indexed* wage contract contains an *escalator clause* that provides workers with additional money wages to compensate for inflation. The additional wage is often referred to as a *cost-of-living allowance* (COLA).

Often, there is a cap on the cost-of-living adjustment, which limits the increase to no more than a specified percentage.

The primary reason for wage indexation is to protect workers from inflation. However, some economists have suggested a second reason: Indexation can increase the flexibility of nominal wages and thus help to break an inflationary spiral. If wage contracts are not indexed, years of abnormally high unemployment may pass before inflation can be sweated out of an economy, as noted in Chapter 15. With wage indexation, the transitional period may be shorter. Instead of negotiating a wage increase of 7.5% during a period when inflation is 6%, workers may settle for a real wage increase of 1.5%; that is, an increase of 1.5% plus the increase in the price index. If initial success is achieved in reducing inflation — from, say, 6% to 4% — then indexing will *automatically* reduce the increase in nominal wages from 7.5% to 5.5%. Upward pressure on prices will be reduced further, and the inflationary spiral broken in a relatively rapid and painless way.

However, indexation is dangerous. It is a two-edged sword; rather than helping, it can make the spiral worse. If inflation begins to increase, indexation makes wages respond more quickly, generating even more inflation.

The danger of escalating inflation can become particularly acute if wages are fully indexed and if other incomes are too—for example, Old Age Security benefits or pensions of government employees. The problem is that the public may be promised more income than the economy can possibly produce. In a non-indexed economy, this problem is solved by inflation. Inflation cheats people out of some of their income, and the public ends up with no more than the economy can actually produce. However, if everything is fully indexed, price increases cause automatic increases in nominal income. If more has been promised than can possibly be delivered, there is no limit to how high inflation can spiral.

The risk of promising more than can be delivered will increase if real production or real income of society falls short of expectations. Two examples might be cited:

1. *The rate of increase of labour productivity slowed down* in the 1970s. The increase in output was less than expected, for reasons that were discussed in Chapter 17. The combination of indexation and weak productivity added to the wage-price spiral.
2. *An external shock* can sometimes reduce the real income in an economy. For example, if the world demand for Canadian export goods declines, the Canadian dollar will depreciate and the Canadian prices of imported goods will rise. With higher import prices, someone's real income has to be reduced: Someone has to bear the burden of the higher cost of imports.

If wages and other incomes remain unchanged in Canadian dollar terms, then each of us will bear the burden of higher import prices. But if some Canadians are protected by indexing, then their wages, and the prices of what they sell, will increase automatically. The burden will be passed along to someone else who is not protected — such as a retired person with a private pension that is fixed in dollar terms.

Thus, in the face of an external shock, indexing leads to two problems: a speeding up of the inflationary effect and an even heavier burden on those "at the end of the line" who are not protected from inflation.

In this regard, Britain had a particularly unfortunate experience. In 1973, Prime Minister Heath encouraged the use of escalator clauses in labour contracts, in the belief that they would make it easier for unions to settle for moderate wage increases and thus help to reduce inflation. The timing could not have been worse. The new indexation clauses added to the inflationary effects when oil prices skyrocketed in late 1973 and 1974.

Because of such problems, some early advocates of indexing have become less enthusiastic in recent years. While indexing undoubtedly contributed to the rapid fall in the rate of inflation in Canada and the United States in the early 1980s, it has in many cases made inflation worse, not better.

The Share Economy

Indexing can make the wage-price spiral worse by making real incomes more rigid (even while it makes nominal incomes more flexible). A more promising policy is to move in the opposite direction, making real incomes *more flexible*.

One way to do this is through **profit-sharing**, with workers being paid a base wage plus a share of the corporation's profits as a bonus. During a recession, firms would lay off fewer workers because the cost per worker (wage plus bonus) would automatically fall as profits fall. Furthermore, with lower costs per worker, firms would be encouraged to cut prices during recessions in order to stimulate sales. This would help to break the inflationary spiral. It might also reduce cyclical fluctuations in output. For example, if the public recognized that car prices were unusually low during recessions, they would be encouraged to buy at that time.

Profit-sharing has been strongly recommended by Martin Weitzman, an economist at the Massachusetts Institute of Technology, who bolsters his case by pointing to the low inflation and low unemployment in Japan, where profit-sharing makes up a sizeable fraction of total labour income. Historically, North American unions have been cool to the idea, since they see it as a way to keep the base wage down.

In Canada, profit-sharing contracts are still uncommon. However, in the United States profit-sharing has begun to take hold in recent years. The United Auto Workers' union has negotiated profit-sharing agreements with GM, Ford, and Chrysler, and the idea has spread to other important sectors, including parts of the steel, aerospace, banking, and telephone industries. One reason is the increasing international competition (partly because of the appreciation of the U.S. dollar in world markets in the mid-1980s), which has provided an incentive to U.S. labour and management to cooperate more closely.

To its supporters, profit-sharing provides workers with a clear and obvious stake in the success of the firm. In order to make the idea more acceptable to labour, it has been renamed: It is often referred to as *gain-sharing* or *pay for performance* rather than profit-sharing, and Weitzman entitles his program *The Share Economy*.[5] Profit-sharing is sometimes combined with a no-layoff policy, making it even more similar to the Japanese system.

Some of the shares have been big enough to really count. Ford's workers received an average bonus of $2,100 in 1987 and $3,700 in 1988.

> With *profit-sharing* or *gain-sharing*, workers receive both a base wage and a share of the company's profits.

EXPECTATIONS WHEN PEOPLE ANTICIPATE POLICIES

An influential group of economists believe that *expectations* are the key to any successful anti-inflationary policy. Because of the way expectations adjust, it may be possible to unwind inflation in a relatively painless way without long periods of abnormally high unemployment.

Large Shifts in the Short-run Phillips Curve

To see how important expectations can be, let us reconsider the accelerationist theory outlined in Chapter 15. If the authorities adopt an expansive aggregate demand policy in an effort to hold unemployment below the natural rate, the result will be an ever-accelerating inflation. To recapitulate briefly: From an initial point of equilibrium G in Figure 19-1, an increase in aggregate demand causes unemployment to decrease and prices to rise. The economy moves to H. But H is not a stable equilibrium. H is on the short-run Phillips curve $PC_{0\%}$

[5] Martin Weitzman, *The Share Economy: Conquering Stagflation* (Cambridge, Mass.: Harvard University Press, 1984).

which is based on the expectation of zero inflation. However, actual inflation is running at 2% per annum. Contracts are adjusted upward to compensate for the 2% inflation, causing the short-run Phillips curve to shift up to $PC_{2\%}$. If the government wants to keep unemployment at the low target rate of U_T, it will increase aggregate demand again, moving the economy from H to J in the next period.

Suppose that we have reached J in this manner, with actual inflation at 4%. What rate of inflation will people expect to occur in the next period? What rate of inflation will unions and businesses expect when they negotiate wage contracts?

The answer, according to the original accelerationist theory, is that the expected rate for the future will be the same as the *actual* rate today—in our example, the 4% rate of inflation that people are experiencing at point J. This is an example of *adaptive expectations*; people's expectations adapt to the inflation they actually experience. If people adjust to the existing rate of inflation of 4%, the short-run Phillips curve will shift up to $PC_{4\%}$. If the authorities want to keep unemployment at the low rate U_T, they can increase aggregate demand enough to move the economy from J to K, just like the earlier move from H to J.

> If expectations of inflation are *adaptive*, they depend on the inflation actually observed.

However, this is not necessarily the correct answer; when the economy is at J, people do not necessarily expect that the actual inflation rate of 4% will continue. The reason is that they have already been fooled twice. They expected zero inflation, but got 2% inflation at H instead. Then they expected 2% inflation, and were wrong again. Inflation rose to 4% as the economy moved to J. Once people figure out the authorities' strong commitment to a low rate of unemployment, they may anticipate further inflationary policies in the future; they may come to expect that future inflation will be *worse* than inflation today. Hence, at J, they may expect that inflation in the future will be *higher* than the 4% that exists today. Suppose, for example, that at J they come to expect that future inflation will be 6%. In other words, when the economy is at J and people have a chance to renegotiate contracts, the short-run Phillips curve does *not* simply shift up from $PC_{2\%}$ to $PC_{4\%}$, based on the current rate of inflation. Instead, it jumps all the way up to $PC_{6\%}$.

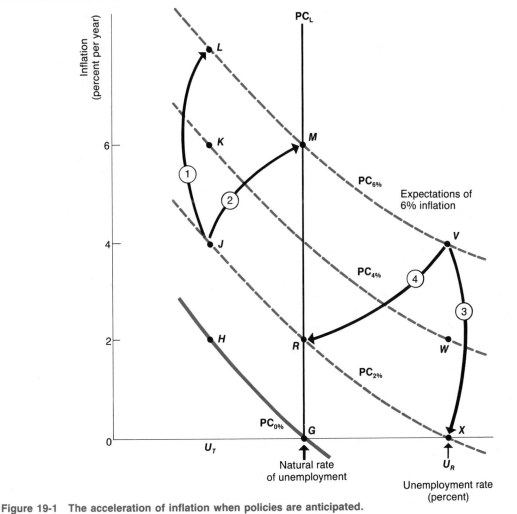

Figure 19-1   The acceleration of inflation when policies are anticipated.

In this example, people are fooled twice by rising inflation —when the economy moves from *G* to *H*, and when it moves from *H* to *J*. In each case, they expected the current rate of inflation to continue when, in fact, it was rising. However, when they get to *J*, they may expect that future inflation will be higher than the current rate of 4%. As a result, the short- run Phillips curve may shift up even more than in the simple accelerationist theory presented in Chapter 15. Similarly, if declining inflation is anticipated at *V*, then the short-run Phillips curve shifts down more rapidly, easing the inflation-unemployment problem.

There are now two possibilities:

1. The authorities remain determined to keep unemployment at the small percentage U_T, and expand aggregate demand at an increasingly rapid rate in order to do so. The economy moves from *J* to *L*, (arrow 1 in Figure 19-1) leapfrogging over *K*. The rate of inflation has jumped from 4% at *J* all the way to 8% at *L*. People have once again been fooled: They expected 6% inflation, but got 8%. No matter what inflation they have anticipated in the past, they

have gotten more. Next time, how much inflation will they anticipate? 15%? 20%? More? The next jump in the inflation rate may be huge.

2. The second possibility at point *J* is that the authorities recognize the danger of runaway inflation and, accordingly, do not expand aggregate demand so rapidly. If they expand demand only enough to create the 6% inflation the public expects but not enough to keep unemployment down to U_T, the economy will move from *J* to *M*. At *M*, the inflation rate is at least

stable. Equilibrium exists: The public expects 6% inflation, and gets it.

In summary:

1. If the public comes to expect that future inflation will exceed current inflation, then the wage-price spiral may explode.
2. If the public correctly anticipates future inflation, then unemployment will return to its natural or equilibrium rate (arrow 2 in Figure 19-1).

The first conclusion was important in the late 1970s. People did begin to fear that inflation was getting out of hand and this fear accelerated the wage-price spiral.

Unwinding Inflation

Now consider what happens if the authorities take a further step and try to unwind inflation by following restrictive demand policies, starting from the equilibrium at M in Figure 19-1.

Chapter 15 has already described what will happen if people have adaptive expectations and, therefore, expect the current rate of inflation to continue. To quickly review: At equilibrium point M, expected inflation is equal to the actual rate of 6%; the economy is not only on the long-run Phillips curve, but also on the short-run Phillips curve $PC_{6\%}$. When the authorities tighten aggregate-demand policy in the fight against inflation, the economy moves down $PC_{6\%}$ from M to V. Inflation drops from 6% to 4%. If people expect current inflation to continue (as assumed in Chapter 15), the next contracts would be written on the expectation of 4% inflation. Thus, the short-run PC curve would shift down to $PC_{4\%}$. If the authorities continue to pursue policies that are tight enough to keep the unemployment rate at U_R, substantially greater than the natural rate, the economy would move to W in the next period; and then, by a similar process, to X. Thus, inflation would be reduced, but very slowly. The unemployment rate would be very high and inflation would come down only 2% each time period. This painful problem is what this chapter is all about.

However, the process need not be this slow. If people figure out what is going on and recognize that the authorities are firmly committed to reducing inflation even at the cost of heavy unemployment, then they will come to expect that future inflation will not be the same as today's inflation, but will instead be less. When they sign contracts based on this assumption, the PC curve shifts down rapidly. For example, if they figure out that

the authorities are committed to an anti-inflationary policy when the economy is at V, they will be willing to sign contracts based on the assumption that inflation will not stay at its current rate of 4% but will instead be lower, say, 2%. Thus, when contracts are renegotiated at V, the short-run Phillips curve will shift all the way down to $PC_{2\%}$.

The authorities then have the option of reducing inflation rapidly, leapfrogging from V over W and all the way to X in Figure 19-1, as illustrated by arrow 3. (Alternatively, they can ease their tight policies, causing a movement along arrow 4 back to the natural rate of unemployment at R.) In short, people's ability to figure out what is going on will make it possible to bring inflation down more rapidly. *Long, costly periods with high unemployment may not be necessary to unwind inflation.*

Credibility

If a policy is to be believed, it should be believable.

William Fellner

Note that the *credibility* of an anti-inflationary policy can be the key to its success. Paradoxically, the way to stop inflation *without* long periods of high unemployment is to convince the public that you *will* tolerate long periods of high unemployment, if necessary. People will be ready to sign contracts based on lower inflation rates only if they believe that inflation will, in fact, come down.

Recent North American history gives some support to this view. In Canada, the inflation rate came down quite rapidly after 1982, as the public came to recognize that the Bank of Canada really was determined to fight inflation, and that the Federal Reserve in the United States was doing the same. Nevertheless, the reduction in inflation was far from costless; during the recession of 1981/82, the unemployment rate rose above 12% — the highest rate since the Great Depression. This suggests that, even when the authorities take a strong anti-inflationary stand, the unwinding of inflation can cause high unemployment. A strong stand can speed the process of adjustment, but not eliminate it.

To sum up the main ideas so far:

1. If people figure out that policy makers are trying to achieve lower unemployment with an inflationary policy, the wage-price spiral may become explosive. The authorities will find that they cannot achieve a lower rate of unemployment for any extended period.

2. If people figure out that policy makers are determined to push down the rate of inflation by following tight aggregate-demand policies, the wage-price spiral may come down quickly, with a relatively low cost in unemployment. *Credibility* is the key to a successful anti-inflationary policy.

In addition, this analysis is based on the key ideas of the original accelerationist theory presented in Chapter 15:

1. When people get the inflation they expected when they wrote their contracts, unemployment will be at the natural rate.
2. When people get more inflation than they expected when they wrote their contracts, unemployment will be less than the natural rate (as illustrated by point *H* or *J* in Figure 19-1).
3. When people get less inflation than they expected when they wrote their contracts, unemployment will be greater than the natural rate (point *V*).

RATIONAL EXPECTATIONS

The idea that the public may anticipate policies has been formalized and extended by ***rational expectations*** theorists, who believe that people make the best forecasts with the information available to them.

> *Rational expectations* are the best forecasts that can be made with available information, including information on (1) what the authorities are doing and (2) how the economy works. People with rational expectations may make mistakes, but they do not make systematic mistakes. The errors in their forecasts are random, chance occurrences.

(To see why the best forecast may nevertheless be mistaken, consider what happens if a coin is tossed 10 times. Clearly, the best forecast is: 5 heads and 5 tails. But when the experiment is actually carried out, 7 tails may come up. The two extra tails have occurred by chance.)

Ineffective Policies?

In the hands of Thomas Sargent and Neil Wallace,[6] rational expectations led to the controversial conclusion

that aggregate-demand policies are *worthless* as a way of reducing unemployment. By adjusting the quantity of money, the monetary authorities can have a powerful effect on prices. But it cannot systematically affect output and employment. To see why Sargent and Wallace come to this conclusion, consider two cases.

Case 1

In the first — admittedly unrealistic — case, the public knows exactly what the central bank is doing. The central bank announces its target for the money stock each period and hits the target precisely.

Suppose that the economy in Figure 19-2 begins at point *G*, an equilibrium on the vertical long-run Phillips curve PC_L. Inflation has been zero for some time. Suppose, now, that the central bank announces that it will increase the rate of growth of the money stock by 5%. People, therefore, expect higher aggregate demand and expect prices to rise by, say, 5% in the future.

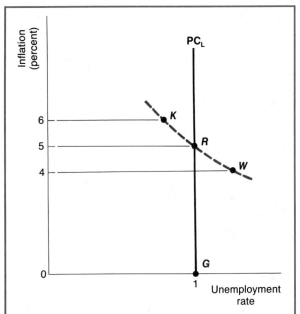

Figure 19-2 Rational expectations.
If expectations are rational, people make the best estimate of inflation. Their errors are random and, therefore, departures from the natural rate of unemployment are random.

For example, if the central bank pursues an inflationary policy when the economy is at *G*, the public will make the best estimate of the inflationary effect of that policy. If the estimate is correct, then the economy will move directly to *R*, with no increase or decrease in unemployment. Since mistakes are random, the economy is as likely to move to *W* as to *K*.

■ ■ ■ ■ ■
[6] Thomas Sargent and Neil Wallace, "Rational Expectations, the Optimal Monetary Instrument, and the Optimal Money Supply Rule," *Journal of Political Economy*, April 1975, pp. 241–54.

According to rational expectations theory, people won't wait until the higher inflation actually arrives before they adjust their contracts upward. While the economy is still at G, people adjust as soon as they see the policies that will cause future inflation. Therefore, the short-run Phillips curve shifts upward to $PC_{5\%}$. If people now get the 5% inflation they *expect*, the economy will stay on PC_L, moving directly from point G to R. In this case, the inflationary policy will cause no change in output or employment *even in the short run*.

However, even though 5% is the *best* estimate of inflation, it is not necessarily *correct*. People do not know exactly how the economy works; they do not know how much inflation will be caused by the faster growth in the money stock. They may get more inflation than they expect—say, 6%. In this case, the economy will end up at K rather than R. On the other hand, they may get less inflation (say, 4%), putting the economy at W. The economy may depart from the point R, but only in a random way; it is just as likely to move to the right as to the left of R.

With rational expectations, notice how easily the rate of inflation may be reduced—*if* the central bank's policies are credible. Suppose the bank announces a reduction in money growth and carries through with an actual reduction. Anticipating a lower inflation, the public will revise their contracts. The economy will move directly to a lower point on the long-run Phillips curve (again, plus or minus a random error). This move is similar to the move from G to R, but in the opposite direction. Inflation falls quickly, with only a random disturbance in the unemployment rate. Rational expectations theorists are hawks in the war against inflation. They believe that inflation can be prevented with little or no cost in terms of high unemployment.

Case 2

In practice, the public does not know exactly what the central bank will do. This complication is taken into account in case 2, where people have two things to figure out—what the bank will do and how the economy will respond. But, once again, rational expectations mean that people will make the best forecasts. Their errors will still be random. However, they are now forecasting two things rather than just one. Therefore, their errors will generally be larger than in case 1, and random departures from the natural rate of unemployment will accordingly be larger.

Consider a hypothetical example. Suppose that, at a time when an election is approaching, the party in power

decides to stimulate aggregate demand in order to increase employment and put people in a good mood when they go to the polls. What will happen? People will figure this out (although they will not do so perfectly; they will make random errors). They will say to themselves, "Now that an election is coming, the authorities will follow an inflationary policy." Workers will demand higher wage contracts in anticipation of this. Wages and prices will increase. But, because the increase in aggregate demand and prices is expected, there will be no systematic (non-random) change in output or unemployment.

The central bank, nevertheless, may be able to push unemployment temporarily below the natural rate by trickery—that is, by misleading the public. For example, the bank might say it was going to reduce the quantity of money but actually increase it. Then inflation would be greater than expected and the unemployment rate less than the natural rate. However, this would be a bad policy. Having been fooled, people would have a hard job figuring out the central bank's policy in the future. They would make larger errors in forecasting inflation, causing larger fluctuations in output and employment.

Rational expectations theorists conclude that, instead of using trickery, the monetary authorities should do the opposite. They should make aggregate demand and prices as stable and *predictable* as possible, in order to reduce the random fluctuations in employment. The best way to do this is to follow a monetary rule, increasing the money stock by a slow, constant rate of (say) 3% per year. Thus, they advocate the same policy rule as the earlier monetarists.

Criticisms

The "policy ineffectiveness" theory of Sargent and Wallace has attracted much attention, but remains a minority viewpoint. Critics raise several objections.

1. The theory assumes that people make detailed calculations of what the central bank is doing and how this will affect the economy. But, as one economist has observed, "It is absurd to assume individuals can make the necessary calculations since most economists still cannot do so."[7]

2. Rational expectations alone are not enough to establish the proposition that policies are ineffective. There is also another assumption imbedded in Figure

■ ■ ■ ■ ■
[7] Stanley Fischer, "Recent Developments in Monetary Policy," *American Economic Review*, May 1975, p. 164.

19-2—namely, that people renegotiate their contracts frequently. But many labour contracts last two or three years. During a two- or three-year period when wages are sticky, the economy is stuck on a short-run Phillips curve. Changes in aggregate-demand policy can affect output and employment, even if expectations are rational.

3. The facts don't fit the theory. The theory predicts that unemployment will fluctuate randomly; it will not remain consistently above (or below) the natural rate for very long. But in fact, unemployment was very high throughout the 1930s. More recently, unemployment was over 10% for four consecutive years (1982–85).

4. There is a problem with the policy conclusion.

Rational expectations theorists say that, to get the most stable, predictable path of aggregate demand and prices, the authorities should adopt a monetary rule. But this is not necessarily so. If the central bank actively manages monetary policy, it may be able to make demand and prices even more stable and predictable. It may be able to offset disturbances in the economy. Rational expectations theory has therefore left macroeconomists facing the same old question: in practice, *can* the authorities stabilize aggregate demand through active management? This, of course, was the key question studied in Chapter 18.

Table 19-1 provides a summary of the similarities and differences between the the rational expectations school and the earlier monetarists of the 1960s.

Table 19-1   Early Monetarism vs. Rational Expectations Theory: A Comparison

Issue	Early Monetarism	Rational Expectations Theory
Key to aggregate demand	Money	Money
Best policy	Monetary rule (steady increase in money stock)	Monetary rule (steady increase in money stock)
Which results in a more stable, predictable demand: monetary rule or discretion?	Rule	Rule
How public forms expectations	Adaptively	Rationally
Public's ability to figure out monetary policy	Unspecified (not a central issue)	Great, if policy is consistent; not great, if central bank resorts to trickery
Price flexibility	Moderately high, but not high enough to prevent sizeable recessions if aggregate demand is unstable	Very high
Long-run Phillips curve	Vertical; no long-run trade-off	Vertical; no long-run trade-off
Short-run Phillips curve	There is a trade-off; inflationary policies cause low unemployment for a time	There is no trade-off with systematic policies, which will be anticipated. Erratic policies (trickery) will increase the random deviations from the natural rate of unemployment

LIVING IN A GLOBAL ECONOMY: WHY IS THE UNEMPLOYMENT RATE SO HIGH IN EUROPE?

Some years ago, economists used to ask: Why is the unemployment rate so much lower in Europe than in Canada or the United States? However, in the early 1980s, unemployment rates in the European countries rose precipitously and, in the middle and late 1980s, European rates remained above 10%, even as unemployment rates in Canada and the United States declined (Figure 19-3). What accounts for the worsening unemployment situation in Europe?

Three possible explanations are debated by European economists:

1. Big Government?

Many blame big government, pointing out that it can inhibit economic adjustment in many ways. For example, generous unemployment insurance reduces the incentives for the unemployed to look for work. Workers who already have jobs can push aggressively for higher wages with little fear of the consequences. Laws restrict the right of employers to fire or lay off workers, and employers are therefore reluctant to hire people in the first place. A prominent critic of big government is Herbert Giersch of Kiel University, who believes that, as a result, the continent suffers from *Eurosclerosis*— a collective hardening of its economic arteries.

One difficulty with this explanation is that there are some obvious exceptions—most notably, Sweden. The Swedish government is the champion spender, reaching a peak of almost 60% of gross domestic product in the early 1980s. (Not all of this represented a direct government claim on the nation's output; transfer payments amounted to 25%.) Yet, in the mid-1980s, when the average unemployment rate in Western Europe was about 11%, it was only 3% in Sweden.

2. Excessive Real Wages?

The second explanation for the high unemployment rate is the high level of real wages in Western Europe. Employers won't hire more workers because they would have to pay them more than they could produce.

Support for this view is provided by the remarkable

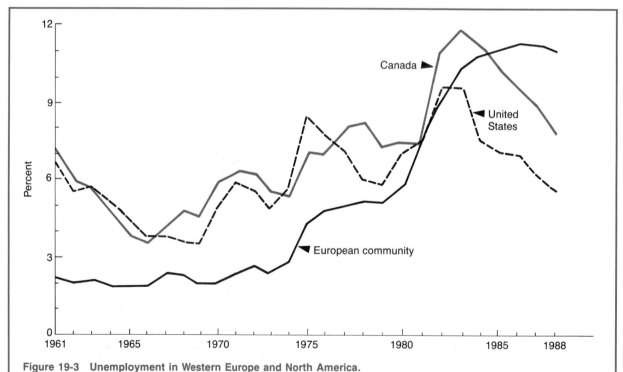

Figure 19-3   Unemployment in Western Europe and North America.
In the 1960s, the European unemployment rate was less than the rate in either Canada or the United States. However, since 1982, it has been higher.

Source: Organization for Economic Cooperation and Development, Main Economic Indicators and the *CANSIM Databank*. (Data for Europe include Belgium, France, Germany, Italy, Luxemburg, the Netherlands, and the United Kingdom, but excludes recently admitted members such as Greece.)

ability of the European labour force to protect its real wage in the face of inflation or other disturbances. European workers have been much more successful in capturing quick compensation for inflation than have their North American counterparts.

However, this explanation also raises difficulties, in particular, these questions: "How have European workers managed to capture and hold such high real wages in the face of competition from unemployed workers? Why haven't employers turned to the unemployed as a source of cheaper labour?"

European economists have offered several answers. The first focuses on the behaviour of those who are still employed and the strong unions that represent them. They are the "insiders" in labour negotiations and in political decisions. The unemployed are "outsiders" and are, in effect, disenfranchised. Unions act in the interest of employed workers who will retain their jobs. Unions push for higher wages, even though they will make it more difficult for the unemployed to find work.

An alternative explanation focuses on the unemployed themselves. People who have been unemployed for long periods may come to be regarded as unemployable; they are perceived as having lost the skills and motivation needed to be productive workers. Whether correct or not, this perception means that the long-term unemployed may gradually become unemployable.

This explanation may be important. Long-term unemployment is quite common in Europe. For example, in 1979/80, 40% of the French and British unemployed had been out of a job for more than 6 months, and 55% in Germany, considerably more than in Canada or the United States.

3. Hysteresis?

If the long-term unemployed do gradually become unemployable, then unemployment can become very sticky. It can gradually build up over many years and be unresponsive to rapid cures. This idea—that current unemployment is the cumulative effect of the past decade or so—has been given the obscure and clinically-sounding name, *hysteresis*. The term is borrowed from physics; hysteresis occurs if a material changes when subjected to an external influence, but then fails to return to its original condition when the external influence is removed. In the economic example, unemployment increases in the face of some economic disturbance, but doesn't fall back to its original level when the disturbance is removed.

Economists have not reached a consensus on which of these three points provides the best explanation of the high unemployment rate. They may all be important.

KEY POINTS

1. A number of suggestions have been made to deal with the inflation-unemployment dilemma:

   (a) Develop labour-market policies aimed at reducing the natural rate of unemployment.

   (b) Use wage and price guideposts or controls to restrain inflation directly.

   (c) Do not depend solely on aggregate-demand restraint as a way to reduce inflation, since it can cause high unemployment. Look for ways to make the transition to lower inflation less painful. Wage indexation is one proposal.

2. Between 1960 and the late 1970s, the natural rate of unemployment increased. Several controversial explanations have been offered for this increase:

   (a) Increases in the percentage of teenagers in the labour force. Teenagers have a higher unemployment rate than older workers.

   (b) Increases in the height and coverage of the minimum wage, which priced some workers with low skills out of the market.

   (c) Improvements in unemployment insurance benefits. They may have increased frictional unemployment, since they reduced the pressures on the unemployed to take jobs quickly.

3. During the 1980s, there may have been a decrease in the natural rate of unemployment. One factor working for a decrease has been the decline in the percentage of teenagers in the labour force.

4. Proposals to reduce the natural rate of unemployment include:

   (a) A two-tiered minimum wage, with a lower wage for teenagers.

   (b) Training programs for the unemployed.

   (c) A program in which the government acts as the employer of last resort.

5. A number of policies have been suggested to ease the transition to a lower rate of inflation, without causing a long period of high unemployment:

   (a) Incomes policies.

   (b) Indexed wages.

   (c) Profit-sharing.

6. Incomes policies were used during 1975–78 by the Trudeau government which created the AIB in an attempt to suppress inflation directly. A limited type of incomes policy concentrating on public-sector wages and government-controlled prices (the 6-and-5 program) was used in the early 1980s.

7. Incomes policies are controversial; they raise several important questions:
   (a) Do they work?
   (b) Do they have an adverse effect on efficiency?
   (c) Can they be effective in an economy with large imports?
   (d) Are they consistent with economic freedom?

8. If the public anticipates what the policy makers are going to do, the inflation rate will become more volatile. An attempt to keep the unemployment rate below the natural rate will quickly lead to very rapid inflation. A tight policy will reduce inflation with relatively little unemployment. *Credibility* is the key to a successful anti-inflationary policy.

9. According to the rational expectations theory, there will be only random deviations from the natural rate of unemployment. Systematic demand management policies will be useless as a way of keeping the unemployment rate consistently low.

10. However, *if* the authorities are able to stabilize aggregate demand, they should do so, thereby reducing *fluctuations* from the natural rate of unemployment.

11. In the 1960s, the unemployment rate was significantly lower in Western Europe than in North America. However, European unemployment rates rose rapidly in the 1970s and 1980s.

KEY CONCEPTS

employer of last resort
incomes policies
guideposts
wage-price freeze
import prices and price controls

tax-based incomes policies
   (TIP)
indexation of wages
escalator clause
cost-of-living allowance

escalator cap
profit-sharing
the share economy
adaptive expectations
rational expectations

PROBLEMS

19-1. Teenagers have a much higher rate of unemployment than older workers. How might this be the result of government policies? In the absence of such government policies, would you expect the teenage unemployment rate to be equal to, above, or less than the rate for older workers? Why?

19-2. For each of the following statements, state whether you agree or disagree, and explain why. If you disagree with the statement, revise it.
   (a) An increase in the minimum wage makes the unemployment rate higher. Therefore, it should not be increased.
   (b) Unemployment insurance also makes the unemployment rate higher. Therefore, it should be abolished.
   (c) The Kennedy-Johnson wage guidepost in the United States provided for an increase of wages of approximately 3%. The objective of this wage increase guideline was to provide labour with a gradually increasing share of national product in order to make up for past exploitation of workers.

19-3. Guideposts and wage-price controls are often opposed both by labour unions and by business executives. Why might labour leaders oppose them, when their objective is to make possible a combination of low inflation and low unemployment? Why might business executives oppose them, when one of their main objectives is to restrain nominal wage increases without having to put the economy through a period of recession and falling profits?

19-4. At the time of the 1974 election campaign in Canada, inflationary pressures were strong. During the campaign, the leader of the Progressive Conservatives declared that if the PCs were elected, they would move quickly to impose a program of wage and price controls. How do you think the announcement influenced inflationary pressures in the months *before* the election? Explain your reasoning.

When the Liberals did implement their anti-inflation controls in 1975, in the first year the program appeared quite successful. Some observers have suggested that part of the reason for its apparent early success was that the controls program had been widely anticipated. Can you explain the logic behind this suggestion?

19-5. In the text it was explained how a depreciation of the Canadian dollar would make it hard to control inflation through an incomes policy, because it would make import prices rise.

A depreciation of the Canadian dollar also tends to increase the prices received by Canadian *exporters* for the goods they sell in foreign markets. Explain what effect (if any) this tendency might have on Canadian inflation.

19-6. Indexed wages can create inflationary problems in the face of a "supply shock," such as an increase in the world price of oil.
(a) Explain why.

(b) Suppose that, at a time when unemployment and inflation are already high, there is a *favourable* supply shock, such as a decline in the world price of oil or a bumper crop. Will indexation make the inflation unemployment problem worse or better in this case? Explain why.

19-7. Would you favour the government's acting as the employer of last resort? Why or why not? If you are in favour, what jobs would you give to those hired under a last-resort program? How much would you pay them? Would you place any time limit on how long they can work for the government under this program?

*19-8. At the end of the previous chapter, we saw that the accelerationist hypothesis was not consistent with what actually happened during the Great Depression of the 1930s. Is the rational expectations theory supported by the events of the Great Depression or not? Why or why not?

Chapter 20

■■■■■■■■■■■■■■■■■■■■■■■■■■■■■■■■■

How Should We Organize the International Monetary System?

As for foreign exchange, it is almost as
romantic as young love, and quite as resistant
to formulae.
H.L. Mencken

Almost every country in the world has a single national currency and a single central bank that acts as a "bankers' bank" and is in charge of the monetary system. This is an efficient arrangement. By acting as a clearing house for the banking system, the central bank facilitates transactions between banks in different parts of the country. Because we have a single Canadian currency and monetary system, trade and investment flows between Canadian provinces and regions are made less risky and more convenient.

But this raises the question: If this is an efficient arrangement for Canada, would it not also be efficient for the whole world economy to have a single currency? In fact, at various times there have been suggestions that there should be one world central bank which would issue a currency that could be used throughout the world.

On the whole, these suggestions have not received much support. National governments do not want to give an international organization control over their monetary systems; they want to continue using monetary policy as an instrument for stabilizing their economies. Moreover, without a national central bank, governments would no longer have automatic access to "the printing press" (credit from the central bank) as a last resort in financing budget deficits.

But even if countries retain their separate currencies, they can still collaborate to create an **international monetary system** to reduce exchange rate instability and exchange risks in international transactions. One

approach is to have a system of fixed (or pegged) exchange rates. This chapter will consider two international systems of fixed exchange rates, namely:

1. The gold standard, on which the international monetary system was based before World War I and for a period in the late 1920s.
2. The International Monetary Fund (IMF) system of pegged exchange rates between 1945 and 1971 (in which Canada participated during 1945–50 and again in 1962–70).

Both the gold standard and the IMF system of pegged exchange rates had defects, and both ultimately broke down. Since the mid-1970s, most industrial countries have allowed exchange rates to float. Through international cooperation countries have continued trying to reduce exchange rate fluctuations since that time. But as this chapter explains, the flexible rate system has not worked as well as was originally hoped: Fluctuations have been substantial, causing disturbances in normal trade and investment transactions. Thus, governments face an important question: Should they consider further changes in the international monetary system, perhaps taking stronger steps to stabilize exchange rates and move part way back toward a pegged exchange rate system?

Finally, the last section of the chapter will consider some of the causes of the *international debt crisis* facing a number of developing countries — a crisis that has placed severe burdens on their economies and introduced a major destabilizing factor into the world economy.

FIXED EXCHANGE RATES UNDER THE GOLD STANDARD

Under the gold standard system, exchange rates were kept stable because national currencies were convertible into gold. That is, central banks (or the government) guaranteed banks and others the right to convert national currencies into gold at fixed prices. But this implied that exchange rates were stable. For example, the U.S. government guaranteed conversion of the U.S. dollar into approximately 1/20th of an ounce of gold. The value of the British pound was guaranteed by the British government to be worth about 1/4 of an ounce of gold; or more precisely, 4.86 times as much gold as the U.S. dollar. But since gold could be traded internationally, this implied that the exchange rate between the pound and the dollar also had to stay close to £1 = $4.86. The reason is that if the exchange rate deviated substantially from this value, one of the governments would quickly lose its gold reserves.

Suppose, for example, that the pound were to appreciate to $5.00 in the exchange market. In this case an investor could make money by buying one pound's worth of gold in the United States (which would cost $4.86), ship it to Britain, exchange it for a pound, and then resell the pound in the exchange market for $5.00. There would be a net profit of 14 cents ($5.00 − $4.86) less the transportation cost for the gold. If the situation were to persist, the United States would quickly lose its whole gold reserve. Under the gold standard, however, it would not persist, as we will now see.

The Adjustment Mechanism of the Gold Standard

The international gold standard provided an automatic *mechanism of adjustment*. It worked to prevent a continuing flow of gold from one country to another. Here's how.

As we just saw, exchange rates that were even slightly out of line with currencies' relative values in terms of gold would cause speculators to ship gold from one country to another. With gold being accepted everywhere, a country's stock of gold served as its *international reserve*; gold shipments represented changes in a country's international reserves in response to balance-of-payments deficits or surpluses. In the previous example, the upward pressure on the British pound that led to the gold inflow from America might have occurred because of rising imports into the United States from Britain, or a capital outflow from the United States to Britain, causing a deficit in the U.S. balance of payments with Britain.

But the gold flow to Britain would cause the British money supply to increase. Gold itself is money; more importantly, more gold in the system would increase the reserves of British banks (including the central bank), since gold also serves as a bank reserve asset. With the additional reserves, banks can expand their loans, thereby causing a further increase in the money stock. With more money and bank loans in Britain, interest rates there would begin to fall, and prices would tend to increase. On the other side, the United States is losing gold. As a result, its money stock automatically falls. Interest rates tend to rise, aggregate demand falls, and prices will fall.

But with rising prices in Britain and falling prices in the United States, British goods would begin to look less attractive to American buyers, and American goods would look more like a good bargain to British buyers. With lower interest rates in Britain and higher ones in the United States, less capital would flow from America to Britain. With British imports rising and exports falling, and a reduced capital inflow, the British balance-of-payments surplus would disappear. As a result, the gold flow from America to Britain would cease.

> An international *adjustment mechanism* is a set of forces that operates to eliminate balance-of-payments surpluses or deficits. That is, an adjustment mechanism works to ensure that one country won't continuously lose large amounts of gold or other reserves to other countries.

Problems with the Gold Standard

The international gold standard provided exchange rate stability during much of the nineteenth century when international trade and investment grew rapidly. But it had two major defects:

1. The process of adjustment could be *very painful*. For example, gold sometimes flowed out of a country that was already in recession. The gold standard caused an automatic reduction in the money supply, further depressing aggregate demand and increasing unemployment. In other words, there sometimes was a **conflict** between the *expansive* policies needed for domestic prosperity and the *decrease* in the money stock required by the gold standard to drive down prices and strengthen the country's ability to compete in the world market.

This problem became especially acute in the early stages of the Great Depression in the 1930s. During World War I, the gold standard had been suspended. In the face of huge government deficits, inflationary monetary policies, and huge expenditures for imports, governments were unable to maintain convertibility of their currencies into gold. However, in the 1920s, attempts were made to restore the gold standard. For example, Britain re-established gold convertibility in 1925, and Canada in 1926. Following the crash in 1929, the system again came under pressure. In attempting to preserve gold convertibility of their currencies in the face of this pressure, a number of countries conducted highly restrictive monetary and fiscal policies, even though aggregate demand was already collapsing and their economies were rapidly moving into a depression. Canada and Britain abandoned the attempt and suspended gold convertibility for good in 1931; the United States followed in 1933. By that time, however, the damage had already been done: The restrictive policies in the preceding years had contributed to making the Depression worse.

2. As we saw in Chapter 12, the gold standard could lead to very **unstable** monetary conditions. Under the fractional reserve system of banking, a large quantity of money was built on a relatively small base of gold. The monetary system, therefore, was vulnerable to a crisis of confidence and a run on the gold stock. This problem came to the fore whenever a country was losing gold because of a balance-of-payments deficit, and a crisis of confidence contributed to the collapse of the gold standard during the 1930s.

THE ADJUSTABLE PEG: THE IMF SYSTEM, 1945–71

The advantage of the gold standard was that it provided stability in exchange rates. Its main disadvantage was that the automatic adjustment mechanism that created this stability had undesirable side effects: It sometimes destabilized the economy.

Following the suspension of the gold standard in the early 1930s, most countries allowed their currencies to float. In the unsettled conditions of the Great Depression, however, exchange rates fluctuated widely. This contributed to the disruption of international trade and investment, and delayed the recovery from the Depression. As nations began to plan for a reorganization of the international economy toward the end of World War II, re-establishing some degree of exchange rate stability was, therefore, a major objective.

In 1944, senior financial officials from the allied countries met at Bretton Woods, New Hampshire. This conference designed a ***pegged-but-adjustable*** system of exchange rates for the postwar world and established a new organization, the International Monetary Fund (IMF), to help make the new system work. (The Bretton Woods conference also established a second important international organization, the World Bank, to provide financial assistance for postwar reconstruction and for economic development.)

The adjustable peg system was designed to provide some of the exchange rate stability of the old gold standard while avoiding its major defects. Specifically, under the Bretton Woods system, exchange rates were normally to be kept stable within a narrow band ($\pm 1\%$) around an officially declared ***par***. For example, between 1962 and 1970 the Canadian dollar was pegged at an official price or par value of C\$1 = U.S.\$0.925.

> Under the IMF system prior to 1971, the *par value* of a currency was the official price of the currency, specified in terms of the U.S. dollar or gold.

As long as exchange rates were pegged at given par values, the IMF system was equivalent to a system of fixed exchange rates. As we saw in Chapter 14, however, when a country is on fixed exchange rates, changing economic conditions will give rise to deficits or surpluses in its balance of payments. Under the gold standard system, such surpluses or deficits led to gold flows which, in turn, caused changes in the money supplies of the countries that were losing or gaining gold. In the IMF system, *there was no such automatic adjustment mechanism*. However, the founders of the IMF recognized that some provision would have to be made for international adjustment in the event of deficits or surpluses. Recall from the discussion in the previous chapter that there are only four major ways for a country, say Britain, to deal with a disturbance in the foreign exchange market. It may:

1. Keep the price of the pound stable by buying surplus pounds with reserves (U.S. dollars, say) or selling pounds in the event of a shortage;
2. Change tariffs or other restrictions on imports or other international transactions;

3. Change domestic aggregate-demand policies in order to shift the supply curve for pounds;
4. Change the exchange rate.

The IMF system represented a compromise, with each of these steps playing a part. Increases in tariffs or other restrictions on imports (option 2) were considered undesirable, since they reduced international trade and made the world economy less efficient. However, they were permitted in emergencies, including the severely disrupted period after World War II. And, while countries were expected in normal circumstances to use a combination of options 1 and 3 to maintain pegged exchange rates, it was recognized that in certain situations this might be too difficult and costly: As we shall see shortly, in such exceptional situations, the IMF agreement allowed countries to change their exchange rates (option 4).

Short-term exchange market disturbances that gave rise to surpluses or deficits in a country's balance of payments were initially to be handled through option 1, as countries were expected to keep their exchange rates stable by using foreign exchange reserves to intervene in the international market for their currency. In some cases, such disturbances may be temporary. For example, they may reflect problems such as strikes, bad weather that affects crops, or other transitory phenomena. In such cases, temporary market intervention by the central bank may be all that is needed, and the deficit or surplus in the balance of payments may disappear by itself. In other cases, however, the disturbances in the exchange market may not be due to short-term transitory factors. In such cases, a commitment to fixed exchange rates will force a country to take more fundamental steps, such as changes in domestic aggregate demand (option 3). For example, if a country is following excessively expansive aggregate-demand policies, the resulting inflation may price its goods out of world markets and cause international payments deficits. A more restrictive demand policy is then appropriate, both to restrain inflation and to improve the country's international payments position.

In either of these situations, an important question for a country experiencing a balance-of-payments *deficit* is how large an amount of reserves it has available to draw on as it attempts to stabilize exchange rates. Even transitory deficits may sometimes be quite large, so that a country may need a large amount of reserves to inter-

vene in the market while it is waiting for conditions to return to normal. And, in the case of a country that is using restrictive aggregate-demand policies to eliminate a balance-of-payments deficit, a large amount of reserves may be needed to maintain pegged exchange rates as the policy makers wait for the restrictive measures to take effect: A country with access to only a small amount of reserves may be forced to implement sudden, sharp policy changes to deal with a deficit, and such policy changes may end up destabilizing the economy.

Thus, it is easier for countries to maintain fixed exchange rates if they have access to relatively large amounts of reserves. In recognition of this, the IMF was empowered to lend foreign currencies to deficit countries; they could then use these "borrowed reserves" to stabilize their own currencies on the exchange markets. (The currencies lent out in this way were provided to the IMF by the member countries.) Thus, "Fund" is an important part of the title of the IMF.

In most cases, a combination of options 1 and 3 are sufficient for a country to maintain pegged exchange rates without too much of a problem. However, in some situations, the disturbances in the exchange market may be so severe that they cannot be handled in this way. No country has unlimited quantities of foreign reserves, and there are limits on the amount the IMF is willing to lend. Moreover, an adjustment in domestic demand is not always a desirable way of dealing with an international payments problem. For example, a deficit country might already be suffering from domestic recession. Restrictive aggregate-demand policies to solve the international payments problem would just make the recession worse.

In such circumstances, where the first three options had been ruled out or proved inadequate, the country was considered to be in a *fundamental disequilibrium*, and the Bretton Woods system approved the only remaining option: Change the exchange rate. For example, in 1949 the British *devalued* the pound from £1 = $4.03 to a new par of £1 = $2.80, and Canada devalued its currency from C$1 = U.S.$1.00 to C$1 = U.S.$0.909. On the other side, the Germans *revalued* the D-mark upward in 1961 and 1969.

A country *devalues* when it lowers the par value (the official price) of its currency.

A country *revalues* when it raises the par value of its currency.

THE IMF SYSTEM: THE PROBLEM OF ADJUSTMENT

For several decades, the IMF system worked reasonably well — well enough to provide the financial framework for the recovery from World War II, and for a very rapid expansion of international trade. But it contained major flaws that ultimately caused its breakdown in the early 1970s.

In practice, there were defects in the policy of changing the par value of a currency to deal with a "fundamental disequilibrium." When a country begins to run a deficit or surplus, it is uncertain whether the deficit or surplus is only temporary — in which case it can be dealt with by buying or selling foreign currency rather than by changing the exchange rate — or whether it represents a fundamental disequilibrium — in which case a change in the par value is appropriate. The IMF agreement itself provided no help in this regard. At no place did it define a fundamental disequilibrium.

Since a fundamental disequilibrium involves a surplus or deficit that will persist, one simple test is to wait and see whether, in fact, it does persist. But waiting can be a nerve wracking experience. In particular, deficits cause a loss of foreign exchange reserves. And, as reserves dwindle, *speculators* add to the problem. As soon as speculators become convinced that the deficits will continue — and the British, say, may eventually be forced to devalue — they have an incentive to sell pounds. For example, if a speculator sells pounds when the price is $2.80 and the British do devalue the pound to $2.40, the speculator can buy the pounds back for $2.40, making a profit of 40 cents on each pound. Speculators may stampede into the market because the pound is such a fat target. Speculators win big if the pound goes down. If the crisis passes without a devaluation, they don't win. But they don't lose much, either (only the cost of buying and reselling the foreign currencies). In such circumstances, the speculator looks on the foreign exchange market as a great place to bet: Heads I win, tails we're even.

A *speculator* is anyone who buys or sells a foreign currency (or any other asset) in the hope of profiting from a change in its price.

Thus, speculators may add a flood of pounds for sale on the foreign exchange market. To keep the pound from dropping in price, the British authorities have to buy up these excess pounds, using their reserves of U.S. dollars to do so. Consequently, the entry of speculators into the market speeds up the loss of British foreign exchange reserves and puts increased pressure on the authorities to devalue. This may then become a case of *self-fulfilling expectations*. The expectation by speculators that the pound will be devalued leads them to take an action (selling pounds) that increases the likelihood that the British authorities will, in fact, have to devalue.

In our example, speculators reap a windfall gain of 40 cents per pound when the British devalue. But this 40 cents represents a transfer from the British authorities, who lose exactly the same amount by fighting the speculators. (When a speculator sells pounds, the British buy these pounds at $2.80. After the devaluation, they sell them back at $2.40, for a loss of 40 cents.) Ultimately, the British taxpayer bears this loss. Why, then, do the authorities fight speculation as it builds up? Why don't they devalue quickly? The answer is that they are still unsure whether a devaluation is really necessary. They hope to end speculation by restoring confidence that the pound will not be devalued.

To restore confidence, the authorities firmly proclaim their determination to defend the pound. Even if they are almost sure that they will have to devalue the pound tomorrow, they must declare today that they will *not* do so. What choice do they have? If they admit that a devaluation is possible — or even if they refuse to comment — speculators will pour pounds into the market and reap even greater profits at the expense of the government when the devaluation does occur.

Once government leaders have staked their reputations on the defence of the currency, it is very difficult for them to back down and change its par value. Therefore, in practice, devaluations tended to be infrequent and long delayed under the IMF system. And, once they came, they tended to be large, so that the government would not have to go through the painful experience again in the near future. Thus, the system of adjustable pegs did not work out as hoped. For long periods the system was one of rigid pegs as officials committed themselves firmly to the existing exchange rates. Then, when the pressures became intolerable and changes had to be made, "jumping pegs" were the result, with drastic adjustments being made. (Speculation can sometimes also cause problems for a country with a balance-of-payments *surplus*. An example of this is the episode of the floating of the Canadian dollar in 1950; see Box 20-1.)

When countries clung desperately to their existing par values, they were pushed back toward the old gold standard system, using domestic aggregate demand as a way to adjust. The British, for example, engaged in a series of stop-go domestic policies, restricting aggregate demand when they were losing foreign exchange reserves, and turning policies to "go" when their international position improved. Thus, a strong destabilizing force was introduced into domestic economic policy.

The lack of a smooth and effective adjustment process was not the only shortcoming of the old IMF system. In that system, the U.S. dollar played a central role, and this created special problems for the United States.

THE U.S. DOLLAR AND THE ADJUSTABLE PEG: THE PROBLEMS OF LIQUIDITY AND CONFIDENCE

Under a pegged exchange rate system, not all countries are equal. It is not possible for every country to have control over its exchange rate. The reason is that there are fewer independent exchange rates than there are countries. In a very simple world of two countries, say the United States and Britain, there is only one exchange rate. (Of course, the rate may be quoted either way. For example, $1 = £0.50$ is just another way of stating that £1 = \$2.) In general, in a world of n countries, there are only n-1 independent exchange rates.[1]

This fundamental fact posed two interrelated questions for the designers of the IMF system:

1. If an exchange rate — such as the rate between the pound and the U.S. dollar—begins to rise or fall, does Britain or the United States have the responsibility of intervening in the foreign exchange market to keep it close to the official par value?
2. In the case of fundamental disequilibrium, the par value might have to be altered. Does the United States

■ ■ ■ ■ ■
[1] In a three-country world — Britain, France, and the United States, say — it may seem that there are three independent exchange rates: one between the pound and the dollar, another between the franc and the dollar, and another between the franc and the pound. But, effectively, there are only two (that is, n-1). Any two exchange rates determine what the third will be. For example, if the pound is \$2 and the franc is 20 cents, the pound must be worth 10 times as much as the franc; that is, the exchange rate must be £1 = 10 francs. (If you are curious why this must be so, look at Box 20-2.)

Box 20-1
■ ■ ■ ■ ■ ■ ■ ■ ■ ■ ■ ■ ■ ■ ■ ■ ■ ■ ■
The Crisis of 1950 and the Floating of the Dollar

After the Bretton Woods conference in 1944/45, Canada followed the example of most other countries and maintained a system of pegged exchange rates. However, in 1950 Canada broke ranks: The Canadian dollar was allowed to float and, as noted in Chapter 14, for the next 12 years Canada followed a policy of flexible exchange rates while other nations continued to use a pegged exchange rate system.

The events in 1950 that induced the Canadian government to abandon the pegged rate system provide a classic example of the difficulties that can occur in such a system when there are large speculative capital flows. What happened was this: Oil had been discovered in Alberta, and Americans had begun to invest in Alberta oil fields. Moreover, with the outbreak of the Korean war in 1950, the U.S. demand for Cana-

or Britain make the decision to alter the par value? And which country chooses the new par?

The IMF solution to the first question was as follows. Other countries tied their currencies to the U.S. dollar, and the United States, in turn, undertook to keep the dollar convertible into gold.[2] This determined the entire set of exchange rates between countries (Figure 20-1). As far as exchange rates were concerned, the United States was the odd man out. Every other country was responsible for its exchange rate. As the nth country, the United States had no such responsibility.

■ ■ ■ ■ ■
[2] That is, the United States undertook to buy or sell gold to foreign central banks and treasuries at the official price of 1 ounce = U.S.\$35. In technical terms, the IMF system was an example of the *gold exchange standard*, which exists when countries peg their currencies either to gold or to another currency — like the U.S. dollar — that, in turn, is pegged to gold.

Although all currencies were thus pegged to gold either directly or indirectly, the old IMF system was a far cry from the classical gold standard. The U.S. government made no commitment to sell gold to the public, and there was no automatic link — in the United States or elsewhere — between gold and the money supply. Furthermore, exchange parities were to be adjustable, not fixed firmly as under the gold standard.

dian raw materials shot upward. For both reasons, the Canadian balance of payments moved strongly into surplus. Speculators began to wonder if the Canadian dollar would be revalued. Their interest was kindled by an incautious statement by C.D. Howe, Minister of Trade and Commerce: "It is true, at the moment, that Canadian funds are at a 10% discount, but that is a temporary situation. The historic position of the Canadian dollar is at par with the United States (that is, C$1 = U.S.$1.00)."* The result was a large capital inflow: The rush to buy cheap Canadian dollars was on. To keep the value of the Canadian dollar down, the Canadian authorities had to sell a large amount of Canadian dollars in exchange for U.S. dollars.

* Note that the term "par" has two meanings: (1) In the IMF system, it means the officially chosen exchange rate, regardless of what that exchange rate may be. (2) In Canada, the word "par" often means the specific exchange rate C$1.00 = U.S.$1.00. (This Canadian meaning of the word "par" is the result of an historical accident: Both the Canadian and U.S. currencies are called a "dollar," and the exchange rate between the two currencies has usually been fairly close to C$1.00 = U.S.$1.00.)

This, in turn, created a major problem in the management of monetary policy. When the Bank of Canada bought U.S. dollars, it paid for them with newly created Canadian dollars. Hence, the Bank's actions eased monetary conditions. But, because of the threat of renewed inflation brought on by the Korean war, the Bank of Canada was trying at the time to move in exactly the opposite direction — toward a more restrictive policy. Therefore, in order to sterilize the increase in Canada's reserves of U.S. dollars, the Bank engaged in the tight monetary policy of selling bonds in the open market.

But the result of the open market sales was lower bond prices (higher interest rates) which made Canadian bonds more attractive to Americans; this, in turn, created an even larger capital inflow, adding once again to Canadian bank reserves and the Canadian money supply. Thus, the attempt to sterilize failed: Canada had lost control of its monetary policy. Accordingly, in 1950 the authorities abandoned the policy of pegged exchange rates and opted instead for a floating rate.

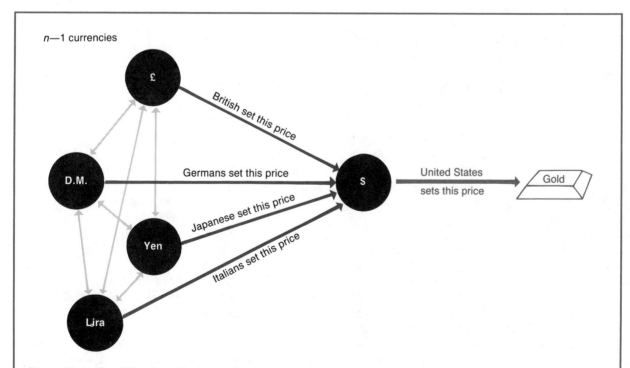

Figure 20-1   The IMF adjustable peg system.

Each of the *n* – 1 countries set its exchange rate with the U.S. dollar (black arrows). These *n* – 1 exchange rates determined all exchange rates, including those in gray. The United States, as the *n*th country, set the price of gold.

The answer to the second question followed from the answer to the first. Since Britain was responsible for keeping the pound pegged in terms of dollars, the ball was in the British court when the decision came to change the parity. However, Britain was to consult other members of the IMF regarding the new parity.

THE BREAKDOWN OF THE ADJUSTABLE PEG SYSTEM, 1971–73

For the United States—with its responsibility to keep the dollar convertible into gold—gold formed the primary reserve. Other countries had the responsibility of stabilizing their currencies relative to the dollar. Even though they also kept small amounts of gold, they held most of their reserves in the form of U.S. dollars, to be used as needed to intervene in the exchange markets.

In his 1960 book, *Gold and the Dollar Crisis*, Robert Triffin of Yale University argued that there was a fundamental problem with the IMF system: As international trade expanded, countries would want more reserves. How could reserves be increased? By digging more gold, or by increasing foreign holdings of U.S. dollars.

The prospects for large increases in the supply of gold were not promising. Thus, if countries were going to get the reserves they needed, their holdings of U.S. dollars would have to increase. But how does another country get more dollars? By running a balance-of-payments surplus with the United States. In other words, *if other countries were to accumulate dollar reserves, the United States would have to have deficits*. But, as American deficits continued and foreign dollar holdings became larger and larger compared with the relatively stable U.S. stock of gold, the ability of the United States to convert the dollar into gold would increasingly come into question. There would inevitably be a crisis of confidence, a run on U.S. gold by foreign governments, and a collapse of the IMF system.

In brief, the IMF system could not last. The United States could eliminate its deficit, giving the world a *liquidity crisis*, with inadequate reserves. Or, the United States could continue to run deficits, with the predictable result of a *crisis of confidence* and a run on U.S. gold.

In 1971, the adjustable peg system came apart. During the early part of that year, the U.S. economy was recovering from a recession. But the recovery was painfully slow, in part because of the large leakage of U.S. demand into imports. There was a growing concern in Washington that imports were increasing so rapidly because the

value of the dollar was too high: American goods had been priced out of the world markets, making it difficult for the United States to reduce its deficit. Yet as the nth country, the United States had little control over this situation. Instead, the value of the dollar in international markets was determined when other countries pegged their currencies to it—as we saw in Figure 20-1. As the U.S. deficit mushroomed in early 1971, doubts grew regarding the ability of the United States to maintain the convertibility of the dollar.

In August 1971, the United States suspended the convertibility of the dollar into gold, and imposed tariff surcharges in order to pressure other countries into raising the prices of their currencies—that is, into lowering the international value of the U.S. dollar. In the uncertainty that followed, a number of countries abandoned their fixed pegs and by 1973, most major currencies had been allowed to float in the exchange markets.

FLUCTUATIONS IN CURRENCY MARKETS SINCE 1973

As countries began allowing their currencies to float, an important question was: How much instability would there be in exchange markets under a floating rate system? Those who favoured floating rates argued that, even if exchange rates were *allowed* to fluctuate, in practice they would remain fairly stable. While a changing world economy might sometimes cause changes in equilibrium exchange rates, it was hoped that these would occur gradually, and that short-term fluctuations would be relatively minor.

As Figure 20-2 shows, in the first several years after 1973, the picture was somewhat encouraging. True, the British pound depreciated by as much as 30% against the U.S. dollar. But the exchange rates between the U.S. dollar, on the one hand, and the West German Deutschmark (or D-mark for short), the Japanese yen, and the Canadian dollar, on the other hand, all remained reasonably stable until 1976.

In the decade 1977-87, however, there was very substantial instability in exchange rates. Between 1977 and 1980, the pound, the D-mark, and the yen all rose sharply in value relative to the U.S. dollar. For example, the D-mark rose from about $0.40 to $0.55 between 1976 and 1980. Of course, the appreciation of these currencies in terms of U.S. dollars meant that the dollar was depreciating. For example, the appreciation of the yen from 33.7 cents to 45.7 cents per 100 yen between

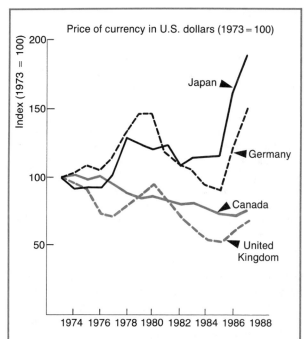

Figure 20-2 **Currency fluctuations since 1973.**

Exchange rates among major currencies have fluctuated widely since 1973. In the first half of the 1980s, most major currencies depreciated rapidly against the U.S. dollar (the U.S. dollar appreciated). In 1985–87, the U.S. and Canadian dollars depreciated rapidly against currencies such as the Japanese yen and the D-mark.

Source: Compiled from data in IMF, *International Financial Statistics*, various issues.

cies. For example, the Canadian dollar appreciated by 55% against the pound and 40% against the D-mark. Since the U.S. dollar continued to rise against the Canadian dollar, it rose even more against these other currencies. Finally, between 1985 and 1987 there were sharp declines in the value of both the U.S. and Canadian dollars against the D-mark and the yen: For example, by 1987 the value of the Canadian dollar in Japanese funds had fallen to 106 yen from 204 in 1985.

Thus, there has been very substantial instability in the exchange rates between some of the world's major currencies in the last decade and a half. Those who were hoping for nothing more than moderate and gradual exchange rate realignments under a floating rate system have been disappointed. The supply and demand curves that determine exchange rates in a floating rate system appear to have been subject to large shifts. What were the reasons for these shifts?

Exchange Rates and Inflation Rates

One clue to the causes of exchange rate fluctuations is provided by the experience of some countries that are not shown in Figure 20-2. Some of the largest exchange rate depreciations in recent history have occurred in countries such as Israel, Brazil, and Mexico. For example, the value of a Brazilian cruzado in 1987 in U.S. funds was less than 0.5% of what it was worth in 1982: The cruzado had depreciated by 99.5% against the dollar. But Brazil, Mexico, and Israel have also been unusual in another respect: They have had very high rates of domestic price inflation. For example, the annual average rate of inflation in Brazil during 1980–86 has been estimated at over 150% per year.

It is no coincidence that the value of a country's currency in the foreign exchange market tends to decline if the country has a high rate of domestic price inflation. As we saw in Chapter 14, inflation causes shifts in the demand and supply curves for a country's currency in the international markets. For example, suppose the exchange rate between the U.S. dollar and the Mexican peso is initially $0.30 per 100 pesos, and suppose wages and prices in Mexico are rising at 100% per year while prices in the United States are constant. The doubling of prices in Mexico means that, this year, 100 pesos buys only half as many goods and services as it did last year. Since (by assumption) the purchasing power of the dollar has not fallen, one would expect that the peso would now depreciate against the dollar. The question is: by how much?

1976 and 1979, is equivalent to a depreciation of the U.S. dollar from 297 yen to 219 yen per dollar between those years.

While the pound, D-mark, and yen rose in value, the Canadian dollar *depreciated* somewhat against the U.S. dollar, falling from U.S. $1.014 to U.S. $0.855 between 1976 and 1980. Because the Canadian dollar declined in value relative to the U.S. dollar, it fell even more than the U.S. dollar relative to other currencies, such as the D-mark and the yen. For example, the Canadian dollar fell from 301 yen to 187 yen per dollar between 1976 and 1980. (Note that if you divide the 187 yen that a Japanese buyer had to pay for a Canadian dollar in 1980 by the 219 yen that a U.S. dollar cost, the result is 0.854, or just about the value of a Canadian dollar in terms of U.S. dollars in that year. This is no coincidence: See Box 20-2.)

In the first half of the 1980s, the U.S. and Canadian dollars appreciated dramatically against other curren-

Box 20-2

■ ■ ■ ■ ■ ■ ■ ■ ■ ■ ■ ■ ■ ■ ■ ■ ■ ■ ■ ■

Exchange Rates and Arbitrage

What is suggested in the text is this: Suppose we know the values of two different currencies in terms of a given third currency. (For example, suppose we know that the value of the Canadian dollar is 187 in terms of Japanese yen, and the value of the U.S. dollar is 219 yen.) Then the exchange rate between the two original currencies will be approximately equal to their relative value in terms of the third currency. (In terms of Japanese yen, the U.S. dollar is worth 1.17 times as much as the Canadian dollar in this example: 219/187 = 1.17.) The suggestion then is that a U.S. dollar will trade for about C$1.17 in the exchange market. But this is indeed what we observed in 1980: If one Canadian dollar is roughly 85.4 U.S. cents, that means that one U.S. dollar is worth about C$1.17 (1/0.854 = 1.17).

Why does this kind of relationship prevail? To see the answer, suppose it didn't prevail. For example, suppose you are reading the financial section of the morning paper, and you see that the U.S. dollar is worth 200 yen, while the Canadian dollar trades for 150 yen. This suggests that the Canadian dollar is worth about 3/4 as much as an American dollar, so that you expect the U.S.-Canadian exchange rate to be C$1 = U.S.$0.75. However, suppose instead the paper says that the Canadian dollar trades for about 85 U.S. cents in the exchange market.

"Interesting," you say to yourself. "If I needed some Japanese yen, it would be cheaper to get them by first buying U.S. dollars and then selling these U.S. dollars for yen. For example, 100 Canadian dollars would get me 85 U.S. dollars which I could exchange for 17,000 yen; if I bought yen directly for Canadian dollars, I would get only 15,000 yen."

Just before you turn to the sports section, another thought occurs to you. If you can start with 100 Canadian dollars and get 17,000 yen, what prevents you from then *selling* these yen for Canadian dollars? Since the paper says that the Canadian dollar trades for 150 yen, your 17,000 yen would get you about 113 dollars (17,000/150 = 113.333 . . .), for a net profit of 13 dollars. Moreover, these transactions could be completed in a matter of minutes over the telephone; and if you can do it with 100 dollars, why not do it with 100 *million* dollars? In a flash, you realize that here, at last, is your opportunity to retire as a multi-millionaire at age 23. Without even finishing your morning coffee, you set out for the bank to negotiate a 100 million dollar overdraft.

The problem, of course, is that you will never discover this kind of opportunity (if you do, it's probably a misprint). In the hypothetical example above, the opportunity to make a profit arose because the U.S. dollar was relatively cheap and the Japanese yen was relatively dear in terms of Canadian funds, given the exchange rate between the yen and the U.S. dollar. Long before the rates would have gotten as far out of line as in this example, foreign exchange dealers who engage in *exchange arbitrage* would have recognized

One possible (and plausible) answer is: by 50%, to $0.15 cents per 100 pesos. At this exchange rate, the attractiveness of Mexican goods to American importers and tourists would remain the same as before. For example, a hotel room that cost 10,000 pesos last year would have cost an American tourist 30 dollars. With an inflation rate of 100%, the hotel room would cost about 20,000 pesos this year (assuming the cost of hotel rooms kept pace with the general rate of inflation). If the exchange rate this year were $0.15 per 100 pesos, the cost of the hotel room would still be 30 dollars. Similarly, a depreciation of the peso by 50% would leave unchanged the relative attractiveness of American goods to Mexican buyers: With U.S. dollar prices remaining constant, a 50% depreciation of the peso would double the cost of American goods expressed in pesos, match-

ing the 100% increase in the peso prices of domestic Mexican goods.

The idea illustrated in this example — that exchange rates between currencies are determined by their relative purchasing power — is referred to as the theory of *purchasing power parity*.

> According to the theory of *purchasing power parity*, changes in the exchange rate between the currencies of two countries will reflect differences in the countries' inflation rates. That is, they will reflect changes in the two currencies' purchasing power.

The principle of purchasing power parity can also be illustrated by introducing the distinction between *nominal exchange rates* and *real exchange rates*. The nominal exchange rate is defined in the standard way as the

Courtesy of Canapress Photo Service/Sadayuki Mikami

this opportunity for making a profit, and would have started selling yen and buying U.S. dollars in the Canadian market. As a result, the price of the U.S. dollar in Canadian funds would have risen, and the price of the yen would have fallen. Arbitrage takes place as soon as there is even the slightest margin for profit, and the effect of the arbitrage itself is to bring about changes in the exchange rates which eliminate the opportunities to make a profit. The result is that in reality, exchange rates are always aligned in such a way that there is little or no profit to be made from these kinds of transactions. If the U.S. dollar costs 200 yen and the Canadian dollar is 150 yen, you can be sure that when you look up the U.S.-Canadian exchange rate, it is going to be very close to C$1 = U.S.$0.75.

price of one currency in terms of another. But when we look at the real exchange rate, we take inflation rates into account as well.

The *real exchange rate* is the nominal exchange rate adjusted for differences in inflation between countries.

As an example, suppose that initially, one U.S. dollar exchanges for one Canadian dollar, and that the United States has a 5% inflation rate while inflation in Canada is 10%. If the real (inflation-corrected) exchange rate is to remain stable, the Canadian dollar has to depreciate by 5% (that is, by the difference in the inflation rates). But this is exactly what the theory of purchasing power parity predicts would happen. Thus, the theory of purchasing power parity suggests that real exchange rates will remain stable.

EXCHANGE RATE FLUCTUATIONS AND CAPITAL FLOWS IN THE 1980s

The purchasing power parity theory can be used to explain why countries with persistently high inflation rates (such as Brazil and Mexico) have seen their currencies depreciate steadily over time. However, in the short run, and when inflation rates differ only moderately among countries, exchange rate changes do not always closely reflect relative inflation rates. The wide swings in the exchange rates of the U.S. and Canadian dollars against other currencies have not simply reflected differences in inflation. Instead, real exchange rates have also fluctuated strongly, causing major changes in the competitive position of Canadian and American goods on overseas markets.

The most important reason that exchange rates sometimes deviate substantially from what the purchasing power parity theory would predict is that exchange markets are also affected by capital flows, as we discussed in Chapter 14. Thus, for example, the substantial appreciation of both the U.S. and Canadian dollars against currencies such as the D-mark and the British pound during 1981-84 cannot be explained by slower inflation rates in the United States and Canada during that period. Instead, it reflected the very high interest rates that prevailed in North America.

In the late 1970s, inflationary pressures were rapidly building up in Canada and the United States. To counteract these pressures, both monetary and fiscal policies were generally moved in a restrictive direction. In the United States, the shift toward restrictive monetary policy was particularly sharp: Inflationary pressures there appeared to have been stronger than in other countries. In 1979, the U.S. Federal Reserve announced a policy of severely limiting money supply growth in order to fight inflation and defend the dollar.

Following his election victory in 1980, the newly elected President Reagan moved quickly to implement his campaign promise to "make government smaller." He tried to do this in part through substantial cuts in the personal and corporate tax rates. The result was a series of very large federal government deficits during the first half of the 1980s.

To finance the deficits, the government had to borrow large amounts in the U.S. capital market. The combination of the increased demand for funds and the restrictive monetary policy of the Federal Reserve (which was limiting the supply of funds) led to exceptionally high interest rates in 1981/82. In countries like Germany and Japan, on the other hand, fiscal policy was much more restrictive, and even though these countries also pursued relatively restrictive monetary policies, interest rates there did not rise as much as in North America.

The result of the differential between U.S. interest rates and those in other countries was striking. Large amounts of capital began to flow in, and the demand for dollars increased. It was this capital inflow that led to the dramatic appreciation of the U.S. dollar against other major currencies. (This appreciation shows up in Figure 20-2 as a fall in the values of other currencies, such as the D-mark and the yen, in terms of American dollars.)

The dollar remained high through the 1982 recession and into the 1983/84 recovery. Even though nominal interest rates fell, inflation also fell and real interest rates

in North America continued to be high. With the U.S. dollar being expensive, overseas buyers had to pay high prices for American goods. At the same time, foreign goods became cheaper to American buyers. The consequence was a profound change in the U.S. economic position in the world. American imports soared, while exports remained stagnant. The current account deficit, which had averaged around $10 billion in 1980-83, rose to more than $100 billion in 1984 and 1985; by 1987 it had reached some 3.4% of U.S. GNP, or $154 billion. The capital inflow—foreign purchases of U.S. bonds and other assets — was being used to finance a huge deficit on the current account, as Americans bought many more goods and services from foreigners than they sold to them. By the late 1980s, U.S. debts to other countries exceeded U.S. assets abroad by a substantial margin; by some estimates the United States had become the world's largest debtor, with a net indebtedness at the end of 1987 in excess of $400 billion.

One of the consequences of the surging imports was a rising tide of protectionism in the United States. As industry after industry clamoured for protection against competition from low-priced imports, the U.S. Congress responded by introducing a comprehensive, highly protectionist, international trade bill that would have created major barriers against various types of imports into the United States.

For a time, it was feared that the Canada/United States free trade agreement was going to be one of the casualties of this protectionist sentiment in the United States. However, the protectionist momentum moderated in 1987/88, and the agreement was approved by Congress and signed by President Reagan in September of 1988. Part of the reason for the change in attitude was the fact that in 1985-88, the U.S. dollar had once again depreciated rapidly against other major currencies. In fact, the depreciation of both the Canadian and U.S. dollars during those years was as large as their appreciation in the first half of the 1980s. As a result, there was a reduction in the pressure on North American industry from Japanese and European competition and a strong recovery in the automotive industry: For the first time in many decades, a few North American cars were even sold in Japan.

Even though the U.S. trade balance ultimately did begin to adjust, it did so with excruciating slowness. The deficit did not begin to decline until 1988 — three years after the U.S. dollar had started to fall in the international exchange markets. Businesses apparently take a long time to respond to more favourable conditions in world markets. Some observers were concerned that the high dollar of the mid-1980s has done lasting damage to parts of North American industry, particularly where firms were driven out of business by severe import competition.

TOWARD A COMPROMISE SYSTEM?

The exchange rate instability and disruption in trade and investment during the 1980s has led to increasing criticism of the flexible rate system, and the question has arisen whether fundamental reforms are desirable. Should we consider some intermediate system, part way between the old adjustable pegs and freely floating exchange rates? Two possibilities are particularly worth noting.

1. Target Zones?

A number of economists have suggested that governments calculate their Fundamental Equilibrium Exchange Rates (FEERs) — that is, the rates consistent with balance-of-payments equilibrium. Because such rates cannot be estimated with any degree of precision, it would not be desirable to try to force exchange rates to the estimated FEERs. However, the suggestion is that governments undertake to keep their exchange rates in a target zone, within 10% of the FEERs. In doing so, they would prevent extreme exchange rate misalignments, such as the overvalution of the U.S. dollar in early 1985. Even though we may not be able to identify equilibrium exchange rates precisely, we can tell when an exchange rate is *far* out of line.

Target zones have, in fact, been considered at meetings of finance ministers, but no firm commitments have been made. If this reform were adopted, countries would be expected to keep within the target zones by exchange market intervention, backed up as necessary with changes in domestic monetary and fiscal policies.

2. Crawling Pegs?

An even more radical reform would be a return to pegged exchange rates, with one big difference from the old IMF system. Rather than keeping the pegs rigid, with periodic jumps, the pegs themselves would be changed gradually. For example, the currency of a deficit country would be devalued by 0.25% per month, or 3% per year, as long as the deficit lasted. Such gradual movements in exchange rates would help to prevent the buildup of deficits and surpluses that occurred under the old IMF system.

It might seem that such predictable changes in parities would present fat targets to speculators, who would rush to sell declining currencies. But that is not necessarily so. A country whose currency is declining steadily at 3% per year could discourage speculators from rushing away from its currency by keeping its interest rate 3% higher than elsewhere. The higher interest rate would offset the change in the exchange rate.

There was considerable support for the idea of crawling pegs within the U.S. government in 1969/70. The idea was shelved when the pegged system broke down in 1971. There has been, however, a revival of interest in crawling pegs in recent years, as doubts about the flexible exchange rate system have intensified.

A number of Latin American countries—such as Brazil—have experimented with crawling pegs from time to time. However, as their inflation rates are often quite high, a change of 3% per year has simply not been enough to maintain equilibrium.Consequently, exchange rate adjustments have been larger; they are sometimes called "trotting pegs" rather than crawling pegs.

THE EUROPEAN MONETARY SYSTEM

A system of pegs—but less rigid than the old IMF system—has been adopted within the European Community, an association of most of the Western European nations. In order to reduce fluctuations in the exchange rates between the European currencies and thus provide a more stable basis for trade and investment flows, they established the **European Monetary System** (EMS) in 1979. The European leaders were, however, mindful of the rigidities that had brought down the IMF's pegged exchange rate system and also led to the breakdown of an earlier attempt to stabilize exchange rates within Western Europe in the early 1970s. They, therefore, allowed for significant flexibility in the EMS. Member nations are encouraged to change their par rates much more quickly than they did under the old IMF system. They also can let their currencies move in wide bands, of as much as 6% around par.

The long-term objective of the European countries is to reduce the degree of flexibility among their currencies, perhaps ultimately developing a monetary union, with a single, unified currency. This objective was highlighted in the Delors Report (1989), which outlined the steps that the members of the European Community would have to take if they were, in fact, to achieve monetary union. Most importantly, they would have to give up their independent national monetary policies. There would be only one, unified policy for the whole community. France would have no more freedom to follow its own monetary policy than does Quebec or British Columbia.

THE INTERNATIONAL DEBT CRISIS

Exchange rate fluctuations and large capital flows between North America and the rest of the world was one set of factors that caused problems in the international monetary system in the 1980s. Another was the debt crisis of a number of less developed countries (LDCs).

During the 1970s and early 1980s, there were large capital inflows into many countries in Latin America, Africa, and Asia. Most of the funds came in the form of loans from public or private sources to governments or state corporations in LDCs. As a result, there was a large increase in their external debt. Taking all developing countries as a group, their medium- and long-term debt increased from less than $150 billion in 1974, to nearly $900 billion in 1986; if short-term debt is included, the total exceeds one trillion dollars (see Figure 20-3). The two largest debtor nations, Brazil and Mexico each have debts of more than $100 billion. Countries such as Argentina, Bolivia, Chile, Venezuela, Peru, the Philippines, and the Ivory Coast, all have external debts that are very large in relation to their GDP.

The 1970s was not the first decade when there were large international flows of capital. For example, before World War I the countries of Europe provided substantial amounts of capital to countries like the United States, Canada, Australia, and a number of nations in Latin America. After World War II, there were large flows of capital from the United States to countries in Europe, Latin America, and Asia; more recently, capital has moved from countries such as Japan and Hong Kong to Europe and North America. Most of these capital movements can be seen as a normal and productive part of the international economy: They represent an efficient reallocation of capital to countries where it is relatively scarce and where there exist many profitable investment opportunities. (We will discuss the effects of such capital flows in more detail in Part 9.)

However, the large flows of capital in the form of loans to LDCs in the 1970s ultimately led to a crisis. In 1982, Mexico became unable to make payments of interest and principal to foreign lenders. After tense negotiations, Mexico's debt was *rescheduled*—that is, there was an agreement to change the terms of some loans

so as to allow a postponement of repayment. In the following months and years, a number of other heavily indebted countries have gone through similar rescheduling exercises. The rescheduling has eased the immediate pressures on the debtor countries to repay. However, they have also made it difficult, if not impossible, for the debtor nations to raise new loans. As a result, the net flow of resources to developing countries—that is, new loans less payments of interest and principal on old loans—has changed from a positive inflow of about $25 billion per year during most of the 1970s, to a net resource *outflow*; according to World Bank estimates, this outflow was more than $30 billion in 1986.

In the following sections, we address two main questions.

1. What were the origins of the debt crisis of the 1980s? Why did the capital flows to the LDCs in the 1970s and 1980s end in a crisis, while large international capital movements in other eras took place without causing serious problems?

2. What can be done to resolve the crisis? Will it be possible to re-establish the normal flow of funds from capital-rich industrialized countries to capital-poor nations in the developing world, without forcing the LDCs to suffer serious hardship as they struggle to rid themselves of the debt burden they incurred in the 1970s?

Origins of the International Debt Crisis

In 1973, the nations of OPEC (the Organization of Petroleum Exporting Countries) entered into an agreement to fix the international market price of oil at a level of about U.S. $12 per barrel—that is, four times the $3 price that had prevailed until that time. In 1979/80, OPEC again sharply raised the oil price until it was well above $30 per barrel.

These increases raised the real incomes of oil-exporting countries. However, for oil-importing LDCs, they created a difficult situation. On the one hand, the higher oil prices in themselves imposed hardship on their populations: Those living in urban areas were faced with higher food prices as the cost of transporting food from the countryside rose, and with higher prices for electricity as the cost of operating oil-burning power plants shot up. Farmers suffered from increases in the cost of artificial fertilizer which is produced by using large amounts of energy.

In addition, however, the increased oil prices threatened to slow down the process of economic growth which

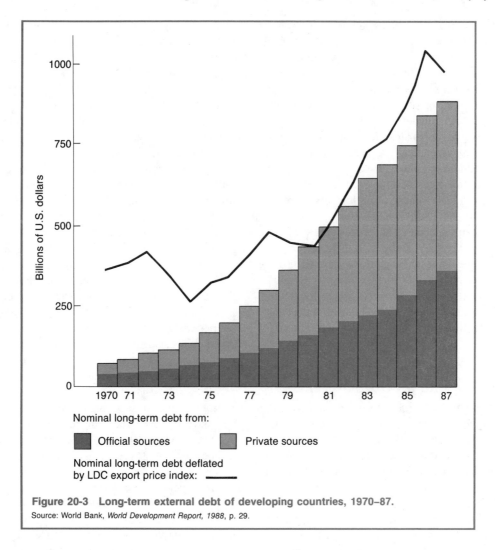

Figure 20-3 Long-term external debt of developing countries, 1970–87.
Source: World Bank, *World Development Report, 1988*, p. 29.

LDCs were trying so hard to speed up. The increased oil prices meant that a large share of the foreign currency they earned from exports had to be devoted to paying for imported oil. As a result, there was less foreign exchange for imports of machinery and other capital goods that were needed for the development process.

Faced with the high price of oil, the LDCs typically borrowed the funds necessary to finance their oil purchases. As a result, their indebtedness grew rapidly.

In part, the borrowing of oil-importing LDCs was indirectly financed by the OPEC nations themselves. The OPEC governments deposited much of their oil revenue in U.S. banks or in *Eurodollar deposits*—that is, deposits denominated in U.S. dollars but held in banks outside the United States. The growth in these deposits was part of

the reason that the banks were actively seeking to increase their lending to LDCs and others during those years.

Ironically, some oil-*exporting* LDCs were also large borrowers. For example, Mexico, Nigeria, and Indonesia are all major producers and exporters of oil, but they were also among the countries with the largest debts in the 1980s. In these countries, the expectation was that oil prices were going to continue rising. Consequently, they embarked on ambitious but costly development projects and, in some cases, allowed consumption to increase at a faster rate than could be supported by their revenues from oil exports.

At first, the increased indebtedness of the borrowing countries created little difficulty. As interest and principal payments fell due, funds were raised by additional borrowing. But in the early 1980s, the system began to come apart. The crisis was precipitated by Mexico which ran into difficulties when the price of oil levelled out in 1982, under the influence of the recession in the industrialized countries. But an even more important part of the explanation for the crisis of the early 1980s had to do with another development in the international capital market: Interest rates in North America, and in the Eurodollar market, rose dramatically. Since many of the loans that the LDCs had taken up were in the form of "floating debt" with variable rates of interest, the interest payments they had to make on their existing debt increased sharply.

As banks became concerned about the borrowers' ultimate ability to repay, they cut back on their new lending and insisted on repayment. When this happened, it rapidly became clear that many countries were facing short-term interest and principal payments which they could not possibly meet without additional loans. But the banks had become unwilling to extend further loans. The crisis was on.

Policies to Deal with the Debt Overhang

As the 1980s progressed, a number of ways were tried to cope with the debt crisis. Not only was the crisis imposing severe hardship on the populations in the debtor nations, there was even concern that the whole international financial system might be destabilized unless solutions were found.

Since 1982, there have been a large number of debt renegotiations between individual debtor countries on the one hand, and consortia of private banks, creditor governments, and international lending institutions, such as the IMF and the World Bank, on the other hand. In the early stages, these negotiations mostly concerned postponement of principal and interest payments, and some provision of new credit. As time went on, there was increasing emphasis on new forms of *debt relief*, such as negotiated reductions in interest rates. In some of the poorest debtor nations, including many in Sub-Saharan Africa, some loans were simply forgiven.

In the case of several "middle-income" debtor countries, some relief from their debt to private banks has been given through new financial techniques, such as *debt-equity swaps*. In a debt-equity swap, the lending bank in the United States, say, may sell its claim on an LDC debtor to a U.S. investor who wants to acquire shares in a company in the debtor country, say, Chile. The investing firm allows the Chilean debtor to repay the loan, sometimes at a reduced face value, in Chilean pesos. These pesos are then used to buy shares in the Chilean company that the American investor wanted to acquire. The end result of the transaction is that there has been a reduction in Chile's dollar-denominated debt. True, there has also been an increase in U.S. ownership of Chilean business, and the future profits that will accrue to the foreign investor is a cost to the Chilean economy. But, in the short term, these profits are likely to be less of a burden than the interest and principal that Chile would otherwise have had to pay on the loan. Another approach to the debt problem has been for the debtor nations to issue bonds that carry interest payments which are conditional on their economy's rate of growth or on the prices of their major export commodities.

Throughout the debt renegotiations, the IMF has played a major role, both as a source of new funds and as a mediator between debtor and creditor nations. In the negotiations with the heavily indebted LDCs, the IMF has insisted on various kinds of *structural adjustment policies*. The purpose of these policies has been to reduce consumption and aggregate demand, so as to decrease inflationary pressures and make possible an improved balance-of-payments performance. Typically, they have involved recommendations for more restrictive fiscal and monetary policies, reduced subsidies, and reduced use of government controls on the business sector.

These policies have been controversial. Those who support them have argued that they are necessary if heavily indebted LDCs are going to repay their debts, and that repayment is essential if LDCs are to continue having access to the international capital market in the future. Moreover, they point to the example of countries, such as South Korea, Indonesia, and Thailand who, by and large, have followed policies of the kind favoured by the IMF. Even though these countries have borrowed heavily in the international market, they have not had the problems of many of the other debtor countries: Their economies have been growing fast enough so that they have been able to manage both payments on their foreign debt, *and* allowing domestic consumption to grow.

On the other hand, the critics of the IMF point out that in practice, debt repayment can only be accomplished through a net capital outflow from debtor nations to creditors. Since the debtors on average are poor countries and the creditors are relatively rich ones, this means a resource transfer from poor to rich. In the critics' view, the groups that would suffer losses if a substantial part of the LDC debt were forgiven (the shareholders in private banks, and the taxpayers in the creditor countries) can well afford to bear this burden.

Developed Country Policies

Certain policies of the industrialized nations have contributed to making the debt crisis worse. In particular, some observers have pointed to macroeconomic policies in North America, particularly the government deficits in the United States during the Reagan administration. The deficits, and the restrictive monetary policies, contributed to keeping world interest rates high, aggravating the debt crisis. Moreover, these policies indirectly con-tributed to the U.S. trade deficit and the intense pressure of international competition on U.S. producers, which led to protectionist policies in North America. But these policies made it more difficult for developing nations to increase their exports of manufactured goods to the developed countries, and earn the foreign exchange they need if they are to service their debt.

What all of this illustrates is that even in a world with flexible exchange rates, domestic economic policies cannot be carried out without considering their international repercussions. When all countries are interdependent through international trade and capital flows, no country is free to focus exclusively on domestic goals, whether exchange rates are fixed or flexible.

KEY POINTS

1. Under the old gold standard, each country fixed the value of its currency in terms of a given quantity of gold. As a result, exchange rates among currencies also remained fixed. For example, if the British pound was worth 4.86 times as much gold as the U.S. dollar, the exchange rate between the pound and the dollar had to be £1.00 = U.S.$4.86.

2. The classical gold standard provided an adjustment mechanism that tended to eliminate balance-of-payments surpluses and deficits through changes in aggregate demand. For example, a country with a balance-of-payments surplus would experience a gold inflow. This flow would automatically increase the quantity of money so that aggregate demand would rise and domestic prices would go up. The increase in the prices of domestic goods would stimulate imports and decrease exports, which would tend to eliminate the initial balance-of-payments surplus.

3. There were two major defects in the classical gold standard:
   (a) The change in aggregate demand caused by an international gold flow might make it more difficult to meet the domestic objectives of full employment and stable prices.
   (b) Because domestic currency was convertible into gold, the monetary system was vulnerable to a crisis of confidence and a run on the available gold stock. This defect contributed to the collapse of the international gold standard during the Great Depression of the 1930s.

4. At the end of World War II, the IMF system was established with pegged but adjustable exchange rates. In the event of a fundamental disequilibrium, a country could devalue or revalue its currency. There were several problems with the IMF system:
   (a) There could be a crisis of *confidence* when a devaluation was expected. Speculators had an incentive to sell the currency before its official price was reduced (that is, before the currency was devalued).
   (b) In order to discourage speculation, authorities generally denied that devaluation was being considered. Once they had made a commitment not to devalue, exchange rates tended to be rigid, leaving the system without an adequate *adjustment* mechanism.

5. The adjustable peg system broke down in the 1971–73 period, leading to the present system of flexible, or floating, exchange rates.

6. The experience since the early 1970s suggests that short-term speculative capital flows may create a problem in a system of floating rates as well as in a pegged rate system. In particular, the high U.S. interest rates in the first half of the 1980s led to a very rapid appreciation of the U.S. dollar. This made it hard for U.S. producers to compete with low-priced imports and contributed to a large U.S. current account deficit.

7. According to the principle of purchasing power parity, exchange rate changes tend to reflect changes in the domestic purchasing power of

currencies. Thus, countries such as Brazil, Mexico, and Israel, who have had very rapid rates of domestic price inflation, have also seen a rapid depreciation in the value of their currencies on the foreign exchange markets.

8. Because of the problems with the international system of flexible exchange rates, some observers have suggested that the system should be changed, taking it part of the way back toward more stable exchange rates. In Europe, the countries belonging to the European Monetary System are trying to reduce fluctuations in exchange rates among the European currencies. The ultimate objective is to move toward a single European currency.

9. Between 1973 and 1982, the external debt of developing nations grew at a rapid, unsustainable rate. In 1982, a number of countries were unable to meet their commitments to pay interest and principal, and debts were rescheduled. Since then, there have been a number of proposals for international action to reduce the debt burden of these countries.

KEY CONCEPTS

gold standard	*speculator*	*nominal vs. real exchange rates*
adjustment mechanism	*ajustment problem*	*interest rates and exchange rates*
adjustable peg	*"stop-go" policy*	*budget deficits vs. trade deficits*
par value	*nth country*	*Eurodollars*
fundamental disequilibrium	*confidence problem*	*debt rescheduling*
devalue	*international liquidity problem*	*debt-equity swaps*
revalue	*purchasing power parity theory*	*European Monetary System*

PROBLEMS

20-1. Under the old gold standard, what prevents a country from continuously losing gold?

20-2. In a system of adjustable pegs, why does there have to be an *n*th country? Why did the United States end up as the *n*th country? What special problems does the *n*th country have?

20-3. What causes a country to follow a "stop-go" policy under a pegged exchange rate system? What are the possible disadvantages of such a policy?

20-4. The text explains why the finance minister of a deficit country would be unwise to admit that a devaluation was being considered under the IMF adjustable peg system. Would the finance minister of a *surplus* country be similarly unwise to admit that a *revaluation* was under consideration? Explain why or why not.

20-5. In an unsuccessful attempt to prevent a revaluation of the D-mark in 1972, West German authorities sold enough marks to speculators to buy 2 million Volkswagens. Explain how the speculators who bought these D-marks gained at the expense of the German government when

the D-mark was finally allowed to rise in the exchange markets.

20-6. The text states that the rapid build-up of LDCs' external debt in the 1973–82 period was "unsustainable"; that is, it could not go on rising indefinitely at that rapid rate. Might a slower build-up be "sustainable," or will any steady build-up lead to a financial crisis sooner or later? If you believe that a slow rate of growth of debt (say, 1% or 2% per year) might be sustainable, explain why. If you think that it must lead to a crisis sooner or later, explain why.

*20-7. (a) If investors try to obtain the highest possible return on their funds, why doesn't all the short-term capital in the world flow to the country with the highest short-term interest rates?

(b) Suppose it is expected that a year from now the exchange rate between the Swedish Krona (Skr) and the Norwegian Krona (Nkr) will be Skr 1 = Nkr 1.15. Suppose short-term interest rates in Sweden are about 6%

per annum, while in Norway they are around 13%. If the value *today* of the Swedish Krona were Nkr 1.10, would you, as an investor, invest your money in Sweden or in Norway? What if the exchange rate were Skr 1 = Nkr 1.05? Looking only at capital flows, what do you think today's equilibrium exchange rate might be?

*20-8. Suppose that at the beginning of the year, one Japanese yen trades for 10 Italian lira in the exchange market. Suppose that during the year, inflation in Italy is 15% and in Japan 5%. Assume also that at the end of the year, the exchange rate is 10.5 lira for one yen.

(a) What has happened during the year to the real exchange rate between the yen and the lira?

(b) If the real exchange rate had stayed constant, how many lira would a yen have traded for at the end of the year?

(c) During this year, would you have expected nominal interest rates to be higher in Italy or Japan? How much higher? Would you have expected capital to flow from Italy to Japan or the other way? Explain your reasoning.

Glossary

■ ■

This glossary provides references to terms included in the combined edition of *Economics*. Therefore, some references will be to terms that do not exist in this paperback "split" volume. Please refer to its companion volume should this occur. Also, not all of these terms appear in the text; some are included here because they occur frequently in readings or lectures.

ability-to-pay principle. The view that taxes should be levied according to the means of the various taxpayers, as measured by their incomes and/or wealth. Compare with *benefit principle.*

absolute advantage. A country (or region or individual) has an absolute advantage in the production of a good or service if it can produce that good or service with fewer resources than other countries (or regions or individuals). See also *comparative advantage.*

accelerationist. One who believes that an attempt to keep the unemployment rate low by expansive demand policies will cause more and more rapid inflation.

accelerator. The theory that investment depends on the change in sales.

accounts payable. Debts to suppliers of goods or services.

accounts receivable. Amounts due from customers.

action lag. The time interval between the recognition that adjustments in aggregate demand policies are desirable and the time when policies are actually changed.

actual investment. Investment as it appears in the GDP accounts; investment including undesired inventory accumulation.

adjustable peg system. A system whereby countries peg (fix) exchange rates but retain the right to change them in the event of fundamental disequilibrium. (In the adjustable peg system of 1945–73, most countries fixed the prices of their currencies in terms of the U.S. dollar; however, during the period 1950–62, Canada was an exception to the rule by allowing its currency to float.)

adjustable rate mortgage. See *variable rate mortgage.*

ad valorem tax. A tax collected as a percentage of the price or value of a good.

aggregate demand. (1) Total quantity of goods and services that would be bought at various possible average price levels. (2) Total expenditures on consumer goods and services, gov-

ernment goods and services, (desired) investment, and net exports.

aggregate supply. (1) Total quantity of goods and services that would be offered for sale at various possible average price levels. (2) Potential GDP.

allocative efficiency. Production of the best combination of goods with the lowest-cost combination of inputs.

annually balanced budget principle. The view that government expenditures should be limited each year to no more than government receipts during that year.

anti–combines legislation. See *competition policy.*

Anti-Inflation Board. Government body charged with overseeing the 1975–78 price and incomes policy.

appreciation (depreciation) of a currency. In a flexible exchange-rate system, a rise (fall) in the price of a currency in terms of another currency or currencies.

arbitrage. A set of transactions aimed at making a profit from inconsistent prices.

arbitration. See *compulsory arbitration* and *voluntary arbitration.*

arc elasticity of demand. The elasticity of demand between two points on a demand curve, calculated by the equation

$$\frac{\Delta Q}{Q_1 + Q_2} \div \frac{\Delta P}{P_1 + P_2}$$

asset. Something that is owned.

automatic stabilizer. A feature built into the economy that tends to reduce the amplitude of fluctuations. For example, tax collections tend to fall during a recession and rise during a boom, slowing the change in disposable incomes and aggregate demand. (Thus, they are an automatic fiscal stabilizer.) Another example is the tendency for imports to rise and fall as national income rises and falls; the leakage into imports also tends to reduce the fluctuations in the aggregate demand for Canadian goods and services.

average cost pricing. Setting the price where the average cost curve (including normal profit) intersects the demand curve.

average fixed cost. Fixed cost divided by the number of units of output.

average product. Total product divided by the number of units of the variable input used.

average propensity to consume. Consumption divided by disposable income.

average propensity to save. Saving divided by disposable income.

average revenue. Total revenue divided by the number of units sold. Where there is a single price, this price equals average revenue.

average total cost. Variable cost divided by the number of units produced.

average variable cost. Variable cost divided by the number of units produced.

balanced budget. (1) A budget with revenues equal to expenditures. (2) More loosely (but more commonly), a budget with revenues equal to or greater than expenditures.

balanced budget multiplier. The change in equilibrium national product divided by the change in government spending when this spending is financed by an equivalent change in taxes.

balance of payments. The summary figure calculated from balance-of-payments credits less balance-of-payments debits, with certain monetary transactions excluded from the calculation. (There are various ways of defining monetary transactions; thus, there are various balance-of-payments definitions. The most common excludes official reserve transactions.)

balance-of-payments accounts. A statement of a country's transactions with other countries.

balance-of-payments surplus (deficit). A positive (negative) balance of payments.

balance of trade (or balance on merchandise account). The value of exports of goods minus the value of imports of goods.

balance sheet. The statement of a firm's financial position at a particular time, showing its assets, liabilities, and net worth.

band. The range within which an exchange rate could move without the government's being committed to intervene in exchange markets to prevent further movement. Under the adjustable peg system, governments were obliged to keep exchange rates from moving outside a band (of 1% either side of parity).

Bank Rate. The interest rate charged by the Bank of Canada on its loans to the chartered banks.

bank reserve. See *required reserves.*

bank run. A situation in which many owners of bank deposits attempt to make withdrawals because of their fear that the bank will be unable to meet its obligations.

bankruptcy. (1) A situation in which a firm (or individual) has legally been declared unable to pay its debts. (2) More loosely, a situation in which a firm (or individual) is unable to pay its debts.

barrier to entry. An impediment that makes it difficult or impossible for a new firm to enter an industry. Examples: patents, economies of scale, accepted brand names.

barter. The exchange of one good or service for another without the use of money.

base year. The reference year, given the value of 100 when constructing a price index or other time series.

beggar-thy-neighbour policy (or beggar-my-neighbour policy). A policy aimed at shifting an unemployment problem to another country. Example: an increase in tariffs.

benefit-cost analysis. The calculation and comparison of the benfits and costs of a program or project.

benefit principle. The view that taxes should be levied in proportion to the benefits that the various taxpayers receive from government expenditures. Compare with *ability-to-pay principle.*

benefits in kind. Payments, not of cash, but of some good (like food) or service (like medical care).

bilateral monopoly. A market structure involving a single seller (monopolist) and a single buyer (monopsonist).

bill. See *Treasury bill.*

blacklist. A list of workers who are not to be given jobs because of union activity or other behaviour considered objectionable by employers.

black market. A market in which sales take place at a price above the legal maximum.

block grant. Grant that may be used in a broad area (such as education), and need not be spent on specific programs (such as reading programs for the handicapped).

bond. A written commitment to pay a scheduled series of interest payments plus the face value (principal) at a specified maturity date.

book value. The book value of a stock is its net worth per share. (It is calculated by dividing the total net worth of the company by the number of its shares outstanding.)

bourgeoisie. (1) In Marxist doctrine, capitalists as a social class. (2) The middle class. (3) More narrowly, shopkeepers.

boycott. A concerted refusal to buy (buyer's boycott) or sell (seller's boycott). A campaign to discourage people from doing business with a particular firm.

break-even point. (1) The output at which costs just equal revenues and therefore profits are zero. (2) The level of disposable income at which consumption just equals disposable income and therefore saving is zero.

broker. One who acts on behalf of a buyer or seller.

budget deficit. The amount by which budgetary outlays exceed revenues.

budget line (or income line or price line). The line on a diagram that shows the various combinations of commodities that can be bought with a given income at a given set of prices.

budget surplus. The amount by which budgetary revenues exceed outlays.

built-in stabilizer. See *automatic stabilizer.*

burden of tax. The amount of the tax ultimately paid by different individuals or groups. (For example, how much does a cigarette tax raise the price paid by buyers, and how much does it lower the net prices received by sellers?) The incidence of the tax.

Bureau of Competition Policy. The government bureau in charge of investigating violations of the Competition Act. Replaced the Restrictive Trade Practices Commission in 1986.

business cycle. The more or less regular upward and downward movement of economic activity over a period of years. A cycle has four phases: recession, trough, expansion, and peak.

Canada Assistance Plan. A plan under which the federal government contributes to provincial and local spending on social welfare assistance to poor individuals and families.

Canada Savings Bonds (CSBs). Federal government bonds issued at attractive rates of interest; CSBs can usually be cashed at face value.

Canada-United States Free Trade Agreement. See *Free Trade Agreement.*

Canadian Labour Congress (CLC). An organization of labour unions to which most of Canada's labour unions are affiliated.

Canadian Wheat Board. A government agency that has a monopoly on the marketing of all wheat, oats, and barley grown in the Prairie provinces.

cap. A limit on the upward adjustment of an indexed wage in response to a rise in the price index.

capital. (1) Real capital: buildings, equipment, and materials used in the productive process that have themselves been produced in the past. (2) Financial capital: either funds available for acquiring real capital *or* financial assets such as bonds or common stock. (3) Human capital: the education, training, and experience that make human beings more productive.

capital account. The account in a country's balance-of-payments accounts that records international transactions in existing assets.

capital consumption allowance. Depreciation, with adjustments for the effects of inflation on the measurement of capital. Loosely, depreciation.

capital flows. Purchases by foreign residents of Canadian assets (inflow), or by Canadian residents of foreign assets (outflow). Sometimes referred to as capital imports or exports. See also *direct foreign investment, portfolio investment.*

capital gain. The increase in the value of an asset over time.

capitalism. A system in which individuals are permitted to own large amounts of capital, and decisions are made primarily in private markets, with relatively little government interference.

capitalized value. The present value of the income stream that an asset is expected to produce.

capital market. A market in which financial instruments such as stocks and bonds are bought and sold.

capital-output ratio. The value of capital divided by the value of the annual output produced with this capital.

capital stock. The total quantity of capital.

cartel. A formal agreement among firms to set price and market shares.

cash reserves. See *required reserves.*

central bank. A banker's bank, whose major responsibility is the control of the money supply. A central bank also generally performs other functions, such as cheque clearing and the inspection of commercial or chartered banks.

central planning. Centralized direction of the resources of the economy, with the objective of fulfilling national goals.

certificate of deposit (CD). A marketable time deposit.

ceteris paribus. "Other things unchanged." In demand-and-supply analysis, it is common to make the *ceteris paribus* assumption; that is, to assume that none of the determinants of the quantity demanded or supplied is allowed to change, with the sole exception of price.

chartered bank. A privately owned, profit-seeking institution that accepts chequing and savings deposits, makes loans, and acquires other earning assets (particularly bonds and shorter-term debt instruments). There are only about a dozen domestic chartered banks in Canada; the five largest ones have as much as 90 percent of total chartered bank assets.

checkoff. The deduction of union dues from workers' pay by an employer, who then remits the dues to the union.

cheque clearing. The transfer of cheques from the bank in which they were deposited to the bank on which they were written, with the net amounts due to or from each bank being calculated.

chequing deposit. A deposit against which an order to pay (that is, a cheque) may be written.

child tax credit. A reduction in the tax payable by families with children. The credit is *refundable*, meaning that it is reduced for families with high incomes.

circular flow of payments. The flow of payments from businesses to households in exchange for labour and other productive services and the return flow of payments fom households to businesses in exchange for goods and services.

classical economics. (1) In Keynesian economics, the accepted body of macroeconomic doctrine prior to the publication of Keynes' *General Theory*. According to classical economics, a market economy tends toward an equilibrium with full employment; a market economy tends to be stable if monetary conditions are stable; and changes in the quantity of money are the major cause of changes in aggregate demand. (2) The accepted view, prior to about 1870, that value depends on the cost of production. In the late nineteenth century, this was replaced with the "neoclassical" view that value depends on both costs of production (supply) and utility (demand).

class struggle. In Marxist economics, the struggle for control between the proletariat and the bourgeoisie.

clean float. A situation where exchange rates are determined by market forces, without intervention by central banks or governments.

closed economy. An economy where exports and imports are very small relative to national product.

closed shop. A business that hires only workers who are already union members.

cobweb cycle. A switching back and forth between a situation of high production and low price and one of low production and high price. A cobweb cycle can occur if there are long lags in production and if producers erroneously assume that price this year is a good indicator of price next year.

coincidence of wants. Situation in which each of the parties involved in a barter has a product that the other wants.

collective bargaining. Negotiations between a union and management over wages and working conditions.

collective goods. Goods that, by their very nature, provide benefits to a large group of people.

collusion. An agreement among sellers regarding prices and/ or market shares. The agreement may be explicit or tacit.

Combines Investigation Act. See *Competition Act.*

commercial bank. A term used in other countries to describe banks similar to Canada's chartered banks.

common property resource. A resource in which nobody has established property rights and which can be used by anyone.

commons. Land that is open for use by all or by a large group of people; for example, commonly owned pasture land.

common stock. Each share of common stock represents part ownership in a corporation.

communism. (1) In Marxist theory, the ultimate stage of historical development in which (a) all are expected to work and no one lives by owning capital, (b) exploitation has been eliminated and there is a classless society, and (c) the state has withered away. (2) A common alternative usage: the economic and political systems of China, the Soviet Union, and other countries in which a communist party is in power.

company union. A union dominated by the employer.

comparable worth. See *equal value, work of.*

comparative advantage. If two nations (or cities or individuals) have different opportunity costs of producing a good or service, then the nation (or city or individual) with the lower opportunity cost has a comparative advantage in that good or service. See also *absolute advantage.*

compensating wage differentials. Wage differences that may result if labour views some jobs as less attractive than others. (Employers have to pay a higher wage to fill the unattractive jobs.)

competition. See *perfect competition.*

Competition Act. An Act passed by Parliament in 1986 to reform Canada's competition policy and replace the earlier Combines Investigation Act.

competition policy. The laws contained in the Competition Act, and other policies designed to limit monopoly power and dis-

courage business practices that reduce competition in the economy.

competitive devaluations. A round of exchange-rate devaluations in which each of a number of countries tries to gain a competitive advantage by devaluing its currency. (Not all can be successful; each must fail to the extent that other countries also devalue.)

complementary goals. Goals such that the achievement of one helps in the achievement of the other. (Contrast with *conflicting goals.*)

complementary goods. Goods that are used together. A rise in the price of one causes a leftward shift in the demand curve for the other. (Contrast with *substitute.*)

complements in production. Goods produced together, as a package. A rise in the price of one causes a rightward shift in the supply curve of the other. Joint products.

compulsory arbitration. In a labour dispute, occurs when the government forces both parties to submit their dispute to an arbitrator, who then decides on a binding settlement.

concentration ratio. Usually, the fraction of an industry's total output made by the four largest firms. (Sometimes a different number of firms — such as eight — is chosen in calculating concentration ratios, and sometimes a different measure of size—such as assets—is chosen.)

conditional transfers. Contributions by the federal government to provincial budgets (or by provincial governments to local governments) which are conditional on the amounts spent by the receiving governments.

conflicting goals. Goals such that working toward one makes it more difficult to achieve the other.

conglomerate merger. See *merger.*

conspicuous consumption. Consumption whose purpose is to impress others. A term originated by Thorstein Veblen (1857–1929).

constant dollars (or real dollars). A series is measured in constant dollars if it is measured at the prices existing in a specified base year. Such a series has been adjusted to remove the effects of inflation or deflation. Contrast with *current dollars.*

constant returns (to scale). This occurs if an increase of x percent in all inputs causes output to increase by the same x percent.

consumer price index (CPI). A weighted average of the prices of goods and services commonly purchased by an average household, as calculated by Statistics Canada.

consumer surplus. The net benefit that consumers get from being able to purchase a good at the prevailing price; the difference between the maximum amounts that consumers would be willing to pay and what they actually do pay. It is approximately the triangular area under the demand curve and above the market price.

consumption. (1) The purchase of consumer good and services. (2) The act of using goods and services to satisfy wants. (3)

The using up of goods (as in capital consumption allowances).

consumption function. (1) The relationship between consumer expenditures and disposable income. (2) More broadly, the relationship between consumer expenditures and the factors that determine these expenditures.

contestable market. A market with only one or a few producers, whose market power is nevertheless severely limited by the ease with which additional producers may enter.

continental union. A Canadian labour union which is affiliated with a union in the United States (sometimes also called an *international union*).

convergence hypothesis. The proposition that the differences between communistic and capitalistic societies is decreasing.

convertible bond. A bond that can be exchanged for common stock under specified terms and prior to a specified date, at the option of the bondholder.

cornering a market. Buying and accumulating enough of the commodity to become the single (or at least dominant) seller, and thus acquire the power to resell at a higher price.

corporation. An association of shareholders with a government charter that grants certain legal powers, privileges, and liabilities separate from those of the individual shareholder-owners. The major advantages of the corporate form of business organization are limited liability for the owners, continuity, and relative ease of raising capital for expansion.

correlation. The tendency of two variables (such as income and consumption) to move together.

cost-benefit analysis. See *benefit-cost analysis*.

cost-push inflation. Inflation caused principally by increasing costs—in the form of higher prices for labour, materials, and other inputs — rather than by rising demand. Contrast with *demand-pull inflation*.

countercyclical policy. (1) Policy that reduces fluctuations in economic activity. (2) Policy whose objective is to reduce fluctuations in economic activity.

countervailing power. Power in one group, which has grown as a reaction to power in another group. For example, a big labour union may develop to balance the bargaining power of a big corporation. A term originated by John Kenneth Galbraith.

Cournot-Nash equilibrium. Equlibrium that exists when each firm assumes that none of its competitors will react to any changes it makes.

craft union. A labour union whose members have a particular craft (skill or occupation). Examples: an electricians' union, or a plumbers' union. Contrast with *industrial union*.

crawling peg system. An international financial system in which par values would be changed frequently, by small amounts, in order to avoid large changes at a later date.

credit crunch. A situation of severe credit rationing.

credit instrument. A written promise to pay at some future date.

credit rationing. Allocation of available funds among borrowers when the demand for loans exceeds the supply at the prevailing interest rate.

creeping inflation. A slow but persistent upward movement of the average level of prices (not more than 2% or 3% per annum).

cross elasticity of demand. The percentage change in the quantity demanded of a good in response to a 1 percent change in the price of a related good.

cross-section data. Observations taken at the same time. For example, the consumption of different income classes in Canada in 1989.

cross-subsidization. A firm's or agency's use of revenues generated in profitable lines of activity to offset losses in other, less profitable lines of activity.

crowding out. A reduction in private investment demand caused when an expansive fiscal policy results in higher interest rates.

Crown corporation. A government-owned corporation, usually one that derives most of its revenue from the sale of goods and services to the public—for example, Air Canada, Ontario Hydro.

currency. (1) Coins and paper money (dollar bills, for instance). (2) In international economics, a national money, such as the British pound or the Japanese yen.

current account. The account in a country's balance-of-payments accounts that records that country's exports and imports of goods and services, as well as unilateral transfers.

current dollars. A series (like GDP) is measured in current dollars if each observation is measured at the prices that prevailed at the time. Such a series reflects both real changes in GDP *and* inflation (or deflation). Contrast with *constant dollars*.

current liabilities. Debts that are due for payment within a year.

customs union. An agreement among nations to eliminate trade barriers (tariffs, quotas, etc.) among themselves and to adopt common tariffs on imports from nonmember countries. Example: the European Economic Community.

cut-throat competition. Selling at a price below cost, with the objective of driving competitors out of the market (at which time prices may be raised and monopoly profits reaped).

cyclically adjusted budget. See *full-employment budget*.

cyclically balanced budget. A budget whose receipts over a whole business cycle are at least equal to its expenditures over the same cycle. Unlike an annually balanced budget, a cyclically balanced budget permits the use of countercyclical fiscal policies. Surpluses during prosperity may be used to cover deficits during recessions.

debasement of currency. (1) Reduction of the quantity of precious metal in coins. (2) More broadly, a substantial decrease in the purchasing power of money.

debt instrument. A written commitment to repay borrowed funds.

declining industry. An industry whose firms make less than normal profits. (Firms will therefore leave the industry.)

decreasing returns (to scale). Occurs if an x percent increase in all inputs results in an increase of output of less than x percent.

deficit. The amount by which expenditures exceed revenues. Contrast with *surplus.*

deflation. (1) A fall in the average level of prices; the opposite of inflation. (2) The removal of the effects of inflation from a series of observations by dividing each observation with a price index. The derivation of a constant-dollar series from a current-dollar series.

deflationary bias. Such a bias exists in a system if, on average, monetary and fiscal authorities are constrained from allowing aggregate demand to increase as rapidly as productive capacity. (The classical gold standard was criticized on the ground that it created a deflationary bias.)

deflationary gap. See *recessionary gap.*

demand. A schedule or curve showing how much of a good or service would be demanded at various possible prices, *ceteris paribus.*

demand deposit. A bank deposit withdrawable on demand and transferable by cheque.

demand management policy. A change in monetary and/or fiscal policy aimed at affecting aggregate demand.

demand-pull inflation. Inflation caused by excess aggregate demand. Contrast with *cost-push inflation.*

demand schedule. A table showing the quantities of a good or service that buyers would be willing and able to purchase at various market prices, *ceteris paribus.*

demand shift. A movement of the demand curve to the right or left as a result of a change in income or any other determinant of the quantity demanded (with the sole exception of the price of the good).

demand shifter. Anything except its own price that affects the quantity of a good demanded.

depletion allowance. A deduction, equal to a percentage of net taxable income, that certain extractive industries are permitted in calculating taxable profits.

deposit multiplier. See *money multiplier.*

depreciation. (1) The loss in the value of physical capital due to wear and obsolescence. (2) The estimate of such loss in business or economic accounts. (3) The amount that tax laws allow businesses to count as a cost of using plant or equipment.

depreciation of a currency. A decline in the value of a floating currency measured in terms of another currency or currencies.

depression. An extended period of very high unemployment and much excess capacity. (There is no generally accepted, precise, numerical definition of a depression. However, none of the economic slumps since World War II has been generally considered a depression.)

derived demand. The demand for an input that depends on the demand for the product or products it is used to make. For example, the demand for flour is derived from the demand for bread.

devaluation. In international economics, a reduction of the par value of a currency.

developing countries. See *LDCs.*

dictatorship of the proletariat. In Marxist economics, the dictatorship that occurs when a revolution has eliminated the capitalist class and power has fallen into the hands of the proletariat.

differentiated products. Similar products that retain some distinctive difference(s); close but not perfect substitutes. Examples: Ford and Chevrolet automobiles, different brands of toothpaste.

diminishing returns, law of eventually. If technology is unchanged, then the use of more and more units of a variable input, together with one or more fixed inputs, must eventually lead to a declining marginal product for the variable input.

direct foreign investment. Occurs when foreign residents establish or invest in firms in which foreign owners have a controlling interest.

dirty float. See *floating exchange rates.*

discounting. (1) The process by which the present value of one or more future payments is calculated, using an interest rate. See *present value.* (2) In central banking, lending by the central bank to a chartered bank or authorized investment dealer.

discount rate. (1) A term used to denote the rate of interest used to calculate discounted present value. (2) In the United States, the interest charged by the Federal Reserve when lending to commercial banks. See also *Bank Rate.*

discouraged worker. Someone who wants a job but is no longer looking because work is believed to be unavailable. A discouraged worker is not included in either the labour force or the number of unemployed.

discretionary policy. Policy that is periodically changed in the light of changing conditions. The term is usually applied to monetary or fiscal policies that are adjusted to meet the objectives of high employment and stable prices. Contrast with *monetary rule.*

disposable (personal) income. Income that households have left after the payment of taxes. It is divided among consumption expenditures, the payment of interest on consumer debt, and saving.

dissaving. Negative saving.

dividend. The part of a corporation's profits paid out to its shareholders.

dividend tax credit. A deduction from the personal income tax payable by someone who has received dividend payments from a Canadian corporation. Intended to offset the income tax already paid by the corporation, to avoid *double taxation* of profits distributed as dividends.

division of labour. The breaking up of a productive process into different tasks, each done by a different worker (for example, on an automobile assembly line).

dollar standard. An international system in which many international transactions take place in U.S. dollars and many countries hold sizeable fractions of their reserves in dollars. Also, other currencies may be pegged to the U.S. dollar.

domestic product. See *GDP, NDP*.

double-entry bookkeeping. An accounting system in which each transaction results in equal entries on both sides. When double-entry bookkeeping is used, the two sides of the accounts must balance.

double taxation. The taxation of corporate profits first when they are earned and second when they are paid out to shareholders as dividends. Has been effectively eliminated in Canada through the dividend tax credit, but still exists in the United States.

dual labour market. A double labour market, where workers in one market are excluded from taking jobs in the other market.

dumping. The sale of a good at a lower price in a foreign market than in the home market—a form of price discrimination.

duopoly. A market in which there are only two sellers.

dynamic efficiency. Efficient change in an economy, particularly the most efficient use of resources, the best rate of technological change, and the most efficient rate of growth.

dynamic wage differential. A wage difference that arises because of changing demand or supply conditions in the labour market. It tends to disappear over time as labour moves out of relatively low-wage jobs and into those that pay a relatively high wage.

econometrics. The application of statistical methods to economic problems.

economic efficiency. See *allocative efficiency, dynamic efficiency*, and *technological efficiency*.

economic freedom. A situation in which people have the right to choose their own occupations, to enter contracts, and to spend their incomes as they please.

economic independence. A situation in which a nation's economy is controlled by its citizens, with relatively little influence by foreign decision makers.

economic integration. The elimination of tariffs and other barriers between nations. The partial or complete unification of the economies of different countries.

economic profit. Above-normal profit; profit after the opportunity costs of capital have been taken into account.

economic rent. The return to a factor of production in excess of its opportunity cost.

economics. (1) The study of how people acquire material necessities and comforts, the problems they encounter in doing so, and how these problems can be reduced. (2) Frequently, a narrower definition is used — the study of the allocation of scarce resources to satisfy human wants.

economies (diseconomies) of scale. Occur if an increase of $x\%$ in the quantity of every input causes the quantity of output to increase by more (less) than $x\%$.

economize. To make the most of limited resources; to be careful in spending.

efficiency. The goal of getting the most out of our productive efforts. See also: *allocative efficiency, dynamic efficiency*, and *technological efficiency*.

effluent fee. A tax or other levy on a polluting activity, based on the quantity of pollution discharged.

elastic demand. Demand with an elasticity of more than one. A fall in price causes an increase in total expenditure on the product in question, because the percentage change in quantity demanded is greater than the percentage change in price.

elasticity of demand. The price elasticity of demand is

$$\frac{\text{Percentage change in quantity demanded}}{\text{Percentage change in price}}$$

Similarly, the income elasticity of demand is

$$\frac{\text{Percentage change in quantity demanded}}{\text{Percentage change in income}}$$

The unmodified term ''elasticity'' usually applies to price elasticity.

elasticity of supply. The (price) elasticity of supply is

$$\frac{\text{Percentage change in quantity supplied}}{\text{Percentage change in price}}$$

elastic supply. Supply with an elasticity of more than one. A supply curve which, if extended in a straight line, would meet the vertical axis.

emission fee. See *effluent charge*.

employer of last resort. The government acts as the employer of last resort if it provides jobs for all those who are willing and able to work but cannot find jobs in the private sector.

employment rate. The percentage of the labour force employed.

endogenous variable. A variable explained within a theory.

Engel's laws. Regularities between income and consumer expenditures observed by nineteenth-century statistician Ernst Engel. Most important is the decrease in the percentage of income spent on food as income rises.

entrepreneur. One who organizes and manages production, makes business decisions, and innovates and bears risks.

envelope curve. A curve that encloses, by just touching, a series of other curves. For example, the long-run average-cost curve is the envelope of all the short-run average-cost curves (each of which shows costs, given a particular stock of fixed capital).

equal value, work of. ''Equal pay for work of equal value'' is a strengthening of the principle ''equal pay for equal work'' in legislation to eliminate pay discrimination between men and women.

equalization payments. Transfers by the federal government to "have-not" provinces, whose low tax base would make it difficult for them to finance adequate levels of public services without federal assistance.

equation of exchange. MV = PQ.

equilibrium. A situation in which there is no tendency for change.

equity. (1) Ownership, or amount owned. (2) Fairness.

escalated tariff. A tariff that is very low (or zero) on resources, but rises as goods become more and more highly processed.

escalator clause. A provision in a contract or law whereby a price, wage, or other monetary quantity is increased at the same rate as a specified price index (usually the consumer price index).

Established Programs Financing Act. The laws that state the amounts to be contributed by the federal government to provincial spending in the areas of health care, post-secondary education, and social assistance.

estate tax. A tax on property owned at the time of death.

Eurodollars. Deposits denominated in U.S. dollars but held in banks in countries outside of the United States (such as Canada or the European countries).

European Economic Community (EEC). A customs union formed in the 1950s by a number of European nations (Britain became a member in the 1970s). The EEC provides for tariff-free trade in goods and services, as well as free flows of investment and a common labour market, among the member nations; its ultimate objective is to move toward some form of political union.

European Monetary System (EMS). An agreement designed to limit fluctuations in the exchange rates between the currencies of the EEC member nations. The ultimate goal is to have a single currency in the EEC.

excess burden of a tax. The decrease in efficiency that results when people change their behaviour to reduce their tax payments.

excess demand. The amount by which the quantity demanded exceeds the quantity supplied at the existing price. A shortage.

excess reserves. Reserves of chartered banks in excess of the legally specified amount, when the banks are subject to a law that prescribes a minimum ratio of reserves to deposits. See also *required reserves.*

excess supply. The amount by which the quantity supplied exceeds the quantity demanded at the existing price. A surplus.

Exchange Fund Account (EFA). A government account in which Canada's foreign exchange reserves are held.

exchange rate. The price of one national currency in terms of another.

exchange-rate appreciation (depreciation). See *appreciation (depreciation) of a currency.*

excise tax. A tax on the sale of a particular good. An *ad valorem* tax is collected as a percentage of the price of the good. A *specific* tax is a fixed number of cents or dollars collected on each unit of the good.

exclusion principle. The basis for distinguishing between public and nonpublic goods. If those who do not pay for a good can be excluded from enjoying it, then it is not a public good.

exogenous variable. A variable not explained within a theory; its value is considered to be given. Example: investment in the simple Keynesian theory.

expansion. The phase of the business cycle when output and employment are increasing.

export (X). Good or service sold to foreign nationals.

export of capital. Acquisition of foreign assets.

export-oriented development. A generally successful strategy pursued by a number of developing countries under which they have tried to achieve higher economic growth rates by concentrating on production for exports rather than for the home market.

external cost. Cost borne by others. Pollution is an example of an external cost (sometimes called a *cost spillover* or a *neighbourhood cost*).

externality. An adverse or beneficial side effect of production or consumption. Also known as a *spillover* or *third-party effect.*

externally held public debt. Government securities held by foreigners.

extra-territoriality. Attempts by a country to apply its own laws to firms owned by its citizens but operating in another country; for example, the attempts by the U.S. government to enforce its anti-trust laws on U.S.-owned firms operating in Canada.

Fabian socialism. Form of socialism founded in Britain in the late nineteenth century, advocating gradual and evolutionary movement toward socialism within a democratic political system.

face value. The stated amount of a loan or bond. The amount that must be paid, in addition to interest, when the bond comes due. The principal.

factor mobility. Ease with which factors can be moved from one use to another.

factor of production. Resource used to produce a good or service. Land, labour, and capital are the three basic categories of factors of production.

fallacy of composition. The unwarranted conclusion that a proposition which is true of a single sector or market is necessarily true for the economy as a whole.

fair return. Return to which a regulated public utility should be entitled.

featherbedding. Make-work rules designed to increase the number of workers or the number of hours on a particular job.

federal-provincial transfers. Transfers of federal government revenue to provincial governments, as equalization payments or as payments under the Established Programs Financing Act.

fiat money. Paper money that is neither backed by nor convertible into precious metals but is nevertheless legal tender.

Money that is money solely because the government says that it is.

final product. Product that has been acquired for final use and not for resale or for further processing.

financial capital. Financial assets such as common stocks, bonds, or bank deposits.

financial instrument. A legal document representing claims or ownership. Examples: bonds, Treasury bills.

financial intermediary. An institution that issues financial obligations (such as demand deposits) in order to acquire funds from the public. The institution then pools these funds and provides them in larger amounts to businesses, governments, or individuals. Examples: chartered banks, trust companies, insurance companies.

financial market. A market in which financial instruments (stocks, bonds, etc.) are bought and sold.

fine-tuning. An attempt to smooth out mild fluctuations in the economy by frequent adjustments in monetary and/or fiscal policies.

firm. A business organization that produces goods and/or services. A firm may own one or more plants.

fiscal dividend. A budget surplus, measured at the full-employment national product, that is generated by the growth of the productive capacity of the economy. (This term was most commonly used during the 1960s.)

fiscal drag. The tendency for rising tax collections to impede the healthy growth of the aggregate demand that is needed for the achievement and maintenance of full employment. (This term was most commonly used during the 1960s.)

fiscal policy. The adjustment of tax rates or government spending in order to affect aggregate demand. *Pure fiscal policy* involves a change in government spending or tax rates, unaccompanied by any change in the rate of growth of the money stock.

fiscal year. A 12-month period selected as the year for accounting purposes.

Fisher equation. The equation of exchange: $MV = PQ$.

fixed asset. A durable good, expected to last at least a year.

fixed cost. A cost that does not vary with output.

fixed exchange rate. An exchange rate that is held within a narrow band by the monetary authorities.

fixed factor. A factor whose quantity cannot be changed in the short run.

flat tax. A tax with only one rate applying to all income. A proportional tax.

floating (or flexible) exchange rate. An exchange rate that is not pegged by monetary authorities but is allowed to change in response to changing demand or supply conditions. If governments and central banks withdraw completely from the exchange markets, the float is *clean*. (That is, the exchange rate is *freely flexible*.) A float is *dirty* when governments or central banks intervene in exchange markets by buying or selling foreign currencies in order to influence exchange rates.

focal-point pricing. This occurs when independent firms quote the same price even though they do not explicitly collude. They are led by convention, rules of thumb, or similar thinking to the same price. (For example, $59.95 for a pair of shoes.)

forced saving. A situation where households lose control of their income, which is directed into saving even though they would have preferred to consume it. This can occur if the monetary authorities provide financial resources for investment, creating inflation which reduces the purchasing power of households' incomes (and therefore reduces their consumption). Alternatively, forced saving occurs if taxes are used for investment projects (such as dams).

foreign exchange. The currency of another country.

foreign exchange market. A market in which one national currency is bought in exchange for another national currency.

foreign exchange reserves. Foreign currencies held by the government or central bank.

Foreign Investment Review Agency (FIRA). An agency set up in the 1970s by the federal government to regulate and restrict direct foreign investment in Canada. When policy toward foreign investment became less restrictive in the mid-1980s, FIRA was renamed *Investment Canada.*

forward price. A price established in a contract to be executed at a specified time in the future (such as three months from now). See also *futures market.*

fractional-reserve banking. A banking system in which banks keep reserves (generally in the form of currency or deposits in the central bank) equal to only a fraction of their deposit liabilities.

freedom of entry. The absence of barriers that make it difficult or impossible for a new firm to enter an industry.

free enterprise economy. One in which individuals are permitted to own large amounts of capital, and decisions are made primarily in markets, with relatively little government interference.

free good. A good or service whose price is zero, because at that price the quantity supplied is at least as great as the quantity demanded.

free-market economy. An economy in which the major questions "What?" "How?" and "For whom?" are answered by the actions of individuals and firms in the marketplace rather than by the government.

free rider. Someone who cannot be excluded from enjoying the benefits of a project, but who pays nothing (or pays a disproportionately small share) to cover its costs.

free trade. A situation in which no tariffs or other barriers exist on trade between countries.

Free Trade Agreement (FTA). A 1988 agreement that provides for elimination of most non-tariff barriers and all tariffs on trade and investment flows between Canada and the United States over a ten-year period, as well as a mechanism to settle some trade disputes between the two countries.

free-trade area (or free-trade association). A group of

countries that agrees to eliminate trade barriers (tariffs, quotas, etc.) within itself, while each country in the group retains the right to set its own tariffs on imports from non-member countries. Compare with *customs union*.

frictional unemployment. Temporary unemployment associated with adjustments in a changing, dynamic economy. It arises for a number of reasons. For example, some new entrants into the labour force take time to find jobs, some with jobs quit to look for better ones, and others are temporarily unemployed by such disturbances as bad weather.

fringe benefits. Benefits other than wages (such as health insurance premiums, subsidized lunches, and employer contributions to employee pension plans) paid as part of the remuneration to employees.

front-loaded debt. A debt on which the payments, measured in constant dollars, are greater at the beginning than at the end of the repayment period. See also *graduated payment mortgage*.

full employment. (1) A situation in which there is no unemployment attributable to insufficient aggregate demand; that is, where all unemployment is due to frictional causes. (2) A situation where all who want to work can find jobs reasonably quickly.

full-employment budget (or high-employment budget). Full-employment government receipts (that is, the receipts that would be obtained with present tax rates if the economy were at full employment) minus full-employment government expenditures (that is, actual expenditures less expenditures directly associated with unemployment in excess of the full-employment level). Similar to *cyclically adjusted budget*.

full-employment GDP. The GDP that would exist if full employment were consistently maintained. Potential GDP.

full-employment rate of unemployment. See *natural rate of unemployment*.

full-line forcing. See *tied selling*.

fundamental disequilibrium (in international economics). A term used but not defined in the articles of agreement of the International Monetary Fund. The general idea is that a fundamental disequilibrium exists when an international payments imbalance cannot be eliminated without increasing trade restrictions or imposing unduly restrictive aggregate demand policies.

futures market. A market in which contracts are undertaken today at prices specified today for fulfillment at some specified future time. For example, a futures sale of wheat involves the commitment to deliver wheat (say) three months from today at a price set now.

gains from trade. Increase in real income that results from specialization and trade.

game theory. Theory dealing with conflict, in which alternative strategies are formally analysed. Sometimes used in the analysis of oligopoly.

GDP. See *Gross Domestic Product*.

GDP (price) deflator. Current dollar GDP divided by constant dollar GDP, times 100. Measures the change in prices of goods and services.

GDP gap. Amount by which actual GDP falls short of potential GDP.

general equilibrium. Situation where all markets are in equilibrium simultaneously.

general equilibrium analysis. Analysis taking into account interactions among markets.

general glut. This occurs when excess supply is a general phenomenon. The quantity of goods and services that producers are willing to supply greatly exceeds the quantity buyers are willing and able to purchase.

general inflation. An increase in all prices (including wages) by the same percent, leaving relative prices unchanged.

generalized purchasing power. Describes anything that can be used to buy any of the goods and services offered for sale: e.g., money.

general price level. Price level as measured by a broad average, such as the consumer price index or the GDP deflator.

Giffen good. A good whose demand curve slopes upward to the right.

Gini coefficient. A measure of inequality derived from the Lorenz curve. It is the "bow" area between the curve and the diagonal line, divided by the entire area beneath the diagonal line. It can range from zero (if there is no inequality and the Lorenz curve corresponds to the diagonal line) to one (if there is complete inequality and the Lorenz curve runs along the horizontal axis).

gold point. Under the old gold standard, an exchange rate at which an arbitrager can barely cover the costs of shipping, handling, and insuring gold.

gold standard. System in which the monetary unit is defined in terms of gold, the monetary authorities buy and sell gold freely at that price, and gold may be freely exported or imported. If central banks follow the "rule of the gold standard game," they allow changes in gold to be reflected in changes in the money stock.

gold sterilization. A gold flow is sterilized when the central bank takes steps to cancel out the automatic effects of the gold flow on the country's money supply (that is, when the "rule of the gold standard game" is broken).

good. Tangible commodity, such as wheat, a shirt, or an automobile.

Goods and Services Tax (GST). A broadly based sales tax proposed to come into effect in 1990, as a replacement for the existing less broadly based manufacturers' sales tax. Will be applied as a *value-added tax* (see that word).

graduated-payment mortagage. A mortgage on which the money payments rise as time passes, in order to reduce front loading. If the money payments rise rapidly enough to keep real payments constant, then the mortgage is *fully* graduated.

greenhouse effect. The gradual warming of the world's climate that is taking place as a result of the increasing build-up of carbon dioxide and other gases in the earth's atmosphere.

Gresham's law. Essentially, "Bad money drives out good." More precisely: If there are two types of money whose values in exchange are equal while their values in another use (such as consumption) are different, the more valuable item will be retained for its other use while the less valuable item will continue to circulate as money.

gross domestic investment (I_g). Expenditures for new plant, equipment, and new residential buildings, plus the change in inventories.

gross domestic product (GDP). Personal consumption expenditures plus government purchases of goods and services plus gross domestic investment plus net exports of goods and services. The basic measure of aggregate economic activity; it comprises the total value of goods and services produced in Canada, excluding double-counting.

gross national product (GNP). GDP less the return to foreign capital in Canada, net of the return to Canadian-owned capital invested in other countries. Approximately equal to the total value of goods and services produced by *Canadian-owned* factors of production.

growth. An increase in the productive capacity of the economy.

Herfindahl index. A measure of concentration. Specifically, the sum of the squared market shares of all the firms.

high-employment GDP. The GDP that would exist if a high rate of employment were consistently maintained. Potential GDP.

holding company. A company that holds a controlling interest in the stock of one or more other companies.

horizontal merger. See *merger*.

human capital. Education and training that make human beings more productive.

hyperinflation. Very rapid inflation.

identification problem. The difficulty of determining the effect of variable *a* alone on variable *b* when *b* can also be affected by variables *c*, *d*, etc.

impact lag. The time interval between policy changes and the time when the major effects of the policy changes occur.

imperfect competition. A market in which some buyer(s) or seller(s) are large enough to have a noticeable effect on price.

implicit (or imputed) cost. The opportunity cost of using an input that is already owned by the producer.

implicit tax. Built into a welfare program. The benefits a family loses when it earns another $1 of income. For example, if its benefits are reduced by 46¢, the implicit tax is 46%.

import (M). Good or service acquired from foreign countries.

import of capital. Sale of financial assets to foreign nationals, or establishment by foreign nationals of firms in the domestic country.

import quota. A restriction on the quantity of a good that may be imported.

incidence of tax. The amount of the tax ultimately paid by different individuals or groups. (For example, how much does a cigarette tax raise the price paid by buyers, and how much does it lower the net price received by sellers?)

income-consumption line. The line or curve traced out by the points of tangency between an indifference map and a series of parallel budget (income) lines. It shows how a consumer responds to a changing income when relative prices remain constant.

income effect. Change in the quantity of a good demanded as a result of a change in real income with no change in relative prices.

income elasticity of demand. See *elasticity of demand*.

income line. See *budget line*.

incomes policy. A government policy (such as wage-price guidelines or wage and price controls) aimed at restraining the rate of increase in money wages and other money incomes. The purpose is to reduce the rate of inflation.

income statement. An accounting statement that summarizes a firm's revenues, costs, and income taxes over a given period of time (usually a year). A profit-and-loss statement.

increasing returns to scale. This occurs if an increase of *x* percent in all inputs results in an increase in output of more than *x* percent.

incremental cost. The term that business executives frequently use instead of "marginal cost."

incremental revenue. The term that business executives frequently use instead of "marginal revenue."

index. A series of numbers, showing how an average (of prices, or wages, or some other economic measure) changes over time. Each of these numbers is called an index number. By convention, the index number for the base year is set at 100.

indexation. The inclusion in a contract or law of an automatic adjustment for inflation. A wage contract is *indexed* if it contains an *escalator clause* providing for an automatic increase in the wage in the event of a rise in the average level of prices (as measured, usually, by the consumer price index). The income tax is *indexed* when tax brackets, exemptions, and other provisions of the tax code automatically increase by the same proportion as the increase in the average level of prices.

indifference curve. A curve joining all points among which the consumer is indifferent.

indifference map. A series of indifference curves, each representing a different level of satisfaction or utility.

indirect tax. A tax that is thought to be passed on to others, and not borne by the one who originally pays it. Examples: sales taxes, excise taxes, import duties.

induced investment. Additional investment demand that results from an increase in domestic product.

industrial union. A union open to all workers in an industry, regardless of their specific craft or skill. Contrast with *craft union*.

industry. The producers of a single good or service (or closely related goods or services).

inelastic demand. Demand with an elasticity of less than one. See *elasticity of demand.*

infant-industry argument for protection. The proposition that new domestic industries with economies of scale or large requirements of human capital need protection from foreign producers until they can become established.

inferior good. A good for which the quantity demanded decreases as income rises, *ceteris paribus.*

inflation. An increase in the average level of prices.

inflationary gap. The vertical distance by which the aggregate demand line is above the 45° line at the full-employment quantity of domestic product.

information cost. See *search cost.*

inheritance tax. Tax imposed on a property received from a person who has died.

injection. Demand for a GDP component other than consumption.

innovation. A change in products or in the techniques of production.

inputs. Materials and services used in the process of production.

interest. Payment for the use of money.

interest rate. Interest as a percentage per annum of the amount borrowed.

interlocking directorate. Situation where one or more directors of a company sit on the boards of directors of one or more other companies that are competitors, suppliers, or customers of the first company.

intermediate product. A product intended for resale or further processing.

internal cost. Costs incurred by those who actually produce (or consume) a good. Contrast with *external cost.*

internalization. A process that results in a firm or individual taking into account an external cost (or benefit) of its actions.

international adjustment mechanism. Any set of forces that tends to reduce surpluses or deficits in the balance of payments.

international liquidity. The total amount of international reserves (foreign exchange, SDRs, etc.) held by the various nations.

International Monetary Fund. An international organization founded as part of the 1945 Bretton Woods agreement, with the task of overseeing the world's monetary and exchange rate system. Played a particularly important role in managing the *adjustable peg* system 1945–73.

inventories. Stocks of raw materials, intermediate products, and finished goods held by producers or marketing organizations.

investment. Accumulation of capital.

Investment Canada. See *FIRA.*

investment dealer. A firm that markets common stock, bonds, and other securities.

investment demand. (Also known as *desired investment* or *planned investment.*) This is the amount of new plant, equipment, and housing acquired during the year, plus additions to inventories that businesses wanted to acquire. Undesired inventory accumulation is excluded. (If undesired inventory accumulation is included, the result is *actual investment.*)

investment, domestic (I). See *gross domestic investment* and *net domestic investment.*

investment good. A capital good. Buildings, equipment, or inventory.

investment tax credit. A provision in the tax code providing a reduction in taxes to those who acquire capital equipment.

invisible. An intangible; a service (as contrasted with a good).

"invisible hand." Adam Smith's phrase expressing the idea that the pursuit of self-interest by individuals will lead to a desirable outcome for society as a whole.

iron law of wages. The view (commonly held in the nineteenth century) that the high birth rate creates a tendency for the supply of labour to outrun the productive capacity of the economy and the demand for labour. As a consequence, it was an iron law of nature that wages would be driven down to the subsistence level. (Any excess population at that wage would die from starvation, pestilence, or war.)

joint products. Goods such that the rise in the price of one causes a rightward shift in the supply curve of the other. Complements in production. Products produced together. Example: meat and hides.

joint profit maximization. Formal or informal cooperation by oligopolists to pick the price that yields the most profit for the group.

key currency. A national currency commonly used by foreigners in international transactions and by foreign monetary authorities when intervening in exchange markets. Examples: the U.S. dollar, and, historically, the British pound.

Keynesian economics. The major macroeconomic propositions put forward by John Maynard Keynes in *The General Theory of Employment, Interest and Money* (1936): A market economy may reach an equilibrium with large-scale unemployment; steps to stimulate aggregate demand can cure a depression; and fiscal policies are the best way to control aggregate demand. Contrast with *classical economics.*

kinked demand curve. A demand curve that an oligopoly firm faces if its competitors follow any price cut it makes but do not follow any of its price increases. The kink in such a demand curve occurs at the existing price.

labour. The physical and mental talents of human beings, applied to the production of goods and services.

labour force. The number of people employed plus those actively seeking work.

labour-intensive product. A good whose production uses a relatively large quantity of labour and relatively small quantity of other resources.

labour participation rate. See *participation rate.*

labour productivity. See *productivity of labour.*

labour theory of value. Strictly, the proposition that the sole source of value is labour (including labour "congealed" in capital). Loosely, the proposition that labour is the principal source of value.

labour union. See *union.*

Laffer curve. A curve showing how tax revenues change as the tax rate changes.

laissez-faire. Strictly translated, "let do." More loosely, "leave it alone." An expression used by the French physiocrats and later by Adam Smith, to describe the absence of government intervention in markets.

land. This term is used broadly by economists to include not only arable land but also the other gifts of nature (such as minerals) that come with the land.

law of diminishing marginal benefit (utility). As a consumer gets more and more of a good, the marginal benefit (utility) of that good will (eventually) decrease.

law of diminishing returns. See *diminishing returns, law of eventually.*

leading indicator. An economic variable that reaches a turning point (peak or trough) before the economy as a whole changes direction.

leakage. (1) A withdrawal of potential spending from the circular flow of income and expenditures. (2) A withdrawal of currency from the banking system that reduces the potential expansion of the money stock.

leakages-injections approach. The determination of equilibrium national product by finding the size of the product at which leakages are equal to injections.

legal tender. An item that creditors must, by law, accept in payment of a debt.

less developed countries (LDCs). Refers to the world's non-industrialized nations with low *per capita* incomes. Most LDCs are in Africa, Asia, and Latin America.

leverage. The ratio of debt to net worth.

liability. (1) What is owed. (2) The amount that can be lost by the owners of a business if that business goes bankrupt.

life-cycle hypothesis. The proposition that consumption depends on expected lifetime income (as contrasted with the early Keynesian view that consumption depends on current income).

limited liability. The amount an owner-shareholder of a corporation can lose in the event of bankruptcy. This is limited to the amount paid to purchase shares of the corporation.

line of credit. Commitment by a bank or other lender to stand ready to lend up to a specified amount to a customer on request.

liquid asset. An asset that can be sold on short notice, at a predictable price, with little cost or bother.

liquidity. Ease with which an asset can be sold on short notice, at a predictable price, with little cost.

liquidity preference. The demand for money—that is, the willingness to hold money as a function of the interest rate.

liquidity preference theory of the interest rate. The theory put forward by J.M. Keynes that the interest rate is determined by the willingness to hold money (liquidity preference) and the supply of money (that is, the stock of money in existence). Contrast with *loanable funds theory of interest.*

liquidity trap. In Keynesian theory, the situation in which individuals and businesses are willing to hold all their additional financial assets in the form of money — rather than bonds or other debt instruments — at the existing interest rate. In such circumstances, the creation of additional money by the central bank cannot depress the interest rate further, and monetary policy cannot be used effectively to stimulate aggregate demand. (All additional money created is caught in the liquidity trap and is held as idle balances.) In geometric terms, the liquidity trap exists where the liquidity preference curve (the demand for money) is horizontal.

loanable funds theory of interest. The theory that the interest rate is determined by the demand for and the supply of funds in the market for bonds and other forms of debt. Contrast with *the liquidity preference theory of the interest rate.*

lockout. Temporary closing of a factory or other place of business in order to deprive workers of their jobs. A bargaining tool sometimes used in labour disputes; the employer's equivalent of a strike.

logarithmic (or log or ratio) scale. A scale in which equal percentage changes are shown as equal distances. For example, the distance from 100 to 200 is equal to the distance from 200 to 400. (Each involves a doubling.)

long run. (1) A period long enough for equilibrium to be reached. (2) A period of time long enough for the quantity of capital to be adjusted to the desired level. (3) Any extended period.

long-run Phillips curve. The curve (or line) traced out by the possible points of long-run equilibrium; that is, the points where people have adjusted completely to the prevailing rate of inflation.

long-run production function. A table showing various combinations of inputs and the maximum output that can be produced with each combination. For a simple firm with only two inputs (labour and capital), the production function can be shown by a two-dimensional table.

Lorenz curve. A curve showing cumulative percentages of income or wealth. For example, a point on a Lorenz curve might show the percentage of income received by the poorest half of the families. (The cumulative percentage of income is shown on the vertical axis. The family with the lowest income is counted first, and then other families are added successively in the order of their incomes. The cumulative percentage of families is on the horizontal axis.) Such a curve can be used to measure inequality; if all families have the same income, the Lorenz curve traces out a diagonal line. See also *Gini coefficient*.

lump-sum tax. A tax of a constant amount. The revenues from such a tax do not change when income changes.

M1. The narrowly defined money stock; consisting of the non-bank public's holdings of currency (coins and paper money) plus demand deposits in the chartered banks. Currency held by banks is excluded, as are deposits owned by banks or by the federal government. This was the definition of money used by the Bank of Canada as an indicator of monetary policy from the mid-1970s to the early 1980s.

M1A. M1 plus daily-interest chequable and non-personal notice deposits in chartered banks.

M2. Defined as M1 *plus* all notice (savings) and personal term deposits in chartered banks. Excludes large term deposits held by corporations; these are included in M3.

M2 + . Defined as M2 plus deposits in trust and mortgage loan companies and *caisses populaires*.

M3. Defined as M2 plus non-personal term deposits, *plus* deposits owned by Canadian residents but denoted in foreign currency, in chartered banks.

macroeconomics. The study of the overall aggregates of the economy, such as total employment, the unemployment rate, national product, and the rate of inflation.

Malthusian problem. The tendency for population to outstrip productive capacity, particularly the capacity to produce food. This is the supposed consequence of a tendency for population to grow geometrically (1, 2, 4, 8, etc.) while the means of sbusistence grows arithmetically (1, 2, 3, 4, etc.). The pressure of population will tend to depress the wage rate to the subsistence level and keep it there, with the excess population being eliminated by war, pestilence, or starvation. A problem described by Thomas Malthus in his *Essay on the Principle of Population* (1798).

managed float. A dirty float. See *floating exchange rate*.

marginal. The term commonly used by economists to mean "additional." For example: *marginal cost* is the additional cost when one more unit is produced; *marginal revenue* is the addition to revenue when one more unit is sold; *marginal utility* is the utility or satisfaction received from consuming one more unit of a good or service.

marginal benefit. The value (in money terms) that an individual would ascribe to having an additional unit of a good or service; that is, the amount of money the individual would be willing to pay for having an additional unit of the good or service. (An individual's marginal benefit schedule for a good or service is equivalent to the individual's demand curve for that good or service.)

marginal cost pricing. Setting price at the level where MC intersects the demand curve.

marginal efficiency of investment. The schedule or curve relating desired investment to the rate of interest. The investment demand curve.

marginal physical product. The additional output when one more unit of an input is used (with all other inputs being held constant). For example, the *marginal physical product of labour* (often abbreviated to the *marginal product of labour*) is the additional output when one more unit of labour is used.

marginal product. (1) Strictly, the marginal physical product. (2) Sometimes, the value of the marginal physical product.

marginal product of labour. See *marginal physical product*.

marginal propensity to consume (MPC). The change in consumption expenditures divided by the change in disposable income.

marginal propensity to import (MPM). The change in imports of goods and services divided by the change in GDP.

marginal propensity to save (MPS). The change in saving divided by the change in disposable income. 1 − MPC.

marginal rate of substitution. The slope of the indifference curve. The ratio of the marginal utility of one good to the marginal utility of another.

marginal revenue. The increase in total revenue from the sale of one more unit.

marginal revenue product. The additional revenue when the firm uses one additional unit of an input (with all other inputs being held constant).

marginal tax rate. The fraction of additional income paid in taxes.

marginal utility. The satisfaction an individual receives from consuming one additional unit of good or service.

margin call. The requirement by a lender who holds stocks (or bonds) as security that more money be put up or the stocks (or bonds) will be sold. A margin call may be issued when the price of the stocks (or bonds) declines, making the stocks (or bonds) less adequate as security for the loan.

margin requirement. The minimum percentage that purchasers of stocks or bonds must put up in their own money. For example, if the margin requirement on stock is 60%, the buyer must put up at least 60% of the price in his or her own money and can borrow no more than 40% from a bank or stockbroker.

market. An institution in which items are bought and sold.

market economy. See *free-market economy*.

market failure. The failure of market forces to bring about the best allocation of resources. For example, when production of a good generates pollution, too many resources tend to go into the production of that good and not enough into the production of alternative goods and services.

marketing board. A legally sanctioned producer organization in agriculture; some boards have the right to fix prices and control production of their product.

market mechanism. The system whereby prices and the interaction of demand and supply help to answer the major economic questions "What will be produced?" "How?" and

''For whom?''

market power. The ability of a single firm or individual to influence the market price of a good or service.

market-power inflation. See *cost-push inflation.*

market share. Percentage of an industry's sales accounted for by a single firm.

market structure. Characteristics that affect the behaviour of firms in a market, such as the number of firms, the possibility of collusion, the degree of product differentiation, and the ease of entry.

Marxist economy. One in which most of the capital is owned by the government. (Individuals may of course own small capital goods, such as hoes or hammers, but the major forms of capital—factories and heavy machinery—are owned by the state.) Political power is in the hands of a party pledging allegiance to the doctrines of Karl Marx.

measure of economic welfare (MEW). A comprehensive measure of economic well-being. Per capita real domestic product is adjusted to take into account leisure, pollution, and other such influences on welfare.

median. The item in the middle (that is, half of all items are above the median and half are below).

mediation (or conciliation). In labour disputes, occurs when major negotiations are deadlocked and an impartial outsider is brought in to suggest a settlement.

medium of exchange. Money; any item that is generally acceptable in exchange for goods or services; any item that is commonly used in buying goods or services.

mercantilism. The theory that national prosperity can be promoted by a positive balance of trade and the accumulation of precious metals.

merchandise trade surplus. The excess of merchandise exports over merchandise imports.

merger. The bringing together of two or more firms under common control through purchase, exchange of common stock, or other means. A *horizontal merger* brings together competing firms. A *vertical merger* brings together firms that are each others' suppliers or customers. A *conglomerate merger* brings together firms that are not related in either of these ways.

merit good. A good or service that the government considers particularly desirable and that it therefore encourages by subsidy or regulation—such as the regulation that children must go to school to get the merit good of education.

microeconomics. The study of individual units within the economy—such as households, firms, and industries—and their interrelationships. The study of the allocation of resources and the distribution of income.

military-industrial complex. A loose term referring to the combined political power exerted by military officers and defence industries; those with a vested interest in military spending. (In his farewell address, President Eisenhower of the United States warned against the military-industrial complex.)

minimum wage. The lowest wage that an employer may legally pay for an hour's work.

mint parity. The exchange rate calculated from the official prices of gold in two countries under the gold standard.

mixed economy. An economy in which the private market and the government share the decisions as to what shall be produced, how, and for whom.

model. The essential features of an economy or economic problem, explained in terms of diagrams, equations, or words—or some combination of these.

monetarism. A body of thought that has its roots in classical economics and that rejects much of the teaching of Keynes' *General Theory.* According to monetarists, the most important determinant of aggregate demand is the quantity of money; the economy is basically stable if monetary growth is stable; and the authorities should follow a monetary rule, aiming for a steady growth of the money stock. Many monetarists also believe that the effects of fiscal policy on aggregate demand are weak (unless accompanied by changes in the quantity of money), that the government plays too active a role in the economy, and that the long-run Phillips curve is vertical. (The most famous contemporary monetarist is Milton Friedman).

monetary base. Currency held by the general public and by chartered banks plus the deposits of chartered banks in the Bank of Canada.

monetary policy. Central bank policies aimed at changing the rate of growth of the money stock; for example, open market operations or changes in required reserve ratios.

monetary rule. The rule, proposed by monetarists, that the central bank should aim for a steady rate of growth of the money stock.

money. Any item commonly used in buying goods or services.

money illusion. Strictly defined, people have money illusion if their behaviour changes in the event of a proportional change in prices, money incomes, and assets and liabilities measured in money terms. More loosely, people have money illusion if their behaviour changes when there is a proportional change in prices and money incomes.

money income. Income measured in dollars (or, in another country, income measured in the currency of that country).

money market. The market for short-term debt instruments (such as Treasury bills).

money multiplier (deposit multiplier). The number of dollars by which the money stock can increase as a result of a $1 increase in the reserves of chartered banks.

money stock (supply). Narrowly, M1 (or M1A). More broadly, M2, M2 +, or M3.

monopolistic competition. A market structure with many firms selling a differentiated product, with low barriers to entry.

monopoly. (1) A market in which there is only a single seller. (2) The single seller in such a market. A *natural monopoly* occurs when the average total cost of a single firm falls over such an extended range that one firm can produce the total quantity sold at a lower average cost than could two or more firms.

monopoly rent. Above-normal profit of a monopoly.

monopsony. A market in which there is only one buyer.

moral suasion. Appeals or pressure by Bank of Canada intended to influence the behaviour of chartered banks.

most-favoured-nation clause. A clause in a trade agreement that commits a country to impose no greater barriers (tariffs, etc.) on imports from a second country than it imposes on imports from any other country.

multinational corporation. A corporation that carries on business (either directly or through subsidiaries) in more than one country.

multiplier. The change in equilibrium real national product divided by the change in investment demand (or in government expenditures, tax collections, or exports). In the simplest economy (with a marginal tax rate of zero and no imports), the multiplier is $1 \div$ (the marginal propensity to save). See also *money multiplier.*

national debt. See *public debt.*

National Energy Program (NEP). A 1980 program outlining the federal government's policy on pricing and taxation of oil and gas, energy exports, and Canadianization of the energy sector. The NEP was largely abolished by the Conservative government in 1984–85.

national income. The return to all factors of production owned by the residents of a nation.

national product. See *gross national product,* and *net national product.*

national union. A Canadian labour union that is not affiliated with foreign labour unions.

natural monopoly. See *monopoly.*

natural oligopoly. See *oligopoly.*

natural rate of unemployment. The equilibrium rate of unemployment that exists when people have adjusted completely to the existing rate of inflation. The rate of unemployment to which the economy tends when those making labour and other contracts correctly anticipate the rate of inflation. The rate of unemployment consistent with a stable rate of inflation.

near money. A highly liquid asset that can quickly and easily be converted into money. Examples: Canada Savings Bonds, Treasury bills, Certificates of Deposits.

negative income tax. A reverse income tax, whereby the government makes payments to individuals and families with low incomes. (The lower the income, the greater the payment from the government.)

neocolonialism. The domination of the economy of a nation by the business firms or government of another nation or nations.

net domestic investment (I_n). Gross domestic investment less depreciation.

net domestic product (NDP). Private consumption expenditures plus government purchases of goods and services plus net domestic investment plus net exports of goods and services. Equals GDP minus capital consumption allowances (depreciation).

net exports. Exports minus imports.

net national product (NNP). GNP minus capital consumption allowances (depreciation).

net official monetary movements. Changes in Canada's official foreign exchange reserves. An increase in reserves appears as a positive entry on the debit side of the balance-of-payments accounts, a decrease as a negative debit.

net worth. Total assets less total liabilities. The value of ownership.

neutrality of money. Money is neutral if a change in the quantity of money affects the price level without affecting relative prices or the distribution of income.

neutrality of taxes. (1) A situation where taxes do not affect relative prices. (2) The absence of an excess burden of taxes.

New Left. Radical economists; Marxists of the 1960s and 1970s.

nominal. Measured in money terms. Current dollar as contrasted to constant-dollar, or real. See also *current dollar.*

noncompeting groups. Groups of workers that do not compete with each other for jobs because their training or skills are different.

non-price competition. Competition by means other than price; for example, advertising or product differentiation.

non-renewable resource. Resource of which a finite quantity exists.

non-tariff barrier. Impediment to trade other than tariffs. Example: an import quota.

normal good. A good for which the quantity demanded rises as income rises, *ceteris paribus.* Contrast with an *inferior good.*

normal profit. The opportunity cost of capital and/or entrepreneurship. (Normal profit is considered a cost by economists but not by business accountants.)

normative statement. A statement about what should be. Contrast with *positive statement.*

notice deposit. A deposit in a chartered bank or other financial institution for which the institution has the legal right to insist on several days' or weeks' notice before being obliged to allow the depositor to withdraw his or her funds. (Though ordinary savings accounts are legally notice deposits, banks and trust companies routinely waive the notice requirement for small depositors.)

official settlements surplus. See *net official monetary movements.*

Okun's law. The observation that a change of 2% to 3% in real GDP (compared with its long-run trend) has been associated with a 1% change in the opposite direction in the unemployment rate. (Named after Arthur M. Okun.)

Old Age Security. A monthly transfer payment by the government to every Canadian or landed immigrant over the age of 65 (provided they meet certain residency requirements).

oligopoly. A market in which there are only a few sellers, who sell either a standardized or differentiated product. A *natural oligopoly* occurs when the average total costs of individual firms fall over a large enough range that a few firms can produce the total quantity sold at the lowest average cost. (Compare with *natural monopoly*.)

oligopsony. A market in which there are only a few buyers.

OPEC (the Organization of Petroleum Exporting Countries). A cartel of oil exporters that brought about the large increase in the world price of oil in the 1970s.

open economy. An economy where exports and imports are large relative to domestic national product.

open market operation. The purchase (or sale) of government (or other) securities by the Bank of Canada on the open market (that is, not directly from the issuer of the security).

open shop. A business that may hire workers who are not (and need not become) union members. Contrast with *closed shop* and *union shop*.

opportunity cost. (1) The alternative that must be foregone when something is produced. (2) The amount that an input could earn in its best alternative use.

output gap. The amount by which output falls short of the potential or full-employment level. The GDP gap.

panic. A rush for safety, historically marked by a switch out of bank deposits into currency and out of paper currency into gold. A run on banks. A *stock-market panic* occurs when there is a rush to sell and stock prices collapse.

paradox of thrift. The paradoxical situation, pointed out by Keynes, in which an increase in the desire to save can result in a decrease in the equilibrium quantity of saving.

paradox of value. The apparent contradiction, pointed out by Adam Smith, when an essential (such as water) has a low price while a nonessential (such as a diamond) has a high price.

Pareto improvement. Making one person better off without making anyone else worse off. (Named after Vilfredo Pareto, 1848–1923.)

Pareto optimum. A situation in which it is impossible to make any Pareto improvement. That is, it is impossible to make any individual better off without making someone else worse off.

partial equilibrium analysis. Analysis of a particular market or set of markets; ignoring feedbacks from other markets.

participation rate. Number of people in the labour force as a percentage of the population of working age.

partnership. An unincorporated business owned by two or more people.

par value. (1) Under the IMF adjustable peg system, the officially specified value of the currency in terms of gold or U.S. dollars. (2) A situation in which the Canadian dollar trades for precisely one U.S. dollar in the exchange market.

patent. Exclusive right, granted by the government to an inventor, to used an invention for a specified time period. (Such a right can be licensed or sold by the patent holder.)

payroll tax. A tax levied on wges and salaries, or on wages and salaries up to a specified limit. Examples: Unemployment Insurance contributions, Canada/Quebec Pension Plan contributions.

peak. The month of greatest economic activity prior to the onset of a recession; one of the four phases of the business cycle.

peak-load pricing. Setting the price for a good or service higher during periods of heavy demand than at other times. The purpose is to encourage buyers to choose nonpeak periods and/or to raise more revenue. Examples: electricity, weekend ski tow.

pegged exchange rates. See *adjustable peg system*.

penalty rate. A discount rate kept consistently above a short-term market rate of interest.

perfect competition. A market with many buyers and many sellers, with no single buyer or seller having any (noticeable) influence over price. That is, every buyer and every seller is a *price taker*.

permanent income. Normal income; income that is thought to be normal.

permanent-income hypothesis. The proposition that the principal determinant of consumption is permanent income (rather than current income).

personal consumption expenditures. See *consumption*.

personal income. Income received by households in return for productive services, and from transfers prior to the payment of personal taxes.

personal saving. (1) Loosely but commonly, disposable personal income less consumption expenditures. (2) More strictly, disposable personal income less consumption expenditures less payment of interest on consumer debt.

Phillips curve. The curve tracing out the relationship between the unemployment rate (on the horizontal axis) and the inflation rate or the rate of change of money wages (on the vertical axis). The *long-run Phillips curve* is the curve (or line) tracing out the relationship between the unemployment rate and the inflation rate when the inflation rate is stable and correctly anticipated.

planned investment. Desired investment; investment demand; *ex ante* investment.

plant. A physical establishment where production takes place.

policy dilemma. This occurs when a policy that helps to solve one problem makes another worse.

portfolio investment. Purchase by a foreign investor of bonds, stocks, or other Canadian financial assets in corporations or other firms which remain controlled by Canadian owners. (May also refer to purchases by foreigners of Canadian government securities.)

positive (or descriptive) statement. A statement about what is (or was) or about how something works. Contrast with *normative statement*.

potential output (or potential GDP). The GDP that would exist if a high rate of employment were consistently maintained.

poverty. Exists when people have inadequate income to buy the necessities of life.

poverty line (or poverty standard). An estimate of the income needed to avoid poverty. In 1988 Statistics Canada's poverty line was approximately $23,500 for a large-city family of four.

precautionary demand for money. The amount of money that households and businesses want to hold to protect themselves against unforeseen events.

preferred stock. A stock that is given preference over common stock when dividends are paid. That is, specified dividends must be paid on preferred stock before any dividend is paid on common stock.

premature inflation. Inflation that occurs before the economy reaches full employment.

present value. The value now of a future receipt or receipts, calculated using the interest rate, i. The present value (PV) of $\$X$ to be received n years hence is $\$X \div (1 + i)^n$.

price ceiling. The legally established maximum price.

price discrimination. The sale of the same good or service at different prices to different customers or in different markets, provided the price differences are not justified by cost differences such as differences in transportation costs.

price-earnings ratio. The ratio of the price of a stock to the annual (after-tax) earnings per share of the stock.

price elasticity of demand (supply). See *elasticity of demand (supply)*.

price index. A weighted average of prices, as a percentage of prices existing in a base year.

price leadership. A method by which oligopolistic firms establish similar prices without overt collusion. One firm (the price leader) announces a new price, confident that the other firms will quickly follow.

price line. See *budget line*.

price maker. A monopolist (or monopsonist) who is able to set price because there are no competitors.

price mechanism. See *market mechanism*.

price searcher. A seller (or buyer) who is able to influence price, and who has competitors whose responses can affect the profit-maximizing price. An oligopolist (or oligopsonist).

price support. A commitment by the government to buy surpluses at a given price (the support price) in order to prevent the price from falling below that figure.

price system. See *market mechanism*.

price taker. A seller or buyer who is unable to affect the price and whose market decision is limited to the quantity to be sold or bought at the existing market price. A seller or buyer in a perfectly competitive market.

price-wage flexibility. The ease with which prices and wages rise or fall (especially fall) in the event of changing demand and supply. Contrast with *price-wage stickiness*.

price-wage stickiness. The resistance of prices and wages to a

movement, particularly in a downward direction.

primary burden of tax. The amount of tax collected. Compare with *excess burden of a tax*.

prime rate of interest. (1) A bank's publicly announced interest rate on short-term loans. (2) Historically, the interest rate charged by banks on loans to their most credit-worthy customers.

prisoner's dilemma. A situation where an agreement or action that would benefit both parties in a transaction will not occur because neither party can trust the other to keep the agreement.

procyclical policy. A policy that increases the amplitude of business fluctuations. (''Procyclical'' refers to results, not intentions.)

producer surplus. Net benefit that producers get from being able to sell a good at the existing price. Returns to capital and entrepreneurship in excess of their opportunity costs. Rents on capital and entrepreneurship. Measured by the area left of the supply curve between the break-even price and the existing price.

product differentiation. See *differentiated products*.

production function. The relationship showing the maximum output that can be produced with various combinations of inputs.

production possibilities curve. A curve showing the alternative combinations of outputs that can be produced if all productive resources are used. The boundary of attainable combinations of outputs.

productivity. Output per unit of input.

productivity of labour. The *average* productivity of labour is total output divided by the units of labour input. The *marginal* productivity of labour is the additional output when one more unit of labour is added, while all other factors are held constant.

profit. In economics, return to capital and/or entrepreneurship over and above normal profit. In business accounting, revenues minus costs. Also sometimes used to mean profit after the payment of corporate income taxes.

profit-and-loss statement. An accounting statement summarizing a firm's revenues, costs, and income taxes over a given period (usually a year). An income statement.

progressive tax. A tax that takes a larger percentage of income as income rises.

proletariat. Karl Marx's term for the working class, especially the industrial working class.

proportional tax. A tax that takes the same percentage of income regardless of the level of income.

proprietors' income. The income of unincorporated firms.

prospectus. A statement of the financial condition and prospects of a corporation, presented when new securities are about to be issued.

protectionism. The advocacy or use of high or higher tariffs to protect domestic producers from foreign competition.

protective tariff. A tariff that is intended to protect domestic producers from foreign competition (as contrasted with a revenue tariff, intended to be a source of revenue for the government).

proxy. A temporary written transfer of voting rights at a shareholders' meeting.

proxy fight. A struggle between competing groups in a corporation to obtain a majority vote (and therefore control of the corporation) by collecting proxies of shareholders.

public debt. The debt owed by governments as a result of previous borrowing to finance budget deficits. Most of Canada's public debt is owed to Canadian holders of government debt instruments such as ordinary government bonds, Canada Savings Bonds, or Treasury bills. However, part of it is held by foreign capitalists.

public good. See *pure public good.*

public utility. A firm that is the sole supplier of an essential good or service in an area and that is regulated by the government.

pump priming. Short-term increases in government expenditures aimed at generating an upward momentum of the economy toward full employment.

purchase and resale agreement. An arrangement by which the Bank of Canada makes short-term loans to investment dealers; by purchasing Treasury bills from the dealers at an agreed price and specifying the price and date at which the dealer has to buy them back, the Bank is in effect making a short-term loan to the dealer.

purchasing power of money. The value of money in buying goods and services. The change in the purchasing power of money is measured by the change in the fraction 1 ÷ the price index.

purchasing power parity theory. The theory that changes in exchange rates reflect and compensate for differences in the rate of inflation in different countries.

pure public good. A good (or service) with benefits that people cannot be excluded from enjoying, regardless of who pays for the good.

quantity theory (of money). The proposition that velocity is reasonably stable and that a change in the quantity of money will therefore cause nominal domestic product to change by approximately the same percentage.

quota. A numerical limit. For example, a limit on the amount of a good that may be imported.

Rand Formula. A famous arbitration ruling which settled a 1945 strike by Fork workers; it included compulsory contribution of union dues by workers and has had a great deal of influence on Canadian labour relations and labour law since that time.

random sample. A sample chosen from a larger group in such a way that every member of the group has an equal chance of being chosen.

rate base. Allowable capital of a public utility, to which the regulatory agency applies the allowable rate of return.

rate of interest. Interest as a percentage per annum of the amount borrowed.

rate of return. (1) Annual profit as a percentage of net worth. (2) Additional annual revenue from the sale of goods or services produced by plant or equipment, less depreciation and operating costs such as labour and materials, expressed as a percentage of the value of the plant or equipment.

rational expectations. Expectations based on available information, including information about the policies being pursued by the authorities. If expectations are rational, people do not consistently make the same mistake.

rationing. (1) A method for allocating a good (or service) when the quantity demanded exceeds the quantity supplied at the existing price. (2) More loosely, any method for allocating a scarce resource or good. In this sense, we may speak of the market *rationing by price.*

ratio (or logarithmic) scale. A scale in which equal percentage changes are shown as equal distances. For example, the distance from 100 to 200 is equal to the distance from 200 to 400. (Each involves a doubling.)

Reaganomics. The economic program of U.S. President Reagan, including (1) tax cuts, (2) restraint in domestic spending, (3) increases in defence spending, and (4) less regulation.

real. Measured in terms of quantity; adjusted to remove the effects of inflation.

real capital. Buildings, equipment, and other materials, including inventories, used in production, which have themselves been produced in the past.

real deficit. The *increase* in the real debt of the government.

real investment. The accumulation of machines and other real capital.

real rate of interest. The nominal rate of interest less the expected rate of inflation.

real wage. The quantity of goods and services that a money wage will buy; the nominal (or dollar) wage adjusted for inflation.

recession. A decline in output, income, employment, and trade, usually lasting six months to a year, and marked by widespread contractions in many sectors of the economy.

recessionary gap. The vertical distance by which the aggregate demand line is below the 45° line at the full-employment quantity of domestic product.

recognition lag. The time interval between the beginning of a problem and the time when the problem is recognized.

refundable child tax credit. See *child tax credit.*

regression analysis. A statistical calculation of the relationship between two or more variables.

regressive tax. A tax that takes a smaller percentage of income as income rises.

rent. (1) In economics, any payment to a factor of production in excess of its opportunity cost. (2) A payment by the user of land to the owner. (3) Payments by users to the owners of land, buildings, or equipment.

replacement-cost depreciation. Depreciation based on the current replacement cost of buildings and equipment rather than their original acquisition cost.

required reserve ratio. The fraction of deposit liabilities that a chartered bank is legally obliged to keep in reserves. Under proposed legislative changes in 1990, the Bank Act will no longer specify a required reserve ratio.

required reserves. The reserves that, by law, the chartered banks had to keep before the 1990s. Chartered bank reserves are typically held as currency and deposits with the Bank of Canada.

resale price maintenance. Practice whereby a manufacturer sets the minimum retail price of a product, thereby eliminating price competition among retailers of that product. The practice has long been illegal under Canadian competition legislation, and has recently been made illegal in the United States as well.

rescheduling of debt. The renegotiation of the terms of the debt, to give the debtor more time to repay, and sometimes including a reduction in the interest rate.

reservation price of a resource. The cost of harvesting the resource today plus the amount necessary to compensate for the reduction in the quantity of the resource available in the future.

resource. Basic inputs used in the production of goods and services, namely, labour, land, and capital. See also *factor of production*.

restrictive agreement. Agreement among companies to restrain competition through practices such as price fixing or market sharing.

Restrictive Trade Practices Commission. See *Bureau of Competition Policy*.

return to capital. See *rate of return*.

revaluation of a currency. In international economics, an increase in the par value of a currency.

revenue sharing. See *federal-provincial transfers*.

revenue tariff. See *protective tariff*.

right-to-work law. Law making it illegal to require union membership as a condition of employment. Equivalent to prohibition of closed shops and union shops. Such laws exist in some states in the United States, but do not exist in Canada.

risk premium. The difference between the yields on two grades of bonds (or other securities) because of differences in their risk. The additional interest or yield needed to compensate the holder of bonds (or other securities) for risk.

roundabout production. The production of capital goods and the use of these capital goods in the production of consumer goods. The production of goods in more than one stage.

rule of the gold standard game. The understanding that each country would permit its money stock to change in the same direction as the change in its gold stock. That is, if a country's gold stock were to rise, it should allow its money supply to increase, and vice versa.

rule of 70. A rule that tells approximately how many years it will take for something to double in size if it is growing at a compound rate. For example, a deposit earning 2% interest approximately doubles in $70 \div 2 = 35$ years. In general a deposit earning x percent interest will double in about $70 \div x$ years.

run. A rush to switch into safer assets; for example, a *run on banks*.

sales tax. A tax charged on the sales of goods and services. Similar to an excise tax, but typically collected as a fixed percentage of the sales value of a broad range of goods and services.

satisficing theory. The theory that firms do not try to maximize profits but rather aim for reasonable target levels of profits, sales, and other measures of performance.

saving. See *personal saving*.

saving function. (1) The relationship between personal saving and disposable income. (2) More broadly, the relationship between personal saving and the factors (like disposable income) that determine saving.

Say's law. The discredited view that supply in the aggregate creates its own demand (regardless of the general price level).

scarcity. (1) The inability to satisfy all wants because they exceed what we can produce with our available resources. (2) A shortage.

SDRs. See *special drawing rights*.

search cost. The time and money spent in collecting the information necessary to make a decision to buy or sell stocks or any other item.

seasonal adjustment. The removal of regular seasonal movements from a time series.

secondary boycott. Boycott against a firm to discourage it from doing business with a second firm, in order to exert pressure on the second firm (which may be in a strong position to withstand other forms of pressure).

secondary reserves. Chartered bank holdings of liquid assets (Treasury bills, etc.) that can readily be converted into primary reserves (currency or reserve deposits).

second best, theory of the. The theory of how to get the best results in remaining markets when one or more markets have defects about which nothing can be done.

secular stagnation. A situation of inadequate aggregate demand extending over many years. Consequently, large-scale unemployment persists, and it may even become increasingly severe.

secular trend. The trend in economic activity over an extended number of years.

sell short. See *short sale*.

seniority rules. Rules giving preference to those who have been longest on the job. Individuals with seniority are typically the last to be discharged or laid off, and the first to be rehired.

shortage. (1) The amount by which quantity supplied is less than quantity demanded at the existing price; the opposite of a surplus. (2) Any deficiency.

short run. (1) The period before the price level has adjusted to its equilibrium. (2) The period in which the quantity of plant and equipment cannot change. (3) The time period before equilibrium can be re-established. (4) Any brief time period.

short-run production function. The table showing the relationship between the amount of variable factors used and the amount of output that can be produced, in a situation where the quantity of capital is constant. For the simple case of a firm with just two inputs — capital and one variable factor — the short-run production function is one row in the long-run production function.

short sale. A contract to sell something at a later date for a price specified now.

shutdown point. The point where the MC curve cuts the AVC curve. If the price is below this point, the firm produces nothing.

single proprietorship. A business owned by an individual person. Contrast with *partnership* and *corporation.*

single-tax proposal. The proposal of Henry George (1839–1897) that all taxes be eliminated except one on land. (George argued that all returns to land represent an unearned surplus.)

slope. The vertical rise in a function divided by the horizontal run.

small, open economy. An economy that has substantial international transactions but is too small to have a substantial influence on the prices of the goods and services that are involved in the transactions.

snake. An agreement among some Western European countries to keep their currencies within a narrow band of fluctuation (the snake). Prior to 1973, they allowed their currencies to move jointly in a wider band with respect to the dollar. (This was called the *snake in the tunnel.*) (Since 1973, the snake has not been tied to the dollar.)

social assistance. Cash payments by local authorities to individuals and families with low incomes; commonly known as "welfare." See also *Canada Assistance Plan.*

social insurance. Government programs such as Old Age Security, Unemployment Insurance, provincial health insurance plans, etc., which provide payments or services to people in specifed circumstances such as old age, unemployment, or illness. Synonym: social security.

socialism. An economic system in which the means of production (capital equipment, buildings, and land) are owned by the state.

special drawing rights (SDRs). Bookkeeping accounts created by the International Monetary Fund to increase the quantity of international reserves held by national governments. SDRs can be used to cover balance-of-payments deficits.

specific tax. A fixed number of cents or dollars of tax on each unit of the good. Contrast with *ad valorem tax.*

speculation. The purchase (or sale) of an asset in the hope of making a quick profit from a rise (fall) in its price.

speculative demand for money. The schedule or curve showing how the rate of interest affects the amount of assets that firms and households are willing to hold in the form of money, rather than in bonds or other interest-bearing securities.

speculator. Anyone who buys or sells a foreign currency (or any other asset) in the hope of profiting from a change in its price.

spillover. See *externality.*

stagflation. The coexistence of a high rate of unemployment (stagnation) and inflation.

standard of value. The item (money) in which the prices of goods and services are measured.

sterilization of balance-of-payments surplus (deficit). Operations by the central bank to prevent a balance-of-payments surplus or deficit from causing changes in chartered bank reserves and, hence, in the money supply.

store of value. An asset that may be used to store wealth through time; an asset that may be used to finance future purchases.

structural unemployment. Unemployment due to a mismatch between the skills or location of the labour force and the skills or location required by employers. Unemployment due to a changing location or composition of jobs.

subsidy. A negative tax.

subsistence wage. Minimum living wage. A wage below which population will decline because of starvation or disease.

substitute. A good or service that satisfies similar needs. Two commodities are substitutes if a rise in the price of one causes a rightward shift in the demand curve for the other. (Contrast with *complementary goods.*)

substitution effect. The change in the quantity of a good demanded because of a change in its price when the real income effect of the change in price has been eliminated. That is, a change in the quantity demanded as a result of a movement along a single indifference curve. See also *income effect.*

sunspot theory. The theory put forward in the late nineteenth century that cycles in sunspot activity cause cycles in agricultural production and, hence, cycles in business activity.

superior good. A good for which the quantity demanded rises as income rises, *ceteris paribus.* A *normal good.* Contrast with an *inferior good.*

supply. The schedule or curve showing how the price of a good or service influences the quantity supplied, *ceteris paribus.*

supply of money. See *money stock.*

supply schedule. A table showing the quantities of a good or service that sellers would offer at various market prices, *ceteris paribus.*

supply shift. A movement of the supply curve of a good (or service) to the right or left as a result of a change in the price of inputs or any other determinant of the quantity supplied (except the price of the good or service itself).

supply shifter. Anything that affects the quantity of a good or service supplied except its own price.

supply side. The view that it is supply factors — such as the quantity of capital and the willingness to work — that are the principal constraints to growth. According to this view, a lack of aggregate demand is not the main constraint.

support price. Agricultural price guaranteed to farmers by the government. (If the market price falls short of the target price, the government pays farmers the difference.)

surplus. (1) The amount by which quantity supplied exceeds quantity demanded at the existing price. Contrast with *shortage*. (2) The amount by which revenues exceed expenditures. Contrast with *deficit*. Any excess or amount left over.

surplus value. In Marxist economics, the amount by which the value of a worker's output exceeds the wage; the share of output appropriated by capitalists.

sustainable yield. The amount of a renewable resource (like fish) that can be harvested while still leaving the population constant.

sympathy strike. A strike by a union that does not have a dispute with its own employer, but is trying to strengthen the bargaining position of another striking union.

syndicate. An association of investment bankers to market a large block of securities.

tacit collusion. The adoption of a common policy by sellers without explicit agreement.

takeoff. The achievement of sustained growth, in which capital can be accumulated without depressing the standard of living below its existing level.

tariff. A tax on an imported good.

tax base. The total amount of income or sales revenue subject to a specific tax (such as the personal income tax or a provincial sales tax).

tax-based incomes policy (TIP). An incomes policy backed up with tax penalties on violators or tax incentives for those who co-operate.

tax credit. A subtraction from the tax payable. (For example, if a $1000 machine is bought, a 10% investment tax credit means that $100 can be subtracted from the taxes that must be paid to the government.)

tax deduction. A subtraction from taxable income. Suppose an individual pays $1,000 in allowable charitable donations. This $1,000 can be deducted from taxable income. For someone in the 36% tax bracket, this results in a $360 reduction in taxes. (Note that the tax saving depends on the tax bracket. Thus, a $1,000 deduction reduces taxes more for someone in the 36% tax bracket than for a person in a lower bracket. Note also that the $1,000 deduction is worth only $360 to this individual, while a $1,000 tax credit is worth the full $1,000 in tax savings.)

tax incidence. See *incidence of tax*.

tax neutrality. (1) A situation in which taxes do not affect relative prices. (2) A situation in which the excess burden of taxes is zero.

tax shifting. This occurs when the initial taxpayer transfers all or part of a tax to others. (For example, a firm that is taxed may charge a higher price.)

technological (or technical) efficiency. Providing the maximum output with the available resources and technology, while working at a reasonable pace. The avoidance of wasted effort and sloppy management.

term deposit. A deposit in a bank or other financial institution which has a specific term to maturity; a penalty is charged if the depositor wants to cash it in before maturity.

terms of trade. The average price of goods sold divided by the average price of goods bought. Often used to refer to the prices of a country's export and import goods.

theory of games. See *game theory*.

theory of public choice. Theory of how government spending decisions are made and how they should be made.

third world. Countries that are neither in the "first" world (the high-income countries of Western Europe and North America, plus a few others such as Japan) nor in the "second" world (the countries of Eastern Europe). Low- and middle-income countries other than those run by communist parties.

tied selling. Transaction in which purchaser is forced to buy another item or items in the seller's line of products in order to get the one that is really wanted.

time preference. The desire to have goods now rather than in the future. The amount by which goods now are preferred over goods in the future.

time series. A set of observations taken in successive time periods. For example, GDP in 1974, in 1975, in 1976, etc.

TIP. See *tax-based incomes policy*.

total cost. The sum of fixed costs and variable costs.

total revenue. Total receipts from the sale of a product. Where there is a single price, total revenue is the price times the quantity sold.

transactions demand for money. The amount of money that firms and individuals want to cover the time between the receipt of income and the making of expenditures.

transfer of government deposits. A technique of monetary control by which the Bank of Canada influences chartered bank reserves by depositing or withdrawing government funds held in the chartered banks.

transfer payment. A payment, usually made by the government to private individuals, that does not result from current productive activity. See also *federal-provincial transfers*.

Treasury bill. A short-term (less than a year, often three months) debt of the Bank of Canada. It carries no explicit interest payment; a purchaser gains by buying a bill for less than its face value.

trough. The month of lowest economic activity prior to the beginning of a recovery; one of the four phases of the business cycle.

turning point. The trough or peak of a business cycle.

turnover tax. A tax on goods or services (whether they are intermediate or final products) whenever they are sold. Compare *value-added tax.*

underemployed. (1) Workers who can find only part-time work when they want full-time work. (2) Workers who are being paid full time but are not kept busy because of low demand for output.

underground economy. Economic activity unobserved by tax collectors and government statisticians.

underwrite. Guarantee by an investment dealer that the whole new issue of stock will be sold. (An investment dealer unable to sell all the underwritten stock must buy the remainder.)

undesired inventory accumulation. Actual inventory accumulation less desired inventory accumulation.

undistributed corporate profits. After-tax corporate profits less dividends paid.

unemployment. The condition of people who are willing to work but cannot find jobs. More generally, the condition of any underutilized resource.

unemployment rate. The percentage of the labour force unemployed.

union. An association of workers, formed to negotiate over wages, fringe benefits, and working conditions.

union shop. A business where all nonunion workers must join the union within a brief period of their employment. Compare with *closed shop* and *right-to-work law.*

unit elasticity. Elasticity of one. If a demand curve has unit elasticity, total revenue remains unchanged as price changes. (The demand curve is a rectangular hyperbola.) If a supply curve has unit elasticity, it is a straight line that would, if extended, go through the origin.

unlimited liability. Responsibility for debts without limit.

utility. The ability to satisfy wants.

value added. Value of the product sold less the cost of intermediate products bought from other firms.

value-added tax (VAT). A sales tax paid by business firms on their gross sales, but with a provision for a refund of the tax that has been paid on the intermediate goods and services bought as inputs from other firms; thus it is effectively a tax on individual firms' value added.

value of marginal product (VMP). Marginal physical product times product price.

variable costs. Any costs that increase as output increases.

variable-rate mortgage. A mortgage which has an interest rate that is periodically adjusted in response to changes in the market interest rate.

velocity of money. The average number of times per year that the average dollar in the money stock is spent. There are two principal ways of calculating velocity. (1) *Income velocity* is the number of times the average dollar is spent on final products (that is GDP ÷ M). (2) *Transaction velocity* is the number of times the average dollar is spent on *any* transaction (including those for intermediate goods and financial assets). That is, total spending ÷ M.

vertical merger. See *merger.*

voluntary arbitration. In labour disputes, occurs when labour and management submit their conflict to an impartial third party and commit themselves in advance to accepting that third party's decision.

wage-price controls. See *incomes policy.*

withholding tax. A tax (generally of about 15 percent) charged (withheld) by the Canadian government on payments of interest and dividends from Canadian sources to foreign investors.

windfall. An unexpected increase in profit that accrues to existing producers in an industry as a result of an unforeseen price increase; an example is the increase in the profits of Canadian oil companies as a result of the rapid rise in the producer price of oil during the 1970s.

workable competition. A compromise that limits monopoly power while allowing firms to become big enough to reap economies of scale. A practical alternative to the often unattainable goal of perfect competition.

World Bank. An international bank founded after the 1945 Bretton Woods conference. Its principal activity is to lend money for economic development projects in Third World countries. Affiliated with the International Monetary Fund.

yellow-dog contract. Contract in which an employee agrees not to become a member of a union.

yield. The annual rate of discount that would make the present value of a stream of future payments equal to the price or present value of an asset. The *rate of return.*

zero-base budgeting. A budgeting technique that requires items to be justified anew ''from the ground up,'' without regard to how much has been spent on them in the past.

Index